BRIEF CONTENTS

CONTENTS

PART I

FRAMEWORKS   1

PART

II

CONTEXTS   125

PREFACE AND ACKNOWLEDGEMENTS

We originally decided to write this book to provide support for modules we designed and taught at different universities in London. Our aim was to develop a book that would combine ethics and corporate social responsibility as it applies to decision making in business organizations operating across borders. We also sought to expand on the issue of corporate social responsibility as, in our opinion, this has not been covered to the same extent as business ethics in existing textbooks.

When we started writing the book, there was discussion about whether ethics and corporate social responsibility would continue to be important issues for business as the economic downturn was tightening its grip. The events of the last year have proved this to be the case. The near collapse of the banking sector shows that lack of ethical awareness and introspection can have substantial negative consequences on individuals, organizations and societies alike. A positive view of business ethics and corporate social responsibility, that places these at the heart of decision making, has been shown to be essential for maintaining an economic system based on trust and shared values.

Business ethics and corporate social responsibility are sometimes seen as overlapping concepts and sometimes as gradually diverging fields. We hope that this book provides clarity on the distinct nature of the two concepts, but also emphasizes their similarities in involving reflection on the boundaries between individual, governmental and corporate responsibility. Indeed, we would argue that business ethics and corporate social responsibility remain topical issues because these boundaries are in a constant state of flux and debate. For example, one individual may argue that markets should be left to determine whether employees are paid bonuses, whilst others would argue that governments should take more responsibility over remuneration practices. Theories of ethics and corporate social responsibility shed light on these types of arguments and thus provide a better understanding of the dilemmas and choices encountered by companies and people who work them, both at corporate and individual levels of decision making.

Writing this book has taken place after normal university hours, but our interest and commitment has been sustained by the enthusiasm of our students. Business and corporate social responsibility are topics that seem to inspire students to produce unusually personal and engaged work. We are indebted to the many students who have shared the classroom and their thoughts with us over the last couple of years.

We would like to thank the anonymous panel of reviewers for their comments that have been invaluable in making this book more comprehensive and better argued. We would also particularly like to thank Tom Rennie who has been an exceptionally helpful and patient editor. Finally, we would like to dedicate this book to our respective partners who have been supportive and understanding of the long hours and absent-minded glances this book has meant for them.

October 2009

In addition to the dozens of international academics who answered online surveys at the start of this project, the Publisher would particularly like to thank the following academics for supplying detailed feedback on the proposal and manuscript which has helped inform the development of this new textbook:

David Campbell, Newcastle University

Jim Chandler, Sheffield Hallam University

Chris Downs, University of Chichester

Mick Fryer, Loughborough University

Miroslav Glas, University of Ljubljana

Jim Hine, University of Edinburgh

Ronald Jeurissen, Nyenrode Business Universiteit

Oliver Marnet, Aberystwyth University

Hugh McBride, Galway-Mayo Institute of Technology

Geoff Moore, Durham University

Mette Morsing, Copenhagen Business School

Piet Naude, Nelson Mandela Metropolitan University

Christian Newman, Webster University Vienna

Louise Preget, Bournemouth University

The publisher also thanks various copyright holders for granting permission to reproduce material throughout the text. Every effort has been made to trace all copyright holders, but if anything has been inadvertently overlooked the publisher will be pleased to make the necessary arrangements at the first opportunity (please contact the publisher directly).

ABOUT THE AUTHORS

Paul Griseri

Paul is head of the Department of Business and Management at Middlesex University Business School. Prior to this he has taught management at all levels, from first line management through to MBA, and he has worked in a range of institutions, most recently at University College London. Paul is co-editor of the journal *Philosophy of Management*, and has published several books and articles on subjects related to this area. He has also trained a large number of professional managers both in formal education and through in-house organization development programmes.

Nina Seppala

Nina has a PhD in Business Studies from University of Warwick. She is now Director of Studies at the Department of Management Science and Innovation, University College London. Previously, she worked for the United Nations and International IDEA in the areas of democracy promotion and preventive diplomacy. Her research interests are in strategy in non-profits, boundaries of corporate responsibility, and business and human rights.

LIST OF FIGURES

LIST OF TABLES

LIST OF CASES

WALK-THROUGH TOUR

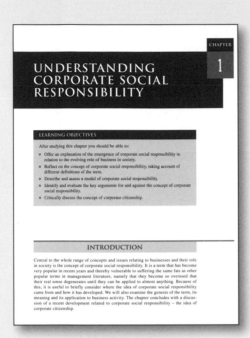

Learning Objectives – appear at the start of every chapter to help you monitor your understanding and progress through the chapter.

Ethics in Practice – short case studies show how various issues are dealt with in real-life scenarios.

Thinking Critically About Ethics – help you to critically assess your understanding of topics.

Ethics and You – an opportunity for you to see how decisions are made and how those decisions affect different outcomes.

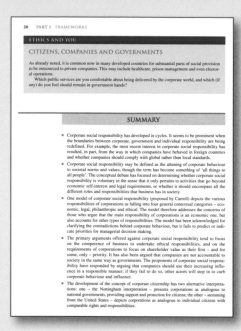

Summary–each chapter ends with a comprehensive summary that provides a thorough re-cap of the key issues in each chapter, helping you to assess your understanding and revise key content.

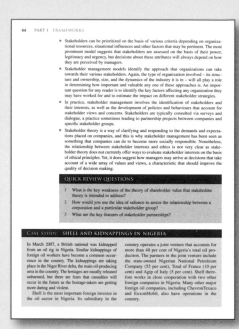

Review Questions–are provided at the end of each chapter to help reinforce and test your knowledge and understanding, and provide a basis for group discussions and activities.

Chapter Cases with Questions–these appear at the end of each chapter to discuss how the main issues are applied in real-life business situations in different types of international and national companies. Each case is accompanied by questions to help test your understanding of the issues.

References–comprehensive references at the end of each chapter allow you to explore the subject further, and act as a starting point for projects and assignments.

COMPANION WEBSITE

Visit the *Business Ethics and Corporate Social Responsibility* companion website at www.cengage.co.uk/griseri to find valuable teaching and learning materials including:

FOR STUDENTS

- Revision questions
- Weblinks to a wide range of study resources
- Online glossary

FOR LECTURERS

- Instructor's manual
- PowerPoint slides
- Additional question and answer material

INTRODUCTION: THE UNDERLYING THEMES OF THIS BOOK

The title of this book needs some explaining, and in doing so we will hopefully make clear the overall focus of our approach. It was not so long ago that the term 'corporate social responsibility' was relatively unknown. In contrast, 'business ethics' for over two decades had been a growing field, covering a range of issues from company legitimacy through codes, governance and bribery, to areas such as duty and virtue.

In recent years the situation with these two terms has been, while not reversed, substantially corrected, so that today there are as many articles and books, if not more, using the terminology of corporate social responsibility as there are of business ethics. This growth, and the legitimation that it has engendered, has led to a gradual diversion of the two fields, to the extent that it has become a fair question to wonder whether there is sufficient connection between them to justify a single text.

Our view is that the two fields are distinct but linked by common themes, sufficiently so to justify a single text for students and professionals. One aim of this text is to make clear our vision of this separate-but-connected relationship between the fields. Later in this Introduction we will put flesh to the bones of this statement.

INTERNATIONAL FOCUS

First, however, we should indicate the main thematic considerations that run through the book. Notwithstanding the economic recession that has gripped the globe during the time we have been writing this text (2008 and the first half of 2009) it is clear that the economically related activity of human beings has become irrevocably worldwide in its operations, its impact, and its cultural and human meaning. So any discussion of ethics or responsibility with regard to business activity cannot, without an international perspective, pretend to cover the full range of issues. This is not quite so simple as it looks. Management theory in the Anglo-Saxon literature until very recently was dominated by US and, to a lesser extent, by UK material. More recently, the expansion of management education in mainland Europe – eastern as well as western Europe – has produced extremely important and innovative thinking beyond Anglo-Saxon traditions. However, both sets of literature have been written in the main by academics reared in those educational cultures, experienced in business in those economic environments, and sustained within academic networks that reflected the same backgrounds. So the material on ethics and responsibility in relation to business has not been able to avoid the colours and flavours of their respective approaches to both business and ethics. Not that there is necessarily anything wrong with these colours and flavours; simply that if these are dominant then they leave a lot of other important thinking out.

We have attempted to correct this potential imbalance, and achieve a degree of international overview, by a variety of means, including the use of cases that have an international dimension to them, using examples in the text drawn from beyond the developed economies, and making some use of research and concepts developed from academic sources other than the literatures referred to above. To write a truly international text on business ethics and corporate social responsibility is an ambitious aim, however, and it would be disingenuous for us to pretend that we have produced a completely international treatment, or that this is a culture-free text. It has been produced by two UK-based academics, written in the English language and with an Anglo-Saxon speaking readership as a primary target. We doubt that a completely international and culture-fair treatment of ethics in business is really possible, but the attempt to produce one will always remain important. This book, therefore, seeks an international, rather than regional, outlook, without pretension to a completely equal treatment of the fields on a worldwide basis.

DECISION-MAKING FOCUS

Another theme is a reflection of the question of whether such discussions should be *about* or *for* responsibility in business. By this is meant the perennial double aspect of management writing, research and education: namely, are we trying to produce as close as we can an accurate picture of this business-related field, or are we trying to develop material that will help practitioners be more effective in their work? To put this more epigrammatically – are we aiming to create truths or tools? Our answer to this is again deliberately ambitious, for we are really trying to address both needs: we are trying to reflect the key issues and problems in the area, while at the same time keeping in clear focus the challenges that these present for professional managers. This means that at times we look at organizational decisions from the inside – discussing cultures, motives, power structures and similar – and at other times we look at them from the outside, asking questions about legitimacy or impact. As a result, in addition to the occasional reference to traditional philosophical issues of right and wrong, there is a thematic undercurrent of the dependence of international practices of corporate responsibility on political concepts and the continuing evolution of international political relationships. This is certainly no more than an undercurrent, but it is no less important for being so, and it would misrepresent the argument of this book to ignore the assumptions and trends in politics that affect many aspects of the topics of this book.

Thematically then, a key perspective in this text is the focus on *decisions*. As with all management and organizational writing, decisions are central to the analysis. All organizational activity is the result of decisions taken individually or collectively by managers and others. The argument of this book is oriented around the nature of ethical decision making, the contexts – internal and external – in which managers and others make ethical decisions, the content of those decisions and their impacts in global as well as local terms.

One primary contextual issue often disregarded in business ethics or corporate social responsibility texts is that for most organizations *survival* is regarded as the overriding economic and practical necessity. And in market economies this is a matter of competing with other organizations for survival in an environment of limited and changing resources. Even where an organization may be flourishing, the uncertainties of markets, of resource availability and of state policy choices means that achievement of objectives is always perceived as a response to threats as much as a seizure of opportunity. In other words, the imagery of failure and extinction is rarely far away from managerial decision making. For this reason organizations are rarely explicitly altruistic – even though the values of their members may well be.

Internally, the survival imperative influences individuals' choices, their perceptions of organizational needs in relation to their values, and their influence over the behaviour of others either within or without the organization. This relates to issues such as value conflicts, peer pressures, the relation of individual values to the context of organizational needs, the management of cultures and the diversity of values. The survival imperative also critically affects how people work together in organizations, and how they are guided, supported and managed – a frequent complaint being that organizational needs take precedence over those of organizational members. Above all it affects the manner in which an organization is run from the very top, and how the overarching intentions of its senior managers influence and can transform – for good or ill – the behaviour and values of organizational members. Central to the manner in which organizations survive without being swamped by this imperative is how far they respect the rights of key stakeholders – internally (workers) as well as the many external stakeholders such as local residents, investors, regulators or customers. Rights figure in several places in this text as a key aspect of how organizations impact on different stakeholder groups.

Externally, individual values, plus the survival imperative of organizations, relate to the interrelationship between organizations – those that act as competitors as well as those that may be contributing as partners or clients. But these also relate to members of the wider community. Furthermore, each organization is also affected, in its turn, by an institutional context – the behaviour of those institutions that can create, modify or even constrain opportunities for an organization. So there are greater or lesser levels of competition, constraints or enablement created by government and other bodies, as well as needs and opportunities presented by non-state organizations. But it is important also to note that an organization has other impacts on a community than simply its stated goods and services; also relevant are how the local or global amenity of resources is exploited, and sometimes possibly reduced or damaged, and also important are the growing ways in which organizations try to 'put something back'.

These are not hermetically sealed arenas, however. Individuals can and do violate their personal values when dealing with external organizations. Equally, an organization trying to enhance its position within its context of institutional forces may well expect its individual members to behave in ways that may clash with their personal values. Internal and external factors interact and influence each other.

This discussion therefore helps us to identify a wide range of elements, all of which have a significant bearing on the responsibility of corporate decisions:

- the basic imperative of most organizations to survive, and the influence of this on corporate actions and attitudes
- individual values
- stakeholders
- rights
- ethical concepts
- the way in which firms are run at the highest levels
- the external and internal resource bases – uncertain and ever-fluctuating
- the ways in which organizational members are managed
- the measurement and management of values
- responsibility in operations
- the interrelationships, both supportive and competitive, between various organizations in the corporate context
- the roles of governments and other non-commercial players that create an institutional context for corporations

- corporate impacts on communities
- fair trading
- corporations putting something back.

These elements are incorporated into the content of this text at several levels. We present ethics and social responsibility in terms of the theoretical frameworks that define the issues, the organizational, institutional and global contexts within which these issues arise, and the business processes that represent the ways in which organizations respond to these issues as they arise in context.

FIGURE A Business ethics and corporate social responsibility in context

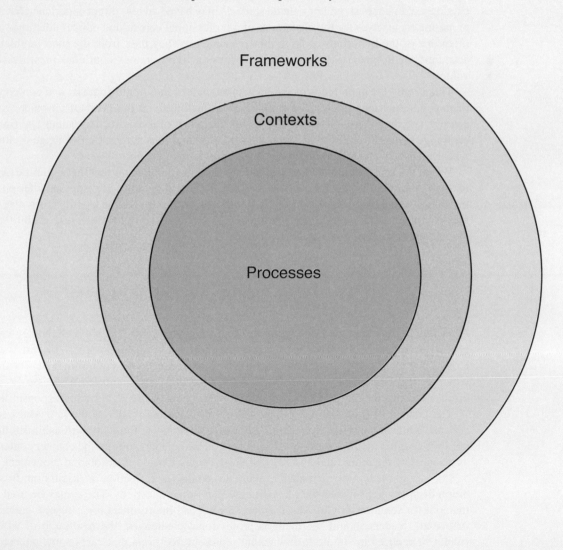

Each Part of the book reflects one of these dimensions, though it is important to acknowledge the inter-relationships that exist between frameworks, contexts and processes. The main intention of the book, then, is to provide the reader with sufficient sense of the context and of the central concepts, so that they can develop thier own formulations of the key issues and design their own responses to these.

WHO THIS BOOK IS AIMED AT

The primary intended readership of this text is the body of individuals studying business ethics and/or corporate social responsibility on intermediate to advanced undergraduate courses or at Masters level. Many individuals on MBA or similar programmes find themselves dealing in the classroom with situations analogous to their day-to-day professional experience. In contrast, undergraduate students may have had less direct experience but are preparing themselves for the challenges of a professional career, and ethical dilemmas are often one of the first kinds of issue they encounter as they pass from the more regulated academic environment into one where business activity creates continual pressures on values.

This is why the main focus of the book is on understanding the contexts and content of managerial decisions in ethical terms. Decision making is at the heart of all managerial activity, and the examination of decisions in the context of issues such as values and rights can range across the entirety of corporate activities, and thus across the full range of areas where managers and others might be called upon to take action.

We do not offer solutions to ethical dilemmas in this book – we feel that organizational reality is too multifarious for set solutions to be appropriate, and, as discussed later on in the book, sometimes situations are just too novel, too unusual, for existing formulae to apply. Instead, what we try to do is bring out the key issues of ethics and responsibility as they might manifest themselves in decisions.

HOW TO APPROACH THIS BOOK

After this Introduction the book is divided into three parts. Part I deals with the key conceptual frameworks of corporate social responsibility and business ethics. In Part II we look at the main contexts – global, political, organizational and environmental – within which ethical decisions may be made. Finally, in the third part – entitled 'Processes' – we discuss some of the more specific organizational aspects of managing with responsibility.

The content of each chapter is intended to introduce the reader to the key issues and debates, while at the same time eliciting critical evaluation of these, as well as illustrating our own position on the issues. We strongly encourage readers to treat the chapter contents as a source of reference, and as a starting point for their own reflection and judgement.

Located in the text of each chapter there are points for reflection or discussion. In addition each chapter finishes with a short case plus some questions. These may be used as material for seminars or class discussions, or even as opportunities for assessed analysis. Above all, readers should see them as professional challenges, the resolution of which cannot be reduced to simple formulae, but represent decisions that carry some degree of risk in professional as well as ethical terms.

FRAMEWORKS

FIGURE A1 Business ethics and corporate social responsibility

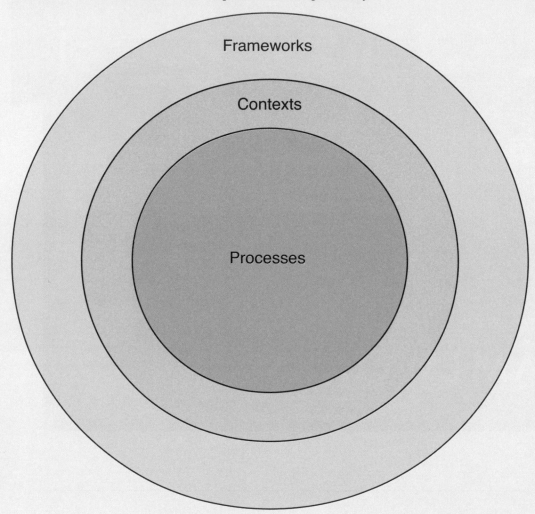

In the first part of this book we are mainly concerned with the key concepts that inform and frame debates and practices relating to ethics and responsibility as they apply in the corporate world. These concepts appear in various forms in succeeding parts of the book, reflecting different ways of implementing practice, different strategies for dealing with ethical or social issues relating to business, and different ways of interpreting the context within which these issues may arise.

The key elements that are presented in Part I are the general issue of responsibility, the characteristic ethical positions that may be adopted, the manner in which the main players in ethical contexts are depicted and, finally, the different approaches taken to the relationship between business and the natural world. Of these, the first two are about how the field as a whole is understood, while the third and fourth are about specific, but highly important, areas for decision.

As indicated in the Introduction, the intention of this book is to place corporate social responsibility and business ethics in a global context. The concepts discussed do not represent comprehensive coverage of every different possible interpretation of corporate social responsibility or ethics. Rather they are intended to generate an understanding of the political, social *and* philosophical bases of the debate. All too often discussions of business ethics or corporate social responsibility are informed by a narrow business-strategic intent, without an understanding of the political context within which social issues are conceived. Or, there is a close attention to the niceties of philosophical debate without a recognition of the social context that gives colour to philosophical considerations. This first part of the book is intended to help the reader bring the various different conceptual frameworks to bear on issues of business in society, bearing in mind that there is no fixed formula for this, and that every professional worker has their own unique take on issues of what is right or wrong in business.

Chapter 1 therefore looks directly at the concepts of corporate social responsibility, and the different meanings and interpretations that have been given to this term. Chapter 2 examines stakeholders and stakeholder management – the primary way in which the key actors of the corporate social responsibility and business ethics' agendas are understood and evaluated. Chapter 3 presents the key ethical positions – the building blocks of debates and arguments over right and wrong in business – while Chapter 4 looks specifically at the contrasting ways of understanding the environment. This latter is less generic than the preceding chapters, but is placed here because it is more properly a conceptual area, distinguishing it from the later chapter on environmental practices.

UNDERSTANDING CORPORATE SOCIAL RESPONSIBILITY

LEARNING OBJECTIVES

After studying this chapter you should be able to:

- Offer an explanation of the emergence of corporate social responsibility in relation to the evolving role of business in society.
- Reflect on the concept of corporate social responsibility, taking account of different definitions of the term.
- Describe and assess a model of corporate social responsibility.
- Identify and evaluate the key arguments for and against the concept of corporate social responsibility.
- Critically discuss the concept of corporate citizenship.

INTRODUCTION

Central to the whole range of concepts and issues relating to businesses and their role in society is the concept of corporate social responsibility. It is a term that has become very popular in recent years and thereby vulnerable to suffering the same fate as other popular terms in management literature, namely that they become so overused that their real sense degenerates until they can be applied to almost anything. Because of this, it is useful to briefly consider where the idea of corporate social responsibility came from and how it has developed. We will also examine the genesis of the term, its meaning and its application to business activity. The chapter concludes with a discussion of a recent development related to corporate social responsibility – the idea of corporate citizenship.

EMERGENCE OF CORPORATE SOCIAL RESPONSIBILITY

Various texts in ancient times included material suggesting that moral obligations existed for those engaging in trade and commerce. In modern times, the first substantial publications on the role of business in society can be traced to as early as the 1930s,[1] but corporate social responsibility emerged as an area of general concern for companies only in the 1960s.[2] The emergence of the new field reflected increasing pressures placed on companies to assume a greater responsibility for correcting the harmful impacts of their operations, a role traditionally performed by society as a whole. Companies, particularly in the United States, experienced public scrutiny regarding a variety of issues, including the support of repressive regimes in Southern America, discrimination against women and other minorities, and product safety.[3] At the same time, the growth of the green movement placed a spotlight on the impact of commercial activity on the natural environment.[4] In this context, corporate social responsibility was seen as a method of self-regulation distinct from both government legislation and managerial ethics.[5] Corporate social responsibility was therefore a way in which the business community reacted to the concerns raised by various groups rather than something imposed on business by external actors.

By the 1980s governments had introduced legislation on many of the issues that had led to the emergence of corporate social responsibility in the 1960s. To take one illustration of this trend, most European and North American countries had passed laws forbidding gender or race discrimination in employment. At the same time, however, and possibly due to this very success, concern for corporate social responsibility seemed to be declining. In contrast, the notion of shareholder value, with its direct emphasis on just one group of stakeholders, began to undermine and supplant the attention to corporate social responsibility evident in the 1960s. The rise of shareholder thinking reflected the era of neo-liberal policies of the Reagan and Thatcher administrations. It also mirrored the fact that during the early 1980s uncertainty in the external environment was caused by economic and financial factors such as deregulation and foreign competition rather than by social and political demands placed on companies.

ETHICS IN PRACTICE

COCA-COLA BUYS INNOCENT

Innocent is a young company selling fruit smoothies and other healthy drinks. It was launched by three Cambridge graduates in the United Kingdom and named Innocent to reflect the healthiness of its product range. The entrepreneurs behind Innocent had difficulties in finding funding for their business idea, but the company soon became successful and held 20 per cent of a market worth £20 million. It also had a reputation of being organic and fun, partially due to its delivery vehicles that are painted to resemble cows. In 2009 it sold 10–20 per cent of its shares to Coca-Cola in order to pay for an expansion in Europe. Critics saw this move as a sell-out to a corporate giant that did not share Innocent's values on natural ingredients. Innocent defended its decision by maintaining that its business principles were not changing; instead, it was given an opportunity to affect the values of a much larger company. What is your view on this? Did Innocent sell its soul?

Source: Sweeney, M. 2009. Innocent drinks sell stake to Coca-Cola. *The Guardian*, 6 April 2009. Available from www.guardian.co.uk, accessed 26 July 2009.

However, if attention on corporate social responsibility was comparatively modest in the 1980s and early 1990s, many factors have contributed to a renewed interest in the topic since the mid-1990s. This interest has been driven by the increased demands voiced by civil society groups, both for the broader distribution of business benefits and for better management of the effects of corporate operations in society. These demands have been placed on companies rather than on governments as the latter have been under pressure to curb their expenses.[6] Vulnerable to reputation damage, companies have provided a convenient target for pressure groups that have used modern communication technologies, including the internet, to promote their arguments.[7]

The most recent wave of interest in corporate social responsibility has been marked by some new developments. First, the debate is now more about how to make substantial commitments rather than whether to make them at all.[8] This shift is illustrated by a number of concrete and specific initiatives on corporate social responsibility including ethical sourcing, social audits, stakeholder dialogue and ranking companies in relation to socially responsible investing criteria (for instance, the Dow Jones Sustainability Index and the FTSE4Good Index). Secondly, there has been an increasing interest in the topic in Europe where not only businesses but also governments have engaged in the debate and launched initiatives on corporate social responsibility. This contrasts with the 1960s when corporate social responsibility was mainly a North American phenomenon.

THINKING CRITICALLY ABOUT ETHICS

THE FUTURE OF CORPORATE SOCIAL RESPONSIBILITY

One implication of the discussion in the first section of this chapter is that a concept such as corporate social responsibility has evolved in parallel with the fortunes of the economy. This could suggest that corporate social responsibility is not a fundamental requirement for business to act ethically, but only a periodically relevant brake on corporate excess.

The counter-argument to this is that it is not that corporate social responsibility is more or less relevant as the economic cycle changes, but simply that attention paid to it varies in time with the changes in economic and social conditions.

However, ideas are only as valuable as the era in which they exist allows them to be. One of the great challenges with corporate social responsibility is to encourage managers and others to have the issue on their agenda in both hard times and good times.

In this section, then, we have seen how corporate social responsibility has evolved and oscillated in influence in response to how economic and social factors have affected business performance. What this implies for further development of the concept is not clear – certainly the continuing emphasis on brand integrity and the impact of modern (i.e. corporately created) life on the environment suggest that the concept is likely to remain embedded as a key element of corporate perception and performance for many years to come.

DEFINING CORPORATE SOCIAL RESPONSIBILITY

One might expect in the light of the discussion above that the concept of corporate social responsibility has been clearly defined, but the field has suffered from the lack of a commonly accepted definition. As will be seen, the conceptual debate reached an impasse in the

1970s with many authors commenting on how the term lacked substance while being used to express general concern over the role of business in society. The impasse was resolved to some extent by Archie Carroll's 1979 model of corporate social responsibility (discussed in the next section). Since then, the emergence of other terms, including sustainability and corporate citizenship, have captured the attention of the research community.

At its broadest level, corporate social responsibility can be defined as the accommodation of corporate behaviour to society's values and expectations. According to Howard Bowen,[9] corporate social responsibility is an obligation that arises from the impact corporate decisions and actions have on the lives of people. Bowen argued that because of this impact, companies should conduct their business in line with the objectives and values of the societies in which they operate. Corporate social responsibility therefore refers to the 'obligations of businessmen to pursue those policies, to make those decisions, or to follow those lines of action which are desirable in terms of the objectives and values of our society'. Defined in this way, corporate social responsibility is about ensuring that corporate activity advances, rather than conflicts with, generally accepted norms.

The view that companies should accommodate their behaviour to societal values and expectations has been challenged by a number of authors who argue that not all demands placed on companies are reasonable and well founded.[10] Others have similarly posited that '[b]eing responsive does not necessarily mean the same thing as being responsible'.[11] Indeed, being responsive to the expectations of certain groups can be deemed as irresponsible by others. The experience of those German companies that complied with the policies of the Nazi regime demonstrates that companies should be critical about the demands placed on them. This is why some authors have insisted that socially responsible corporate behaviour needs to rest on principles that 'express something fundamental that people believe is true'.[12] On this view, then, companies should be responsive only to those expectations and demands that are consistent with some commonly recognized moral principles.

Researchers have also argued that corporate social responsibility refers to corporate behaviour that extends beyond economic motives and legal requirements. This view suggests that corporate social responsibility concerns the acceptance of voluntary or additional responsibilities beyond those motivated by economic interests and the law.[13] Davis, for example, defined corporate social responsibility as 'the firm's consideration of, and response to, issues beyond the narrow economic, technical, and legal requirements of the firm'.[14] Nevertheless, a debate still exists as to whether corporate social responsibility pertains to *all* corporate activity or only activity that is driven by other than economic interests and legal requirements.[15] No consensus therefore has emerged on the nature of the behaviour that should be considered as corporate social responsibility.

ETHICS IN PRACTICE

AL JAZEERA PRESENTS *CORPORATIONS ON TRIAL*

Al Jazeera is a news network based in Qatar. Its willingness to broadcast dissenting views has made it popular in the Middle East and, more recently, worldwide. Al Jazeera gained international recognition after the terrorist attacks of 11 September 2001 in the United States for broadcasting video statements by Osama bin Laden and other terrorist leaders. Despite this, Al Jazeera is seen as a politically independent news network that produces cutting edge documentaries and news programmes.

In 2009, Al Jazeera showed a five-part series on lawsuits brought against multinational companies. The lawsuits demonstrate how a relatively small number of lawyers can challenge the way in which companies operate in foreign countries.

The topics covered in the series varied from environmental dumping in Ivory Coast to killings of labour union activists in Colombia. Juliana Ruhfus, the reporter behind the series, says that Al Jazeera decided to focus on the topic to show how lawsuits can change corporate behaviour on a global scale. The makers of the series also believe that the cases will have important implications on how companies operate around the world.

One of the documentaries focuses on Chiquita's links to the killings and disappearances carried out by paramilitary groups in Colombia. Chiquita has admitted making payments to paramilitaries and was fined US$25 million by the US government for funding a terrorist organization. The company has defended its payments by claiming that the paramilitaries threatened to kill its employees, but paramilitary commanders have denied this and alleged that Chiquita made payments in order to provide security for their banana plantations. In the Al Jazeera documentary, one paramilitary leader confesses to murdering 70 people in one year to avert strikes and disruption among plantation workers. It is alleged that over 3000 people were killed by the Banana Block that provided security for Chiquita. The company has now sold its subsidiary in Colombia, but it has been sued by family members who lost their relatives in the killings.

The *Corporations on Trial* series is available on YouTube.

Source: Al Jazeera (2009). Available from http://english.aljazeera.net/programmes/peopleandpower/2009/05/200951912718478492.html, accessed 21 July 2009.

The lack of a commonly shared conceptual basis has led to a wide and non-specific use of the terminology, which in turn has led to a degradation of the concept as a management and research tool. Sethi, for example, noted that '[t]he phrase *corporate social responsibility* has been used in so many different contexts that it has lost all meaning', while Clarkson highlighted this weakness further by stating that corporate social responsibility and its related concepts, social responsiveness and social performance, 'carry no clear meaning and remain elusive constructs'.[16] Zenisek (1979) summed up the multitude of meanings given to the concept as follows:

The term means something, but not always the same thing, to just about everyone. To some it conveys the idea of legal responsibility or liability; to others it means socially responsible behaviour in an ethical sense; to still others the meaning transmitted is that of 'responsible for' in a causal mode; many simply equate it with 'charitable contributions'; many of those who embrace it see it as a mere synonym for 'legitimacy'; a few see it as a sort of fiduciary duty.[17]

The definitional debate on corporate social responsibility peaked in the 1960s and 1970s. Thereafter, other related concepts have appeared and generated discussion of the role of business in society. In the 1980s researchers focused on developing the notion of 'corporate social performance',[18] while in the late 1990s the concept of 'corporate citizenship'[19] emerged to mark a renewed interest in the relationship between business and society. However, despite the rise of the new concepts and lack of shared conceptual basis, the term corporate social responsibility is still widely used and serves as a reference point for the more recently introduced concepts. Perhaps its very strength is that variety of meanings that Zenisek and others critiqued, as this provides opportunities to link it with many different aspects of business.

CARROLL'S PYRAMID OF CORPORATE SOCIAL RESPONSIBILITY

One of the most popular definitions of corporate social responsibility was presented by Archie Carroll in 1979. According to Carroll, corporate social responsibility involves the *expectations* that society has of business. As the expectations placed on companies evolve over time and across countries, social responsibility becomes a continuous process of the accommodation of corporate behaviour to societal expectations. Any corporate activity

ETHICS AND YOU

BOUNDARIES OF CORPORATE SOCIAL RESPONSIBILITY

How far can expectations of corporate social responsibility go? Where should one draw the line between what is a reasonable requirement of corporate social responsibility and what is not? These questions go to the heart of the corporate social responsibility debate – opponents suggest that corporate social responsibility is a voluntary concept, while adherents sometimes speak as if businesses have to comply with ethical requirements to obtain a 'licence to operate'.

should therefore be assessed against the expectations placed on companies. Carroll also argued that a definition of corporate social responsibility should encompass the entire range of expectations placed on companies, including economic, legal, ethical and philanthropic responsibilities:

- **Economic responsibilities.** The primary responsibility of companies is to produce goods and services in a way that is profitable to their owners. Companies also offer employment and career opportunities and in this way form the basic economic unit of modern society. All the other responsibilities are underpinned by this economic role of business in society.

- **Legal responsibilities.** While assuming their fundamental economic role, companies are expected to comply with the laws and regulations that reflect society's values and norms. Legal expectations apply to companies as juristic entities that can act as persons for some purposes, but also to individuals in their role as employees irrespective of the responsibilities they have in an organization.

- **Ethical responsibilities.** Businesses are also expected to abide by the ethical norms of society. Carroll argues that because these norms are not written in law, they are more ambiguous than legal requirements and therefore more difficult for companies to anticipate and follow. Nevertheless, there is an inherent link between legal and ethical responsibilities because ethical expectations can be seen to underpin and predict the emergence of new laws and regulations. For example, social movements including the ones promoting women's rights and the natural environment have advocated values that have been later codified into law.

- **Philanthropic responsibilities.** Finally, business may engage in activities that go beyond the expectations of society. These activities include volunteer work, sponsorship of philanthropic projects, and donations to public and non-profit organizations such as sports clubs. Even though lack of engagement in discretionary activities is not perceived as irresponsible, it is quite common for companies to carry out such roles in society, particularly in local communities.

Carroll (1991) himself presented the four different types of responsibilities in the form of a pyramid as shown in Figure 1.1, but the responsibilities are not in any way consecutive or cumulative, nor are they mutually exclusive. It is therefore possible that a company satisfies the ethical expectations placed on it, but fails to meet its legal responsibilities that are lower down in the pyramid. Moreover, any single action by a company may embody or conflict with more than one of the responsibilities. For example, a decision to pull out from a repressive regime may meet the ethical expectations placed on a company, but be against its economic interests. Carroll's four-part model is therefore useful in distinguishing and clarifying the motives and contradictions behind corporate behaviour, but it would not work to predict corporate behaviour or indicate priorities for decision making.

Carroll's intention with his model of corporate social responsibility was 'to bring into the fold those who have argued against social responsibility'.[20] One of the most influential arguments against corporate social responsibility at the time was presented by Milton Friedman,[21] who argued that managers should 'make as much money as possible while conforming to the basic rules of society, both those embodied in law and those embodied in ethical custom.' Even though Friedman acknowledged that 'ethical custom' should be taken into account, he

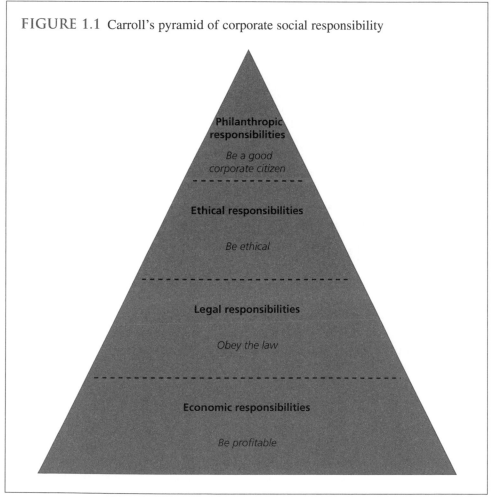

FIGURE 1.1 Carroll's pyramid of corporate social responsibility

Philanthropic responsibilities

Be a good corporate citizen

Ethical responsibilities

Be ethical

Legal responsibilities

Obey the law

Economic responsibilities

Be profitable

Source: Carroll (1991).

was seen to challenge the idea of corporate social responsibility by promoting the view that the main social responsibility of companies was to maximize profits – thus placing him squarely in the camp of those who advocated shareholder value as the key aim of business activity. Carroll's definition of corporate social responsibility addressed Friedman's challenge by acknowledging the primacy of profitability, but also accommodated views that saw social responsibility as something that went beyond economic and legal considerations. His four-part model can therefore be seen as successfully encompassing a range of concerns and definitions of social responsibility, and to an extent bridging the gap between those in favour of corporate social responsibility and those with misgivings over the idea.

Despite the popularity of Carroll's four-part model, it has some limitations. First, the boundaries between the categories are not always clear. For example, it is difficult to use the model to analyse a company that carries out philanthropic activities with the expectation of improving its reputation and thereby economic performance. Should these activities therefore be categorized as satisfying economic rather than philanthropic responsibilities? Secondly, the model does not indicate what to do when different types of expectations conflict. For example, what should a company do when one set of stakeholders is asking it to allow its workers to organize in a country where unions are banned and therefore illegal? Should it comply with the social expectations that reflect international standards and best practice or local legislation? Carroll's model does not give us an answer. Also, the model does not provide ethical principles against which societal expectations or corporate behaviour can be assessed, and can therefore be criticized for allowing behaviour that is generally seen as unethical (think about the example of companies collaborating with the Nazi regime). Finally, the model does not seem to separate out corporate social responsibility from other types of corporate behaviour. For example, the model could be interpreted as allowing us to refer to profit-seeking as socially responsible activity. This, however, goes against what is generally meant by the term corporate social responsibility. Carroll's model therefore, although useful in terms of categorizing aspects of business activity, fails to shed light on the specific nature of corporate social responsibility and does not sufficiently acknowledge that distinct but related concerns are often raised when companies prioritize economic interests to other motives.

ARGUMENTS FOR AND AGAINST CORPORATE SOCIAL RESPONSIBILITY

Many corporate social responsibility activists like to dismiss the arguments presented against corporate social responsibility. For example, Simon Zadek, the head of London-based AccountAbility, says that 'the "whether in principle" conversation about corporate social responsibility is over. What remains is "What, specifically, and how?"'[22] Nevertheless, the recent publication of various articles and books that consider arguments against corporate social responsibility shows that the debate is very much alive.[23] Historically, discussion on the benefits and drawbacks of corporate social responsibility was particularly strong in the 1970s when Milton Friedman and others representing the free-market right criticized the idea. The debate re-emerged in the mid-1990s when a number of corporate scandals gave rise to renewed interest in corporate social responsibility.

Many arguments presented for and against the concept refer to the impact of corporate social responsibility on corporate performance. Others are based on more normative statements about the role of business in society. The following sub-sections identify some of the main areas of disagreement about the effects of corporate social responsibility on individual companies and society at large.

Profit maximization

As noted earlier, Milton Friedman and others advanced the idea of shareholder value being in conflict with corporate social responsibility. According to their view, companies are misusing the resources entrusted to them if they engage in corporate social responsibility. Social involvement is costly and may dilute companies' focus on economic activity and hence their productive role in society. In contrast, others[24] have argued that it is in the interest of business and its owners to comply with societal values and take an active role in society as this is in line with the long-term interest of business. Companies that are responsive to the expectations of various societal groups will, on this alternative view, benefit from resulting goodwill and attract high-quality employees; furthermore, corporate social responsibility has a positive effect on reputation, through which companies can gain more customers, employees and other benefits.

Resource fit

A second area of dispute is the role of business in addressing social problems. It may be argued that business has valuable resources that could be used to tackle social problems. For example, business is credited with generating management talent and innovation, two resources not traditionally associated with the provision of social services. These resources could be used to address social problems, for example by helping with the management of operational performance. It has however been argued in opposition to this that while companies may possess significant competences, they lack the *specific* knowledge, skills and experience needed to deal with societal problems – knowledge such as the particular technical expertise to communicate effectively with highly disadvantaged clients. As two writers put it, social initiatives by companies are like 'using a dishwasher to wash clothes'.[25]

Lack of accountability

Because of their ownership structure, companies are mainly accountable to their shareholders rather than to society at large. The public cannot therefore hold companies to account in the same way as they may with democratically elected governments. This is why some have argued that companies should not engage in social activities and why business should focus on pursuing economic profit rather than performing other roles in society. By engaging in well-meaning corporate social responsibility, companies merely become paternalistic, unaccountable rulers. The proponents of this view have therefore argued that corporate social responsibility undermines democracy – part of this argument being that in the case of unethical or irresponsible practice by business, it is the responsibility of the prevailing government to reform those regulations that have allowed companies to misbehave in the first place.[26] According to this view, corporate social responsibility is bad not because it prevents the free operation of markets, but because it diverts attention from government, which is the body that should control the markets for the benefit of society.

The 'Iron Law of Responsibility'

Finally, Davis has propounded what he called the 'Iron Law of Responsibility',[27] which suggests that companies will lose their power if they do not act responsibly. For him, social power and social responsibility go hand in hand – the underpinning idea here being that power needs to be exercised in a certain way for it to be retained. It is therefore in the interest of businesses to use their power in a way that satisfies other societal actors. Should they

THINKING CRITICALLY ABOUT ETHICS

WHEN DOES CORPORATE SOCIAL RESPONSIBILITY PAY OFF?

A common argument presented by many who support corporate social responsibility and the value of business ethics is that 'good behaviour is good business'. Using examples such as damage to reputation and trust, some would argue that an irresponsible organization eventually loses the support of its key stakeholders, and therefore suffers. Davis' argument on power mentioned earlier is a version of this. There is an important assumption here, though, that what can be argued in the long term can be applied to short-term situations. In reality, some unethical behaviour may not get its just deserts within a normal lifetime, and only long afterwards is there any retribution for what has been done.

   Does this mean that the principle is not worth bothering with? If we cannot see it apply over the timescale of ordinary individual careers, does it have any value?

not do so, other groups will move to restrain the power of business to operate in a way that is seen as harmful by other groups in society. In this context, corporate social responsibility can be seen as a way for business to avoid government regulation and other limitations to their flexibility. The vast majority of business leaders regard the ability to respond quickly to changes in the commercial environment as central to their survival, and therefore anything that might restrict flexibility can appear as a threat. Such limitations can also be costly as companies may be expected to implement new measures to comply with regulatory or other initiatives. For example, it has been estimated that the US financial and governance regulations generally known as the Sarbanes-Oxley Act cost one large firm over US$1 million in the year 2003 alone.[28]

SOCIAL RESPONSIVENESS AND PERFORMANCE

We have seen in this chapter that many authors have engaged in the conceptual and normative debate on corporate social responsibility, but what do companies actually *do* to behave responsibly? The concept of social responsiveness emerged in the 1970s to highlight the shift in focus from the earlier normative and conceptual interest in corporate social responsibility to one that considered what companies were actually doing in this respect. Responsiveness is therefore about doing something rather than discussing what should be done, and the concept of social responsiveness complements the normative concept of corporate social responsibility by adding an action dimension to it.

   There are several examples of the way in which corporate social responsiveness may be elaborated. For example, Carroll (1979) defines responsiveness as 'the managerial processes of response' and identifies a number of processes that contribute to the degree of a company's overall responsiveness – planning and social forecasting, social decision making and social policy, and organizing for social response. The extent to which companies engage in these processes and hence social responsiveness can thus be described on a continuum from doing nothing to doing much. Similarly to Carroll, Wartick and Cochran (1985) have defined social responsiveness as 'the approach to realising social responsibility'. However, rather than looking at components of this, they proposed a typology of different approaches: (1) reactive, (2) defensive, (3) accommodative and (4) proactive. Wartick and Cochran thus view responsiveness

ETHICS IN PRACTICE

APPLYING WARTICK AND COCHRANE IN PRACTICE – FOUR EXAMPLES

- **Reactive** – McDonald's rigidly adhered to a policy of not offering vegetarian burgers for several decades; only when the 'mad cow' health scare of the mid-1990s affected customer demand for beef products did they relent.

- **Defensive** – Several tobacco firms have aggressively attempted to undermine the well-established scientific links between smoking and cancer in a bid to avert public disapproval, at least to a sufficient degree to enable them to switch their marketing to countries where the relevant knowledge is less well recognized within the population.

- **Accommodative** – Firms in many countries in Europe have ensured that their employment policies conform to the various protections required under EU legislation (within Europe, that is). In other areas of the world they adopt different policies, depending on how restrictive local legislation is.

- **Proactive** – Toyota has developed the 'Prius' model, which runs on hybrid fuel, much cleaner than any petrol or diesel-powered car. The model was not initially successful and has hardly met its costs, but the firm has persisted in the belief that this is a car for the future.

as a company's general approach towards corporate social responsibility, whereas Carroll attempts to specify the actual processes and activities involved in responsiveness.[29]

Social responsiveness has figured in the development of the related concept of corporate social performance. Discussions of corporate social performance tend to organize the field of corporate social responsibility around a variety of themes, thus providing a framework for assessing corporate behaviour against criteria.[30] In this context, corporate social responsibility is viewed as a normative concept that provides a basis for the evaluation of corporate action and its outcomes. As a result, social performance can be related to the manner and extent to which a company makes use of processes of responsiveness to realize principles of corporate social responsibility. Social responsibility and responsiveness can therefore be seen as concepts that are inherently interconnected. Relatively little research exists in this area, but Donna Wood[31] has identified three types of observable outcomes that can help demonstrate how companies perform in the area of corporate social responsibility. Taken together, the outcomes contribute towards a theory of how corporate social responsibility might be measured in organizational practice:

- **Corporate social policies** are formal statements or informal practices and ways of behaving that reflect organizational values and principles. As will be seen in Chapter 10, many companies have adopted formal policies in the areas of ethics and corporate social responsibility. The way in which informal policies emerge from organizational culture and other organizational, individual and situational factors is discussed in Chapter 11.

- **Social programmes** concern the allocation of corporate resources to some activity that the company views as socially desirable. Such programmes can include one-shot ventures, longer-term projects or institutional arrangements that promote social goals. For example, Nokia provides training in information technology for young people in Colombia. Even though this training is linked to the company's product portfolio, it also facilitates access to education and thereby contributes to social development.[32]

THINKING CRITICALLY ABOUT ETHICS

MEASURING SOCIAL RESPONSIVENESS

We shall look in more detail at the question of measurement later, but for the moment it is worth noting that measurement is not a neutral activity, but a highly political one, in any organization. It is critically affected by:

- who decides to make the measurement
- what is selected for measurement
- when the measurements are made
- how the measurements are made (and can they be subverted)
- what account is taken of the measurements.

So the Wood model, while a useful guide, is itself still subject to the various political pressures that affect all organizational processes.

A more extreme example of this may be seen with some companies whose very business idea promotes a social rather than a financial goal. Ethical trade, for example, is based on the principle of making trade more profitable for the producers in developing countries.

- **Social impacts** refer to the effect of corporate behaviour on society. Following Wood, we can see this as a cycle through which issues come to public awareness and give rise to concerns over corporate behaviour; eventually this creates pressure on corporations, and as a result they respond by behaving more responsibly. Once the cycle is completed, public concerns focus elsewhere and so the process continues. However, although this is theoretically a logical sequence, in practice the problem with considering the impact of business activity on society is in *isolating* the impact of business from the impact of other actors and events. Social events are complex, with a tangled mesh of antecedents and consequences, and for some of these it may not be clear even whether they have some causal relationship or not.

CORPORATE CITIZENSHIP

The term 'corporate citizenship' emerged in the mid-1990s and was first used by business leaders to refer to their activities in local communities.[33] It therefore initially pertained to philanthropic activity and community relations rather than a broader set of corporate responsibilities and roles in society. It has been particularly popular among the business community in the belief that it has a more positive connotation than the notion of corporate social responsibility.

The introduction of fresh terminology such as 'citizenship' has not made the field clearer. In many cases the language of corporate citizenship has not replaced the language of corporate social responsibility. Instead, the term is often used in the same sense as corporate social responsibility, which has resulted in an unclear relationship between the two concepts. What is more, other concepts, including sustainability, have gained popularity at the expense of the older terms. Consequently, 'citizenship' is increasingly used as a metaphor in corporate publications and the press but as a theoretical construct in academic literature.

The concept of citizenship has been applied to companies in two principal ways. Researchers from the United States have developed the concept of corporate citizenship on the basis of viewing companies as actors that share characteristics with natural persons.[34] In contrast, researchers at Nottingham University have developed an analysis of the idea of corporate citizenship based on the observation that businesses are increasingly assuming roles that have been traditionally performed by governments.[35] This school of thought therefore compares the role of companies with that of governments rather than with individual human beings. In the following two sub-sections, these two main ways of interpreting the concept of corporate citizenship are reviewed in more detail.

Companies as individual citizens

The concept of citizenship defines the relationship between the individual and the state.[36] Accordingly, the individual has rights that are protected and maintained by the state against other individuals and actors. For example, individuals can be argued to have the right to own private property and the corresponding duty to respect the same right held by other members of society. It has been argued that similarly to individuals, companies have a set of rights and duties as members of communities.[37] This interpretation of corporate citizenship is based on viewing companies as actors that are similar to human beings. Several legal systems have granted 'person' status to companies, most notably the United States and, in a slightly different way, the United Kingdom. As artificial persons, the rights and duties of a firm are however limited and differ from those of natural persons. For example, companies cannot really have a right to life in the same way as human beings.

Whether the rights and duties of companies go beyond what is required by the law is a similar discussion to the one that has taken place with regard to corporate social responsibility. It appears, however, that that there is a tendency to define the term in a narrow sense according to which companies are expected to obey the law and pay their taxes, but where their contribution to solving social problems is voluntary and therefore praised as being over and above their specific duty when it happens.

Wood and Logsdon have promoted a more substantial interpretation of citizenship in the context of business organizations by introducing the terminology of 'business citizenship'. As can be seen in Figure 1.2, this term refers to companies as global rather than local or national actors. Because the rights and responsibilities of companies are likely to vary from one country to another, Wood and Logsdon argue that there is a need for 'hypernorms' (see box) that take precedence over local and national norms. Companies that operate globally should comply with these hypernorms rather than national norms if the

'HYPERNORMS'

Coined by Thomas Donaldson, the term 'hypernorm' refers to a fundamental 'global' value that is culture-independent, so that it can act as a criterion for evaluating more localized values and ethical principles.

FIGURE 1.2 Four states of citizenship

		Level of analysis	
		Local or national	Global or universal
Unit of analysis	The individual person as citizen	**The individual citizen** Relationship of the person to the state; rights and duties of citizens; national and cultural identity	**The universal citizen** Common humanity; interdependence; universalism; based on philosophical ideas instead of laws
	The business organization as citizen	**The corporate citizen** Business a responsible player in its local environments; organization's rights and duties in and for the community	**The business citizen** Business as a responsible local and global actor; rights and duties within and across national borders; hypernorms

Source: Wood & Logsdon (2001).

two are in conflict, and thereby avoid accusations of 'bad citizenship' outside their home countries. Human rights standards as defined in the Universal Declaration of Human Rights could be, for example, regarded as a basis for such hypernorms. The Universal Declaration and its criticism is discussed in more detail in Chapter 7.

Companies as state-like providers of rights

The Nottingham school argues that companies are increasingly performing roles that have been traditionally linked to governments. This is particularly happening when governments fail to fulfil their functions with regard to the protection and enabling of rights held by individuals. Instead of aligning companies with individual citizens, the Nottingham school therefore views companies as state-like bodies that protect and provide rights conventionally administered by governments: the 'definition reframes CC away from the notion that the corporation is a citizen in itself as individuals are, and towards the acknowledgement that the corporation administers certain aspects of citizenship for those individuals.'[38]

The implication of this position is that even though governments are still the main protectors and providers of citizenship rights, companies have taken over significant responsibility for supplying such rights. This trend has occurred in both developed and developing countries, though for slightly differing reasons. In Western countries the change has taken place in the context of the neo-liberal policies of the 1980s that focused on diminishing the role of governments in providing welfare, as well as on privatizing and outsourcing public services to private sector organizations. In developing countries, on the other hand, companies have often acted because governments have been unable or unwilling to guarantee citizenship rights.

Rights are themselves a much debated concept, but they are often associated with the ideas of positive and negative freedom – the positive indicating *freedom* to do something, the negative being *freedom from* some restriction. In what follows, we can see illustrations of how companies contribute to the enjoyment of social, civil and political rights. The examples relate to the activities of a French oil company, Total, in Burma/Myanmar:[39]

- **Social rights** provide individuals with the *freedom to* realize their human potential and aims in life. They include the right to education, health and general welfare as well as the right to work. Companies can play a role in the provision of social rights by carrying out activities that enable individuals to access services in the areas of healthcare, education and cultural events. Many companies have run social programmes that have facilitated such access. For example, notwithstanding the well-publicized abuses of human rights conducted by the Burmese government, the social programme operated in Burma by Total has seen the renovation of 50 schools, the building of health centres, a series of campaigns on vaccination, the drilling of some 800 wells to improve the quality of drinking water, and the financing of animal farming and crop production aimed at developing economic activity in the country. In this way, Total has contributed to the social rights of the villagers living in the area covered by the social programme.

- **Civil rights** protect the individual against interference that makes them unable to enjoy their rights. This absence of restraint is, as referred to above, *freedom from* activities or restrictions that prevent people from exercising their rights. Civil rights include the right to own private property, freedom from torture and other degrading treatment, and freedom of speech. Companies can play a role in enhancing the provision of civil rights by facilitating the enjoyment of these rights by individuals. For example, Total provided assistance to Burmese villagers whose property had been appropriated by the Burmese army. This assistance involved both monetary donations and in-kind contributions such as boats and buffalo carts to replace the property requisitioned by the army. The company also asked the army to change its behaviour towards those inhabiting the vicinity of the pipeline, thereby helping people to enjoy their rights to personal freedom and private property.

- **Political rights** enable people to participate in the political process and governance of a society. They include the right to vote, stand in elections and hold office. In terms of these rights, companies are an additional channel through which individuals can exercise the rights. For example, in countries where the right to participate has been violently repressed, companies have enabled people to exert some impact on how their community is governed. Western oil companies operating in Burma, for instance, have set up committees through which local villagers can influence how social programmes funded by the companies are run.

Even though companies may be increasingly performing roles traditionally assumed by governments, as argued by the Nottingham school, it is states – governments – that are *responsible* for the promotion and protection of human rights within their territory.[40] Accordingly, governments have been held responsible for the human rights violations committed by companies, as it has been seen as their failure to ensure that human rights are respected on their territory. States have also been held responsible for protecting companies against the violation of certain rights that businesses have been argued to possess, including, for example, the rights to property, free speech, fair trial and privacy. It is therefore clear that under international laws, national governments are the bodies that have the ultimate responsibility for guaranteeing the respect of rights for individuals and companies alike, and arguably this is an expectation that many citizens will also have of their rulers.

CITIZENS, COMPANIES AND GOVERNMENTS

As already noted, it is common now in many developed countries for substantial parts of social provision to be outsourced to private companies. This may include healthcare, prison management and even electoral operations.

Which public services are you comfortable about being delivered by the corporate world, and which (if any) do you feel should remain in government hands?

SUMMARY

- Corporate social responsibility has developed in cycles. It seems to be prominent when the boundaries between corporate, government and individual responsibility are being redefined. For example, the most recent interest in corporate social responsibility has resulted, in part, from the way in which companies have behaved in foreign countries and whether companies should comply with global rather than local standards.

- Corporate social responsibility may be defined as the attuning of corporate behaviour to societal norms and values, though the term has become something of 'all things to all people'. The conceptual debate has focused on determining whether corporate social responsibility is voluntary in the sense that it only pertains to activities that go beyond economic self-interest and legal requirements, or whether it should encompass all the different roles and responsibilities that business has in society.

- One model of corporate social responsibility (proposed by Carroll) depicts the various responsibilities of corporations as falling into four general contextual categories – economic, legal, philanthropic and ethical. The model therefore addresses the concerns of those who argue that the main responsibility of corporations is an economic one, but also accounts for other types of responsibilities. The model has been acknowledged for clarifying the contradictions behind corporate behaviour, but it fails to predict or indicate priorities for managerial decision making.

- The primary arguments offered against corporate social responsibility tend to focus on the competence of business to undertake ethical responsibilities, and on the requirements of corporations to focus on shareholder value as their first – and for some, only – priority. It has also been argued that companies are not accountable to society in the same way as governments. The proponents of corporate social responsibility have responded by arguing that companies should use their increasing influence in a responsible manner; if they fail to do so, other actors will step in to curb corporate behaviour and influence.

- The development of the concept of corporate citizenship has two alternative interpretations: one – the Nottingham interpretation – presents corporations as analogous to national governments, providing support and protection for citizens; the other – stemming from the United States – depicts corporations as analogous to individual citizens with comparable rights and responsibilities.

QUICK REVIEW QUESTIONS:

1 What do you think were the key factors in the development of corporate social responsibility during the 20th century?

2 How does Carroll's model take account of the objections to corporate social responsibility raised by Friedman and others?

3 How far is corporate citizenship a concept that is distinct from corporate social responsibility?

CASE STUDY: GOOGLE – 'DON'T BE EVIL'

Google has been one of the most successful internet companies in the world. In 2007, more than half of the searches on the internet were conducted through Google sites, which include YouTube and Gmail. Google's success is based on PageRank, an algorithm used by its search engine to rank web pages. The company has also been popular because it has kept its site as simple as possible. For example, it has had a strong position against pop-up windows and other features that tend to annoy the end-user. Visits to the company's sites are matched with its financial success; in 2007 Google's revenue grew by 60 per cent compared with the previous year, to $16,594 million. It has used its income to invest in innovation and acquisitions, and it employs almost 17,000 people in offices around the world.

Google's motto, 'Don't be evil', refers to its goal of serving its users by providing them with unbiased access to information. This is why the company flags advertising as 'sponsored link' and makes a pledge of not manipulating the ranking of search results. At a more general level, Google seeks to play a positive role in society by acting in an ethical manner. In the Google Code of Conduct, the company encourages its employees to take personal responsibility for ensuring that high standards of ethical behaviour are respected: 'Each of us has a personal responsibility to incorporate, and to encourage other Googlers to incorporate, the principles of the Code into our work.' Whistle-blowing is also endorsed: 'If you see something that you think isn't right — speak up!'

Google has gone beyond its 'Don't be evil' policy by committing significant resources to philanthropic activity. By 2008 it had given out more than $75,000 million in grants and investments to diverse causes. The philanthropic activity is a result of the commitment made by Google's founders, Larry Page and Sergey Brin, to contribute at least 1 per cent of the company's equity and profits to address some of the world's problems. This work is done through Google. org that gives grants for societal causes, but also invests in for-profit projects aimed at finding innovative solutions to the world's ills. Moreover, through its Google Grants programme, the company gives free advertising to non-profit organizations working in the areas of poverty, human rights, environment and other societal problems.

Despite the 'Don't be evil' policy and charitable activity, Google has been criticized on various counts. In 2007, *Harper's Magazine* censured the company for using large amounts of energy without being clear about how it would offset this by clean power and carbon credits. According to the magazine, Google's servers in the United States require as much electricity as 82,000 American homes. In general, data centres consume more power than televisions but there is little awareness of the energy consumed by internet companies, which are often seen as more environmentally friendly than more traditional businesses.

Moreover, along with other internet search engines such as Yahoo!, Google has been criticized for its decision to block access to certain sites on the basis of a list of keywords provided by the Chinese government. For example, no search results involving the Tiananmen Square demonstrations or the independence movement of Tibet are brought up when the search engine is accessed through its Chinese site. Google argues that the cause of free speech is better served by a limited access rather than no access to its search engine. It also informs users of the content that has been removed by posting a message at the bottom of the search results page. The critics of Google's policy have, however, taken action against the company. In 2006, for example, some of them boycotted the company on Valentine's Day to show their disapproval of Google's policy in China.

China is not the only country where Google filters search content. Sites are also removed from search results when they are in conflict with the German law that bans hate speech and anti-Semitism. The blocked search results are however listed at the bottom of the results page with links to a site where the decision is explained and the addresses of the filtered sites provided. Users are therefore still able to access the removed sites, even though they do not appear in Google results.

STUDY QUESTIONS

1 How would you characterize Google's policies and behaviour by using Carroll's pyramid of corporate social responsibility?

2 Are there any conflicts between the four types of responsibilities defined by Carroll? What are the implications of this for the usefulness of Carroll's pyramid?

3 Is there any difference between blocking search content in China and Germany? Why?

SOURCES

Google Code of Conduct. Available from http://investor.google.com/conduct.html, accessed 31 March 2008.

Google.org. Available from http://www.google.org, accessed 31 March 2008.

Google Watch. Available from http://www.google-watch.org, accessed 31 March 2008.

Strand G. Keyword: Evil. *Harper's Magazine*, March 2008. Available from http://www.harpers.org/media/slideshow/annot/2008-03/index.html, accessed 31 March 2008.

Who's afraid of Google? *The Economist*, 30 August 2008. Available from http://www.economist.com, accessed on 31 March 2008.

This case study was prepared using only publicly available sources of information for the purposes of classroom discussion.

NOTES

1. Cf. Carroll (1999).
2. See, for example, Ackerman (1975), pp. 6–7; Preston (1986); Vogel (1996).
3. As discussed in Vogel (1986).
4. As evidenced by Rachel Carson's groundbreaking book *Silent Spring,* published in 1962 (by Houghton).
5. Wood & Logsdon (2001).
6. Matten *et al.* (2003); Reich (1998).
7. Spar (1999).
8. Smith (2003).
9. Bowen (1953), cited in Carroll, 1999.
10. Henderson (2001).
11. Wartick & Cochran (1985), p. 703.
12. Wood (1991) p. 695.
13. For example, McGuire (1963); McWilliams & Siegel, 2001; Sethi 1975.
14. Davis (1973), p. 312.
15. McWilliams & Siegel (2001).
16. Sethi (1975), p. 58; Clarkson (1995), p. 92.

17. Zenisek (1979), p. 359.
18. For example, Carroll (1979); Wartick & Cochran (1985); Wood (1991).
19. For example, Matten *et al.* (2003); Windsor (2001); Wood & Logsdon (2001).
20. Carroll (1979), p. 500.
21. Friedman (1970),
22. In search of the good company. *The Economist,* 6 September 2007.
23. Some of the relatively recent discussion may be seen in Henderson (2001).
24. See Davis (1973).
25. Margolis & Walsh (2003), p. 272.
26. Reich (2007).
27. Davis (1973).
28. Nyber (2003). Also cf. Chapter 9 on corporate governance.
29. A similar analysis may be found in Sethi (1979).
30. For example, Carroll (1979); Sethi (1975); Wartick & Cochran (1985); Wood (1991).
31. Wood (1991).
32. Nokia (2008). See http://www.nokia.com/link?cid=EDITORIAL_73183, accessed 24 February 2008.
33. Wood & Logsdon (2001).
34. Including, for example, Jeanne Logsdon and Donna Wood.
35. Moon *et al.* (undated).
36. Wood & Logsdon (2001).
37. For example, Andriof & McIntosh (2001); Logsdon & Wood (2003); Windsor (2001); Wood & Logsdon (2001).
38. Moon *et al.* (undated), p. 13.
39. Information for these paragraphs derived from du Rusquec (2003) and from corporate material of Total (2003).
40. See Muchlinski (2001) from which much of this paragraph is derived.

REFERENCES

Ackerman, R. W. 1975. *The Social Challenge to Business*. Cambridge, MA: Harvard University Press.

Carroll, A. B. 1979. A three-dimensional conceptual model of corporate performance. *Academy of Management Review*, Vol. 4, No. 4, 497–505.

Carroll, A. B. 1991. The pyramid of corporate social responsibility: Toward the moral management of organisational stakeholders. *Business Horizons*, July–August, 39–48.

Carroll, A. B. 1999. Corporate social responsibility: Evolution of a definitional construct. *Business & Society*, Vol. 38, No. 3, 268–295.

Clarkson, M. B. E. 1995. A stakeholder framework for analyzing and evaluating corporate social performance. *Academy of Management Review*, Vol. 20, No. 1, 92–117.

Davis, K. 1973. The case for and against business assumption of social responsibilities. *Academy of Management Journal*, Vol. 16, No. 2, 312–322.

du Rusquec, J. 2003. Interview de Jean du Rusquec, chargé de mission Myanmar chez Total. Available from http://www.sri-in-progress.com, accessed 2 March 2004.

Friedman, M. 1970. The social responsibility of business is to increase its profits. *New York Times Magazine*, 13 September 1970.

Henderson, D. 2001. The case against corporate social responsibility, *Policy*, Vol. 17, No. 2, 28–32.

Logsdon, J. M. and Wood, D. 2002. Business citizenship: From domestic to global level of analysis. *Business Ethics Quarterly*, Vol. 12, Issue 2, 155–187.

Margolis, J. D. and Walsh, J. P. 2003. Misery loves companies: Rethinking social initiatives by business. *Administrative Science Quarterly*, Vol. 48, No. 2, 268–305.

Matten, D., Crane, A. and Chapple, W. 2003. Behind the mask: Revealing the true face of corporate citizenship. *Journal of Business Ethics*, Vol. 45, No. 1, 109–120.

McGuire, J. 1963. *Business and Society*. New York: McGraw-Hill.

McWilliams, A. and Siegel, D. 2001. Corporate social responsibility: A theory of the firm perspective. *Academy of Management Review*, Vol. 26, No. 1, 117–127.

Moon, J., Crane, A. and Matten, D. (undated). *Can Corporations be Citizens?* Second edition. No. 13-2003 ICCSR Research Paper Series: ISSN 1479-5124.

Muchlinski, P. T. 2001. Human rights and multinationals: Is there a problem? *International Affairs*, Vol. 77, No. 1, 31–47.

Nyber, A. 2003. Sticker shock: The true cost of Sarbanes-Oxley compliance. *CFO: Magazine for Senior Financial Executives*, September, 2003.

Preston, L. E. 1986. *Social Issues and Public Policy in Business and Management: Retrospect and Prospect.* College Park: University of Maryland.

Reich, R. B. 1998. The new meaning of corporate social responsibility. *California Management Review*, Vol. 40, No. 2, 8–17.

Reich, R. B. 2007. *Supercapitalism: The Transformation of Business, Democracy, and Everyday Life.* Knopf Publishing Group.

Sethi, S. P. 1975. Dimensions of corporate social performance: An analytical framework. *California Management Review*, Vol. 17, No. 3, 58–64.

Sethi, S. P. 1979. A conceptual framework for environmental analysis of social issues and evaluation of business response patterns. *Academy of Management Review*, Vol. 4, No. 1, 63–74.

Smith, N. G. 2003. Corporate social responsibility: Whether or how? *California Management Review*, Vol. 45, No. 4, 52–76.

Spar, D. L. 1999. Foreign investment and human rights. *Challenge*, Vol. 42, No. 1, 55–80.

Total 2003. *Corporate Social Responsibility Report.* Available from http://www.total.com, accessed 4 May 2004.

Vogel, D. 1986. The study of social issues in management: A critical appraisal. *California Management Review*, Vol. 28, No. 2, 142–151.

Vogel, D. J. 1996. The study of business and politics. *California Management Review*, Vol. 38, No. 3, 146–165.

Wartick, S. L. and Cochran, P. L. 1985. The evolution of the corporate social performance model. *Academy of Management Review*, Vol. 10, No. 4, 758–769.

Windsor, D. 2001. Corporate citizenship: Evolution and interpretation. In Andriof, J. and McIntosh, M. (eds) *Perspectives on Corporate Citizenship.* Sheffield: Greenleaf Publishing.

Wood, D. J. 1991. Corporate social performance revisited. *Academy of Management Review*, Vol. 16, No. 4, 691–718.

Wood, D. and Logsdon, J. M. 2001. Theorising business citizenship. In Andriof, J. and McIntosh, M. (eds) *Perspectives on Corporate Citizenship.* Sheffield: Greenleaf Publishing.

Zenisek, T. J. 1979. Corporate social responsibility: A conceptualisation based on organisational literature. *Academy of Management Review*, Vol. 4, No. 3, 359–368.

STAKEHOLDER MANAGEMENT

LEARNING OBJECTIVES

After studying this chapter you should be able to:

- Critically analyse the implications of different stakeholder definitions.
- Prioritize stakeholder groups using appropriate criteria.
- Evaluate different theoretical models of stakeholder management.
- Elaborate on what stakeholder management involves in practice.
- Draw out implications of the relevance of stakeholder theory for ethics and corporate social responsibility.

INTRODUCTION

Even though the idea of corporate social responsibility has been widely accepted, it has not always been clear what companies can actually do to behave in a more responsible manner. In this chapter we introduce stakeholder management as a way of managing corporate social responsibility. Accordingly, corporate social responsibility is about identifying and managing relationships to key stakeholders. We will first look at the emergence of stakeholder thinking before moving on to discuss a range of ways in which the concept can be conceived depending on circumstance and managerial decisions. We will also look at different approaches to the management of stakeholders. In addition, partnership projects between companies and non-governmental organizations are briefly reviewed to gain a better understanding of how companies can collaborate with stakeholders.

FROM SHAREHOLDER VALUE TO STAKEHOLDER THINKING

Stakeholder thinking has emerged over the last 25 years as a popular way of framing corporate behaviour. It is underpinned by the assumption that values applicable to business, and the expectations derived from these, can be identified with the common interests of specific individuals and groups; each of these, therefore, has a 'stake' in the performance of a business. Responsible organizations, on this approach, take into account stakeholder concerns and accommodate their behaviour accordingly.

Stakeholder thinking epitomizes the criticism that has been presented about the priority given to shareholders at the expense of other groups. While it may be an oversimplification to say that many corporations, past and present, have been overly focused on achieving profits for the benefit of their shareholders, organizations are often depicted as mechanisms to generate benefits for those who own them, be these original entrepreneurs or shareholders who invest in the company. The legal accountability of a limited company to shareholders is another element that adds to the emphasis often given to shareholders. In contrast, the stakeholder perspective regards a much wider range of interests as relevant to how organizations are managed. As one author states:

> A socially responsible firm is one whose managerial staff balances a multiplicity of interests. Instead of striving only for larger profits for its stockholders, a responsible enterprise also takes into account employees, suppliers, dealers, local communities, and the nation.[1]

This focus on shareholder value was particularly evident in the 1980s when the Reagan and Thatcher administrations promoted deregulation of the markets. During this period, uncertainty in the external environment was caused by foreign competition rather than

ETHICS IN PRACTICE

PROCTER & GAMBLE PARTNERS WITH LOCAL NON-PROFITS

Procter & Gamble is one of the largest manufacturers of consumer products in the world. It is perhaps best known for its range of detergents and beauty products, but it also sells pet food and prescription medicine. In 2000 it launched a new product, a water purifying powder named PUR. The product was targeted at emerging markets where clean water was scarce, including countries such as Mexico and Pakistan. PUR was sold in sachets of powder that could be mixed with dirty water turning it into drinkable water. Even though the product was effective, market tests from across the world showed that it was not commercially viable. Given the public health benefits of water purification, Procter & Gamble was however reluctant to terminate the product and opted for another strategy involving non-profit organizations. In Haiti, for example, the company worked together with a social marketing organization that sold the product at prices sufficient to cover production and distribution costs. Procter & Gamble also sells the product at cost to Care, a humanitarian organization that distributes it for free in disaster areas. By 2006 Procter and Gamble had sold over 18 million sachets, and though the product is still not commercially viable, the company sees it as an important part of its contribution to society.

Source: Hanson, M. 2007. Pure Water. *Management Today*, 1 April 2007. Available from www.managementtoday.co.uk, accessed 23 July 2009.

social and political demands placed on companies.[2] As a result, companies centred their attention on attracting and keeping investors, these having become, in general, increasingly mobile and more likely to focus on short-term gains.

More recently, many developments have contributed to increasing demands that companies broaden the distribution of business benefits to a wider set of stakeholders, not only shareholders.[3] Further pressure has come from academics such as Henry Mintzberg, who has criticized the focus on shareholder value, noting that even though shareholders need a fair return on their investment in order for the capital markets to work, an unbalanced focus on shareholder value creates a wedge between shareholders and other stakeholders and is therefore 'bad for business and bad for capitalism'.[4] Accordingly, the latest interest in corporate social responsibility represents a way to criticize the priority given to shareholders at the expense of other stakeholder groups. Moreover, corporate social responsibility is about arguing that corporations are not only legal-economic entities; rather, responsible companies also seek to contribute to the societies in which they operate. Overall, then, a significant degree of pressure has come to bear on organizations to take account of a much wider range of actors than simply their owners or shareholders.

WHAT ARE STAKEHOLDERS?

Stakeholders comprise individuals, or sometimes groups, with similar interests in a particular organization.[5] For example, shareholders are mainly interested in gaining adequate return on their investment. A variety of groups, including shareholders, employees, customers and suppliers, are typically identified as stakeholders. It is often meaningful to separate groups of stakeholders into sub-categories with similar, but not identical interests. For example, one set of shareholders may seek a sustainable return in the long term while another looks for quicker gains. Because of their slightly different interests, the two types of shareholders are likely to have different expectations of corporate behaviour. Similarly, some employees may have a high degree of commitment to their company, while others have less – hence, as well as their obvious shared desire for good pay and conditions, there may be differences in attitude to the long-term survival of the employer.

It should also be noted that the same individual or group may have multiple interests in an organization and therefore belong to various stakeholder clusters. For example, an employee of a big supermarket chain such as Tesco or Carrefour is also likely to be a customer of the retailer. Stakeholder groups, then, should not be considered as mutually exclusive categories, but sets of shared interests that people have in particular organizations.

The stakeholder concept was popularized by Edward Freeman in his landmark book, *Strategic Management: A Stakeholder Approach*, published in 1984. According to Freeman, '[s]takeholders include employees, customers, suppliers, stockholders, banks, environmentalists, government and other groups who can help or hurt the corporation'.[6] This quote from Freeman stresses the role of those groups that can enable or hamper the achievement of organizational goals. However, stakeholders also include groups that are only affected by the organization's operations without being able to influence the organization. For example, future generations can be regarded as a stakeholder group that cannot act on its own behalf. Stakeholders can therefore be defined as 'individuals or groups of individuals who can affect or are affected by the achievement of an organization's objectives'.[7]

Stakeholder groups can be categorized in many ways. A distinction is often made between internal and external stakeholders, distinguishing those who form the organization from those who just interact with it. However, this distinction simply locates the groups involved

WHO CAN REPRESENT THE INTERESTS OF NON-SOCIAL STAKEHOLDERS?

Inevitably the management of non-social groups is problematic: for one thing they often have no authentic voice (the World Wildlife Fund is a proxy for future generations but can only guess at what will matter to the latter); for another, it is difficult to even imagine what exactly are the interests of, say the impala species.

So, how far can we make sensible choices affecting non-social groups when the representation and knowledge of their interests is so uncertain?

and tells us little about the nature of the interests that the stakeholders have in the company. Another distinction can be made between social and non-social stakeholders.[8] Non-social stakeholders differ from social stakeholders because they cannot be communicated with directly. They include the physical environment, non-human species and future generations. The interests of non-social stakeholders can be represented by special interest groups. The World Wildlife Fund (WWF), for example, has a mission to 'stop the degradation of the planet's natural environment, and to build a future in which humans live in harmony with nature'.[9] The way in which organizations can or should deal with the interests of non-social stakeholders will be discussed in later chapters on environmental ethics.

Stakeholder groups can also be categorized on the basis of strategic environments.[10] Categorizing stakeholders in this way begins to indicate the kind of approach that an organization should take to how each of these is managed. As seen in Figure 2.1, *core* stakeholders include those individuals and groups that are vital for the existence and success of the company. These stakeholders form the principal resource base for the company and include investors, employees and customers. Successful companies maintain and improve their ability to draw on the resources held by their core stakeholders. In contrast, the second group relates to the company's competitive position within a particular industry and market. This group of stakeholders includes business partners, unions and regulatory authorities. The main challenge for the company with this group of stakeholders is to establish and sustain relationships that improve its competitiveness in compliance with laws and regulations. The third and final group comprises stakeholders in the company's social and political environment, including governments, communities and private organizations. With regard to these stakeholders, the company is challenged to foresee and respond to any new developments that might enhance or interrupt its business operations.

Even though companies have more frequent interactions with their core stakeholders, and the support of these stakeholders is therefore essential for the running of profitable business operations, any stakeholder from the three groups may become the most critical on a particular issue. Take the example of a company such as Shanghai Airlines: while investors, suppliers of services such as aircraft maintenance, and customers are critically important for the day-to-day success of the firm, there will be times when the approval of a regulatory body (say for increasing numbers of flights or for expanding services to different regions) will be paramount, and other situations where the support of the local community may be the priority (e.g. where a pool of ancillary staff is retained to deal with fluctuating levels of operations).

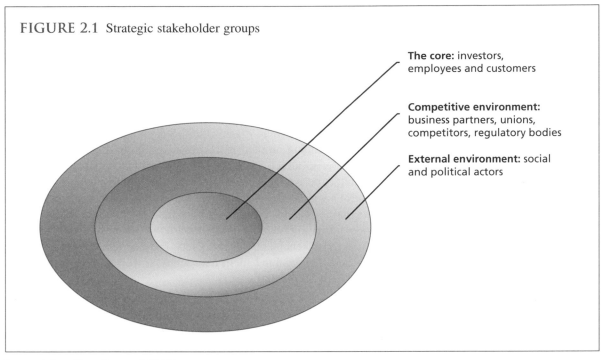

FIGURE 2.1 Strategic stakeholder groups

The core: investors, employees and customers

Competitive environment: business partners, unions, competitors, regulatory bodies

External environment: social and political actors

Source: Adapted from Post *et al.* (2002).

Categories of stakeholders naturally have different levels of relevance depending on the organization type. A smaller organization has little opportunity to influence government policy, but may have much closer relationships with individual customers than the large corporation. Similarly, a public service organization may have less discretion on customer relationships but have a more detailed involvement in policy and regulation.

CONFLICTING INTERESTS AND STAKEHOLDER IMPORTANCE

There are inevitably situations where the interests of stakeholders conflict. Such a conflict may exist when employees ask for a salary increase and other benefits, while shareholders put pressure on the management to cut costs of production and labour. Companies thus need to *prioritize* stakeholders, often because of resource limitations. This process is a critical decision for any organization, and can have a major impact on specific stakeholder groups, as well as setting the ethical image of the organization in the public eye.

Various criteria can be used to prioritize stakeholders and their importance to a particular organization. Stakeholders can, for example, be divided into *primary* and *secondary* stakeholders on the basis of how essential they are for the achievement of the organization's objectives.[11] Primary stakeholders are stakeholders without whose participation an organization would cease to exist. These stakeholders include employees, shareholders and customers, and their support is critical for the continuation of business activities. Secondary stakeholders are individuals or groups that are not essential for a firm's survival, but may still be in a position to interfere with and damage a company's business. Such groups include competitors and the media. The distinction between primary and secondary stakeholders sheds light on the importance of stakeholders, but provides little basis for prioritization as the interests of stakeholders belonging to the same main group can conflict. Shareholders and employees, for example, are both primary stakeholders and cannot be prioritized on the basis of this categorization.

A more sophisticated way to determine the importance of stakeholders involves their categorization on the basis of *salience*, defined with regard to the following three attributes:[12]

- **Power** of a stakeholder to influence an organization. Stakeholders derive their power from a mix of sources depending on their resources and relationships.[13] Some stakeholders have *formal* power to affect corporate policies and behaviour. Investors and governments, for example, derive their power from legal or contractual arrangements that allow them to have some degree of influence. Other stakeholders, including customers and suppliers, have *economic* power over corporate performance. Stakeholders may also have *political* power to express and put forward their interests. Political power arises from the position the stakeholder holds in society. For example, the power of civil society groups arises from their goal to benefit the society as well as their credibility in the eyes of other actors (e.g. the media).

- **Legitimacy** of the stakeholder's relationship with the company. Legitimacy pertains to the perception that the stakeholder's goals and activities are in line with generally accepted values and norms in society. For example, the lawsuits brought against McDonald's for contributing to the obesity of two teenagers have been perceived as illegitimate because decisions about eating habits are seen to fall into the sphere of individual rather than corporate responsibility.

- **Urgency** of the stakeholder's claim on the company. Urgency calls for immediate attention on the basis of two conditions: (1) time sensitivity – the degree to which a delay in dealing with the claim is intolerable to the stakeholder; and (2) criticality – the importance of the claim or relationship with the company to the stakeholder. For example, an oil spill requires urgent action so that any damage to the environment can be limited, while a call for the protection of non-endangered species of wildlife may seem less pressing.

A highly salient stakeholder possesses all three attributes to a high level while a stakeholder with low salience holds none of them to any great degree (see Figure 2.2). The attributes are dynamic in the sense that a stakeholder may become more or less important for a company as a result of a change in the extent to which they possess one or more of these attributes. For example, a shareholder may acquire more power by buying additional shares in a company, while a non-governmental organization may increase its power by mobilizing the interest of the mainstream media. It should also be noted that the attributes do not exist objectively. Different actors may hold conflicting views over, say, the legitimacy of stakeholder claims. Ultimately, it is the *perception* of managers that determines which stakeholders are regarded as salient and are therefore given management attention. As with the categorization of stakeholders, the degree of salience will vary depending on the type of organization making the analysis.

An inevitable question that arises in a manager's mind is which of these two approaches (primary/secondary, salience) should they use to identify and categorize stakeholders? Both have their advantages and disadvantages. As with many management models, the answer to this is less a matter of one being simply superior to another, and more a matter of understanding what the implications may be of *using* one rather than another. The salience approach is arguably more sound intellectually, but it may take more reflection and

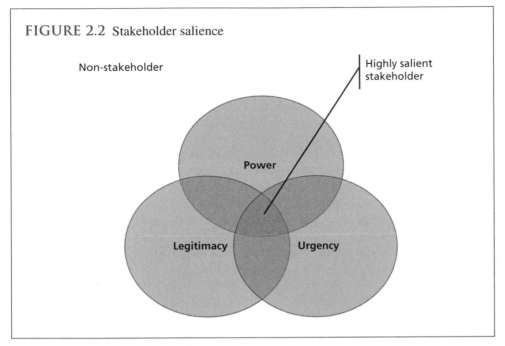

FIGURE 2.2 Stakeholder salience

Source: Adapted from Mitchell *et al.* (1997).

interpretation of information to be really useful – and this all takes time. A manager may well choose the simpler primary/secondary division, but it is important for them to recognize the limitations of such a choice.

STAKEHOLDER THEORY

Stakeholder theory posits the company as a hub of relationships between diverse actors. These relationships were initially portrayed as a two-way influence between the company and a range of stakeholder groups, although it was recognized that stakeholders are interconnected and that coalitions of stakeholder groups may emerge to help or oppose a company on a particular issue.[14] More recently, researchers have viewed stakeholder relationships as more complex and interrelated, rather than just a collection of one-to-one relationships between the

THINKING CRITICALLY ABOUT ETHICS

CHOOSING A MODEL IS A TELLING SIGN

One object lesson here for managers and students of management is that thinking is not a neutral act, but often represents a choice or action in its own right. Deciding to adopt a less sophisticated model reflects a choice to devote fewer resources to social responsibility decisions, while deciding to adopt a more complex approach demonstrates an acceptance of a longer timescale for decisions, something which may well affect the level of satisfaction among a particular stakeholder group.

company and its various stakeholders.[15] The company is now regarded as part of a *stakeholder network* in which its position in the centre of the net is not taken for granted.[16] In this network, each stakeholder possesses its own stakeholders, but relationships may exist between the company's various stakeholders. In the field of management studies, the focus is on companies as entities through which diverse actors pursue multiple purposes in the network of stakeholder relationships.[17] Research in the area has focused on managerial decision making, although it has also included the study of the behaviour of stakeholders other than the company, and the examination of the entire network of relationships between stakeholders without a particular emphasis on the role of the company or the manager.[18]

Stakeholder theory has been argued by some to be a normative rather than explanatory or predictive theory of management.[19] The proponents of this view argue that managers *should* take into account the interests of all stakeholders because of the intrinsic value that each stakeholder possesses. Accordingly, stakeholders have legitimate interests in companies for their own sake, rather than because they can further the achievement of some organizational goals.[20] This contrasts with the predictive view that managers do in fact take account of different stakeholders by virtue of their impact on organizational performance and achievement of corporate targets. Our view is that, in its current form, stakeholder theory is indeed normative – there is no guarantee that managers do consider the interests of other than those of critical stakeholder groups. In order to develop stakeholder theory further towards a *predictive* theory of management, models that explain the behaviour of firms and its stakeholders need to be identified and tested in the field.[21] Ultimately, stakeholder theory should be able to describe the processes of stakeholder relationships and predict their outcomes for the company and its stakeholders,[22] but this is likely to be a highly complex matter, involving perceptions of the full range of primary stakeholders, interrelationships between stakeholders (and potentially in some cases even with non-stakeholders) and the highly problematic issue of measured organizational performance. For the moment, therefore, it is better to see it as a useful tool rather than a confirmed explanation of corporate behaviour.

STAKEHOLDER THEORY AS AN ALTERNATIVE THEORY OF THE FIRM

Conventionally, companies have been viewed as organizations that managers control for the benefit of the owners, or as black boxes that transform inputs provided by investors, employees and suppliers into outputs for the benefit of customers. However, stakeholder theory has been seen as an alternative to this theory of the firm. In stakeholder theory, companies are presented as organizations through which a diversity of actors accomplish multiple and sometimes conflicting purposes.[23] Researchers have also sought to integrate stakeholder theory with other theories of the firm. For example, it has been combined with the contractual theory of the firm to present the firm as a nexus of contracts between managers and other stakeholders.[24] The modern business organization can therefore, on this view, be seen as a series of multilateral contracts among stakeholders: 'the interests of a multiplicity of stakeholders interact to form the modern corporation'.[25]

Approach to strategic management

Stakeholder theory has also been advanced as an approach to strategic management.[26] Researchers in this field have argued that in contrast to other theories of strategic management, stakeholder theory takes into account the social and political environment in which companies operate. This is important because in addition to the company's base of resources and competitive position within a particular industry, strategic threats and opportunities arise from the claims and expectations placed on the company by various social and political actors. It is therefore the management of relationships with critical stakeholders, together with the accumulation of conventional assets, that determines the company's capacity to survive and create wealth in the long term.[27] The stakeholder view provides managers with a framework that allows them 'to more effectively handle turbulent external environments'.[28] In this context, stakeholder theory can be seen as a substitute for the PEST (political, economic, social and technological) analysis and other frameworks that provide structure for the examination of the strategic threats and opportunities arising from the external environment.

Framework of corporate social responsibility

Stakeholder theory has been advanced as an increasingly popular way of conceptualizing corporate social responsibility.[29] Authors in this field see a natural fit between the concepts of corporate social responsibility and stakeholders, because the stakeholder concept provides a way to frame and assess society's values and expectations of business. Researchers have also found that managers seem to understand the concepts of stakeholder management, whereas they 'do not think or act in terms of the concepts of corporate social responsibilities and responsiveness, nor of social issues and performance'.[30] According to this view, corporate social responsibility can therefore be more easily analysed through the relationships that companies have to their constituent groups than in direct terms of issues or values.

THEORETICAL MODELS OF STAKEHOLDER MANAGEMENT

Stakeholder management involves the process by which managers reconcile the objectives of a company with the claims and expectations of various stakeholder groups. The development and maintenance of stakeholder relationships is considered essential for successful stakeholder management, which implies that organizations need to develop capacity for doing this. Little has been demonstrated in academic research about the resources and competences required for interacting with stakeholders but they have been broadly defined

THINKING CRITICALLY ABOUT ETHICS

DIFFERENCE AND EQUALITY

Of course, each stakeholder group has its own features. Some, such as local communities, have little power but are highly vulnerable to any errors made by the company. Others, such as government regulators, have a substantial amount of power but are rarely affected by individual corporate failure.

Each of these groups, therefore, involves different kinds of transaction with a company, and thus requires distinct management processes.

One ethical issue that follows from this is how fair it is for an organization to deal with one stakeholder group in one way, and a different group in another way.

as the organization's understanding of its map of stakeholders, the processes of dealing with these stakeholders, and the transactions that take place between the organization and its various stakeholders.[31]

There are various strategies that companies can pursue in order to manage their relationships with stakeholders.[32] Strategies put forward by different authors share few characteristics, although most refer to the degree of involvement with stakeholders: some assume a high degree of cooperation whereas others are characterized by the avoidance of any interaction. The strategies are also in the main generic, in the sense that they do not specify the exact nature of the related activities. For example, collaboration, a strategy put forward by Savage and his colleagues (1991), may involve an array of arrangements from informal information sharing to profit-seeking ventures with considerable investment from the participating organizations. When these models of stakeholder management are applied to analyse real-life situations, specific activities need to be identified under each major category of strategy in order for them to apply in practice. Three overall types of focus have been outlined, as explained in the following sub-sections:

- focus on the generic approach towards a stakeholder
- focus on the relationship
- focus on the stakeholder network.

Focus on the generic approach towards a stakeholder

Savage *et al.* (1991) argued that strategies for managing stakeholders should be based on two assessments:

1 the stakeholder's potential to threaten the organization
2 the stakeholder's potential to cooperate with the organization.

These assessments depend on at least four factors that have an impact on the level of threat or cooperation posed by stakeholders: possession of resources needed by the company; relative power of the stakeholder; willingness of the stakeholder to take action; and the likelihood of the stakeholder to form coalitions. For example, the likelihood that the stakeholder forms coalitions with other stakeholders increases its potential for threat and decreases the potential for cooperation, while its likelihood of forming an alliance with the company has the opposite effect.

Based on the assessment of the stakeholder's potential for threat and cooperation, four separate strategies for managing stakeholders can be identified (see Figure 2.3). These strategies are essentially generic approaches that organizations can have towards a particular stakeholder on a particular issue:

- *Involvement* concerns the inclusion of stakeholders into decision making and other activities in organizations. Companies can, for example, involve their suppliers in the development of new production processes.
- *Monitoring* refers to the consideration of particular stakeholder groups when important decisions are being made. Such stakeholders typically include issue-specific organizations that have a limited interest in the company. The objective of monitoring is to ensure that the interests of stakeholders do not at any stage conflict with those of the organization.
- *Defence* involves attempts to decrease the power that the stakeholder has over the company. For example, companies may seek to establish exclusive relationships with suppliers in order to fight off a competitor.

FIGURE 2.3 Approach to stakeholders

Stakeholder's potential for threat to the organization

		High	Low
Stakeholder's potential for cooperation with the organization	**High**	Mixed blessing stakeholder: **Collaborate**	Supportive stakeholder: **Involve**
	Low	Non-supportive stakeholder: **Defend**	Marginal stakeholder: **Monitor**

Source: Savage *et al.* (1991).

- *Collaboration* refers to partnerships and other collaborative ventures established between the organization and its stakeholders. Such partnership projects are discussed in more detail below.

Focus on the relationship

Friedman & Miles (2002) suggested that strategic actions taken by organizations and their stakeholders depend on two variables that characterize relationships between them:

1 the compatibility of their interests

2 the nature of the connections between them.

First, the interests of companies and their stakeholders can be compatible or incompatible. For example, the interests of shareholders and the organization are typically compatible because the top management is expected to manage the organization in the interests of the shareholders. Secondly, the connections between organizations and their stakeholders vary from necessary to contingent depending on whether the two parties recognize that a formal relationship exists between them. If both parties recognize that such a relationship exists, the connection is necessary. If it is not recognized, or only exists momentarily in special circumstances, the connection is contingent. So, for example, the interests of a group of employees may happen to coincide at a particular time with those of a group of local residents, perhaps when there is a risk of a major pollution event, but at other times they may be opposed, for example where a firm decides to develop a 24-hour operation in one particular factory, potentially creating noise in the middle of the night.

Based on the two variables, stakeholder relations can be grouped into four categories (see Figure 2.4). Each category corresponds to a particular type of strategic action by companies. First, companies may *defend* a relationship they have to a stakeholder. This action is typical when the company and its relevant stakeholders expect to benefit from the existing relationship. Secondly, companies may behave opportunistically

FIGURE 2.4 Nature of stakeholder relationships

| | | Connections between stakeholders | |
		Necessary	Contingent
Stakeholder interests	Compatible	**Defend:** Shareholders Top management Partners	**Form relations:** The general public Companies connected through trade associations
	Incompatible	**Compromise:** Trade unions Customers Suppliers Some NGOs	**Eliminate:** Some NGOs Aggrieved/criminal members of the public

Source: Friedman & Miles (2002).

to *form a relationship* with a stakeholder if they believe that this will further their interests. It is also possible that stakeholders will advance the company's goals even without a formal relationship as their interests are compatible with those of the company. Thirdly, companies may be pushed to *compromise* in order to reconcile incompatible interests between themselves and some stakeholders. For example, adverse publicity and possible punitive action from unions encourages companies to find a way to respond to the demands of their employees. Finally, companies may seek to *eliminate a relationship to a stakeholder* with which they compete in some way or with which their interests conflict. For example, companies may choose to cut their relations to a non-governmental organization with which they cannot engage in a constructive way.

Focus on the stakeholder network

A third approach is provided by Rowley (1997), who argued that individual stakeholder relationships cannot be used to explain corporate responses to stakeholder pressures because companies respond to the entire network of stakeholder relationships. He posited that the way in which companies respond to stakeholder pressures depends on the variation of two factors:

1 the centrality of the company in the stakeholder network and
2 the density of this network surrounding the organization.

The first factor, centrality, refers to the number of contacts the company has to other actors in the stakeholder network. It therefore determines the extent to which the company can control the flow of information between different stakeholders. The more contacts the company has, the more able it is to resist stakeholder pressures. The second factor, network density, pertains to the number of ties that link actors in a stakeholder network. The maximum number of ties can be calculated on the basis of the total number of ties that exists if each actor in the network is tied to every other actor. As the network density increases, the ability of stakeholders to constrain the company's actions increases. This is because the ties between stakeholders result in shared behavioural norms and communication that can be used to monitor the company's behaviour.

Depending on the variation of the two factors, companies can have four roles in the stakeholder network, as depicted in Figure 2.5. Unlike the strategies described before, the roles do not relate to any particular stakeholder relationship; instead, they characterize the general role or posture that the company tends to have *vis-à-vis* its stakeholders. First, a *compromiser* has a central position in a well-connected network of stakeholders. It is therefore susceptible to stakeholder pressures, but also able to resist them by being in a position to negotiate for an arrangement that satisfies all parties. A compromiser is, however, likely to encounter a continuous series of negotiations with stakeholders that are capable of putting collective pressure on the company. A *commander* is in a central position in a stakeholder network with few connections. It is therefore able to exert control over the behaviours and expectations of other stakeholders in the network. Criminal organizations including drug cartels and terrorist organizations are examples of such networks characterized by sparse ties. Due to secrecy and the limited knowledge that actors have of each other, the focal organization is able to impose its will on the network. Thirdly, a *subordinate* lacks power because it has only a few connections to other stakeholders that are well organized and linked to each other. Because of this, it complies with established norms and the expectations that more powerful stakeholders may have. An example of this type of organization is an isolated supplier of produce to just one company. Finally, a *solitarian* experiences few pressures because it encounters only some demands from its stakeholders that share few linkages with each other. It can also attempt to distance itself from others through hermit-like behaviour. For example, a number of companies operating in free-trade zones in developing countries have been criticized for restraining the freedom of movement and speech of their employees in order to cut all but necessary connections to outside groups.

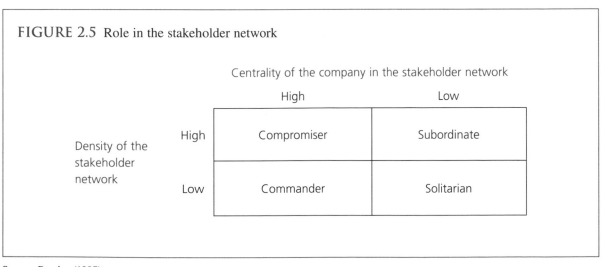

FIGURE 2.5 Role in the stakeholder network

		Centrality of the company in the stakeholder network	
		High	Low
Density of the stakeholder network	High	Compromiser	Subordinate
	Low	Commander	Solitarian

Source: Rowley (1997).

CHOOSING BETWEEN STAKEHOLDER MANAGEMENT MODELS

All three approaches are variants of conflict management models. As such, they depict the potential relationships between organization and stakeholder in terms of different forms of conflict.

How would you decide between these three approaches? As indicated before, the choice of which analytical tool one uses is not a neutral act, but one that carries significant implications for how an issue will eventually be resolved.

Associated with this is the question of what features of an organization would help you decide which approach to use? Is size an important variable, for example? Or speed of operations? Or degree of complexity of processes? There is no simple answer to these questions – they are the kind of decision that managers have to make for themselves.

STAKEHOLDER MANAGEMENT IN PRACTICE

In practice, stakeholder management encompasses the identification and analysis of stakeholder groups as well as the development of organizational policies and practices that are aimed at addressing the expectations of these groups. Several household name companies have conducted a detailed analysis and plan of stakeholder management. British American Tobacco (BAT), for example, has substantial negative features of its business – being a producer of a cancer-causing drug. This firm has therefore carried out an extensive stakeholder 'dialogue' to map out its stakeholders and respond to their concerns. While it is difficult to see how BAT could address all of these, it is still possible for the firm to deal with many, such as the concerns of their employees. Needless to say, for reasons of resourcing alone, not all companies engage in such a comprehensive process of stakeholder mapping and consultation.

Stakeholder management can be regarded as a set of techniques that organizations can use to better understand and manage stakeholder concerns. Three such techniques are described in this section: (1) stakeholder mapping; (2) surveys and stakeholder dialogue; and (3) partnership projects between companies and non-governmental organizations. The first two of these involve the identification and assessment of stakeholder concerns, while the third is an increasingly common way of responding to stakeholder pressures.

Stakeholder mapping

Stakeholder mapping involves the identification of the organization's stakeholders and its current relationships to these stakeholders. It is typically conducted at the outset of the process of stakeholder engagement, though it can also be drawn for any specific issue of concern. Stakeholder mapping can be divided into several steps:

1 Identification of stakeholder groups including those that are in a position to affect the company and those that are affected by the company's operations.

2 Classification of stakeholders into categories and sub-categories that are likely to share interests and characteristics.

3 Naming of specific stakeholder groups and analysis of the company's relationship to them.

Once stakeholders have been identified, their concerns and expectations can be examined. At this stage, companies may also prioritize some stakeholders relative to others. They should however avoid doing this before reaching an adequate understanding of each of the stakeholders and their readiness to take action.

Stakeholder surveys and dialogue

Surveys and stakeholder consultation are techniques through which companies can identify and analyse the interests, concerns and opinions of stakeholders. Even when companies have not systematically mapped out their stakeholders, they can seek to better understand a specific constituent group. Numerous consultancy firms have emerged to provide companies with services in this area. Using such suppliers has many benefits for companies that may lack appropriate internal expertise to carry out surveys and stakeholder dialogue, but the use of suppliers makes it more difficult for managers to build a good understanding of the stakeholders as the process may be moved away from the company. Also, in order to gain maximum benefit from stakeholder dialogue, companies should actively take part in the dialogue process as the purpose is to enhance mutual understanding through direct interaction.

Surveys involve the gathering of stakeholder views on a particular company and its activities. Both qualitative and quantitative techniques can be employed. Focus groups, for example, are typical for gauging the opinions and attitudes of consumers, while questionnaires are often used for collecting the views of investors and employees. Inevitably these run the risks standard to such methods of data collection – researcher bias, poor instrument design and poor sampling are all potential shortcomings that those responsible for conducting such surveys must guard against.

Dialogue/consultation involves active engagement with stakeholders to explore their concerns and exchange views over relevant issues. Dialogue can take many forms, but it typically entails informal discussions between a single company and stakeholder over a period of time. For example, a company manager may have a series of conversations with a representative of Amnesty International over the impact of corporate activities on human rights in a particular country. Dialogue can also include more than one stakeholder group. Such multi-stakeholder dialogue often focuses on a specific topic that is of concern to the company and its stakeholders. For example, Nike and other retailers have engaged in a multi-stakeholder dialogue with governmental and non-governmental organizations to address the issue of child labour in Pakistan.

Even though companies are aware of 'consultation fatigue' experienced by some stakeholders, they have set up permanent structures through which they engage with specific constituent groups. For example, some companies have established village-level consultation committees in local communities in developing countries.[33] These committees were initially created to explore the needs of local communities, but they have become regular communication channels between villagers and foreign companies. Again, there are potential shortcomings when collecting information in this way. For example, stakeholder intimidation might be a problem.

Partnership projects

Many larger companies first became aware of non-governmental organizations because of campaigns launched against their products or operations. As a result, relationships between companies and non-governmental organizations have often been adversarial. This has changed over recent years as an increasing number of companies and non-governmental

ETHICS IN PRACTICE

MCDONALD'S AND MOMS

McDonald's is a successful company with about 60 million people eating at its restaurants every day. The company has more than 31,000 branches in almost 120 countries and it is one of the most recognised brands in the world. In 2009, the Financial Times ranked it as the fifth most valued brand in the world making the 'golden arches' worth more than Disney, Amazon and BMW together.

McDonald's has enjoyed exceptional success since it was founded in 1940, but it has also encountered an array of challenges. In 2001, customer satisfaction surveys showed that McDonald's was falling behind its closest rivals because of unclean restaurants and indifferent service. The negative surveys coincided with increasing social concerns over junk food and its impact on health and McDonald's was directly criticised for contributing to the problem of obesity and unhealthy eating habits. For example, two teenage girls sued the company in the United States for making them obese. At the same time, a film, 'Super Size Me', showed how eating 'McFood' can make you ill and gain weight. As a result, the company's financial performance suffered and led to a quarterly loss in 2002.

McDonald's responded to the loss in profits by changing its strategy. As part of this change, it consulted various stakeholders paying particular attention to its core customers consisting of mothers and their children. McDonald's was concerned that a mother would buy a Happy Mean to her children, but only a coffee for herself. By introducing healthier items including salads and sandwiches on its menu, the company simultaneously responded to social concerns over junk food and had an offering that appealed to mothers. As a consequent, the order value per customer has increased and the company is profitable again.

McDonald's has built on its successful consultation with mothers by creating a group of 'moms' that brings together the company's core customers and concerns over healthy diets because it is often mothers who pay attention to what their families eat. The McDonald's club of moms consists of six mothers from different parts of the United States. The company gives them special access to its facilities by organising trips including presentations and visits to production sites. In return, the moms give their views to the company and report about their experiences on a dedicated website maintained by McDonald's. To date, the entries written by the moms have been very positive.

Examples of entries by McDonald's moms:

'It was amazing to see how the toy goes from just an idea to its actual roll out in the restaurant. The whole process is about 24 months and from day one, safety is the main focus. I found out why these toys are so safe and durable. They do a lot of research and out the toys through a lot of safety tests before its final approval.' Monica

'In the past, I would have never considered McDonald's a contender when it came to healthy selections. The quality and taste of the produce wasn't even a consideration; they didn't exist as far as I was concerned. Burgers, chicken and fries were all that mattered. I'm grateful to have learned through this experience that McDonald's has a lot more to offer. Not only does their produce taste good, but it's fresh and safe. Like the beef, produce is held to a strict set of standards, and all of McDonald's suppliers must comply. Produce selection is not a haphazard process but one where careful planning and consideration are ongoing.' Gilda

Critics have pointed out that McDonald's moms do not seem particularly concerned about issues that the company is usually criticised for, such as what chickens are eating or how animals are slaughtered. Instead, the moms have focused on cleanliness and other quality issues. As a result, the club of moms is being seen by many as a promotional exercise rather than genuine stakeholder consultation.

Sources: *The Economist, "McDonald's turned around", Special report, 16 October 2004.*
Financial Times,"Global brand"s, Special report, 29 April 2009.
Gilbert, S. 2008. Moms defend 'victimised food': McDonald's marketing program is working. Available from http//:www.walletpop. com, accessed 20 November 2009.
McDonalds 2009. Available from http://www.mcdonaldsmom.com, accessed 20 November 2009.

organizations have become interested in working in collaboration with each other.[34] Partnerships have been particularly successful in situations where both parties have been able to achieve their goals by bringing together their core expertise and resources.[35] In addition to non-governmental organizations, popular partners have been industry associations, the United Nations and other international organizations, labour unions and government agencies.[36]

Partnerships are typically defined as projects where the parties work together to carry out specific tasks or to address an issue of concern by contributing some skills and resources as well as sharing the risks of the project. Sponsorship of development projects without any direct involvement from business is therefore often excluded from the definition of partnerships and regarded as a charitable activity.[37] Partnership projects can include a variety of activities from information sharing, research and advocacy to technical assistance and delivery of development projects including the building of schools and health centres.[38] They are sometimes categorized into three types of partnerships.[39]

- **Process-orientated** partnerships where non-governmental organizations become part of activities within companies. Such partnerships include training provided by non-governmental organizations to company staff on, for example, human rights.
- **Project-orientated** partnerships where the parties collaborate to carry out a task outside the company. These partnerships include a variety of development projects from vaccination programmes to the building of infrastructure.
- **Product-orientated** partnerships focus on the development of a specific product or its endorsement. An example of such a partnership includes the development of a water purification system by Norwegian Church Aid and Hydro Polymers.

Companies find collaboration with non-governmental organizations beneficial because they may lack appropriate internal resources, and because they can expect to improve their reputation via the association with civil society organizations, while non-governmental organizations, on the other hand, will enter such partnerships with the expectation to access additional resources and influence the way in which companies interact with their environments. A more detailed list of benefits typically sought by companies and non-governmental organizations from partnership projects is provided in Table 2.1. Ultimately, a partnership, to be successful, should deliver benefits for both parties – if it does not deliver on this mutual benefit, then its prospects for continuance are minimal.

Despite the increasing number of partnerships, many concerns still exist over their advantages. The most common ones are listed in Table 2.1. As can be seem, they reflect the different goals and cultures of companies and non-governmental organizations. The latter have been particularly apprehensive about the negative effect that association with companies can have on their neutrality and reputation. This is why well-known advocacy organizations, including Amnesty International and Human Rights Watch, have been careful about their contacts with companies. Advocacy organizations have also felt that engagement with companies is consuming their resources to an extent that prevents them from focusing on their core activities. From this it follows that the non-governmental organizations that enter into partnerships with companies tend to be those that deliver development projects on the ground. Still, research shows that the decision to enter a partnership is often made by an individual who sees that the benefits of such projects exceed their risks.[40] These individuals may

TABLE 2.1 Partnership benefits and concerns

| Non-governmental organizations | | Companies | |
Benefits	Concerns	Benefits	Concerns
Funding – partnerships are a source of income	Extra work and costs	Heading off confrontation	Identifying the wrong partner
Management and technical expertise – companies have skills that NGOs may not possess	Co-option	Developing markets – partnerships help to identify business opportunities	Legal risks
Inside knowledge – partnerships provide a better understanding of companies	Credibility – concerns over conflict with staff and fundraising base	Branding	Waste of time
Chance to change an industry – partnerships may initiate change beyond partner companies	Splits among groups of activists	Media relations	Information leakage – NGOs may share the information they have gained about the company through a partnership
New solutions – NGOs are disenchanted with governments; companies provide a new solution	Fulfilling role of appeasers – fear that the company is mainly after public relations benefits	Financial benefits	Potential fall-out in the press
Credibility in the eyes of governments	Stagnation – partnerships can introduce additional bureaucracy and formality	New types of products and services	May be costly and decrease competitiveness
	Culture change	Skills and contacts Communicating values	

Source: Schiller (2003).

have to fight against internal resistance to push their organization to enter into a partnership.

As with other kinds of partnerships between organizations, including strategic alliances, there are some critical factors that can greatly enhance the prospects of success, such as:

■ a key champion of the partnership on both sides

■ direct support in principle from senior management

■ frequent and multi-channel communications between parties.

IMPLICATIONS ON CORPORATE SOCIAL RESPONSIBILITY

Issues management and stakeholder management can be seen as alternative approaches to how society's values and expectations are framed. The issues perspective depicts society's values and expectations in terms of the key issues that companies can anticipate, assess and respond to. Stakeholder management, in contrast, places more emphasis on relations to stakeholders and it is stakeholders who represent and express society's values and expectations of business. The quality of relationships to particular stakeholders and the overall network of stakeholder relations is then taken into account in decisions about particular issues.

Over time, the focus has shifted from issues management to stakeholder management, which has become increasingly popular among business and society scholars following the publication in 1984 of Freeman's book on the stakeholder approach to strategic management. Indeed, the role of stakeholders has been considered so central in the development of issues that some researchers believe that the main challenge for issues management is 'to bring a more coordinated, proactive, and sustained approach to the management of an organization's relationships with its stakeholders'.[41]

Many researchers regard issues management and stakeholder theory as complementary rather than alternative ways of identifying and addressing society's values and expectations. Freeman (1984), for example, views the identification and prioritization of issues for each stakeholder group as an essential element of stakeholder analysis (p.p. 113–114). There is still, though, some disagreement about where the focus of analysis should lie. Savage *et al.* (1991), for example, argued that the relevance of stakeholders for the organization is issue-specific and that the willingness and opportunity of stakeholders to act relates to particular issues. Conversely, Wood (1991) puts the focus on the stakeholder concept by arguing that stakeholder management emphasizes the role of actors, whereas issues management focuses on assessing the various interests of those actors.

So far as a practising manager is concerned, the key choice of approach will be based on a variety of organization-specific factors – features of the industry, for example, may well indicate that certain key issues are of overriding importance. For example, financial service companies are sufficiently regulated in most post-industrial nations that regulation, as an issue, subsumes reference to key stakeholders. Organization culture may also be a determining factor. In many public sector organizations, careful attention is paid to key stakeholders, such as funding bodies or elected representatives, so that the main issues are defined directly in terms of the interests and needs of these groups.

SUMMARY

- Stakeholders have been defined as individuals or groups that can influence or are influenced by organizational activity. Stakeholders are normally seen to include employees, suppliers, communities and other groups that have similar interests in the organization. This does not mean, however, that stakeholders would act in concert or form uniform groups. Instead, stakeholders are often loose groupings of actors that may be brought together and stirred into action by some specific circumstances.

- Stakeholders can be prioritized on the basis of various criteria depending on organizational resources, situational influences and other factors that may be pertinent. The most prominent model suggests that stakeholders are assessed on the basis of their power, legitimacy and urgency, but decisions about these attributes will always depend on how they are perceived by managers.

- Stakeholder management models identify the approach that organizations can take towards their various stakeholders. Again, the type of organization involved – its structure and ownership, size, and the dynamics of the industry it is in – will all play a role in determining how important and valuable any one of these approaches is. An important question for any reader is to identify the key factors affecting any organization they may have worked for and to estimate the impact on different stakeholder strategies.

- In practice, stakeholder management involves the identification of stakeholders and their interests, as well as the development of policies and behaviours that account for stakeholder views and concerns. Stakeholders are typically consulted via surveys and dialogue, a practice sometimes leading to partnership projects between companies and specific stakeholder groups.

- Stakeholder theory is a way of clarifying and responding to the demands and expectations placed on companies, and this is why stakeholder management has been seen as something that companies can do to become more socially responsible. Nonetheless, the relationship between stakeholder interests and ethics is not very clear as stakeholder theory does not currently offer ways to evaluate stakeholder interests on the basis of ethical principles. Yet, it does suggest how managers may arrive at decisions that take account of a wide array of values and views, a characteristic that should improve the quality of decision making.

QUICK REVIEW QUESTIONS:

1 What is the key weakness of the theory of shareholder value that stakeholder theory is intended to address?

2 How would you use the idea of salience to assess the relationship between a corporation and a particular stakeholder group?

3 What are the key features of stakeholder partnerships?

CASE STUDY: SHELL AND KIDNAPPINGS IN NIGERIA

In March 2007, a British national was kidnapped from an oil rig in Nigeria. Similar kidnappings of foreign oil workers have become a common occurrence in the country. The kidnappings are taking place in the Niger River delta, the main oil-producing area in the country. The hostages are usually released unharmed, but there are fears that casualties will occur in the future as the hostage-takers are getting more daring and violent.

Shell is the most important foreign investor in the oil sector in Nigeria. Its subsidiary in the country operates a joint venture that accounts for more than 40 per cent of Nigeria's total oil production. The partners in the joint venture include the state-owned Nigerian National Petroleum Company (55 per cent), Total of France (10 per cent) and Agip of Italy (5 per cent). Shell therefore works in close cooperation with two other foreign companies in Nigeria. Many other major foreign oil companies, including ChevronTexaco and ExxonMobil, also have operations in the country.

The kidnappings are carried out by militant groups that are seeking greater control over the revenue derived from oil in the delta. The militants, under the umbrella Movement for the Emancipation of the Niger Delta (Mend), criticize the government for using the revenue to develop other parts of the country while the residents of the region live in poverty. They also allege that oil production has resulted in environmental damage and that oil has created unemployment by destroying the livelihood of local farmers and fishermen. As a result, kidnappers have, on several occasions, demanded jobs rather than money for releasing their hostages.

The situation in the delta region is escalating. Attracted by the ransom payments, criminal gangs without political goals have copied the kidnappings. They also steal oil to sell it in the black market with the protection of dishonest military officials and politicians. Some of the oil is sold to eastern Europe in exchange for arms. As a result, the local militants and criminal gangs have become better equipped and are using speedboats, machine guns and rocket-propelled grenades in their operations. In addition to kidnappings, the groups have attacked oil installations and pipelines, at times bringing oil production to a halt.

Nigeria is the 12th largest producer of oil in the world. From this follows that any interruptions in production affect the international price of oil, particularly in the context of the war in Iraq and nuclear proliferation in Iran. Oil is also an important source of income for the Nigerian government, which receives 85 per cent of its revenue from oil-related payments.

The Nigerian government has taken a variety of measures in response to the kidnappings and other attacks. First, it has increased the number of army troops in the delta region, but the militants have enjoyed the support of the local population who have been alienated by the heavy-handedness of the army. Secondly, the government has promised to create new jobs and build infrastructure in the area. The government has also held talks with the militants, but these negotiations have failed to end the violence in the region. Finally, the government has warned the oil companies against paying ransoms for the release of their workers and thereby escalating kidnappings.

STUDY QUESTIONS

1 What are the key issues underpinning the conflict in the Niger delta?

2 Who are the main stakeholders of Shell in this context?

3 How should Shell approach each of these stakeholders? Use a model of stakeholder management to shape your answer.

SOURCES

BBC News 2008. Nigeria 'shock' after oil attack, 20 June. Available from http://news.bbc.co.uk/1/hi/world/africa/7465766.stm.

Shell 2006. *Shell Sustainability Report 2006*. Available from http://sustainabilityreport.shell.com/2006/servicepages/search.php?q=kidnappings&pageID=18352.

Walker, A. 2008. 'Blood oil' dripping from Nigeria, 27 July. Available from http://news.bbc.co.uk/1/hi/world/africa/7519302.stm.

This case study was prepared using only publicly available sources of information for the purposes of classroom discussion.

NOTES

1. Johnson, 1971, p. 50 (cited in Carroll, 1999, p. 273)
2. Vogel (1986).
3. Warhurst (2000).
4. Mintzberg *et al.* (2002). It is useful to recall in this context that, in many countries (the original corporation charters included a reference to the need to serve society.
5. Clarkson (1995); Donaldson & Preston (1995); Key (1999).
6. Freeman (1984), p. vi.

7. Freeman (1984), p. 46.
8. For example, Wheeler & Sillanpaa (1997), p. 168.
9. WWF Mission Statement, available from http://www.wwf.org.uk/core/about/whoweare.asp, accessed 9 July 2007.
10. Post *et al.* (2002).
11. For example, Clarkson (1995); Savage et al. (1991).
12. Mitchell *et al.* (1997).
13. Freeman & Gilbert (1987).
14. Freeman (1984), p. 25, 58.
15. Key (1999); Post *et al.* (2002); Rowley (1997).
16. Rowley (1997).
17. Donaldson & Preston (1995).
18. For example, Rowley (1997).
19. Donaldson & Preston (1995); Key (1999).
20. Donaldson & Preston (1995).
21. Key (1999).
22. Jones & Wicks (1999).
23. Donaldson & Preston (1995), p. 70.
24. Similarly, Hill & Jones (1992); Freeman & Evan (1990).
25. Freeman & Evan (1990).
26. For example, Freeman (1984); Post *et al.* (2002).
27. Post *et al.* (2002).
28. Freeman (1984), p. 8.
29. For example, Clarkson (1995); Wood & Jones (1995).
30. Clarkson (1995), p. 98.
31. Freeman (1984), p. 73.
32. For example, Friedman & Miles (2002); Harrison & St. John (1996); Rowley (1997); Savage *et al.* (1991).
33. See http://burma.total.com/.
34. World Economic Forum (2005).
35. Norwegian Business and Industry (2003).
36. United Nations (2006).
37. Schiller (2005).
38. Parker (2003).
39. Norwegian Business and Industry (2003).
40. Elkington & Fennell (2000).
41. Nigh & Cochran (1987), p. 4.

REFERENCES

Carroll, A. B. 1999. Corporate social responsibility: Evolution of a definitional construct. *Business & Society*, Vol. 38, No. 3, 268–295.

Clarkson, M. B. E. 1995. A stakeholder framework for analyzing and evaluating corporate social performance. *Academy of Management Review*, Vol. 20, No. 1, 92–117.

Donaldson, T. and Preston, L. E. 1995. The stakeholder theory of the corporation: Concepts, evidence, and implications. *Academy of Management Review*, Vol. 20, No. 1, 65–91.

Elkington, J. and Fennell, S. 2000. Partners for sustainability. In Bendell, J. (ed) 2000. *Terms for Endearment: Business, NGOs and Sustainable Development*. Sheffield: Greenleaf Publishing.

Freeman, R. E. 1984. *Strategic Management: A Stakeholder Approach*. Boston: Pitman/Ballinger.

Freeman, R. E. and Evan, W. 1990. Corporate governance: A stakeholder interpretation. *Journal of Behavioral Economics*, Vol. 19, No. 4, 337–359.

Freeman, R. E. and Gilbert Jr., D. R. 1987. Managing stakeholder relationships. In Sethi, S. P. and Falbe, C. M. (eds) *Business and Society: Dimensions of Conflict and Cooperation*. Lexington: Lexington Books.

Friedman, A. L. and Miles, S. 2002. Developing stakeholder theory. *Journal of Management Studies*, Vol. 39, No.1, 1–21.

Harrison, J. S. and St. John, C. H. 1996. Managing and partnering with external stakeholders. *Academy of Management Executive*, Vol. 10, No. 2, 46–60.

Hill, C. W. L. and Jones, T. M. 1992. Stakeholder-agency theory. *Journal of Management Studies*, Vol. 29, No. 2, 131–154.

Jones, T. M. and Wicks, A. C. 1999. Convergent stakeholder theory. *Academy of Management Review*, Vol. 24, No. 2, 206–221.

Key, S. 1999. Toward a new theory of the firm: A critique of stakeholder 'theory'. *Management Decision*, Vol. 37, No. 4, 317–328.

Mintzberg, H., Simons, R. and Basu, K. 2002. Memo to: CEOs. *Fast Company*, Issue 59, p. 117. Available from http://www.fastcompany.com/online/59/ceo.html, accessed 16 July 2007.

Mitchell, R. K., Agle, B. R. and Wood, D. J. 1997. Toward a theory of stakeholder identification and salience: Defining the principle of who and what really counts. *Academy of Management Review*, Vol. 22, No. 4, 853–886.

Nigh, D. and Cochran, P. L. 1987. Issues management and the multinational enterprise. *Management International Review*, Vol. 27, No. 1, 4–12.

Norwegian Business and Industry 2003. *Cooperation for Development*. Norwegian Business and Industry, the Norwegian Agency for Development Cooperation, Save the Children Norway, Veidekke, WWF-Norway, Norwegian Church Aid.

Parker, R. A. 2003. Collaboration with multinational enterprises. In Doh, J. P. and Teegen, H. (eds) *Globalization and NGOs: Transforming Business, Government, and Society*. Westport, Connecticut: Praeger.

Post, J. E., Preston, L. E. and Sachs, S. 2002. Managing the extended enterprise: The new stakeholder view. *California Management Review*, Vol. 45, No. 1, 6–28.

Rowley, T. J. 1997. Moving beyond dyadic ties: A network theory of stakeholder influences. *Academy of Management Review*, Vol. 22, No. 4, 887–910.

Savage, G. T., Nix, T. W., Whitehead, C. J. and Blair, J. D. 1991. Strategies for assessing and managing organizational stakeholders. *Academy of Management Executive*, Vol. 5, No. 2, 61–75.

Schiller, B. 2005. *Ethical Corporation Report: Business-NGO Partnerships*. Available from http://www.ethicalcorp.com/londonpartnership/FINAL_REPORT_Jan_10.pdf.

United Nations 2006. *Draft Interim Report of the Secretary-General's Special Representative on the Issue of Human Rights and Transnational Corporations and Other Business Enterprises*, E/CN.4/2006/97, February 2006.

Vogel, D. 1986. The study of social issues in management: A critical appraisal. *California Management Review*, Vol. 28, No. 2, 142–151.

Warhurst, A. 2000. *Tri-sector Partnerships for Social Investment: Business Drivers*. Working Paper No. 4. Business Partners for Development, Natural Resources Cluster. Available from http://www.bpd-naturalresources.org/media/pdf/working/work4.pdf, accessed 15 January 2004.

Wheeler, D. and Sillanpaa, M. 1997. *The Stakeholder Corporation: A Blueprint for Maximizing Stakeholder Value*. London: Pitman Publishing.

Wood, D. J. 1991. Corporate social performance revisited. *Academy of Management Review*, Vol. 16, No. 4, 691–718.

Wood, D. J. and Jones R.E. 1995. Stakeholder mismatching: A theoretical problem in empirical research on corporate social performance. *The International Journal of Organizational Analysis*, Vol. 3, No. 3, 229–267.

World Economic Forum 2005. *Partnering for Success: Business Perspectives on Multistakeholder Partnerships*. World Economic Forum in cooperation with International Business Leaders Forum and Harvard University John F. Kennedy School of Government.

THEORIES OF ETHICS

LEARNING OBJECTIVES

After studying this chapter, you should be able to:

- Assess the various roles of theories and theorizing in business ethics.
- Identify the key features of a representative range of theories of ethics.
- Critically evaluate the application of these theories in a business context.

INTRODUCTION

In this chapter we look at some of the most important theories of ethics. The treatment is of necessity selective, given that ethics has a history stretching back over 2000 years. The theories that we discuss all reflect characteristic perceptions of, and responses to, business challenges on the part of managers and other stakeholders of an organization. Ethics, the study of right and wrong, is not only the foundation of business ethics but also underpins the key arguments and concepts of corporate social responsibility. The latter is concerned with, among other things, how organizations act *responsibly*. Hence the arguments considered in this chapter reflect not only individual issues but also corporate policies and strategies.

THEORIZING ETHICS

There are two connected issues relating to the idea of a theory of ethics in business that need to be discussed before looking at any theories proper. One of these is the tension between ethical ideas as (i) *tools* for decision making and as (ii) *ways to depict, explain or reflect* the decisions we make independently of theory. The other issue is the question of what exactly a theory of ethics tells us about right and wrong.

The first of these, then, is the contrast between theories of business ethics as instruments to help managers formulate decisions or as explanations of the decisions managers make. This leads to a systematic ambiguity in the use of ethical theories, an understanding of which is critical for establishing what such theories can do. One example of this ambiguity is the question whether ethical theory is intended to help us *understand* what ethics and moral claims are and what they mean, as opposed to helping us *want* to be more ethical (i.e. helping us see how ethically right choices are preferable over ethically wrong ones). As long ago as 1912 the philosopher David Pritchard titled a famous paper 'Does moral philosophy rest on a mistake?'[1] in which he outlined this ambiguity. One response to this might be to decide that theories of ethics in future can only do one of these tasks – that is either to understand what ethics is, or to attempt to make ethics seem more desirable. However, one can argue against the dichotomy that this position presents, because understanding certain things makes us more or less disposed towards them: for example if I understand the deeper implications of a policy on equality it is likely to affect my feelings towards adopting this in practice; similarly if I am strongly committed to a certain value then this is often manifest in behaviour such as trying to establish different ways it may be implemented. So the differentiation between understanding ethics and wanting to be more ethical can at least be questioned.

Another version of this ambiguity is the question of how business people might *use* ethical theories – are they tools to justify decisions, so that one can try now one, now another, as seems appropriate to the situation? Or are they ways to illuminate our ethical instincts and intuitions, helping us reflect on choices we make anyway – that is, independently of our knowledge of theory – and see what is involved in making them? More recently, Bruce MacFarlane has brought these questions into a wider debate, with his discussion of the tension between the study *of* business ethics as a phenomenon in its own right, potentially emancipatory or even 'subversive', and the study of ethics *for* business, as a mechanism for introducing business values into the management education curriculum.

This is not an empty issue – in some way or another ethical theory should have an influence on how people act, otherwise it would be a purely intellectual study with no relevance to business. How someone's choices and actions are informed by their access to ethical theory is therefore crucial for understanding how the study of ethics can impact upon business decisions. If someone regards these theories as tools then it suggests that they may use them to try justifying choices they *already* have formulated, while if they see theory as a reflection of their ethical instincts then they will look to these to *help* them formulate choices. So this ambiguity is reflected in practical terms in the way in which ethical theories might be used by an individual – in an exaggerated opposition we could think of this as ethical theory operating at an earlier (option-generating) phase of decision making or at a later (choice-justifying) phase.

The second issue, before looking at ethical theories, is that we should ask what such theories are *for*? What is achieved by the formulation of a theory of ethics such as consequentialism?[2] What do such theories tell us? There are at least three different things that theorizing ethics *might* accomplish:

- An analysis of key ethical terms and concepts that *informs* a manager's future ethical choices.

- A statement of norms or standards that function as the *grounding* of a manager's ethical decisions.

- A fundamental ethical value that is the *basic starting point* for ethical decision making.

These represent a scale of intensity. The weakest relationship would be where a manager's decisions are in some way structured or influenced by their knowledge of a certain theory. A stronger link might be where a manager refers his or her choices back against a theory as a sort of test of ethical soundness. Perhaps with the strongest connection, a theory provides a specific value or principle that acts as the first step in any chain of ethical decision making. We see here again a manifestation of the ambiguity discussed earlier – the weakest link identified in the list above reflects the idea that theories illuminate for us the structure and nature of ethical concepts and values, whereas the strongest provides a foundation stone that purportedly is acceptable to any manager placed in an ethical decision-making situation. There is no simple formula that will necessarily link one ethical theory with one or other of these kinds of outcome. Rather, the reader should bear them in mind as we discuss the representative examples of different types of theory.

One final preliminary point about ethical theories. These are not sociological, in the sense of studying patterns and trends that are evident in people's thinking and behaviour, as measured for example by using observation, surveys or focus groups. Rather, they aim towards the establishment, critique and evaluation of ethical claims by argument, debate and examples. The difference is crucial – a sociological study discovers what people *happen to think* about a subject such as ethics in business, whereas this kind of enquiry[3] attempts to establish how people *must think* about that subject. This difference will be seen in the use of examples to illustrate possibilities, rather than to indicate what may typically occur, and in the use of argument and the analysis of concepts as the primary means of moving forward. Furthermore, on occasion such an argument is not so much analysing what an ethical concept actually represents or means, as it is proposing a particular meaning: in other words sometimes the argument is not meant to *show* how we must think but to *suggest* how we should think.

Turning to the theories themselves, there are several ways of categorizing these. Many texts classify theories into classical and modern, but this is not especially accurate (many theories were originally suggested in ancient times but have been resurrected in a more precise form in recent decades) and in any case only indicates the chronology of their origin. More illuminating is to relate them to the nature of ethical choice, as below.

One can distinguish a range of different elements in an ethical decision or choice:

- The personality features that prompt an individual to make a certain choice.
- The nature of the rationale or motive for the choice.
- The outcomes that result from the choice.
- The situation of those affected by the choice.

Each of these has become a focus of emphasis of ethical theories, and will form the basis of the next four sections. We will not pretend that the discussion is exhaustive – instead we shall cover as much as will provide a good representation of the particular kind of theory in each case. We will also consider at the end of this chapter how far such theoretical

ETHICS AND YOU

ETHICAL THEORIES – TOOLS OR EXPLANATIONS?

Consider how ethics is managed in an organization that you are familiar with. How far do managers in that organization use ethical theories as part of the training and development of staff? And how far is that use based on theories as tools or as explanations?

positions can be seen as providing 'the' truth about ethics as opposed to providing one kind of perspective on the subject.

ETHICAL EGOISM AND SUBJECTIVISM

Before embarking on a detailed discussion of the main theories that have influenced discussions of corporate social responsibility or business ethics, the majority of which are in some way or another concerned with altruistic values, it is important to note theories that on the face of it would operate against altruism and would rather favour self-interest.

Ethical egoism is the view that what is right is simply what is in one's own interests. This however, is ambiguous – it can often be taken to mean that what I perceive as in my interest at any moment is what is right, as opposed to the idea that what is right is what is in my long-term interest. What I think at a certain moment to be in my interest could easily be wrong, of course. I might think that it is in my interest to cheat a supplier at that moment that I carry out the action of cheating, but if it turns out that the supplier successfully sues me, or decides in future not to supply me, or negotiates much harder terms in the future, then arguably the outcome that I sought for – namely an improvement in my own circumstances – has not materialized. So a key issue is what difference is reflected in the meaning of 'long term.'

A rational egoism is self-oriented, but may still lead to results that may be compared to more altruistic theories. Business is intrinsically social in nature, and therefore the inter-relationships between individuals are critical to success. Behaviour that severs someone from this social nexus, such as immediate short-term acquisitiveness at the expense of others, is thus not in their long-term interest, and so not rationally egoist.

This argument is particularly relevant for business, in that the actions of organizations, rather than individuals, are often overtly self-oriented. The goal of a company is to succeed in a competitive environment where other companies may be hostile. The legal responsibility of managers is to secure positive returns for their shareholders, not for those of other companies. It would be going too far to draw the conclusion from this that companies are intrinsically anti-altruistic, but it is clear that this is a potential trend. However, the need to secure cooperation from key stakeholders requires that organizations look beyond their most immediate narrow interests. In line with this, then, one key argument often advanced in support of the need for corporate social responsibility is that it represents the rational course in the long term. Organizations may be egoist, but their rational interests require some degree of social responsiveness.

A different version of this style of attitude was advanced by Ayn Rand, who argued that altruism is misplaced, and that the true moral value is to act for oneself.[4] While this looks very like an egoist view, her argument was based on different premises. Her view was that humans are rational beings, and thus the most logical source for their ethical choices must be their own rationality. Self-interest implies a sense of responsibility to oneself. Rand argued that the pursuit of self-interest would not necessarily lead to conflicts between individuals, as potentially human needs and productiveness can be harmonized.

Rand – a refugee from the Russian Revolution – has been very influential in the United States, due mainly to the compatibility between her views and the development of the liberal market orthodoxy in American politics and economics. However, her confidence in the harmonizability of human interests, and the consequent suggestion that interests need not conflict, looks more like an article of faith than a practical claim.

Subjectivism is a more extreme view – the idea that there are no objective considerations regarding morals, and that each individual's ethical position is not subject to rational

THE VALIDITY OF EGOISM

In debates on ethics and responsibility in business, one often encounters justifications for an egoist-like position, based on comments such as 'The market requires people to act in their own interest. If you tried to be socially minded in a market context you would be out of business in no time.'

How valid is this as an argument, in your view? How far does it really support an egoist approach to ethics? And would you try to counter this attitude in a work situation (and if so, how)?

criticism from others. This can take different forms: the idea that ethical statements are really expressions of personal choice, or expressions of emotion, or represent the choices or attitudes of groups of individuals but without any claim to be universal. On this view there is no rational basis for argument or debate about ethics at all. However, in practice few people consciously adopt this position – the mere fact that we will feel resentment at the behaviour of others is sufficient to indicate that most of us regard ethical debate as a valid practice. This does not mean we are all altruistic all the time, or even often. But it shows that we do recognize altruism as a criterion by which we will evaluate the acts of others. If we did not, then we would have no basis for resenting the actions of others: if someone hurt us or caused us some loss, we might not like this, but we would have to simply accept that everyone is selfish, all the time.

Subjectivism and egoism do not necessarily imply that someone acts selfishly – they may see their own interest as rooted in the well-being of others (egoism) or they may simply feel a high degree of sympathy for others and thus act unselfishly (subjectivism).

VIRTUE ETHICS: ETHICAL CHOICES AND THE PERSONALITIES OF THOSE WHO MAKE THEM

Virtue ethics is often traced back to the writings of the ancient philosophers – most notably Aristotle[5] and other thinkers such as Confucius. The central feature of the Greek-inspired version of virtue ethics is the idea that the attempt to understand the rightness or wrongness of an *individual action* is misplaced, and that it makes more sense to look at the idea of a good *life*, considered overall. What makes someone's life a good one is best understood by considering their character; that is, by looking at specific features of their personality – which is what leads them to live the good life. This is where the term 'virtue' comes in.

By 'virtue' is generally meant a feature of an individual that prompts them to act in a certain way: kindness is a virtue because it prompts people (i.e. makes them more likely) to act in a kind manner in the right situation. A virtue does not compel someone to act in a certain way – rather it makes them more likely to do so, for example by giving them a certain perspective on issues. There have been many lists drawn up of 'the' virtues, including features such as honesty, integrity, kindness, fairness and prudence. We can extrapolate from this the idea of a good life in business as being the kind of management style evident in the actions of someone whose virtues are evident in their work behaviour and choices. Many of the virtues that have been traditionally associated with this approach seem to have a direct application to work: managerial integrity is perhaps the best known of these,[6] though the linked idea of honesty has also often been a source of attention, and virtues such as prudence have also been discussed in the context of business.

One of the key questions with this approach is settling what features should figure in a list of virtues.[7] Is courage always a virtue – or is it sometimes recklessness (consider the Anglo-Saxon saying 'it is better to fight and run away, and live to fight another day')? Equally, for those of a religious persuasion, piety would likely be an important virtue, while those who are atheistic would find this irrelevant. This is not a fatal flaw with the idea of virtue ethics, however. One important distinction that needs to be made here is between a *person being virtuous*, and a person *displaying specific virtues*. Aristotle in particular made clear that 'virtue' and the idea of a good life needed to be conceived not simply in terms of specific acts that arise from specific motives. Rather he made clear that being virtuous represented a particular way of living your life. A good life was one that was lived in accordance with the specific nature of human beings – what he called fulfilling their particular kind of 'excellence'. In other words, Aristotle claimed that being ethical was directly related to a particular idea of what it is to be human. This in turn, though, implied that a person living a good life *avoided extremes* – such a life represented moderation in choices and motives. Virtue for Aristotle was explicitly contrasted with vice in this respect: a virtuous person deals with a certain issue (such as the management of danger) in a balanced manner, while an unbalanced approach – overly or inappropriately heedless of danger – would manifest the vice of recklessness (and thus in doing so would detract from the individual reaching their fulfilment or a state of excellence). So while many writers have in recent times looked at specific lists of virtues, the basic Aristotelian approach was to indicate that there was an underlying pattern to how a virtuous person deals with their life, one based on moderation, on finding the mean between extremes, which would assist an individual to be truly fulfilled.

Put in this manner this sounds deceptively simple – and it probably is deceptive, for moderation itself could as easily be seen as at times appropriate and at other times inappropriate. For example, in the midst of a business crisis, such as impending bankruptcy, it would be casual to the point of negligence to be moderate in one's response – a radical, dynamic and possibly risky response is probably more suitable. But underlying this is the idea that good business behaviour is not simply good because someone demonstrates a range of specific personal attributes in what they do, but because the personal qualities evident in their behaviour reflect an *overall approach* to issues. Aristotle thought of this overall approach as being one of moderation in all things, but it is open to other possibilities, such as maintaining a coherence between one's choices – taking integrity as the overarching virtue. And there are doubtless other ways to conceive of virtues as arising from a specific conception of human nature and human fulfilment. Whatever the specifics here, common to these is a sense that the virtues are not just a discrete list of qualities, but that in some way they reflect a certain kind of *unity* within an individual.[8]

There are many advantages to considering someone's character when thinking of ethics in business. Business and organizational management is a dynamic environment in which not only are specific elements changing but where the very nature of the field can change, sometimes rapidly and fundamentally. An individual equipped with rules and principles may find these become redundant. Equally some dilemmas may be too involved to easily fall under a set of principles. In such circumstances, what matters will surely be the basic integrity and orientation to value that an individual professional may demonstrate – how they act when the rules no longer determine the right response, and they have to make their own mind up. This element to the theory is critical – for virtues, like any sources of ethical evaluation, can at times conflict, and therefore some basis is required on which to make a decision in such cases.

ETHICS IN PRACTICE

WHOSE VIRTUES?

Traditional European virtues in the main stem from Christianity, and include concepts such as honesty, kindness, prudence, charity, mercy and humility. Traditional Chinese virtues are greatly influenced by Confucius, and are based around concepts of benevolence, honesty, loyalty, wisdom, integrity and propriety. Arguably, when considered collectively, these appear very similar, but their interpretation can lead to greatly varying practice.

How might you use these two conceptions of virtue when working with a team containing individuals from both European and Chinese cultures?

Clear practical implications of virtue ethics can be drawn out that can be applied directly to business. If character is what is important, then the development of professionals and managers in terms of the kinds of judgement they make, the kinds of attitudes they hold, becomes an important organizational goal. Equally, organizational cultures that reflect a virtue-ethical orientation are likely to focus less on blame (for actions) and more on self-evaluation (for character). And finally, the implication of the *unity* of virtues should, if taken to its logical conclusion, indicate a coherence between internal organizational values and the values inherent in the goods or services produced or delivered. An organization that produces chemical weapons, which are then sold to a government that is known to use them to violate the human rights of their citizens, will find it difficult to set this practice alongside a virtue-ethical approach to their business, not simply because their business develops products that can be harmful to individuals, but because the possibility of these products causing harm cannot be made consistent with an underlying unity of the virtues. Whether in terms of human flourishing, or in terms of moderation in all things, once a potentially harmful product has been sold on to a separate party that has malign intentions, then the fact that the manufacturer can no longer guarantee that virtues such as consideration or avoidance of harm will be upheld counts against them, if not as seriously as for the government using them, then at least as a willing collaborator.

We see here a potential linkage between ethics and corporate social responsibility, as explained in the two previous chapters. For here the strategic choices of the firm are open

ETHICS AND YOU

LAW AND ETHICS

How far would you go in condoning actions of your employer that may be legal but you feel are nevertheless immoral? For example, how would you react to the following:

- Exploiting a weak workforce by paying them low wages?
- Selling goods that are accepted to be sub-standard and overpriced?
- Dealing with suppliers who refuse to disclose the sources of their materials?
- Supporting a government that represses political dissent?

THINKING CRITICALLY ABOUT ETHICS

APPLYING VIRTUE ETHICS

Suppose you start working as a manager in a small marketing firm, specializing in brand consultancy. Your new boss says to you, 'I want this firm to become known as honest, considerate and responsible, and I want to build our reputation for integrity. I expect all my managers to start putting this into practice forthwith.'

How would you try to put this into practice? How far is it a realistic aspiration, and what are the potential dangers or risks?

to evaluation directly in terms of consistency with given virtues. The above discussion is, of course, idealistic in tone. This provides a strong clue as to the kind of theory that virtue ethics is best considered to be: for this is neither a simple analysis of key concepts, nor a step in an ethical argument. Rather it is a reflection of the kinds of judgement and the kinds of person we aspire to. This is less theory as a tool and more theory as a depiction – an attempt at explanation of what we are like, rather than a model that we can directly use in our day-to-day decisions. But over and above this, it is an aspirational theory, one that aims not simply to indicate what our ethical attitudes are, but to change these in a certain direction. We shall come across this orientation to change in a later section.

This, however, puts a finger on the main shortcoming of virtue ethics. For while it can help people understand more about ethics and values in their work, it is not helpful once we are faced directly with a dilemma. If I cannot already answer the question 'What is the honest thing to do here?' when, say, offered a bribe, then I cannot easily answer the question 'What would an honest person do here?' Indeed, one version of a virtue ethic would have it that the virtuous person would simply not find a bribe tempting – arguing that to the extent that someone does find it tempting they are not really virtuous at all. It is as if virtue ethics is very useful for offline reflection, but less helpful when we go online and have to confront conflicts and temptations. In the next sections we will consider approaches that do have a more immediate bearing on practical situations that may confront a manager.

To summarize this discussion, virtue ethics is an approach to right and wrong that focuses on the character or personality of the individual concerned. It considers those qualities of an individual that can lead people to act in certain ways (virtues), and in more sophisticated versions also considers what might be the underlying basis for such ranges of virtues. As a theory that aims at reflecting the attitudes we have (and to some extent that aims to modify these) it is most valuable for developmental work, but is of less help when an individual is confronted with immediate, pressing dilemmas.

DEONTOLOGICAL THEORIES: THE ETHICS OF THE ACT ITSELF AND ITS RATIONAL MOTIVATION

We have discussed how virtue ethics – the idea that ethics is best seen in terms of the character of individuals making choices – helps us to understand patterns and trends in people's behaviour, but it does not furnish a tool to help people make decisions in an ethically acceptable manner. One alternative approach, which arguably can help the making of decisions, is to consider whether *features of actions themselves* can function as a basis for deciding what to do, by identifying duties and obligations arising from the nature of an action. Hence the ungainly term 'deontology' – derived from Greek terms for 'duty' and 'explanation'.

By far the best known example of a deontological theory of ethics is that of the 18th century German philosopher, Immanuel Kant. However, while we will discuss his approach in detail below, it should be noted that this is one of several examples of deontology, not the sole version.[9] In particular there is an element of absolutism about Kant's views, which is not a necessary aspect of deontology: it is quite possible to identify ethically relevant aspects of actions and their motives that carry a degree of relativity, depending on other factors such as an individual's personal circumstances. Kant, in contrast though, did attempt to outline a theory of ethics that was absolute, and operated independently of particular circumstances.

Kant's approach to ethics is to focus on what humans can be fully responsible for, which is essentially our motives and intentions: we cannot be responsible entirely for the consequences of our actions because these may be affected by fortuitous circumstances. But although in his later writings he did discuss an aspect of character as a feature of ethics (specifically what he called people's overall disposition towards ethics) his most influential arguments relate to the idea that some actions can be demonstrated to be *intrinsically* ethically worthwhile.[10] Essentially, Kant argued that a pure ethical choice – an action done out of a sense of duty – has a certain kind of form. An ethical choice is expressible in *universalizable* terms. By this, Kant meant that if I do something for a certain reason it must be possible for anyone else to adopt the same reason. Take the idea of lying; Kant argued that this cannot be universalizable because if everybody lied then the whole practice of communication via statements of what is intended to be true would break down. The wrongness of lying is therefore that it cannot be adopted by all as a principle of action. In contrast, the keeping of a promise is universalizable in that it is perfectly possible for everyone to keep their promises – the practice would be strengthened and reinforced by promise-keeping behaviour in exactly the opposite manner to which a practice of lying would be self-defeating.

Kant's best known expression of his ethical approach lies in what he called the categorical imperative. By this he meant an imperative that applied to a rational actor no matter what the circumstances and no matter what that individual's particular desires and needs (we see an element of the absolutism referred to earlier). Kant contrasted hypothetical and categorical imperatives – a hypothetical imperative would be of the form 'if you want to achieve x , then do y', whereas the categorical imperative states 'do z'. In other words it applies no matter what your personal desires or wishes, but rather applies to any rational actor in any circumstances.

Much is made by some writers of three different formulations that Kant made of the categorical imperative, especially one version where he talked of treating rational nature as an end and never as a means. This could be construed as a theory of how humans use their rationality, and thus a theory of what people can expect as a *right* in respect of their rationality. But it is not a blueprint for human rights in any detailed sense. Rather Kant was trying to express the idea that if an action was a duty for *one* rational individual, it would apply to *any* – and therefore we have to accept the rationality of others as being of equal importance to our own, and not as something to be dismissed. In effect what Kant was suggesting is that since we – humans – are all rational, then we have the same rational ends (though of course we may have many non-rational ends, based on desires, that we do not share). So if something is a duty for one person, it will be a duty for all.

One of the great merits of Kant's approach is that, despite some of his more abstract reasoning, the theory contains a straightforward test of whether something is ethically acceptable or not, a test which it would appear that any individual, in professional or personal life, can easily apply. Faced with a dilemma, such as whether or not to accept a bribe in order to win a contract that will save jobs, a manager can quickly reflect on whether acceptance of the bribe is a motive that could be applied by anyone in any context. And they would find that it cannot be consistently maintained: if taking a bribe to win a contract were adopted by all as an open principle of action, then trust in business would quickly break down, individual purchasing managers could not be relied upon to get the best deal, and in all transactions it would be assumed that the negotiators were acting in their personal interest (in offering or accepting a bribe) and not in the interests of the business. In which case it would not be possible to give them the task of negotiating supplier contracts. And then business to business trade would cease to be viable.[11]

The organizational implications of such an approach include a need to develop in individuals sufficient self-knowledge that they can recognize their own intentions clearly, in order to be able to evaluate these on the universalizability test. But in addition it would require professionals and managers to *care* about what their duty is. While in one sense this is virtually a truism (if asked we would all want to do the right thing) in another it is anything but – much business decision making is founded on uncritical acceptance of organizational goals, and on aims defined by classical microeconomics, which do not incorporate any sense of what one's duty is, but rely instead on the universal pursuit of self-interest. Even where managers query organizational goals there is immense pressure on them to stifle their misgivings.

So there is a practical drawback to a deontological approach to managerial decision making: to be really effective it requires managers to have a keen sense of rightness and wrongness, one which is not often encouraged in modern business practice.

There are other shortcomings of deontology (at least in Kant's version of this approach). For example, Kant makes assumptions about what counts as a consistent practice: it would seem logically open to someone simply to say 'So what if everybody broke their promises? I don't support the idea of promising anyway so I will simply profit from everyone else's naivety at the moment.' Kant seems to suggest in cases such as honesty and promising that what underpins these is an acceptance of a given practice, and that the collapse of such a practice would be self-defeating. While this might be a strong argument if someone adopted a principle of breaking promises whenever it benefited them, it would be less so if someone simply rejected the practice of promising altogether.

ETHICS IN PRACTICE

EQUALITY AND THE CATEGORICAL IMPERATIVE

Perhaps the clearest example of the categorical imperative being put into practice is provided by the growth in processes and policies relating to equality of opportunity. The principle behind these policies is the treatment of all individuals as being equal, not simply in the sense of being equally needy, but also as being equally valuable to an organization.

The development of diversity policies is a case in point – diversity management is where an organization tries to make the fullest use of the demographic diversity of its workforce, for example by making sure that speakers of minority languages are rewarded for their occasional value in communicating with a client or customer who spoke the language in question. Where this goes beyond Kant's own views is that he focused on people's rationality as the basis for treating them equally – he argued that it is in virtue of our ability to think logically that our reasons merit being taken seriously by others. Diversity suggests that our capacity to make uniquely valuable contributions to society also marks each of us out as of equal merit.

THINKING CRITICALLY ABOUT ETHICS

THE LIMITS TO HONESTY

One of the clearest dilemmas arising from a Kantian approach is the conflict between what seems to be a principle of duty, such as telling the truth, and a highly damaging prospective outcome, such as the revelation of something embarrassing. Kant's absolutism suggests that one should tell the truth no matter what the consequences, but in practice most of us tell 'white lies' – small untruths that are not especially serious. But where does one draw the line?

A related shortcoming of the universalizability concept is the possibility of *fanaticism*: superficially at least, one can imagine an individual who maintains a consistent principle, even if this led to disproportionately harsh consequences, for the individual themselves as much as for others. Suppose, for example, that a senior manager said, 'Anyone who presents a false expenses claim should be sacked', and when challenged about the possibility of honest error says, 'No matter what the reason, false expenses claims are gross misconduct and should be dealt with accordingly.' This would be a consistent, but overly stringent principle. Most people would want to temper such a principle with some kind of qualification such as 'except when the falsity arises from a genuine error' or similar. But on the Kantian approach the extreme principle is as ethically sound as a more lenient one, if adopted and progressed consistently, on the basis that the individual saw it as a principle of duty. This runs counter to our instincts, where the gravity of consequences is a key factor to be taken into account when deciding what to do. In practice the stronger principle would itself probably lead to some kind of breakdown in the practice of making expense claims, but on Kant's view it is as sound as a less demanding principle. In the next section we will look at a theory that focuses specifically on outcomes and consequences.

What kind of theory is the deontological approach? A tool for decision making, or an explanation of what a right decision should look like? In its pure form this is intended as an explanation of what it is for an act to be ethically right, though within this there lies a test of rightness that could be used as a tool for decision makers. However, this is not a take it or leave it approach that can be ignored if it does not yield the answer desired – in that respect it is less a tool and more a proposal as to how ethical decisions ought to be arrived at, if we were more consistent in our thinking.

To summarize: we have discussed Kant's view as the best known and most clear example of a deontological approach; this provides a clear explanation of what it is to act out of a sense of duty, and also gives us a clear test of whether a principle is ethically acceptable or not; however, the test does not eliminate extreme counter-examples.

CONSEQUENTIALIST THEORIES: EVALUATING CHOICES IN TERMS OF THE OUTCOMES THEY BRING ABOUT

We move a step along the process of action, to the view that the ethics of an action is to be evaluated in terms of the *consequences* it carries. As with the other theories considered in this chapter, this stems from a natural instinct that we have – in this case to look at what results from an act before judging it. For example, at the time of the Barings Bank collapse, there may have been other financial traders who were doing similar things to Nick Leeson. If so, they were lucky, and have escaped the universal opprobrium that Leeson experienced. But even if they were now discovered, the actions that they performed, while representing breaches of trust and to a significant extent to be condemned, would still not bear the vast responsibility that Leeson's acts do – for the simple reason that his led to the collapse of a bank and theirs did not. In other words, one act is made much worse because of its consequences.

This formulation of the view pitches it in direct contrast with deontology, where some acts are wrong no matter what the consequences. While it is true that the most well-known versions of consequentialism can indeed be presented in opposition to deontological ethics, it is also true that the two approaches share many assumptions. For example, both can be seen as an attempt to provide a mechanism for decision making, so that the individual caught in a dilemma as to what to do could (supposedly) use one of these approaches to help fix on a choice of action that is ethically acceptable. And behind this is another assumption – that there is a solution to every ethical problem, that an individual can always find a choice that is the best (or at least, the least worse) available in the circumstances. Related to this is the idea that 'ought' implies 'can' – in other words, that the right action can actually be carried out. Furthermore, both approaches make the assumption that we can act in as full a knowledge of the situation as is relevant – that everything that I need to know, I *can* know in order to make a decision.

By far the best known example of consequentialism is utilitarianism, the view that an action is right if it promotes the greatest good for the greatest number of people. While some echoes of this were evident in ancient times, it was developed in its modern forms during the 17th to 19th centuries by a line of British philosophers, including Locke, Hume, Jeremy Bentham and, most influentially, John Stuart Mill.[12] Essentially the position comes down simply to the claim that in any situation there is one right action, and that is the one that will bring the greatest benefits, this being defined as the greatest good of the greatest number. Different explanations have been given of what 'good' here should mean. Mill tried to identify it with pleasure, though this has been argued against on the basis that it fails to distinguish between so-called 'lower' pleasures, such as the satisfaction of basic appetites, and 'higher' ones such as the contemplation of great art. While such a distinction may be a little idealistic,[13] there is certainly a burden to be placed on the idea of what 'good' is in this theory. Another idea that has been offered is that the good is happiness – so the principle becomes the greatest happiness of the greatest number. However, this is also subject to criticism, being itself not a simple concept, and subject to serious variation between different individual and social and cultural groups.

Be that as it may, the idea behind consequentialism is that once one has identified what is regarded as absolutely good – happiness, pleasure and perhaps one could add fulfilment to this list – then actions are evaluated in terms of how far they contribute towards or detract from achievement from this good. Utilitarianism is the specific version of this view that the kind of achievement to be used as the criterion for evaluation of actions is that of a maximum across the whole population. But alternative forms of distribution may be considered – for example, actions could be evaluated in terms of whether they brought about the highest results for each individual affected.

A recent[14] refinement of utilitarianism in particular, has been a distinction between applying the 'greatest happiness' principle to individual *acts*, as opposed to particular *rules*. The traditional, act-utilitarian view presented evaluation as being made of a specific choice made by an individual at a particular point. The rule-utilitarian approach, on the other hand, states that evaluation should be made not of individual actions but of the rules that we

THINKING CRITICALLY ABOUT ETHICS

CONSEQUENTIALISM IN NOVEL SITUATIONS

Consequentialism assumes that we can collect sufficient relevant information to make a reasonable estimation of what the likely results of our actions will be. One drawback to this is that some situations are novel to us, where we do not know exactly what the key underlying aspects of the situation are, because it is outside of our previous experience and knowledge. How would you evaluate the potential consequences in such a situation?

follow. Blurring the difference between deontology and consequentialism, this approach has been criticized on the basis that it does not tell us what to do in any specific situation (should one follow a justified rule even when in this specific instance it leads to undesirable results?). Furthermore, it fails to acknowledge the issues of when rules, justified in themselves, conflict – one rule suggesting one course of action and another a different one.

Consequentialist theories have a familiar ring to many professionals when they encounter theories of ethics, as they do bear a passing resemblance in certain respects to some models of decision making. For example, Vroom and Yetton[15] posited that managers should use a range of decision strategies, each of which is suited to specific combinations of circumstances. The reasoning here is that in a situation requiring the taking of a decision there are critical questions to be resolved (such as how much information is needed to make the decision, and whether a manager has enough to make it autonomously or needs others to be involved). According to Vroom, in each such combination the best results will follow from the adoption of a certain kind of strategy (such as taking the decision oneself after gaining advice from staff). Even greater similarity with consequentialism may be seen in Vroom's account of career motives, which has been elaborated to become the original version of the expectancy theory of motivation in general. Vroom's version of expectancy presented a decision as a choice between alternatives, each of which would be evaluated in terms of what outcomes it led to and how far each of those outcomes contributed to a specific property. So the decision would be made in favour of which option had the greatest total amount of that property when all its outcomes were summed together.

This similarity is striking, as it almost repeats verbatim one form of utilitarianism. However, it must be borne in mind that this is a theory not of ethics but of motivation and choice, one for which there is significant and substantial evidence collected from field research.[16] Having said this, it puts a finger on a couple of clear pragmatic advantages that consequentialism has over other approaches to ethics, namely that managers can use it easily to choose between alternatives, and that it is easily comprehended by someone with a basic business knowledge.

Problems with consequentialism

However, there are several weaknesses with consequentialism. The main weakness of this approach is the failure to adequately explain what counts as the basic value against which all actions are to be evaluated. We have seen that happiness and pleasure are difficult to explain properly. No more straightforward is the concept of satisfaction – one traditional counter-argument to this (stemming from Plato) is the choice of whether you would prefer

SACRIFICES FOR THE GREATER GOOD

One implication of consequentialism already alluded to is the idea of sacrificing one party's interests for the sake of the greater good. This happens often in business – laying off some staff so that a firm can stay in business, for example. But how far can this go? At what point does sacrifice become unacceptable?

to be a satisfied pig or a dissatisfied philosopher?[17] The ultimate degeneration of the use of satisfaction as the key value in utilitarianism is in the classical possessive individualism that states that whatever an individual desires or seeks is thereby a source of satisfaction and therefore relevant to the ethical evaluation of actions. On this view, utilitarianism would become no more than a calculation of wants.

A second problem with consequentialism is that, in parallel with deontology, it can have its own fanatics, for this is the view that 'the end justifies the means'. In other words, if an action will lead to a justifiable end then it is itself automatically justified, even if it has undesirable consequences of its own.[18] So, for example, if a business needs to resolves a trade union dispute, and finds that the quickest way is to blame a certain manager and sack them (perhaps even when they are in fact innocent of any wrongdoing) then this will be justified if it succeeds, for the hardship of the individual manager is more than offset by the success of the business and the securing of wages by the workers returning to work.

Yet a third issue is a whole raft of counter-examples over consequences and their distribution. One example of this is the gruesome idea that a medical firm could save many lives by taking one healthy child and butchering it for spare parts – thus saving perhaps many lives for the sake of one sacrifice. Clearly no one could accept such a move, though it would appear to be right under utilitarianism. Another type of objection is that in some cases the arithmetical summation of satisfaction may simply not work – as Raimond Gaita puts it, how to differentiate between a bomb that kills one million people and a bomb that kills seven million.[19] Of course the latter is worse than the former, but in fact both are so utterly dreadful that one could never simply say that one is 'better' than the other, as if choosing the smaller bomb rather than the larger is morally OK.

To sum up, consequentialism, particularly in its utilitarian version, is likely to be familiar to many business people as it has resonances with models in decision making (as well as economics). It provides a superficially straightforward method for making choices, though underlying this are serious difficulties in identifying what is valuable absolutely. In addition, the approach encounters several kinds of counter-example that suggest that ethically right acts have some degree of egalitarianism in the distribution of outcomes.

JUSTICE AND RIGHTS-BASED THEORIES: EVALUATING CHOICES IN TERMS OF THEIR SOCIAL IMPACTS

It is somewhat artificial to put together approaches to ethics based on rights and on justice, as these are really quite distinct approaches. However, they share certain features, in particular both having a more politically focused perspective on ethical choices, as well as the related aspect that they both place emphasis on long-term, social outcomes of choices (rather than the calculation of immediate results envisaged by many consequentialists). The corollary of the second of these points is that these theories move away from individual actions towards wider policies and strategies – the emphasis being therefore less on individual choices and more on broader trends in decisions.

Rights

First, what might be meant by an 'ethics of rights'? From the outset it must be recognized that what is meant here are not legal or political rights, which are enshrined in the constitutions and systems of law in each nation-state. Nor even is it meant to refer to moral rights, for these are essentially an alternative formulation to duties that may be underpinned by any one of several different ethical theories. Rather the term here is intended to refer to a much more evasive concept – the idea of *human rights*. In other words, the idea that there are some rights that people have solely by virtue of their being human.

Before we turn to what such rights might be, we need to consider a more basic question: what does it mean to say that someone has a 'right' to something? How does having a right to a certain amenity such as freedom of speech differ from simply saying that it is right that all people enjoy such freedom? What makes it a *right*?

A parallel with political rights would suggest that if someone has a human right to x then they arc justified in taking specific steps to assert that right, for example by acting in a manner that assumes that this right exists, or by seeking to use decision processes such as state legal apparatus to enforce their right. While this is a useful analogy, and while indeed there have been many legal and quasi-legal attempts to make human rights more like political rights,[20] the fact remains that someone would have a human right to x even if no legal or social system in the world acknowledged this. Indeed many of the most acute dilemmas in corporate ethics occur where a firm operates in a country in which a fundamental human right is denied by the legal system of that country (for example where a country prevents one sector of the population from participating freely in political processes, or suppresses a particular religion).

Shaw[21] identifies four useful properties of human rights, as indicated in the accompanying text box. However, these describe how the concept of human rights works – they do not define exactly what a right *is*. Perhaps the easiest way of thinking of rights is to go back to the Aristotelian idea that a human being has a natural state of excellence, and therefore human rights are those amenities that enable someone to attain such a condition.

SHAW'S PROPERTIES OF HUMAN RIGHTS

- **Universal application** – everyone has the same human rights.
- **Equality of application** – everyone has the same human rights to the same extent; there are no individuals who are 'more equal than others'.
- **Non-destructibility of rights** – you cannot sign away human rights, nor can any other party negate them; we have such rights in perpetuity.
- **Independence of social or political institutions or practices** – we all have human rights irrespective of what any or all governments, organizations, political parties or social institutions or traditions include or exclude.

In this discussion an important distinction to be drawn is that between negative and positive rights. Negative rights are those that release the individual from restrictions, such as the right to be free of religious persecution, or the right to be free to express one's political beliefs publicly. Positive rights are those that indicate benefits that each individual can expect from society and governments, such as rights to education or healthcare.[22] How far these create obligations for governments, how far for civil society organizations, and how far for corporations is a substantial matter of political theory. But what is clear is that an ethics based on the concept of human rights developed in this way is not addressed simply to corporations and their employees in the manner that, say, deontology or consequentialism is. For the latter approaches to ethics apply in the same manner whether decisions are taken by individuals, firms or regulatory bodies. With the matter of rights a decision made by a corporation has to take account of what actions are taken by relevant governments and civil society organizations. In a country where healthcare is not provided or supported to any great degree by government actions, then a corporate decision to offer free healthcare to its employees is a major contribution towards the fulfilment of their human rights. In a country where there is substantial free healthcare publicly available then the same corporate act has far less ethical significance.

This argument, however, applies more obviously with positive rights than with negative. The latter, involving issues such as freedom from harassment, or freedom from intrusion on private personal life, can be more straightforwardly applied to corporate action without consideration of the behaviour or policies of governments. The obligation for corporations to respect privacy, or to provide a reasonable degree of personal safety in the workplace, for example, are more closely tied to the nature of the transactions companies involve themselves in, with employees, customers and other stakeholders, than positive rights, which relate more closely with national social policy.

It should be clear that attention to rights is a key plank of much of corporate social responsibility, especially in the manner in which corporations based in affluent northern and eastern developed countries operate in poorer economies in the south. It is not clear, however, that an ethic based on rights, negative or positive, can fully encompass the range of duties and obligations that are commonly expected of a corporation. For example, the expectation that a corporation should provide work that is developmental for employees, avoids drudgery and contributes to an individual's personal fulfilment, does not seem to be in any way a *right*. And while this is not universally accepted as an obligation, it is certainly accepted by some.[23] Given that it is at least arguable that this is not a human right, then it seems that there are some obligations for organizations and managers that are not based on human rights. So human rights appears to be an important but incomplete basis for the ethics of business.

Despite this, it is equally clear that the acceptance of certain potential benefits as human rights does create some obligation for organizations, as already considered in earlier chapters on corporate social responsibility, and as will be considered at further length in later chapters.

What this underlines again is the intimate linkage between business ethics and corporate social responsibility, conceived of as distinct aspects of management action and of the study of business. While ethics at first sight, and as presented in the Introduction to the book, is primarily concerned with individual actions and choices, and corporate social responsibility is correspondingly conceived of in terms of the overall impact of corporate behaviour on social fabric, we continue to see connections between the more local decisions made by managers (and which might be more properly regarded as ethical issues) and broader policy and strategic issues that would naturally sit more comfortably within corporate social responsibility.

In parallel with the discussions of virtue ethics and consequentialism, there is naturally a potential dispute about which specific benefits should be regarded as a human right, as opposed to being simply desirable in some weaker sense. The fact that there is likely to be variation across cultures but also across political ideologies does not diminish the importance of the concept of human rights, but it does underline the difficulties of applying it in concrete situations.

Similarly, there are also issues concerning conflicts of rights: the right to free expression of political views is often cited as a human right, but what if this conflicts with, say, the right to be free from discrimination on the grounds of sexual orientation, as when one employee in a workplace expresses critical views about gays and lesbians? Or what of the conflict between the right of employees to enjoy personal privacy (e.g. when making personal communications by telephone or email) and the rights of customers to expect financial details used to make payments for goods or services to be kept secure. Of course these are soluble in different ways. But the point is that the resolution is not simply 'read off' from a definition of human rights, but represents an additional element to the theory.

One potential addition is the concept of proportionality.[24] This is the idea that it could be justifiable that human rights may be ethically violated, where there are cases of conflict between them, in proportion to the seriousness of the issue under consideration. Thus someone would be justified in eavesdropping on employee's personal phone calls if the damage done by not doing so were to seriously threaten the security of the business – say if there were some apparent evidence that customers' bank details were being leaked to third parties. The proportion involved here might be that it would be reasonable to eavesdrop on individuals who had access to such data, and for a period during which the suspicion remained that customers' rights might be violated. It would not, however, justify a blanket assertion of the company's right to access all and any personal communications.[25]

Turning to the role of justice as a theoretical basis for business ethics, we see again the balance between organization-specific and society-wide issues, and the interplay between corporations and governments in terms of their provision and responsibilities. The close connections between justice and rights, as well as the linkage between justice and the operation of state legal processes, means that there is a strong link with political concepts. On the other hand, it is also clear that obligations based on justice apply to corporations and other organizations at least as much as they might do to individuals.

Justice

Justice has been debated since the time of Socrates, with many different interpretations having been proposed, though in modern times it tends to be equated with the idea of the fair and equal application of laws and moral codes and rules. However, too close an examination of this can suggest its own difficulties. 'Fair' seems to indicate that individuals receive what they deserve, while 'equal' means that all get a comparable share of social benefits and goods. While this is only an apparent problem (in practice fairness is usually explained as all members of society receiving an equal opportunity to partake of available social benefits) it points up that justice is not to be easily explained away in terms of more basic concepts.

Concepts of justice are often differentiated on the basis of whether or not they refer to *processes* or *outcomes*. The former (known unsurprisingly as procedural justice) points to how laws and organizational rules operate, and how they ensure that all members of a given institution are treated equally (and thus with equal degree of fairness) by such rules.

JUSTICE AND SENIOR MANAGERS' REMUNERATION

A common argument made in favour of senior managers being treated differently from other organizational members is that they often have to devote a greater proportion of their life to their job, can often run substantial personal career risks depending on the kinds of decision they make, and by their actions can often add – or subtract – a huge amount of value to (or from) the organization. Hence, many private companies will pay their most senior executives percentage salary increases well beyond those of other staff, while public sector organizations may allow senior staff access to much more generous benefits than other employees, including 'golden hello' and 'goodbye' starting and termination pay premiums, enhanced pensions and privileged expense allowances.

How far is this compatible with principles of natural justice? How far can this be justified in terms of equality, fairness or deservingness? How would you present your position to a group of chief executives who have themselves benefited from such arrangements and practices?

The just treatment of employees, for example, requires that all are subject to the same set of organizational regulations, and that exceptions are not made in favour of, say, more senior employees.

In contrast, justice focused on outcomes is often referred to as *distributive* justice (i.e. the justice of how social benefits are distributed to all). It is impossible to discuss distributive justice in any detail without venturing into substantial issues of political theory, and thus of political ideology. This is often overlooked in texts on business ethics and corporate social responsibility, where issues are presented as if in a politics-free environment, as if they would apply no matter what the dominant political ideology. Unfortunately this is a serious oversimplification of the basis of distributive justice. Of the many versions of this concept, we shall very briefly consider three: a libertarian approach, an approach based on the idea that society is a kind of contract between its citizens, and a radical approach based on the idea that there are distinct and opposing groups in society.[26]

The libertarian approach sees distributive justice as no more than the outcomes resulting from procedurally just operations. The main modern proponent of this view, Robert Nozick, takes lawful possession of property as the primary feature of human society, and transactions are evaluated in terms of how lawful are the transfers of property and value between individuals. This is clearly a strongly free-market view of human society, and given that no nation currently operates in this manner, it is clear that there is as much aspiration here as analysis of what is right or wrong. While there is much that can be said in favour of this approach, it is clear that societies exist with quite differing ideas about what counts as private property and what counts as public amenity. Consider just two examples. First, the collaborative project of academic learning, dating back over 2000 years in Europe and possibly longer in parts of Asia, relies on the idea that knowledge is a public amenity, not owned by its originator or sponsor. Once knowledge is produced, it is presented to the academic community – which has been global in nature for more than 1000 years, involving scholars from European, Arabic, Chinese and Indian traditions – where it is critiqued, developed, extended and adapted as far as is intellectually valid, all of which is open to the public, and from which the public may develop technologies and systems of social organization and production. It would of course be open for scholars to lay claim to ownership of the knowledge they produce – as, for example, some American researchers have attempted to 'copyright' genetic coding, by claiming the tests used to identify DNA strings as intellectual property. But this is simply not how most academic knowledge has worked for many centuries.

A second example is the varying approaches to land adopted by different pre-industrial societies. There are as many traditions that see land as a common amenity to be stewarded by its current occupants[27] as there are those who regard land as property to be taken and held for private benefit. Of course, the libertarian might write the former off as not being just societies at all, but this would be a strange conclusion, given that in these communities land is made equally and freely available to all who are deemed citizens. So the libertarian approach is not a true reflection of what all different societies actually regard as just distribution, and arguably it can be seen as an expression of a modern capitalist ideology.

The social contract approach is best typified by the highly influential views of John Rawls. Summarizing brutally, Rawls suggested that we should try to imagine society as if it were today to arise from nothing; further, he suggests that we imagine that no one actually knows what position they will occupy in society, from the lowest to the highest – he talked of each of us making the choice of our social position under a 'veil of ignorance'. In such a situation, what would make society as fair (for Rawls this is virtually equated with just) as possible? Rawls turns this question around, however, and actually asks – what would each of us do to try to get as good a result for ourselves as possible, given that we do not actually know what position we will occupy in this brave new world? Rawls talked of this as a 'veil of ignorance' – a lack of knowledge about one's specific position in society. Based on this question of self-interest, each of us, Rawls claims, would choose a society in which the fate of the lowest was tolerable (for who knows which of us would actually end up having such a fate). A just society, then, for Rawls, is one where the worst position is still morally acceptable. The other side to this is that if a society exists where we regard the fate of its lowest members as intolerable, then that alone makes it unjust.

There are faint echoes of Kantianism in this argument, notably the idea that each of us will judge what is a just society on the same basis – reflecting Kant's view that a rational end for one human being is a rational end for any. But there is also a reflection of consequentialism in the focus on the idea that what is right is measured in terms of society-wide outcomes.

Criticisms of Rawlsian social contract theory have focused on several areas. One is the sheer implausibility of the hypothesis – we do not live in a primitive non-social situation and therefore the idea of a choice is deeply misleading. Rawls would counter this by arguing that such a thought experiment helps us not to construct a new society but to understand what we mean when we say this society is fair or not. Perhaps a more difficult argument is the objection that here, in analogous fashion to Nozick, there are social assumptions built in to this approach, masquerading as analytic concepts. For the very idea of what is a tolerable life, and whether we would choose it or not, is a presumption that is

ETHICS AND YOU

RAWLS IN PRACTICE

If faced with the 'veil of ignorance' test, what would be your bottom line? What kind of life would be the minimum that you could regard as acceptable? How far do you think this would be shared by others?

What does this say about Rawls' argument?

not demonstrated even in developed economies: 'give me liberty or give me death' is an oft-quoted phrase that undermines the idea of what is tolerable in material terms by suggesting that some aspects of life are beyond measurement. In general, political opposition to repressive regimes often involves individuals sacrificing far more than they, as individuals, would gain from the political freedoms they seek. So 'a tolerable life' is not easily measurable. Further, why should we use self-interest as the basis for defining a society, when it is clear that it is not the universal basis for choices and decisions? Indeed, a latter-day Kantian, Thomas Nagel, has argued that *all* decision making that deserves to be called rational is necessarily altruistic in nature.[28]

The final version of distributive justice to be mentioned, rather more briefly, is that of Karl Marx. Marxism is based on an elaborate model of society comprising opposed social groups or classes, economies that gradually become ever more unstable over the decades, social ideas and philosophies that build up as a reflection of the material relationships between the various classes, especially on which class is dominant at any one time. It is also notorious as having been used – some would say misused – as the basis for communist regimes in eastern Europe in the 20th century, now discredited and replaced with market systems. However, within Marxism is also a vision of a certain kind of distributive justice, expressed in the dictum 'from each according to their abilities and to each according to their needs'. While currently this view is not much seen in its pure form, it underpins (as well as classical communism) mixed economics, the idea that market economies need also to incorporate some degree of welfare in order to ensure that the least well-off still enjoy a modicum of social support adequate to enable them to participate in the economy (by the sale of their labour power in employment) so that they can generate income to acquire at least some of the benefits of modern economic production.

But while this finds some reflection in national social policies, it is a far cry from the idea of justice to be found in organizations. True, some corporates have HR policies that take account of specific needs of certain groups such as some categories of disabled workers (indeed in the EU this is required by law). But these tend to be exceptions to the rule, which is that needs and abilities are elements that are traded on the labour market (not exactly a free market given that on one side the individual needs to work to live) and therefore subject to market conditions and forces, especially availability, demand and price. Maybe Marx would simply say that this is another manifestation of the unjust nature of a market or mixed economy, but for us, living in such economies, the more pragmatic answer is that his approach to justice is not a model for our times, however useful some aspects of it may be.

This discussion of rights and justice has been at greater length than earlier theories, partially because it incorporates several contrasting elaborations, and partially because it continues to demonstrate the integration between the ethics of individual choice and the obligations of corporations to act responsibly. What we have seen here is that while rights

THINKING CRITICALLY ABOUT ETHICS

RAWLS APPLIED TO ORGANIZATIONS

To what extent can we apply Rawls' theory to organizations, and treat them as an analogue of societies as a whole? And if we did do this, how far could this go: would or should senior managers modify their package of rewards so that even the worst job in the firm would be acceptable to all?

theories and theories of justice focus on important fragments of the way we think about ethics in business, they represent neither effective tools for decision making (being too broadly focused on society), nor do they accurately reflect or describe the way we do actually think about the morality of business.

CULTURAL RELATIVISM

We have already seen allusions to cultural variations on ethical concepts in earlier sections. However, this has also been developed into a full-scale theory of ethics in itself. Put in its most pointed terms, cultural relativism is the idea that the values embodied in different cultures can only be understood in their own terms. This indicates that all ethical positions need to be understood as arising out of dominant cultural assumptions and styles of thinking and acting. Therefore, no practice specific to a culture can be validly critiqued from the point of view of any other culture. The importance of this view for managers is that the growth of the global dimensions of many businesses has led to many hitherto 'local' business practices now acquiring a global dimension.

In a discussion of culture and management, one has to bear in mind the dual nature of this term: as indicating the dominant set of customs, perceptions and practices or a definable *national or ethnic group* in society, or as referring to the internal idiosyncratic style of a *particular business* ('the way we do things round here'). In general, discussions of cultural relativism begin from a presumption that each identifiable national or ethnic social unit has some right to follow its own set of practices and customs.[29] However, no such right is generally seen as attaching to organizational cultures, even though these can often operate almost as a microcosm of the wider society. What this suggests is that cultural relativism is a *political* concept at root, rather than an organizational one: it rests on an acceptance of the rights of cultures to determine their own ways of living, while not accepting that organizations have quite the same kind of right.

Taken to its extreme, cultural relativism would appear to suggest that any defined ethnic or national group can rebut any critical ethical assessment made by an 'outside' party. While this is rarely encountered, the real question is how far such a view may be taken? What are its limits? Many writers[30] distinguish cultural variations in *practice* from variations in *principle*. Different customs between national cultures are impossible to ignore and can affect almost every aspect of life: eating, clothing, social rituals, how personal relationships develop, approaches to authority, conduct of family life and many other examples. However, it is not a simple matter to separate out customs that are 'merely' practice from those that betoken a deeper issue of values. The value element may be obvious in matters such as the treatment of death or the conduct of family life. But it is not easy to identify other features of social customs that carry no element of value with them. Few social phenomena are as simple as the decision whether to drive on the right or the left-hand side of the road. Clothing, for example, expresses assumptions about the value placed on a range of demographic elements by a society, including age, gender differences and professional standing.

National customs reflect social assumptions. So, to take another example, a tradition of hospitality to visitors from abroad may demonstrate a value for supporting and helping strangers, for instance. Customs, therefore, such as giving presents to a distant acquaintance on their visit to one's country, or inviting them to your home, or offering to accompany them on social events while they are visiting the country, all reflect this sense of value.[31] This is more than simply a matter of recognizing that for some important phenomena there are different views – it may be a question of what people actually count as valuable or not. It is not possible to separate out the value-neutral aspects of the different customs relating to hospitality in different national cultures, from the value-dependent aspects. This can mean that what matters and has significance for one culture may seem to be trivial to another.

Yet a further issue is that in some national cultures there are aspects that cannot even be properly represented in others. The contrast between European and Japanese concepts relating to respect for others is often expressed in the English language as the avoidance of 'losing face'. However, the Japanese concept is richer than this, and connects with values such as respect between generations and acceptance of social unitarism, which are not implicated in the 'western' idea. So it is misleading even to talk about western and Japanese concepts of 'losing face', for the latter is not the same thing, even though it overlaps with the concept of 'face' substantially. This should provide a major note of caution in the interpretation of the well-known models of dimensions of national culture developed by Hofstede[32] and others: arguably, these are measures of how far non-European cultures compare with European ones, not independent culturally neutral methods of analysing cultures.

All this emphasizes that there are differences between national cultures. But it does not help us decide when it is legitimate to question values of individuals from other cultures, and when this is inappropriate. The theoretical extreme – pure cultural relativism – would have it that no evaluation is possible, and that no matter what an individual or an organization based in another culture does, we are not justified in criticizing them. However, whatever the theoretical arguments may be, it is clear that people do actually evaluate the acts of those from other cultures, so in some sense we do regard the ethics of different cultures as comparable, to a degree at least.

More importantly, the theoretical extreme takes a narrow view of a 'culture' as being a fixed terrain that has clear boundaries that separate it from other cultures, so that someone is unequivocally 'in' one national culture to the exclusion of others. As Amartya Sen has argued forcefully,[33] human beings are members of a wide range of different kinds of social groupings, each with their own allegiance, and each of which, therefore, may be regarded as a legitimate part of their identity, and therefore have a good claim to be reflected in their values and ethical attitudes. An individual may be born in one country, with parents from another country, they are male or female, they have a certain position on religion, they may be members of a certain profession, and so on. Each of these demographic features of the individual will have some bearing on their values. So they cannot be simply seen as 'in' one culture to the exclusion of others.

One can take this further and point to the phenomenon often characterized as 'acculturation' – the tendency of individuals to modify attitudes drawn from their original culture when in foreign environments. Put simply, we often change our attitudes when placed in novel situations. Further, whole national cultures also gradually change as their members mingle with others: for example, the polarized approaches to the roles of women in society represented within European (primarily secular) cultures as opposed to those of some Muslim cultures evident in the second half of the 20th century have begun to slowly erode, so that in many of the more economically developed Muslim countries there is a growing flexibility in attitude towards women that encompasses some professional and personal independence from husband or father, while in Europe there is a corresponding growth in recognition that different women may choose their own lifestyle, even ones that may involve apparently less liberation than the feminist writers of the 1960s and 1970s envisaged. Then, of course, there are the directly exported cultures of migrant populations: so that a great deal of modification and combination of cultural elements has occurred with the

CULTURE AND TOLERANCE

Imagine you are the training officer for a large global business. You have been asked to run a development programme intended to build strong team relationships as a part of a major new change initiative for wider global expansion of the business. However, you find that the group you are training comprises a wide range of different ethnicities, and many have very strong attitudes, which, while not exactly racist, imply substantial intolerance towards the norms and values of people from other ethnic groups. The company code of ethics states clearly '… we should show respect for all our colleagues, regardless of race, nationality, religion, gender, ability, orientation or other major demographic or biographical features.'

How far are you justified in attempting to modify the values of these members of staff, and how far should you aim solely to restrain the more explicit expressions of intolerance?

substantial expatriate communities of the world – the Chinese in Malaysia, for example, the Hispanic populations of the United States, or the 'Britishtanis' (Pakistanis who have moved to the UK and become integrated into British society).

As a principle of caution in how we debate the values of others, cultural relativism is a useful tool. As an overall theory of ethics, however, it is not defensible. The simplest counter-argument echoes one advanced earlier with respect to egoism: if cultural relativism were true then we would never be justified in expressing any kind of critical comment on the values of those whom we perceive as being from another culture. The sheer fact that we can express such evaluations of the values of others demonstrates that, even though there may be substantial cultural aspects of values that require greater understanding, the values of others are open to us to discuss, debate and even ultimately to share.

POSTMODERNITY AND CRITICALITY IN ETHICAL THEORY

The classical theories discussed in the previous sections have been presented as arising out of different points of emphasis in the process of making a decision, be this the character of the individual making the decision (virtue ethics), the kind of motive prompting the decision (deontology), the outcomes of the decision (consequentialism), or the social impact of the decision (justice and rights). In contrast to classical theories there is a growing body of thought that looks less at an aspect of the decision-making process and more at the social context within which a theory itself has been developed. This kind of approach arose during the 20th century, and is often associated with the movement in social studies known as 'critical theory'. Do not be misled by the label for this approach: all theories that are of any value will inevitably include some element of critical evaluation. By the use of the term 'critical' is intended the idea that *a theory is self-critical about its social origin.* So such approaches do not just focus on and provide some kind of analysis – in our case, about what is right or wrong when taking business decisions. They also take account of how our present society allowed such a theory to come about and be sustained by discussion and analysis. In other words, this approach looks as theories as social phenomena needing an explanation of their social existence as much as a justification of their key statements.

Critical theory is associated with a number of writers, and it would be a great oversimplification to try to isolate a single source of the idea. It is often associated with a political ideology whereby understanding the social origins of theories helps emancipate individuals by showing them how even quite pure categories of thought (such as ethics) may be influenced by social traditions and power structures.

There are many manifestations of this trend of thought, including ones that look at the impact of social inequalities on theory,[34] and others that look at particular ways for individuals to achieve freedom.[35] We shall look very briefly at two of these – feminist ethics and postmodern ethics.

Feminist ethics is, as the name suggests, based on the idea that ethics in general has been developed within a male-dominated society, and reflects male-oriented perceptions, stereotypes and implicit beliefs that elevate certain aspects (such as autonomous choice) over others (such as interpersonal sensitivity). Annette Baier has underlined this argument, by pointing out that the transactional approach behind most theories of moral choice only works by making unrealistic assumptions that all relevant parties are in an equal position with respect to choice, in terms of knowledge, opportunity and power.[36] This critique leads to what Carol Gilligan has called the ethics of care,[37] where the key concerns of ethics are modelled in terms of care for others, relationships, collaboration and shared responsibility, as opposed to the (male-oriented) approach that sees the key ethical problem as being about how a free, potent individual can arrive at the right, independent choice which they can put into practice and for which they can take personal responsibility.

One way of looking at this is that what we have here is a development out of virtue ethics, one which takes some of the traditional virtues – such as kindness and consideration – and draws out the fullness of their implications for ethics. Like virtue ethics as a whole, this focuses less on the phenomenon of ethical choice and more on the nature of those who choose. However, unlike virtue ethics, this is a distinctively *critical* theory (in the sense outlined above) in that the approach demonstrates one set of traditional social frameworks within which ethical theories are constructed, as well as indicating how a greater understanding of the idea of an ethics of care helps individuals to recognize how far their thinking may be dominated by stereotypes encouraged by those social frameworks.

There are several ways in which this approach may be applied to ethical issues in business. It is not a question of the numerical fact that most senior managers in organizations tend to be male, but rather that organizational concepts themselves are framed in male terms (and often in militaristic language – for example 'strategy', 'campaigns' and 'chains of command' – all derived from military leadership).[38] Furthermore, the economics of business encourages a transactional approach to many aspects of work – for example, the idea of employment as a contract where one free individual offers the use of their labour power in return for financial and other benefits is often a gross fictionalization of realities where opportunities to change from one employer to another may be highly limited.

It is probably misplaced to discuss this approach in terms of arguments for or against, still less to try to come to a summary evaluation of benefits and drawbacks. Having said that, it is not clear how far this is intended as a complete theory of ethics (whether in business or in life generally) as opposed to being a critical balance to the dominant ideological perspective on ethics. Indeed, a feminist position would probably suggest avoidance of a direct pro–con orientation to ethical theories. Nevertheless, it is not out of place to note that some contexts in business – such as whistle-blowing – are less easy to present in terms of the ethics of care, and rather easier to explain in terms of choice.

The other approach to mention in this context is the less clear but influential perspective of postmodernism. This view has impacted on a wide range of different disciplines, including sociology, philosophy, and management theory.[39] The essence of postmodernism is that the concept against which it reacts – modernism – attempts to solve problems and issues by rationality, though in fact this latter concept is itself blind to its role within social structures. One writer sometimes seen as postmodern, Michel Foucault, argued that each historical period had dominant ways of thinking, which he called *epistemes*, that conditioned what would be accepted as valid argument.[40] Postmodernists would therefore see the present era as dominated by an episteme based on the belief that rational processes can answer each question, and that the application of these processes can generate as much knowledge and understanding as is necessary to function successfully. The flaw in this, they would argue, is that reality often resists the simplification required by rational modelling. As a leading postmodern ethicist, Zygmunt Bauman, puts it, 'Human reality is messy and ambiguous – and so moral decisions, unlike abstract ethical principles, are ambivalent.'[41]

This approach is less easy to apply in any simple manner to business. Most business activity is indeed based on at least a modified idea of rationality – as being the best tool around for solving business problems, even if it is not perfect in all cases. Most technological innovation (upon which modern societies depend so very heavily) has been generally explained in terms of the application of rational methods of research and development. So the postmodern argument is an argument against the current social conditions of production of goods and services. Perhaps many postmodernists would welcome this; however, it is a barrier to the use of postmodern ideas in establishing what it is right to do in business.

Related loosely to feminist ethics and to critical theory is the idea of an approach called the 'ethics of discourse'.[42] This term refers to the creation of an environment in which values and different positions can be expressed and examined collaboratively rather than in an adversarial manner. Such an approach requires something rather like what in Europe[43] would be described as a liberal political ideology: acceptance of the supremacy of rational processes as the basis for decision making, encouragement of openness, tolerance of dissent and respect for diversity. This is however not really a theory of ethics itself, so much as a view of what kind of context is most conducive to good ethical practice. As such we will reserve discussion of this to later chapters on the organizational context.

So, are these tools to help us make ethical decisions or explanations of what we do when we make decisions? By and large they are not especially useful as tools. Feminism and its related approaches such as race theory or queer theory do present alternative

THINKING CRITICALLY ABOUT ETHICS

ORGANIZATIONS AND ETHICAL POSITIONS

Critical theory states that ethical theories need to be understood as social phenomena, and that dominant intellectual positions reflect the general dominance of certain social groups. Organizations often identify themselves with certain theoretical approaches, as a part of their culture. So, many financial institutions will self-consciously adopt a *transactional* approach to management in general and ethics in particular. In contrast, in a state social care provider, such as a housing project for people with disabilities, workers may quite deliberately focus on issues such as *rights*.

How far is the ethical position of an organization a part of its business, and to what extent can or should it be open to modification?

options in a very broad sense, but they do not help us address specific concrete cases. Postmodernism is even further away from particular decisions, being a general critique of the dominance of rationality in ethical discussions.

MAKING SENSE OF THEORY

Having looked at a range of theories now, it makes sense to consider what we have gained from them. It is clear that some (such as deontology) can be used as tools to help specific choices, and it is equally clear that others (such as virtue ethics or postmodernism) can less do so. But, as we indicated earlier in this chapter, it would be oversimplifying to the extreme to isolate particular kinds of issue and say that one approach will work for one kind of issue and another approach will help with something else.

On the other hand, business is about making decisions, and therefore theories are only helpful when they contribute in some way or another to decision making. A theory, however, can make such a contribution in a way other than simply providing a step in ethical reasoning: it may, for example, focus someone on long-term policies and practices, without necessarily helping with an immediate problem; or it might lead someone to reflect on their behaviour and integrity, again even when there is no direct immediate action-guiding outcome.

As we suggested early on in this chapter, one way to categorize ethical theories is to consider their position in the process of decision making. Despite its distance from decision making, it is still possible to relate critical theory to this, in that it claims to include the entire process. Table 3.1 summarizes this.

The value of considering ethical theories in this way is that it indicates a potential for integration of the different approaches. They are often presented by philosophers as if they are in mutual competition – as if one of these is 'the' most fundamental concept and the others are to be derived from it. Our position is that while some of these theories overlap in some places, they are complementary, and therefore to some extent one can and should take account of all of them. This does not lead to a list of questions for each of which one of these theories is appropriate to provide an answer, so much as a range of features of ethical choice and action, which raise their own questions. The bad news for managers is that any of these theories could present a challenge when one needs to make an ethical decision. The good news is that they do not form a mechanical whole that forces one to go through a pre-defined series of steps. Rather like strategic models, the skill is in exercising one's judgement as to which questions to pay more attention to and which can safely receive less. In the next chapter we look in more detail at how ethical reasoning works in specific contexts, taking these theories as given.

TABLE 3.1 How theories of ethics link together

The character of someone taking an ethical decision	Virtue ethics
The kind of ethical action taken	Deontology
The outcomes of an ethical decision	Consequentialism
The social impact of a decision	Rights theory, theories of justice
The social context that sustains these theories	Postmodernity, critical theory, cultural relativism

SUMMARY

- Ethical theories may be categorized in terms of their focus on particular aspects of the process of decision making.
- Virtue ethics focuses of the character of individuals and how this may influence action.
- Kantian deontology focuses on the idea of a duty being rationally based, and thus such a decision applying equally for all actors.
- Consequentialist theories such as utilitarianism attempt to measure the rightness of actions in terms of the total outcomes they bring about.
- Rights and justice theories look at the social impact of ethical policies in the long term.
- Cultural relativism asserts that values can only be understood by those within the specific culture from which these emanate.
- Critical theory takes a view on ethical theories as products of their social context, with the intention of liberating actors.
- These theories are best regarded as complementary, raising questions in their own right but not integrated in a mechanistic way.

QUICK REVIEW QUESTIONS:

1   What is the principle of the greatest happiness of the greatest number?
2   How does feminism critique current business ethics theories?
3   What does Rawls mean by the 'veil of ignorance'?
4   What does the categorical imperative state?
5   How does Aristotle try to integrate the different virtues?

CASE STUDY: MITSUBISHI AND FORCED LABOUR

The Mitsubishi Group consists of over 500 companies employing close to 54,000 people around the world. It is one of the largest Japanese *keiretsus,* a cluster of interlinked companies backed up by cross-holdings of shares. The first Mitsubishi company was a shipping firm established in 1870, but it soon diversified into coal mining to ensure access to fuel that was used in its ships. Since then, the group has played a central role in the Japanese economy as its businesses have expanded into numerous industries including banking, insurance, real estate, oil, paper and car manufacturing.

Mitsubishi also holds one of the best known Japanese brands at home and abroad.

In 2003, Mitsubishi Material Corp., a member of the Mitsubishi Group, was sued for using forced labour in its coal mines during the Second World War. Similar lawsuits have been brought against other Japanese companies for forcing civilians and prisoners of war to work long hours in harsh conditions without compensation or sufficient nutrition. Mistreatment and lack of attention on health and safety resulted in a high number of injuries, accidents and fatalities. The poor working conditions were encouraged by the government 'Guidelines for Controlling Imported Chinese Labourers' in which companies were told to give foreign labourers inferior clothing, limited medical care, and primitive sleeping and sanitary facilities. The instructions were aimed at curtailing the security risk provided by the presence of young enemy males on Japanese territory.

Japanese companies employed involuntary labour mainly from China and Korea, though they also forced allied prisoners of war to work in plants and infrastructure projects. In the lawsuit against Mitsubishi Materials, the Chinese plaintiffs accused the company of operating two coal mines that forcibly employed a total of 2709 Chinese labourers. The workers were abducted or conscripted under false premises in China and brought to Japan where they were forced to work in harsh conditions without pay. According to a government report compiled after the war, the death rate for Chinese workers in one of the mines was 25 per cent. One of the plaintiffs in the case alleged that he worked 12-hour shifts and was beaten for resting, while a rice ball filled with vegetables formed the daily diet.

To date, Mitsubishi has not paid compensation to the alleged victims of forced labour. In general, companies in Japan and Europe have evaded compensation claims by arguing that they were compelled by their respective governments to use involuntary labour. German companies accepted responsibility for the use of forced labour only in 2000 when a foundation aimed at restituting victims of the Nazi regime and their families was established by a law enacted by the national parliament. The German government and more than 6000 German companies consequently provided funds for the foundation that paid financial compensation to more than 1.7 million victims living in almost 100 countries. The companies that donated money for the fund received protection from further legal action even though the payments made to the victims were regarded as symbolic rather than reparatory (€2500–7500). Nevertheless, the law on which the foundation was based acknowledges the suffering of the victims and can therefore be seen as a step towards reconciliation.

Reparation payments have been a controversial issue for Japan. Some companies made cash payments to Chinese work unit leaders when Japan surrendered, but the leaders did not always share the money with their team members. Companies also gave out payment vouchers that could be redeemed in China, but many workers had difficulties in cashing the vouchers in the context of post-war disorder. Some compensation payments were also made immediately after the war as a result of the Tokyo trials, but only a few companies were prosecuted as the focus was on rebuilding the economy. Japanese governments have in general argued against reparation payments in reference to the peace treaties negotiated after the war. The Japanese interpretation of the treaties has received support from the US State Department. For example, the State Department has argued that the San Francisco Peace Treaty precludes individual claims against Japanese companies. However, as an exception to the stance of the Japanese government, the Asian Women's Fund was set up in 1995 to compensate for military sexual slavery of Korean women during the war.

During the war, the wages of the forced labourers were directed to special accounts and later moved to government accounts. They are still held by various state agencies including the Bank of Japan and regional customs offices. According to the Japanese government, poor records make it difficult to match the deposits with individuals or their heirs. The lack of records is a result of the order given by the government after the war to burn documentation held on forced labourers.

Mitsubishi has typically based its defence against compensation claims on the provisions of peace treaties and time limits for making reparation claims. It has also argued that it was not in a position to resist a policy applied by the Japanese government. More recently, it has denied that any forced labour took place in its mines on the basis of its own site reports from 1946.

The relations between China and Japan have been negatively affected by the Chinese perception that Japan has not taken sufficient action to acknowledge and atone wartime atrocities. Even though several Japanese governments have apologized for the treatment of foreign workers during the war, public and private behaviour of state officials has been seen to negate the apologies. For example, annual visits by the former Japanese Prime Minister, Junichiro Koizumi, to the Yasukuni shrine that honours Japanese nationals including 14 convicted war criminals were perceived by the Chinese as symbols of Japanese patriotism and militarism. As a result, the Chinese refused to hold meetings with Koizumi. The relations have improved since Koizumi stepped down to the extent that the Chinese Prime Minister hailed the progress in December 2007: 'Prime Minister Fukuda said the spring has come in our relations, and after two-and-a-half hours of talks, I truly feel that the spring of China–Japan relations has arrived.' Nevertheless, six months earlier the Chinese head of state called for Japan to match its apologies for wartime atrocities by concrete actions. The feeling is mirrored in other Asian countries that were occupied by Japan during the Second World War.

Any action by the Japanese government and industry, including Mitsubishi, will arrive late for many of the victims as only about 10 per cent of them are still alive. Calls for retribution have therefore included plans for foundations that would grant funds for the descendants of the victims. Other means of compensation have also been discussed. For example, part of the money from the German foundation was used to launch social programmes among the communities that had suffered from forced labour.

STUDY QUESTIONS

1 Apply one theory of ethics to assess whether Mitsubishi's position can be regarded as ethical.

2 What problems occurred when applying the theory of ethics to the case? Do these relate to the criticism presented on the theory?

3 Given the position of the Japanese government, what should Mitsubishi do to behave ethically?

SOURCES

BBC News 2007. China PM seeks war reconciliation, 12 April. Available from http://www.bbc.co.uk, accessed 25 March 2008.

BBC News 2007. China and Japan PMs hail progress, 28 December. Available from http://www.bbc.co.uk, accessed 25 March 2008.

BBC News 2006. Japan's controversial shrine, 15 August. Available from http://www.bbc.co.uk, accessed 25 March 2008.

Reuters AlertNet 2007. Germany ends war chapter with 'slave fund' closure, 12 June. Available from http://www.alertnet.org, accessed 25 March 2008.

Schmidt, P. 2000. Japan's wartime compensation: Forced labour. *Asia-Pacific Journal on Human Rights and the Law*, Vol. 2, 1–54.

Underwood, W. 2006. Mitsubishi, historical revisionism and Japanese corporate resistance to Chinese forced labour redress, *Znet*, 11 February 2006. Available from http://www.zmag.org, accessed 20 March 2008.

This case study was prepared using only publicly available sources of information for the purposes of classroom discussion.

NOTES

1. Pritchard (1912).
2. The view that actions are ethically evaluated in terms of their consequences; a position considered later in this chapter.
3. Essentially philosophical in tone.
4. Rand (1964).
5. Primarily in his book of lectures on ethics, which is today called the *Nichomacean Ethics* (Aristotle).
6. See for example Connock & Johns (1995).
7. With one of the liveliest contributions in this respect coming from Alistair Macintyre (1985), who suggests that virtues need to be understood, not simply in respect of one conception of 'the good life' but in relation to the community within which a certain kind of life may be regarded as good.
8. A point brought out by Chryssides and Kaler (1993) pp. 140 ff.

9. For example, an alternative may be found in the views of W. D. Ross (1930).

10. The discussion below is drawn primarily from Paton (1976), to which the reader is referred for further explanation of Kant's best known ethical views.

11. It is important to recognize that this is not an argument stating that people cannot violate principles of trust – clearly they do, and sadly quite often. Rather, the argument is that one cannot make a *universal principle* that such trust be violated – this is what would break down.

12. Whose extended essay 'Utilitarianism' is still regarded as the clearest introduction to the view – Mill (1863).

13. And potentially highly parochial, if not even elitist.

14. Mainly in the 20th century – cf. Brandt (1992) – though there were hints of this approach in some 19th century treatments.

15. A convenient source for this and Vroom's formulation of expectancy theory discussed a little later is Handy (1998), though other standard textbooks on organizational behaviour will also cover these theories.

16. Though not unequivocal in all respects – see Mitchell (1974).

17. Just in case anyone is in doubt, the presumption is that the life of the philosopher, even when dissatisfied, is preferable to living a satisfied pig's life. But maybe one could even argue over this…

18. With the important proviso that the means are not so wrong as to outweigh the value of the end.

19. See Gaita (1982).

20. Two of the best known and most influential, which have been mentioned already and will be discussed again in later chapters, are the United Nations 1948 Charter of Human Rights and the European Union's 2000 Charter of Fundamental Human Rights.

21. Shaw (2005), p. 66.

22. It should be emphasized that the existence of such rights does not automatically imply a certain kind of social system – for example it does not necessarily mean that governments should provide education or healthcare via public service delivery, supported by taxation. Rather it means that governments, corporations and other organizations should ensure that such rights are fulfilled *in some way or another*. This is quite compatible with a right-wing free-market agenda where rights to equal access to employment create sufficient opportunity for individuals to accrue personal wealth to purchase healthcare or education from private providers.

23. And, indeed, elements of this are enshrined in some legislative systems, such as in The Netherlands, where explicit protections for employees are built in to avoid excessive exposure to repetitive operations at work.

24. Which has been incorporated into certain legislative codifications of human rights, such as the UK's Human Rights Act of 1999.

25. This example relates to issues of privacy. It assumes that there are not other concerns about staff personal communications, such as wasting time when work should be done.

26. Origins of the libertarian approach may be found in Nozick (1974), of the social contract approach in Rawls (1971) and the radical approach in Marx (1848).

27. For example, this was observed in Celtic pre-industrial communities, among some native American tribes, in several African areas and in the attitude towards land held by native Australians.

28. Nagel (1970).

29. Though there are some intractable differences, such as the difficulty of Europeans, with traditions of equality and growing uniformity of expectation between the sexes, accepting some Asian traditions where the two genders have distinct and separately defined roles.

30. For example, see Chryssides & Kaler (1993), p. 81.

31. Crucially, of course, all these impact substantially on business relationships in the modern globalized economy.

32. Hofstede (2003).

33. Sen (2005).

34. Including certain kinds of feminist studies, race theory which looks at the way in which theories may reflect racial stereotypes, and so-called 'queer theory' looking at the way in which heterosexualism influences intellectual thought, to name but a few.

35. Including at the individual level psychoanalysis, and at the macro level 'world systems' theory (which tries to move beyond theories that may reflect assumptions closely related to particular countries or nations to a theoretical basis that is nation-neutral) and some versions of ecological philosophy.

36. And, one might add, in terms of personal commitment to others, both at work and away from work. Baier (1994).
37. Gilligan (1982).
38. See Simpson & Lewis (2007) for further illustrations of the lack of gender neutrality in organizations.
39. Where it is often associated with the critical management studies movement.
40. Foucault (1970).
41. Bauman (1993).
42. Cf. Habermas (1990).
43. But not in the United States, where the term has different connotations; and note also that this is *political* liberalism, a centre left approach, not *economic* liberalism, which is right wing in nature.

REFERENCES

Baier, A. 1994. *Moral Prejudices*. Cambridge, MA: Harvard University Press.

Bauman, Z., 1993. *Postmodern Ethics*. Oxford: Blackwell.

Brandt, R. B. 1992. *Morality, Utilitarianism, and Rights*. Cambridge: Cambridge University Press.

Chryssides, G. and Kaler, J. 1993. *An Introduction to Business Ethics*. London: Chapman and Hall.

Connock, S. and Johns, T. 1995. *Ethical Leadership*. London: IPD.

Foucault, M. 1970. *The Order of Things*. UK translation: Pantheon Books.

Gaita, R. 1982. Better one than ten. *Philosophical Investigations*, Vol. 5, No. 2, 87–105.

Gilligan, C. 1982. *In a Different Voice*. Cambridge, MA: Harvard University Press.

Habermas, J. 1990. *Moral Consciousness and Communicative Action*. Cambridge, MA: MIT Press.

Handy, C. 1998. Understanding Organisations. Fifth edition. Harmondsworth: Penguin.

Hofstede, G. 2003. *Culture's Consequences*. London: Sage.

MacIntyre, A. 1985. *After Virtue*. London: Duckworth.

Marx, K. 1848 (original publication). *The Communist Manifesto*.

Mill, J. S. 1863 (original publication). *Utilitarianism*.

Mitchell, T. 1974. Expectancy models of job satisfaction. *Psychological Bulletin*, Vol. 81, No. 12, 1053–1077.

Nagel, T. 1970. *The Possibility of Altruism*. Oxford: Oxford University Press.

Nozick, R. 1974. *Anarchy State and Utopia*. New York: Basic Books.

Paton, H. J. 1976. *The Moral Law*. An edited commentary including the text of Kant's Groundwork of the metaphysic of morals. London: Routledge.

Pritchard, H. A. 1912. Does moral philosophy rest on a mistake? *Mind*, Vol. 21, 21–37.

Rand, A. 1964. *The Virtue of Selfishness*. New American Library.

Rawls, J. 1971. *A Theory of Justice*. Cambridge, MA: Harvard University Press.

Ross, W. D. 1930. *The Right and the Good*. Oxford: Clarendon Press.

Sen, A. 2005. *Identity and Violence*. Harmondsworth: Penguin.

Shaw, W. 2005. *Business Ethics*. Belmont: Thompson Wadsworth.

Simpson, R. and Lewis, P. 2007. *Voice, Visibility and the Gendering of Organizations*. London: Palgrave.

ENVIRONMENTAL ETHICS

LEARNING OBJECTIVES

After studying this chapter you should be able to:

- Evaluate the scale of environmental issues as they affect industries.
- Identify the key parties to the environmental debate and their agendas.
- Critically evaluate different conceptions of environment and sustainability.
- Identify some of the key arguments relating to sustainability and the environment.

INTRODUCTION

This is the first of two chapters on environment and sustainability. We include a chapter here, in Part I of the book, to cover the ethical importance of this issue for business, and the conceptual foundations of the various arguments and practices relating to the environment. In this chapter, then, we will look at the *concepts*: the origin and meaning of the terms 'environment' and 'sustainability', the areas of philosophical consensus and those of disagreement, and the manner in which these ideas have come to play so large a role in our current thinking about economic development and our relationship with the natural world. In Part III we will return to the environment, looking at issues of *practice*, including some of the more controversial approaches to dealing with environmental problems.

THE CURRENT IMPERATIVE

The current pervasiveness of concern over the environment, climate change and sustainability can easily distort our awareness of these issues in human history. There is no doubt that human activity has had significant impacts on the natural world since at least the beginning of recorded history. There is evidence, for example, that Ancient Greece suffered serious soil erosion problems and maybe even some change to climate as a result of farming methods adopted at the time.[1] Many plant and animal species have been extinguished due to human activity in the past – for example the extinctions on the Pacific islands as human beings spread across the world.[2] What has changed, however, is the scale of threat, which has become substantially more acute. While issues such as metropolitan air pollution and domestic waste disposal, and even to a limited extent agricultural matters such as soil degradation, create significant problems for humans, it is the impact of climate change that has created the biggest threat not only to the human race but to many other species of life as well.

Climate change is expected to involve increased temperatures over the next century of between 2° and 6° Celsius.[3] So far as the impact of this on species extinction is concerned, estimates range up to the possibility that 50 per cent of all animal species may become threatened by 2100. Further, this degree of increase may lead to greater levels of desertification in some of the poorest parts of the world, as well as greater climatic turbulence such as increased incidence of hurricanes, torrential rainstorms, excessive heatwaves or even spells of cold weather in some regions. It may also undermine agriculture in many countries, as methods that have been developed over hundreds or even thousands of years of relative climatic stability become redundant as weather changes.

However, the imperative is still not at all well understood. Part of the reason for this is the excessive complexity of weather systems and weather forecasting. Not only are there very many variables affecting weather conditions, but also the historical variation of weather can only be understood over very long periods of time. Evidence suggests that there have been many eras with much greater levels of climatic volatility than during the period of recorded history. Equally, there are many interacting weather cycles and periodicities that impact on the global climate at any time – for example, as well as the well-known El Niño phenomenon of increased temperature in the south-eastern Pacific every few years, there are similar events such as the Arctic and North Atlantic oscillations, which lead to variations in air pressure and, via wind behaviour, to warmer or cooler weather on both sides of the Atlantic Ocean. Add to these the cycles of sunspot activity, minor fluctuations in the earth's orbit, the time lags for changes in temperature or energy to work their way through different parts of the ecosphere, and other periodically recurring phenomena such as rapid global temperature fluctuations,[4] and it is clear that even without any human intervention the weather would be difficult to predict.

ETHICS AND YOU

SURVIVAL

In the Introduction to this book we talked of the *survival imperative* – the common perception, especially in the for-profit sector, that organizations are under a near-constant threat of extinction, and therefore need to continually work to ensure that they will not be forced out of business. A natural expression of this would be for a company to reject non-binding requests for greater environmental responsibility on the ground that it will erode its competitive position unless all of its main rivals do the same.

In the light of the content of this section, how can an organization's environmental champion counter this natural resistance? How would you deal with internal arguments in a firm that while environmentally protective measures are desirable they would threaten the future of a company?

It is now generally acknowledged that human activity has *some* kind of influence on the eco-system. The primary contributory causes are the so-called greenhouse gases – carbon dioxide, methane and others that serve to strengthen the heat-conserving properties of the atmosphere to an excessive degree. Since the 18th century the production of these has been steadily rising, so that today it stands at an historically unprecedented level.[5] This results in part from the actions of the more successful industries of the developed world. High levels of pollution have come from activities such as the production and use of motor vehicles, as well as from some forms of agricultural production, such as the high levels of lean meat consumed in the West, especially beef. Additional effects on the atmosphere have come from practices such as the use of CFCs – gases that until the 1980s were used as propellants in aerosol sprays – that have been found to contribute to the holes in the ozone layer of the atmosphere, which protects us from too much ultra-violet radiation. However, until relatively recently there was controversy over the causes of the current growing changes in the climate, with some alleging that these human impacts were negligibly small compared with the greater naturally occurring forces that can influence weather.

What further complicates the understanding of the environmental imperative is the complex of different agendas of the various players. The dominance of the United States over the global economy in recent decades has led to a degree of protectionism and conservatism on the part of successive US governments over any responses that might undermine that country's competitive advantages (and thus lead to politically unpopular diminution of living standards). Similarly, the rapid growth of the so-called 'BRIC'[6] economies has created an ambition among these, to which the idea of restrictions on their activity (for the purpose of better environmental effects) is a threat. Another agenda is the obligation of managers of limited companies to protect the interests of their shareholders, which provides a motive for them to try to offset, minimize or rebut arguments that corporate activity should be regulated or curtailed (as this is generally seen as a cost to the business). Finally, there are academic and corporate interests that see climate change as an opportunity to support technologies and systems that might contribute to environmental solutions. Interestingly, such arguments have been advanced not only for technological solutions that are typically seen as more 'green', such as electronic cars or paperless books, but also for some approaches that in public opinion are more controversial, such as nuclear power or GM crops. Nuclear energy has been argued to be an effective short-term resolution of the need to produce the energy necessary for current growth while other renewable energy sources are developed, and GM crops have been argued to be a food source that involves less eco-harmful elements such as use of pesticides. All of these agendas have provided differing impetus for these players to sponsor research that might inhibit or counter the arguments of environmentalists, at least partially succeeding in creating a degree of doubt in public attitudes. Table 4.1 summarizes the roles of the key players in this debate.

Table 4.1 does not cover a complete set of stakeholders. What it indicates, though, is that these players have competing interests. With the best wills in the world – and often at least some of these do not have such wills – these groups are not likely to easily agree on the main issues. But more difficult is the pact that most of these parties to the debate *themselves* have conflicting objectives, quite apart from any difference with other groups. For example, the scientific community has an interest in receiving sufficient governmental and industry support to continue to carry out research, as well as an interest in finding out what is really going on and communicating this to society at large. The Putszai affair in the United Kingdom,[7] however, has demonstrated that good science, and the motive of researchers to produce it, can often be undermined by sectional interests even from within their own ranks.

TABLE 4.1 Players and interests in the debate

Player	Interest
Government of more developed country	Maintenance of competitive position; protection of party esteem in public opinion
Government of less developed country	Economic growth; equal rights in decision making
Environmental lobby groups	Protection of the natural world; education of the public
Large corporations	Protection of shareholders' interests; maintenance of market position
Industry representative group	Enhanced status of the industry; control over member behaviour
Regulators	Control of firms in accordance with legislation
Public opinion(s)	Information on threats; protection and security; maintenance or improvement of living standards
Scientific community	Objective conclusions; dissemination of true picture; resourcing and permission to continue to conduct research
International organizations	Cross-border collaboration

The main lesson to learn from this is that organizational strategies with respect to the environment sit within a shifting balance of forces of different institutions and bodies that define the possibilities as well as the constraints of activity in this area. As lobby groups develop, so too do the arguments in favour of specific practices. Similarly, as different

THINKING CRITICALLY ABOUT ETHICS

ENVIRONMENTALISM AND GOVERNMENT

Ideas evolve and find the space to be developed and discussed, in part because social forces allow the appropriate space to exist. This is as true of environmentalism as it is of other social concepts such as equality or human rights.

The discussion in this section indicates some groups with the potential to create or inhibit discussion of environmental issues. For reasons mentioned earlier, industries that have up until now been heavy polluters find the arguments on climate change threatening. As a result, they tend to be opposed to these arguments. Governments are generally unwilling to allow movements that have arisen spontaneously in civil society to have too great a voice that is expressed independently of the organs of the state, seeing it as the rightful job of elected representatives.

Given this, how far would you describe the environmental movement as a protest against big business and government? To what extent does it serve the interests of governments, in particular, to allow environmentalism to flourish?

funding institutions support research in certain areas, then opportunities arise for the exploitation of new technologies. Finally, as government and inter-government policies change, this in turn changes the challenges and incentives for organizations to act with greater environmental responsibility.

A corollary of this is that dispute and debate about the environmental threats to the globe are unlikely to dissipate, even as scientific knowledge continues to increase. In later sections we shall see some of the assumptions and arguments that give intellectual sustenance (though not necessarily validity) to these differences. In addition, though, we can see that the debates are not disinterested: positions are taken, not because of the soundness of the arguments in their favour, but in some cases rather on the basis of how far they support the interests of this or that group.

THE DEVELOPMENT OF THE CONCEPT OF 'ENVIRONMENT'

Origins

While the term 'environment' is a relatively new concept in its global ecological sense, there are many longstanding cultural traditions relating to the relationship between humans and the natural world. Islam, for example, contains implications for how humans interact with nature.[8] Other religions, such as Sikhism, depict the purpose of humanity as to live in harmony with nature. Also, many pre-industrial cultures, such as native Australians or native North Americans, have elaborate intellectual systems that present people as integrated into the natural world.[9]

The idea of 'the environment', as an explicit concept, has changed over time as the detailed issues have developed. Earlier phases focused on the loss of amenity as human activity affects the natural world. Rachel Carson was one of the first to draw attention to the potential of human actions to destroy parts of nature, though the era in which her groundbreaking book *Silent Spring* was published (the 1960s) was far more concerned with the potential impact of all-out nuclear war on the globe rather than with the effects of industrial activity.[10] Her arguments were concerned with the impact of agricultural practice on species extinction. At that time there was no indication of any long-term impact on climate, so the key issues were related to flora and fauna, with a view to the consequences for human consumption.

In the next decade, the Club of Rome's report, *The Limits to Growth*,[11] identified a range of trends, which, they argued, would lead to serious social problems if not directly addressed. Their main areas of interest were resource utilization, population growth and food availability. Pollution was discussed and analysed, but again there was no scientific evidence at the time to take climate change into account. However, arguably this discussion raised the issue of sustainable civilization, even if the terminology was not directly employed, as one of their main arguments was that key resources, such as oil or coal, would run out within decades if the trends identified at the time continued unchecked. *The Limits to Growth* did not attempt to make concrete predictions, but rather to illustrate trends as a basis to inform policy. Its assumptions about oil supply, technological progress and resource utilization were soon made obsolete by new discoveries of resources, changed usage patterns and technological progress. Nevertheless, the underlying message, that there are indeed limits to growth, and that resources are not infinite, has framed much of the debate since that time.[12]

Sustainability was also a key theme of E. F. Schumacher's groundbreaking work on alternative economics, *Small is Beautiful*, published within a year of the Club of Rome's report.[13] Its argument was based around the idea that use of non-renewable resources was rather like living off capital instead of income – progressively one depletes the capital until there is none left to generate the necessary income. This sat within a broader critique of capitalist society, which included the claim that when considered from a total resource and utility perspective, industrial production was less efficient than intermediate technologies, as well as the philosophical argument that modern economics erroneously depicted consumption as the end of all human activity. Again the prime concern with the environment at this point was still the ability of human civilization to maintain its current standard of living given the limited resources available. But a new theme was also emerging – environmentalism, not simply as a critique of practice but as an alternative social philosophy.

At almost the exact same time that Schumacher's book was published, scientists Frank Sherwood and Mario Molina were beginning experiments into the effect of CFCs on ozone depletion. As with other early work on ecology, their views were heavily criticized by industry, including chemical giants such as DuPont, but their theoretical predictions in the 1970s were strongly supported by the discovery by the British Antarctic Survey of a hole in the ozone layer in that region in 1985. Two years later, the Montreal Protocol represented the first attempt at international collaboration to deal with a climate change issue.

By this time, the 'green' movements in Asia and Europe had become significant political players, with strong electoral support in elections in several countries. Although none achieved a controlling position in government, many refocused political agendas, and some were minority members of coalition governments. As already hinted, and as we will see in more detail later on in this chapter, environmentalism as a political movement becomes a kind of diluted average of different positions that may join together as much because of their opposition to other political groups as for the extent of their joint agreements.[14] So although the growth of these movements added a strong spur to the debate, they did not necessarily in themselves clarify or develop the ideas involved. In fact we shall see that there has been a somewhat confusing proliferation of different environmental approaches.

Rio, Kyoto and beyond

Since that time, the concept of environment has been steadily focused on the themes of climate change, species extinction, non-climatic waste and pollution impacts on living conditions, deterioration in agricultural land and loss of amenity value of nature. Further international agreements have been formulated[15] to deal with atmospheric pollution, sustainable development, and the balance between controls on growth and the needs of poorer countries to improve standards of living. The most important of these was probably the Earth Summit in Rio de Janeiro in 1992, which led to a number of far-reaching agreements on the environment and international cooperation in development matters. One of the key outcomes of Rio was a statement of 27 principles for sustainability in development (see the accompanying text box[16]), enshrining a link between environmental responsibility and the need for an international perspective on development and control, recognizing that poorer countries have some right to develop, even while richer ones may have to hold their own growth in check.

THE 27 PRINCIPLES OF THE RIO DECLARATION (HEADINGS ONLY)

1 The role of humans
2 State sovereignty
3 The right to development
4 Environmental protection in the development process
5 Eradication of poverty
6 Priority for the least developed
7 State cooperation to protect eco-system
8 Reduction of unsustainable patterns of production and consumption
9 Capacity building for sustainable development
10 Public participation
11 National environmental legislation
12 Supportive and open international economic system
13 Compensation for victims of pollution and other environmental damage
14 State cooperation to prevent environmental dumping
15 Precautionary principle
16 Internationalization of environmental costs
17 Environmental impact assessments
18 Notification of natural disaster
19 Prior and timely notification
20 Women have a vital role
21 Youth mobilization
22 Indigenous peoples have a vital role
23 People under oppression
24 Warfare: protection for the environment in times of armed conflict
25 Peace, development and environmental protection
26 Resolution of environmental disputes
27 Cooperation between state and people

Source: United Nations Environment Programme.

The Rio Principles are highly aspirational in tone. One underlying theme is the inter-relationship between environmental protection and economic development. Behind this are two issues. The first is the desire on the part of less-developed economies to maintain an impetus for growth, which might be undermined by environmental regulation. While regulations or agreement covering greenhouse gases, for example, would have an impact on the economic performance of the well-established economies such as Japan or the United States, they would have a much greater impact on those emerging economies such as Brazil or South Africa. These economies have therefore argued that the developed countries should take a lead in environmental protection.

The second issue is the pattern of exploitation of natural resources in less-developed countries by companies based in more affluent economies. What this can lead to is that economically weaker countries are less able to combat environmental degradation. Often, too, this impacts negatively on the least advantaged groups of people in such countries. The legal requirement for a company to act in the best financial interests of its shareholders means that it may not have as a priority the needs and interests of less influential stakeholders such as members of a local community. One of the key challenges for environmental managers is to develop an appropriate sensitivity towards the impact of corporate actions on vulnerable stakeholders. As we have discussed in previous chapters, stakeholder management requires organizations to look beyond the most immediately influential actors and take into consideration the full range of those affected, especially those who have low levels of information and influence, though are highly vulnerable to the effects of corporate actions. One argument that is telling in this respect is to reflect on *long-term* consequences: while a particular group of stakeholders may be less influential currently, there is always the possibility that in the future they may acquire greater influence, and then may be able to retrieve some of their earlier losses.

Ethical theory can have a bearing here. Taking an analogy with the Rawlsian 'veil of ignorance' approach, it could be argued that the responsible corporation should look at the least advantaged group of stakeholders and decide whether that would be a tolerable situation. The basis for this would be that in the long term it is not clear how successful or influential any firm might be, and hence it may well itself be subject to disadvantage. Therefore it is preferable to ensure that account is taken of the least advantaged as well as of the most advantaged. This is not a pure application of Rawls, for it compares companies with stakeholder groups. However, the general principle is comparable: to base decisions on ensuring that the least advantaged position that results is still tolerable.

Perhaps of even more importance than the Rio Principles was the Framework Convention on Climate Change. In this, the parties to the Rio Earth Summit agreed to commit to an ongoing process of developing and implementing reductions in the use of greenhouse gases (GHGs), to be achieved through a continuing series of further conferences.[17] The most important of these subsequent conferences, in Kyoto, Japan, led in 1997 to the so-called Kyoto Protocol.

This Protocol took the non-binding agreement of the Rio Earth Summit and made this a formal commitment of signature nations. The Protocol introduced several new elements, including:

- Formal reporting on progress towards reductions in GHGs, with explicit targets for each signature country.
- Emissions trading systems.
- 'Clean development mechanisms' that enable green technologies to be transferred between countries (notably to help developing countries benefit from advances made in the developed world).
- Joint implementation of GHG reduction projects in more than one signature country.
- Adaptation funding for projects.

Although, by end-2008, 178 countries (plus the European Union as a distinct entity over and above its member states) have ratified the Protocol, it has generally been regarded as of limited impact due to the non-cooperation of the United States, by far the largest polluter. Neither the Clinton nor Bush administrations showed much interest in the Kyoto Protocol – Bill Clinton signed it but only in the last few weeks of that administration, leaving no time for it to be implemented, and it was explicitly rejected by George W. Bush in 2001. Australia for some years also would not ratify, but eventually did so in 2007. Further weaknesses have emerged in the slow progress of most countries towards their agreed targets: large European industrial nations such as Germany, the United Kingdom and France have not met their targets. And some of the most rapidly industrializing nations, notably Brazil, India and China, are without agreed reduction targets, even though their emissions of GHGs are predicted to rise within a very few years to the levels of the 36 countries that already have targets.

It is clear that there has been resistance to the development of greater environmental regulation by the most industrialized nations, as well as by some of the most powerful corporations. What is less clear is the nature and justification for such resistance. As we shall see in the following section, there is a legitimate environmentally sympathetic position that is based on an optimistic view of technological progress, such that future technological developments may lead to cleaner fuels and energy sources, reduced atmospheric and sea pollution, and generally much more efficient and less ecologically damaging production.

Developments in areas such as the oil industry lend support to this view, as companies such as BP and Shell have expanded their production of greener forms of petrol and of cleaner fuels such as LPG. However, this trend is not universal, and many large firms have sought to retain their existing methods of production, as change would potentially be very costly and might erode their competitive position. There is little in the way of direct corroborated evidence regarding corporate lobbying, but the question might be raised whether those most established and powerful corporations might use their influence through the lobbying process to delay changes in environmental legislation until such time as they have identified ways to maintain or enhance their competitive advantages. Explicit warnings from aluminium producers in the early 2000s that they would move from Australia should that country ratify Kyoto have been given as an explanation for Australia's reluctance to ratify.

Again, we might see here the concern with sheer survival overcoming longer-term considerations. However, while other ethical issues, such as corporate approaches to equality, might arguably be comparable in scale with the need for corporate survival, the matter of the environment differs, in that it may threaten the survival not just of companies but of humanity in general. So in this debate the argument is less justifiable. A company is not valuable in the way that human beings are, and therefore its survival or demise is less a matter of concern than that of humans.

The main lesson to be learned from this discussion is that the idea of 'environment' has slowly changed, as the science has brought new issues to light, but also as the balance of priorities has evolved. The early emphasis on protecting nature and on resource depletion gave way to the more immediate, and potentially more disastrous, impacts of climate change brought about by human over-production of GHGs. But this in turn has been modified to take account of the balance between developed and developing countries and their differing needs. And recalcitrant remains the world's largest industrial economy, supported by a raft of major global companies. The parties to the debate, as presented in Table 4.1, have remained reasonably stable, though their interactions and positions have modified over the decades.

ETHICS AND YOU

LIMITS OF ENVIRONMENTALISM

The discussion here highlights that the concept of the environment has changed in the last 50 years as scientific knowledge has increased, and as the relative balance of power between developed and developing countries has shifted.

This does not, though, indicate what is the most appropriate concept to use. The following are all elements that at one point or another have been brought into the environment debate. How far, and how many, do you see them as relevant to business activity, and where (if anywhere) should business organizations draw the line? Should firms include a consideration of all these in their strategic plans?

- climate change
- rising sea levels
- agricultural production
- pollution and toxic emissions
- species extinctions in general
- the loss of particular species such as tigers or beetles
- the rights of poorer nations to enjoy increased standards of living
- over-consumption by richer nations
- the rights of all humans to benefit from the fruits of the land
- the avoidance of poverty in poorer nations.

COMMON RESOURCES, INDIVIDUAL AND COLLECTIVE RESPONSIBILITIES

Underlying the whole set of debates regarding the environment are some fundamental questions of how human beings relate to the natural resources of the globe. In the next section we will look at conceptions of the environment, but in this section we will introduce the issue of how humans should take responsibility for the world's natural resources.

Natural resources are in one sense free to all. This is obvious in the case of the open seas or the air we breathe. Activity of individuals or corporations impacts on the ecosphere, on these natural resources. A key issue is who should be responsible for ensuring the protection of these natural resources. One can identify several positions, including:

- Governments should take the lead in protecting the environment by legislating to provide a sound regulatory framework. The responsibility of corporations is to follow such frameworks, working within them.
- Corporations should take initiatives to protect the environment, working with governments and other bodies such as NGOs to develop appropriate frameworks.
- Individuals and corporations should take responsibility for what they own, and governments should only intervene with respect to impact on common resources.

A well-known concept in respect of the third of these positions is the so-called 'tragedy of the commons'. This phrase originated in the writing of Garrett Hardin,[18] though the idea has been discussed for some centuries. Imagine a piece of common grazing land. Each herder taking cattle on to that land benefits from the use of that land. But if the land is over-grazed it will eventually lose its ability to support grazing at all. So the collective long-term interest of the herders would be to take steps to control the amount of grazing, so that the land is not exhausted. However, for each individual there remains a benefit for them alone to continue to graze on the land. So all herders might continue to over-graze the land until it is exhausted. One might see this solely as a metaphor were it not for the fact that this kind of phenomenon has been observed with fish stocks in the open seas, which continue to be depleted by the actions of individual fishers and by separate governments supporting their national fisheries at the expense of the common amenity.

The key issue is that, given the potential of individuals acting in their self-interest to deplete common resources, what is the most appropriate response. Opinions diverge as to whether this idea implies that collective – i.e. government – regulation is necessary to prevent such tragedies occurring, or whether this shows that common resources are always prone to this weakness, and would be better being privatized (i.e. made no longer common). These in turn reflect ideological preferences, for example in favour of free-market libertarianism as opposed to state planning. However, there are direct implications for business activity. We shall see these in the next sections, when discussing approaches supporting and contesting the argument for environmental protection.

APPROACHES TO ENVIRONMENTAL ISSUES

In the previous sections we have looked at the challenge presented by the environment, as well as the background to the current level of debate and policy evolution. In Part II we will explore further the policies and practices of the various institutional players in this field. But in order to understand the nature of the debates, and the underlying justification of different arguments, it is necessary to recognize the wide range of different ways that 'the environment' may be conceptualized.

The underpinning concepts behind environmentalism and environmental ethics have been variously categorized. Adherents of environmental values are often represented on a scale that includes 'deep' or 'dark' greens, 'light' greens, and 'bright' greens, suggesting different points on a continuum between an extreme deontological value placed on the environment in itself, through to a consequentialist balance between the rights and needs of different groups of humans, as well as the rights of other animals. While this is a convenient device, it can suggest that each environmental position is characterized by the same set of issues, only taken to greater or lesser extremes. This is misleading, as we shall see. It is also important to understand those different kinds of conception of the human-to-nature relationship that may be generally seen as *opposed* to environmentalism, for these too fall into different classes, and are not simply more or less strong in their antipathy to environmental ethics. We shall consider these as well.

The environmental movement has, as stated earlier, a wide range of different subgroups, some of which differ from each other almost as much as they differ from the non-environmental positions. There has been a tradition of trying to locate these different positions on a scale, using ever more puns on the image of green as the colour of nature. Some of these are described in the following list:

- **Deep green** – or sometimes called deep ecology. This is the view that we should not look at the environment from a human-centred perspective, but rather consider nature as a whole, with humans simply occupying one of many positions in it. One originator of this view, philosopher Arne Naess, claims that the sense of 'deep' that he intended was partly to reflect the need to pursue ever deeper questions about our views on how people integrate with the rest of the environment, and partly to contrast with what he called 'shallow environmentalism', an approach concerned with finding the right tools for humans to live sustainable lifestyles, but not with the question of exactly how humanity should co-exist with the rest of nature.[19] Supporters of the 'deep' approach have also been attracted by the holistic views of James Lovelock, who regards the Earth as a whole as a single self-managing system, which he calls 'Gaia':[20] originally described as an hypothesis, this has come to be regarded more as a conviction or an overall philosophical article of faith by some. The implication of this latter view is that the earth-system is able to correct imbalances on its own – so if humans push it too far in a certain direction the spontaneous correction by the Gaia may well undermine or even eliminate humanity.

- **Dark green**. Whereas the 'deep' approach relates to spiritual ideas about humans and their place in the universe, the 'dark' approach emphasizes the political – their view is that environmental problems have been caused by the market-oriented industrial form of human life, and that the root solution is to change society to make it less obsessed with consumerism and growth. Some 'darks' would also associate themselves with the 'deep' philosophy, but this is not an inevitable link. However, both views agree on the removal of humanity from being the centre of life, and the acceptance of all living forms as having an independent value.[21] Allied to this is eco-feminism, the idea that our problems with the ecosphere are a result of the dominance of human life, and of the natural world, by the male gender and by 'male' values.

- **Light green**. This is a more restrained approach to the environment, that emphasizes the role and responsibility of individuals rather than of large-scale changes in society. The approach places confidence in the capacity of society to make incremental changes to benefit the eco-system, and thus it focuses on the details of how consumer lifestyle choices can be adapted to reduce environmental damage to a manageable limit. The key engine of this is change internally within each individual.

- **Bright green**. The proliferation of 'green' variants has recently included the idea that the drivers for the necessary social change to achieve sustainability are technological in nature. This approach believes that new technologies, better design, and alternative forms of social organization[22] can resolve the current environmental problems. This approach shares with the technological anti-environmentalist position a confidence in the progress of technology (see below). The main difference here is that this progress is projected as being explicitly and deliberately focused on environmental improvement, while the anti position presumes that such improvement would result naturally from technological progress.[23]

It should be clear from the above discussion that some of these approaches treat the value of the natural world *deontologically* – as part of what it actually is to be an ethical human being – while some see it in more *consequential* terms, as contributing to human well-being, but needing to be balanced against other considerations. Another aspect of this range of views is the extent to which a spiritual element is involved. Some deep ecologists see the universe in quasi or even explicitly religious terms (one interpretation of Gaia treats it as more a matter of belief than of scientific evidence). Interestingly many of the traditional environmentally related philosophies such as *Ubuntu* also have religious connections.

A further dimension of these different views is the degree of politicization. The deepest green approaches call for a radical change in the very nature of society. Other 'dark' or deep green views look for a change in the structure of society but retaining that aspiration, originating from the enlightenment, that greater knowledge will bring greater emancipation from illness, poverty and manual toil. The so-called 'lighter' approaches look to reforms in society and industry that enable greater progress in technology as well as a change in cultural expectations of individual consumption.

Most of these positions are at a fairly abstract level of socio-political thought. The key issue, when looking at corporate social responsibility, is how they relate to business behaviour and strategy. Inevitably there are difficulties connecting the deep green

ETHICS IN PRACTICE

THE CHIPKO MOVEMENT

In the 1970s, a group of women in Uttaranchal, in northern India, took direct, non-violent action to prevent the cutting down of trees in their region – trees that represented part of their traditional way of life and were seen as part of their rights to use the land for subsistence. Following the example of an historical figure, Amrita Devi, the women physically hugged the trees, making it impossible for the loggers contracted by the Forestry Department to cut down the trees without harming the women.

From one village the protest spread to others, in most cases only communicated by word of mouth. Encouraged by their slogan, 'What do the forests bear? Soil, water and pure air', the Chipko protesters eventually succeeded in persuading the then Prime Minister of India, Indira Gandhi, to ban all tree felling in the region for 15 years, a move that was later replicated in several other states of India.

After this success, the movement went on to protest about mines and dams, and led to a movement known as Save Our Seeds, which continues to the present day. The movement was awarded the 'Right to Livelihood' Award in 1987 (sometimes called the 'alternative Nobel').

A key feature of this example is the link between ecological preservation and local economic development. Closely allied to this is also the impact of self-determination and non-violent protest. Finally, it has been often quoted as an example of eco-feminism, where women were able to protect the environment without recourse to 'male' strategies such as violent conflict.

Source: Ministry of Health and Welfare, India.

arguments with current commercial activity, since the logical conclusion of the deep green approach is that modern commerce is wrong. The so-called 'light' approach is less challenging, but its vision of a more restrained, less consumerist, population does not square with the current market-driven economies where growth of market penetration, market share and absolute sales volumes are central to their operation. The 'bright' green approach is most easy to make compatible with current market economies, focusing as it does on progress that comes with more focused and more targeted technological growth.

THINKING CRITICALLY ABOUT ETHICS

BUSINESS AND DEEP GREEN

Arguably, the more radical approaches to the environment cannot be made compatible with current market-driven or even mixed economic structures.

One argument might be to ignore them, as being too idealistic. Another might be to see if it is possible for businesses to work with these ideas, by asking what kinds of transformation would be necessary, and how could we get to these from where we are today?

Consider a company you know well. What changes could you envisage that might represent a move towards the 'deep, dark' green versions of the environmentalist position, that are both realistic for businesses, and also would be acceptable for people in developed as well as developing countries? Or do you think that the gap is too great to bridge?

OPPOSITION TO ENVIRONMENTALISM

The environmental movement is just that – a movement, with distinctive groupings, identities and characteristic positions. In contrast, opposition to environmentalism does not come in the form of specific anti groups, so much as in an array of different arguments offered against. Some of these arguments are directed at specific points, though the different views are not generally associated with specific groups or parties. As was indicated earlier, it is arguable that many of these positions have been adopted less as convictions on the part of, say, major polluting companies, so much as moves to stave off changes that those companies see as damaging to their commercial success.

Among the views that are commonly seen as anti-environmental, one can distinguish three quite different responses:

1 **Scientific scepticism**. While in general this has abated, with the vast majority of the academic scientific community accepting that human activity has to some appreciable extent adversely affected the climate, there remain pockets of uncertainty about the degree of change, the capacity of the earth to sustain these ecological shocks and recover from them, and more significant areas of debate about the nature of the impact of the changes in different regions of the globe and in different dimensions of weather.

2 **Free-market environmentalism.** This position does not directly dispute the science, but rather the social assumptions about change. It comes from the same root as the general free-market economics of Freidman and others, and essentially posits that individuals in society, when left to themselves without government interference, will gradually adapt their choices as the costs and benefits of different practices become more apparent. Eventually the pursuit by individuals of their own interests will lead to environmentally the best outcome, one that reconciles the needs of different groups in society with the capacity of the natural world to sustain human life to an acceptable degree.

3 **Technological progress.** Adherents of this approach draw sustenance from the story of the Club of Rome's work: the predictions in detail made by that group were confounded, in part, by the advances made in technology. Ever cleaner and more efficient technologies are continuing to be developed, by means of more careful targeting of activities, use of nano-technologies that consume much lower levels of energy in operation, smarter ways of reusing 'waste' products for other purposes, as well as the identification of more effective methods for cleaning and storing unwanted gas emissions. The sum total of these should therefore be sufficient to offset the worst effects of climate change and other environmental problems in the long run.

These positions do not dispute the fundamental ethical assumptions of the environmental movement – that if human activity is causing substantial change to the climate then this is wrong and we should change our ways of producing and consuming goods. Rather, they focus on different aspects of the facts and probabilities. Probably the last of these has most validity: scepticism about the science continues to be resolved, and usually in favour of the environmental position; the free-market approach rests on the assumption that market mechanisms can operate before the damage to the environment is irreparable. The technological position approaches the 'bright green' vision of technology and smart design as key means to offset and reduce environmental damage.

In addition, the technological position does not retard debate about what should be done, in the way that the other two positions might. For it is reasonably clear what should be done by companies, regulators, and those who commission and fund research. In practice this approach is most consistent with what is actually happening: companies are responding to public and governmental pressure by developing new technologies that retain good commercial prospects, but piecemeal tend to reduce or offset environmental damage. This is not universal, and some of the largest firms still espouse the belief that it is the role of government to set the framework for corporate responsibility. However, that confidence in government has been undermined from a different direction, namely the failure of the major governments to control the financial sector prior to the crash of 2008. The argument for the initiative to come from all players, be they governments, companies, scientists or pressure groups, has become part of the current consensus on how to deal with climate change.

GREENWASHING

Public opinion has been continually favourable to at least some aspects of the environmental case since the late 1970s. This has therefore had a significant impact on consumer behaviour. Organic food has enjoyed a steady and substantial rise in popularity, for ecological as well as for health reasons. Non-chlorine household cleaning agents, energy-saving electrical items and rechargeable batteries are all examples of goods that have seen an increase in demand due in part to the greater desire of the public to buy more environmentally responsible products. At the same time, recycling and recyclable products have become extremely popular in many countries – not just the big developed economies but also in many that are still in the process of development.

Many producers of domestic goods have latched on to this. From the 1980s onwards there has been a vast emphasis on almost any aspect of a product that could be conceivably described as 'green', covering items such as washing powders, wind-up radios, energy-saving computers, petrol for cars and supermarket own-brand food products, to name but a few. These have often been promoted by the same firms that have actively opposed aspects of the environmental movement. For example, almost all the major oil firms today offer a 'green' fuel, even though simultaneously they have been in conflict with groups like Greenpeace over issues such as location of pipelines, disruption to local rural resources and disposal of old oil rigs. There are, of course, arguments both consequential and deontological about the merits of such actions. But many in the environmental movement have regarded a great deal of the green marketing today as no more than a cynical way to exploit idealism for the purpose of generating more sales, often with little or no real ecological benefit. Such an attitude has been dubbed 'greenwashing' – rather like whitewashing, it does not actually clean out environmental problems, but rather covers them up with a veneer of ecological 'value' that is often little more than colours and logo.

There is, however, the alternative view that for a company in a highly competitive business context it is essential to project the key features of a product. If a product does, in comparison with its rivals, have more ecological benefit (or is less ecologically harmful) then it would seem reasonable to communicate this to the market. In principle, then, some form of 'green' advertising is potentially justifiable. But note that this assumes that the product in question genuinely does have such ecological benefits, and that the promotional activity does in fact present the real balance of such benefits. Whether this is actually realized in the 'green' advertising campaigns of many companies is unproven in our view, though readers are invited to form their own judgement on this issue.

ETHICS AND YOU

GREENWASHING IN PRACTICE

Imagine that you work for a company whose operations represent a substantial negative impact on the ecosphere. The board are sympathetic to environmental arguments, but they feel that the changes necessary to satisfy these will have to take several years. In the meantime, to protect their brand as they slowly move towards a more responsible production method, they propose to develop a greater 'green' image, preparing their market for the changes to come.

   Is this greenwashing in your view? How would you respond to this when asked by the managing director for your view?

SUSTAINABLE DEVELOPMENT

Sustainable development has been described as that which 'meets the needs of the present without compromising the ability of future generations to meet their own needs'.[24] However, it involves also the balancing of the needs of different present groups, in particular the relationship between the richer and poorer nations and the fate that befalls the citizens in the two different kinds of country. The UN has recognized this as involving three different aspects (which it describes as the 'pillars' of sustainable development): economic development, social development and environmental protection.[25] We can see much of the preceding complex of different views on environmentalism as representing different approaches to dealing with these three 'pillars'. The more radical green approaches tend to look mainly at environmental protection and, in some cases, to social reorganization, while opposition comes from those who want to advance the economic side of development.

   Philosophers have found some difficulty with the concept of the interests of future generations. If someone does not now exist (and of course might never exist if events go in one way rather than another) how can we talk of their rights? Feinberg has argued that whoever does exist in the future, and however they may have come into being, we can already identify at least some of their rights and needs.[26] However, this is not a conclusive position. For one thing, how far into the future should one go in evaluating a potential decision? Future prediction is uncertain, and the further forward one looks the less certain it gets. So while we might have some idea about impact on people who are born in the next 300 years, do we have much of an understanding of what will matter to those born in, say, 10,000 years' time? This undermines, incidentally, the use of stakeholder theory to help resolve ethical issues, for in theory one could argue that all and any who come after us have some kind of stake in what we do, but we have progressively diminishing ability to identify what that stake might be and how we can help to support it. Be that as it may, there is clearly some meaning to talking about the needs of those who might be born in the next few decades at least, and the scale of environmental threat facing the world today may mean that these next decades are the most crucial in our future planning.

   There is a further problem, here, though. It is generally believed that we can only be held responsible for actions that we had some influence over or capacity to affect, an idea summed up in the phrase that 'ought implies can'.[27] How can I be responsible for the future impacts of what I do now, when there will be countless events that will happen that will alter the exposure of future generations to these impacts? Some events may exaggerate

WHERE TO DRAW THE LINE?

Some industries, such as mining or other forms of primary production, have clear and relatively immediate long-lasting implications for future generations. Others have potentially significant effects that may or may not come to pass. For example, the most efficient forms of storage of nuclear waste are predicted to remain secure for several thousand years. However, if at the end of that time the storage facilities fail, the waste will still be radioactive, and will still be harmful to human beings (who are extremely unlikely to have evolved in such a short time to be resistant). Is this an argument against storing the waste at all? Should we try to leave written or graphic communications at the point of storage to alert future generations to the risk? Or should we work on the bases, either that technology will have developed to a point where this is harmless, or assume that the population will take account of the threat and adjust their lifestyles to stay away from affected areas?

dramatically what I counted to be rather small risks, so what level of responsibility should I have for these unforeseen losses? In practice there may be no simple solution to this – some risks are foreseeable and slight in probability though great in impact, others may be simply unpredictable. But the distant impact of a decision taken now is the result of a *process*, which carries through several generations of human beings. So the responsibility of those who act now may need to be regarded as a step in a chain of generations: the prime issue would be how to pass on to the next generation sufficient resource and information that they can take their own decisions to ensure that what is passed on by them is acceptable. 'Leave it as you found, or would like to find it' may be the moral principle here.

SUMMARY

In this chapter we have looked at some of the theories and concepts underlying the debate over the environment. This has been discussed at a socio-political level, and has not addressed business practice. Sustainable environmental practices at a business level, such as 'fairtrade', carbon trading and environmental reporting, will be discussed in Part III.

The key points of this chapter are:

■ The arguments over the environment represent political positions as much as evaluations of the extant knowledge about the environment.

■ There is a range of different environmental approaches – often characterized as 'deep', 'dark', 'light' or 'bright' green.

■ There is a corresponding range of opposing arguments – scepticism over scientific results, confidence in the ability of technological progress and free-market liberalism.

■ Sustainability is the need to allow the natural world to refresh itself while providing sufficient resource for human life; this should be regarded as a dynamic balance rather than a static one.

■ Arguments over the environment and sustainability reflect not only economic and technological standpoints but in some cases spiritual values and also the political imperative for poorer nations to develop economically.

QUICK REVIEW QUESTIONS:

1   Which of the different 'green' positions is most compatible with standard business activity?
2. How do spiritual values sometimes influence the environmental debate?
3. What is free-market environmentalism, and can it be reconciled with more traditional environmental positions?

CASE STUDY: CEMENT SUSTAINABILITY INITIATIVE

The Cement Sustainability Initiative (CSI) was launched by the World Business Council for Sustainable Development. It is an industry body with membership from North America, South America, Europe, and southern Asia. Members companies sign up to a charter that commits them to a range of actions, including formulating a policy on business ethics, developing a climate change mitigation strategy and creating stakeholder engagement programmes.

The cement industry produces approximately 5 per cent of all global emissions of CO_2, hence any action that reduces the industry's levels of pollution has a substantial impact on global atmospheric levels. It has been estimated that in the period 1990–2006, in part as a result of the CSI charter, while cement production has increased by over 50 per cent CO_2 emissions attributable to it have only increased by 35 per cent.

A substantial focus of the CSI is in the engagement with emerging economies. These are identified as the primary consumers of cement in the coming decades, as these countries build factories, houses, public buildings and transport infrastructure. The Initiative has implemented a series of actions that are targeted on cement production in China and India, identified as the two countries likely to lead cement production in the coming decades (China is already the world's largest producer). CSI explicitly acknowledges the central role of construction in economic development, and of concrete as the building material of choice in many applications. A key principle of the Initiative is that all countries have the right to develop economically and relieve poverty.

Central to CSI's development is the acceptance of its CO_2 Accounting and Reporting Protocol. This is a measuring system that calculates CO_2 emissions from cement production processes, and thus can put flesh on reduction targets. The main members of CSI have all committed to double-digit percentage reductions in CO_2 production over the next few years, as well as identifying potential means of reducing nitrogen oxide and sulphur oxides.

While there are a number of global players in this industry, small firms still account for over half the production. Cement, being a heavy material, is not economic to transport great distances by road, and hence there are many local producers, especially in landlocked countries. Cement involves high levels of mineral quarrying, which inevitably diminishes the amenity value of surrounding land.

Concrete, the product of cement, is a highly efficient building material, heat-conserving, highly durable and light-reflective (hence reducing city heat). It is also fire resistant and has a long lifetime before any maintenance is needed. Above all, it is a relatively cheap material to produce.

While, then, cement is in absolute terms a very large carbon producer, in relative terms it may still represent good value-for-emission. Alternative materials – bricks, metals, plastics – all consume much greater levels of energy per tonne, as well as having shorter lifespans. Although it is unlikely that 'deep' green adherents will be convinced of the utility of cement, there is a strong argument that this can, if properly managed, make a strong positive contribution to reducing GHG emissions.

STUDY QUESTIONS

1 Which of the philosophies of the environment would seem closest to the work of this Initiative?

2 Compare an evaluation of the work of CSI as based on a consequentialist approach with one based on a deontological approach. Which of these would be most compelling, in your view?

3 What might be the arguments for, and against, a cement producer becoming associated with CSI?

SOURCE

World Business Council for Sustainable Development. See http://www.wbcsdcement.org.

NOTES

1. Cf. for example Hughes (1994), Chapter 5.
2. As described in Martin & Klein (1984).
3. IPCC (2007).
4. Dansgaard-Oeschger events – sudden increases in temperature, typically a 5°C change in only about 40 years, measured via Greenland ice cores, that occur every 2000 years or so. Cf. Schultz (2002).
5. It is worth noting the theory that human-driven climate change may have happened in ancient Greece around 500 BC (cf. Runniman 2005); however, this view is controversial, and in any case seems to apply only to a small part of the eastern Mediterranean, whereas the current increase in temperature appears to be having worldwide effects.
6. Brazil, Russia, India, China; four relatively less-developed countries with large landmass and resources, large populations and a reasonable-sized educated middle class – all key components for economic growth.
7. In the 1990s Dr Arpad Putszai conducted research into the effects of GM potatoes on the immune systems of rats. His conclusions suggesting a link led to his summary dismissal, legal prevention of him discussing his views publicly, and later, when many eminent scientists supported his findings, the Royal Society – the UK's oldest and most renowned scientific body – threatened reprisals against even the editors of *The Lancet*, the country's leading and most respected medical journal, for having supported Dr Putszai. See Mayer (2002).
8. cf. Dien (2000).
9. Another interesting example of how traditional philosophies depict an alternative conception of humanity and nature is the widespread African idea of *Ubuntu*. See Lutz (2008).
10. Carson (1962). Rachel Carson was another scientific writer who was subject to vilification following the publication of *Silent Spring*, though this was largely ineffective, as the debate sparked by her book eventually led to the banning of the pesticide DDT.
11. Meadows *et al.* (1972).
12. There have been two updates to the original report, at a 20-year and 30-year anniversary, each of which acknowledges that subsequent events have confounded the Club's assumptions, though as indicated in the text not the main logic of their argument.
13. Schumacher (1973), and revised 1999.
14. A feature of political parties generally, as true of the various Social Democratic parties in Europe, or of the Indian National Congress Party.
15. Though sadly all too often either dishonoured or ignored.
16. The box text only lists the 27 headings. The reader is advised to consult the UNEP website for the text of these principles: http://www.unep.org
17. At the time of writing the next of these will take place in 2009 in Denmark.
18. Hardin (1968).
19. Naess (1989).
20. See Lovelock (1990). 'Gaia' – the Ancient Greeks' name for the earth mother goddess.
21. See Singer (1995) for a philosophical expression of the equality of all living forms.

22. Such as 'closed loop' resource systems, where a defined group of humans can sustain their chosen lifestyle without relying on external sources of resource.
23. Sub-divisions exist even here – 'viridian' theorists emphasize the benefits of smart design in bringing environmental benefits, as opposed to 'leaf' greens who emphasize more natural developments. Perhaps this brings us to the limits of the colour metaphor.
24. United Nations (1987), commonly known as the Brundtland definition, after its originator.
25. WHO (2005).
26. Feinberg (1983).
27. Although perhaps not applying in every example. See Griseri (1987).

REFERENCES

Carson, R. 1962. *Silent Spring*. Houghton Mifflin.

Dien Mawil Izzi *et al.* 2000. *The Environmental Dimensions of Islam*. James Clarke & Co.

Feinberg, J. 1983. The rights of animals and unborn generations. In Beauchamp, T. and Bowie, N. (eds) *Ethical Theory and Business*. New York: Prentice-Hall.

Griseri, P. 1987. Can a dead man be harmed? *Philosophical Investigations*, Vol. 10, No. 44, 317–329.

Hardin, G. 1968. The Tragedy of the Commons. *Science*, Vol. 162, 1243–1248.

Hughes, D. 1994. Deforestation, overgrazing and erosion. Chapter 5 in *Pan's Travail: Environmental Problems of the Ancient Greeks and Romans*. Baltimore: Johns Hopkins University.

IPCC 2007. *Climate Change 2007: The Physical Science Basis*. Contribution of Working Group I to the Fourth Assessment Report of the Intergovernmental Panel on Climate Change (IPCC), Solomon, S. *et al.* (eds). Cambridge: Cambridge University Press.

Lovelock, J. E. 1990. Hands up for the Gaia hypothesis. *Nature*, Vol. 344 (6262): 100–102.

Lutz, D. 2008. *African Ubuntu Philosophy and Global Management*. Conference paper: Philosophy of Management International Conference, Oxford.

Martin, P. and Klein. R. (eds) 1984. *Quaternary Extinctions: Prehistoric Overkill*. Tucson: University of Arizona Press.

Mayer, S. 2002. Agricultural biotechnology hanging in the balance: Why the anti-GM food campaign has been so successful. In Jones, I. and Pollitt, M. (eds), *Understanding How Issues in Business Ethics Develop*. London: Palgrave.

Meadows *et al.* (1972). *The Limits to Growth*. Club of Rome.

Naess, A. 1989. *Ecology, Community and Lifestyle*. Cambridge: Cambridge University Press.

Runniman, W. 2005. *Plows, Plagues and Petroleum: How Humans Took Control of Climate*. Princeton University Press.

Schulz, M. 2002. On the 1470-year pacing of Dansgaard-Oeschger warm events. *Paleoceanography*, Vol. 17, No. 2, 1014.

Schumacher, E. F. 1973 / 1999. *Small Is Beautiful: Economics As If People Mattered*. Hartley & Marks Publishers.

Singer, P. 1995. *Practical Ethics*. Cambridge: Cambridge University Press.

United Nations 1987. *Report of the World Commission on Environment and Development* (commonly known as the Bruntland Commission). New York: United Nations.

World Health Organisation 2005. *World Summit Outcome Document*. WHO.

WALKING THE WALK: PUTTING SOCIAL RESPONSIBILITY INTO ACTION AT THE WHITE DOG CAFÉ

Ivey

Richard Ivey School of Business
The University of Western Ontario

BY DIANE M. PHILLIPS AND JASON KEITH PHILLIPS*

On April 22, 2007, Judy Wicks was sitting at her desk in her upstairs office at the White Dog Café, pondering what to do next. Wicks ran her small, upscale restaurant with a strong social responsibility philosophy, but was clearly at a crossroads. The restaurant was doing very well and her various social responsibility initiatives were making a big difference. However, she wondered how much longer she could keep up the frantic pace and whom she might appoint as a successor when she was finally ready to step down. Today was Earth Day, and Wicks had a full slate of activities planned. She would have to work out these details later.

Background

The name White Dog Café originated from the story of Madame Helena P. Blavatsky, who lived at the restaurant's present location in West Philadelphia during Philadelphia's Victorian era in the late 1800s. This was a time when many great intellectuals were debating the meaning of life, the role of science, and the interaction of humanity and nature. Madame Blavatsky was an author and a spiritualist who promoted "universal brotherhood" as a way to better conceptualize the needs and the rights of all individuals. Blavatsky was a core figure in the

*Diane M. Phillips and Jason Keith Phillips wrote this case solely to provide material for class discussion. The authors do not intend to illustrate either effective or ineffective handling of a managerial situation. The authors may have disguised certain names and other identifying information to protect confidentiality. Copyright © 2007, Ivey Management Services

One time permission to reproduce granted by Ivey Management Services on 1st March 2010.

movement of these universal human rights and held many meetings at her home.

After suffering a bad fall in 1875, Blavatsky's doctor recommended amputation of one of her legs. Instead of heeding her doctor's advice, she decided to take matters into her own hands and had a friend's dog — a white dog — sleep on her leg each night. Blavatsky had a strong belief in the power of nature and the spirit world. After a few nights of this treatment, the leg was fully healed. More than a century later, Judy Wicks, inspired by Madame Blavatsky's spirit and commitment to others, named her new restaurant the White Dog Café.

The White Dog Café opened in January 1983, as a take-out coffee and muffin shop on the first floor of Blavatsky's former home. The current owner of the property, Judy Wicks, had two young children and wanted to make a living close to home. The café was a hit, and soon after opening, the menu started to expand with the addition of soups and sandwiches. As the restaurant began to gain a loyal following, Wicks purchased the house next door to add dining space for her customers. By 1985, the White Dog Café had acquired a liquor license and had started crafting a social responsibility philosophy as a way to guide its many business decisions. Today, the White Dog Café serves its customers wonderful meals in a comfortable, inviting atmosphere. It has achieved a four-star rating in the Zagat Survey and is described as offering an international and eclectic fare. The restaurant serves approximately 138,000 customers per year, employs 110 individuals and grosses approximately $5 million a year.[1]

White Dog Café's Social Responsibility Philosophy

Soon after opening her restaurant, Wicks decided to develop a social responsibility philosophy in order to serve as a guide for the sometimes difficult managerial decisions that needed to be made. Wicks was one of a handful of business leaders who originally attempted to ground their businesses in strong social or environmental awareness principles. She believed that it was possible to make money and also "do the right thing" for the broader community. Little did she know it, but at around the same time, two other businesses were starting up with leaders who had similar philosophies: Ben & Jerry's and The Body Shop. Today, these organizations are hailed as outstanding examples of businesses that are very successful both at making money and, importantly, at making a difference to their communities. Unfortunately, these two businesses have also experienced recent growing pains.

Wicks felt compelled to articulate her philosophy so that her employees and business partners would have a clear understanding of what the White Dog Café was trying to achieve. The result was White Dog Café's four-part philosophy:

1 Serving Customers . . . with delicious and nutritious food, good service, a friendly atmosphere that is clean and smoke free, as well as by providing educational programs to benefit customers. These educational programs include table talks, storytelling, community tours, and international tours.

2 Serving Our Community . . . through encouraging staff and customer volunteer projects, making before-tax profit donations of 20 per cent to the White Dog Café Foundation, matching donations by employees to charitable organizations, actively speaking out against war, promoting education with high school mentor programs, celebrating diversity, and fostering economic justice.

3 Serving Each Other . . . by creating a workplace environment that is respectful, trustworthy and very team-work oriented. Employees are encouraged to share knowledge, humor and ideas with each other. The White Dog Café pay scale is based on a livable wage of $9.00, as opposed to the current minimum wage of $6.25. The White Dog Café also has a computer loan program for its full-time employees. [Wicks was tired of the stereotype of restaurant jobs not being "real" jobs; she classified her employees at the White Dog Café as real full-time employees and provided them with the benefits that any full-time job would provide.]

4 Serving Earth . . . through a variety of strategies such as the use of alternative energy sources (100 per cent of the electricity is generated by renewable sources such as wind and solar power). Many of the restaurant's food products and supplies are purchased from local organic farms and 100 per cent of the meat and poultry is from small farms that practise humane treatment of animals. The White Dog Café recycles everything possible and reduces its total food waste by sending it to a composting site, which was started by the restaurant and is now used by five local restaurants. This compost is used in landscaping the University of Pennsylvania campus. The restaurant also supports an employee-run group called the "Green Team" which works to protect the environment.

It is interesting to note that this four-part philosophy was not posted in any public areas of the restaurant where the customers might see it. The menu itself included a brief history of the restaurant and described the importance that the restaurant placed on the environment and social causes. Most customers, however, visited the restaurant for its great food and atmosphere. Very few knew about the philosophy of the restaurant and its staff.

Perhaps the most unusual thing about the White Dog Café was that, unlike other organizations that are much more impersonal, customers and employees who became a part of the White Dog "family" found that they became fully integrated into the fabric of the company's mission and philosophy. The White Dog Café was more than just a nice place to work; it was a place where people with similar values and passions about the environment and social issues could come together and share their passions. It was a safe haven, a gathering place, a launching pad.

Many businesses create a social responsibility philosophy and post the philosophy in the lobby of the corporate offices or print it on the front cover of the annual report. For the White Dog Café, the social responsibility philosophy was a part of the everyday operations at the restaurant. It was not unusual for the executive chef to use his day off to drive to Philadelphia's surrounding countryside to meet with an organic pork farmer to ensure that the animals were being treated humanely. Similarly, it was not unusual for the director of marketing to spend his day off making final arrangements for the White Dog Café's upcoming speaker, who would be discussing recent federal funding cuts for HIV/AIDS research. In other words, the White Dog Café didn't just "talk the talk" of social responsibility, it also "walked the walk."

White Dog Café's Projects and Programs

In support of its four-part social responsibility philosophy, the White Dog Café continued to actively engage in a number of different programs. Each of its programs was designed to address one or more of the four overriding objectives in the social responsibility philosophy.

The Sister Restaurant Project

This project began in 1990 with the intention of gaining support for minority-owned restaurants in different areas of Philadelphia through the development of relationships among the restaurants themselves. Customers were encouraged to visit neighborhoods they would normally not visit in order to build understanding, awareness and a city-wide community mentality. The White Dog Café had formed relationships with six restaurants in six different sections of the city. It regularly promoted these restaurants in its newsletter and even hosted community events at the sister restaurants.

The White Dog Café also operated a sister restaurant program internationally with the slogan, "Table for 6 Billion Please." This program formed relationships between the White Dog Café and restaurants in areas of the world that had poor relationships and/or conflicting views with the United States. Table for 6 Billion Please strived to develop a better understanding of the world community by opening the lines of communications, starting with the mutual interest of food. Currently, there are eight international sister restaurants in Vietnam, Cuba, Lithuania, Mexico, Israel, Nicaragua, the Netherlands and Palestine. Customers and staff

from the White Dog Café visit these international restaurants in order to learn more about the cultural, political and economic environments of these locations. The focus is on greater mutual education and understanding.

Mentoring program

Launched in 1992, the mentoring program provided workplace experience, community service participation, field trips to purveyors and family farms, and recreational and cultural activities for students from a variety of local high schools. Students learned how to manage a restaurant business and helped to put on a special event at the end of the semester. A $1,000 scholarship was awarded to one graduate each year, to be applied to culinary school.

Community tours

Through these tours, participants witnessed and experienced different issues in Philadelphia neighborhoods first-hand. The tours increased a sense of community and encouraged active citizen engagement.

- Community Wall Murals and Community Garden Tours illustrated the importance of gardens and murals in the inner city community.
- Affordable Housing Tours visited housing projects in various stages of development.
- Prison Garden Tours allowed participants to meet inmates and work on a mural dedicated to victims and survivors of violent crimes.
- Eco-Tours provided first-hand experience with environmental issues, such as recycling, energy conservation and water purification.
- Child Watch Visitation Programs allowed people to experience the lives of inner-city children through visits to child and family service centers, such as schools, juvenile detention centers, shelters and recreation centers.

Annual multicultural events

These events, such as Noche Latina, Native American Thanksgiving Dinner, Rum & Reggae and MLK Dinner, celebrated diversity within the community.

Whole World Products

Located on the premises of the White Dog Café, The Black Cat Gift Shop sold merchandise made from recycled materials and products made by disadvantaged workers throughout the world.

Table Talks

These talks featured speakers who led a discussion of a current issue of public concern, such as health care reform, the environment, or crime and violence.

Storytelling

On select Monday nights, the White Dog Café provided an opportunity to hear the life stories of active Philadelphians and gave voice to under-represented groups, such as gays, youths, homeless people, senior citizens and ex-offenders.

Community Service Days

Community service days were held for employees and customers throughout the year and included activities such as rehabilitating houses and building community gardens.

Take a Senior to Lunch

On Saturdays, White Dog Café patrons were encouraged to bring a senior to lunch or be matched with a senior who would like to get out more often. Participants were rewarded with a half-priced bill.

Opposition to War Activities

The White Dog Café raised awareness of the terrible realities of war and organized trips to anti-war protests.

The Culture of the Restaurant

A typical consumer who walked into the White Dog Café for a nice lunch in the dining room or a quick drink at the bar probably had little knowledge of all the activities that occupied the management and staff of the restaurant. However, there were many stories about the commitment that went on behind the scenes. One story had its origins in the desire to locate reliable food suppliers. Several years ago, before organic and fairly-traded products were easily ordered from restaurant-supply companies, the White Dog Café's owner traveled to Chiapas, Mexico to work with an indigenous coffee cooperative to help them export their coffee. In the process, the White Dog Café loaned the cooperative $20,000 to help them plant trees, purchase supplies and organize their operations for exporting.

Another story shared around the White Dog Café was that of the employee who had his bicycle stolen. Since the bicycle was his only source of transportation to and from work, he needed to replace the bicycle quickly. The staff and the restaurant donated money to help their co-worker purchase a new bicycle (and lock!) so that he would be able to continue working. This prompted the establishment of the "Sunshine Fund" to help anyone at the restaurant who had an emergency. Each month, the restaurant donated $50 and the employees each donated $1 to the fund. Individual employees pulled from $500 to $1000 from the fund for events like the birth of a new baby, a broken leg or a house fire. This philosophy of caring for the community and the environment transformed the White Dog Café's philosophy of social responsibility into a lived experience.

Other Socially Responsible Businesses

The White Dog Café was not alone in working to develop a business that infused all of its operations with a social responsibility philosophy. Two other businesses were Ben & Jerry's and The Body Shop. Both, however, had recently experienced significant growing pains.

The Ben & Jerry's Buyout

In April of 2000, due to pressure from both Unilever and Ben & Jerry's stockholders, Ben & Jerry's of Vermont was bought out by Unilever for $326 million, or $43.60 per share, which was a 25 per cent overvaluation of the current trading price. Ben & Jerry's became an independent subsidiary of Unilever with one member of Unilever on the board of directors. Unilever vowed to continue the socially responsible programs that were the hallmark of Ben & Jerry's and even hired Ben Cohen and Jerry Greenfield to design the company's social responsibility policy and maintain the Ben & Jerry's Foundation.

Although the takeover was not what Ben & Jerry's initially wanted, and many outside observers believed that the buyout would be detrimental to the company's social responsibility program, Ben & Jerry's seemed to have received some benefits from the buyout. The buyout was not widely publicized to the general public. In fact, the majority of Ben & Jerry's customers had no knowledge of the buyout and still viewed the company as a very socially responsible organization.

Sales have increased and Ben & Jerry's products have traveled to new locations. Several downsides, however, have resulted from the buyout. Unilever quickly did away with Ben & Jerry's long-standing policy of donating 7.5 per cent of pre-tax profits to charitable organizations and instead, made a flat annual donation of $1.1 million to these causes. With Cohen and Greenfield no longer in leadership positions, the organization also experienced several problems with the management team. Recently, the company's former chief financial officer (CFO) was accused of embezzling several hundred thousand dollars in company stock.

The Body Shop Problem

The Body Shop was founded in 1976 by Anita Roddick, who began retailing homemade, naturally inspired products with minimal packaging. She started a small shop in Brighton, on the southern coast of England, and sold an assortment of 25 handmade products to a worldwide network of shops. By 1978, The Body Shop began franchising and was rapidly expanding throughout the world. Not only were The Body Shop products expanding globally, but the organizational campaigns and social responsibility programs were also becoming more well-known across the world. The company focused on campaigns that promoted human rights, the protection of animals and the environment and the elimination of stereotypes produced by cosmetics companies. To date, The Body Shop Foundation has donated more than £8 million in grants and gift-in-kind support, assisting the work of numerous worldwide organizations.

The Body Shop, known for its ethical business practices, was in the final stages of a buyout by the French cosmetics giant, L'Oreal. L'Oreal would have to pay an estimated $1.1 billion dollars for the company. Simply as a result of the news of the potential buyout, Body Shop shares rose by 18 per cent, to $4.52 per share, giving the company a value of $975 million. The buyout would result in a significant net profit for shareholders; founders Anita and Gordon Roddick alone would profit by $118 million if the buyout goes through.

L'Oreal already appeared to be making adjustments to its business operations to become more in line with the values held by the Body Shop. L'Oreal had banned animal testing and spent $24 million dollars last year to fund alternative ways to test its cosmetic products. The buyout of The Body Shop would quickly revamp the image of L'Oreal and bring significant attention from former critics of the company's animal testing policies; however, it was still too early to tell how many of The Body Shop's ethical practices would be adopted by L'Oreal if the deal went through. Industry experts predicted significant changes with the Body Shop's ethical agenda if the buyout occurred. Just as Ben & Jerry's donation of 7.5 percent of pre-tax profits died quickly after its buyout, it was speculated that the "Body Shop will quietly drop their 'Against Animal Testing' commitments."[2]

Ben & Jerry's situation was clearly similar to The Body Shop's situation. Both companies had strong social responsibility philosophies and business practices. However, both companies found that as their businesses grew and as their founders made decisions to take a less active role in the day-to-day activities of the business, the transitions to new management teams and organizational structures were troublesome.

White Dog Community Enterprises

A real turning point occurred when Judy Wicks realized that, despite the success of her business, a single business enterprise that had a strong social responsibility philosophy wasn't nearly enough to make a strong and lasting impact at the local or even regional level. What Wicks wanted was for change to happen at the regional, national and even global level. According to Wicks, the philosophy of her business "needed to change from one that worked competitively, to one that worked co-operatively" with other businesses to achieve a common goal. She realized that "my real security laid not only in a strong business, but in a strong local economy filled with other socially responsible businesses." One of the first projects after this realization was to offer free consulting to her competitors on how to develop similar, socially responsible business models.

One of the next steps was the development of the non-profit White Dog Community Enterprises. The White Dog Café furthered the social impact of its philosophy through this non-profit. The purpose of White Dog Community Enterprises was to help build a local living economy in the Greater Philadelphia area. Each year, 20 per cent of the White Dog Café's pre-tax profits were donated to its own and other non-profit businesses. Each year, approximately $8,000 to $12,000 was donated by the café to organizations such as Action AIDS, Bread and Roses Community Fund, Habitat for Humanity and Greenpeace. Food was regularly donated to non-profit events, and gift certificates were given to fundraising events for these non-profit organizations. In addition, the café

matched any donation to a non-profit organization that employees wished to allocate from their paychecks. The café also worked to raise funds for current situations, such as the Hurricane Katrina disaster, by asking patrons to add an extra dollar to their bill, to go towards the cause. See Exhibit 1 for data from one of the café's recent financial statements.

As a point of comparison, a 2005 study by the National Restaurant Association and Deloitte found that for similar, full-service restaurants, the median income before taxes was 3.2 per cent of total sales and the median total cost of sales was 33 per cent of total sales.[3]

Moving On

Judy Wicks certainly had reason to sit back and feel satisfied with what she had accomplished. Evolving from a small coffee shop to a fully functioning, profitable, socially responsible organization was no small feat. However, there was little time to be complacent. In Wicks's mind, a key problem was not so much the development of a social responsibility philosophy or incorporating that philosophy into the day-to-day operations of the restaurant. Instead, the real challenge for the future was how to sustain the growth of the restaurant and the commitment to social causes in the long term. Judy Wicks was the visionary behind the White Dog Café phenomenon. What would happen when the day eventually came when she was no longer able to continue her role as the leader of this organization?

EXHIBIT 1 White dog café financial statements

Item	Oct 2005	Oct 2006
Sales Food	$316,420	$318,219
Sales Liquor	24,875	31,647
Sales Draft Beer	19,742	26,011
Sales Btl Beer	3,866	4,397
Sales Btl Wine	41,102	35,798
Comps	(22,743)	(28,592)
Total Sales	383,262	387,480

EXHIBIT 1 (Continued)

COGS Food	97,739	89,714
COGS Liquor	6,519	9,032
COGS Draft Beer	4,361	5,156
COGS Btl Beer	1,310	1,014
COGS Btl Wine	12,285	13,471
Purchase Discount	(1,183)	(1,405)
Total COGS	121,031	116,982
GROSS PROFIT	262,231	270,498
Payroll & Benefits	130,843	143,866
Direct Operating	10,994	7,200
Music & Entertainment	1,400	1,800
Advertising	6,046	1,902
Utilities	10,217	9,880
Admin & General	14,515	15,178
Social Resp	2,566	1,577
Repairs & Maint	5,635	5,272
Occupancy Cost	21,045	21,347
Other	2,138	1,916
TOTAL EXPENSES	205,399	209,938
NET PROFIT	$56,832	$60,560

SOURCES

David Goodman, "Culture Change," Mother Jones, January/February 2003, available from http://www.motherjones.com/news/feature/2003/01/ma_209_01.html, accessed July 30, 2007.

David Gram, "Ben & Jerry's to Be Acquired by Multinational Unilever," The Post [Ohio University], April 13, 2000, available from http://thepost.baker.ohiou.edu/archives3/apr00/041300/news10.html, accessed July 30, 2007.

"L'Oreal Buy Out The Body Shop," ScouseVeg-Liverpool Vegetarians and Vegans, available from http:www.scouseveg.co.uk/2006/03/17/loreal-buy-out-the-body-shop/, accessed July 30, 2007.

"L'Oreal Considering Approach for The Body Shop," Birmingham Post, February 24, 2006, Business Section.

National Restaurant Association and Deloitte, Annual Report, pp. 72–95.

"Potential Takeover Has Body Shop Sitting Pretty," The Canberra Times, February 25, 2006, p. A24.

Stephen Taub, "Ben & Jerry's Ex-CFO Sent to the Cooler," CFO.com, April 19, 2006, available at http://www.cfo.com/article.cfm/6823121?f=search, accessed July 30, 2007.

"Unilever Fat and Thin — Ben & Jerry's, Slim-Fast Acquired," The Economist, April 15, 2000, pp. 63–65.

Notes

1. All funds in US$ unless otherwise stated.
2. "L'Oreal Buy Out The Body Shop," ScouseVeg-Liverpool Vegetarians and Vegans, available at http:www.scouseveg.co.uk/2006/03/17/loreal-buy-out-the-body-shop/, accessed July 3, 2007.
3. National Restaurant Association and Deloitte, Annual Report, 2005. pp. 72–95.

GLAXOSMITHKLINE AND DEVELOPING COUNTRY ACCESS TO ESSENTIAL MEDICINES

"Shareholders will be aware that the creation of GlaxoSmithKline has coincided with an upsurge of public comment and concern on two issues in particular: the use of animals in the discovery and testing of medicines and access to medicines in the developing world."

— J P Garnier & Sir Richard Sykes Joint Statement by the Chief Executive Officer and Chairman[1]

On January 17 2000, the Boards of Glaxo Wellcome (Glaxo) and SmithKlineBeecham (SmithKline), two of Europe's leading pharmaceutical companies announced proposed terms of a merger; a deal that would create the second largest research-based pharmaceutical and healthcare company in the world, with a global workforce in excess of 100,000 and a combined market capitalisation of £114 billion. Only US-based pharmaceutical giant Pfizer would be in a position to rival GlaxoSmithKline's (GSK) £18.1 billion ($27.5 billion) in global sales, R&D capabilities, extensive development pipeline, and product range (see Exhibit 1 for GSK overview).

The strategic logic behind the merger appeared clear. Both companies had a number of country-level operations, offering a merged GSK significant scope to reduce costs and to benefit from potential synergies in areas such as marketing, administration,

Source: *Journal of Business Ethics Education* 2(1): 97–122. Copyright © 2005, NeilsonJournals Publishing. Permission has been granted to include this case study.

Anne Duncan, NatWest Ph.D. Fellow prepared this case study under the supervision of Professor N. Craig Smith, as a basis for class discussion rather than to illustrate either effective or ineffective handling of an administrative situation. Financial assistance provided by Accenture for the development of this case study is gratefully acknowledged.

Reproduced with permission from NeilsonJournals.

and R&D. The proposed cost savings from the merger, combined with savings from manufacturing restructuring efforts that were already underway within the two companies, were estimated to reach around £1.6 billion ($2.28 billion) by 2003. The aim was to reinvest those savings in the critical area of R&D, which would in turn enhance the merged company's product pipeline.

On December 27 2000, Glaxo and SmithKline officially became one company, with Glaxo and SmithKline shareholders holding approximately 58.75% and 41.25% of the share capital of GSK respectively. Dealings in GSK shares commenced on the London Stock Exchange on the same day. On January 11 2001, the new CEO, Jean-Pierre Garnier, made his first in-house speech broadcast by satellite to employees around the world. Describing his aspirations for the company, Garnier said: "The pharmaceutical industry today sells 80% of its products to 20% of the world's population. I don't want to be the CEO of a company that only caters to the rich. . . . I want those medicines in the hands of many more people who need them."

Garnier's statement struck a chord with GSK employees, many of whom wanted to work for a company committed to improving the health and lives of *all* of the world's people. However, it was becoming more and more difficult to see how any pharmaceutical company could deliver on such a promise in the evolving socio-political and competitive business environment.

GSK: A new company facing new challenges

A personal reminder for GSK employees of the increasingly cynical view that some people held of the pharmaceutical industry was often revealed in negative reactions in social situations when they mentioned the name of their employer. Indeed, within the first week of the new company's existence, GSK had effectively become *the* primary target of activists intent on vilifying the pharmaceutical industry. Oxfam International, a confederation of twelve non-governmental organizations (NGOs) formed in an effort "to find lasting solutions to poverty, suffering, and injustice," was

EXHIBIT 1 GSK: Mission and key facts

Mission:

GlaxoSmithKline – one of the world's leading research-based pharmaceutical and healthcare companies – is committed to improving the quality of human life by enabling people to do more, feel better and live longer.

Overview:

Headquartered in the United Kingdom and with major operations based in the United States, GSK is one of the industry leaders, with an estimated seven per cent of the world's pharmaceutical market.

GSK also has leadership in four major therapeutic areas – anti-infectives, central nervous system (CNS), respiratory and gastro-intestinal/metabolic. In addition, it is a leader in the important area of vaccines and has a growing portfolio of oncology products.

The company also has a Consumer Healthcare portfolio comprising over-the-counter (OTC) medicines; oral care products and nutritional healthcare drinks, all of which are among the market leaders.

Based on 2000 Annual Results, GSK had sales of £18.1 billion ($27.5 billion) and profit before tax of £5 billion ($8.1 billion). Pharmaceutical sales accounted for £15.4 billion ($23.5 billion), 85 per cent of the total.

GSK had four products with sales of over $1 billion and a total of 16 products with sales in excess of $500 million.

GSK has over 100,000 employees worldwide. Of these, over 40,000 are in sales and marketing, the largest sales force in the industry.

R&D:

GSK R&D has over 16,000 employees based at 24 sites in 7 countries. The company has a leading position in genomics/genetics and new drug discovery technologies. The GSK R&D budget is about £2.4bn/$4bn.

Global manufacturing & supply:

GSK has 104 manufacturing sites in 40 countries with over 42,000 employees. The sites within the GSK manufacturing network . . .

- supply products to 191 global markets for GSK
- produce over 1,200 different brands
- manufacture almost 4 billion packs per year
- produce over 28,000 different finished packs per year
- supply around 6,000 tonnes of bulk active each year
- manage about 2,000 new product launches globally each year

GSK 'In time':

Every second, more than 35 doses of vaccines are distributed by GSK.

Every minute, more than 1,100 prescriptions are written for GSK products.

Every hour, GSK spends more than £277,000/$450,000 to find new medicines.

Every day, more than 200 million people around the world use a GSK brand toothbrush or toothpaste.

Every year, GlaxoSmithKline donates more than £55 million/$90 million in cash and products to communities around the world.

Source: GlaxoSmithKline (as of 1 October 2002).

preparing to launch a new campaign entitled 'Cut the Cost' aimed at pressuring pharmaceutical companies to make HIV/AIDS treatments available and affordable for people in least developed countries (LDCs).

The day before Garnier's January 11 speech, Oxfam had provided GSK with a draft of a briefing document criticising GSK and inviting it to comment. The briefing, intended to be launched alongside the Cut the Cost campaign, argued that enforcement of global patent rules had the effect of keeping drug prices high in LDCs; that this situation was wrong; and that GSK could and should do more to resolve the situation. Focusing on the HIV/AIDS crisis in LDCs, Oxfam challenged GSK to develop and deliver a comprehensive access to essential medicines policy that would help address the imbalance between treatment in the developing and the developed world.

In response to Oxfam's challenge, GSK's policy staff reviewed the draft briefing and alerted Oxfam to a number of errors that they believed existed within the document. However, Oxfam had already contacted one of GSK's institutional investors, Friends Ivory & Simes (FI&S), which expressed concerns at the contents of the Oxfam briefing and invited a response from Garnier. On February 12 2001, earlier than GSK had expected and two days before FI&S was due to host a meeting for Oxfam, GSK, and other institutional investors to discuss the Oxfam briefing, Oxfam made its report public. The report received significant media attention and now anything GSK did would seem to be in response to the challenges by Oxfam in its report. It was becoming increasingly apparent that Oxfam, together with other prominent NGOs such as the Nobel Prize-winning Médecins Sans Frontiéres and Treatment Action Campaign (a leading NGO on the access issue in South Africa), intended to mount a campaign challenging the pharmaceutical industry's traditional business model.

The South African court case

Events came to a head in a Johannesburg courtroom on March 5 2001, when opening arguments began in a high profile court case between South African President Nelson Mandela (as well as other parties) and a consortium of 40 pharmaceutical companies, including GSK. The case, which had been filed in April 1998, originally arose from disputes between the industry and the South African government over the 1997 Medicines and Related Substances Control Amendment Act. The industry had criticised the legislation over key issues such as labelling requirements, compulsory licensing of generic drug substitutes and parallel importing (imports of drugs sourced from other countries and not authorised for distribution by the manufacturer), and had claimed that it provided inappropriate discretionary powers to the South African Health Minister. By 2000, AIDS activists and public opinion viewed the dispute as primarily involving a conflict between intellectual property (IP) rights and access to essential drugs. The South African government, under intense public pressure and facing a devastating HIV/AIDS epidemic, had responded by empowering the Health Minster to allow generic versions of patented drugs to be manufactured or imported and distributed in South Africa, though the government stated that it did not have the financial resources to buy HIV/AIDS drugs itself at this time, even at generic prices.

Activists suggested that the prices of generic drugs that might become available for sale in South Africa could be 98% below those of the U.S. patented versions (that were averaging $12,500/patient/year). The industry consortium argued that the South African government would be acting in violation of the World Trade Organisation's (WTO) *Trade-Related Aspects of Intellectual Property Rights* (TRIPS) agreement. As a signatory to the agreement, South Africa was among the countries where the TRIPS rules would be going into force in 2000. In addition to concerns about the regulatory environment within South Africa, the industry consortium believed that any action that might weaken the wider establishment and enforcement of IP protection would threaten the industry's business model by cutting the financial incentives necessary to ensure pharmaceutical innovation. It feared that the government's intention to allow the distribution of generic versions of patented drugs could start a chain reaction involving other countries that would render the TRIPS agreement meaningless.

For several years, AIDS and anti-poverty activists had been trying to focus the world's attention on the price of HIV/AIDS drugs in LDCs. They argued that patent protection resulted in premium prices that restricted access to essential drugs and thus perpetuated unnecessary suffering and deaths of millions of AIDS-affected people in the developing world. Since 1997, Glaxo had tried to be responsive to these pricing concerns by offering lower prices for its AIDS drugs in Africa. In May 2000, the company helped create the Accelerating Access Initiative (AAI), a partnership involving four other pharmaceutical companies, the World Health Organisation (WHO), and the United Nations Joint Program on HIV/AIDS (UNAIDS). As part of the AAI, Glaxo had worked voluntarily with LDC governments to progressively reduce prices on HIV/AIDS drugs on a country-by-country basis. It even published its discounted price list, while other companies kept their lists confidential.

However, these actions had proved insufficient to stem the criticism directed at Glaxo and other pharmaceutical companies. Critics argued that the price reductions were small and did not constitute a long-term framework that would ensure that essential drugs reached the world's poor. Graphic photographs showing sick and dying men, women, and children with HIV/AIDS were being used to bring home the human cost of AIDS and were capturing the attention of people around the world. Public health experts framed the issue as one of ensuring universal "access to essential medicines", even though they realised that solving the HIV/AIDS crisis and ensuring universal access involved much more than drug prices. Support was increasing for the activists' message that wealthy drug companies were letting people suffer and die just to preserve their profits.

Garnier knew that the South African court case could mark a major turning point both in terms of the battle between business, government and NGO leaders over how to address the international HIV/AIDS crisis and in defining the nature of the relationship between the pharmaceutical industry and society. Prior to the merger, Garnier had asked Howard Pien, then President of SmithKline's worldwide pharmaceuticals business, to take executive responsibility for the access issue within GSK. Pien's familiarity with many of the issues involved in the access debate would prove critical to the development of GSK's future policy (Pien became head of GSK's international pharma division after the merger). Pien believed that the intersection of the HIV/AIDS crisis with the access issue could prove to be the biggest challenge ever faced by the pharmaceutical industry and that determining how to respond would have profound strategic implications for GSK and the industry as a whole. As Pien explained: "There was a clear business imperative for doing good. Our ability to do well as a company was predicated on the perception that we were capable of doing good."

HIV/AIDS and access to essential medicines

First identified in the 1970s, Human Immunodeficiency Virus (HIV), the virus that can lead to Acquired Immune Deficiency Syndrome (AIDS), was believed by scientists to have crossed over to humans from chimpanzees in the 1940–1950s in the Republic of Congo. Infection occurred when HIV was passed from one person to another through blood-to-blood or sexual contact. Pregnant women infected with HIV could also pass the virus to their child during pregnancy, delivery, or breast-feeding, a form of infection known as 'mother-to-child transmission'. As an example of a 'retrovirus' (from the Latin 'retro' meaning 'reverse'), HIV's genetic information was stored on single-stranded 'RNA' rather than the double-stranded 'DNA' found in most organisms. In order to replicate, HIV used an enzyme known as 'reverse transcriptase' to convert its RNA into DNA, enabling the virus to enter the nucleus of the host's healthy cells, insert itself into the cell's DNA, and instruct the cell to make copies of the original virus. Having identified the mechanism for replication, researchers began to search for ways to interfere with this process. The first "anti-retroviral" drugs aimed to prevent the replication of the HIV virus by either binding directly onto the reverse transcriptase enzyme, thus preventing the conversion of RNA to DNA, or by incorporating themselves into the DNA of the virus, thereby stopping the building process.

Although it could take several years, most people who became HIV infected would ultimately develop full-blown AIDS, resulting in eventual death as the body's immune system became unable to function properly or fight off the daily attacks from even the most common bacteria and viruses such as the common cold. There was no cure for AIDS and like other pandemics such as the global influenza pandemic of 1918–1919 (that may have killed as many as 40 million people), HIV/AIDS spread rapidly, aided by the extent and ease of global movement of people. By 1995, 14,500 new cases of HIV were occurring daily, particularly in the developing world, with 95% of HIV/AIDS sufferers living in the least developed countries that represented only 10% of the world's population. By 2001, it was estimated that more than 53 million men, women and children had been infected worldwide and in 2001 alone five million people became infected with HIV, three million died of AIDS, and forty million were living with the AIDS virus on a daily basis.[2] Two-thirds of those infected lived in sub-Saharan Africa.

As a slow killer, AIDS was taking a devastating toll, both on afflicted individuals and their families and on the societies in which they resided. The toll on LDCs was particularly acute, crippling their economies and destroying communities by depriving them of millions of productive employees and making orphans out of millions of children.[3] The virus represented the most significant threat to the long-term growth prospects and social progress of countries in the developing world. James Sherry, director of programme development for UNAIDS commented: "I can't think of the coming of any event which was more heralded to less effect… In terms of real redeployment of resources, it hasn't changed. The bottom line is, the people who are dying from AIDS don't matter in this world."[4]

HIV/AIDS in the developed world

In the United States, the HIV/AIDS crisis began to emerge in the 1980s, when outbreaks of two rare illnesses typically affecting older men (*Pneumocystis carinii* pneumonia, a respiratory illness and *Kaposi's sarcoma,* a cancer) were found to be increasing among young homosexual males. Medical professionals also started to notice a number of mysterious deaths, primarily among gay males. By 1984, researchers had isolated the virus and identified the disease. However, developing ways to treat its symptoms would take time and money; finding a cure could take decades. Gay activists argued that HIV was receiving insufficient attention because of its label as a "gay man's disease". But by the mid-1980s, wider concern intensified when statistics indicated the rate at which the virus was spreading, across the country and to heterosexual as well as homosexual Americans.

As politicians, health experts, and NGOs in the United States and increasingly in Europe rallied behind the call for more action, millions of dollars were being poured into developing drugs to treat and eliminate HIV and AIDS. In March 1987, the anti-retroviral (ARV) treatment drug, zidovudine (AZT), was introduced by Wellcome (prior to its merger with Glaxo) under the brand name Retrovir. It was licensed for patients with advanced AIDS. Other anti-retroviral drugs followed. In the United States, each received fast track regulatory approval from the Food and Drug Administration (FDA), though this meant that the potential benefits and risks of these drugs could only be known after they were on the market. Further clinical trials in less sick patients were conducted and in 1995 a study showed that administering AZT during pregnancy and to the newborn infant, reduced the risk of mother-to-child HIV transmission by up to two-thirds.

Between 1995 and 1997, Roche, Merck and Abbott Laboratories introduced new drugs and data emerged indicating that drug combinations delayed the onset of AIDS for those with HIV and reduced the symptoms for those with full-blown AIDS. By 2001, the FDA had approved some 23 HIV/AIDS drugs aimed at increasing the quality and duration of life for HIV-infected individuals. However, the drugs alone cost $10,000–15,000/patient/year and their administration also required ongoing medical supervision—particularly for the complex "triple drug cocktails." The expense involved was an enormous financial burden for health care providers, insurance companies, and governments, even in wealthy developed countries and while many developed world victims of HIV/AIDS had access to drugs, this was not guaranteed. Nonetheless, the cost of HIV/AIDS treatments seemed entirely out of reach to those living in LDCs. According to the UN, more than 1.2 billion people, 291 million in Sub-Saharan Africa alone, were living on less than $1/day.[5] Less than one percent of HIV/AIDS victims in need of antiretroviral treatment in Sub-Saharan Africa were receiving it.

A pandemic of tragic proportions

Experts agreed that treatment of HIV positive patients was only a temporary measure—for most, death remained the ultimate consequence of infection. For those who lacked access to the expensive treatments, death could occur within six months of infection. Efforts at finding a long-term solution needed to focus on prevention and cure. Medical experts believed that it would take at least ten years before a preventative vaccine would be discovered and finding a cure would take even longer. Educating people to take responsibility for preventing their own infection remained the only proven method to ensure safety. Prevention was also the most cost effective means of forestalling the spread of HIV/AIDS. With so many people around the world still lacking access to basics such as food, clean water and adequate shelter, governments and institutions such as the World Bank were reluctant to channel precious resources into expensive AIDS treatment regimes. They considered preventative approaches to be more cost effective over the long term. As a former head of the U.S. government's overseas AIDS assistance programme remarked: "Our experience, and I think *the* experience, is that treatment always drives out prevention. We were afraid that if we opened the door on treatment at all, then all of our money would be drawn away. You get into paying for commodities that have to be supplied, supplied, supplied, to the end of time."[6]

The attention finally being directed at HIV/AIDS in the developed world meant that it was no longer considered a disease that attacked only the poor or homosexual communities. HIV was

recognised as posing a real threat to the social and economic prospects of people around the world, including those in developed countries. The U.S. government declared the crisis to be a threat to international security. The sheer scale of the pandemic was also beginning to be quantified. Pien observed that "the problem of HIV/AIDS is going to peak at the current trajectory in 2060 . . . and that is going to impact upwards of 60% of the world's population. This is what is harrowing to me... if we are not going to see the crescendo of the crisis in our own lifetime, our children will."

While the scale of the crisis served to capture attention, development experts recognised that saving people from HIV/AIDS would be futile if other major killers such as malaria and tuberculosis (TB) were ignored (see Exhibit 2 for data on infectious diseases). With increasing global awareness of the health conditions of people in the developing world, even pharmaceutical companies that were not active in the HIV/AIDS category found they had to consider their position on the access issue.

HIV/AIDS in South Africa

The emergence of the South African HIV/AIDS crisis was perhaps the most significant catalyst in the shift of global public opinion about the role of pharmaceutical companies in the advancement of human health and welfare. Only 1% of the adult South African population was believed to have been HIV infected in 1990. By 2000, that number had increased to 20%. More than four million people—the largest number of any country in the world—were infected, though only a small number were aware of their HIV status. UNAIDS/WHO estimated that 250,000 deaths in South Africa in 2000 were attributable to HIV/AIDS. The South African Medical Research Council projected in 2000 that, absent more substantive interventions, approximately six million South Africans would die of AIDS by 2010. However, for economic and complex socio-cultural reasons, a frequent response within South Africa had been to ignore the looming crisis.

Many South Africans were uncomfortable talking about the disease or methods of prevention.

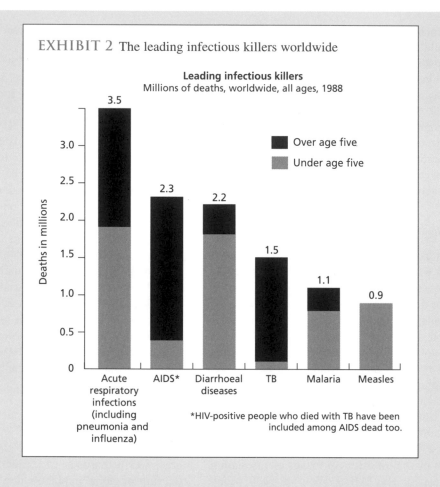

EXHIBIT 2 The leading infectious killers worldwide

Leading infectious killers
Millions of deaths, worldwide, all ages, 1988

Legend:
- Over age five (black)
- Under age five (grey)

Values by category:
- Acute respiratory infections (including pneumonia and influenza): 3.5
- AIDS*: 2.3
- Diarrhoeal diseases: 2.2
- TB: 1.5
- Malaria: 1.1
- Measles: 0.9

Y-axis: Deaths in millions

*HIV-positive people who died with TB have been included among AIDS dead too.

For cultural reasons, many HIV-infected South African men refused to wear condoms and thus knowingly infected their wives, partners, prostitutes and even rape victims. The myth that having sex with a virgin could cure AIDS drove men to engage in unprotected sex with girls. Infants might avoid infection from their HIV-positive mother during pregnancy and birth. However, the public shame associated with failing to breast feed one's own child led many mothers to do so regardless of the risk of HIV infection (and despite the alternatives of a non-infected wet nurse or bottle feeding with formula). It was clear that efforts to increase access to HIV/AIDS drugs would be insufficient without corresponding efforts to address certain cultural and behavioural issues.

The problem was exacerbated by the fact that many South African leaders appeared to share these cultural beliefs. At the UN Conference on HIV/AIDS held in Durban, South Africa in June 2000, South African President (and former Health Minister) Thabo Mbeki angered many people by appearing to support the theory, circulated over internet rumour pages, that HIV did not cause AIDS. However, UN delegates remained undeterred and UNICEF called for a worldwide "mobilisation" to address the AIDS crisis. An International Labour Organization report released for the conference predicted that by 2020 the economic growth rate in certain sub-Saharan countries would be cut by 25% as a result of AIDS. South African employers were also concerned about the significant negative impacts that the epidemic would have on their workforce. Even South Africa's leading research institution, the Medical Research Council, believed the government's approach was unconscionable. Its research found that AIDS was the leading cause of death in South Africa.

The context for the court battle had been set before the government came to power. In 1995, officials from Glaxo and the British Government provided assistance to the African National Congress (ANC) as it developed its ideas on the type of healthcare system that could be created in South Africa. However, when the ANC was elected, many of those suggestions were not adopted and the new government dismantled many drug licensing laws and the drug safety testing council.

As South African AIDS activists started mobilising under the banner of the NGO, Treatment Action Campaign, they lobbied the government to disregard patent rights of specific AIDS drugs to allow generic copies to be made in South Africa, even though this would contravene the TRIPS agreement that was to take effect from 2000. Sympathetic government officials grumbled that any changes in government policy would have little effect on South Africa's capacity to treat AIDS sufferers; this was simply out of the question for the debt-ridden South African economy. Thus activists' attention turned to the pharmaceutical industry, focusing not only on the price of drugs but also the claim that it was a social responsibility of the industry to help ensure universal access to essential medicines.

The pharmaceutical industry

The pharmaceutical industry had global sales of more than $220 billion in 1999. Forty-one percent of sales and 60% of industry profits came from the United States, where health care was largely based on market principles and drugs expenditures covered mostly by private sector insurers.[7] The industry was intensely competitive with no one company capturing more than 7% of the global market.[8] Nonetheless, it was one of the most profitable; according to *Fortune*, the pharmaceutical industry in 2001 continued to hold the top ranking position with an average industry profit of 18.5% as a percentage of revenues, compared to a median 5% return for all industries surveyed.[9]

The pharmaceutical industry was highly regulated and its business model was based on strict enforcement of IP rights. Industry and economic experts argued that this highly institutionalised legal and market-based structure benefited consumers and society at large because it provided incentives for innovation. Pharmaceutical companies could take advantage of monopoly rights on the sales of their patented products over a 20-year period. The equation was simple: the high risk associated with drug development was balanced by assurances of greater profit potential. A healthy, profitable pharmaceutical industry could attract capital to be invested in continuous innovation. The incentives-based structure benefited society by providing a constant stream of new drugs, treatments, and cures that enhanced and saved lives.

Countering this logic, critics argued that while innovation was clearly desirable, the industry enjoyed excess profits at the expense of many of the most vulnerable people in society. Some asserted that the length and universality of many of the patents were indirectly infringing on the universal human right to good health. They suggested that drug prices were far higher than they should be, resulting in access to the drugs being limited to those with good health care coverage in the world's richest countries. Even those critics who agreed that some form of market-based system was necessary acknowledged that the costs of most drugs put them out of reach of most of the world's people.

The General Assembly of the United Nations adopted and proclaimed the *Universal Declaration of Human Rights* on December 10, 1948. Several articles of the Declaration were offered as the basis for the argument that people have a right to good health, including Article 25, of which Paragraph 1 stated: "Everyone has the right to a standard of living adequate for the health and well-being of himself and of his family, including food, clothing, housing and medical care and necessary social services, and the right to security in the event of unemployment, sickness, disability, widowhood, old age or other lack of livelihood in circumstances beyond his control." Paragraph 2 stated: "Motherhood and childhood are entitled to special care and assistance. All children, whether born in or out of wedlock, shall enjoy the same social protection."

The industry was doing its part to address the access issue, according to trade associations such as the Pharmaceutical Research and Manufacturers of America (PhRMA), who pointed to the philanthropic activities supported by pharmaceutical companies over many years. In particular, the industry supported foundations investing in research and basic health initiatives and it donated drugs for programmes targeted to treat the poor. As well, companies typically charged less for drugs sold in developing countries and as some drugs moved through the commercial life cycle and new ones were launched in their place, pharmaceutical companies would often significantly reduce prices in LDCs to levels at, or in some cases below, cost. While PhRMA and others argued that the industry was doing what it could to help bring drugs to people who needed them, they also asserted that the problem was one for governments and society, not the industry, to solve. In any event, as noted by many health care professionals as well industry representatives, the most serious constraint that prevented the provision of adequate healthcare for the world's poor was the severe lack of health care infrastructure in LDCs. For example, in 2000, the WHO *World Health Report* reported that nearly three million children died each year from diseases that could have been prevented with available vaccines and that nearly 30 million of the 130 million children born every year were not receiving vaccinations of any kind (see Exhibit 3 for more background on the healthcare challenges of LDCs). The financial cost of a drug was only one potential obstacle to patient treatment. In fact, 95% of the drugs on WHO's list of essential drugs were not even under patent. Despite their lower prices, many patients in LDCs remained untreated because of the lack of an infrastructure to deliver and administer these non-patented medicines.

Drug development and industry profitability

Drug development involved a significant degree of failure—the average approved drug required more than 10,000 molecules to be vetted before a single molecule emerged successfully from the development process. Only 1 in 5000 compounds ever

reached the market as a finished product and only 30% of those would turn out to be commercially successful.[10] An approved drug took an average of thirteen years from the time of initial molecular screening through clinical developments and approval processes before finally reaching its market. Thus, while patent protection generally ran for 20 years, patent protected exclusivity on marketing and sales averaged only 10–12 years.

Bringing a new drug to market was capital intensive, costing an estimated $400–$800 million on average, including expenditures on drug development, marketing and regulatory approval and the sunk costs associated with drug failures.[11] Critics disputed the upper limit of the industry estimate, claiming that it did not take account of various tax deductions and government research contributions common to many drugs that reached the market. NGO Public Citizen asserted that the out of pocket drug development cost figure was actually closer to $240 million since 50% of the Tufts Report total ($399 million) used in the industry estimate was the opportunity cost of capital, which Public Citizen considered a debatable "theoretical calculation of what R&D expenditures might be worth if they were invested elsewhere."[12] Critics also asserted that the costs of bringing a drug to market were not the same for all drug categories and that many costs were the result of the industry's own actions. To illustrate the point, critics attacked marketing expenses and the shift towards a "pull" strategy which involved targeting consumers with television advertising (where legally permissible) that encouraged asking consumers to ask their doctor about a drug treatment. However, even at the lower end estimates, the fact remained that drug development was expensive.

During the 1990s, demand for new drugs combined with major scientific advances presented the industry with fresh challenges. Emerging DNA-based approaches to treatment had led to venture capitalist backed biotechnology firms outside the more established industry. The large pharmaceutical companies believed that they needed to invest heavily in these new areas to remain competitive. Profits from existing portfolios of drugs were critical to the ability of the industry to generate

EXHIBIT 3 Healthcare challenges of LDCs

The most deprived one in six

A baby girl born in one of the least developed countries in 1993 can expect to live barely 44 years—2 years more than a baby boy born in the same year. Her problems begin before birth since her mother is likely to be in poor health. If she is born in southern Asia, she has 1 in 3 chance of being underweight, a greater chance of dying in infancy and a high probability of being malnourished throughout childhood. She has a 1 in 10 chance of dying before her first birthday and a 1 in 5 chance of dying before her fifth. In some African countries her chance of being vaccinated is less than 1 in 2. She will be brought up in inadequate housing under insanitary conditions contributing to diarrhoeal disease, cholera and tuberculosis. She will have a 1 in 3 chance of ever getting enough schooling to learn how to read and write. She may be circumcised at puberty with consequent effects on her life as a woman and a mother. She will marry in her teens and may have 7 or more children close together unless she dies in childbirth before that. Ancient traditions will prevent her from eating certain nutritious foods during her pregnancies, when she most needs building up, and dangerous practices such as using an unsterile knife to cut the umbilical cord and placing cow-dung on the stump may kill some of her babies with tetanus.

She will be in constant danger from infectious disease from contaminated water at the place where she bathes, washes clothes and collects her drinking-water. She will be chronically anaemic from poor nutrition, malaria and intestinal parasites. As well as caring for her family she will work hard in the fields, suffering from repeated attacks of fever, fatigue and infected cuts. If she survives into old age she will be exposed to the same afflictions as women in the rich countries: cardiovascular disease and cancer. To these she will succumb quickly, having no access to proper medical care and rehabilitation. She will not be able to pay anything herself: her country currently has less than $9 a year to spend on her health.

Some 24 million babies, one-sixth of the world total, were born in the least developed countries in 1993 and too many of them will grow up in miserable conditions of life and health. Equity demands that the situation of these deprived infants be improved without delay.

Source: WHO, *World Health Report*. Geneva: WHO, 1995, p. 5.

capital for long-term investments in new drugs. Thus, any weakening of IP rights was seen as likely to erode profits and prevent the industry from continuing to invest in necessary R&D.

Drug pricing, generics and parallel trade

Drug prices varied around the world. Even within the developed world, variations were significant due to different pricing mechanisms. In the United States, drug prices tended to be set by the market. In Canada, Mexico and most European countries, state-funded health care systems meant that prices were usually negotiated at the national level. In the United Kingdom, the government placed limits on the overall allowable level of profit made by a pharmaceutical company on drug sales to the National Health Service. In other countries such as France and Japan, prices were regulated on a product-by-product basis. In LDCs, private and public funds were limited and drug prices were heavily influenced by the priorities, tendering processes and the subsequent aid provided by international donors, including national aid agencies, global health organizations such as WHO, and private sector foundations and NGOs like Oxfam and Médecins Sans Frontiéres.

Drug prices also reflected the competitive pressures of generic products, substitutes, and parallel trading. Once a drug's patent expired, generic drug manufacturers, who did not face the same lengthy and expensive R&D costs as the original manufacturer, would quickly enter a market at lower prices. In countries that did not honour IP rights, generic versions of patent-protected drugs were manufactured or imported and sold at deeply discounted prices. These lower prices often outweighed possible concerns about the quality of generic drugs, some of which were not monitored and thus their safety and efficacy was less certain.

Drugs were frequently misappropriated or purchased by a client or government at a discounted price and rather than being used to treat the intended population, were instead resold at a higher price to generate cash. Frequently, there was both a domestic and an export market for this parallel trade and the amounts resold were often significant. In South Africa, GSK estimated that 30% of drug stocks in the National Health Service was stolen and sold into the private sector.

International trade rules: TRIPS

The events that led to the South African court case were to some degree by-products of the liberalisation of international trade that had occurred under the General Agreement on Tariffs and Trade (GATT) and associated WTO rules. Attempting to use "free trade" as the primary catalyst for lifting developing countries out of poverty had dominated much of economic development thinking and efforts over the past decade. Experts argued that both developing and developed countries stood to benefit from greater openness of their markets to competition. However, as open trade policies began to take effect, respected analysts and NGOs challenged the assumption that "free trade" should dominate all other agendas. They pointed to imbalanced outcomes for many countries. For example, some international trading rules such as those involving IP rights could generate benefits, but also unfair outcomes for poorer countries coerced into accepting the rules by the threat of being prevented from trading with other countries. Often labelled "anti-globalisation activists", not all NGOs were against global trade, but many wanted to ensure that overall social, health, economic, and environmental impacts were considered in parallel with economic free trade objectives.

The South African court case presented an early opportunity to test provisions in TRIPS. The TRIPS agreement had emerged from the 1986-1994 Uruguay round of international trade negotiations and was designed to provide an international standard for the laws and enforcement of IP rights. When future trade disputes over IP rights would arise, it was intended that the WTO dispute settlement system would be used to determine outcomes. However, the WTO rules did not provide the flexibility to consider the merits of other needs that a country might have beyond international trade. Only a vague provision in TRIPS allowed a country to waive IP rules in the case of a 'national emergency', under which the country could invoke 'compulsory licensing'; in effect, licensing low cost manufacturers to ignore patents and produce generic versions of essential drugs.

What constituted a national emergency under TRIPS was undefined. In 1997, Brazil launched a controversial programme invoking the provision and authorised state laboratories to manufacture generic versions of all but four of the twelve leading patented HIV/AIDS drugs. The government threatened to license the manufacture of the four remaining drugs unless the pharmaceutical companies radically reduced their prices. The outcome was that the price of HIV/AIDS anti-retroviral treatment was reduced by two-thirds to an average of $4,500 per patient, saving Brazil $472 million in just three years. While there were positive health (and economic) results for Brazil, the United States filed a WTO complaint against the Brazilian government for its actions. Even so, other countries soon became interested in following Brazil's example, determined not to allow international trading rules to override public health concerns.

In addition to compulsory licensing, it was also possible to purchase generic versions of patented drugs from companies operating in countries that had not yet implemented TRIPS. Cipla, one of India's generic pharmaceutical companies was among the most prominent of these "pirate companies", manufacturing copies of patented HIV/AIDS drugs and selling them at around 2% of the cost of the U.S. patented versions.

NGOs were particularly concerned at the potentially unfair outcomes that could result from international trading rules. Many believed that pharmaceutical companies had a *moral* duty to do more to fulfil their societal obligations. Some organisations acted with protests. In March 2000, activists from American NGO, ACT UP (The AIDS Coalition to Unleash Power) stormed the New York offices of Pfizer CEO Bill Steere, demanding that the company provide South Africans with cheap access to Diflucan, a drug used to treat cryptococcal meningitis, one of the diseases associated with AIDS. The following day, Pfizer announced that it would supply the drug free of charge to South African patients.

Other NGO's such as Médecins Sans Frontier and Oxfam had been lobbying governments to address the negative impacts of trade rules long before the widely publicised disruption of the 1999 Seattle meetings of the WTO by anti-globalisation protestors. These NGOs wanted the ambiguity within TRIPS to be clarified at the follow-up WTO meetings in Doha, due to be held in November 2001. In late 2000, just before the powerful WTO trade rules were to come into force in many countries, a bloc of NGOs joined together to challenge the pharmaceutical companies to radically reduce drug prices or to waive drug patent rights to allow generic copies of essential medicines to be supplied by low cost manufacturers within developing countries.

The evolution of GSK's access policy

Both Glaxo and SmithKline had long histories of philanthropic activities prior to their merger. However, many employees felt that little credit had been given to the success of these efforts. One particularly significant programme was a partnership formed in 1997 between the WHO and SmithKline targeted at eliminating *lymphatic*

filariasis (LF) by 2020. LF, caused by a parasitic worm found mainly in the developing world, was a crippling and disfiguring disease commonly known as "elephantiasis" that could lead to the arms, legs, or genitalia swelling to several times their normal size. With more than 120 million suffering from LF in 1997, the disease was the second leading cause of permanent disability in the world. By 2001, the LF Global Alliance, now involving GSK, the WHO, and 28 other organisations, was a major initiative, having brought about the most significant drug donation in history and working to create effective distribution systems to reach affected populations once a year for five years. It was estimated that GSK would provide five to six billion treatments to prevent LF infection as part of this programme.

Building upon programmes like the LF Global Alliance, GSK's Global Community Partnerships function, led by Justine Frain (see Exhibit 4 for GSK organisation chart), was working to expand GSK's Positive Action programme. Initiated in 1992, Positive Action had been transformed into an international programme of HIV education, care and support, in partnership with community groups, healthcare providers, governments, international agencies and others.

Glaxo and HIV/AIDS

At the time of the merger, GSK held a dominant position in the global market for HIV/AIDS therapies with a 40% market share. This was due largely to Glaxo's purchase of Burroughs Wellcome in 1995, which brought with it the ground breaking AZT treatment. Glaxo and Wellcome also had collaborated on Epivir, an enzyme blocker that prevented the AIDS virus enzyme from replicating itself. After Glaxo and Burroughs Wellcome merged, the new management had considered dropping out of the AIDS market because of its potential political ramifications (not least as a result of protests over LDC pricing of AIDS drugs). However, internal lobbying from the clinical products division resulted in a rethink and the newly merged Glaxo Wellcome continued to develop, market, and sell HIV/AIDS treatments. In May 2000, GlaxoWellcome joined

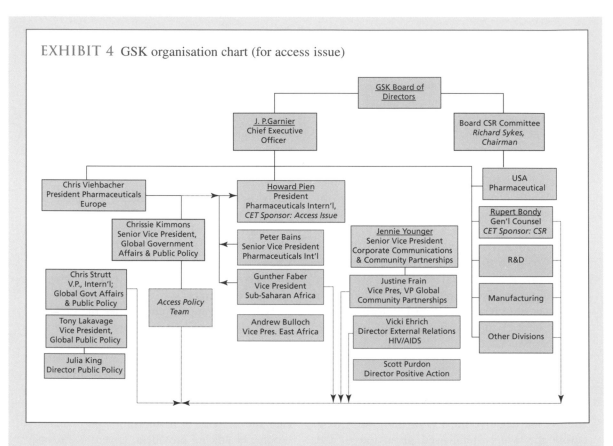

EXHIBIT 4 GSK organisation chart (for access issue)

five other companies in a partnership with WHO and UNAIDS to create the Accelerating Access Initiative. The aim was to enhance access to HIV/AIDS drugs in LDCs by creating a tri-sector platform to establish national and local level HIV/AIDS treatment plans and delivery systems, to improve access to essential drugs, and to lower the ultimate cost of treating more people.

As manufacturing costs came down, so did the prices of Glaxo's HIV/AIDS drugs. However, price was only one factor. The need for lifelong therapy and the scale of the HIV/AIDS pandemic meant any successful long-term AIDS treatment programme would have to take into account the complex process of ongoing treatment and patient management by trained clinicians. As Howard Pien explained: "HIV and AIDS is a problem that will not go away for a long time. It is a problem that is far bigger than any national government, and is therefore far bigger than any multinational company. The only way to address it is through the involvement of all of us."

Pre-merger: Evaluating options and building bridges across the two companies

Garnier was favourably predisposed to addressing the HIV/AIDS crisis and the issue of access generally. As the incoming CEO of the merged GSK, he inherited a portfolio of HIV/AIDS medicines from Glaxo and he wanted to make the most of that opportunity. During his tenure at SmithKline, the company had introduced a tiered pricing model for many of its vaccines, selling them at a market price in countries where health care systems could afford to pay for them, and providing them heavily discounted in LDCs. Vaccines were very different from long-term treatments, but the success of the vaccines pricing model had been acknowledged.

In advance of the merger, Garnier took a keen interest in the views of various stakeholders including public health experts and NGO leaders, to gain a better understanding of their concerns, together with related analyses from his SmithKline corporate policy team, headed by Chrissie Kimmons. The policy team, working closely with other divisions of SmithKline, had been tracking the HIV/AIDS and global trade rules issues, and representing the company's interests at various international forums, including the Seattle WTO meetings. Protests at Seattle and subsequent events suggested that the new company's reputation could be threatened and it might have to act in response to direct action pressure rather than out of strategic choice. Nonetheless, Kimmons, like Pien, believed that both SmithKline and Glaxo were industry leaders in developing approaches to the access problem, even though this had not been widely recognised.

Garnier asked Kimmons to bring together a team to further analyse the situation and propose specific approaches that GSK could take. Briefing papers developed by the team discussed the access issue, stakeholder and activist concerns, and broader issues associated with corporate social responsibility and global trade. These documents provided a basis for engaging senior managers within both SmithKline and Glaxo in a conversation about these issues in the merged company.

In August 2000, Garnier invited the proposed GSK Corporate Executive Team (CET) to meet and identify key issues that would require management's attention once the merger took place. Corporate social responsibility, including the access issue, was identified as one of the top six topics for attention. GSK would assume global R&D and market leadership in drugs for the three leading diseases in LDCs: HIV/AIDS, tuberculosis and malaria. The CET agreed that GSK's approach to access could thus have significant strategic, commercial, operational and reputation impact.

It was at this meeting that Garnier had asked Pien to lead efforts to develop a GSK access policy that would be responsible and sustainable. Pien observed that the CET "came to recognize that the ultimate creation of the merged company required among other things, shareholders' support, regulatory authorities' approval and articulation of the vision of what this company was about—things we couldn't do without the encum-

brance of the huge amount of pressures that were coming in our direction. I give a huge amount of credit to JP [Garnier] for crystallizing the issue; namely, the moral legitimacy of the innovation-based pharmaceutical industry." Noting that NGOs had been quick in writing to Garnier as the CEO presumptive and asking to meet with him, Pien said, ". . . and did he do it! In contrast to the bunker mentality of many CEOs, he was very active in engaging these people and thinking through the issues. He became the force that made this a paramount issue for GSK as a new company."

Garnier and Pien were keen to advance some of the more radical ideas recommended in the internal report on the access issue, released prior to the meeting of the CET presumptive. Garnier thought the industry could do more in partnership with governments and he wanted GSK to be at the forefront of such an initiative. He saw an opportunity in a speech he was to make to the European Union's High Level Roundtable on HIV, Malaria and Tuberculosis on September 28, 2000. Kimmons and her colleagues were asked to develop a policy statement for the speech. Their draft was not as far-reaching as Garnier had intended. It reiterated the view that drug prices were only one part of the problem. Garnier wanted to suggest a significantly new approach for GSK that would set the company and the industry on a different path. Infrastructure and funding problems in LDCs notwithstanding, Garnier believed that prices were still a serious issue, impacting directly on the ability of governments and NGOs to treat people, and indirectly in preventing resources from being reallocated towards building necessary infrastructure.

In his speech to the EU Roundtable, Garnier, as CEO of SmithKline and GSK's CEO presumptive, made an unprecedented offer. He signalled a desire to consider a new way forward including a willingness on the part of GSK to reduce prices in LDCs to a not-for-profit level. Garnier stated that in return, governments would need to ensure the innovation-based industry's viability by agreeing to protect the existing IP rights and pricing mechanisms in the lucrative North American, European, and Japanese markets.

It was the first time that such an offer had been made by the CEO of a leading pharmaceutical company and Garnier's statement opened the door for discussions about a new industry-wide approach. However, these ideas were not universally welcomed within the industry and some pharmaceutical companies resolved to defend the prevailing industry position.

Post-merger: Developing a detailed and sustainable policy

Garnier, Pien and the rest of the incoming CET had agreed that GSK's access policy needed to be in place within six months of the merger being completed. But until the merger became official in December 2000, it had not been possible to engage in the detailed discussions and sharing of product and pricing information that was critical to any specific policy GSK would put in place. That month, Garnier and Pien signed off on the creation of the Access Policy Team, to be sponsored by Pien as a member of GSK's CET. Kimmons, now GSK's Senior Vice President, Global Public Affairs & Public Policy, was made responsible for the policy's development along with a team of key people from across the newly merged company. On the commercial side, Gunther Faber, Vice President of Sub-Saharan and South Africa and Peter Bains, Senior Vice President of Commercial Development International, assumed responsibility for working out how the policy would be implemented. Chris Strutt, a Vice President and Access Alignment Master, reported to Kimmons and would be responsible for coordination, to ensure the alignment of specific activities and functional areas. Other managers involved included Julia King, Director of Public Policy and CSR, Justine Frain, Vice President, Global Community Partnerships, Vicki Ehrich, Director of HIV External Relations and a former Glaxo spokesperson in South Africa, together with other team members from manufacturing, legal, corporate communications, IP, and R&D. Unable to share critical information prior to the merger, the team now had six months in which to develop a specific company-wide policy which could be announced to the world.

The team debated the best approach. Should GSK radically reduce prices and/or donate HIV/AIDS drugs even though there was inadequate healthcare infrastructure in South Africa and other poor countries to support distribution and long-term monitoring? Should it ignore patent infringements in South Africa given that so little profit was derived in such countries anyway? What would be the effect of such decisions on GSK's operations in other countries and on the existing business model? Would pressure continue no matter what the company did? How would the company finance new drug innovation if the existing patent regime could be selectively ignored? Over the long term, should GSK consider withdrawing from the developing world entirely, abandoning expensive operations in LDCs or reducing R&D on developing world diseases?

GSK's tuberculosis and malaria drugs made the company an easy target for activists who had widened the access issue beyond HIV/AIDS drugs. A major concern was that even if GSK continued to reduce prices in the developing world, what was to stop activists in the United States or Europe from exerting pressure on their own politicians to force down prices to match those in LDCs, and not just for the HIV/AIDS category? Could they argue that the best interests of shareholders ultimately would be served by the access policy?

On February 21, 2001 as part of the announcement of GSK's first results, Garnier responded to the charges in the Oxfam report, released just days earlier, that the company was not doing enough. He stated that GSK, a new company, had been working out details of a sustainable pricing model and that it was "determined to build a long-term viable framework which will enable GSK to offer our best prices in developing countries on a sustainable basis". He promised that GSK would make further specific announcements in June 2001.

Withdrawal from the South African court case

The ongoing case in South Africa, combined with a joint WTO-WHO conference in Norway, gave many of the activists and NGOs such as Oxfam an ideal platform from which to press their views. On

March 13, 2001, facing rising criticism and reflecting the new approach within GSK, Garnier contacted his counterparts at Roche, Boehringer Ingelheim and Merck to explore how they might withdraw their case against the South African Government, even though other companies wished to proceed. The industry coalition was no longer united and there were now alternative views on how to proceed on the access issue.

On April 5, 2001, UN Secretary General Kofi Annan hosted a meeting of seven pharmaceutical company CEOs, along with the heads of WHO and UNAIDS. Annan's intention was "to establish a new and constructive partnership with the research based industry." The meeting opened a dialogue, with the company leaders signalling a willingness to drop their case in South Africa and Annan indicating his intention to try to focus UN member governments' and the world's attention on the need for vastly more resources for the treatment of HIV/AIDS in LDCs. Two weeks later, the drug companies dropped their case. Considered a victory for industry critics, this was seen in the industry as a major setback in its defense of IP rights. The *Boston Globe* commented, "With their boardrooms raided and their executives being hounded in the streets, 39 of the world's largest drug makers caved to public pressure. . . . It was hailed as a stunning triumph for the developing world: A $360 billion industry was brought down by a country that represents just half of one percent of the pharmaceutical market."[13] Pien observed that "the geographies have become intermingled and the South African court case made it so. Opinion leaders in the U.S., Europe and the developing countries have shifted their focus of concern. Availability of a drug was not the core of the problem, but how a company behaved as a corporate citizen. That was the real problem."

Justine Frain described the South Africa case as the pharmaceutical industry's "Brent Spar" (alluding to the controversy over Royal Dutch/Shell's attempt to dump an oil platform in the North Sea). The South African court case had originally started in 1998 as a dispute about the framework and enforcement of drug licensing and regulatory systems in South Africa. However, by April 2001, the case had come to be seen as being exclusively about HIV/AIDS drugs, patent infringements and life or death choices for sick people. It appeared to mark a turning point for the industry, offering a new scenario with far less predictable consequences. As Pien commented, "what seemed like a long time ago, this issue was principally a staff issue—to do with communication and social responsibility—rather than a business issue. Now it was both."

Both GSK and Merck announced significant price reductions on their HIV/AIDS drugs to LDCs (though their prices were still two-to-three times those of generic equivalents selling at around $250–$350/person/year). GSK had signalled its intentions to deliver on Garnier's earlier promise of action. Announcing Merck's price reductions, Raymond Gilmartin, Merck's CEO, reiterated the industry-wide concern that lowering drug prices in LDCs might trigger pressure to lower prices in the developed world, thus rendering the tiered pricing model unsustainable. In a worst case scenario, he suggested, those reductions might trigger a downward spiral, destabilising the industry's business model, threatening innovation, and challenging the viability of the industry. At the very least, the radical cuts could prove to be a double-edged sword, forcing pharmaceutical companies out of controversial areas of health treatment into more neutral and potentially lucrative areas such as "lifestyle drugs" (e.g., Prozac, Viagra). Gilmartin's remarks largely echoed the concerns that Garnier had expressed at the EU Roundtable six months previously and in February. With GSK's leadership, the industry had been the first to give way. Would governments, NGO's and other stakeholders keep up their end of the deal?

A welcome response to the withdrawal of the South African court case came from Kofi Annan. He used the occasion to emphasize the need for shared responsibility for tackling the HIV/AIDS pandemic. Rather than focusing on drug prices, Annan called for governments, intergovernmental organisations, NGO's and businesses to vastly expand the resource pool and to work in partnership to address the global HIV/AIDS crisis. Addressing a forum of African leaders in Abuja, Nigeria, Annan called for the creation of global HIV/AIDS and health fund, with an annual "war chest" of $7–10 billion to address HIV/AIDS, tuberculosis and malaria in LDCs. This figure (which was similar to the $7.5 billion/year previously suggested by policy analysts Amir Ataran and Jeffrey Sachs of Harvard University) represented little more than 1% of global military expenditures, according to Annan. However, the world had never united to fund any public health initiative on this sort of scale. Moreover, Annan's announcement and the withdrawal of the court case did not mean that pressures on GSK and the rest of the industry to do more on access would disappear.

Defining a detailed access policy

GSK's managers remained acutely aware that the industry's business model and its reputation remained under threat. While the long-term hope (at least with respect to HIV/AIDS) continued to be the discovery of an HIV vaccine, in the short term GSK needed to come up with a detailed access strategy and to implement it in a way that would meet GSK's business and ethical imperatives whilst also protecting the company's image and reputation. In early May 2001, just five months after the merger, Kimmon's Access Policy Team was preparing to submit final and specific recommendations to Garnier, Pien and the CET.

Notes

1. *GSK Annual Report*, December 2000, p. 3. The terms "developing world" and "developing country" are used to refer to the world's poorest countries. The United Nations Conference on Trade and Development maintains a list of Least Developed Countries based upon criteria such as GDP per capita of less than $800/year; low life expectancy, literacy and caloric intake; and low levels of economic diversity. As of 2001, the UN had designated 49 countries as developing countries, 34 of which were located in Africa.

2. International AIDS Vaccine Initiative (IAVI), 2001.

3. "UN Highlights AIDS Orphans," BBC News report, 1 December, 1999 at http://news.bbc.co.uk/1/hi/world/545518.stm

4. Barton Gellman (2000), "The Belated Global Response to AIDS in Africa," *Washington Post*, July 5 2000, p. A1.

5. *United Nations Basic Facts*, December 2000.

6. Jeffrey R. Harris, of the Center for Disease Control and formerly of USAID, quoted in Barton Gellman, "An Unequal Calculus of Life and Death," *Washington Post*, December 27, 2000.

7. *Financial Times* September 1999; *Economist* industry survey, 21 February 1998.

8. Based upon 2000 data. "Pfizer Still Ahead Following GlaxoSmithKline Merger" IMS Health, 4 January 2001. London.

9. *Fortune*, April 15, 2002. The pharmaceutical industry performed well ahead of other profitable industries including commercial banks, ranked second at 13.5% return on revenues, diversified financial institutions (10.5%), mining and crude oil producers (8.6%) and computers, office equipment and computer/data services (2.3%).

10. PhRMA 1997 Annual Report.

11. PhRMA, *Pharmaceutical Industry Profile 2000*, p. 20; DiMasi, Joseph A., et al., "Tufts Center for the Study of Drug Development Pegs Cost of a New Prescription Medicine at $802 million," 30 November, 2001.

12. Public Citizen (2002) "Pharmaceuticals Rank as Most Profitable Industry Again." Washington DC.

13. Kurt Shillinger, "AIDS Drug Victory Sours in South Africa: Government Still Refusing to Supply AZT," *The Boston Globe*, 23 April, 2001, p. A8.

CONTEXTS

FIGURE AII Business ethics and corporate social responsibility

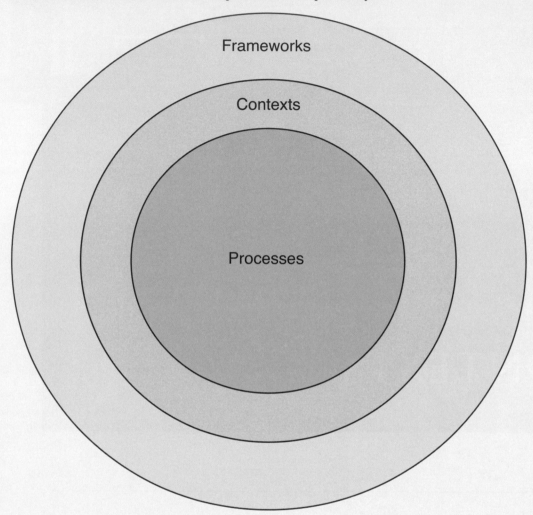

In Part I we looked at key frameworks – of corporate social responsibility, of ethical theory and of the environment. In this part of the book we will consider the contexts within which decisions relating to ethics or responsibility are made.

The contextual basis of any managerial decision is a critical factor that can often be the determinant of success or failure. What works extremely well in one set of circumstances may be disastrous in others. The issues of responsibility and ethical right or wrong bring several different kinds of contextual issue that are relevant to business decisions. Most immediate is the internal context of how people are organized, how they behave collectively, and what perceptions and attitudes are influenced or even developed as a result of this. Very many cases of ethical scandals have been attributed, in part, to the culture and general work attitudes of those working in the organization, rather than to any specific moral flaws. Often a small number of powerful individuals can distort decision making so that even a majority of people wishing to avoid an ethical calamity are unable to do so, due to power relationships, reporting lines or even sheer motivations of the key actors.

As well as the specific internal behavioural context, there is the global economic and corporate context – the fact that we live in a world where telecommunications and transport have made every part of the globe, every industry, every locality, accessible (in principle at least) to any other. As is well recognized, with the globalization of economies, and all the benefits that this has brought to some, has also come new and intractable problems that have created fresh difficulties for others. This is not solely an economic dimension, for international politics also plays a substantial role in areas such as the balance of international trade, third world development, and the speed and trajectories of technology transfer.

In addition to the politico-economic global context, there are other external factors that are important for the success of corporate social responsibility and ethical actions and initiatives. One of these is the network of civil society organizations that operate nationally and internationally, and how these relate to business as well as to governments, in terms of collaborating in services, as well as critically evaluating corporate activity. This sector has seen significant growth in recent years, to the point where it has become a key player in the development of the global economy.

Another is the context of understandings of, and attitudes towards, human rights. Few countries can boast that they respect fully the rights of all, and even the developed Western democracies have continued to be criticized due to failures in the treatment of some groups of individuals. This intersects with the global and political contexts, for it is when corporations operate with ever more global reach that they are confronted with disparities between the values expressed in one region as compared with those evident in others. The result can present some of the most difficult dilemmas of corporate strategy: how far to respect one culture but stay true to the firm's original sense of values? How far to treat such differences as learning points or as points of conflict?

THE BEHAVIOURAL CONTEXT

LEARNING OBJECTIVES

After studying this chapter you should be able to:

- Identify and explain differences in terms of ethical decision making in different organizational forms, including SMEs, family-owned businesses, not-for-profit organizations and partnerships.

- Evaluate how ethics and responsibility in business are affected by organizational structures and cultures.

- Analyse the different factors that can influence the ways that individuals conceptualize ethics and make ethical choices.

INTRODUCTION

In this chapter we will discuss the organizational and behavioural contexts within which ethics and corporate social responsibility issues are considered, and how far these contexts influence the policies and acts of corporations and of the individuals who work in them. This chapter will primarily look at the collective patterns of behaviour, beliefs and ways of conceptualizing values and ethics, as well as the ways in which attitudes and cultural assumptions can often vary depending on the type of organization involved. We will make use of a range of concepts and theories drawn from management and organizational behaviour, but the intention here is to demonstrate how these connect with ethics and social responsibility.[1] It is not a comprehensive discussion but intended to make the reader aware of the breadth of the issues that can affect ethical decision making.

THE BEHAVIOURAL COMPLEX AFFECTING ETHICAL DECISION MAKING

In general, people's decisions are influenced by many factors – motives, their current state of knowledge, their values, emotional states and other personality-related items. When operating collectively further issues come into play, such as the perception of the norms of the group, the manner in which an organization is structured, power relations between individuals and groups, collective patterns of behaviour, and the kinds of arena for discussion and debate that exist. Also highly relevant is the nature of the organization – who owns it and how do they influence choices made by teams and individuals. These all can interact, so that someone's personal values can be heavily influenced by the values and behaviour of others with whom they identify, such as members of the same working group. Figure 5.1 illustrates the relationship between these factors. We shall focus in this chapter on some of these individual and collective factors in so far as they can influence ethical choices.

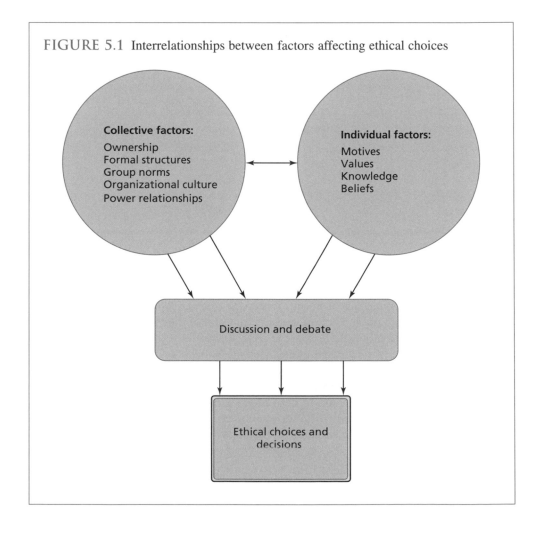

FIGURE 5.1 Interrelationships between factors affecting ethical choices

Collective factors:
Ownership
Formal structures
Group norms
Organizational culture
Power relationships

Individual factors:
Motives
Values
Knowledge
Beliefs

Discussion and debate

Ethical choices and decisions

OWNERSHIP AND MANAGEMENT

Ownership may seem at first sight to be more of a strategic external context than a behavioural one. In fact, however, the question of who owns and/or controls an organization, and how they do so, is central to how individuals take ethical considerations into account when making decisions. We shall see the results of this in Chapter 9 on governance. However, as ownership and management critically influence the actions of those further inside an organization it is appropriate to consider this aspect as part of the behavioural context.

As well as limited companies, there are several other forms of ownership and management of an organization, and each can have a distinct kind of influence on ethics and responsibility:

- SMEs – small and medium-sized enterprises
- family-owned businesses
- partnerships
- 'third way', voluntary organizations – NGOs, charities
- government or neo-government bodies

We will look briefly at ethical challenges of each of these.

Small and medium-sized enterprises

Traditionally, small business was defined as a company with no more than 250 employees. However, more recent definitions put the bar much lower, often identifying a 'small' business as one with 50 employees or fewer.[2] We shall focus on smaller firms in this sense, in particular looking at so-called micro-businesses that may employ less than 25 staff.

It is often supposed that all owners of small businesses are entrepreneurs, but as Moore and Spence point out,[3] entrepreneurs generally have a specific business strategy involving high growth and maximizing profitability. In contrast, many small businesses operate on a less dynamic model, aiming at a stable and reasonable level of return rather than at rapid high growth. A related misconception is that micro-businesses are necessarily young, and will either grow or fail. For many firms, however – e.g. local retail or small building firms – a stable position in a local mature market can provide a business with solid returns but without major opportunities for growth.

Small businesses are often characterized by lower profits, a small resource base, a small range of customers/clients, tactical planning rather than strategic, and with little spare capacity in the case of a serious reversal. Consequently decisions tend to be short term in nature and businesses are highly conservative when it comes to indirect business costs. Classical ethical issues, such as openness in deal negotiation, can often then be regarded as an additional cost for businesses, without the immediate return that they look for.

However, small businesses by definition have short lines of communication, and decisions can often be made very quickly. Many people start up a business because of a keen sense of value in what they propose. Hence a small business can reflect key values of the owner/manager, which can quickly diffuse through the business. The small business may be more dependent on the values of its senior management than larger organizations, but it is more fluid and able to respond rapidly to events. So there is a balance between the risks of short-termism or limited governance, and the relative ease with which a smaller firm can operate ethically.

Family ownership

It has been estimated that between 65 per cent and 80 per cent of all businesses worldwide are family owned,[4] so any specific features of such firms that are relevant to ethics and responsibility are likely to have wide application in many different industries and economies.

Gallo[5] has pointed out that family businesses can often involve distinct behavioural features in comparison with non-family businesses: a wider range of interconnected stakeholders; power is exercised more intimately at least in the early phases of a family business; equity partners have a greater level of commitment to the business; and the growth and development of the business relates to the perceived needs of the family, rather than in its own right. Vallejo[6] has expanded this by linking family business culture to the phases of their development, indicating that the main differences are indeed cultural and behavioural, rather than in terms of capital structure or business risk.

One aspect of family business behaviour is the overall attitude towards a business. A family business can often represent the fruit of labour of possibly several generations, the potential inheritance of children, the primary source of economic wealth for an extended group of dependents, and also the symbolic manifestation of the identity and achievements of the family members. Unlike a public corporation, the business may well be seen by family members as 'theirs' even when the family no longer has voting control on the board of directors. Loyalty to the company among family members often therefore goes beyond the normal loyalty that an employee has towards a large corporation.

Hence, where a business is owned or controlled by family members, the attitude to profitability is different from how it is perceived in companies whose shares are listed on an exchange, where maintaining a high level of profitability is a key requirement for most investors. In contrast, the long-term sustainability of the business is often most important for a family company. Equally, termination of a public company, by acquisition, merger, or dismemberment through asset-stripping, will normally be determined by economic criteria. But a family business is much more likely to strive to remain in its original form, and resist moves to merge or to sell off resources.

Another feature of a family business is the role of family and non-family members. As Belak has shown, often members of the family will see each other as engaged in a common project,[7] to which they have a special loyalty that is not expected of non-family members. One aspect of this is the presumption of family loyalty, which then translates into loyalty to the business. This can then create pressures on family members to support the firm even when something unacceptable has happened – hence a family member who acts as a whistle-blower over some unethical practice would be regarded as not only having violated loyalty to the firm but also that to the family. Of course, families are not always stable, loving collaborations: the tensions, rivalries and even close hatreds that families can entertain can also be present in business disputes.

In contrast, even highly effective non-family managers may see their views overruled for reasons of family solidarity and support. Strategic decisions are taken, not for the objectively best business reasons, but for the benefit of the family, which in some cases could be to the detriment of minority investors. Paradoxically, employees in long-standing family-owned businesses are often treated with a positive degree of paternalism that is not generally encountered in public companies, where a more cost-driven approach to human resource management tends to formalize employer–employee relationships. However, where an employee has a grievance against a specific member of management, it can be much more difficult than in a public company to get this resolved satisfactorily.

THINKING CRITICALLY ABOUT ETHICS

FAMILY EMPLOYEES

Family firms often employ other family members even when the latter are not shareholders. Arguably, however, this represents a type of nepotism – a form of discrimination against others who may be as suitable for employment but happen not to be related to the owners.

Are there any circumstances where it would be ethically justifiable to decide to discriminate in favour of family members?

Professional partnerships

Professional partnerships are for-profit organizations that can range from just two individuals up to global players with tens of thousands of employees and dozens if not hundreds of partners. They often work in many ways like public companies, but a key difference is that each partner has a more direct share in the firm, in the sense that they are part-owners. All profits and value in the firm is thus directly in the possession of the partners. Often also the partners are without the limitation on liability that characterizes a company. So in theory the partners in such a firm might be personally liable for the entirety of losses due to any error they make (though in practice professional partners will take out a special insurance policy to indemnify themselves against such losses and subsequent litigation). This makes the governance of the firm quite different from a company owned by shareholders, for in that case the managers are stewards of someone else's interests, whereas in a partnership they are conducting business for themselves.

While this more personal aspect of governance eliminates the gap between manager's and owner's interests, it accentuates the tension between the interests of owners and those of other stakeholders such as employees or clients.

Many partnerships operate in the professional services field. Partnerships in industries such as law or accounting are governed by codes of professional practice that in theory should enhance responsible practice. However, the influence of professional codes has been critiqued as being ineffective.[8] Additionally, it could be argued that codes of professional practice protect an industry rather than its clientele. In professional services, conflicts of interest can often occur in more accentuated forms than with other industries. The larger players in industries such as accounting have diversified over time, so that they offer a range of different services, including, for example, accounting, auditing, management consultancy, IT and asset management. A client receiving a range of services from a professional practice can become vulnerable to manipulation. For example, the management consultancy arm of a professional service organization may recommend that the client company should adopt a certain information system, which coincidentally the same consultancy's IT division happens to be able to provide at a special rate. This issue is not specific to the nature and governance of partnerships, so much as to the industries in which they often operate, but it is convenient to note the matter here as part of the context in which ethical issues arise.

To prevent such conflicts many industries (and some governments) have attempted to build in safeguards involving internal restrictions on communication between different divisions of the same partnership about a certain client.[9] Inevitably this remains based on a great deal of trust, and many larger companies have in recent years chosen to split their reliance on professional services between different providers, a signal that they do not always believe in the security of such safeguards.

Not-for-profit 'third sector' organizations

The so-called 'third sector' is that category of organizations that are independent, self-governing entities but which are not operated for profit. In the main these are organizations set up for social or charitable purposes, such as collecting and distributing aid relief in regions of the world with high levels of poverty, or to research key social issues and lobby politicians to support changes in policy, or in some cases to sponsor worthy causes such as medical research.

These 'voluntary' organizations[10] are generally governed by a board of trustees or managers, who are usually nominated by other members when a place on the board becomes vacant. In many developed countries they benefit from government grants, can enjoy certain tax advantages, and are usually subject to significant levels of government regulation. An important sub-class of the voluntary sector are civil society organizations (CSOs) – also known as non-governmental organizations (NGOs). These tend to be politically inspired (but usually non-aligned in terms of specific party allegiances) and focused on broad social ends such as poverty alleviation or promotion of human rights. Although they work often in partnership with governments and pan-national bodies such as the UN, they remain independent, and thus structurally they still have similar features to more narrowly focused or locally based voluntary bodies such as housing cooperatives. We will discuss CSOs/NGOs in more detail in a later chapter.

Governance has traditionally been one of the weak points of third sector organizations. Trustee boards are often self-perpetuating entities, where each new appointment is made on recommendation rather than on an objective evaluation. As a result there was often in the past a question as to the competence of such governors. In more recent years many governments have legislated to control their behaviour, for example by requiring members of boards to be appointed following objective procedures designed to identify expertise rather than being based on social networks and friendships.

Voluntary organizations often experience conflicts of interest, as individuals can take the roles of trustee, supplier or even beneficiaries.[11] A related flaw of governance is the vulnerability of the voluntary organization to abuse of privileges. Particularly at the board level, the checks and balances that the private sector enjoy – mainly driven by the continuing demand of shareholders to receive a good return on their investments – are absent. While most countries have some external auditing checks, these are less well developed than the simple market-driven checks of the private sector.

ETHICS AND YOU

A DILEMMA FOR NGOS

An acute dilemma for some NGOs is the question of compromise with repressive regimes – for example, in order to do any work in a certain country an organization may have to turn a blind eye to violations of human rights. An irrigation project in a desertified country, for example, might be carried out while there is direct harassment of minority ethnicities.

If placed in this dilemma how would you resolve it? Withdrawal? Direct confrontation? What alternative solutions might be available to you?

As stated above, the general presumption is that this category of organization is in some way dedicated to some kind of social enhancement, be this research support, political lobbying or the provision of welfare. However, the processes of regulation of these organizations do not guarantee that all have ethically worthy ends. It is possible for a political organization to be disguised as simply a social lobby research group, for example. Equally, members of a particular social group might form a charitable organization that then wins government funds, which are then used by those who set up the organization for their own personal needs. A larger issue, developed in a later chapter, is the extent to which third sector organizations do actually achieve their ends, or might they actually contribute to consolidating the underlying structural issues that give rise to social problems.

State or neo-state organizations

The state in almost every country is its biggest economic player. It is generally the largest employer – with armed forces, medical provision, security and policing, infrastructure and many more functions. It also is usually the largest individual investor. And it is the regulator of the country's financial systems, especially with respect to its currency, interest and exchange rates.

'State' in this context does not necessarily mean solely 'government'. Many operations are set up and funded by a government but operate independently; sometimes these are described as neo-state or para-state bodies, or more informally as quangos.[12] These arm's-length governmental operations suffer from the problems of distance we discussed earlier, but also have some of the weaknesses experienced by third sector organizations, such as poor governance.

In general, many of the ethical problems experienced in this sector are evident elsewhere – for example corruption of officials or inequity of public service delivery. It has been argued that the public sector is more vulnerable to practices such as bribery than the private.[13] An additional issue of responsibility is the temptation for a government body to use the rule of law for ends other than social order. For example, political dissent is often treated as criminality – not difficult when in many cases a political minority may only get the opportunity to have a public voice by means of some kind of violation of the law. Many governments are alleged to use their legal systems to harass opponents of the political status quo and to condone violations made by those friendly to the regime.

Additionally, government bodies have a great deal of control over information, especially about their own activities. State security, maintenance of good civic order, or keeping financial markets stable, are often used to justify the restriction of information to avoid embarrassment or diplomatic awkwardness. Usually this is based on a consequentialist argument that the end is great enough to justify the means of suppression of information. This is not specific to governments – the really large public limited companies have similar issues – but the former exhibit this issue to the most extreme degree.

A further issue is that of vulnerability to corruption. High-ranking government officials rarely receive financial reward comparable to their counterparts in business. Usually this approach to pay is justified in terms of expecting a commitment to public service, of the security that government employment usually brings, and of the general prospect of a stable retirement pension. Be that as it may, there is the potential for a senior government employee to see the difference between their salary and, say, an old college friend in the private sector, as unfair – and out of such perceptions is born the temptation to accept a bribe.

A broader issue of social responsibility is the perception that in countries with popular elections of representatives and of the political leadership, much of what government does is intended not so much for the good of the country but more for the public image of the

DOES THE THREAT OF TERRORISM JUSTIFY VIOLATIONS OF HUMAN RIGHTS?

A common position of governments in the 21st century is to justify much of their law and order policies on the basis of the threat of terrorism. Many nations around the world have seen restrictions on free speech, travel and access to government documents all justified on this basis. This has reportedly gone beyond legitimate governing and included illegitimate or even illegal actions. Government officials have been reported to have justified violations of rights, even illegal activity, on the same basis.

If you worked for a major government department, where would you draw the line? In response to what kind of threat would you feel justified, say, in lying to journalists? Or lying in a courtroom? Or lying to elected representatives?

ruling party. Hard decisions that might lead to short-term difficulty but long-term gain are thus given lower priority to decisions that are immediately popular, but not necessarily in the best long-term interest of the nation.

In this section we have looked at a selection of different types of organizations – SMEs, family businesses, partnerships, state and third sector organizations. The intention has been to provide an indication of the kind of variation in issue relating to ethics or social responsibility that each sector may experience. What we have seen here is that these different forms of ownership and control raise related but distinct issues – of governance, of internal influence, of bias and potentially of corruption. Whether people act in certain ways is of course their personal responsibility, but factors such as organizational ownership create the conditions that define people's options for action – in short, they provide opportunities for good or bad actions. In the next section we shall start looking at some of the internal factors affecting ethics and corporate responsibility.

ORGANIZATIONAL STRUCTURES

The familiar models of organizational structure are often construed as definitions of the formal operations of an organization. True, they can often depict the way in which an organization formally defines its operations, but they are rarely fixed, and as often as not there are shadow, informal organizational channels that have a high level of influence on decisions and policies.

As Mullins[14] points out, the whole idea of 'a' structure can mislead one into thinking that structures fulfil a single clear purpose – for example, the delineation of authority. In practice, however, a structure such as a tree diagram or matrix mapping may fulfil several functions, including the formulation or justification of the following:

- The hierarchy of authority – who has to ask whom for permission to do something.
- The hierarchy of responsibility – who takes credit or blame for organizational actions.
- The logical division of operations into functions, service/product types, projects, or areas.
- The hierarchy of status – the higher the placing in a tree, for example, then often the more prestigious the role.
- The hierarchy of capability – the assumption that managers have to have a greater level of ability than those they manage.

- The hierarchy of pay levels – embodying the assumption that the higher you go the more you get paid.
- The standard career track for most professional workers – assuming that these employees are motivated by money, success, status and power.

Maybe no one organization treats its structure in all these ways, and often several of these are unspoken assumptions without much basis in fact. But the point is that simply to state that a certain organization is a product-line based structure, for example (as some motor manufacturers are), is to oversimplify how different stakeholders will view the structure of the firm. For example, many external stakeholders will assume that the organizational structure may represent, in part at least, a means of controlling the behaviour of employees. However, *internally* the structure may be regarded more as a means of dividing up tasks and functions, with the result that there may grow up greater levels of psychological distance between manager and managed than is supposed by, for example, customers.

One of the most prevalent aspects of organizational structure that is relevant to ethics and responsibility is how a structure can *disengage* employees from their moral instincts. The blurring of authority, responsibility and capability that can occur with a structure can lead to loss of a sense of responsibility by employees. This can happen in different ways: one is where a tall structure, with many levels, creates in employees a sense that they do not have any responsibility for a decision, as there are many above them who will be responsible. Another is where the sheer complexity of the operation distributes responsibility around many parts of an organization, and in consequence staff move from thinking they have *little* responsibility to regarding this as *no* responsibility. Kenneth Goodpaster[15] talks of ethical wrongdoing in business as resulting from fixation with certain goals, rationalization of these goals and a consequent detachment from individual values. This is accentuated in contexts where the complexity of operations makes it difficult for individuals to perceive their contribution to tasks or to overall emergent ethical outcomes.

Another key ethical issue arising from the nature of organizational hierarchy is the manner in which a structure provides for the control of employees. Ethical distance may grow up in two directions – the wider the span of control of the manager, the less they can keep a detailed view of any individual employee, but the narrower the span of control, the more levels of hierarchy that communication needs to go through, with the consequent dilution or even distortion of the meaning of the communication.

However, the other side to management control is management trust in employees. Delegation, and the trust that goes with it, encourages employee satisfaction and commitment, and conversely a failure to delegate is perceived negatively by employees. One principle that is relevant here is that of subsidiarity – the idea that decisions should be taken at the lowest appropriate level. As Mele has argued, such a principle should be seen not as a solution in its own right but in concert with other factors.[16] If a manager leaves decisions to her or his subordinates, this will not enhance ethical decisions unless there is a strong sense of values to support this. However, where there is a consistency of values, subsidiarity can preserve these by avoiding the confusions that many levels of management can lead to.

In several well-known organizational scandals, structural factors such as the nature of the relationship – or maybe better expressed as *distance* – between manager and employee has been a key issue. In 1995 Barings Bank, one of the longest established British banks, was brought to bankruptcy by the actions of one of its traders, Nick Leeson. Leeson was able to carry on a string of highly risky financial transactions, with the final outcome that the bank was ruined when his risks did not pay off. One of the key findings of the subsequent enquiry was that Leeson was not properly managed, partially because the distance between him and his managers was based on a division of *tasks* rather than on the need for direct *control* – in short, Leeson was allowed to make his mistakes because his managers did not regard it as important to control what he was doing.[17]

Also important is the development of 'virtuality' in an organization's structure – that is to say, how much of an arm's-length approach is taken with respect to an organization's upstream and downstream activities. For example, a company might only carry out a core function of its business, with the rest being controlled through outsourcing, detailed specifications for suppliers and after-sales care. One ethical risk of greater virtuality (in this sense) is the potential for corporate distance to create knowledge gaps. A supplier may be unclear what has been promised to end-users, and thus produce components that are unsuitable for their final use. Alternatively, the company may be unclear as to the origin of certain supplies – for instance a food retailer labelling products as organic when they are not.

A significant ethical problem with outsourcing and virtual organizations is the nature, quality and volume of information that passes along the supply chain. Often it is difficult to specify with complete precision exactly how supplies are to be used, so that informal agreements and trust have to be relied on to assure an appropriate outcome. In the 1980s pellets of cobalt-60, a highly radioactive material, were taken from a refuse site in Mexico and transported across the border into the United States, where some of it then ended up being reprocessed in a metal factory, so that office furniture, factory equipment and even school desks containing some traces of the radioactive material were resold in the developed world.[18] The distributed nature of the operation of waste disposal, and the distance created by the process of outsourcing, meant that those who knew enough to understand the risks and the burden of responsibility, were far away from the point where decisions were made regarding the waste. During the late 1990s and early 2000s there have been several further cases of organizations with a high level of outsourced operations discovering that suppliers have not always met the expected levels of ethical performance: many clothes firms such as Nike have discovered to their cost that assumptions they have made about activity on the part of suppliers have not been justified.

With organizations operating at an international or global scale, there are further aspects of structure that affect ethics and responsibility. One aspect is simply the intensification of the issues of distance outlined above, where local managers may be on a different continent from the corporate HQ. Another key issue is how far an international firm tries to maintain its original style and culture, as opposed to flexing its approach depending on each country in which it is operating – sometimes called the 'global–local' dilemma. The company that maintains a strong sense of its 'home' country when operating elsewhere will generally need to have a structure that is consonant with this strategy, for example by developing a structure that retains key functions at the home location, or by placing home managers at the head of each country subsidiary, or – more determinately – by creating a *group structure* where, although the operation in each country is technically a distinct company, in practice the directors of the holding company maintain tight control over financial and other targets. The distance that this creates, however, further emphasizes the gaps in understanding and moral awareness that can grow up in larger organizations.[19]

With international organizations there are further ethical issues relating to organizational structure – too much central control looks like neo-colonialism, while too much decentralization can lead to behaviour that the 'home' country of the organization might regard as unacceptable. For example, in many developing nations it is common practice for children to work and contribute to the family income. In the developed world this is often seen as unacceptable, on the basis that children have a right to a childhood of play and growth rather than be committed at too young an age to having to work to earn a living. For the international firm that gives a high level of discretion to local management this is a dilemma – satisfy home customers and public opinion, or support the local economy in the way that they understand and can accommodate in their normal way of life? This dilemma can be resolved in different ways – such as allowing young people to work but ensuring that an appropriate level of schooling is also provided – but the point is that the structure provides a context that gives rise to the dilemma. We will look in more detail at ethics in a global management context in a later chapter.

THINKING CRITICALLY ABOUT ETHICS

COMPLEXITY AND DISTANCE

Modern products and services are steadily becoming ever more complex, involving the interaction of professionals from different disciplines, sometimes from different organizations, and with high levels of specialized knowledge. As work becomes more technical and more knowledge-driven, and as any one service or good becomes increasingly the responsibility of more and more participants in the process, the underlying basis for all such activity – the provision of a benefit to the customer or client – can easily be lost. Modern international outsourcing only accentuates this pattern.

Morally, the promise that any organization gives to its clients is that it can meet their needs. But is the increasing complexity of organizational structures undermining this promise?

GROUP FACTORS AFFECTING ETHICAL DECISION MAKING

Organizations, being collections of individuals, are subject to processes of socialization. Work becomes not merely a sequence of tasks but a set of interactions between people. Group dynamics, power and internal cultures thus play a very important role in organizational decision making.

Before looking at these internal aspects of ethics and decision making, it is worth noting that the cultures that people *bring* to organizations are also highly relevant. Demographic features such as national identity, race and ethnicity are commonly linked, and sometimes incorrectly presumed to be identical, as influences on managerial behaviour and decision making. Well known are models that attempt to map out the trends in people's thinking and decision making depending on their national origin, the most widely disseminated of these being that of Geert Hofstede.[20] Equally, many studies have indicated differences in ethical behaviour between individuals from different countries.[21]

Such differences do not necessarily stem from different patterns of behaviour as such. They may reflect different kinds of belief, stemming maybe from nationally accepted religions for example. Or they might reflect conventions that are not so much different styles as alternative ways of dealing with issues: for example, in some countries verbal agreements are treated as binding, while in others nothing is regarded as real unless it is backed up by a written contract, and in still others there is ambiguous, inconsistent behaviour in this respect. These differences do not always reflect deep underlying differences of world-view; they can often as easily demonstrate simply a different tradition of approaching a problem.

Turning to the internal collective processes affecting decisions in organizations, there are several key factors, including:

- the internal culture and sub-cultures in an organization
- pressures to conform to group
- the use of sources of power.

HOFSTEDE'S DIMENSIONS OF NATIONAL CULTURE

Hofstede identified five dimensions of behaviour that varied across national cultures:

- **Power distance** – how far social relations are based on power and status.

- **Individual/collective** – how far decisions and responsibility are individually focused or group focused.

- **Uncertainty avoidance** – how tolerant (or not) a culture is to risk.

- **Masculinity/femininity** – the degree to which some features traditionally seen as 'feminine' (e.g. relationships, communication) are valued as opposed to 'masculine' features (e.g. power, achievement, wealth).

- **Long-term/short-term orientation** – the prevalence of virtues that encourage a longer- or a shorter-term outlook; longer-term ones including perseverance, and shorter including personal stability.

On the basis of these dimensions, Hofstede was able to draw a wide range of broad conclusions, such as the Italians being more individualistic than the French, or the Chinese having a longer-term orientation than Pakistanis.

Organizational culture – often summarized as 'the way we do things around here' – can be a substantial influence on people's behaviour and choices. These cultures arise out of a range of underlying factors, such as the size and dispersion of the workforce, the commercial pressures on the organization, and the values placed on individuals and tasks. As with nationality, there are several established models of organization culture. Charles Handy categorizes cultures on the basis of their dominant value – task, roles, people and power.[22] Deal and Kennedy[23] focus on the key operational elements – speed of feedback on decisions and level of risk.

From the perspective of ethics and corporate responsibility, the key issue is how culture influences decisions and behaviour. Organizations vary in the degree to which conformity with the culture is expected – some are high-profile cultures where explicit standards are expected, while others tolerate a wider degree of behaviours. Organizational cultures also embody or express certain values. Organizations with strict dress codes, for instance, make a statement about the value of their presentation to the customer.

An organizational culture can encourage ethical behaviour, for example by the encouragement of discussion and debate. A focus on task fulfilment can also be a positive factor,

ETHICS AND YOU

CULTURAL APPROACHES TO EQUALITY

Inevitably differences in the way people characteristically are thought or expected to behave in different countries can create substantial ethical dilemmas.

Consider a company from a country with high levels of equality between the genders visiting a client from a country that is generally thought of as less egalitarian. Should the normal sales team arrive, with equal numbers of men and women? Or should the firm avoid the possible difficulty and send only men?

where this is associated with all tasks and not just those that have a high profile. But equally, cultures can work against good ethics. A company where blame is the first reaction to organizational shortcomings is likely to encourage a range of negative reactions from staff, such as:

- concealment of errors
- reduced transparency
- scapegoating of weaker members of staff
- avoidance of responsibility.

What is noticeable about these is that the customer drops out of consideration, and organizational efforts are directed more to internal matters than to external. This kind of blame culture is accentuated when allied to certain kinds of structure. A blame culture can more easily be accommodated within taller structures with many divisions and narrow spans of control, where there are ample opportunities to operate without transparency and where power differences are magnified.

A further problematic aspect of culture, as opposed to official rules of behaviour, is that it is by definition tacit and not open to overt managerial control. This can mean that poor ethical behaviour is uncorrected, not because people think that it is right but because there is no formal, official means of changing attitudes. Behaviours may be legislated for by company rules, but attitudes and styles cannot be.

Jackall[24] and others have identified a general 'business' culture where executives become progressively more identified with business values to the extent that their own personal values are subverted. Many popular TV series and novels have dealt with the gradual erosion of personal values by corporate cultures.[25] Conformity is one important aspect of this – especially for a new, young or relatively powerless member of staff, there are substantial pressures to conform to what are presented as the norms of behaviour. Long hours is an example: in some organizations it is regarded as a sign of a lack of commitment to leave work at the end of one's official hours; in others it is seen as a sign of lack of competence to have to stay working late. This may reflect a professed cultural symbol, or it might stem from tacit assumptions about how involved in an organization someone ought to be.

A related aspect of collective influences on behaviour is the nature of the group of which one is a member. The extent to which a group is aware of its own identity and values can often be an important factor in behaviour. For example, tightly knit groups under great pressure from external threats can develop a 'siege' mentality where preserving the integrity and unity of the group become a key aim. Any actions that appear to diminish this can therefore be strongly inhibited and disapproved of. So a whistle-blower is portrayed as disloyal and even 'one of the enemy' if they make public any concerns over unethical practice. The well-known phenomenon of 'groupthink'[26] is a related influence tending towards conformist behaviour. In groupthink there is pressure to agree with a perceived consensus, often on the basis that the group's self-image is of a high degree of expertise. In groupthink, decisions tend to be more risky, because no individual feels themselves to be individually responsible. The discouragement of discussion and debate means that unethical decisions can easily go unchallenged. Criticism is inhibited, not because it is seen as a threat, but because the group's ideas are perceived (by them) as being so high quality that no alternative viewpoint is valuable. The phraseology often applied to financial traders in the biggest global investment banks encapsulates this attitude – 'masters of the universe'.

Cultural norms in organizations, and group pressures, are generally enforced by the use of different kinds of social power. Power in an organization can stem from one's official position, from one's control over certain resources, from being close to those in senior

ETHICS IN PRACTICE

MOTOROLA AND OPEN COMMUNICATIONS

As part of a systematic ethics programme, Motorola encourages direct reporting of ethical issues via its 'Ethics line' – a phone line that can be used anonymously, where employees or others can report areas of concern. The company also encourages employee suggestions as a means of enhancing corporate performance in all areas, including ethics.

positions, or from the ability to give or withhold rewards. Groups can also exercise power simply by choosing to include or exclude individuals socially. Also, intimidating individuals use bullying tactics to force acquiescence, either physically or psychologically. A further extension of this is group bullying – sometimes called mobbing – where a number of individuals adopt intimidatory behaviour on a systematic basis to force someone to comply with their desired norms.[27]

Faced with these various influences – power, cultural norms, group pressures – it is not surprising that many people do not stand by their personal values in organizations. Many cases on unethical actions happen because individuals' personal convictions are challenged by the collective environment they find themselves in – the pressure on a junior member of staff to turn a blind eye to a more senior manager offering a bribe to a client, for example, or the group pressure on an individual to condone racist language. The difficulty in managing these is that often the collective pressures to preserve unethical behaviour also involve a degree of concealment of the reality of what is happening. The merits of an open discursive environment in this context are that attitudes and behaviours are made transparent – though those who wish to retain poor behaviours will often attempt to subvert transparency. Argyris talks of the 'undiscussability of the undiscussable' – in other words, the refusal of some to allow any consideration at all of an issue, even of *the fact* that they will not discuss it.[28]

The management of groups and group processes is intrinsically problematic – much cultural content and group norming is left tacit, which means that even those who practice these may not be fully aware of them. In practical terms it is probably discourse ethics that offers the best managerial solutions. Other approaches, such as the cultivation of good levels of personal virtue, are desirable but represent substantial personal change, whereas the creation of open discussion and debate is more easily facilitated within the organization.

INDIVIDUAL FACTORS AFFECTING ETHICAL DECISIONS

In terms of the ethical dimensions of decisions made in organizations, it should be clear that individual differences play a substantial part. People's motives, their perceptions and their emotions will all play a major role. In this final section we look at two key individual issues and how they affect ethics and corporate responsibility.

Values and ethical ideologies

Our values come from many different sources. For those with religious convictions this tends to be a clear origin of people's values. In many countries people are brought up with some contact with a religion that then is rejected as they reach adulthood – this early connection with religion may also play a role in people's values. However, individual values are based on many other factors, primarily their experiences, as well as the values they encounter in those close to them. Values are very close to our sense of identity, so much so that they are often difficult to clearly analyse.

One aspect of this is that we sometimes are not clear even ourselves about what is most important in value terms. For example, in some cases we have very strong views about a particular kind of example, so that we feel that x should happen, even when we cannot fully articulate the reason, whereas in other cases we have strong feelings about certain general principles but are prepared to change our minds easily over specific examples.

A further complication is that different protagonists in an ethical debate may start from very different positions, yet fail to recognize that a difference exists – if they agree with each other's final conclusions about what to do they may not realize that their views are based on very different premises. Each individual is a complex of a number of different values, which have subtle interrelationships that are not easily comparable with how others see the same issues, even when they appear to be committed to the same values. One important aspect of the structure of ethical arguments is *how* we hold a certain value.

Forsyth[29] uses the term 'ethical ideology' for the way in which we hold values. He has categorized the way in which values are held into four different types, based on two dimensions of deliberation (how idealistic someone is over an issue; how far their views would be relative to circumstances):

- absolutist – little relativism but a lot of idealism
- exceptionist – little idealism or relativism
- situationist – a lot of both relativism and idealism
- subjectivist – a lot of relativism, little idealism.

Forsyth classifies agents as belonging to one or other of these types. An individual who has strong ethical views, and does not accept qualifications or modifications to them, is what Forsyth would describe as an absolutist, whereas, for example, someone who has the same degree of idealism but can see that their ideals have to accommodate different circumstances, would be on Forsyth's view a situationist. This is not the only way to classify an individual's orientation to ethics.[30]

These types that are presented as features of different kinds of personality may be adopted by the same person for different issues. Each of us has some values that are very dear to us – issues that might be regarded as close to our sense of our own identity. Equally, for most of us there are other values that we hold but less strongly. So for one issue someone might think and argue as a situationist, while for another they may be subjectivist, and for still another they may be more of an absolutist.

The key point to note in this context, however, is that people often do not recognize that others are approaching an issue from a different standpoint. Just as we saw that someone may not realize that their opponent in a debate over ethics may be making different factual assumptions, so they may also fail to recognize that that opponent may be adopting a more or less relativistic stance, for example. Indeed, for an absolutist, it may be difficult to recognize that greater levels of relativism are still compatible with some degree of idealism, and at the other extreme it may be difficult for a subjectivist to understand that some idealism is not a commitment to a hard and fast absolutist position.

DEALING WITH ABSOLUTES

The most difficult ethical debates to handle are ones where an individual holds an absolute value. By definition they are unlikely to accept a compromise. People may hold absolute values over many issues, including those such as corporate gifts, equality or rights to express one's religion publicly. Absolutism is on the face of it difficult to reconcile with corporate behaviour, where response to ambiguous situations with something to be said on both sides is commonplace.

How would you manage individuals who appeared to hold certain values in an absolute manner?

Perception and cognition

Two individual factors are highly relevant to how they respond to ethical situations. First is someone's attitude to risk. If we look back to the Barings case discussed earlier, one of the key issues there was that Nick Leeson was initially very successful, but continued with a highly risky strategy. A common phenomenon in cases of corporate scandals and other cases of criminal behaviour is the belief that someone will not get caught. One way in which unethical behaviour can be reduced is for organizations to continue to operate monitoring systems that detect unethical behaviour. By regularly demonstrating that unethical actions do get found out and dealt with, this undermines the belief that someone might be able to get away with wrong actions without loss. This is in line with theories of motivation that depict choice as determined by desires in combination with beliefs as to what actions will succeed.[31]

The second factor to note is the imagination of individuals. Moral imagination refers to our ability to think of different ways to resolve a situation, as well as to our ability to view situations in a different light. Patricia Werhane[32] has indicated the ways in which ethical choices may be affected by imagination. For example, a line manager may act in a bullying manner to staff because she cannot think of another way to improve productivity. Similarly, a director of marketing may decide that sustaining a certain kind of publicity would be 'unthinkable' – i.e. a state of affairs that he cannot reconcile with existing strategic imperatives. In both cases a failure of imagination has occurred. Explanations of action such as 'I had no choice' or 'There is no alternative' may often be signs of this failure.[33] Werhane's argument is that this lack of imagination leads to a substantial number of ethically unacceptable actions.

A slightly different elaboration of this argument may be seen in the writing of the philosopher-journalist Hannah Arendt, whose discussion of the trial of Adolph Eichmann, the Nazi officer responsible for very many of the deaths in the gas chambers, is subtitled 'the banality of evil'.[34] Arendt's point is not the same as Werhane's. She is concerned to show that people who carry out even the most ghastly evil acts are not necessarily fantastic demons, but sometimes very ordinary, selfish, even *dull* people into whose hands are placed technology – for which one could read 'weapons' – of extraordinary power. But in both cases the argument is based around the notion that unethical behaviour is often founded on an intellectual failing.

Clearly, one way to resolve this managerially is to encourage a culture that helps develop greater imagination in organizational members. This is an effective long-term strategy. More problematic is the short-term dilemma: for example, a situation where an immediate response is required, yet some of those in positions of influence demonstrate a lack of imagination, or of empathy with others, or of some other intellectual faculty that contributes towards ethical choice.

SUMMARY

As stated earlier, the contents of this chapter are not intended to be comprehensive. They are meant to provide an indication of the breadth of issues that can be involved in the behavioural context of ethical decision making. Above all, the discussion of this chapter has underlined the need for organizations to adopt processes of discussion, debate and openness wherever possible, as a means of understanding values, of formulating solutions to problems and of reducing the opportunities for unethical behaviour by bringing issues out into the open.

What we have seen, then, is that:

■ Organizational structure rarely creates ethical risks of itself, but tends to exaggerate ones that are already evident.

■ SMEs, and family businesses, often operate to different owner-strategies and have different objectives compared with the wider stakeholder strategies of larger organizations; these therefore manage ethics in a more intimate, but also potentially a more personally focused manner.

■ Not-for-profit organizations, whether state or voluntary sectors, tend to have potential weaknesses in governance.

■ Organizational culture, group norms, and organization power can all create pressures towards group conformity in ethical choice, for good or bad.

■ Individuals conceive values in distinct ways, which render ethical discussion and debate more problematic than is generally realized, as agreement in judgements is often taken to indicate agreement in starting points.

QUICK REVIEW QUESTIONS:

1 An implication of models such as Hofstede's is that different cultures have different views about the role of human beings in nature. How would this affect the way a business responds to the environmental arguments encountered in the previous chapter?

2 What steps can a manager in a small business take to minimize the risk that employees might act unethically?

3 Civil society organizations generally exist to promote a widely based benefit to society. Yet being essentially voluntary organizations they can suffer from the problem of self-replicating governing bodies (where as soon as one member of the governors leaves, another is appointed from among the friends or social networks of the board). How would you try to avoid this weakness in governance?

CASE STUDY: WE'RE ALL ACTIVISTS NOW

BY ANDY MIAH

From recycling to mass protests on social networks like Facebook, having an ethical conscience is becoming part of our daily lives. Now it's the turn of governments and companies to change, writes Andy Miah.

Amid all the great changes afoot in the world, a trend is emerging that is as pervasive as it is critical. I call it an 'ethical turn', a surge in popular activism, broad democratic demands and institutional reforms that mark a new era of ethical concern in our daily lives.

The furore over bankers' financial arrangements and the need for tighter monetary regulations is just one area where the ethical turn has come to light. Everyone from the rightfully indignant public to ministers and celebrities has joined calls for greater accountability. With luck, we are now on the cusp of truly ethical economic reform.

The ethical turn has emerged as a powerful movement in popular culture. Celebrity chefs such as Jamie Oliver have attempted to transform society by urging schools to provide nutritious meals, meanwhile teaching the rest of the nation to cook for ourselves. We are encouraged to ditch fast food, TV dinners and pre-chopped, pre-cooked supermarket foods, and to rediscover the joys of cooking.

In doing so, we will regain not only the pleasure of making meals for ourselves, but the social benefits that come with it. We may even find our sense of taste again.

Reality television has now been joined by ethical television. In BBC3's recent show, 'Kill it, Cook it, Eat it', participants and viewers were asked to re-engage with their inner carnivore by taking part in the slaughter and butchery of animals before feasting. The underlying message is clear: by facing up to the realities of the food we buy and eat, we develop a more finely honed morality towards animals.

Others are taking up the idea. Artist and activist John O'Shea is developing what he calls the 'Meat Licence Proposal', which requires people to have killed an animal before they are allowed to eat one. The licence works on a species level. If you've killed a fish, you can eat fish, but if you want to eat beef, you need first to have killed a cow.

The environmental movement is surely the most public arena where the ethical turn has come into play, and here, the sense of public conscience is growing. Today, failing to recycle is stigmatized, but tomorrow, we may feel ashamed of how many flights we take, a shift that would transform our view of the well-travelled citizen.

Dealing with climate change is clearly a pressing obligation, but speaking at the first Natural Economy Northwest Green Lecture recently at the Foundation for Art and Creative Technology in Liverpool, green campaigner Jonathon Porritt emphasized how much more we have to do in the UK to come close to being ethical in this field.

Of course I'm not trying to claim the ethical turn is only at work in Britain. President Obama's emphasis on 'mutual responsibility' encompasses the development of science and technology. From stem cell research to internet privacy, there has been a tremendous backlash against moves to limit our freedoms.

In the recent controversy over Facebook's new 'terms of service', ethically aware members appealed to the ideology of social media and convinced Facebook to revert to its original policy. It worked this time, but ethical issues will arise again in the world of social media.

Overwhelmingly, the ethical turn seems a force for good, but there are substantial hurdles it is likely to encounter. Undoubtedly, we must take responsibility as individuals for making the world a better place, but too often, governments and companies undermine individual actions by doing too little themselves.

For individuals to have their greatest impact, those in power need to radically rethink how they can make it easier for us. It is neither adequate nor reasonable for us simply to use fewer plastic bags when shopping for groceries. We need to distinguish between what individuals can do, and what governments and companies must enact to allow us to make a difference.

We need to democratize ethics and find a way to put it at the heart of our organizations and daily lives. We need transparency to understand the labels on our food, the privacy settings on our computers, and the difference between fair trade and ethical trade. Above all, we need to cultivate an ethical awareness that can identify bad practice before it becomes catastrophic.

A middle class ethical crisis will do wonders to raise awareness of broader social injustices. It might even help us find the right moral ground for our times, which will be critical when science and technology create fresh ethical dilemmas that cut across society in fundamental ways.

Inevitably, an ethical conscience has already found its way into the branding of multinational corporations. That alone should tell us that a new era of ethical vigilance is upon us. However, if we are not careful, we will empty ethics of its value.

This is why the ethical turn cannot be about ethics for ethicists. It involves recognizing the many ways in which an ethical conscience is becoming a part of our daily lives, from what we wear and who made it, to asking fundamental questions about emerging technologies and their implications.

STUDY QUESTIONS

1 What is meant by 'the ethical turn'? Give examples from outside the case to demonstrate the phenomenon.

2 What has contributed to the emergence of the ethical turn?

3 Is the ethical turn sustainable or will it become another fad that quickly disappears?

SOURCE

guardian.co.uk, Friday 20 March 2009.

NOTES

1. It is assumed that readers already have some familiarity with the basic management theories relating to organizational culture, business strategy, organizational structures and similar. If not, then they are advised to consult either Mullins (2004) or Boddy (2008).
2. European Commission (2003).
3. Moore & Spence (2006).
4. Worley & Cummings (2004) p. 579.
5. Gallo (1995).
6. Vallejo (2008).
7. Belak (2005). Cf. also Dyer & Whetton (2005) for research on family firms and corporate social responsibility.
8. For example, Brecher (2004).
9. Often known by the misleading term of 'Chinese walls' – based on the structure of many Chinese homes of the past involving quite thin internal walls, which meant that families developed a culture of speaking quietly and discreetly if they wanted to keep something secret.
10. A misleading term, though it stems from the fact that some of the key roles in such organizations, in particular governance, are undertaken voluntarily and usually attract little or no financial reward.
11. Cf. Macdonald *et al.* (2002).
12. Quango is an acronym with several different expansions – quasi autonomous neo-governmental organizations is one of several related to what in the United States is called a quasi-governmental organization. In other countries, such as Australia, it refers to 'quasi autonomous *non*-governmental organizations' – for example the Red Cross provides a national blood bank service in that country. But all refer in some way to organizations that carry out government business without actually being formally part of the elected government.

13. Berkman (1992).
14. Mullins (2004).
15. Goodpaster (2006).
16. Mele (2005).
17. Readers unfamiliar with the case can find a reasonable – if somewhat subjective – account in Leeson's own book (Leeson, 1997).
18. J. R. Croft, review of IAEA Dijon Conference, paper supplied to the Third UK and Irish Conference on Nuclear Hazards, Newcastle, Co Down, 13–14 April 2000.
19. Velasquez (1995) gives an interesting account of how this occurred with the development of the aluminium industry in Jamaica.
20. Hofstede (2005).
21. To take just one example out of many, see Chung *et al.* (2008).
22. Handy (2005).
23. Deal & Kennedy (1982).
24. Jackall (1988).
25. Among these many, one recent example is the TV series 'Mad Men', depicting the decline in morality of a US advertising executive during the 1950s and 1960s.
26. A term associated with the work of Irving Janis (1972).
27. Cf. Cemaloglu (2007).
28. Argyris (1992).
29. Forsyth (1980).
30. We shall discuss in detail in a later chapter the ethical psychology of Laurence Kohlberg, who categorized individuals in terms of how closely attuned their ethical views are with established conventions.
31. A model that is philosophy goes back a least to the work of David Hume, and in social psychology is often called the expectancy model of motivation.
32. Werhane (1999).
33. But – arguably – not in all cases.
34. Arendt (1965).

REFERENCES

Argyris, C. 1992. *On Organisational Learning.* New York: McGraw-Hill.

Arendt, H. 1963. *Eichmann in Jerusalem: A Report on the Banality of Evil.* New York: The Viking Press.

Belak, J. 2005. Business ethics of a family enterprise. *Naše Gospodarstvo* (Our Economy) Vol. 3–4, 111–115.

Berkman, Ü. 1992. Bureaucracy and Bribery: A Conceptual Framework. *International Journal of Public Administration*, Vol. 15, No. 6, 1345–1368.

Boddy, D. 2008. *Management: An Introduction.* Fourth edition. London: FT Prentice-Hall.

Brecher, B. 2004. Against professional ethics. *Journal of the Philosophy of Management*, Vol. 4, No. 2, 3–8.

Cemaloglu, N. 2007. The exposure of primary school teachers to bullying: An analysis of various variables. *Social Behavior and Personality*, Vol. 35, No. 6, 789–802.

Chung, K. Y., Eichensher, J. and Taniguchi, T. 2008. Ethical perceptions of business students: Differences between east Asia and the USA. *Journal of Business Ethics*, Vol. 79, 121–132.

Deal, T. E. and Kennedy, A. A. 1982. *Corporate Cultures: The Rites and Rituals of Corporate Life.* Harmondsworth: Penguin Books.

Dyer, W.G., Jr. and Whetton, D.A. 2006. Family firms and social responsibility: Preliminary evidence from the S&P 500. *Entrepreneurship Theory and Practice*, Vol. 30, 785–802.

European Commission 2003. http://ec.europa.eu/enterprise/enterprise_policy/sme_definition/index_en.htm.

Forsyth, D. 1980. A taxonomy of ethical ideologies. *Journal of Personality and Social Psychology*, Vol. 39, No.1, 175–184.

Gallo, M. 1995. *La Empresa Familiar.* Praxis.

Goodpaster, K. 2006. *Conscience and Corporate Culture.* Wiley Blackwell.

Handy, C. 2005. *Understanding Organisations.* Fourth edition. Harmondsworth: Penguin.

Hofstede, G. 2005. *Cultures and Organizations: Software of the Mind.* Second revised edition. New York: McGraw-Hill.

Jackall, R. 1988. *Moral Mazes.* Oxford: Oxford University Press.

Janis, I. 1972. *Victims of Groupthink.* Houghton Mifflin.

Leeson, N. 1997. *Rogue Trader.* Sphere Books.

Macdonald, C., Macdonald, M. and Norman, W. 2002. Charitable conflicts of interest. *Journal of Business Ethics*, Vol. 39, 67–74.

Mele, D. 2005. Exploring the principle of subsidiarity in organisational forms. *Journal of Business Ethics*, Vol. 60, 293–305.

Moore, G. and Spence, L. 2006. Responsibility and small business. *Journal of Business Ethics*, Vol. 67, 219–226.

Mullins, L. 2004. *Management and Organisational Behaviour.* London: FT Prentice-Hall.

Schein, E. H. 2005. *Organizational Culture and Leadership.* Third edition. Jossey-Bass.

Vallejo, M. 2008. Is the culture of family firms really different? *Journal of Business Ethics*, Vol. 81, No. 2, 261–279.

Velasquez, M. 1995. *Business Ethics* (teaching and learning classroom edition). London: Pearson.

Werhane, P. 1999. *Moral Imagination and Management Decision Making.* Oxford: Oxford University Press.

Worley, C. and Cummings, T. 2004. *Organisational Development and Change.* Thomson South-Western.

ETHICS AND CORPORATE SOCIAL RESPONSIBILITY IN A GLOBAL CONTEXT

LEARNING OBJECTIVES

After studying this chapter you should be able to:

- Explain how conflict affects business and give examples of how business can contribute to conflict prevention and management.
- Identify and assess the challenges faced by companies in selling their products and services to the poor.
- Outline and evaluate the ways in which corruption affects the economy and business.

INTRODUCTION

Developing countries provide profitable business opportunities for multinational companies in terms of natural resources, low-cost labour and markets, but companies also risk being associated with problems arising from scarcity and weak governance. In this chapter we explore some of the main challenges encountered by companies operating in developing countries. The focus is on issues that cannot be internalized and dealt with in this way by companies. For example, issues related to the workplace will be discussed later in Chapter 12 because companies can adopt and implement internal policies to comply with labour standards. Companies cannot, however, escape the impact of more systemic issues such as corruption, poverty and violent conflict. In what follows we explore each of these problems in some detail to better understand how they affect business operations and can be managed by companies.

THE GLOBAL CONTEXT OF BUSINESS ACTIVITY

The corporate scandals of the 1990s had a profound effect on the development of the fields of business ethics and corporate social responsibility. The scandals took place in the context of globalization – the enhancement of links between people and cultures to an extent that the world can be regarded as a single unit. Indeed, the hyper-globalists would argue that we now live in a 'global village' characterized by homogenous values and instant communication across the globe. Others would oppose this view and assert that the world is still composed of local communities with their own values, beliefs and ways of organizing. Even though there are contrasting views on whether globalization is really happening, it can be separated into three distinct processes:

- globalization of economic activity
- globalization of culture
- globalization of politics.

Globalization of economic activity

Globalization involves increasing amounts of investment flow to developing countries. The emerging economies of east Asia have been the main beneficiaries of growing rates of trade and foreign investment, but many other countries have also become more closely integrated with the world economy. Globalization of business activity stimulates economic growth and has had a positive impact on living standards in many countries, but it has also focused attention on a number of ethical and corporate social responsibility issues including corruption, labour standards and product safety. These issues present challenges for international companies by requiring them to be aware of the political and social situation in far-away countries. Companies are also expected to have control over their operations in distant locations. A number of issues relating to these aspects of globalization will be discussed later in this chapter.

Globalization of culture

Globalization has also meant that values and norms have become increasingly homogenous across countries and regions. This development has enabled companies to sell similar products from New York to Dar es Salaam, but the services and products sold globally are also affecting the values on which culture is based. Even though it seems that certain aspects of culture have become global, globalization of culture is often superficial; using the same products and services does not mean that we are using them in the same way and give them similar meanings. For example, reggae may have become popular across the world, but it has lost its connotation of being anti-government protest music. Nevertheless, it does seem that cultures are in closer contact with each other than ever before. In terms of business ethics and corporate social responsibility, companies have struggled to reconcile expectations placed on them when operating across national borders. On the one hand, they have been seen as a source of innovation and international standards with positive effects on local culture including workplace practices. On the other hand, they have been criticized for imposing foreign values in the form of codes of conduct and corporate social responsibility policies.

Globalization of politics

Finally, globalization of politics involves the growth of cooperation between governments at international levels. This growth has involved different forms of cooperation from trade and investment to security and enforcement of human rights standards. Two recently established international bodies illustrate the extent of inter-governmental cooperation. First, the World Trade Organization shows that governments are increasingly willing to join organizations that have power to impose their decisions on their member countries. Even though the United Nations has had some powers to do this, they have been evoked rarely and are limited to the areas of international peace and security. Secondly, the International Court of Justice shows that governments allow international organizations to make judgements on issues that have traditionally fallen under the sphere of national sovereignty, including the prosecution of those who perpetrate gross human rights violations. The globalization of politics provides concerns and hope for business ethics and corporate social responsibility. It is a concern because economic issues have been prioritized over social ones, especially within the World Trade Organization. The globalization of politics provides hope because international organizations offer guidance on standards that makes it easier for companies to comply with ethical principles without becoming less competitive vis-à-vis their less responsible rivals.

Globalization of business, culture and politics has had an effect on the study of business ethics and corporate social responsibility. Even though theories of ethics and corporate

ETHICS IN PRACTICE

BLOOD DIAMONDS

Blood Diamond is a film about conflict diamonds in Sierra Leone, where an internal war is destroying the country. Leonardo DiCaprio plays a smuggler who learns about a rare pink diamond and befriends a local fisherman whose son has been kidnapped to become a child soldier. The film portrays the damage that civil war, fuelled by illicit trade in diamonds, can cause.

The term 'blood diamonds' refers to diamonds that are sold illegally to raise funds for armed groups that often oppose the government. Diamonds are particularly suitable for smuggling because of their small size and high value. Once polished, their origin is difficult to establish, making them ideal for illegal trafficking.

Blood diamonds have played a part in many conflicts in Africa. In Angola, about 20 per cent of diamonds were sold for illegal purposes before the United Nations placed Angola under sanctions, while in the Democratic Republic of the Congo, blood diamonds have served as a source of income for numerous armed groups. More recently, the production and smuggling of diamonds in Zimbabwe has raised concerns over the impact of diamond trade on conflict and civil unrest.

The diamond industry has sought to stop the sale of conflict diamonds through the Kimberley Certification Scheme. The Kimberley process involves the certification of diamonds so that their origin can be established. Participating countries are expected to establish procedures for diamond certification, but this has been challenging for governments that may lack administrative capacity and political will.

The Kimberley process is an example of an industry-led solution to a social and political problem. Even though it is governments that are mainly responsible for implementing the process, it was the business community that initiated the scheme and that enforces it by expecting all diamonds to come with a certificate of origin. The film, *Blood Diamond*, has also played a role by raising awareness of the issue among the general public.

social responsibility can be seen as universal, they reflect the values and norms of the context in which they were developed. For example, ethical theory has often been criticized for being based on a masculine understanding of the world. Similarly, the development of the concept of corporate social responsibility can be seen to reflect the concerns and issues faced by business in the United States and Europe. Globalization has introduced both new topics (e.g. conflict diamonds) and concepts (e.g. corporate citizenship, complicity) to the study of business ethics and corporate social responsibility.

OPERATING IN CONFLICT ZONES

Many companies avoid involvement in armed conflict due to the additional risks and costs arising from operating in conflict zones. There are, however, situations where the private sector has become entangled in conflict. Consider the following examples:

- Elf, a French oil and gas company that has now merged with Total, allegedly supplied arms and other assistance to Sassou N'Guesso to stage a coup d'état in Congo-Brazzaville in the 1990s. According to allegations, the company supported the opposition leader in order to secure the future of its investments in the country. Its conduct was later investigated and condemned by a French parliamentary commission. The incident was also linked to one of the biggest political and corruption scandals in France, *l'affaire Elf*.[1]

- A United Nations report on the exploitation of the natural resources and other forms of wealth in the Democratic Republic of the Congo from 2001 named over 120 companies and individuals for contributing to violent conflict and the squander of gems, coltan, gold and other natural reserves in the country. The report alleged, for example, that a Ugandan-Thai forest company, DARA-Forest, collaborated with a rebel group to extract and export timber from the country. Satellite images reveal that large areas of forest were logged after government authorities had denied the company a lawful concession. As a result, the Congolese government was not only denied revenue from the logging of timber, but a rebel movement was able to finance its anti-government activities.[2]

In both of the above situations, foreign companies played a clear role in exacerbating or profiting from conflict. Such opportunistic behaviour is relatively rare; most companies become involved in conflict without a deliberate decision to do so. When businesses do choose to invest in challenging environments, they expect higher than average returns to offset the risks and additional costs arising from the investment. In what follows, we first look at how conflicts have changed over time to have a better understanding of how business is exposed to conflict. We then identify the main risks and costs of operating in conflict zones, and finish by reviewing some of the ways in which the private sector can have a positive role in preventing and ending violent conflict.

Changing nature of conflict

The number of armed conflicts has declined since the end of the Cold War. As can be seen from Figure 6.1, the number of conflicts increased until 1992, but has fallen since then by about 40 per cent. The decreased number of conflicts is a result of two important developments. First, the majority of proxy wars in developing countries have come to an end as the warring parties have lost the support of the United States and Soviet Union/Russia. Concurrently, the major powers have made less frequent use of their veto power in the

FIGURE 6.1 Conflicts by region, 1946–2006

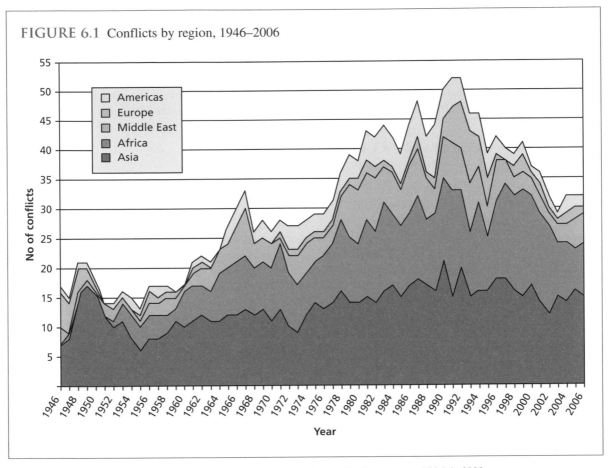

Source: Uppsala Conflict Data Program, Uppsala University, www.ucdp.uu.se/database, accessed 29 July 2008.

Security Council to block peacekeeping operations. As a consequence, the UN has been able to play its intended role as the peacemaker in conflict areas and the world is a more peaceful place than it has been for some time.[3] Nevertheless, there is still an important number of armed conflicts, especially in Asia and Africa.

It is not only the number of conflicts that has varied over time – the nature of conflict has also changed from interstate wars to internal armed struggle.[4] While many recorded conflicts before the Second World War took place between states, they have now been replaced by internal disputes over land and resources. These internal conflicts are often associated with countries where the central government lacks military and moral authority. Geopolitical and ideological disputes between states have therefore become rare with only a few exceptions. Most of today's conflicts involve dissatisfied groups challenging government power through armed struggle. Also, an increasing amount of violence is caused by international terrorism in defiance of national borders.

The recently ended Maoist rebellion in Nepal is a good example of an internal conflict taking place within a country rather than between states. Disillusioned with Nepalese politics, the Maoists took up arms in 1996 to improve the plight of the rural poor and other disadvantaged groups. Despite being poorly armed and organized, they gained sufficient support from the lower castes, who saw the Maoists as an alternative to the old order, and were able to mount a serious challenge to existing authority. As a consequence, the government entered into peace talks with the rebels and in 2006 the Maoists gave up arms and agreed to take part in democratic elections to form a new government. By then the war had left at least 12,000 people dead and 100,000 displaced. As is typical for today's armed clashes, the conflict had its sources in internal strife and discontent rather than disputes between states. No surrounding country took an active part in the civil war, though they were affected via flows of displaced people and general instability in the region.

Business risks and costs

With the exception of defence and security companies, few industries gain from armed conflict. Zones of conflict are normally a source of risk and additional expenses for the private sector. Nevertheless, there are companies that continue to operate in conflict areas due to their previous investments, intense global competition and lack of alternatives. This is particularly the case for the extractive sector exploiting oil, timber, minerals and other natural resources. These industries experience strong competitive rivalry and are tied to the locations where reserves have been found. The main risks and costs arising from conflict are often operational, but may also have an effect on company valuation as discussed next.

Security costs Foreign investment is often an important source of revenue and international standing for governments. Because of this, many insurgent groups regard the workers and assets of foreign companies as legitimate targets in their struggle against the central government. An increasing number of attacks by insurgents have led to serious incidents and, in some cases, fatalities. For example, four workers of the UK-based Granger Telecom were kidnapped and later killed by Chechen gunmen in 1998 despite being protected by more than 20 security guards.[5] Many others have died in Iraq and Afghanistan after the US invasion in these countries. Faced by the violence, companies have spent more on security arrangements to protect their staff and physical assets. According to *The Economist*, oil firms in Algeria allocated almost 10 per cent of their budgets to security in 2000.[6] Most of the money is used for fences, alarm systems and guards, but companies have also hired firms staffed with ex-soldiers to provide them with security in particularly challenging environments.

Material losses Companies also suffer material losses and disruption of activities as a result of attacks against their assets and general infrastructure in conflict areas. For example, UK-based Lonrho spent £2 million per month to cover material losses and security costs during Mozambique's civil war. The indirect consequences of material loss have involved high insurance costs and, in some cases, a total withdrawal of insurance coverage. In order to offset the additional costs and risks, companies have found innovative ways to deal with unexpected disruptions. For example, South African Breweries paid a local fire brigade to transport water and hose it into beer vats when water supply in conflict-ridden Mozambique was interrupted.[7]

Impact on share price Investing in conflict zones can have a harmful impact on share price and access to capital. PetroChina's initial public offering on the New York Stock Exchange provides an example of the discrimination experienced by companies operating in conflict zones. Due to the company's investments in Sudan where it was allegedly benefiting from violence perpetrated by government forces and private militias, a coalition of human rights groups and labour associations lobbied investors not to buy its shares. As a consequence, several major investment funds decided against investment in PetroChina and the company raised less capital than it had expected.[8] A company's share price may also remain undervalued because of exposure to reputational and material risks associated with conflict countries. Companies are therefore often faced with questions about the overall profitability of their activities in conflict zones. Instead of selling their assets, they may put their operations on hold and wait for the situation to improve. This has been the answer arrived at by a number of oil companies in the southern parts of Sudan.

Litigation costs Operating in conflict zones can also give rise to important litigation costs. Unocal, for example, is said to have paid several million dollars to settle a case in the United States for allegedly turning a blind eye to human rights violations in Burma. The attorney fees for the case have been estimated at US$15 million on the basis of the lawsuit that the company filed against its insurers to cover the costs of the initial litigation process.[9] Similar lawsuits have been pursued in the United States and Europe. Even though few of them have been solved in favour of the plaintiffs, the cases show that companies can face expensive legal processes at home for their behaviour in foreign countries.

What can business do?

The private sector may play an important role as a source of revenue for the main actors in armed conflicts, but its role in preventing and ending conflict is less obvious. Companies

---

ETHICS IN PRACTICE

SOURCES OF CONFLICT

Paul Collier,[10] an economist well-known for his theories on the causes of conflict, argues that civil wars are more likely to be caused by greed than grievance. By this he means that civil wars create economic opportunities for a small but influential group of actors that benefit from conflict and have no reason to end it. Collier argues, based on his research, that even though grievance may be the root cause of many civil wars, economic opportunities often become the main reason for their continuation. For example, the insurgency movement in Colombia has turned from an anti-elitist, leftist rebellion to an economy based on coca trade and kidnappings.

Despite the rhetoric often presented by rebel groups, Collier claims that many civil conflicts are caused and upheld by access to resources that become the main driver of the conflict. Primary commodities are particularly lootable for rebel forces as their remote location gives rebels opportunities to impose their taxes on the trade. Because the origin of primary materials is more difficult to establish than that of manufactured and branded products, they are also easier to sell on international markets. Diamonds are an exceptionally convenient source of money for illegal activities as they can be easily smuggled and their origin is not immediately evident.

Collier's research further suggests that the proportion and availability of young men in society also increases the risk of civil war as most recruits to rebellions are young men. The willingness of these men to join a rebellion depends on the other opportunities they have in life. Collier found that low levels of education increase the willingness of young men to join a rebellion. Conversely, each year of education reduces the risk of conflict by around 20 per cent.

In sum, Collier argues that there are opportunistic businessmen, criminals and rebel organizations that do well out of war and this sustains armed conflicts. Rebel groups will claim narratives of grievance as they are not so naive as to admit greed as a motive. Nevertheless, the end of hostilities would threaten their sources of income and they hence have a reason to sustain conflict.

have only rarely been involved in diplomatic efforts to bring about peace and many observers are of the view that the private sector does not have the legitimacy to engage in peacemaking because of the business relationships companies may have with conflict parties. Instead, the business community has been encouraged to support the efforts of other actors at different stages of the conflict cycle. As seen next, companies can have a role in the main intervention strategies of mediation, sanctions and peacekeeping. In addition, they can contribute to post-conflict reconstruction and reconciliation.

Mediation seeks to bring parties to a potential conflict around the same table to discuss the sources of grievances and aggravation. Such mediation is often led by senior statesmen or UN personnel, though religious organizations and others have also been involved. Companies are not usually viewed as suitable mediators because of the business relationships they may have with one of the parties. Their involvement can also be harmful if the parties use the abundance of willing mediators to gain leverage in negotiations. Companies may still play a positive role by providing a venue, funding or other support for mediation efforts. For example, the private sector supported the negotiations between the ANC and the governing National Party in South Africa by taking members of both sides on fishing trips to facilitate the building of personal relationships across parties.[11]

Arms embargos and economic sanctions may be placed on individuals, groups, or countries to sanction unwanted behaviour. The private sector should uphold any sanctions introduced by legitimate actors, especially the United Nations. This may, however, have effects on competitiveness as the positions of different countries and organizations may not be consistent. The French government, for example, has not banned investment in Burma and has actively lobbied other European countries to prevent the EU from introducing further sanctions on the military dictatorship. Other governments, especially the United States, have applied stricter sanctions with a result of their companies losing business to French companies.

Finally, peacekeeping operations may be deployed to stop tense situations from escalating into a full-blown conflict. They necessitate a situation where the conflicting parties are committed to a peaceful solution to address their grievances. When such commitment has been absent, peacekeeping operations have been unsuccessful as the massacre in Rwanda shows. The private sector has held a minimal role in peacekeeping, but some companies have found ways of engaging in peacekeeping efforts. For example, local entrepreneurs and businesses in the Democratic Republic of Congo assisted the UN peacekeeping mission in the country by facilitating relations to rebel groups and providing information on routes used for smuggling military equipment.[12]

ROLE OF BUSINESS IN POVERTY ALLEVIATION

Many initiatives have been launched over the past ten years to raise awareness and mobilize various actors to help the world's poor. For example, in 2000, the United Nations set forth the Millennium Development Goals, aiming to halve the number of people living in absolute poverty by 2015. Supported by celebrities, the Make Poverty History campaign from 2005 put further pressure on governments to do more for eradicating poverty. The focus of the campaigns has been on governments and international financial institutions, but the private sector has also been called upon to participate in efforts to alleviate poverty. In this section we explore the concept of poverty and the role that business can play in poverty alleviation.

What is poverty?

Poverty is humiliation, the sense of being dependent, and of being forced to accept rudeness, insults, and indifference when we seek help.

– Latvia

Don't ask me what poverty is because you have met it outside my house. Look at the house and count the number of holes. Look at my utensils and the clothes that I am wearing. Look at everything and write what you see. What you see is poverty.

– A poor man from Kenya

Poverty is pain; it feels like a disease. It attacks a person not only materially but also morally. It eats away one's dignity and drives one into total despair.

– A poor woman from Moldova

These quotes highlight the main characteristics of poverty as defined by the poor themselves. The quotes are taken from the discussions that the World Bank held with over 40,000 poor people worldwide.[13] The purpose of the discussions was to listen to the poor and explore poverty from the viewpoint of the poor themselves. The consequent report entitled *Voices of the Poor: Can Anyone Hear Us?*, draws five conclusions about the nature of poverty:

1 **Poverty has physical, material, and psychological dimensions**. Experiences of poverty vary on the basis of location, season and gender, but poverty is always underpinned by the lack of adequate resources to live a meaningful life. The bottom line of poverty is hunger, but the poor also lack access to basic infrastructure and services including clean water, healthcare, education and transportation. The lack of one often leads to the lack of others; for example, illness resulting from the lack of affordable healthcare leads to the lack of income and, over time, food. In addition to material scarcity, poverty has psychological dimensions as illustrated by the above quotes. The poor often feel ashamed by their condition and experience dependency, humiliation and powerlessness.

2 **The state has been ineffective in helping the poor**. The poor encounter rudeness, harassment and stonewalling in their dealings with public officials and are especially defenceless against the corruption and brutality of police forces. Women find it particularly challenging to interact with state institutions due to social norms in many cultures, and it is often men who form the contact with the state while women rely on their informal networks. All in all, the poor believe that government interventions have done little to improve the quality of life for the least advantaged.

3 **The poor depend on friends and informal networks**. The poor rely on informal networks for survival. Such networks provide help and support when needed, but are less efficient in lifting the poor out of poverty. Perhaps surprisingly, the poor have relatively little to do with non-governmental organizations and have mixed views of these organizations. In some environments NGOs serve a positive role while in others they are criticized for being irrelevant, self-serving and corrupt. Overall, it seems that even the largest and most successful charities fail to reach the majority of the poor who are hence left to depend on their friends and communities.

4 **Families suffer under the tensions of poverty**. Many households unravel as poverty questions traditional roles held by men and women. Women often become important

breadwinners by taking up jobs that may be demeaning. Unable to cope with the changing distribution of power and the 'failure' to provide for their family, some men resort to alcoholism and domestic violence. As a result, household structures and families break down and make the situation even harder for the poor to bear.

5 **Social network and support mechanisms are unravelling**. The social fabric that has traditionally provided the poor with a source of support is disintegrating as the stronger and more internally cohesive groups become more self-sufficient and reduce their ties with other groups. The breakdown of connections between groups is enforced by economic scarcity and national politics that abuse ethnic and other differences among the population. Because the poor rely on informal networks and solidarity, the disintegration and division of society affects the poor more than the more affluent groups.

To summarize, poverty is a multifaceted phenomenon that escapes easy solutions. The poor often feel unaffected by government efforts to help them. Instead, they rely on personal contacts that are slowly unravelling in the context of the growing divide between societal groups.

The bottom of the pyramid – who are they?

The World Bank estimates that about 1 billion people live in extreme poverty on less than US$1 per day. The proportion of the world's population living in poverty is however expected to drop if living standards continue to rise across regions. The percentage of people living under the US$1 poverty line has already decreased from 29 per cent of global population in 1990 to 18 per cent in 2004. According to poverty projections, only 10 per cent will live on less than US$1 a day in 2015. Despite the relative decrease in poverty, the absolute number of poor will drop less due to population increases. As a result, the number of poor is forecast to be 624 million in 2015 against 970 million in 2004.[14]

Most of the world's poor live in Asia, but rapid economic growth in the region has resulted in sharp drops in poverty, particularly in China and other countries in east Asia. Poverty has also fallen in south Asia though India has the highest absolute number of poor in the world due to the country's slower economic development and a large population. In contrast, poverty rose from 41 per cent in 1981 to 46 per cent in 2001 in sub-Saharan Africa. Even though the percentage has now started to decrease, the absolute number of poor will increase due to population growth widening the gap between the region and the rest of the world.[15]

At the moment, approximately 4 billion people in the world live on less than US$2 a day. This group of people is increasingly referred to as the bottom of the economic pyramid.[16] The bottom of the pyramid concept was introduced in its current form by C. K. Prahalad and Stuart Hart (2002). They divided the world population into four tiers based on annual per capita income, as seen in Figure 6.2. The top tier is the smallest in numbers but has the most to spend; it consists of middle and upper income people in developed countries and the elites in developing countries. Tiers 2 and 3 include the low-income people in developed countries and the middle classes from developing nations. The fourth and bottom tier consists of the majority of the world's population with an annual capital income of less than US$1500 US dollars. Most companies target the top tiers of the pyramid as their main markets due to the low spending power of the bottom tier. As explained in the next section, it has been argued that the bottom tier can also provide a viable business opportunity for companies across the world.

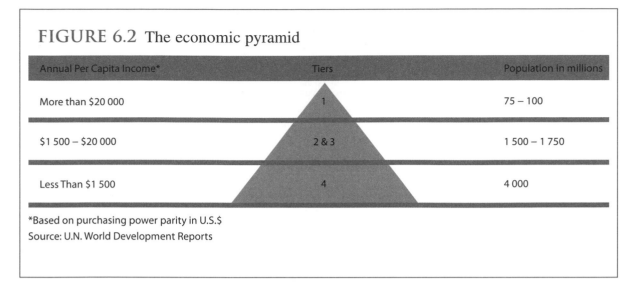

FIGURE 6.2 The economic pyramid

Annual Per Capita Income*	Tiers	Population in millions
More than $20 000	1	75 – 100
$1 500 – $20 000	2 & 3	1 500 – 1 750
Less Than $1 500	4	4 000

*Based on purchasing power parity in U.S.$
Source: U.N. World Development Reports

Helping the poor through business

Prahalad and Hart (2002) argue that the poor provide a business opportunity that has remained largely untapped. The poor do not only represent a large pool of potential customers, but they offer a testing ground for developing environmentally friendly technologies and new products for more affluent markets. Such gains are important in the context of limited natural resources and maturing markets. However, in order to target the poor, businesses are required to change their thinking about market attractiveness, margins, cost and distribution channels. More specifically, the poor are a market where profits are driven by high unit sales and capital efficiency instead of lofty margins.

Prahalad and Hart further argue that targeting the poor does not only bring benefits to companies, it also helps the poor to access services and to reduce their cost of living. For example, many poor communities lack access to affordable banking and financial services, but micro-credit programmes introduced by innovative banks have allowed the poor to avoid moneylenders who sometimes charge more than 10 per cent interest per day. Similarly, providing the poor with a choice of products and services lowers the high prices that they now pay. According to Prahalad and Hart, basic necessities and services like water, food and medication are often more expensive to the poor than to the middle classes due to lack of competition and infrastructure. For example, in the capital of Peru the poor may pay 20 times more than the middle class for water as municipal reserves cannot be accessed from areas inhabited by the poor.

How can businesses then reach the poor? Prahalad and Hammond (2002) identify distribution and adaptation of products and services as the key for reaching the bottom of the pyramid. Distribution is important because poor communities are often physically isolated from the rest of society, and companies have found it difficult to extend their distribution channels to the poor. Creative thinking and innovative solutions are needed to overcome this barrier. An Indian company, Arvind Mills, developed such a solution by introducing a new distribution system for selling jeans. They launched a pack consisting of denim, zipper, rivets and a patch that could easily be stitched together into a pair of jeans. The kit was distributed through a network of tailors who saw a self-interest in marketing the kit in their communities because it would bring them business. In this way, the company cut costs in both distribution and production and was able to sell the jeans kit for about US$6.

In addition to new thinking on distribution, products and services require additional adaptation to be sold to poor families. The poor rarely buy in large quantities as they lack money and space to store household items. As a consequence, products need to be packaged and sold in smaller quantities to make them affordable for the poor. For example, shampoo, tea and medicine can be sold in single-servings rather than in mega-packs. Selling in low volume has, however, negative side-effects. One of these is the larger amount of waste created by single-serve packaging. Also, buying in small quantities tends to be more expensive than buying in large packs as more is spent on packaging and distribution. As a result, companies may be able to reach the poor, but the poor still pay more than the middle class for the same products.

ETHICS IN PRACTICE

HINDUSTAN LEVER – SELLING WASHING POWDER TO THE POOR IN INDIA

More than 70 per cent of India's 1 billion people live in rural areas. Hindustan Lever, a subsidiary of Unilever, has sought many ways to extend its reach to remote villages and communities in rural India. In 2000, it launched a campaign to sell its products to a rural market of 0.5 billion people living in villages spread over large areas with poor transport connections. The rural market was becoming increasingly important as competition for the urban markets was tightening. As a result, the company designed a programme to overcome the difficulties of distributing and selling products in rural communities. The programme was named Shakti, 'strength', to emphasize the empowering role it was expected to play among rural women.

Shakti is a partnership programme between Hindustan Lever and an existing network of self-help groups in rural areas. The self-help groups consist of 10–15 women who contribute money towards a common fund. Once a certain threshold is reached, participating women can apply for micro-credit from a public sector bank or another sponsoring agency. In its research of the rural markets, Hindustan Lever found that women in self-help groups often lacked investment opportunities despite qualifying for micro-credit. As a result, the company partnered a number of self-help groups with the dual objective of providing women with entrepreneurial opportunities and selling products in rural communities.

A Shakti entrepreneur borrows money from a self-help group for purchasing Hindustan Lever products at a reduced rate. She then sells the products in her village to local shops or directly to consumers. The entrepreneurs are supported by sales promoters who coach the Shakti women to create viable businesses. A large proportion of the sales come from sachets of shampoo, detergent, skin cream and other products. The introduction of sachets has been a learning point for Hindustan Lever because until sachet packaging was introduced, penetration of the company's products in poor communities was low as very few could afford to buy them in larger quantities.

In sum, the Shakti programme enables rural women to earn an income and to get business experience and skills. For Hindustan Lever, it provides a distribution channel that is built around women who are the main household decision makers for buying cleaning products and food. Women are also valuable in creating brand-awareness for the company's products as people in poor communities tend to base their decision making on word-of-mouth rather than advertising in mainstream media. Project Shakti broke even in 2004, four years after its initiation, and covers today more than 50,000 rural villages.

Sources: Rangan, V. K and Rajan, R. 2007. *Unilever in India: Hindustan Lever's Project Shakti – Marketing FMCG to the Rural Consumer.* Harvard Business School 9-505-056, Boston, MA, USA.

Vemuri, K. 2004. *Rural Marketing: Indian Experiences.* ICFAI Business School Case Development Centre 504-042-1, Hyderabad, India.

The idea that multinational companies should target the poor has not been received without challenge. Critics have argued that targeting the poor may be a new market for companies, but it provides few benefits for the poor. How, for example, does selling jeans to the poor lessen poverty? Selling to the poor does not necessarily alleviate poverty and improve the quality of life in poor communities. In fact, companies may be creating artificial needs instead of lifting people from poverty. Selling to the poor is not the same as responsible business.[17]

CORRUPTION: FROM BUSINESS AS USUAL TO ECONOMIC MALAISE

A Shell employee recently told a conference on anti-corruption that while he was on a business trip in Nigeria to ensure that his company was taking measures to tackle corruption, he was forced to pay US$20 to a gunman who stopped his car on the way back to the airport. The anecdote highlights some of the dangers and difficulties of fighting corruption. Unwillingness to give bribes or to make other illicit payments may not only close business opportunities, but it can also be physically unsafe. Moreover, corruption can be endemic, extending its reach from everyday interactions to important business deals.

Corruption has been described as a malaise that undermines efforts to pursue economic growth. The World Bank, for example, views corruption as one of the worst obstacles to economic and social development.[18] The Bank believes that corruption is particularly detrimental to the well-being of the poor who are least able to pay the costs of bribery and misuse of power. The United States has also taken a strong stance against corruption. In the context of this denunciation of corruption, it is easy to forget that it was until recently regarded as 'business as usual' to the extent that many European companies were able to claim tax deductions at home in compensation for the bribes they paid in foreign countries. The fight against corruption only took air since the end of the Cold War when the international community came to see it as one of the main obstacles to development.

Corruption is often defined as the misuse of public office for private gain.[19] Dishonesty of public officials has been viewed as particularly detrimental to social and economic

ETHICS IN PRACTICE

BUSINESS AS USUAL?

Until recently, corruption was seen as a normal part of business by many. Adolf Lundin, a successful oil entrepreneur from Sweden, described an intervention with the Emir of Qatar as follows:

> There were delays getting the agreement signed. One day, I told the emir I could predict the weather, and that it would rain the following day at exactly 5:00 o'clock. He laughed and told me that was impossible, so I bet him a million dollars that it would. I lost the bet, he got a million dollars, and I got my oil concession. We drilled the first well on that offshore Qatar concession in 1976. That well hit what is perhaps the biggest gas field in the world: the North Dome field.

Source: *Casey Research Featured Explorer: Adolf Lundin.* Available from http://www.caseyresearch.com/displayExplorer.php?id=107, accessed 29 August 2008.

development. Bribery in the private sector has not been regarded as equally harmful to society. For example, paying a tip to a bouncer to get entry into a busy nightclub is not usually seen to be as damaging as paying a bribe to a customs official to import forbidden goods to a country. One of the reasons for this is that whenever public office is misused, a broader societal goal may be compromised for the benefit of some, while corruption in the private sector is likely to have a more limited impact in society. Also, it is difficult for the private sector to be clean if the government is corrupt and unwilling to uphold the principles of transparency and open competition.

Corruption is sometimes paralleled to taxation. Accordingly, a bribe is like a tax added on a business transaction. Unlike taxes, however, bribes do not raise revenue for the central or local government, but an individual or a group of individuals holding government office. Moreover, deals that have been made through corrupt practices cannot be enforced by law. Corruption hence involves a high degree of uncertainty about the outcomes of corruption. For example, companies may need to make repeat payments in order to maintain the advantage they have obtained through bribery. In some instances, corrupt officials have waited until a company has made expensive infrastructure investments and then gone back to ask for more money. Corruption also distorts competition and the functioning of the free markets by giving an invisible advantage to companies that are ready to pay a bribe or enter into some other illicit arrangement. Nevertheless, a number of arguments have been presented about the benefits of corruption. Some of these will be reviewed below, but first a set of theories explaining levels of corruption is reviewed. The section on corruption concludes with a review of regulation and voluntary initiatives that have emerged to eliminate corruption.

Why are some countries more corrupt than others?

The Ethics in Practice panel shows that some countries are more corrupt than others. A range of explanations has been offered to better understand why levels of corruption differ from one country to another. Some of these explanations are reviewed in the following sub-sections, but it is a combination of factors rather than just one factor that explains the variance in corruption across countries.

Regulatory power of state Some liberal economists argue that corruption is possible when public servants hold power over licences, taxes and other forms of regulation. Conversely, the less power the public sector has, the fewer are the opportunities for corruption available for public sector officials. Because of this, deregulation has been part of the anti-corruption agenda promoted by international agencies such as the World Bank. Others have however pointed out that deregulation may only move corruption from the public sector to the private sector. Moreover, it seems that some countries have become more corrupt after the introduction of market reforms. For example, corruption appears to have increased rather than decreased in post-Soviet Russia. From this it has been concluded that deregulation and other market reforms only work when they are combined with other anti-corruption measures including the example set by political leadership and penalization of corrupt officials.[20]

Economic development It has been noted that countries with lower levels of income are more corrupt than countries with higher levels of income, though there are some exceptions. Evidence from academic research provides consistent support for the relationship between corruption and a country's GDP.[21] Researchers have however struggled to explain the logic behind the relationship. Some have argued that institutions develop in response

WHICH COUNTRIES ARE CORRUPT?

Transparency International ranks countries by levels of corruption (see Figure 6.3). The Index is based on the perceptions held by local business leaders and country experts from risk rating agencies and other independent institutions. Countries that rank lowest in the Index tend to be failed states like Somalia and Iraq, while countries that rank near the top are often Nordic countries. Some Asian countries, including Singapore and Hong Kong, have also ranked well. In general, industrialized countries with high levels of income perform better than developing and post-Soviet countries. Exceptions to this rule include Chile and the Czech Republic, which are ranked as less corrupt than Greece and Italy.

STUDY QUESTIONS

1   Are you surprised by the ranking of any particular country?
2   What are the possible failings of the Index?
3   What are its strengths?
4   How can the Index be used by businesses?

FIGURE 6.3   TI Corruption Perceptions Index 2008

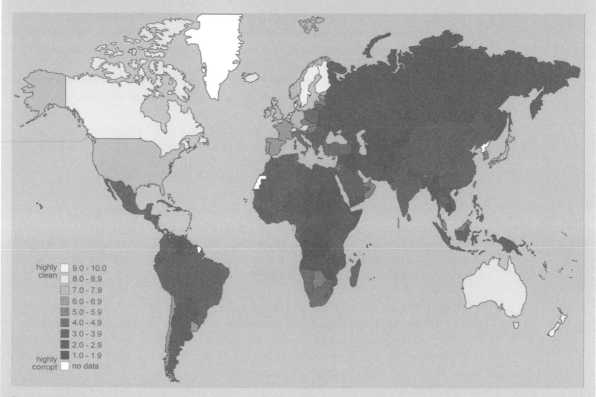

Source: Transparency International.

to a country's income level suggesting that economic growth is the best medicine against corruption.[22] Others have questioned the direction of the relationship by asking whether it is the absence of corruption that makes economic growth possible in the first place. On the whole, however, corruption and economic development are clearly correlated.

Education and human capital The human capital theory suggests that education and corruption are connected because levels of education affect the quality of governmental institutions. For example, standards in legal education have an impact on the efficiency of courts. A certain level of education is also needed in order for the public to keep the government accountable. Findings of academic research support this view on the causes of corruption by showing that corrupt countries have lower levels of human capital measured by years of schooling.[23] Education therefore seems to partly explain why corruption varies from one country to another, but because improving levels of education requires long-term planning and investment, it is rarely included in anti-corruption measures.

Public sector wages Many observers have viewed low wages in the public sector as one of the main causes of corruption.[24] According to this line of reasoning, the less that bureaucrats are paid, the more likely they are to top up their salaries by asking for bribes. In order to address the problem, officials in the Ch'ing dynasty in China were paid extra 'money to nourish honesty'. More recently, countries fighting corruption have introduced a wage premium for public servants to raise their pay above private sector salaries. In some situations, however, higher pay may make public officials ask for higher bribes and in this way amplify the burden of corruption on businesses and private citizens. Research on the issue suggests that wage incentives work only when they are carefully thought out and coupled with other anti-corruption measures. It is particularly important that anti-corruption policies are enforced by an independent body that monitors the public sector. Moreover, it is essential to find an effective penalty for bribe-givers and bribe-takers. This penalty should be important enough to make corruption so costly that it becomes unattractive.

Culture and social norms Sociologists have explained differences in degrees of corruption by reference to social norms. For example, exchange of gifts is in many countries a recognized part of business relationships. Similarly, allegiance to family or ethnic group may in some societies take priority over work roles and responsibilities. It is thus accepted and often expected that holders of public office use their position for the benefit of their own group.[25] Explaining corruption by way of social norms has its limitations. Also, culture changes slowly and makes corruption seem inevitable. Nevertheless, there are examples of how a culture of corruption can be uprooted relatively quickly. For instance, the government of Lee Kuan Yew was able to reduce corruption in Singapore in a period of less than ten years in the 1960s.

Expectations on corruption Finally, some economists have argued that corruption is most likely when a sufficient yet not too high a number of people are believed to be corrupt.[26] Accordingly, corruption does not pay when only a few members of society are corrupt or when most of society is corrupt. In the first situation, it may be difficult to locate the corrupt officials and even though potential gains are high, so are penalties from getting caught. In a situation where most public officials are corrupt, institutions become so weak and ineffective that they cannot be used for even corrupt purposes. Corruption hence depends on the perception that people have of the pervasiveness of dishonesty in society and the public sector.

THINKING CRITICALLY ABOUT ETHICS

WHAT IS THE ROLE OF BUSINESS IN FIGHTING CORRUPTION?

Corruption is often linked to the qualities of a particular country and society. This is why measures to fight corruption reflect this focus on national level action, but is there anything that business can do to discourage corruption? What might be the barriers for this and how can they be addressed?

But is corruption really so bad?

It has been taken for granted until now in this chapter that corruption has negative consequences for the social and economic development of societies. Some observers have argued, however, that there are situations where corruption is not that bad for market efficiency and economic growth. Samuel P. Huntington (1968, p. 386), for example, is of this view: 'In terms of economic growth, the only thing worse than a society with rigid, over-centralized, dishonest bureaucracy is one with a rigid, over-centralized, honest bureaucracy.' According to Huntington, a corrupt government may actually be more efficient than a non-corrupt one. In what follows, some of the arguments presented on the positive effects of corruption are critically reviewed for gaining a better understanding of how dishonesty in the public sector influences business.

Some observers have argued that corruption improves allocation efficiency. This is arguably the case when, for example, a government contract is awarded to the highest bidder who is able to offer the highest bribe as a result of having the lowest production costs.[27] The problem with this argument is that it does not apply to situations where bribery is used to limit competition. For example, a company may pay a corrupt tax inspector to harass a competitor. Moreover, it does not take into account the quality of the goods provided as the lowest bidder may supply goods that are below the desired quality. This may, in turn, eat away the investments made in important public projects. For example, the World Bank has in several instances found that it has funded projects where contractors have used sub-standard materials and technology to build roads that are then wiped out with torrential rain.

It has also been argued that corruption may speed up the slow process of government bureaucracy for those who are willing and able to pay. Bribes paid for this purpose have been referred to as 'speed money' because they help companies and private citizens to overcome cumbersome regulations and inefficiency in the public sector. However, instead of speeding up the wheels of administration, corrupt officials typically slow down the bureaucratic machine.[28] As noted by an Indian official: 'if you want me to move a file faster, I am not sure if I can help you; but if you want me to stop a file I can do it immediately.'[29] Moreover, a study by Kaufmann and Wei (2000) showed that the managers of firms that pay more bribes also spend more rather than less time in dealing with government officials. Moreover, many companies have experienced that officials may demand another bribe in order to keep their side of the deal. Outcomes of corruption are therefore unpredictable and uncertain and do not necessarily speed up the bureaucratic process in the long term.

Finally, some economists have argued that corruption has less adverse consequences when it is centralized as opposed to when it is decentralized.[30] This proposition explains why deregulation and other market reforms exacerbated rather than reduced the negative effects of corruption in post-Soviet Russia. Accordingly, corruption under the Communist Party was effective as the collection of bribes was centralized. A business would hence

ARE LITTLE GIFTS CORRUPTION?

Some students give their lecturers little gifts at the end of the year. Why would some regard this practice as corruption? In your opinion, should the practice be banned or regulated in some way and, if so, how?

only need to pay a bribe once to advance its interests. In contrast, corruption in new Russia is decentralized and therefore less effective and predictable. Companies may need to pay several officials, and even then the outcome is uncertain because the bureaucratic system is less well coordinated.

Fighting corruption: Regulatory measures and voluntary initiatives

Ever since attention and the fight against corruption intensified in the 1990s, an increasing number of measures have been taken to tackle corruption. The international efforts to fight corruption were highlighted by the adoption of the United Nations Convention against Corruption in 2003. By signing the Convention, states can take a stance against corruption and make a commitment to introduce legal and other changes to tackle corruption. Business is also expected to take part in the fight against corruption, which was emphasized by the inclusion of anti-corruption as the tenth principle of the Global Compact in 2004. These developments show that 'corruption is no longer business as usual'.[31] In what follows, measures taken against corruption are discussed as (i) regulatory standards endorsed by governments and (ii) voluntary initiatives launched by businesses and other non-state actors.

Regulatory standards are adopted and enforced by governments. It was the United States that enacted seminal anti-corruption legislation in 1977 through the Foreign Corrupt Practices Act (FCPA) that prohibits companies from bribing foreign officials. The FCPA emerged in response to scandals involving the bribery of government officials in countries like Japan and Italy by major American companies. The penalties provided by the FCPA are serious. For example, Lockheed was given a fine of US$24.8 million in the 1990s for conspiracy to violate provisions of the FCPA, and one of its vice-presidents was also imprisoned for 18 months.[32] Other governments waited until the 1990s to follow the US example of anti-corruption legislation. As a consequence, US companies have been estimated to have lost business deals worth billions of dollars, while less scrupulous foreign competitors gained competitive advantage through bribery and other corrupt practices. Examples of regulatory measures include:

- **US Foreign Corrupt Practices Act (FCPA)**, enacted in 1977, which prohibits US companies from providing anything of value to foreign officials for obtaining or retaining business.

- **EU Convention on Corruption**, adopted in 1997, which considers bribes paid inside and outside the European Union criminal and in this way provides for the prosecution of civil servants from the EU and its members states.

- **OECD Convention on Combating Bribery of Foreign Public Officials in International Business Transactions** from 1999 requires participating countries to introduce and enforce laws that make it a crime for domestic companies to 'offer, promise, or give any undue pecuniary advantage, whether directly or through intermediaries, to any foreign public official' to gain advantage in business relations.

Voluntary initiatives are policies and standards of behaviour that companies and other actors adopt without being obliged to do so. Unlike regulatory measures, voluntary initiatives are discriminatory in the sense that they are often developed and adopted by a small group of like-minded actors. For example, the Extractive Industry Transparency Initiative (see box) was initially launched by an alliance of a few governments, companies, and non-governmental organizations. This is why voluntary initiatives are often seen as examples of 'best practice' or tests of how policy innovations can be implemented in practice. They play an important role in attempting to find innovative solutions to problems stemming from corruption and other issues encountered by multinational companies operating in diverse business environments. Also, voluntary initiatives are often more timely than regulation introduced through the lawmaking process. Examples of voluntary initiatives include:

■ **The Global Compact**, a voluntary initiative set forth by the United Nations, invites companies to 'work against corruption in all its forms, including extortion and bribery' through the development of policies and concrete programmes.

ETHICS IN PRACTICE

EITI: CURBING CORRUPTION IN THE OIL BUSINESS

Many of the largest oil, gas and mining companies in the world have been associated with bribery and facilitation payments in countries where accountability of public institutions and office holders is weak. In 1999, Global Witness, a London-based non-profit organization, published a report called *A Crude Awakening* on the involvement of the international oil and banking industries in the misuse of state assets in Angola. The report called on companies to disclose information about the payments they made to the Angolan government. Inspired by the report, more than 200 non-governmental organizations got together a few years later in 2000 to launch the 'Publish What You Pay' campaign asking companies to make public the payments they made to governments in resource-rich countries. The campaign was formally opened by George Soros, a well-known financial speculator and philanthropist, which stressed the high visibility of the campaign.

The Extractive Industry Transparency Initiative (EITI) was launched in response to the Publish What You Pay campaign. It encourages governments and companies to publish information about the taxes, royalties and fees paid by oil, gas and mining companies to host governments in developing countries. Disclosure of similar information is already common practice in developed countries. The Transparency Initiative was launched by UK Prime Minister Tony Blair in 2002 and can be seen as an effort by the international donor community to promote transparency and good governance in resource-rich countries. It has also received backing from companies that find corruption detrimental to their business interests. As of July 2006, more than 20 governments had endorsed or were actively implementing the Initiative.

Civil society organizations have criticized the Initiative because it relies on governments to take the lead. By doing this, it is likely to exclude the most corrupt countries because civil servants of these economies will avoid committing to a voluntary project that limits their ability to amass financial and other benefits.[33] Civil society organizations have also argued that more focus should be placed on home governments that have an important role to play in encouraging companies to disclose information about their payments in foreign countries. For example, Canadian companies are some of the most transparent companies in the world because it is mandatory for them to disclose information on financial payments on a country-by-country basis.[34]

■ **International Chamber of Commerce Rules against Extortion and Bribery** promote cooperation between governments and companies with an objective to target large-scale corruption involving politicians and senior officials.

■ **The Extractive Industry Transparency Initiative (EITI)** seeks to tackle corruption through encouraging governments to make public the payments made by companies as taxes and fees.

SUMMARY

■ The poor are increasingly seen as a promising market segment. In reaching the poor, companies have encountered challenges in the areas of distribution and product adaptation.

■ Corruption distorts competition and functioning of the free markets by giving an invisible advantage to companies that are ready to pay a bribe. In general, corruption compromises social and organizational goals for the benefit of the few. Outcomes of corruption involve a high degree of uncertainty as deals pursued through bribes and other illicit measures cannot be enforced by law.

■ Few industries gain from violent conflict. Zones of conflict are normally a source of risk and additional expenses for companies. Nevertheless, there are companies that continue to operate in conflict areas, especially in the extractive sector exploiting oil, timber and other natural resources. Such companies have increasingly sought to play a positive role in preventing and ending conflict.

QUICK REVIEW QUESTIONS:

1 What is meant by 'the bottom of the pyramid'? Why is it increasingly seen as a business opportunity?

2 What are the main risks arising from operating in a conflict country?

3 Have you ever given a bribe? Provide details and discuss the wider implications of the bribe on society.

CASE STUDY: CURBING CORRUPTION AT SIEMENS

Siemens is a large engineering and electronics company based in Germany. It is well known to consumers for a wide range of products from dishwashers to computers. In addition to consumer appliances, its businesses cover energy, healthcare, automation and communication technologies. With almost half a million employees and revenues of €72.448 billion in 2007, Siemens has been a role model for German industry and a contributor to the country's reputation of organization, efficiency and quality.

Because of Siemens' reputation, the unfolding of a series of corruption scandals has come as a surprise to the German society. In 2007, two former executives were convicted of bribery. The executives paid about €6 million between 1999 and 2002 to officials of Enel, an Italian energy company, to win a contract valued at €450 million. A year later in 2008, another manager was convicted for diverting company funds into secret bank accounts that were used for bribery. In a separate case, Siemens is alleged to have channelled funds to a friendly labour union that could have 'lamed and tamed' another, less like-minded union. Siemens is also being investigated by the US Securities and Exchange Commission. Unless the company shows that it is taking action to eradicate corruption, it could face high fines in the United States. As a whole, the incidents suggest that corruption has been widespread within Siemens.

The defendants in the Enel case based their defence on arguing that because Enel managers were not public officials, the payments to them do not constitute bribery. In contrast, the prosecutors regarded Enel managers as public officials because the Italian state had a controlling stake in the company at the time when the payments were made. The issue should not arise in the future as Germany has passed a new law to extend the prohibition of bribery to cover people working for all types of organizations including public and private companies.

As a result of the scandals, several senior executives have resigned. Mr. Kleinfeld, Chief Executive Officer, and Mr. von Pierer, Chairman of the supervisory board, both stepped down in 2007, but denied any knowledge of corruption at the company. They have now been sued by Siemens for failing to perform their supervisory responsibilities. In an unprecedented step in German history, the company has filed a lawsuit against altogether 11 former executives who have held a position on the company's management board. The executives are former and current CEOs of major German companies including Deutsche Bank, Allianz and ThyssenKrupp. Because of the high profile of the executives, Siemens is likely to stay in the headlines until the case is closed.

The decision to sue Siemens' executives signals a change in corporate governance in Germany. It suggests that board members will be held personally accountable for ensuring that companies do not engage in corrupt practices. The decision also mirrors the feeling in German society that mistakes made by senior executives should not be paid for by workers while top management is paid unprecedented salaries. Even the conservative parties have suggested that executive pay be restricted.

STUDY QUESTIONS

1 Given that corruption at Siemens came as a surprise to German society, how credible is the Transparency Corruption Index that is based on the perception of business leaders and other observers on the state of corruption in a given country?

2 Siemens has sued its senior managers for failing to carry out their supervisory duties. In your opinion, should senior executives be held personally responsible for corruption that takes place under their management? Would this make corruption less likely?

3 Given that corruption appears to have been institutionalized, what can Siemens do to eradicate this culture?

SOURCES

Boston, W. 2008. Siemens sues its own managers. *Time*, 30 July 2008. Available from http://www.time.com, accessed 5 August 2008.

Dougherty, C. 2007. Bribery trial deepens Siemens woes. *International Herald Tribune*, 13 March 2007. Available from http://www.iht.com, accessed 29 August 2008.

Sims, G. T. 2007. Two former Siemens officials convicted for bribery. *New York Times*, 15 May 2008. Available from http://www.nytimes.com, accessed 29 August 2008.

This case study was prepared using only publicly available sources of information for the purposes of classroom discussion.

NOTES

1. Aubert (1999).
2. Global Policy (2009).
3. Mack (2005).
4. Uppsala Conflict Data Program (2008).
5. http://news.bbc.co.uk/1/hi/world/europe/230215.stm.
6. Risky Returns (2000).
7. Nelson (2000), p. 21.
8. Nelson (2000), p. 23.
9. http://www.thenation.com/doc/20050509/eviatar.
10. Collier (2000).
11. Tripathi & Gündüz (2008), p. 4.
12. Tripathi & Gündüz (2008), p. 4.
13. Narayan (2000).
14. World Bank (2008a).
15. Ibid.
16. Prahalad & Hart (2002); also see Collier (2007).
17. Landrum (2007).
18. World Bank (2008b).
19. Bardhan (1997); Svensson (2005); Treisman (2000).
20. Kaufmann (1997); Rose-Ackerman (1999), pp. 49, 71.
21. Mauro (1995); Sandholtz & Koetzle (2000).
22. Lipset (1960).
23. Svensson (2005).
24. See Bardhan (1997) for a review of the research literature on this topic.
25. Rose-Ackerman (1999), p. 91.
26. Bardhan (1997).
27. Lui (1985).
28. Myrdal (1968).
29. Bardhan (1997).
30. Bardhan (1997).
31. http://www.oecd.org/department/0,2688,en_2649_34855 _1_1_1_1_1,00.html, accessed 4 June 2008.
32. Corr & Lawler (1999).
33. Beyond the Rhetoric (2005a), p. 1.
34. Beyond the Rhetoric (2005b), p. 2.

REFERENCES

Aubert 1999. *Rapport d'Information déposé en application de l'article 145 du Règlement par la Commission des Affaires Etrangères sur le role des companies pétrolierès dans la politique internationale et son impact social et environnemental.* No. 1859. Enrègistre à la Présidence de l'Assemblée national, 13 October 1999.

Bardhan, P. 1997. Corruption and development: A review of issues. *Journal of Economic Literature*, Vol. 35, No. 3, 1320–1346.

Beyond the Rhetoric 2005a. *Measuring Revenue Transparency: Company Performance in the Oil and Gas Industries.* London: Save the Children UK.

Beyond the Rhetoric 2005b. *Home Government Requirements for Disclosure in the Oil and Gas Industries.* London: Save the Children UK.

Collier, P. 2000. Doing well out of war: An economic perspective. In Berdal, M. and Malone, D. M. (eds) *Greed and Grievance: Economic Agendas in Civil Wars.* Lynne Rienner/IDRC.

Collier, P. 2007. *The Bottom Billion.* Oxford: Oxford University Press.

Corr, C. F. and Lawler, J. 1999. Damned if you do, damned if you don't? The OECD Convention and the globalization of anti-bribery measures. *Vanderbilt Journal of Transitional Law*, Vol. 32, 1249–1344.

Global Policy, 2009. Available from http://www.globalpolicy.org/security/natres/diamonds/2001/0412 report.pdf, accessed 12 July 2009.

Huntington, S. 1968. *Political Order in Changing Societies*. New Haven: Yale University Press.

Kaufmann, D. 1997. Corruption: The facts. *Foreign Policy*, No. 107, 114–131.

Kaufmann, D. and Wei, S.-J. (2000). Does 'Grease Money' Speed Up the Wheels of Commerce? *IMF Working Paper*, Vol. 1, 1–22. Available at SSRN: http://ssrn.com/abstract=879552.

Landrum, N. E. 2007. Advancing the 'base of the pyramid' debate. *Strategic Management Review*, Vol. 1, No. 1, 1–12.

Lipset, S. M. 1960. *Political Man: The Social Bases of Politics*. Garden City, NY: Anchor Books.

Lui, F. T. 1985. An equilibrium model of bribery. *Journal of Political Economy*, Vol. 93, No. 4, 760–81.

Mack, A. 2005. Peace on earth? Increasingly, yes. *The Washington Post*, 28 December 2005. Available from http://www.washingtonpost.com, accessed 13 August 2008.

Mauro, P. 1995. Corruption and Growth. *Quarterly Journal of Economics*, Vol. 110, 681–712.

Myrdal, G. 1968. *Asian Drama: An Inquiry into the Poverty of Nations*. New York: Pantheon Books, Twentieth Century Fund.

Narayan, D. 2000. *Voices of the Poor: Can Anyone Hear Us?* Oxford: Oxford University Press.

Nelson, J. 2000. *The Business of Peace: The Private Sector as a Partner in Conflict Prevention and Resolution*. International Alert, Council of Economic Priorities, The Prince of Wales Business Leaders Forum.

Prahalad, C. K. and Hammond, A. 2002. *What Works: Serving the Poor, Profitably: A Private Sector Strategy for Global Digital Opportunity*. World Resources Institute.

Prahalad, C. K. and Hart, S. L. 2002. The Fortune at the Bottom of the Pyramid. *Strategy + Business*, 26.

Risky Returns 2000. *The Economist*, 20 May 2000.

Rose-Ackerman, S. 1999. *Corruption and Government: Causes, Consequences, and Reform*. Cambridge: Cambridge University Press.

Sandholtz, W. and Koetzle, W. 2000. Accounting for Corruption: Economic Structure, Democracy and Trade. *International Studies Quarterly*, Vol. 44, No. 1, 31–50.

Svensson, J. 2005. Eight questions about corruption. *Journal of Economic Perspectives*, Vol. 19, No. 3, 19–42.

Treisman, D. 2000. The causes of corruption: A cross-national study. *Journal of Public Economics*, Vol. 76, 399–457.

Tripathi, S. and Gündüz, C. 2008. A Role for the Private Sector in Peace Processes? Examples, and implications for Third-party Mediation. OSLO Forum 2008 – The OSLO Forum Network of Mediators. Available from http://www.osloforum.org/OSLO%20forum%202008%20-%20Background%20 papers, accessed 17 August 2008.

Uppsala Conflict Data Program, 2008. Uppsala University. Available from www.ucdp.uu.se/database, accessed 29 July 2008.

World Bank 2008a. *Issue Brief: Poverty*. Available from http://go.worldbank.org/RQBDCTUXW0, accessed 23 July 2008.

World Bank 2008b. Available from http://go.worldbank.org/K6AEEPROC0, accessed 3 June 2008.

THE BUSINESS OF HUMAN RIGHTS

INTRODUCTION

Human rights are exceptional in the sense that there is worldwide consensus on a set of rights that are seen as fundamental for the dignity and worth of human beings. Nevertheless, interpretation and respect of human rights varies across countries. Because of this, more pressure has been applied on companies to observe international rather than local standards. In this chapter, we first examine the concept of human rights and the pressures placed on companies to take a more prominent role in advancing human rights. The chapter then turns to assess the ways in which the private sector has sought to ensure that it is complying with international human rights norms.

FROM REGULATORY VACUUM TO HUMAN RIGHTS AS A MANAGEMENT ISSUE

Businesses have been increasingly pressured to consider their role in the promotion and protection of human rights. The attention on companies has taken place against the background of globalization that has given companies more freedom to choose the countries in which they invest. As a result, the power of governments to regulate the private sector has become more limited, and some have argued that companies operate in a situation where markets are global, but human rights standards are not.[1] The absence of common standards has also been referred to as a regulatory vacuum.[2] Accordingly, trade agreements that prioritize free trade to social and environmental concerns have left companies to set their own standards that may conflict with what is expected from them at home.

A number of developments signal the narrowing of the regulatory vacuum. As already seen in the previous chapter, several companies have been sued in the United States and Europe for human rights violations perpetrated abroad. Moreover, state and city governments in the United States and Australia have enacted purchasing laws that prohibit or sanction business interactions between government bodies and companies that operate in countries in which gross human rights violations occur. For example, the Massachusetts Burma law issued in 1996 gives a 10 per cent preference for bids from companies that avoid investing in Burma.[3] Even though some of the purchasing laws have been disputed at the World Trade Organization for forming a constraint to free trade, their introduction has pushed companies to review their approach to human rights.

The United Nations has also taken steps to identify and clarify standards of corporate responsibility with regard to human rights. Notably, it launched the Global Compact that engages companies in ten principles on human rights, labour standards, environmental practices and anti-corruption. By 2006 more than 2300 companies from all over the world had signed up. Another development that highlights the importance given to the topic within the United Nations was the appointment of Secretary-General's Special Representative on the issue of human rights and business in 2005.[4] It is likely that the United Nations will introduce some measures through which concerns can be raised about the behaviour of individual companies even though none have yet been introduced.

As a result of these developments, human rights have become an issue that is taken into account in managerial decision making. According to a survey conducted by the Ashridge Centre for Business and Society, 36 per cent of the largest 500 companies in the world have abandoned a proposed investment and 19 per cent have disinvested from a country because of human rights concerns.[5] Results of another study suggest that many of the largest companies in the world are aware of their human rights responsibilities and think about them in a systematic manner.[6]

WHAT ARE HUMAN RIGHTS?

Human rights are entitlements that one holds by virtue of being a human being.[7] They are therefore held equally by everybody irrespective of gender, nationality, religion, ethnic background or any other attribute that people may have. The equality of human rights may today seem obvious, but it has not always been so. Human rights were first associated with wealthy men who had claimed a right to own property against the monarchic states of early modern

Europe. Accordingly, women, 'savages', servants and wage labourers were excluded from the group of justified rights-holders. Over time, however, an increasing number of groups have claimed their rights. Working men, women, people from countries under colonial rule, and racial, ethnic and religious minorities have all pressed for the recognition of their rights as equal members of society. Human rights have consequently been documented in various declarations and constitutions such as the Declaration of the Rights of Man and the Citizen by the French National Assembly in 1789.

The United Nations Universal Declaration of Human Rights is the most widely accepted collection of human rights standards in the world. It was unanimously[8] adopted by the United Nations General Assembly in 1948 soon after the formation of the United Nations. One of its main purposes was to protect individuals against state abuse, of which the Nazi regime had been an example.[9] Nevertheless, even the Universal Declaration of Human Rights has given rise to debates about the rights it sets forth. For example, the Soviet bloc argued during the Cold War that economic and social rights should be prioritized to civil and political rights because the latter can only be exercised when a certain level of economic development is reached.[10] Today, the opposite view is implied by the continuing refusal of the United States to become party to the International Covenant on Economic, Social and Cultural Rights. The refusal reflects the fact that only a few Americans regard social problems as human rights issues.[11] The Universal Declaration has also been questioned in the name of 'Asian values', which are argued to prioritize community interests and public order over individual rights on which the Universal Declaration is based.[12] In spite of the criticism, the Universal Declaration is regularly evoked by people across the world to call for social and political change (see Table 7.1).

The Universal Declaration and other human rights instruments adopted within the United Nations are not usually seen to provide direct obligations for companies. It is states that are responsible for observing internationally agreed human rights standards in line with the principle of national sovereignty and international law. Still, human rights are not defined in the Universal Declaration with regard to a specific duty-holder.[13] Instead, the Universal Declaration calls on 'every individual and every organ of society [...] to promote respect for these rights and freedoms' (Universal Declaration, 1948). As organs of society, companies and other actors are therefore invited to observe and advocate the human rights standards identified in the Universal Declaration. In practice, companies are accountable only indirectly through laws and regulations introduced at the national level. Nonetheless, the Universal Declaration and the other documents carry moral authority that makes human rights relevant for the private sector.

STATE FAILURE TURNS THE FOCUS ON COMPANIES

Even though the Universal Declaration provides a common standard on human rights norms, the ways in which states interpret, implement and enforce these norms varies. Companies operating in more than one country are faced with a situation where complying with local laws and practice in one country may conflict with what is expected in other countries. The situation seems to be particularly challenging for multinational companies headquartered in Western countries. These companies are pressured to comply with the standards at home when competing with companies from countries such as China, Ukraine and Malaysia that do not encounter similar pressures. Companies have also pointed out that complying with international standards may put them into a situation where they break

TABLE 7.1 Shortened version of the Universal Declaration of Human Rights

Basic rights

Article	1	Right to equality
Article	2	Freedom from discrimination
Article	3	Right to life, liberty, personal security
Article	4	Freedom from slavery
Article	5	Freedom from torture, degrading treatment

Rule of law

Article	6	Right to recognition as a person before the law
Article	7	Right to equality before the law
Article	8	Right to remedy by competent tribunal
Article	9	Freedom from arbitrary arrest, exile
Article	10	Right to fair public hearing
Article	11	Right to be considered innocent until proven guilty
Article	12	Freedom from interference with privacy, family, home and correspondence

Civil and political rights

Article	13	Right to free movement in and out of the country
Article	14	Right to asylum in other countries from persecution
Article	15	Right to a nationality and freedom to change it
Article	16	Right to marriage and family
Article	17	Right to own property
Article	18	Freedom of belief and religion
Article	19	Freedom of opinion and information
Article	20	Right of peaceful assembly and association
Article	21	Right to participate in government and in free elections

Social and economic rights

Article	22	Right to social security
Article	23	Right to desirable work and to join trade unions for the protection of interests
Article	24	Right to rest and leisure
Article	25	Right to adequate living standard
Article	26	Right to education
Article	27	Right to participate in the cultural life of community
Article	28	Right to social order assuring human rights
Article	29	Community duties essential to free and full development
Article	30	Freedom from state or personal interference in the above rights

Source: Human Rights for All 1991, Lawyers for Human Rights (South Africa) and National Institute for Citizen Education in the Law (USA).

local laws. This has been the case in countries where collective action in the workplace is prohibited.

It is the community of human rights activists that has pushed companies to comply with human rights standards. Companies have been under the spotlight especially when host governments have neglected their responsibility to promote and protect human rights. The focus has been on situations where foreign companies have invested in countries where the government has been responsible for systematic human rights violations documented by the United Nations. For example, human rights activists have called on companies to withdraw from Sudan where the government is responsible for gross violations of human rights against ethnic and religious minorities in Darfur and other parts of the country. Such cases emphasize the controversial role of states as the principal protectors and violators of human rights. They also illustrate the pressures placed on companies to take a clear stance on human rights.

Governments have been unwilling to regulate multinational companies domiciled in their country. One reason for this unwillingness stems from the negative effect of regulation on the competitive position of companies.[14] For example, as seen in the previous chapter, anti-corruption legislation enacted in 1977 in the United States put companies incorporated in the country at a disadvantage in comparison to companies domiciled elsewhere. Governments have also been reluctant to apply national laws extraterritorially because it can be seen to violate the sovereignty of other states and, as a result, lead to diplomatic conflict and retaliation.[15]

HUMAN RIGHTS ISSUES VARY BY INDUSTRY

Although most industries have been associated with some human rights concerns, extractive and labour intensive industries have been at the centre of the debate on business and human rights. The human rights concerns encountered by the companies that operate in these two industries have however differed.

In the labour intensive industries, particularly in the textiles and apparel sectors, companies have been linked to human rights abuses in the workplace, including the minimum wage, freedom of association, and health and safety issues.[16] The abuses reflect the important role that labour costs play when companies make decisions about the location of their investment. This phenomenon has been referred to as 'the race to the bottom'.[17] Accordingly, companies relocate from one country to another in the search for low labour costs, which makes governments unwilling to enforce human rights standards. As a result, countries providing low-cost labour get involved in a cycle that weakens rather than strengthens the respect for human rights. Critics have however drawn attention to the fact that many countries have avoided the race to the bottom by using a pool of low-cost labour as a stepping stone for economic and political progress. South Korea and Malaysia are often given as examples of countries that have successfully used low-cost labour as a road to economic growth.

In the extractive industries, companies have often been accused of complicity in the human rights violations perpetrated by host governments. This criticism stems from what is seen as a strong relationship between extractive companies and state institutions. The relationship is strong because companies seek to foster and maintain contacts with host government authorities who control access to natural resources. The relationship is also strong because foreign investment by extractive companies is the main source of income for many resource-rich governments. As a result, the interests of companies and host

ETHICS IN PRACTICE

NIKE AND HUMAN RIGHTS

Nike was heavily criticized in the 1990s for buying footballs from companies that used child labour in Pakistan. The company's initial reaction was to withdraw from the country, but it later decided to stay and established measures to ensure the respect of labour standards in its supply chain. Despite these measures, there have been concerns over the continuing use of child labour and breaches of other labour rights in Pakistan. In 2006, Nike reacted to the concerns by shifting its football production to China and Thailand. This, however, had a harmful effect on employment in the area where football production takes place in Pakistan. A local newspaper commented on the decision as follows: 'By severing its contract with the local company, Nike scored moral points with its customers in the West at the expense of 20,000 families who were affected, since 70 per cent of local workers relied on Saga Sports for employment.' Since then, Nike has reviewed its decision and contracted with another supplier from the same region after receiving assurances from the Pakistani government and the new supplier that labour standards would be respected.

Sources: Business and Human Rights Resource Centre 2009. Nike, available from http://www.business-humanrights.org/Categories/Individualcompanies/N/Nike, accessed 3 July 2009.
    Fazl-e-Haider, S. 2007. Nike bounces back in Pakistan. *Asia Times Online*, available from http://www.atimes.com/atimes/South_Asia/IE31Df02.html, accessed 3 July 2009.

governments have been seen to collide and companies have been associated with human rights violations committed by state organs. The violations have included forced labour, forcible relocation of people, and any human rights violations perpetrated by government forces providing security for foreign companies.

IMPACT OF FOREIGN INVESTMENT ON HUMAN RIGHTS

Foreign investment has often been seen to have a negative influence on human rights in developing countries. Notably, Stephen Hymer argued in 1976 that multinational companies ally with repressive regimes to maintain their financial dominance and to keep the poorest groups in these countries in a position where they cannot challenge the prevailing system. Hymer's argument was supported by the behaviour of a number of multinational companies that colluded with repressive regimes in the 1970s and early 1980s: United Fruit assisted in overthrowing the government in Guatemala, ITT played a role in ousting the Allende government in Chile, and several oil and gas companies forged relationships with dictatorships in Africa.[18]

The changes in the scope and nature of foreign investment since the 1970s have made Hymer's argument obsolete. Many companies now invest abroad in the search for new customers that have sufficient buying power to purchase their products. Such companies gain from the economic and social development of all segments of the society, making Hymer's argument outdated. Moreover, a number of authors have argued that, in general, foreign investment has a positive impact on the condition of human rights. Debora Spar (1999), for example, contends that foreign investment in developing countries influences

SHOULD COMPANIES WITHDRAW FROM REPRESSIVE REGIMES?

Many companies have been called upon to withdraw from countries where the government is responsible for systematic violations of human rights. Such calls are based on the belief that foreign investment provides financial and moral support for repressive governments. For example, argued the Karen Human Rights Group about the role of foreign companies in Burma:

> [I]n the case of Burma, foreign investment directly leads to suffering. [...] The profits from these joint ventures stay with the military and are used to expand the Swiss bank accounts of junta members and to expand and arm the grossly oversized Army, which exists in the absence of any foreign threat, only to crush its own people.

Other human rights advocates have asked companies to use their power in other ways to put pressure on the government. For example, Christian Aid has asked companies operating in Sudan to suspend their operations in the country in order to apply pressure on the government and in this way to promote the respect for human rights:

> Christian Aid is not calling for the operational oil companies to sell their concessions, nor to relinquish their investment in the Sudanese oil industry. But they must send a clear message to the government of the Sudan that it is unacceptable to violate human rights and humanitarian law in order to assist the production of oil.

Many companies have withdrawn in response to such arguments, while others have insisted that their activities set an example on international standards for the repressive authorities. For example, Premier Oil in one of its annual reports stated:

> In any global business, judgements have to be made about doing business in countries that have political systems that are criticized by the international community. [...] However, we believe that the development of an emerging country's energy resources is one of the prime requisites for long-term economic growth. We believe that the high standards of employment and welfare we set are seen as an example of what can be achieved and what is globally acceptable.

Companies have also presented other arguments about their positive impact on human rights. Total, for example, has argued that the presence of international companies is the best way of enforcing the process of normalization and respect for human rights in regimes where systematic human rights violations occur. Companies have also asserted that economic development is a step towards the respect for human rights; Talisman Energy has expressed this argument in the following way:

> The Canadian Government has expressed the view that 'trade leads to development, and development leads to respect of human rights and leads to respect of democracy'. We believe that this will be the case in Sudan.

Sources: Christian Aid 2001. *Scorched Earth*. Available from http:www.christian-aid.org.uk, accessed on 15 June 2006.
Karen Human Rights Group 1995. *Conditions in the Gas Pipeline Area*. Available from http://www.ibiblio.org/freeburma/humanrights/khrg, accessed on 26 February 2004.
Premier Oil 1998. *Annual Report and Accounts 1998*. Available from http://www.premier-oil.co.uk, accessed on 18 August 2002.
Talisman 2000. *Corporate Social Responsibility Report*. Available from http://www.talisman-energy.com, accessed on 2 August 2006.
Total 2002. *Sharing Our Energies: Corporate Social Responsibility Report*. Available from http://www.total.com, accessed on 5 June 2004.

the local environment in a positive way because the working standards of Western companies are nearly always higher than those of the host country. Positive changes may also result from the public scrutiny exercised by human rights activists and the media. For example, after being criticized for excessive use of water in its factories, Coca-Cola has now launched programmes to secure access to fresh water in several communities in Africa and Asia.

Recent case studies on the impact of foreign investment on human rights suggest that companies need to take special measures to ensure that their influence on human rights is positive, and even then foreign investment may worsen the condition of human rights.[19] Manby (1999), for example, posited on the basis of his study of how Shell and Chevron became associated with human rights violations in Nigeria that multinational companies need to adopt substantive measures to ensure that their presence enhances the respect for human rights. Idahosa (2002) went further by arguing that companies cannot make a meaningful contribution to development or human rights in the absence of democracy and conflict. His argument was based on the analysis of the effect of Talisman Oil on human rights violations in Sudan. He concluded that foreign investment can provide a repressive government with a reason and financial means to violate human rights.

BUSINESSES AS HUMAN RIGHTS ADVOCATES

Given that the current debate on business and human rights is more than ten years old, attention has increasingly been shifting from whether companies have a role to play in human rights advocacy to what they can actually do to advance human rights. Some of the most commonly used approaches include the adoption of human rights policies, human rights impact assessments and the monitoring of human rights.

Human rights policies

Companies are increasingly stating their commitment to human rights in their general business principles and specific human rights policies. A study conducted in 2006 found that nearly 80 per cent of the Fortune Global 500 companies had incorporated human rights principles into their policies or management practice.[20] These policies often refer to the Universal Declaration of Human Rights and other documents developed by the United Nations and its agencies. For example, Nokia refers to several international agreements in its code of conduct:

> *Nokia will respect and promote human rights. Nokia recognizes, with the international community, that certain human rights should be considered fundamental and universal, based on accepted international laws and practices, such as those of the United Nations Universal Declaration of Human Rights, International Labour Organization and Global Compact principles.[21]*

Human rights impact assessment

Impact assessments are carried out to determine the effect of proposed investments on human rights before final investment decisions are made. They involve the identification of the main human rights issues that may be encountered in a particular operational environment as well as the assessment of actual and potential human rights impacts of the proposed project. In 2006, 40 per cent of the largest 500 companies in the world routinely conducted human rights impact assessments and a slightly higher number did so occasionally.[22] Impact assessments have resulted in companies deciding against proposed investments,[23] but they have also been used to introduce measures to reduce the negative impact that an investment may have. For example, an oil company may decide to move the route of a pipeline if this helps it to avoid impacting a community's right to ancestral land.

Human rights monitoring

Human rights monitoring refers to a system through which companies monitor the state of human rights in a particular geographical area. According to the above-mentioned study of Fortune Global 500, nearly 90 per cent of the companies that have adopted human rights policies have in place an *internal* system of monitoring and reporting.[24] Companies may also employ *external* organizations for the monitoring, or use a combination of internal and external monitors. The use of external monitors is popular because they bring in experience that businesses may not have and increase the credibility of the monitoring. British Petroleum, for example, set up a committee consisting of both internal and external actors to monitor the human rights performance of the Colombian military units that provide security for the company's operations in Colombia.

VOLUNTARY STEPS TOWARDS HUMAN RIGHTS

A large number of voluntary initiatives including principles, certification schemes and financial indices have been launched since the mid-1990s. Over 200 such initiatives making reference to human rights were identified in 2005.[25] In what follows, we review some of the most important initiatives: the Global Compact; the OECD Guidelines for Multinational Enterprises; and the ILO Tripartite Declaration of Principles Concerning Multinational Enterprises. The three initiatives carry considerable authority because of the intergovernmental character of the organizations that are behind them. They also have a spill-over effect as a number of financial indices and certification schemes require companies to make a statement of commitment to at least one of them. The Global Compact Office has deliberately sought to enhance the spill-over effect by engaging stock markets and financial market analysts in their efforts.[26]

The United Nations Global Compact

The Global Compact initiative was launched in 2000 by Kofi Annan, then Secretary-General of the United Nations. It is currently the most popular voluntary initiative in the area of business and human rights with about 3000 company participants. It is designed for promoting and sharing good practice in relation to ten principles derived from international treaties and declarations in the areas of human rights, labour standards, the environment and anti-corruption. Participation by companies signals a commitment to the improvement of performance over time rather than a full realization of the ten human rights principles.

Principle two of the Global Compact asks companies to make sure that they are not complicit in human rights abuses. This has given rise to a debate on what corporate complicity in human rights offence involves. The discussion has focused on situations where companies have assisted in, benefited from, or failed to use their power to oppose the human rights violations carried out by host government authorities. It has also involved the boundaries of responsibility between companies and their sub-contractors or suppliers. In general, the inclusion of the concept of complicity in the Global Compact demonstrates that corporate responsibility for human rights is increasingly considered to extend beyond the immediate acts of companies to the behaviour of other connected actors.

The participating companies are expected to report on their progress in implementing the principles. Failure to do so results in the company being publicly listed as a 'non-communicating company'. Companies are therefore pressured through the watchdog role of the media and non-governmental organizations to report on the steps that they have taken in support of the Compact (see Figure 7.1). This has not satisfied critics who allege that some of the participants join the Compact to 'bluewash'[27] their image without a serious commitment to human rights.[28] The Compact has also been criticized for the lack of an effective monitoring system as the current system makes it possible for companies to report on the issues of their own choice even if they are performing poorly in another area of the Compact.

In sum, the Global Compact is designed for promoting and sharing good practice rather than introducing binding obligations on companies. It invites companies to consider how they can take account of human rights instead of setting out specific provisions for companies. The Compact is therefore an essentially promotional tool with limited specificity on rights. At its best, the Compact represents the vanguard of companies that seek to translate internationally recognized human rights standards into corporate practice.

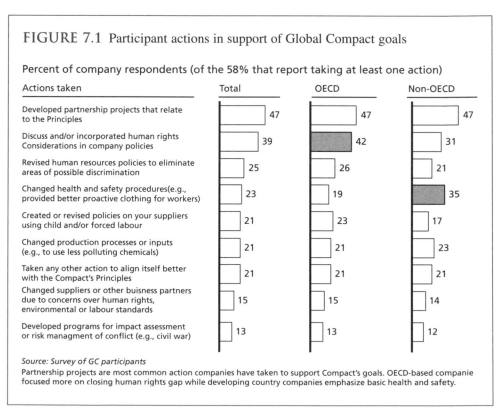

FIGURE 7.1 Participant actions in support of Global Compact goals

Percent of company respondents (of the 58% that report taking at least one action)

Actions taken	Total	OECD	Non-OECD
Developed partnership projects that relate to the Principles	47	47	47
Discuss and/or incorporated human rights Considerations in company policies	39	42	31
Revised human resources policies to eliminate areas of possible discrimination	25	26	21
Changed health and safety procedures(e.g., provided better proactive clothing for workers)	23	19	35
Created or revised policies on your suppliers using child and/or forced labour	21	23	17
Changed production processes or inputs (e.g., to use less polluting chemicals)	21	21	23
Taken any other action to align itself better with the Compact's Principles	21	21	21
Changed suppliers or other buisness partners due to concerns over human rights, environmental or labour standards	15	15	14
Developed programs for impact assessment or risk managment of conflict (e.g., civil war)	13	13	12

Source: Survey of GC participants
Partnership projects are most common action companies have taken to support Compact's goals. OECD-based companie focused more on closing human rights gap while developing country companies emphasize basic health and safety.

Source: McKinsey (2004).

The popularity of the Compact among companies suggests that the business community finds it useful. Yet, the Compact remains contentious in the eyes of human rights groups that advocate binding regulation rather than voluntary initiatives. Indeed, as Figure 7.1 shows, the Compact seems to promote human rights standards among companies that have already decided to take into account human rights standards.

The OECD Guidelines for Multinational Enterprises

The Guidelines are recommendations by governments to multinational companies. They were first launched in 1976, but reviewed and relaunched in 2000 with significant changes. They encompass a broad range of issues from competition to sustainable development. In terms of human rights, they require companies to 'respect the human rights of those affected by their activities consistent with the host government's international obligations and commitments'. They also make reference to a number of labour rights including freedom of association and abolition of child labour.

The Guidelines do not only apply to companies incorporated in the 38 adhering OECD countries. The renewed Guidelines extended the coverage from companies operating *in* OECD countries to also include companies operating *from* OECD countries. This means that the Guidelines apply to the behaviour of OECD companies wherever they operate in the world. Moreover, the renewed Guidelines ask companies to encourage their business partners and sub-contractors to observe the Guidelines. In this way, the Guidelines also apply to companies from non-OECD countries when these are in a business relationship with a company from an OECD country. The extension of the coverage of the OECD guidelines therefore made them relevant for scrutinizing the behaviour of Western multi-nationals in developing countries.

The promotion of the Guidelines takes place through National Contact Points that are also responsible for gathering information on experiences with the Guidelines, discussing related matters, assisting in solving problems that may arise and dealing with enquiries relating to the Guidelines. Moreover, any individual or organization can ask the National Contact Points to investigate 'specific instances' relating to the behaviour of companies in relation to the Guidelines. By 2004, the National Contact Points had considered 79 such instances. Critics[29] have however noted that the National Contact Points do not provide sufficient information on the investigation of specific instances to build confidence in the implementation of the Guidelines. Critics have also alleged that few of the National Contact Points are actively promoting the Guidelines.

The inclusion of new human rights principles and the expanding coverage of the OECD Guidelines demonstrate that companies are increasingly expected to consider the impact of their operations on human rights and abide by human rights standards. Even though the Guidelines are not solely focused on human rights, they provide some clarification on what is expected from companies in terms of human rights and make available a channel for enquiring into the behaviour of companies with respect to human rights.

The ILO Tripartite Declaration of Principles Concerning Multinational Enterprises

This Declaration is addressed to multinational enterprises and all three types of ILO members, including governments and employer's and worker's organizations. It makes specific reference to the Universal Declaration: 'All the parties concerned by this Declaration ... should respect the Universal Declaration of Human Rights and the corresponding international

IMPOSING VALUES?

Some developing countries have argued that Western countries are enforcing their values on other coun-tries through instruments such as the OECD Guidelines. Accordingly, by requiring companies to behave in a certain way anywhere in the world, Western countries are imposing their values on other countries.

What is your view on this? Are there situations where this is acceptable and others where it is not?

Covenants adopted by the General Assembly of the United Nations' (para 8). Its main body covers the four fundamental labour rights identified in the ILO Declaration on Fundamental Principles and Rights at Work (1998): (1) freedom of association and the right to collective bargaining; (2) the elimination of forced or compulsory labour; (3) the abolition of child labour; and (4) the elimination of discrimination in respect of employment and occupation.

The implementation procedure consists of three elements: a periodic survey whereby the permanent members of the ILO provide information on their experiences in imple-menting the Declaration; a clarification procedure for interpreting the Declaration; and promotional and research activities. It therefore enables the permanent members of the ILO, including worker's organizations, to scrutinize and document the behaviour of com-panies with regard to key labour standards. These reports are made publicly available, but only after the names of companies have been taken out.

Like the OECD Guidelines, the ILO Declaration is a normative instrument that shows that companies are expected to abide by internationally recognized human rights stand-ards. Focused on labour rights, it is a more specialized initiative than the OECD Guide-lines, but covers a wider number of countries and other actors including employer's and worker's organizations. Overall, it has attracted less attention than the OECD Guidelines, which may reflect the decision to exclude outside actors, including human rights organiza-tions, from using the implementation procedures.

In sum, voluntary initiatives shed light on emerging standards and practice in the area of business and human rights. They set forth principles on corporate behaviour and, with the exception of the Global Compact, cover a variety of issues, not only human rights. The substance of the initiatives frequently overlaps. For example, the Global Compact and the ILO Tripartite Declaration of Principles Concerning Multinational Enterprises both include principles on the fundamental labour standards as identified in the ILO Declaration on Fundamental Principles and Rights at Work (1998). All the initiatives specify proce-dures for implementation, but, because of their non-binding nature, express what is expected from companies rather than signal strict monitoring of compliance.

SUMMARY

- Human rights are entitlements considered fundamental for the dignity and worth of human beings. The most widely known collection of human rights, the Universal Declaration of Human Rights, represents consensus among states on standards that apply to all human beings without discrimination.

- Countries interpret and implement their human rights obligations through national legislation. Because laws and their enforcement vary from one country to another, expectations placed on companies also differ. High-profile scandals involving Western companies in developing countries have drawn attention to the behaviour of companies that have been increasingly called upon to comply with international best practice rather than local standards.

- The impact of foreign investment on human rights in developing countries is not clear. On the one hand, there is evidence to show that foreign companies have colluded with repressive regimes and exploited local populations for the benefit of international elites. On the other hand, foreign companies are argued to have a positive impact on human rights as they usually apply higher human rights standards than local businesses.

- Companies have introduced human rights policies and monitoring to ensure that they are complying with internationally recognized human rights standards. In addition, businesses are increasingly assessing the impact of proposed investment projects on human rights. Companies have also joined voluntary initiatives to enhance their reputation and share experiences on human rights policy and practice.

- The Global Compact is currently the most popular voluntary initiative in the area of human rights. It has brought together companies from the industrialized and developing world with the exception of American businesses. Other initiatives with worldwide relevance and important enforcement mechanisms include the OECD Guidelines for Multinational Enterprises and the ILO Tripartite Declaration of Principles Concerning Multinational Enterprises.

QUICK REVIEW QUESTIONS

1 Given that the main responsibility for the protection of human rights rests with governments, to what extent can companies be expected to promote and protect human rights?

2 What is the impact of foreign investment on human rights?

3 Compare the strengths and weaknesses of the different voluntary initiatives that have been launched in the area of business and human rights.

CASE STUDY: NOT MARRIED? YOU ARE FIRED!

Iranian newspapers reported in 2008 that a large state-owned company had asked its employees to marry or risk redundancy. The company, Pars Special Economic Energy Zone Company, is reported to have stated in a directive that marrying is a job requirement: 'As being married is one of the criteria for employment, we are announcing for the last time that all the female and male colleagues have until September 21 to go ahead with this important and moral religious duty.' Observers believe the directive reflects worries about the number of prostitutes in the area of the Gulf coast where the company operates. The ruling can also be seen as a way to enforce Iranian law that forbids sexual relations outside marriage.

The directive was reported on the BBC's website and received an array of comments from readers. One reader reported a similar experience with an Iranian company even though he is based in Berlin, Germany: 'I have one month to get married although I have no girlfriend.' Another one wrote that he had married a girl as a result of receiving a similar note from his employer, but regretted his decision as he was fired for other reasons some time after the marriage.

Requiring employees to have a particular marital status is discrimination as defined by the Universal Declaration of Human Rights. The declaration specifically states in its Article 2 that rights and freedoms apply to everybody 'without distinction of any kind, such as race, colour, sex, language, religion, political or other opinion, national or social origin, property, birth or other status.' Setting rules on marital status is also against the spirit of Article 16, which sets out the right to marry and found a family. The article states that 'marriage shall be entered into only with the free and full consent of the intending spouses'. Marriage entered under pressure of redundancy is not free in the sense implied by the Universal Declaration.

In contrast to the request of the Iranian company, many companies expect their workers to be unmarried and not to have children. For example, factories employing low-cost labour in developing countries often prefer to employ young, single women who can work longer hours and may be in a weak position to claim their rights. The problem is not limited to developing countries. Alan Sugar, a businessman who features in the British version of *The Apprentice*, has questioned the law that forbids employers in the United Kingdom from asking interview candidates whether they plan to marry or have children. Sugar believes it is better for women to be open about the topic rather than to leave the interviewers guessing whether a candidate's home life will disrupt her work.

Discrimination based on marital status has recently been addressed by the Chinese government, which enacted a new employment law in January 2008. The law prohibits employers from discriminating against women as regards their getting married or bearing children. Most Western countries have similar legislation in place though it is not always followed by employers. Nevertheless, when discriminated against, women have access to employment tribunals that have penalized employers on the basis of sex discrimination. For example, a female sales executive in the United Kingdom was recently granted up to £200,000 for being told by her boss that she would be 'useless' because of her pregnancy.

STUDY QUESTIONS

1 Iran has not signed the Universal Declaration of Human Rights. Does this mean that Iranian people do not have the same rights as people from states that are signatories?

2 In what situations do companies prefer to employ people who are married/unmarried?

3 Do you feel uncomfortable about revealing your marital status in a job interview? Why is this?

SOURCES

Cochrane, K. 2008. You're fired. *The Guardian*, 23 April 2008. Available from http://www.guardian.co.uk/money/2008/apr/23/worklifebalance.discriminationatwork/print, accessed 4 September 2008.

Executive was told she was 'useless' pregnant 2008. *The Telegraph*, 8 January 2008. Available from http://www.telegraph.co.uk/news/uknews/1574918/Executive-was-told-she-was-'useless'-pregnant.html, accessed 4 September 2008.

Marry or lose job, says Iran firm 2008. *BBC News*, 10 June 2008. Available from http://news.bbc.co.uk/1/hi/world/middle_east/7447227.stm, accessed 4 September 2008.

MOLLS issues new rules on Chinese labour employment 2007. ChinaCSR.com, 12 November 2007. Available from http://www.chinacsr.com/en/2007/11/12/1844-molss-issues-new-rules-on-chinese-labor-employment/, accessed 4 September 2008.

NOTES

1. Leighton, Roht-Arriaza & Zarsky (2002), p. 5.
2. Cragg (2000).
3. Amnesty International and the Prince of Wales International Business Leaders Forum (2002), 81–82.
4. United Nations (2006).
5. Wilson & Gribben (2000).
6. United Nations (2005).
7. Donnelly (1998) p. 18.
8. Out of the 56 member states that the United Nations had in 1948, 48 voted in favour of the Universal Declaration and eight abstained (Saudi Arabia, South Africa and the Soviet Union, together with four east European countries and a Soviet republic; Steiner & Alston, 2000, p. 138).
9. See, e.g., Muchlinski (2001).
10. See, e.g., Donnelly (1998), p. 7; Muchlinski (2001).
11. Donnelly (2003).
12. Steiner & Alston (2000), pp. 334–335.
13. Clapham (2006), p. 34.
14. Forsythe (2001); Joseph (2000).
15. Muchlinski (1999), p. 111.
16. Spar (1999); United Nations (2006).
17. Spar (1998).
18. Spar (1998, 1999).
19. Manby (1999); Wheeler *et al.* (2002); Idahosa (2002).
20. United Nations (2006).
21. Nokia Code of Conduct. Available from http://www.nokia.com/A4254189#Human_Rights, accessed 8 September 2008.
22. United Nations (2006).
23. Wilson & Gribben (2000).
24. United Nations (2006).
25. United Nations (2005).
26. McKinsey (2004).
27. The term refers to the colour of the UN logo.
28. For this and other criticism of the Global Compact, see Williams (2004).
29. OECD Watch (2003).

REFERENCES

Amnesty International and the Prince of Wales International Business Leaders Forum 2002. *Business and Human Rights: A Geography of Corporate Risk*. Available from http://www.humanrightsrisk.org, accessed 18 August 2003.

Clapham, A. 2006. *Human Rights Obligations of Non-State Actors*. Oxford: Oxford University Press.

Cragg, W. 2000. Human rights and business ethics: Fashioning a new social contract. *Journal of Business Ethics*, Vol. 27, No. 1/2, 205–214.

Donnelly, J. 1998. *International Human Rights*. Boulder: WestviewPress.

Donnelly, J. 2003. *Universal Human Rights in Theory and Practice*. Second edition. London: Cornell University Press.

Forsythe, D. P. 2001. *The Political Economy of Human Rights: Transnational Corporations*. Available from http://www.du.edu/humanrights/workingpapers/papers/14-forsythe-03-01.pdf, accessed 4 April 2001.

Hymer, S. H. 1976. *The International Operations of National Firms: A Study of Direct Foreign Investment*. Cambridge, MA: The MIT Press.

Idahosa, P. 2002. Business ethics and development in conflict (zones): The case of Talisman Oil. *Journal of Business Ethics*, Vol. 39, No. 3, 227–246.

Joseph, S. 2000. An overview of the human rights accountability of multinational enterprises. In Kamminga, M. T. and Zia-Zarifi, S. (eds) *Liability of Multinational Corporations Under International Law*. The Hague: Kluwer Law Publishers.

Leighton, M, Roht-Arriaza, N. and Zarsky, L. 2002. *Beyond Good Deeds: Case Studies and a New Policy Agenda for Corporate Accountability*. San Francisco: Nautilus Institute for Security and Sustainable Development.

Manby, B. 1999. The role and responsibility of oil multinationals in Nigeria. *Journal of International Affairs*, Vol. 53, No. 1, 281–301.

McKinsey 2004. *Assessing the Global Compact's Impact*. Available from http://www.unglobalcompact. org, accessed 18 June 2006.

Muchlinski, P. T. 1999. *Multinational Enterprises and the Law*. Oxford: Blackwell Publishers.

Muchlinski, P. T. 2001. Human rights and multinationals: Is there a problem? *International Affairs*, Vol. 77, No. 1, 31–47.

OECD Guidelines for Multinational Enterprises 2006. Available from http://www.olis.oecd.org/olis/ 2000doc.nsf/LinkTo/daffe-ime(2000)20, accessed 20 July 2006.

OECD Watch 2003. Review of National Contact Points June 2002–2003, 20 June 2003. [Online.] Available from http://www.oecdwatch.org/docs, accessed 8 September 2008.

Spar, D. L. 1998. The spotlight and the bottom line: How multinationals export human rights. *Foreign Affairs*, Vol. 77, No. 2, 7–12.

Spar, D. L. 1999. Foreign investment and human rights. *Challenge*, Vol. 42, No. 1, 55–80.

Steiner, H. J. and Alston, P. (eds) 2000. *International Human Rights in Context: Law, Politics, Morals*. Second edition. Oxford: Oxford University Press.

United Nations 2005. Report of the United Nations Commissioner on Human Rights on the responsibilities of transnational corporations and related business enterprises with regard to human rights, E/CN.4/2005/91, 15 February 2005.

United Nations 2006. *Draft Interim Report of the Secretary-General's Special Representative on the Issue of Human Rights and Transnational Corporations and Other Business Enterprises*, E/CN.4/2006/97, February 2006.

Wheeler, D., Fabig, H. and Boele, R. 2002. Paradoxes and dilemmas for stakeholder responsive firms in the extractive sector: Lessons from the case of Shell and the Ogoni. *Journal of Business Ethics*, Vol. 39, No. 3, 297–318.

Williams, O. F. 2004. The UN Global Compact: The challenge and the promise. *Business Ethics Quarterly*, Vol. 14, Issue 4, 278–286.

Wilson, A. and Gribben, C. 2000. *Business Responses to Human Rights*. Ashridge: Ashridge Centre for Business and Society.

CIVIL SOCIETY ORGANIZATIONS

After studying this chapter you should be able to:

- Critically appraise the different meanings of the term 'civil society organization'.

- Discuss the functions of civil society organizations in relation to those of the state and the market.

- Elaborate on the relationships that civil society organizations have with the business sector.

- Describe and give examples of the tactics that civil society organizations use to influence companies and other actors.

- Categorize the different ways in which companies have responded to issues raised by civil society groups.

INTRODUCTION

We have seen in the preceding chapters how contextual influences affect business activity. In this chapter, the focus is on civil society organizations and how they have challenged the way in which corporate operations are run. As discussed in the case study at the end of the chapter, Nestlé was one of the first companies to experience civil society pressure, but similar scrutiny is now commonplace and applied to many companies. The chapter begins with a general discussion of civil society to shed light on the legitimacy and power of civil society organizations. It then moves on to discuss the tactics used by such groups to influence corporate behaviour, before concluding with a summary of corporate responses to civil society pressure.

Civil society organizations (also called non-governmental organizations, or NGOs for short) encompass associations ranging from sports clubs and religious groups to campaign and advocacy organizations such as the World Wildlife Fund and Friends of the Earth.

The expansion of democracy after the end of the Cold War has enabled civil society organizations to flourish not only in the 'old' democracies of the West, but also in other regions, such as in Russia and eastern Europe. At the same time, civil society groups have become increasingly skilled in putting pressure on governments, international organizations and corporations alike. The focus on the corporate sector has been driven by non-governmental organizations such as Greenpeace and Amnesty, which are experienced in influencing governments and have more recently turned their attention to companies. As a result, business organizations have been pushed to consider their roles and impacts in society, both at home and abroad.

Progress in communication technology has enhanced the connections between civil society organizations located in different countries, and thus made corporations more vulnerable to charges of misconduct in far-away places. The internet has been particularly important in increasing the reach and scope of those civil society groups that previously functioned locally, without the means to communicate their concerns to larger audiences.[1] Today, companies are scrutinized by networks of activist groups that are in contact with each other and capable of mobilizing media coverage for issues of their choice. One British Petroleum manager has stressed the extent of this scrutiny by saying that 'there is nowhere to hide'.[2]

The attention of non-governmental organizations has centred on multinational companies, which have been pressured to bring their operations in foreign countries into conformity with internationally agreed standards and best practice at home. Moreover, the scrutiny exercised by NGOs has focused on multinational companies domiciled in Western countries rather than on companies based in developing countries.[3] As a result, some Western companies have felt that their competitiveness is being eroded because of the standards they have to follow, while companies from emerging economies are using the situation to their advantage.

At the same time, non-governmental organizations have also come under some pressure. This is because most of the organizations with worldwide reach come from Europe and the United States, and the legitimacy of the values they represent has been questioned, especially in developing countries.[4] Even organizations providing humanitarian aid and medical expertise have been critiqued for advocating the 'interests of the West' and challenging the authority of governments in developing countries.

In this chapter, the focus will be on civil society groups that base their activities on moral causes and the collective good. Less attention is therefore paid to interest groups, for example trade unions, that promote the specific interests of their members.[5] Even though these groups are often seen as a part of civil society, their relationship to companies is different from other civil society groups due to their more established position and inclusion in corporate and governmental decision-making structures.

THREE MEANINGS OF CIVIL SOCIETY

Adam Seligman (1992) found that the term 'civil society' is used in three distinctly different ways. The first involves the use of the concept as a political slogan to criticize government and corporate policy. This interpretation relies on the positive connotations of the term and the trust placed on civil society organizations as actors that are seen as altruistic rather than self-serving. When employed in this way, the term is an appeal to the legitimacy of those groups that seek to advance the causes and interests of individual citizens and the environment against the established policies and power of the state and the market. In the context of corporate social responsibility and business ethics, the phrase 'civil society' is often used in this way to criticize what can be regarded as the selfish motives and behaviour of companies.

DOES SOLIDARITY EXIST ANYMORE?

Seligman (1992) argues that solidarity is diminishing because we cannot see how our individual interests are related to those of the societies in which we live. Do you agree with this view? Can you remember examples of situations where your interests have been different from those of your community? And conversely, are there examples of the reverse?

The second meaning is the analytical concept used by social scientists to explain social and political phenomena. For example, civil society activity has been seen as essential for the development of citizens who hold democratic values and have a good understanding of how to advance their interests within a democracy. Accordingly, civil society activity serves as a school of citizenship creating trust and skills necessary for a well-functioning democracy. Seligman (1992) acknowledges the importance of civil society for democratic societies, but in his view it adds little to the debates that have taken place in the field of political science around the concepts of democracy and citizenship.

The third and final meaning involves the use of the term in a normative way to describe a vision of the good life and society. Employed in this way, the concept of civil society refers to an ideal world where autonomous individuals form a community characterized by solidarity. According to Seligman (1992), the problem with this understanding of the concept lies with the challenge of combining individualism with a sense of community. This problem is particularly acute in industrialized societies where individuals seem to lack a sense of how their particular interests can be integrated with the more general interests of the society in which they live. As a result, people may be more autonomous than ever before, but have little solidarity towards any particular community to which they belong.

CHARACTERISTICS OF CIVIL SOCIETY ORGANIZATIONS

Civil society has been defined as the 'space of uncoerced human association and ... the set of relational networks – formed for the sake of family, faith, interest, and ideology – that fills this space'.[6] Accordingly, civil society is the space where individuals seek to realize their potential and pursue their interests outside the political and economic structures of society. As such, civil society complements and provides a counterbalance to the other spheres of social activity – the state and the market – and is therefore often referred to as 'the third sector'. At the same time, the boundaries between civil society, the state and the market are not always clear, as civil society groups may play a role in the implementation of government policy or pursue commercial activity to finance their operations. Despite the activities that seem to overlap with the other two sectors, civil society groups differ from political parties and business organizations because they do not seek public office or pecuniary gain as their core activity.[7]

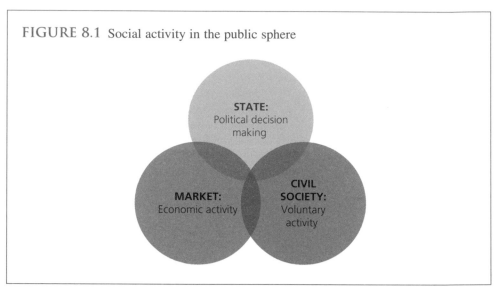

FIGURE 8.1 Social activity in the public sphere

Source: Authors

Civil society groups may not always have a formal structure, but they are more institutionalized than short-lived gatherings of people. As such, they will have some degree of organizational structure, activities and goals that persist over time, though note that participation in civil society groups is voluntary in the sense that it is not mandated by law or enforced in any other way. Moreover, civil society groups control their own activities and can make decisions that may be against the interests of their funders, including governmental agencies and companies. Also, even though civil society organizations may engage in profit-seeking activity, the resulting revenue is intended for use in achieving organizational goals rather than generating profits for the founders or members.[8]

Civil society groups provide employment for a significant number of people worldwide. According to one study, the sector had almost 40 million full-time workers across 35 countries in 2003, or an average of 4.4 per cent of the population in those countries. The same study shows that the size of the sector varies from one country to another, from 14 per cent of the economically active population in The Netherlands to 0.4 per cent in Mexico. In general, the sector employs a relatively higher number of people in industrialized countries than it does in developing countries. The relative number of paid staff and volunteers also varies across countries, but volunteers are an important resource for the non-profit sector as a whole.[9]

Civil society organizations have formed international networks that bring together groups and movements from different countries. They also include organizations that

ETHICS AND YOU

DO YOU BELONG TO A CIVIL SOCIETY ORGANIZATION?

Many of us belong to more than one civil society group. List the civil society groups such as sports clubs, religious associations and other organizations that you may belong to. Do any of these groups have links to business and, if so, what is the nature of this relationship?

operate at the international level, in parallel to governmental organizations like the World Trade Organization. The number of international civil society groups has grown since the 1970s and accelerated from the mid-1990s onwards.[10] This rise of international groups has been seen as a positive development by many and they are now integrated into the consultation structures of the United Nations and other inter-governmental forums. Despite this institutionalization, the groups have kept pressure on governments, companies and international organizations to further social and environmental goals.

ADVOCACY AND SERVICE ORGANIZATIONS

Civil society groups encompass a wide variety of organizations that are often fiercely independent, but may otherwise have little in common in terms of their mission and structure. This variety of civil society organizations makes it difficult for companies to develop a uniform approach towards them. In this section, we discuss the nature of two particular types of civil society organizations – advocacy and service organizations – in order to understand how they relate to companies in the context of corporate social responsibility and business ethics.

When analysed on the basis of their principal activities, two-thirds of civil society organizations are involved with the provision of services, as can be seen in Figure 8.2.[11] Service organizations focus on the delivery of education, health and other social services, and also include organizations working in the area of development aid. For example, Macmillan Cancer Support supports cancer sufferers and their families,[12] while Médecins Sans Frontières delivers medical assistance in developing countries where public provision of health services is weak.[13] In many countries, these organizations have held an important role in supporting and complementing services provided by governments. Similarly, it has been natural for companies to donate money and work in collaboration with service organizations, though there are also service organizations that have been concerned about being linked to companies and their interests.

In contrast to service organizations, advocacy groups involve only about 6 per cent of the whole civil society sector, despite being often the more visible and vocal groups among civil society organizations.[14] Even though they represent only a small proportion of civil society activity, they are important in the context of corporate social responsibility and

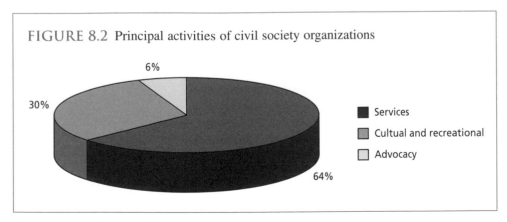

FIGURE 8.2 Principal activities of civil society organizations

6%

30%

64%

■ Services
■ Cultual and recreational
□ Advocacy

Source: Anheier & Salamon (2006).

business ethics as organizations that scrutinize and keep companies accountable. Advocacy work involves the articulation of positions on issues and the mobilization of support for them via dissemination of research, contacts with the media and other campaign work. For example, environmental groups have formed positions on climate change and sought the support of like-minded scientists, politicians, and other influential individuals and groups to promote their views. It should also be noted that many service organizations carry out advocacy work parallel to their core activity. For example, Médecins Sans Frontières is well known for raising awareness of situations that present a danger to vulnerable populations.[15]

Advocacy groups would normally argue that they represent the interests of the general public and underprivileged groups in contrast to the better organized and more powerful institutions of society.[16] Critics have however challenged the ability of civil society groups to represent and promote the public interest and have asked why advocacy groups would have any special insight on the matter. The critics also argue that the public interest is advanced when a broad set of views are expressed, and advocacy should therefore be about ensuring pluralism rather than promoting specific interests.[17] On this view, civil society should therefore not be seen as a magic potion for the ills of the state and society; it has its own values and divisions that create inequality and instability, not different from those caused by state and corporate action.[18]

Collaboration between companies and service organizations is not new, but it is only since the 1990s that companies have engaged with advocacy groups. One of the main reasons why companies have traditionally been more familiar with service organizations is that many advocacy groups have focused their scrutiny on governments rather than companies. Amnesty International, for example, was established in 1961 to defend freedom of opinion and religion in countries such as Nigeria where it targeted public officials with letters and other forms of pressure.[19] Since the mid-1990s, however, non-governmental organizations have directed some of their attention to the corporate sector in which they found a target that appeared to be more responsive to bad publicity than repressive regimes.[20] As a result, there have developed greater connections between companies and advocacy groups. Nevertheless, most partnership projects still take place between companies and service organizations as collaboration between these organizations does not share the same concerns over legitimacy and hostility as cooperation between companies and advocacy groups (see Chapter 2 on stakeholder management concerning the costs and advantages of collaboration).

ETHICS IN PRACTICE

EARTHRIGHTS INTERNATIONAL: TWO ACTIVISTS TAKE ON INTERNATIONAL OIL

Katie Redford returned to Thailand as an intern for Human Rights Watch, an international human rights advocacy group, during the first summer break from university. Her work in Thailand involved the documentation of human rights abuses, especially the use of forced labour by the Burmese military. This is when she first met Ka Hsaw Wa, who was collecting information about the human rights violations in Burma, and who was to become the other founder of EarthRights International. Ka Hsaw Wa was a son of a doctor from one of the ethnic minority groups in Burma, the Karen. He became involved in student politics at university and was arrested and tortured when government forces repressed pro-democracy demonstrations in 1988. He fled the country after being freed, but returned to Burma for the purpose of documenting environmental destruction and human rights abuses. Many of the abuses were connected to the construction of the pipeline that was being built across an area inhabited by the Karen in southern Burma.

Redford and Ka Hsaw Wa travelled for three weeks in Burma interviewing people who had suffered from human rights abuses. Redford contracted malaria, but kept on working because 'it was like everyone I was interviewing had malaria and they'd been raped and tortured'. After the summer, Redford returned back to her studies in the United States and wrote a research paper on the role of foreign companies in Burma and the possible use of a legal statute that had been barely employed since it was enacted in the 18th century. She also secured a grant of US$30,000 for raising awareness of the abuses in Burma. As a result, Redford launched EarthRights International together with Ka Hsaw Wa and another fellow law school graduate from the United States.

EarthRights International is best known for bringing a legal case against Unocal, a US oil company, and its top managers for alleged human rights abuses in Burma. The case was filed in California in 1997 and gave jurisdiction to a United States court over corporate activities in a foreign country, Burma. Seen as a precedent of extraterritorial application of law, the case was closely followed by business and advocacy organizations. It was recently settled out of court for a reported US$35 million.

Source: English, B. 2003. Katie Redford's pipe dream. *The Boston Globe*, 22 October 2003.

FUNCTIONS OF CIVIL SOCIETY

Civil society organizations have their own goals and purposes, but they also perform other functions in society. One of these functions is to provide a substitute for government action. The government produces decisions and services that are desired by the majority, while civil society organizations play a complementary role by providing for the minorities. The behaviour of many governments reflects this way of thinking as they increasingly delegate responsibilities to non-profit organizations. Governments benefit from this outsourcing because the level of satisfaction among potential voters increases. At the same time, civil society groups also benefit because their activities and funding expand. Critical voices have however noted that the increasing provision of publicly funded services through civil society organizations may direct civil society activity towards governmental priorities, blur the boundaries between the government and civil society, obscure relationships of accountability and distort understanding of how tax revenues are spent.[21]

Civil society has also been seen to teach values and skills that are desirable, if not essential, for a democratic society. For example, Robert Putnam (1993) found in his study of Italy that the regions with rich associational activity were also the regions with the highest degree of political stability, governmental effectiveness and economic growth. The same argument was made earlier by Alexis de Tocqueville in his study of democracy in the United States.[22] According to de Tocqueville, civil society activity shapes the preferences and interest of individuals and enables them to become citizens who can make effective demands on the government. Civil society can therefore be seen as a 'school of citizenship' where individuals form their interests and learn democratic skills. Proponents of this view

MOVING FROM ONE SECTOR TO ANOTHER

It is typical in many countries for people to change employment from business to government and back. For example, many people in the Obama administration in the United States have a business background. People working in government and business may also be involved in charitable work, but they seem to rarely seek permanent employment in the non-profit sector.

What might be the implications of these trends for relationships between the different sectors?

regard civil society activity as essential for maintaining a vibrant democratic society where citizens participate in civic and political life.

Critics of the 'school of citizenship' argument have noted that civil society groups enhance democracy only if they cultivate democratic values and skills,[23] and not all civil society organizations are based on values that are in line with these. For example, there are religious groups acting as if women were less valuable than men and therefore sustaining ideas that are contrary to the principle of equality that underpins the concept of democracy. These groups may educate their members about civic skills and other values that are essential for democratic government, but they also promote ideas that are fundamentally inconsistent with democracy. Another example of non-democratic behaviour is animal rights activists who break the law when freeing mink and other animals that are kept in captivity for their fur.

Moreover, civil society organizations may not be participatory in the sense suggested by those who argue that civil society groups serve as schools of citizenship. This is because the non-profit sector has moved from the mobilization of large numbers of volunteers to the hiring of specialized staff. Indeed, it seems that the larger and wealthier the organization, the fewer opportunities for participation and democratic socialization it offers because professionally managed civil society groups tend to recruit people who already have relevant skills and background. It therefore seems that the opportunities for developing democratic virtues are more available in organizations that *lack* human and other resources. In general, professional and well-resourced organizations have become increasingly efficient in their work but do not perform the function of civic education to the same extent as organizations with more limited resources.[24]

INFLUENCE TACTICS

As already discussed, the power of civil society groups derives from the altruistic nature of their goals. In contrast to the more traditional forms of power available to governments and companies, civil society groups draw their influence from the moral and social power coming from information, ideas and principles. Moreover, the power of civil society groups is often based on their ability to mobilize other actors, and public opinion, behind their causes. In comparison with state and market actors, civil society groups have limited resources and need to be innovative about building leverage vis-à-vis these actors. The power of civil society groups is therefore different from the political and coercive power that governments have as sovereign authorities, but it is also different from the economic power that companies hold as the providers of employment and economic growth.

TABLE 8.1 **Influence tactics**

Influence tactic	Description
Information politics	Supply of information to provide an alternative to other sources such as governmental or company-originated
Symbolic politics	Use of powerful events to draw attention and support to specific causes
Leverage politics	Mobilization of powerful allies and public support to gain material or moral leverage
Accountability politics	Use of public scrutiny to monitor and pressure companies to comply with their commitments and good practice

Source: Keck & Sikkink (1998).

Margaret E. Keck and Kathryn Sikkink (1998) developed a typology of four influence tactics from their research on civil society networks (see Table 8.1). All the tactics are similar in the sense that they seek to alter the information and value contexts on which companies and other actors base their behaviour. The tactics are depicted in some detail in the following sub-sections. In general, they involve only a small number of activists from advocacy organizations and the general public, thus demonstrating the cost-efficiency of civil society activity.

Information politics

Information politics refers to the influence advocacy groups obtain by collecting and supplying information that provides an alternative to the more established sources of information. For example, when the World Wildlife Fund carries out research and publishes it to challenge the impact of industrial practices on threatened species of animals, it is using information politics to protect the species.

The use of information politics is not new, but the development of information technology has enabled civil society organizations to challenge the monopoly that governmental actors and the media have held over information flows in the past. The internet has been particularly important in making it easier for civil society groups to share information in a timely manner. What might have taken weeks and months to accomplish before the internet, may now happen in seconds with increased reliability, flexibility and opportunities for interaction. The internet also has the advantage of involving fewer intermediaries than other channels of communication. In this way, the internet has enhanced direct contacts among civil society groups and lessened the distortion of information caused by intermediate parties.

In order to be credible, information needs to be well documented and based on reliable sources. Because of this, many civil society organizations have established meticulous procedures for collecting data and verifying their findings. Despite these procedures, there is often a degree of uncertainty surrounding information that on occasion may be inconclusive, sensitive or collected in environments where freedom of expression is restricted. From this it follows that advocacy groups often find themselves in situations where they fight over 'the facts' with another actor that relies on different sources of information or just interprets events in a different way. The 'Ethics in practice' box provides an example of a situation where information produced by Human Rights Watch is challenged by government authorities in Ethiopia.

ETHICS IN PRACTICE

DISAGREEMENT OVER FACTS

The debate over the human rights situation in the Ogaden region in Ethiopia illustrates the way in which advocacy groups seek to gain influence through the collection and provision of information and how other actors challenge the information produced by the groups. Such debates are typical when free travel and flow of information are restricted or made difficult due to an armed conflict, lack of infrastructure, or other conditions.

Human Rights Watch, a non-profit organization based in the United States, published a report in which it accuses the Ethiopian government of human rights violations including the killing and torture of villagers in the Ogaden region of the country. The human rights group also alleges that government forces have prevented humanitarian organizations from delivering food and other aid to certain areas in the Ogaden resulting in famine, disease and deaths. The report also draws attention on the humanitarian emergency in the region.

The Ethiopian government has denied the allegations made by Human Rights Watch and published its own report to provide an alternative version of the situation in the Ogaden region. The report discusses the allegations made by the human rights group, arguing that they are unfounded and based on the propaganda of the separatist Ogaden National Liberation Front. The report also criticizes Human Rights Watch for writing its report without visiting the region and denies blocking independent journalists from travelling freely.

Source: Ethiopia: A row over human rights. *The Economist*, 7 February 2009.

Information supplied by civil society organizations is often dramatic because it seeks to attract attention. Civil society organizations may, for example, use personal testimonies to present a human side to more technical and statistical information. They also use powerful language and present story lines that appeal to our values and sense of right and wrong. For example, as described in the case at the end of this chapter, the Third World Action Group published a pamphlet entitled 'Nestlé Kills Babies' as part of the campaign that sought to draw attention to the effects of the use of breast-milk formula in developing countries.

Because of their limited resources, civil society organizations seldom have presence in more than a small number of key countries and tend to rely on contacts with other groups for receiving information and support for their activities. These contacts are essential for even large and well-known organizations like Amnesty International because they allow these organizations to access information at low cost. They also enhance the credibility of international NGOs that are sometimes criticized for being distant from the beneficiaries of their work. In return, grassroots organizations gain from their contacts with international groups by getting publicity and, in some instances, protection for their work.

Symbolic politics

Symbolic politics refer to the attempts of advocacy groups to use powerful events to draw attention to and support for their purposes. In order to gain influence, the groups frame events in a way that serves their objectives. For example, advocacy groups have used the attention raised by Al Gore's film on climate change, *An Inconvenient Truth*, to put pressure on companies to introduce sustainability policies. The natural catastrophes in Thailand

ETHICS IN PRACTICE

AL GORE AND CLIMATE CHANGE

Al Gore is former vice-president and presidential candidate in the United States. He retired from main-stream politics when he lost the election of 2000 to George Bush Jr., but he has remained active in promoting social causes in other ways. In 2006, he starred in a film on global warming and climate change. The film, *An Inconvenient Truth*, became a box office hit and focused considerable attention on the issue of climate change. As a result, Gore was awarded the Nobel Peace Prize in 2007 for his contribution in the dissemination of information on environmental issues.

and New Orleans gave additional weight to the concerns of the advocacy groups and were used to sustain pressure on companies. Indeed, it is often a series of interrelated events that make people see situations in a new light. Such events also contribute to the growth of civil society organizations and their support base.

Leverage politics

Leverage politics involves the use of powerful allies or public opinion to influence companies and other actors. Leverage politics often involves the mobilization of the media, but it can also draw on the membership of advocacy groups. Amnesty International, for example, has been successful in mobilizing its members in large-scale mailing campaigns that have often taken business leaders by surprise. In general, a large membership base provides leverage for advocacy groups because it represents potential customers for companies and votes for governments. As discussed below, advocacy organizations can seek *material* or *moral* leverage over the targets of their campaigns.

Material leverage involves the use of financial and other concrete incentives in effecting change. For example, advocacy groups may ask institutional investors to boycott the shares of companies with undesired policies and behaviour. Material leverage may also involve economic sanctions, the closing of access to loans and loss of public sector contracts. For example, some environmental groups have been successful in pressuring government agencies to apply environmental criteria in the selection of suppliers. Similarly, advocacy groups have encouraged governments to introduce economic sanctions on countries that violate international human rights standards. Material leverage may also involve measures that are targeted directly at companies via consumer boycotts and similar campaigns instead of pressure placed on other actors with indirect consequences on companies.

Moral leverage has been referred to as the 'mobilization of shame'. It emphasizes the use of public opinion in leverage politics. The effectiveness of exposure to public scrutiny depends on how much value the target actor places on reputation and good image. Most governments are sensitive to public criticism, with the exception of a small number (e.g. North Korea) that seem to care little about world opinion. The business community seems equally, if not more responsive to moral leverage. Companies selling consumer products with well-known brands are particularly responsive to moral leverage as their brands are easily tarnished with negative associations. An example of this is Nestlé that has found it difficult to disassociate its name from the pamphlet theme of 'killing babies in Africa'. The degree to which companies are vulnerable to this kind of pressure varies and depends on a range of factors including whether they are well known and sell directly to consumers.

ETHICS IN PRACTICE

CORPORATE WATCHDOGS

The past 20 years have seen the emergence of groups that focus on scrutinizing corporate behaviour. For example, CorpWatch was founded in 1996 to mobilize support for campaigns on corporate accountability. Some of the groups monitor the corporate sector as a whole, while others focus on a single company. For example, Coalition against Bayer Dangers only scrutinizes the behaviour of Bayer, a German chemical and pharmaceutical company.

These groups acting as corporate watchdogs are different from the civil society organizations that promote certain values or principles. For example, Amnesty International advocates human rights and puts pressure on any organization that may play a role in the protection and promotion of human rights.

Accountability politics

Accountability politics involves the use of public scrutiny to make companies and governments accountable for their commitments and commonly agreed standards. Accountability politics is based on the information collected by advocacy groups to expose gaps between corporate policy and behaviour. This information can then be used to put pressure on companies. For example, if a company has made a commitment to, say, sustainability, advocacy groups may remind the company of its commitment if they find that the company's performance lags behind its policy.

While information is the foundation of accountability politics, mechanisms for keeping companies accountable vary from one political and cultural context to another. In the United States, for example, the legal system has been central for challenging state and private actors about their behaviour, which explains the large number of advocacy groups specializing in litigation. In other countries, advocacy groups have used less confrontational tactics and relied more on the embarrassment stemming from public exposure.

CORPORATE RESPONSE

Many debates between civil society organizations and companies seem to be a result of the different ways in which events and situations can be interpreted. For example, when a civil society group in February 2009 criticized adverts on cosmetic surgery in the London underground railway system and claimed for 'the right to be natural', the concerned company defended its business in reference to the freedom of choice and information. The role of interpretation in the emergence of disagreements between companies and their stakeholders has been highlighted by researchers who have studied the development of social problems[25] and corporate issues.[26] These researchers have argued that disagreements occur because it is possible to interpret the same phenomenon in many different ways.

When civil society groups and companies have conflicting interpretations over an issue, companies have used three distinct strategies to communicate their views and influence other actors: (1) information strategies, involving the provision of information and opinions from the company viewpoint; (2) leveraging strategies, concerning attempts to increase the trustworthiness of the information and viewpoints provided by companies; and (3) stakeholder

TABLE 8.2 **Corporate response strategies**

Strategy	Description
Information strategy	Provision of information and perspectives with a view to change opinions
Leveraging strategy	Appeals to actors with authority to increase trustworthiness
Stakeholder engagement strategy	Two-way communication aimed at increasing mutual understanding between companies and their stakeholders

engagement strategies, referring to attempts to increase mutual understanding between companies and their critics. The strategies are not mutually exclusive; companies can use more than one of them at any one time to address the same concerns. The strategies are summarized in Table 8.2.

Irrespective of the motivation of companies to engage in different strategies, civil society groups may perceive them negatively as attempts to manipulate the public debate, to exclude diverging voices, and to use divide-and-rule tactics.[27] Civil society groups have been particularly suspicious about companies that have engaged in large-scale discussions without altering their positions. When this has happened, companies have been challenged to show that their engagement with other societal actors is genuine and not merely an attempt to appease critics and benefit from the association with civil society.

Information strategy

Information strategy[28] involves attempts to influence corporate stakeholders through the provision of information that reinforces corporate viewpoints. Information strategies are often targeted at particular actors. Companies may, for example, seek to rally the support of like-minded parties in order to have more influence over the way in which a particular issue is framed. Companies may also target relevant government officials to ensure that decision makers are aware of their positions. It is also typical for companies to engage in large-scale leafleting to influence opinions. For example, McDonald's often distributes leaflets in neighbourhoods where it plans to open a new restaurant. The purpose of the leaflets is to advertise the opening and, at the same time, provide a response to the citizen groups that tend to oppose restaurant openings because of concerns over the consumption of fast food on health.

Information strategy is most effective when other actors do not have preconceived ideas about the issue concerned and when companies are able to frame the situation from their perspective. The strategy can also help companies to obtain the support of their shareholders when issues of corporate responsibility arise. Information strategy is less effective with actors who have researched and formed positions on the issue concerned. This is especially the case when the issue involves matters of opinion.[29] For example, the use of bonuses in executive compensation can give rise to a wide range of arguments, but these arguments cannot be justified in the same way as more logical problems.

Companies use two main types of communication channels to pursue an information strategy. First, they engage with different actors to provide information and viewpoints. As will be seen later, the way in which companies engage with stakeholders varies from informal contacts to structured consultation processes. In addition to stakeholder engagement, companies present information and viewpoints through communication channels

WHO DO YOU TRUST?

Companies and non-governmental organizations often describe situations in different ways. Which account would you trust more and why?

that offer no or little opportunity for interaction, but reach larger audiences. Corporate publications including websites and annual reports play a particularly important role in such communication, but a one-way information strategy may include anything from specific reports prepared for one influential public official to large-scale mailing campaigns reaching thousands of consumers.

Leveraging strategy

Leveraging strategy refers to attempts to increase the credibility of the information and viewpoints provided by companies. These strategies are pursued to enhance the objectivity and authority of the information presented by companies. The main aim of the leveraging strategy is therefore to address the lack of credibility that companies might have in the eyes of some actors. Companies have three main measures at their disposal to address this lack of trust: (1) external verification of their statements; (2) appeals to the views of other actors who possess some form of authority; and (3) reference to regulations, guidelines and laws.

External verification This is where companies use external sources of verification to increase the credibility of the information they make available in corporate publications. For example, companies that publish sustainability reports often employ external organizations to provide assurance that what they say is reliable and balanced. Similarly to information strategy, external verification works best when it is used to provide factual information on contested issues. Verification is less effective in addressing issues that are based on conflicting beliefs and opinions, which are not verifiable in the same way as issues on which concrete evidence can exist. This is exemplified in corporate statements such as the following from Talisman, a Canadian company, as follows: 'We have retained PricewaterhouseCoopers to verify those elements of the report which are capable of objective independent verification [...]. Unverified portions of this report generally relate to background information or our beliefs, opinions or intentions where verification is not always possible'.[30] Nevertheless, despite the external support, verification does not mean that information provided by companies is not challenged by other actors.

Appeals to experts or other actors Another way in which companies seek to increase the credibility of their arguments is through appeals to other actors who possess some form of authority or are seen as more neutral than companies. The effectiveness of appeals to other actors depends on the credibility and expertise of the actors referred to. For example, companies may name the civil society groups they have consulted on a particular issue. This has in some cases resulted in the civil society group claiming that they have not authorized the use of its name and the implied support for arguments made by companies. Such denunciations demonstrate the sensitivity of the relationship between companies and non-governmental organizations and the concerns that the latter have about the negative impact of their association with companies.

Reference to regulation and laws The reference that companies make to regulation and laws in support of their views can be seen as another form of leveraging strategy. Total, for example, stressed in its first corporate social responsibility report that its investment in Burma did not violate any regulation introduced by the United Nations, the European Union or the French government, and was therefore legitimate.[31] In addition to regulation and laws, companies also make reference to guidelines and principles on ethical business, corporate social responsibility and human rights to justify their policies and conduct. References to extant laws or practice do not, however, satisfy the critics who allege that the responsibility of companies goes beyond the law.[32]

Companies tend to categorize civil society groups into those with which they can have meaningful interaction and those with which engagement seems unproductive. Some communication may take place between companies and the organizations of the latter type, but managers often find such engagement futile. The following quote from an executive working for a Swedish oil company, Lundin, illustrates the sentiment of the company managers (Batruch, 2004):

Lundin's experience with special-interest NGOs was more difficult. In many cases, views about the situation in Sudan were so very different that discussions rarely went beyond each side trying to convince the other of the correctness of its views. This was particularly true with respect to religious-based organizations, which characterized the conflict as an attempt by Muslims to eradicate the Christian population in the south of Sudan in order to gain access to the oil there. Although the company responded to their claims, in discussions and in writing, it felt that not much would be gained from this effort.

Stakeholder engagement strategy

Stakeholder engagement involves two-way dialogue that aims to increase mutual understanding between companies and other actors. A stakeholder engagement strategy is typically pursued via discussions and activities that seek to enhance understanding between the company and its stakeholders; these may be both formal and informal as the situation demands. Stakeholder engagement may also take place via annual general meetings and other more formal channels.

THINKING CRITICALLY ABOUT ETHICS

COMPANIES AND CIVIL SOCIETY GROUPS CAUTIOUS OVER COLLABORATION

Relationships between companies and civil society organizations are not always transparent to the public. Many civil society organizations have avoided contact with companies in order to protect their reputation and credibility, which could be negatively affected by association with companies. Civil society groups may also be concerned about giving legitimacy to corporate positions and behaviour. As a result, discussions between companies and civil society organizations are not always made public.

Companies are increasingly fostering contacts with civil society groups. A growing number of civil society organizations is also willing to have contact with companies, even though they may remain critical about the underpinning motivations. Companies often seek to collaborate with international civil society organizations, which is sometimes explained by the fact that only a few local organizations exist, but companies also seem to find it easier to work together with organizations that are familiar with the drivers of corporate policy and behaviour at the international level.

Companies can adopt a range of processes to consult stakeholder groups or provide them with an opportunity to interact with relevant people from the company. Companies can, for example, set up structures to engage with the local communities in which they operate. In general, consultation structures vary from permanent to temporary, and may involve multiple stakeholders or just one particular group. One company, for example, has established committees in the villages surrounding its facilities as part of its community development programme.[33]

In addition to consultation, companies can set up committees that facilitate internal and external stakeholders to make enquiries about corporate policy and conduct. Such committees serve several functions. One purpose could be to offer employees an opportunity to request advice in confidence. The committees can also be responsible for contacts with civil society groups and prepare communications relating to ethical issues towards international, governmental and non-governmental organizations.

Finally, companies can engage with their stakeholders in a less permanent way via, for example, focus groups or questionnaires.

SUMMARY

- Civil society embraces a broad set of organizations ranging from professional associations, religious congregations and charities to cultural institutions and sports clubs. Civil society activity is not driven by political and economic motives, even though it may involve aspects of both.

- Civil society organizations play a complementary role to the government by providing services and other social goods. They can also serve as schools of citizenship, an essential element of democratic societies.[34]

- Companies have relationships with many different types of civil society organizations. From among these organizations, advocacy groups have called on companies to comply with certain standards, while service organizations have offered opportunities for concrete collaboration.

- The power of civil society groups derives from their ability to mobilize the public opinion behind their causes. They often rely on information and principles to draw attention to corporate behaviour and in this way influence the way in which corporate activity is perceived.

- Companies have responded to civil society tactics by providing information from their point of view and engaging with important actors. They have also sought to increase the credibility of their views by reference to other actors with authority.

QUICK REVIEW QUESTIONS:

1   Why are civil society organizations important for understanding ethics and corporate social responsibility?

2   What types of interactions are companies likely to have with advocacy and service organizations?

3   What are the similarities in the strategies companies and civil society groups use to influence each other?

CASE STUDY: NESTLÉ AND MARKETING OF BABY-MILK SUBSTITUTES

The case of Nestlé and the marketing of baby-milk substitutes is one of the classics in the area of business ethics and corporate social responsibility. It is often evoked to illustrate how ethical issues emerge, gain publicity and develop over time. It also demonstrates the ability of civil society groups to put pressure on companies and the tenacity of some of these groups in scrutinizing corporate behaviour.

There is substantial scientific evidence to show that breast-feeding is an ideal source of nutrition for babies. Breast milk is an important source of antibodies offering a degree of protection against illnesses. In the context of poverty, there are additional reasons why breast-feeding is preferred over substitutes to milk. First, most infant formulas come in powder format and need to be mixed with water. Due to a lack of clean water in many developing countries, the use of infant formula can cause diseases such as diarrhoea, which remains one of the most prevalent causes of infant death worldwide. Another problem is that poor mothers dilute the formula in order to make it last longer. This practice has led to the inadequate nutrition of infants. As a result, the World Health Organization recommends that babies be breast-fed until the age of six months. Thereafter, milk needs to be complemented with other foods for meeting the nutritional needs of infants.

The history of Nestlé is tied to the invention of infant formula. It was Henri Nestlé, founder of the company, who developed the modern form of baby-milk substitute over 100 years ago. The formula was first targeted at upper-middle-class women in Europe who were seen as too fragile to breast-feed, but its promotion was so successful that by the end of 1960s only a quarter of babies born in North American hospitals were breast-fed when their mothers returned home. The rates of breast-feeding have now gone up, but the earlier decline has been seen to result from (i) weak awareness over the benefits of breast-feeding among the general population and (ii) the promotion of the practice by doctors.

As birth rates began to decrease in industrialized countries, developing countries became an attractive market for the infant food industry. The first concerns about the impact of baby-milk substitutes and their promotion in developing countries were raised by health professionals working in Africa. A Dutch paediatrician, for example, wrote an article about the topic for the *Journal of Tropical and Geographical Medicine* in 1969. She was concerned about the way in which Nestlé was promoting one of its products in Nigeria as something better than breast-feeding: 'Mother watch the health of your baby, and give him the best, give Lactogen'.

Health workers initially believed that they could collaborate with the industry to change advertising messages and practices, but companies were unresponsive to their concerns. Disappointed with the corporate response, they asked the United Nations Protein Advisory Group to hold a meeting to discuss the issue. The consequent statement published after the meeting was, however, unsatisfactory in the eyes of those who were concerned about the connection between the marketing of infant formula and the health of babies in developing countries.

In 1973, an article on 'the baby food strategy' was published in the *New Internationalist,* a reputable magazine focusing on international development. Two child health specialists argued in the article that Nestlé and other companies were causing malnutrition with the negligent marketing of infant formula in developing countries. Soon after, similar allegations were made in a booklet entitled *The Baby Killer* and published in the United Kingdom by War on Want, a non-governmental organization. The leaflet was also translated into other languages with the result that Nestlé sued a German publisher for libel. Following considerable media attention, the company offered to settle the matter out of court, but the defendant refused in the belief that the trial would raise awareness and in this way benefit the public interest. The case was duly processed and decided in favour of Nestlé because the judge was of the view that criminal law could not be applied to hold the company responsible for infant deaths.

▶

Nonetheless, he advised the company to change its advertising practices in order to avoid similar allegations.

The libel case brought many activists together and resulted in the creation of a network that collected and exchanged information on the marketing of baby-milk formula. Among other actors, many religious organizations in the United States became aware of the issue and filed related shareholder resolutions as important investors in large companies. The infant food industry reacted to the attention by introducing a code of ethics, which was received as a positive step by many, but there were also some non-governmental organizations that criticized the code for being a public relations exercise designed to silence the critics without really addressing the concerns raised by health workers.

A few years later, in July 1977, a boycott was launched against Nestlé by a group of civil society activists. They chose Nestlé because the company had an important share of the infant food market and because Nestlé was seen as particularly unresponsive to criticism. The company responded to the boycott in the United States by mailing 300,000 copies of a leaflet that explained Nestlé's position on the issue. As a result, marketing of baby-milk formula received such widespread attention that, in 1978, Senator Edward Kennedy organized a special Senate hearing on the issue.

Senator Kennedy also contacted the head of the World Health Organization (WHO) to seek an international rather than national solution to the issue. A meeting was consequently held with representation from civil society groups, governments, the UN, industry and experts. After the meeting, the WHO and UNICEF were requested to draft an international code on the marketing of breast-milk substitutes. The code was formally launched in 1981 as a WHO regulation with nearly unanimous support from member countries. The aftermath of the original meeting also saw the formation of the International Baby Food Action International (IBFAN), a network of campaigners who sought to monitor and share information on corporate practice.

Today, IBFAN consists of over 200 groups in 100 countries. It encompasses a wide range of organizations from those specialized in infant food to consumer associations, development organizations and mother support groups. Its main offices are based in Switzerland where the WHO and UNICEF also have their headquarters. IBFAN carries out a range of activities to fulfil its mission:

- Networking worldwide to build and provide support for partners with similar interests.
- Advocacy at national and international level via publications, the media and grassroots activity.
- Training courses targeted at NGOs, consumers and policy makers.
- Coordinating campaigns, including the Nestlé boycott.
- Policy development and advocacy towards governmental actors.

Hundreds of universities and other institutions have banned the sale of Nestlé products on their premises because of the controversy surrounding the advertising of baby-milk. Nestlé has responded via a website dedicated to the issue of infant formula where it addresses concerns raised about its policy and behaviour. It also engages with diverse groups about the issue, including government agencies, health workers, civil society groups and industry organizations. Nestlé and other companies do not deny the superiority of breast milk as a source of nutrition and protection against illnesses. Nestlé, for example, states on its website that 'breast milk is the ideal food for healthy growth and development of babies'. The issue it needs to address has remained the same over time: how to market a product responsibly when its misuse by ill-informed, illiterate and poor users may result in illness and death.

STUDY QUESTIONS

1 What is the ultimate dilemma for Nestlé about the marketing of infant formula?

2 How could Nestlé have avoided the escalation of the issue?

3 What can Nestlé do at this stage?

SOURCES

IBFAN 2005. *What Is the Problem? Action Pack.* International Baby Food Action International.

Nestlé 2007. Available from http://www.babymilk. Nestlé.com, accessed 12 October 2008.

Richter, J. 2001. *Holding Corporations Accountable: Corporate Conduct, International Codes, and Citizen Action.* London: Zed Books.

NOTES

1 Ratner (2001); Spar (1999).
2 Rice (2002).
3 Broadhurst (2000).
4 Dovi (2002 in Clemens, 2006).
5 Tesh (1984).
6 Walzer (1998), p. 291.
7 Scholte (2001).
8 Salamon & Anheier (1997).
9 Anheier & Salamon (2006).
10 Ibid.
11 Ibid.
12 Macmillan Cancer Support (2009).
13 Médecins Sans Frontières (2009).
14 Anheier & Salamon (2006).
15 Médecins Sans Frontières (2009).
16 Jenkins (2006).
17 Ibid. (2006), p. 308.
18 Kumar (1993).
19 Amnesty International (2006).
20 Spar (1999).
21 Pierson (1994 in Clemens, 2006).
22 de Tocqueville (1966) (reprinted).
23 Clemens (2006).
24 Ibid.
25 Daft & Weick (1984); Hilgartner & Bosk (1988).
26 Dutton & Jackson (1987); Lamertz, Martens & Heugens (2003).
27 Richter (2001).
28 The strategy is similar to Hillman and Hitt's (1999) corporate political strategy of the same name, but unlike with Hillman and Hitt's strategy, information does not need to be useful for the targeted actors. Instead, information is provided with the objective of clarifying and explaining the corporate viewpoint on the relevant issue.
29 See Spar (1999).
30 Talisman (2000).
31 Total (2003).
32 EarthRights International (2000).
33 Total (2003).
34 Clemens (2006).

REFERENCES

Amnesty International 2006. Amnesty International, London. Available from http://web.amnesty.org/pages/aboutai-timeline-1960s-eng, accessed 29 September 2006.

Anheier, H. K. and Salamon, L. M. 2006. The nonprofit sector in comparative perspective. In Powell, W. and Steinberg, R. (eds) *The Nonprofit Sector: A Research Handbook*. Second edition. New Haven and London: Yale University Press.

Broadhurst, A. I. 2000. Corporations and the ethics of social responsibility: An emerging regime of expansion and compliance. *Business Ethics: A European Review*, Vol. 9, No. 2, 86–98.

Clemens, E. S. 2006. Collaboration between corporations and nonprofit organizations. In Powell, W. and Steinberg, R. (eds) *The Nonprofit Sector: A Research Handbook*. Second edition. New Haven and London: Yale University Press.

Daft, R. L. and Weick, K. E. 1984. Toward a model of organizations as interpretation systems. *Academy of Management Review*, Vol. 9, No. 2, 284–295.

de Tocqueville, A. 1966. *Democracy in America*. New York: Harper & Row.

Dutton, J. E. and Jackson, S. E. 1987. Categorizing strategic issues: Links to organizational action. *Academy of Management Review*, Vol. 12, No. 1, 76–90.

EarthRights International 2000. *Total Denial Continues. Earth Rights Abuses Along the Yadana and Yetagun Pipelines in Burma*. EarthRights International, May 2000. Available from http://www.earthrights.org, accessed 5 February 2004.

Hillman, A. and Hitt, M. 1999. Corporate political strategy formulation: A model of approach, participation and strategy decisions. *Academy of Management Review*, 24, 825–842.

Hilgartner, S. and Bosk, C. L. 1988. The rise and fall of social problems: A public arenas model. *The American Journal of Sociology*, Vol. 94, No. 1, 53–78.

Jenkins, J. G. 2006. Nonprofit organizations and political advocacy. In Powell, W. and Steinberg, R. (eds) *The Nonprofit Sector: A Research Handbook*. Second edition. New Haven and London: Yale University Press.

Keck, M. and Sikkink, K. 1998. *Activists Beyond Borders*. Ithaca: Cornell University Press.

Kumar, K. 1993. Civil society: An inquiry into the usefulness of an historical term. *The British Journal of Sociology*, Vol. 44, No. 3, 375–395.

Lamertz, K., Martens, M. L. and Heugens, P. P. 2003. Issue evolution: A symbolic interactionist perspective. *Corporate Reputation Review*, Vol. 6, No. 1, 82–93.

Macmillan Cancer Support 2009. Available from http://www.macmillan.org.uk, accessed 6 July 2009.

Médecins Sans Frontières 2009. Available from http://www.msf.org, accessed 6 July 2009.

Putnam, R. 1993. *Making Democracy Work: Civic Traditions in Modern Italy*. New Jersey: Princeton University Press.

Ratner, S. 2001. Corporations and human rights: A theory of legal responsibility. *Yale Law Journal*, Vol. 111, 443.

Rice, D. 2002. Human rights strategies for corporations. *Business Ethics: A European Review*, Vol. 11, No. 2, 134–136.

Richter, J. 2001. *Holding Corporations Accountable: Corporate Conduct, International Codes, and Citizen Action*. London and New York: Zed Books.

Salamon, L. M. and Anheier, H. K. 1997. Defining the nonprofit sector: a cross-national analysis. In Salamon, L. M. and Anheier H. K. (eds) *Johns Hopkins Nonprofit Sector Series*. Manchester: Manchester University Press.

Scholte, J. A. 2001. *Civil Society and Democracy in Global Governance*. CSGR Working Paper No. 65/01, Centre for the Study of Globalization and Regionalization, University of Warwick.

Seligman, A. B. 1992. *The Idea of Civil Society*. New York: The Free Press.

Spar, D. L. 1999. Foreign investment and human rights. *Challenge*, Vol. 42, No. 1, 55–80.

Talisman 2000. Cor*porate Social Responsibility Report*. Available from http://www.talisman-energy.com, accessed 2 August 2006.

Tesh, S. 1984. In support of single-issue politics. *Political Science Quarterly*, No. 99, 27–44.

Total 2003. *Corporate Social Responsibility Report*. Available from http://www.total.com, accessed 4 May 2004.

Walzer, M. 1998. The civil society argument. In Shafir, G. (ed.), *The Citizenship Debates: A Reader*. Minneapolis: University of Minnesota Press.

MICROSOFT'S PARTNERSHIP WITH UNHCR: PRO BONO PUBLICO?

BY NINA MARIE NICOLAS & DR GABRIELE SUDER EDITED BY ELENA BONFIGLIOLI, DIRECTOR OF CORPORATE CITIZENSHIP, MICROSOFT EMEA

"Using Microsoft's core business competencies and expertise enhance UNHCR's technological capacity, bringing the benefit of technology solutions closer to refugee communities and at the same time providing support for UNHCR's general mandate – awareness raising and advocacy for refugees."
– Joosten Frauke, Associate External Relations Officer for Private Sector Fundraising and Public Affairs Service at UNHCR.

"The system handles a broad range of demographic information – the number of men, women, and children – the age of people, the mortality rate, where people come from and what their protection needs are," he said. *"It's recorded their medical status and details on food and nutrition. It's a scorecard of sorts, that helps you plan and make sure you have the right material and help available to provide refugees with the services they need."*
– Patrick De Smedt, Former Chairman of Microsoft Europe Middle East and Africa.

Source: ECCH Case study, Awarded the Philip Law Scholarship 2006–2007, Copyright © CERAM Sophia Antipolis. The authors would like to thank J.P. Courtois, President, Microsoft International, E. Bonfiglioli, Director, Microsoft EMEA Corporate Citizenship, Olivier Delarue, Head of Corporate and Foundation Partnership Unit at UNHCR, J. Frauke, Associate External Relations Officer for Private Sector Fundraising and Public Affairs Service at UNHCR, Uli Holtz, Microsoft EMEA, Human Resources Director, and the many other sources of support and information at Microsoft Corp. and at UNHCR that made this case study possible.

Printed with permission from the authors and www.ecch.com

Kosovo, 1999

It was in 1999, at the time of the Kosovo crisis. For days people across the world had been watching the events unfold, following desperate Kosovars fleeing the Serbs bundled with as many belongings as possible leaving their home behind. Microsoft employees were watching the news together during lunchtime. However, this time a particularly strong shared feeling of empathy arose for those affected by the conflict, which in turn led to a sincere desire to reach out to the many distressed people that filled the TV screen and take action. How could they make a difference to this terrible humanitarian disaster?

Meanwhile, Jean-Philippe Courtois, then CEO of Microsoft Europe, Middle East and Africa, also followed the crisis closely. He began to consider how a company such as Microsoft could contribute to improve these situations by using its particular skills and expertise instead of resorting to regular charity or the typical philanthropy.

At the time philanthropy was widespread among companies, foundations and institutions particularly in the United States. Corporate social responsibility however, was still an unfamiliar term. In Europe one could find a social awareness as well as random examples of equivalents to corporate citizenship, which has since evolved and increased in visibility, expertise and practice throughout the corporate, NGO and political world.

Corporate Social Responsibility or Corporate Citizenship – as the latter is commonly defined in Microsoft – was not explicitly stated as corporate strategy or as a set of activities within the company before 1999. However, a team of Community Affairs professionals were in charge of handling Microsoft's various social investment and philanthropic activities.

Given the urgency of the situation, a small team of employees was formed to handle societal initiatives and community contributions like this one. Employees were brought in from the Community Affairs' team, the business development team, as well as a business manager working for Jean Philippe Courtois. They assessed the different strategies for action in order to aid the victims of the Kosovo crisis through leveraging the company's expertise, its talents and the personal motivation of its employees.

The Microsoft team asked how the company could be actively useful for the UNHCR. Upon analysis of refugees' needs, it was found that beyond the most basic ones – the people in the region were left without homes and identity papers. As a result they were completely unprotected.

UNHCR suggested that Microsoft could help resolving these problems, by providing technology software and hardware with which a refugees' registration system could be created and through collaboration with NGOs, with UNHCR and organisations that were taking care of the many displaced victims.

This was the beginning of what was to become an important partnership for both UNHCR and Microsoft. One of the Microsoft Executives, who had followed this initiative from the very first lunch, had the opportunity to visit one of the refugee camps in Albania during the planning process:

"It was probably the most horrific thing I had ever seen. There were probably 5000 people in this camp."

– Frank Schott, Microsoft EMEA

Other Microsoft volunteers had similar experiences. Women, children and men were crammed together in small tents. By talking to the refugees directly the Microsoft volunteers were able to experience first hand how these were people just like them selves, people with homes and jobs who suddenly were forced to leave everything behind. Their home was no longer theirs and fleeing from the Serbs they had not only lost their possessions but also part of their identity.

"It's very hard to go to a refugee camp and leave without thinking, 'We've got to do something'"

– Frank Schott[1]

Given clear objectives and fuelled by a strong motivation to bring about change, Microsoft employees initiated a project that would become wide cross-sector collaboration and provide the foundation for the future partner-

ship. The employees were also encouraged by their success, to bring in other technological companies with complementary expertise. And so they did. Microsoft decided to go into partnership with Compaq as well as other technology companies and together the taskforce went on to provide assistance and consultancy to the UNHCR. The UNHCR chief technology officer at the time was working side by side with the taskforce to achieve the best result. Loyal to its field of competence, Microsoft donated cash, software, technology assistance and volunteers' working hours.

The first phase of the UNHCR partnership which lasted two years (1999–2001) was driven by the urgency of a deep humanitarian crisis. However, as things stabilized, the establishing of a more formal understanding of the evolving partnership was needed. In Kosovo the involved companies worked pro bono to establish the refugee registration scheme called Project Profile –which by then had become the real solution to UNHCR's very first problem analysis. The second phase started in 2003–2004 when UNHCR wanted to expand the pilot version of Project Profile into a mainstreamed solution. At that point Microsoft Consulting Services (MCS) helped draft the specifications of the technology solution for UNHCR. Having assisted pro bono to the development of the specs, MCS decided not to bid for the UNHCR tender to develop the software solution. The bid was awarded to a local company based in Geneva called ELCA.[2] Microsoft partnered with ELCA to help implement the mainstream version of Project Profile, it assisted UNHCR in the overall project management pro-bono and provided pro bono time from employees to help roll out the technology in various refugee camps.[3]

In December 2003, the partnership was renewed and framed in a Memorandum of Understanding co-signed by Jean Philippe Courtois and the UNHCR High Commissioner at the time, Ruud Lubbers. The Letter of Understanding (LoU) set in writing the important framework of the partnership. Below is an extraction of the LoU detailing the major elements of the co-operation:

". . . Whereas the co-operation consists of three major elements outlined herewith:

1) leadership and support in the establishment of Community Technology Learning Centres for mutually selected refugee populations within the scope of enhancing UNHCR's contribution to personal development, education and protection activities;

2) provision of technical expertise for UNHCR Project PROFILE;

3) opportunities for raising awareness of UNHCR's mission and activities among the general public and aimed toward increasing the support of individuals for UNHCR"[4]

Since 2003 Microsoft has constantly increased its engagement to what is known throughout the company today as Corporate Citizenship.

Thus the question arises as to why a company, this particular company, would engage into activities of citizenship and community work? Is doing good for doing well a necessity for market leaders?

Microsoft Corporation

Known around the globe and used by the vast majority of the computerized world, Microsoft Corporation is a software technology company that was founded by Paul Allen and Bill Gates in 1975. More than 30 years later the company earns revenues of $44.28 billion and employs 71,553 people. As a world leader in its field, the company faces competitive challenges on many levels, in the software, internet and the home entertainment domain. On the legislative level, Microsoft faces anti-trust cases and engages into intellectual property, websecurity and webdomain protection cases. At the time of the Kosovo crisis in 1999, the share value of Microsoft peaked, but soon dropped severely, and Microsoft's external image was suffering. There was an increasingly obvious missing link between engineering potential and consumers' demands which paired with high excess reserves of cash and lack of investment opportunities can be seen as key reasons to the fall in share value.[5] At the time, Microsoft being a market leader was easily related to and yet also thought of

as an impersonal giant swallowing its competitors, expressed in the allegations of monopoly powers in the US at the time.

"The power of computing enables people to pursue their passions and realize their potential, no matter who they are. Through global citizenship efforts and local partnerships, one of the ways we are helping to strengthen communities is to extend the benefits of technology to the people that can benefit most."

– Bill Gates about Microsoft global citizenship efforts.[6] Bill Gates, Microsoft Chairman and Chief Software Architect

Microsoft's Global Citizenship activities

The time period in which Microsoft's Corporate Citizenship initiatives were born also corresponds with the launch period of the Melinda & Bill Gates Foundation, which is positioned well outside of the company sphere. A new awareness of the stakeholder model also developed during this period. Was the company only to be responsive to shareholder expectations for profits, as Friedman prominently argued, or did it need to take other actors into account, such as the community around it, employees, civil society, governments, customers and partners? Is it possible to sustain longer term business success and even shareholder value in today's marketplace without a proper management of stakeholders' expectations?

Is it feasible to marry the two in a complimentary manner; to satisfy those vital shareholder expectations and to engage into activities going further than the development, production, marketing and distribution of a product or service?

The World Business Council for Sustainable Development action team created the CSR definition stating that *"Corporate Social Responsibility is the sustainable commitment by business to contribute to development and to the well-being and the improvement of the quality of life of employees, their families and the community at large."[7]* Critical events in the corporate world, amongst those, Shell Brent Spa (1995), the Nike child labour case (1995), and the Asian Financial Crisis (1997) rose awareness of the fact that time and space were shrinking rapidly for international business and citizens: Globalization had started to leave its marks. The Seattle protests at WTO meeting were a wake up call for the multilateral organizations and led to the creation of the UN Global Compact. At the same time in Europe, the Heads of State and Government appealed *"companies for a new sense of corporate responsibility"*. For the first time ever, CSR was clearly written in the core recommendations of an EU policy document, the Lisbon Strategy setting targets and objectives towards 2010 and reinforcing Europe's twin objectives of competitiveness and inclusion.

Very soon the world was forced to realize the effects of 9/11/2001 which meant finance and business had globalized as well as risks. This called for yet further development and understanding of corporations' role in society and in the larger community. Terrorism had started to attack the very foundations of international values and exchanges: the major corporations' economic foundations and system. The link between poverty, lack of education, wealth polarization and terrorism started to take new and clearer shapes than ever before.

In the same time period, the progressive development of partnerships, ISO and Social Accountability norms and the Triple Bottom Line concept (1998) had started to influence a generation of business leaders. It became increasingly clear that good citizenship would need to be closely connected to the corporate mission and not be an "add-on". At the very same time, Microsoft went through a revision of its own corporate mission and values. It was at that point that the firm's global citizenship activities were to be based on the global corporate mission: *"to enable people and businesses throughout the world to realize their full potential."*[8]

The Corporate Citizenship team of Microsoft was staring to take shape in 2003 within the Corporate Affairs team and in collaboration with various other teams, from Communications to Public sector and other parts of the business. The terms corporate citizenship and corporate social responsibility became synonyms. The company refers to its corporate citizenship initiatives as its "Global Citizenship" activities. It was to be defined

and to be given a content and a body of practice that would reach across shareholders and stakeholders, through specific projects and initiatives with business and societal relevance.

The Chief Executive Officer (CEO) of Microsoft Europe, Middle-East and Africa, Jean-Philippe Courtois, had been a major player in the creation of this vision. His efforts were to engage Microsoft as a responsible leader, servicing the public good through partnerships with customers, governments, local communities and other stakeholders in order to provide economic and social growth.

In short the following three areas of responsibility can summarize thus. First of all, this means to practice responsible business, throughout all processes and with all stakeholders. Secondly it involves addressing the challenges and opportunities that lie in the broad societal impact of the rapidly evolving software technology sector. This means in particular addressing security, privacy, and online child safety issues through investments in collaborative agreements to enhance a safe computing experience for all. Finally, it involves making sure that the benefits of the knowledge economy involves everyone and be spread across the world.

Looking at its various areas of responsibility, Microsoft chooses to specify ambitious targets for success. In the knowledge economy area, it commits to broaden technology skills and reach a quarter billion people world-wide, underserved by technology by 2010. This target applies to Europe with the bold goal to help provide technology opportunities, content, IT skills training to 20 million people through the creation of the European Alliance on Skills for Employability and the investments of the Unlimited Potential Community Technology Skills Program. When the mission refers to help people realize their potential, and when we look at the most disadvantaged, it is clear why Microsoft saw the opportunity to make social investments relating to education and training. In this framework they decided to educate refugees and give them life opportunities. Training and education, humanitarian relief support and responsible capacity building can be seen as long-term business investments and enabling the most underserved to benefit from technology and realize their full potential. Aligning global citizenship to its core business, the social investments made by Microsoft were based on the core expertise, competences and resources of the company.[9]

Building upon the company focus on the provision of education and technology skills training to the most disadvantaged, Microsoft top management decided that the partnership with UNHCR would be a strategic part of its corporate citizenship, and compatible with the knowledge economy programs. The Unlimited Potential Community Technology Centres were used to drive forward the provision of training for refugees as the UNHCR partnership became a grantee of the Unlimited Potential program launched in 2003. At the same time, the refugees' registration kit called project Profile became a core part of the emergency response program: the first practical example of how to combine Microsoft's citizenship efforts with its core competencies as a technology and innovation developer. It was conceived to give refugees an identity card providing access to health care and education as well as the possibility to be reunited with family members. In the follow-up, an extension of this work led to numerous employees volunteering and sent to remote places in Africa to work with UNHCR.[10]

Today Jean-Philippe Courtois reflects upon the lessons learned from the corporate citizenship developments within the company; what these developments have meant for the company, its employees, the community and Microsoft's partners, all cooperating in this effort to work out synergies. Has the partnership with UNHCR been the most efficient to undertake as a strategy? What has each organisation gained from the partnership and what ethical assumptions have each partner been making when agreeing to cooperate? While it is possible to argue that Microsoft's motives are strictly pro-bono and humanitarian, the cynic could perceive the possibility of commercially-beneficial publicity being gained offsetting some negative and widely held perceptions of a dominant company.

Conversely, one could argue that UNHCR decision to take advantage of Microsoft's support to further its important humanitarian aims were responsible whilst others may be less sympathetic, arguing for example that all UN agencies properly

receive non-partisan governmental support for what they do, and shouldn't risk the possible 'taint' of commercial sponsorship in any form, particularly if that might encourage governments to reduce their commitments to it, or citizens that then feel that their consumer perceptions influence their opinion on UNHCR projects.

The United Nations High Commissioner for Refugees

United Nations High Commissioner for Refugees (UNHCR) is headquartered in Geneva, Switzerland and was established in 1950 by UN General Assembly after several earlier international institutions had been established to provide protection for refugees. It was first called the League of Nations (UN) and launched with the appointment of the Norwegian scientist and explorer Fridtjof Nansen as its first High Commissioner in 1921. In 1999, at the time when UNHCR entered into partnership with Microsoft the High Commissioner post was held by Sadako Ogata, followed by António Guterres 2005-2009. Originally UNHCR was given a three year mandate, under the Geneva Convention of 1951 by the United Nations, to help settle the refugees of the Second World War, though due to the continuous new conflicts and therefore also refugees, it was changed in 2003 giving a mandate lasting until the refugee problem is solved. Overall UNHCR has helped an estimated 50 million people, earning two Nobel Peace Prizes. There are 6,540 people working for UNHCR in 116 countries[11] helping 20.8 million people.[12]

The UNHCR mandate based on the 1951 Geneva Refugee Convention and the 1967 Protocol involves coordinating international efforts to protect and aid refugees. The aim of UNHCR is to shield and help the 8.4 million refugees bring their lives back to a normal situation. A refugee is defined according to Geneva Convention 1951 § 1 A2 as: *"people who are outside their countries because of a well-founded fear of persecution based on their race, religion, nationality, political opinion or membership in a particular social group, and who cannot or do not want to return home."*[13] The mandate also covers assistance to asylum seekers. Basic help provided by UNHCR consists mainly of shelter, food, water, sanitation and medical care. UNHCR also provides help for approximately 6.6 million internally displaced people: These are people who have fled their homes, but not crossed any country borders. Because this group is not covered by their mandate, the international community is working to help this group in a more appropriate and complete way.[14] In addition UNHCR looks after 2.4 million stateless people, 1.6 million returnees and 773,000 asylum seekers. The remaining 960,000 are refugees of other concerns.[15]

Funding partners

UN subsidises a little less than two percent of the UNHCR regular budget for administrative costs. The total UNHCR budget is of $ 1 billion annually (2004 figures).

In terms of funding, UNHCR is hence mainly dependent on donations made by countries, institutions, corporations and individuals. (For more information about direct contributions and annual budgets visit the www.unhcr.org.) Cooperative partnering institutions include; World Food Program, World Health Organisation, UN Development Program, International Committee of the Red Cross and the International Federation of the Red Cross and the Red Crescent among others. These partnerships, therefore, are essential for the achievement of the goals of UNHCR.[16]

UNHCR's partnership with Microsoft is one of the strategic corporate partnerships, which UNHCR had agreed to engage into at various levels of depth. Other main partners are Armani Group, Fuji Optical, Marionnaud, Nestlé, Nike, Schneider Electric, Merck & Co. Inc, PricewaterhouseCoopers, Manpower and Statoil.

In their partnership with UNHCR, corporations agree to the UNHCR Corporate Code of Conduct, meaning that the corporations involved have to abide to the code both in principle and in practice: The intentions are that a code of conduct will lead to enduring and transparent relationships. UNHCR enters into partnership with the goal of fulfilling its mandate, not for personal financial gains. This is explicitly described to corporate partners.

Further UNHCR seeks to engage with corporations that are socially responsible and which do not engage in irresponsible operations as described in the three criteria for responsible operations set forward by UNHCR;

1 Manufacture or sale of weapons or components
2 Child labour
3 Operations in countries subject to UN sanctions

Under these criteria, UNHCR is free to choose not to engage with any partner which has a public image reflecting the above mentioned three criteria. It is the responsibility of the corporation to inform of their previous and present business activities. In this, the partnership between Microsoft and UNHCR was an obvious choice for both parties.

The criteria also demand an engagement to operate with transparency and that all partnership information should be available to the public. UNHCR maintains its right to the sole decision power over its operations and the partnership should not compromise the integrity of UNHCR or its partner. This is also why the agency does not grant exclusivity to any corporation in terms of partners, use, preference of promotion of any products and services. Finally, it was to be considered that the use of the UNHCR logo is allowed only when predetermined in writing for a particular activity and only during the time of the contract. For other uses specific authorisation had to be granted from the UNHCR agency.

Choosing UNHCR

During the past decades we have seen an increase in the number of companies, non-governmental organisations, institutions and foundations as well as intergovernmental organisations, which work for the public good. The competition for resources has become fierce and as a result business will have to choose with whom to collaborate.

UNHCR claims that it is in the own interest of business to invest in the work of UNHCR and refugees. The reason is that due to crisis and war, markets experience a negative impact; instability and insecurity, while businesses prosper in communities that are viably stable and safe. This includes the work of UNHCR.

UNHCR offers the framework of a global institution, with experience and expertise in its field operating across the world, as well as a being a proud winner of the NOBEL Peace Prize, twice. One of the most important factors is that 90% of donations are directly used for the target market. It makes a difference, indeed to numerous institutions and NGOs that have been criticised for using a high percentage of donations for administrative costs. Finally also, it made a difference that UNHCR works with capacity building and durable solutions in their work to protect the refugees, which appeared of importance to the business side of Microsoft in its decision process.

Common Ground

After the first phase of the emergency response project, during the Kosovo crisis, the partnership was to be based on a common ground in order to develop and survive; with goals and objectives laid down in the Letter of Understanding. At the base lie the objectives to improve the livelihoods of refugees, through technology support and transfer of know-how used to raise the awareness and advocacy on Refugees' needs and potential. Microsoft's support with employee involvement, education and IT skills training was key to demonstrate the "human face of technology". The partnership was therefore to be based on commitment and core competences as well as trust and public relations.

For Microsoft and UNHCR these aspects were essential. For Microsoft it involved a substantial amount of resources, both in kind and cash to invest in humanitarian response and community building projects; and in principle, without a direct or immediate return on investment. For UNHCR the essentials lie in the fact that it is an intergovernmental organisation –and a non-partisan organisation. A failure to keep the partnership would lead to loss of specific expertise and opportunities for developing pro bono innovation, direct cash grants and in kind support for training of UNHCR refugees. This again, would have a direct impact on refugees' livelihoods. For Microsoft a failure could lead to loss of reputational capital as well as employee pride and morale.

Upon the decision to work together, UNHCR and Microsoft engaged into a durable relationship that stimulated the enlargement and institutionalization of the firm's corporate citizenship staff.

Amongst these growth stimuli, the recruitment of several professionals in the area of Corporate Citizenship, Community Affairs and strategic partnerships were essential to structure global citizenship. As a vital part of this Elena Bonfiglioli, today Director of Corporate Citizenship at Microsoft EMEA, was brought in to apply the most efficient contemporary strategies in the field. Mrs Bonfiglioli previously worked at CSR Europe – the European Business Network on Corporate Social Responsibility (www.csreurope.org) where she had worked with several companies on CSR programs and strategies. Amongst numerous initiatives she has also worked with the creation of the European Academy of Business in Society (EABIS).

Outcomes: The case of Project PROFILE

At the time, in 1999 Microsoft employed about 31, 575 persons and had a net revenue of $ 19.75 billion an equivalent of 29% growth. Seven years later, in 2006 these numbers had accumulated heavily. Microsoft employed 71,172 persons and earned net revenues of $ 44.28 billion. Microsoft began with a dream of a PC on every desk and in every home. Thirty years ago that seemed impossible. Today, for the more than one billion people, life has changed profoundly: information is more readily available; connections are more easily made; commerce is achieved quicker; and success is closer than ever.

Initiated by Microsoft's employees, the Project PROFILE is an example of the technology innovation and skills-for-humanity – initiatives of the company. The Project Profile registration system, the "Refugee Field Kit" is a self-contained transportable registration system which includes basic refugee bio-data and a digital photo of each refugee. The kit produces an ID card and a signature is taken from the refugee. The card also contains a two-dimensional bar-code which includes the coded refugee bio-data. The system keeps track of refugees, but also helps UNHCR identify their needs. During the Kosovo crisis, Microsoft donated 100 "registration kits" to UNHCR and the project was rolled out in over a dozen countries worldwide. Subsequently the kit has been adapted and upgraded to cope with other situations. The field kit was developed as a card-producing solution which does not include identification elements, except for the photo and the signature. These ID cards are primarily used for quick identification and as a protection document. The production of this type of card can be done by relatively inexpensive off-the-shelf computer equipment. The standardized system has proved very useful for UNHCR and it has had a major impact on refugees. The ID cards provide refugees with protection from forcible recruitment, arbitrary arrests and detention. It also ensures basic rights, family reunification and identification of special needs.[17]

John Bankuwiha, Burundian refugee in the UNHCR Refugee Camp, Lukole "B" Camp expressed the vital importance of the registration kit and why the refugees prize the registration system:

"By confusion I had registered for voluntary repatriation to Burundi. Realizing my mistake I ran over to the registration centre. Showing my ration card I hoped that they could find my name in the system. To my great relief my picture came up on the screen and the UNHCR staff could verify my status and my right to food." John explained. "Once we are registered, we refugees are sure that our records in the computer will not be tampered with. This way our rights as refugees are protected and we can get all the assistance we are entitled to in the camps and once we return to our home country."

– John Bankuwiha, Burundian refugee, Tanzania.[18]

Innovating upon success: Unlimited Potential and the Community Technology Skills Program (CTSP)

The Unlimited Potential Community Technology Skills Program (CTSP) is part of a community initiative aimed to bring computer skills and training to the most disadvantaged, in this case to refugees and asylum seekers. It is part of Microsoft's Unlimited Potential initiative (UP) designed to help five billion people realize new opportunities, learn, connect, create and improve life by using the power of software. By partnering with governments, NGOs, educators and academics Microsoft aims to take an innovative approach to enabling new ways of social and economic empowerment for the underserved populations of the world.

The first centre to train refugees was created in St. Petersburg, Russia in collaboration with UNHCR and Red Cross. Computer literacy is becoming increasingly important in everyday-life. The aim is to help refugees live a normal life after repatriation, pursuing higher education and employment.

"The UNHCR and Red Cross do vital work and make a real difference to the lives of millions of people in need. The St. Petersburg Learning Centre marks another significant milestone in our long-term partnership with UNHCR, and the start of an exciting new partnership with the Red Cross. Our employees have a genuine passion and commitment for putting information technology to work to overcome big challenges and we are proud and honoured to support them and our partners, here in St. Petersburg and around the world."
– Jean-Philippe Courtois at the opening ceremony 15th April 2004.[19]

The Centre provides refugees as well as the local community with sources of learning, distance education and Internet access and external sources of support for entrepreneurial projects. A new centre was developed in Tanzania, and was launched in September 2006.[20]

The St. Petersburg centre is equipped with personal computers, a server, software and community staff trained by Microsoft employees to deliver an IT curriculum designed to provide students at the Centre with basic and advanced IT skills, as well as provide support for self-study and other community-building activities.

"This is a unique and important initiative. As the world's first such community learning centre for refugees, it is a defining moment on the road to a truly inclusive information society, and in our five-year partnership with Microsoft. Working with

committed, passionate and innovative people from the business community is enabling UNHCR to really solve problems and provide modern, lasting solutions."

– Dennis Blair, UNHCR Deputy Representative in the Russian Federation, at the opening ceremony.[21]

The UNHCR Council of Business Leaders

As the years progressed, UNHCR started to realize the potential of its various corporate partners. Some of the partner companies also pressed UNHCR to bring forces together and facilitate exchange and synergies amongst its various partners.

In January 2005, stimulated by discussions with Microsoft and Nike, UNHCR spear-headed the creation of the UNHCR Council of Business Leaders. It was launched in Davos, by the UNHCR High Commissioner together with executives from Microsoft, Nike, Manpower, Merck and PwC. The Council aims to create more solid avenues for leveraging the value from various business partnerships. The Council seeks to provide organizational support to UNHCR, capacity building on UNHCR activities like branding and PR, and also to provide the structure for an end-to-end approach to companies' investments for the refugees cause.

Its structure and organisation is so that corporate partners can mobilize the expertise of their executives, assess opportunities for direct or joint funding to UNHCR, and/or donate other resources such as tools, equipment and/ or volunteers. Companies are also encouraged to use their external media and communication tools to reach customers and partners to promote the image and cause of UNHCR. Internally the use of companies' network consisting of suppliers and employees is important as well to raise funds for UNHCR.

Entering into a partnership with UNHCR was an important choice at the time. It was the first time the company entered in a partnership with a UN Agency trying to find joint solutions for a common cause. The company learnt over time to mobilize all its assets: cash and software donations through the Community affairs team, the time, competencies and expertise of its volunteers to deliver real technology innovation through

Microsoft Consulting Services, the management skills of its executives and its online marketing strategy through MSN.

Over time, the relationship started to be managed jointly by Corporate Affairs and the Global Strategic Accounts (GSA) team, which now manages other UN partnerships.

"Working with UNHCR was a great opportunity to see how the company's core business intelligence could make a real difference to society in very unexpected ways. It is an example of what Porter today calls the 'INSIDE OUT' and 'OUTSIDE IN' model of CSR."

– Elena Bonfiglioli, Director of Corporate Citizenship at Microsoft.[22]

Commitment and core competences

UNHCR and Microsoft categorised their efforts and projects around core commitments, which appears to allow for complementary action while being exclusive in nature (Figure 1). Microsoft's expertise and technology support has been used to create the projects and initiative commonly, based on the functional needs of UNHCR and the competitive advantage of Microsoft. Subsequently this involves IT capacity building and application development.

Jean-Philippe Courtois remembers that employee volunteering had always played a very important role in the partnership, for both partners. Those Microsoft employees participating in the volunteering program were very passionate about helping fellow humans. In turn Microsoft excelled in citizenship practices, employee benefits, research and development and accessibility work.

On the other hand, during an internal study conducted for the company, Price water house Coopers found, in 2004, that there was little awareness and understanding of the company's citizenship initiative among Microsoft employees. As Microsoft began to structure its work more thoroughly, the challenge was to implement citizenship programs consistently in all of the worldwide subsidiaries and countries while being locally relevant and efficient. It was essential for Microsoft to put sufficient focus on key performance indicators, to develop appropriate metrics, and external reporting. There is still a

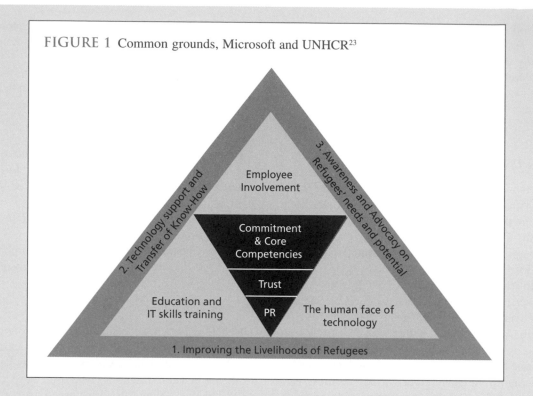

FIGURE 1 Common grounds, Microsoft and UNHCR[23]

lot yet to be done within and beyond the specific UNHCR partnership

Microsoft had enabled UNHCR to use advanced and complex systems making their work more efficient.

"Using Microsoft's core business competencies and expertise enhance UNHCR's technological capacity, bringing the benefit of technology solutions closer to refugee communities and at the same time providing support for UNHCR's general mandate – awareness raising and advocacy for refugees."
– Joosten Frauke, Associate External Relations Officer for Private Sector Fundraising and Public Affairs Service at UNHCR.

Technology systems have been placed or improved at UNHCR headquarters, for UNHCR field offices and onsite in refugee camps, serving, again, both parties in the partnerships and the community involved.

In order to help refugees more directly, Microsoft moved rapidly into training grants through its global community investment program; Unlimited Potential. But also, the investment mentioned above, in Calks in St. Petersburg and Tanzania; are efforts to improve the refugees' livelihood through access to education and opportunities.

But another very important aspect of the partnership became the public relations (PR) and branding exposure of UNHCR to promote the awareness of the UNHCR cause and brand amongst the general public. The budget of UNHCR still relies heavily on donors, and it does not always stretch to cover all expenditures. Especially within the business community it is important to leverage the exposure and the brand of UNHCR. This is done by public relations and / or third party advertorials focusing on raising the awareness of refugees.

Evolution and progress

Transitional phase 2002–2003

Despite the ambitious and enthusiastic beginnings with the Kosovo crisis, the partnership underwent a flex point, as organizational transition took place

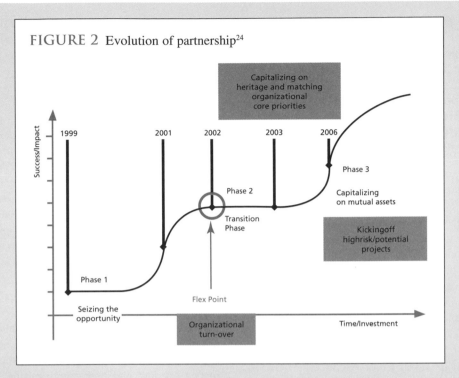

FIGURE 2 Evolution of partnership[24]

in 2002 and 2003 both in UNHCR and in Microsoft. The partnership managers in both organizations moved on to new challenges and the partnership (Figure 2), still in its piloting phase, was left with no direct owner. People managing the partnership changed. As a result the progress in the partnership slowed down in the short run.

Consolidation phase 2003–2005

In the aftermath of the transition period at Microsoft and in UNHCR, the years 2003 and 2004 brought a consolidation phase and new spirit. In December 2003 a formalization of the partnership took place as a three year contract was signed. The technology solution created for the Kosovo crisis was now further developed and rolled out to different refugee camps in Europe, Middle East and Africa (EMEA) region. Some improvements were now adopted to make the registration kit more adaptable, flexible and interoperable, in particular to language differences. However the system proved to be efficient and UNHCR decided to adopt it in all its operations.

The Project PROFILE was rolled out in the summer months of 2004 in various camps and Microsoft employees were encouraged to volun-

teer. The President of Microsoft EMEA at the time, Michel Lacombe e-mailed employees across the region, seeking volunteers. Out of the 5000 contacted, over 400 employees were ready to contribute with their competences and time. Those who, for whatever reason, could not participate were supportive and proud of the initiative:

"This is a fantastic initiative! I really felt proud of Microsoft when I read your email. Running a profitable business is big, delivering innovative products that change the way people work and behave is bigger, but doing all this and still without ignoring countries hit by war or other catastrophes is huge".

– Microsoft employee to CEO Jean-Philippe Courtois.[25]

In less than two weeks 250 employees responded, of which 12 were selected as technology experts in the fields of server systems; database and access management and sent to various refugee camps for periods of 2–3 weeks.[26] The first pilot project to bring IT skills training opportunities to refugees was initiated in April 2004. The Community Technology

Centre in Russia, St. Petersburg proved successful and was, in 2006, undergoing an assessment period to determine the outcomes of the project at the same time of the launch of a centre in Tanzania.

Expansion and the future of a global leader: How to adapt to the diversity of stakeholders?

Yet, Jean-Philippe Courtois reflected, more needs to be done . . . with the partnership expanding in time and size, the creation of a team with credible resources was essential in order to achieve the objectives laid down in the framework. Top-management and world leaders gathered at the World Economic Forum in Davos in 2005 and created the Council of Business Leaders.

An expansion in the partnership took place. A briefing analyzed for UNHCR to note what and where further possibilities lay. Based on the core competencies of the member companies, this Council of Business Leaders, under the management of Bill Gates, Chief Architect, Microsoft, Angelina Jolie, goodwill ambassador, UNHCR, and Wendy Chamberlin, Deputy High Commission, UNHCR was established. The recognition of the communication resources and the network available to Microsoft and other partners, was used to promote the cause of UNHCR, which was turned into a major campaign; ninemillion.org.

Nonetheless, Microsoft reached a point of re-assessment of several projects. While global citizenship had become an integral part of the company, it was urgent to define if this field was to be expanded and how.

Both Project Profile and the building of the centre in St. Petersburg served as milestones to evaluate the effectiveness, capacity and impact of Microsoft's support. The creation of the Council was a milestone as it brought together a distinct partnership approach and it also led to the support of MSN to help raise awareness on the UNHCR brand which was crystallized in the www.ninemillion.org fundraising campaign with Nike and Right to play on the World refugee Day on June 20, 2006

As of hcre, would the company he able to explore the most efficient and effective strategies, initiatives, innovations and markets? Would it not benefit from the recruitment of managers of yet other fields, from private and public sector,, bringing fresh thinking from external minds into a company that came to the market lead three decades ago?

It was stated, and can be read on www.microsoft.com that:

"At Microsoft, we believe that constructive stakeholder engagement improves our business decision-making processes and helps us anticipate and address the changing expectations of society. We understand that our reputation outside the company is a direct reflection of how we demonstrate our corporate values. Engagement with customers, partners, shareholders, NGOs, governments, and other stakeholders will be essential in helping us identify and manage key issues that will test how successfully we live our values."

Is "partnership" the answer and can the company leverage all its asset to contribute pro bono publico? Is it creating the right partnerships to complement its market opening and opportunity raising? Was that lunchtime initiative, in 1999 during the Kosovo crisis, a sign for this vast multinational to serve the challenges of diversity internally and externally? Was it an incident that Microsoft's corporate citizenship initiatives were formed at the very same time as the company's share value fell and anti-trust cases multiplied? Can a company explain its corporate citizenship activities as investments in the future?

Notes

1. *Financial Times Weekend* (31st December, 2004) "Office Angels".
2. UNHCR (2006), "UNHCR and Microsoft Partnership", Toyota Meeting, UNHCR's Corporate Partnership Programme, Belgium.
3. *Financial Times Weekend* (31st December, 2004) "Office Angels".
4. Letter of Understanding between Microsoft Corporation EMEA and United Nations High Commissioner for Refugees, pp. 1, December, 2003.
5. Suder / Payte (2006), "Microsoft – A Case in Cross Company Transformation", *Thunderbird International Business Review*, Vol. 48(4), pp.555–569, July-August Issue.
6. Citizenship Report 2005, pp.4 Bill Gates, Microsoft Chairman and Chief Software Architect, www.microsoft.com/mscorp/citizenship.

7. Regelbrugge (1999), "Promoting Corporate Citizenship – Opportunities for Business and Civil Society Engagement", CIVICUS World Alliance for Citizen Participation, p.32.

8. http://www.microsoft.com/about/corporatecitizenship/citizenship/about/mission.mspx, 12.08.06.

9. Bonfiglioli, E., Director of Corporate Citizenship, Microsoft EMEA, interviewed 07.07.06.

10. http://www.microsoft.com/about/corporatecitizenship/citizenship/knowledge/emergencyresponse.mspx, 29.07.06.

11. http://www.unhcr.org/cgi-bin/texis/vtx/basics, 28.07.06.

12. UNHCR (2006) "2005 Global *Refugee* Trends", Field Information and Coordinated Support Section, Division of Operational Services, UNHCR Geneva, http://unhcr.org/statistics

13. Wilkinson for UNHCR (2001), "The Wall Behind Which Refugees Can Shelter", *Refugees*, Vol. 2, N. 123, Italy.

14. http://www.unhcr.org/cgi-bin/texis/vtx/basics, entered 28.07.06.

15. http://www.unhcr.org/cgi-bin/texis/vtx/events?id= 3e7f46e04 09.08.06.

16. UNHCR (2005), "UNHCR's Mid-Year Financial Report for 2005", found on http://www.unhcr.org, entered 20.07.06.

17. Joosten, Frauke, Associate External Relations Officer for Private Sector Fundraising and Public Affairs Service at UNHCR, written interview 24.08.06.

18. "Microsoft and UNHCR team up to better protect refugees", 10.04.05 http://www.unhcr.org/cgi-bin/texis/vtx/partners?id= 3d8f1be44.

19. "Hi-tech hope for refugees in Russia, thanks to UNHCR, Red Cross and Microsoft initiative", St. Petersburg, Russia 15.04.04 http://www.unhcr.org/cgi-bin/texis/vtx/partners/opendoc.htm?tbl=PARTNERS&page=home&id=40e2c66b4.

20. Joosten, Frauke, UNHCR, 24.08.06.

21. "Hi-tech hope for refugees in Russia, thanks to UNHCR, Red Cross and Microsoft initiative" 15.04.04.

22. Harvard Business Review, December 2006.

23. UNHCR Council of Business Leaders (2006), "Partnering for Impact".

24. UNHCR (2006), "Toyota Meeting" UNHCR's Corporate Partnership Programme, Bruxelles, 19th January 2006.

25. UNHCR (2006), "UNHCR and Microsoft Partnership", Toyota Meeting, UNHCR's Corporate Partnership Programme, Belgium.

26. Bonfiglioli, E., Director of Corporate Citizenship, Microsoft EMEA, interviewed 07.07.06.

IKEA'S SOCIAL AND ENVIRONMENTAL RESPONSIBILITY INITIATIVES

"IKEA is a leader in setting high environmental standards for its product. That means employing strict manufacturing methods and supply processes so that materials, technologies and transportation have the least damaging effects on the environment."[1]

– Rene Hausler, Partner,
IKEA-San Diego Franchisee.

"We consider IKEA to be setting an excellent example for other corporations to follow. IKEA is prepared to go further than just saying 'no' to a supplier who exploits children. The company is showing a genuine interest in bringing about improvement for children by assuming a responsibility for child labour issues."[2]

– Ingvar Hjartso, UNICEF
Representative.

A socially responsible company

In April 2005, Sweden based Inter IKEA Systems BV (IKEA), the global furniture retail giant, received the Outstanding Sustainable Style Achievement (OSSA)[3] Award for eliminating the usage of Polybrominated Diphenyl Ether (PBDE),[4] a toxic fire suppressor used in manufacturing furniture. Earlier, in 2004, IKEA had received the BUPA Healthy Communities award for Excellence,[5] an award funded by the Ministry of Health, UK. The company was given this award for initiating programs to curb crime and to tackle the issue of unemployment in the neighborhood of its Eastville store in Bristol, UK.

Source: This case was written by Komal Chary, under the direction of Vivek Gupta, ICMR Center for Management Research. It was compiled from published sources, and is intended to be used as a basis for class discussion rather than to illustrate either effective or ineffective handling of a management situation. Copyright © 2006, ICMR. All rights reserved.

Reproduced with permission from ICMR Center for Management Research.

IKEA is the world's largest furniture retailer that specializes in stylish but inexpensive Scandinavian designed furniture (Refer Exhibit I for IKEA Facts). IKEA's success is attributed to its vast experience in the furniture retail market, its product differentiation and cost leadership. The company's furniture was sold in kits to be assembled by its customers at home. In addition to furniture, it also sold utility items such as utensils, hooks, clips, stands and more. IKEA's founder Ingvar Kamprad (Kamprad) had built an international furniture chain of 226 stores in Europe, Africa, Asia and the US. For fiscal year 2004–05, IKEA generated revenues of US$ 17.9 billion, a 15% increase over the previous fiscal year.

Most IKEA furniture was made of wood, which the company sourced from different countries. Acquiring this wood often involved large-scale cutting of trees from forests. Some of IKEA's suppliers used to exploit children in the manufacture of goods for IKEA. These problems made IKEA's

---

EXHIBIT I Facts on IKEA

TURNOVER OF IKEA

YEAR	TURNOVER (In Euro million)
1954	1
1964	25
1974	169
1984	1216
1994	4396
1999	8220
2005	15212

NUMBER OF IKEA CATALOGUES

YEAR	IKEA CATALOGUES DISTRIBUTED (In millions)
1954	0.5
1964	2
1974	6.8
1984	35
1994	72
1999	96
2005	160

EXHIBIT I (Continued)

NUMBER OF PEOPLE WHO VISITED IKEA STORES

YEAR	IKEA VISITORS (In thousands)
1954	52
1964	1,644
1974	8,161
1984	52,114
1994	125,595
1999	219,353
2005	453,791

NUMBER OF IKEA STORES

YEAR	IKEA STORES
1954	0
1964	2
1974	9
1984	52
1994	114
1999	152
2005	226

WORLD'S BIGGEST PURCHASERS OF IKEA PRODUCTS

COUNTRY	PERCENTAGE
Germans	19
Americans	11
British	11
French	9
Swedish	8

Source: www.ikea.com.

management decide to reorganize the company's business policies and introduce stringent rules to ensure better social and environmental practices, both within the company and with business partners. Commenting on IKEA's decision, the company spokesman Marty Marston said, "At IKEA, we're moving toward a way of thinking based on the philosophy that everything we take should be used, reused and recycled, either by ourselves or nature, in such a way that causes the least possible harm to the environment."[6] Being socially and environmentally responsible made good business sense too - as Anders Dahlvig, President of IKEA Group said, "Done in a sensible way, social and environmental work is good for business. It is good for business because our customers will feel reassured that they are doing business with a company that shares their views and values. And it is good for business because it can also support cost efficiency. Using resources and raw material efficiently, saving energy, improving working conditions at our suppliers and through that getting more motivated people, will have a positive effect on costs and therefore support our business objectives."[7]

About IKEA

Kamprad established IKEA in 1943 at the age of seventeen. He came up with the name IKEA by combining the first letters of his name (Ingvar Kamprad), followed by the first letters of the farm and village he grew up in (Elmtaryd and Agunnaryd). IKEA began in a shed that was just two square meters in size. Kamprad started his business by buying pens, Christmas cards, matches, cigarette lighters, nylon stockings and other items in bulk. He sold these items to the residents of Smaland[8] at a reasonable price, but still made healthy profits. To save more money, Kamprad would piggyback his packages on milk delivery trucks. IKEA soon started making money. In 1945, Kamprad started promoting business through mail order catalogues as conducting individual sales calls became impossible.

Furniture was introduced in IKEA's product portfolio in the year 1947. By 1951, the furniture sales had increased so much that Kamprad decided to discontinue all other products and concentrate solely on selling furniture that was stylish but low priced. In the same year, the first IKEA furniture catalogue was issued and the first IKEA furniture shop was opened in 1953 at Almhult in Sweden. The first IKEA showroom was opened at Almhult in 1958. The opening of the showroom was an important milestone in the growth of IKEA as customers could, for the first time, see and touch the furniture before placing an order. By visiting the showroom, customers could review three dimensions of its products–function, quality and low price before making their purchases.

IKEA began its overseas foray in 1963 with the opening of its store in Norway. In the same year, IKEA designed the MTP bookcase that went on to become a classic. In building this and other wood products, IKEA forged good relations with Polish suppliers in the 1950s and 1960s. These relationships provided a basis for maintaining prices at levels that the majority of people could afford. With the success of the Norway store, IKEA began venturing into other neighboring countries like Denmark in 1969 and Switzerland in 1973 (Refer Exhibit II for a list of countries in which IKEA established its presence).

IKEA did not have its own manufacturing facilities. Instead, it used subcontracted manufacturers all over the world for supplies. All research and development activities were, however, centralized in Sweden. No matter how beautiful a design, it would not be put up for sale if it could not be made affordable. To achieve this affordability, IKEA engaged 12 designers at Almhult in Sweden, along with 80 freelancers to work in tandem with the production teams to identify materials and suppliers.

IKEA's corporate social responsibility (CSR) initiatives began in the 1970s. The company increased its focus on social and environmental issues in the early 1980s. IKEA's CSR involved three main areas – children, better living and the environment. According to IKEA, it focused on children, as they were the future. The company wanted to give children an opportunity to learn, develop in a safe environment and to be educated.

In the early 1980s, IKEA was criticized for using toxic chemicals such as formaldehyde,[9] polyvinyl chloride (PVC)[10] and PBDE. In 1981, the Dutch Government found that some of the IKEA furniture contained more than the stipulated amount of formaldehyde. The matter was immediately referred to Russel Johnson (Johnson), Head of Quality for IKEA. Johnson said, "If people see IKEA as a company that is polluting the environment, creating wastes or emissions, or wasting resources, then we are not living upto our mission. That's a very strong matter. We are meeting customers face-to-face everyday. As a company built on the mission to create a better everyday life for the majority of people, of course we must take environmental issues seriously."[11]

IKEA then decided to work towards eliminating the usage of all toxic chemicals that were harmful to the environment, its customers and its employees. However, instead of looking for short term solutions, the company sought long term solutions to this problem. IKEA started out by conducting seminars for

EXHIBIT II	IKEA's foray into foreign countries
1963	Norway – Oslo (Nesbru)
1969	Denmark – Copenhagen (Ballerup)
1973	Switzerland – Zürich (Spreitenbach)
1974	Germany – Munich (Eching)
1975	Australia – Artamon
1975	Hong Kong – Hong Kong (Tsim Sha Tsui)
1976	Canada – Vancouver (Richmond)
1977	Austria – Vienna (Vösendorf)
1978	Netherlands – Rotterdam (Sliedrecht)
1978	Singapore – Singapore
1980	Spain – Gran Canaria (Las Palmas)
1981	Iceland – Reykjavik
1981	France – Paris (Bobigny)
1983	Saudi Arabia – Jeddah
1984	Belgium – Brussels (Zaventem and Ternat)
1984	Kuwait – Kuwait City
1985	United States – Philadelphia
1987	United Kingdom – Manchester (Warrington)
1989	Italy – Milan (Cinisello Balsamo)
1990	Hungary – Budapest
1991	Poland – Platan
1991	Czech Republic – Prague (Zlicin)
1991	United Arab Emirates – Dubai
1992	Slovakia – Bratislava
1994	Taiwan – Taipei
1996	Finland – Esbo
1996	Malaysia – Kuala Lumpur
1998	China – Shanghai
2000	Russia – Moscow (Chimki)
2001	Israel – Netanya
2001	Greece – Thessaloniki
2004	Portugal – Lisbon
2005	Turkey – Istanbul

Source: www.ikea.com.

the top management and focused on the company's relationship and commitment to the environment. The company also associated with environmental groups such as Greenpeace[12] to identify and address environmental issues. By working with such organizations, IKEA successfully reduced the usage of formaldehyde, PBDE and other harmful chemicals in its products. IKEA also adhered to the German standards of quality requirements (which were the most stringent in the world) for its products.

IKEA has been especially concerned about child labor being used by some of its suppliers in some countries. The company stepped up its action against child labor after 1995, when a 12 year old boy Iqbal Masih (Iqbal), a child laborer working for one of IKEA's suppliers in Pakistan, was murdered. Iqbal had been sold into bonded labor to a carpet manufacturer, at the age of four by his parents, for the repayment of a loan. Iqbal was made to work 12 hours a day. He was finally rescued by the Bonded Labor Liberation Front of Pakistan (BLLF-P).[13] Iqbal even traveled to the US and Europe to tell his story. He went on to become a crusader against child slavery. He also received international recognition and awards such as the Reebok Human Rights Award[14] for his brave efforts. However, on April 16, 1995, he was shot and killed in his village while riding his bicycle. Although his assassin was never caught, it was widely believed that Iqbal had been murdered by the Pakistani carpet mafia to silence him from speaking out against child slavery. This incident brought to light the deplorable conditions under which people worked for manufacturers. In response, IKEA resolved to work more strenuously towards eradicating the problem and also to ensure that it never again did business with manufacturers who exploited their employees.

Social responsibility

IKEA undertook several projects for community development. Most of its projects were centered on children. IKEA purchased carpets from India. In August 2000, IKEA initiated the Child Rights Program in India in association with UNICEF.[15] The project was started in the Indian state of Uttar Pradesh (UP).[16] The aim of the project was to prevent child labor in 'the carpet belt'[17] of UP, by addressing root causes such as poverty, illiteracy and ill health. The project was started in nearly 200 villages with a population of more than 400,000 people. By 2004, there were a total of 500 villages with a population of about 1.3 million people under the project. UNICEF conducted school enrolment drives to educate the villagers about the benefit of schooling and education for children. Alternative Learning Centers (ALCs) were also set up. As a result of this project, over 80% of the 24,000 children who were previously out-of-school in the 200 villages, were attending primary school by 2004.[18] The remaining 20% of children were enrolled with the 99 ALCs that had been set up. The ALCs aimed at enlightening children and ultimately persuading them to enter into mainstream education.

The root cause of the bonded labor of children was their parents' extreme poverty. Most families were burdened with debt, which was passed on from generation to generation. To overcome this problem, IKEA and UNICEF established nearly 450 self-help groups (SHGs) for women. The SHGs helped the women find income generating opportunities such as embroidery, pottery and weaving. These groups helped them put aside small amounts of money every month, thus creating their own funds. These funds were saved by the SHGs in nationalized banks.

Through the SHGs, women also gained access to micro credit schemes through which they could pay their medical bills, start their own businesses, spend money on weddings in the family and conduct other important activities, instead of depending on borrowing money from local money lenders who charged exorbitant interest rates. Through this project, more than 6,000 women and their families managed to come out of the vicious circle of debt. It also meant freedom from money lenders. The status of the women, both in their families and in the local community, had been given a boost. The women gained confidence and had more decision-making authority. The SHGs also taught women to read and write. They educated the women on children's rights and gave them assistance on health and nutrition related matters. As a result of their empowerment, more and more children were enrolling into schools.

With the success of this project, IKEA and UNICEF, together with the United Nations World Health Organization (WHO),[19] initiated a five-year immunization program in UP. Started in 2002, the objective of the project was to provide protection to babies up to age of one year against the most common childhood diseases such as hepatitis, poliomyelitis, measles, mumps and influenza. Vaccination was also provided to pregnant women. During this five-year period, over 140,000 children and 150,000 pregnant women from 3000 villages were vaccinated. This immunization program was initiated upon the realization that illnesses and diseases in the family were often responsible for financial difficulties of most of the villagers. These financial hardships led people to send their children to work so as to earn for the family. IKEA, UNICEF and WHO hoped that child labor would be reduced, because of the success of the vaccination program.

IKEA and UNICEF also collaborated with Indian agencies such as the Center for Rural Education and Development Action (CREDA)[20] to especially work towards education of girls. The objective of CREDA was to put small girls who were working in villages into schools, to empower the girl child and to build a network of non-governmental organizations to eliminate child labor through education (Refer Exhibit III for achievements of this project).

EXHIBIT III Achievements of IKEA-Unicef-Creda Project

- Removal of 113 girls from hazardous industries.

- Education of girls: 500 adolescent and younger girls completed two years of non-formal education.

- Regular village level meetings.

- Formation of social mobilization groups.

- Women's participation (39% at all meetings that were conducted).

- Adult education for 250 adult women was arranged through five literacy centers.

Source: www.crin.org.

IKEA had been associated with UNICEF since the mid 1990s. Besides major country projects, the company supported UNICEF through the sale of UNICEF greeting cards & products. IKEA supported UNICEF programs through 'in-kind' assistance as well. For instance, IKEA had donated tables for use in schools and health centres in Liberia and Burundi. After the devastating Asian tsunami[21] of December 26, 2004, IKEA stores in Canada, Denmark, Germany, France, Hungary, Netherlands, Norway, Poland, Sweden, US and other countries carried out various promotions to support UNICEF relief operations in the tsunami-affected areas. IKEA donated quilts and sheets to survivors in Indonesia and Sri Lanka. The company also initiated long term rehabilitation programs in the affected areas.

In 2003, IKEA introduced the 'Brum' Teddy Bear project. This project was launched by UNICEF Goodwill Ambassador Roger Moore.[22] It was IKEA's fundraising initiative for children affected by conflict in Africa. Two euros from the sale of each 'Brum' bear in 22 countries was donated to UNICEF's 'Right to Play' projects in Angola and Uganda. The 'Brum' bear had flexible arms and legs and children could use their imagination to make the bear sit, stand, walk, wave, and nod, take a nap, or give a bear hug. At the launch of this project, Roger Moore said, "This is a brilliant initiative. By buying the toy Brum bear you can help give children back their childhood. Many children in Angola and Uganda are still missing out on their right to play in a safe environment. IKEA is setting new standards in corporate responsibility and further increasing its support to protect children's rights with this campaign."[23] Through this project, IKEA and UNICEF worked with the government of Angola, to set up education centers for nearly 1.9 million children. Similarly, in Uganda, IKEA's contribution helped launch awareness campaigns about the dangers of HIV and AIDS,[24] which was rampant in the continent of Africa. By August 2005, IKEA had sold more than 500,000 'Brum' bears, generating over one million euros.

Besides UNICEF, IKEA is associated with other organizations like 'Save the Children.'[25] On November 19, 2005, IKEA launched the '$1 is a fortune. . . . a child's smile is worth so much' campaign, together with UNICEF and Save the Children. The campaign ran between November 19 and December 24, 2005. IKEA donated one US$ for every soft toy that was sold during this period. The funds generated were used for different programs in countries like Nigeria, Chad, Vietnam and Romania. Laurence Martocq, National Communications and Public Relations Manager for IKEA Canada commented, "One dollar goes a long way to helping children in so many countries of the world today. Not only is IKEA Canada offering customers a great range of soft toys, perfect for holiday gift giving, but also an opportunity to support the valuable work of UNICEF and Save the Children."[26]

Environmental responsibility

After the formaldehyde incident came to light, IKEA took a fresh look at its stand on environmental issues. In 1989, Anders Moberg (Moberg), the then president of IKEA instructed Johnson to identify environmental issues that were relevant to IKEA and conversely how IKEA impacted the environment. Moberg told Johnson, "Environment is not just a new fashion, it will not fade away, it is the new reality and we have to adapt to it."[27] Johnson, in association with Karl-Henrik Robert[28] initiated The Natural Step (TNS) environmental program in IKEA in 1990 (Refer Exhibit IV for more information about the TNS).

IKEA's environment policy was based on TNS. With the help of TNS, IKEA identified transportation and distribution, forestry, waste management and energy consumption, as the key areas for bringing in environmental conservation. IKEA devised an action plan that was termed 'Green Steps' to tackle environmental issues (Refer Exhibit V for some of 'The Green Steps' taken by IKEA). The three important aspects of IKEA's environmental policy were: the efficient use of resources so that less waste and emissions were created; extensive use of wood for IKEA products as wood could be recycled, decomposed organically and renewed; and training employees to work on environmental issues (Refer Exhibit VI for environmental initiatives taken by IKEA at its Renton Store).

Transportation and distribution

IKEA depended heavily on transportation through trucks and trailers for the distribution of its prod-

---

EXHIBIT IV The natural step

Dr. Karl, in association with other eminent scientists, laid out four guidelines that form the basis of 'The Natural Steps.' Based on these guidelines, TNS determines the areas of concern for an organization, and works towards evolving methods to curb the problem.

The guidelines are:

- Substances from the Earth's crust must not systematically increase in the biosphere. This implies that natural resources like fossil fuels should not be extracted at a rate greater than they can be replaced by the natural cycle of photosynthesis and sunlight.

- Substances produced by society must not systematically increase in the biosphere. The implication here is that human-created substances must not be produced at a rate greater than natural systems can absorb.

- The physical basis for the productivity and diversity of nature must not be systematically deteriorated. This implies that trees and plants, which conduct photosynthesis and thus maintain a balance of carbon dioxide and oxygen in the atmosphere, must be protected.

There should be fair and efficient use of resources with respect to human needs.

Source: The Natural Step, http://repo-nt.tcc.virginia.edu/book/chap4/chapter4sec5.htm, July 14, 1999.

---

ucts to its stores and also for delivering furniture from stores to its customers' homes. The company's transportation and distribution activities thus had a significant impact on the environment through emission of gases like carbon dioxide into the atmosphere (Refer Exhibit VII for CO_2 emissions in IKEA's transport and distribution operations).

One of the first initiatives IKEA took to reduce environmental impact of transportation was to introduce smart packaging. Packing more products into a single trailer was not easy. Factors like the weight of each product were needed to be considered. IKEA made conscious efforts to make

---

EXHIBIT V Green steps taken by IKEA

- "Trash is Cash" program: Establishing a recycling center at the IKEA store in Gotenborg, Sweden and selling materials like wood, cardboard, metal and paper that would have otherwise been thrown away. This resulted in a better bottomline for the store and a cleaner environment.

- IKEA worked with Greenpeace to reduce the environmental impact of its catalog, which used over 40,000 metric tons of paper. IKEA eliminated the use of chlorine in creating its catalog, and prohibited the use of any paper made from old growth forests.

- IKEA joined the U.S. Environmental Protection Agency's 'Green Lights' Program. The objective was to reduce kilowatt/hours in North American IKEA stores by at least 15%. IKEA made use of fluorescent lighting to achieve the target. These new lights required less energy to operate, lasted longer and generated less heat.

Source: The Natural Step, http://repo-nt.tcc.virginia.edu/book/chap4/chapter4sec5.htm, July 14, 1999.

EXHIBIT VI IKEA's environmental initiatives at Renton

IKEA Renton participated in a local energy conservation program to upgrade lights at the facility. The facility reduced its energy usage by approximately 213,200 kilowatt-hours per year, representing $12,060 in annual energy cost savings.

To conserve paper and reduce pollution, IKEA reduced the size of its catalog to 4" x 5.5", and prints only on non-chlorine bleached paper.

To conserve landfill and disposal costs, IKEA's 'As Is' program salvages returned furniture items for spare parts rather than ship goods back to the manufacturer or discard them. Employees reassemble the products to be sold 'As Is.' The IKEA-Green Steps estimates that this program prevents the land filling of approximately 1,000 tons of solid waste per year.

Taking this program one step further, IKEA-Renton actually redesigns and rebuilds returned or damaged items and resells them as 'Green As-Is' items. This program reduces the store's wood waste by 80-85% with an estimated cost savings per week of over $1,000 in disposal costs.

Through the Holiday 'Rent a Tree–Plant a Tree' program, during Christmas, IKEA encourages customers to rent a 69 foot fir tree for a small deposit and fee; after the holiday, customers return the tree, get their deposit back and IKEA mulches the tree. Resulting compost is either kept by the customer or given to the local municipality; in conjunction with the National Arbor Day Foundation, IKEA then plants another tree in its place.

Source: www.epa.gov.

---

better use of the space that was available in each trailer. Better designing and flat packaging helped IKEA to transport more products in each shipment. This resulted in less shipments and hence, a reduction in total emissions. Fewer shipments also resulted in reduced transportation costs. IKEA used various modes of transport like rail, road and sea. However, road was the most used. Since the early 2000s, IKEA made conscious attempts to reduce its dependence on road transportation (Refer Exhibit VIII for different modes of transportation used by IKEA). It also moved towards a combination of train and road for distances greater than 200 km, rather than using only road transportation.

IKEA's internal studies revealed that about 57% of total CO_2 emissions came from the transportation of products between IKEA stores and its customers' homes. The studies also revealed that barely 10% of its customers used public transport;

EXHIBIT VII	Carbon dioxide emission from IKEA operations in Europe	
	2004	2003
Customer Journeys	57%	53%
Freight transport	26%	28%
Electricity consumption	15%	16%
Fuel use	2%	3%

Source: IKEA Social and Environmental Responsibility Report, 2004.

EXHIBIT VIII	Mode of transport employed by IKEA in Europe
Mode of Transport	Percentage of Products Transported (2004)
Road	76%
Rail	10%
Sea	3%
Combined (Rail and Road)	11%

Source: IKEA Social and Environmental Responsibility Report, 2004.

EXHIBIT IX	IKEA's public transport requirements

- Public transport, preferably rail, must be available from an IKEA store to the city center or to a regional transport hub
- There must be an embarkation/disembarkation point within 150 meters of the store
- Public transport timetables must be clearly displayed in the store, especially at the entry and the exit gates
- There must be at least one trip in each direction every hour during the opening hours of the store

Source: IKEA Social and Environmental Responsibility Report, 2004.

most preferred to use personal vehicles. This prompted IKEA to consider opening new stores in locations where public transport was efficient and easily available (Refer to Exhibit IX for IKEA's public transport requirements). IKEA also introduced car pooling facilities for customers and its employees. In December 2005, IKEA partnered with Zipcar[29] to introduce car sharing for its store at Stoughton in Massachusetts, US. IKEA believed that this would help reduce traffic and car emissions and in utilizing the parking space optimally. IKEA Stoughton became the first major retail chain in the US to reserve parking spaces for car sharing vehicles. On its partnership with Zipcar, Frank Briel, the Store manager of IKEA Stoughton said, "With Zipcar, we are reaching a portion of our customers who either do not have a means of transportation to shop at IKEA Stoughton or are utilizing this service to help conserve the environment. Not only is this a great way to reach customers, our 500+ coworkers will also benefit from this program for business and personal use."[30]

IKEA planned to introduce similar services at other stores. The company also asked its suppliers to adhere to its transportation norms. According to Anders Dahlvig (Dahlvig), President of the IKEA Group, cutting down on the environmental impact due to transportation proved to be a big challenge for the company. He said, "We are already trying to move more products per shipment and to expand the use of trains. IKEA customers visit our stores by cars so we have to do our utmost to create the conditions that will enable more clients to visit IKEA by public transportation. One thing is clear. We still have a long way to go."[31] For the benefit of the customers, IKEA also introduced home delivery facilities. This service was contracted to independent transport companies which were asked to follow IKEA's environmental policies.

Forestry

According to IKEA, about 75% of the raw materials for its furniture, catalogs and packaging came from timber. Hence, conservation of forests was an important environmental issue. IKEA worked with groups such as Greenpeace to formulate policies for sustainable forestry. IKEA was also a member of the Forest Stewardship Council (FSC).[32] As a result of consultations with these organizations, IKEA banned the usage of timber from intact natural forests, except those forests that had been certified by the FSC in its products, in

EXHIBIT X Top five countries supplying
raw material to IKEA

Supplier Countries	Percentage of Raw Material Supplied (2004)
China	19%
Poland	12%
Sweden	8%
Italy	7%
Germany	6%
Others	48%

Source: www.ikea.com.

EXHIBIT XI Project activities initiated by
IKEA AND WWF in China

- Forest mapping and identification of High Conservation Value Forests (HCVFs). HCVFs are defined by the FSC as forests with environmental, biodiversity, landscape or socio-economic values of critical importance.

- Promoting legal compliance by working with other environmental agencies, the Chinese government and suppliers.

- Communication and Education/training outreach to potential suppliers.

Source: www.wwfchina.org.

November 1999. IKEA's ultimate aim was to source all its timber from well-managed forests.[33]

In 2002, IKEA partnered with World Wildlife Fund (WWF)[34] to promote responsible forestry across the world. The major countries they focused on were China, Russia, Bulgaria and Romania. One of the major countries that supplied timber to IKEA was China (Refer Exhibit X for IKEA's major suppliers). In 2004, China supplied about 10% of IKEA's timber requirements. Most of this came from the Xing An and Cang Bai mountain regions of Northeast China and Inner Mongolia. According to WWF studies, China's forests had been overutilized, and as a result they had been converted into low quality forests. Over utilization resulted in loss of biodiversity, soil erosion, frequent flooding, decrease of natural forest area and shortage of forest products like furniture and wood for construction of houses and buildings. WWF revealed that in 2003, China consumed about 130 million cubic meters of timber. However, it had a shortfall of 75 million cubic meters of timber, which was imported from other countries like Russia. Hence, IKEA and WWF's priorities in China were to ensure that the remaining forests were protected for future generations (Refer Exhibit XI for forest conservation activities initiated by IKEA and WWF in China).

Another major activity of IKEA that used wood was the making of its catalogs. IKEA catalogs were among the highest circulated catalogs in the world. IKEA worked in conjunction with Greenpeace since 1991 to find solutions to this problem. To conserve paper and reduce pollution, IKEA reduced the size of its catalog and printed it on chlorine-free paper.[35] IKEA did not use wood from old growth forests[36] in the production of its catalogs. All its suppliers of paper and pulp were required to follow environment friendly practices. IKEA also started collecting old and outdated catalogs to be recycled and used for different purposes.

In 2000, IKEA donated US$ 2.5 million to launch Global Forest Watch, an institute that was established to collect information about the remaining intact natural forests or old growth forests in the world. IKEA made its purchasing decisions based on the information provided by this institute. For instance, Global Forest Watch had mapped the extent of the natural intact forests in Russia's 289 million hectares of total forest land as in 2003. Based on this mapping, IKEA determined the forest land from where its timber would come. The company did not purchase any timber that came from the natural intact forests of Russia.

In 1998, IKEA signed an agreement with the Yayasan Sabah Foundation in Malaysia an organization that promoted health, education, better living and conservation of nature. They jointly initiated an environment project called 'Sow a Seed.' The aim was to rehabilitate burned and degraded rainforests in the state of Sabah in Borneo, Malaysia. By 2004, nearly 4,600 hectares of land had been planted out of the total project area of 18,511 hectares. By 2008, IKEA hoped to double the number of trees in this region. It was also decided that trees in this region would not be felled for at least 50 years.

In December 2004, three California-based IKEA stores, donated money from the sale of Christmas trees to American Forests[37] for replanting forest areas in the US that had been devastated by fire. The stores donated US$ 1 for every Christmas tree sold, thus helping in the planting of nearly 7,500 trees. In addition, in early January 2005, IKEA issued gift certificates of US$ 20 to every customer who returned their Christmas trees to IKEA. For every tree that was returned, IKEA again contributed US$ 1 to American Forests. IKEA supported numerous other tree-planting and environmental education programs that were conducted by American Forests. Since 2001, IKEA had also been funding a one-year course on sustainable forest management in the Baltic countries of Latvia, Lithuania and Estonia. Every year about twenty students from the Baltic countries as well as Poland and Russia received scholarships for this course.

Waste management

Reducing the waste it generated and the management of that waste were important issues for IKEA. The company has been moving towards these goals by recycling wastes, repairing damaged products and reusing packaging material (Refer Table I for the Percentage of Wastes that are recycled or reused for energy production in IKEA). This helped not just in saving resources, but also bringing in considerable monetary savings for the company. Each IKEA store had an 'environmental coordinator' who worked towards waste recycling and energy conservation, and also trained employees on environmental aspects. In addition, the environmental coordinator organized educational programs for IKEA customers to understand the importance of the environment and to showcase IKEA's contribution in this area.

Each IKEA store had a separate compactor[38] for collecting non-recyclable waste such as cardboard and plastic. Once these wastes were segregated, they were sent to the production department to see how they could be reused. According to Joseph Roth, IKEA's spokesman, "During 2003 we recycled or reclaimed 73 percent of the waste coming out of our stores. Our goal is to get that number up to 90 percent by the end of 2005."[39] Products that were damaged during transportation were repaired. They were then either used as spare parts for making other products or were put up in one section of the store to be sold at a heavy discount. IKEA stores also collected and isolateed fluorescent light tubes, which contain traces of mercury.[40] This was done to ensure that mercury, a heavy metal, did not enter the waste stream and pollute the environment further. The company had in fact set a limit for the amount of mercury content in the compact fluorescent light (CFL) bulbs it sold. It then invited bids from CFL manufacturers and purchased the bulbs from the manufacturer who offered an economically-priced CFL that met the minimum mercury content requirement.

In its efforts to reduce toxic wastes, IKEA cut down its usage of substances such as PVC, formaldehyde and PBDE. Instead of using these materials, IKEA brought in alternative materials and methods of conducting its business. For instance, instead of using glue that contained formaldehyde to bind different cork parts (stoppers), IKEA heated the cork parts so they would bind. Several IKEA stores made use of non-wood partitions to display furniture. These partitions were made from grains that could be used as animal feed. Flax waste was also used in making these wall panels. Flax was a plant used in paints and varnishes, and was rapidly renewable. IKEA also used other plants such as bamboo that were rapidly renewable to manufacture furniture.

TABLE I Wastes recycled for energy production in IKEA (in %)					
Year	Europe	North America	Asia	IKEA Warehouses	All IKEA Stores
2003	77	57	59	78	73
2004	85	54	73	80	77

Source: IKEA Social and Environmental Responsibility Report, 2004.

Energy conservation

IKEA consumed a huge amount of energy for electricity, heating and air conditioning of its stores and warehouses. The company was trying to consciously reduce its energy consumption. In 2003, IKEA launched a 'Kill-a-Watt-Energy Saving Competition.' The competition was open to all IKEA stores across the world. IKEA aimed to achieve reduction in energy consumption and also to create awareness among employees regarding electricity costs. By the end of the competition, IKEA had saved energy equivalent to providing electricity to 2,000 households, or two IKEA stores for a year. The competition was won by the IKEA store at Ho Chi Minn City in Vietnam. This store reduced its electricity consumption by 33%. It did so by installing a system that automatically switched off electrical appliances and shut down air conditioning systems after working hours.

IKEA also made use of alternative energy sources to obtain electricity. The store in Pittsburgh, US had solar electric panels on the roof. For this project, IKEA teamed up with the Green Mountain Energy Company[41] and Sun Power Electric[42] in October 2001 to convert solar power into pollution-free electricity. About 175 solar electric panels were set up on the roof of the store. A special public display was introduced at the store's main entrance. This display informed customers about the benefits of the solar panels, specifically the reduction in CO_2 emissions. Jim Anastos, Store Manger at IKEA Pittsburgh commented, "We're excited about playing a role in this new progressive approach toward implementing clean renewable energy, which will benefit our community and the environment. As a socially responsible company, IKEA recognizes that every proactive effort for our environment today can make a big difference for our future."[43] Similarly, in Calgary in Canada, IKEA made use of electricity that was produced by wind generators.

IKEA used heating, ventilating, air conditioning (HVAC)[44] units that did not deplete the ozone layer[45]. In the US, IKEA purchased the HVAC units from Lennox Industries[46] (Lennox). A US government mandate required all HVAC equipment manufacturers to stop manufacturing equipment with R-22 refrigerant by the year 2010 and refrigerant[47] manufacturers to stop producing R-22 by 2020, and shift to using R-410A refrigerants. Though there was plenty of time to conform to this requirement, IKEA wished to incorporate it at the earliest. Hence, it requested Lennox to introduce R-410A refrigerant that was not harmful to the ozone layer. According to Lennox's National Account Manager Curt Picard (Picard), "When I originally approached IKEA construction project manager George Ferrara, he said he would only consider Lennox rooftop units if they had R-410A refrigerant. I then went to our engineers at the product development and research facility and proposed trying to get R-410A units manufactured for clients such as IKEA."[48] Lennox was the first HVAC manufacturer to develop a rooftop unit using R-410A refrigerant. IKEA was the first company in the US to install this refrigerant in its HVAC units. This system had been installed at most IKEA stores by August 2002.

Extending CSR to the suppliers

IKEA had a global web of 2,000 suppliers spread across 55 countries. To further its commitment towards the environment and society, IKEA launched 'The IKEA Way on Purchasing Home Furnishing Products (IWAY)' in September 2000. The IWAY established the 'code of conduct' for IKEA's suppliers to adhere to (Refer Table II for more details on Code of Conduct for suppliers). The IWAY focused on legal compliance, working conditions of employees and environmental compliance. To initiate the process, the suppliers were first required to answer a questionnaire to ascertain how environmentally and socially conscious they were.

IKEA also gave the suppliers, a list of substances that were not to be used in any IKEA product. The substances included wood preservatives like copper chrome arsenic (CCA), antimony compounds and PVC (with the exception of electrical cables as there was no alternative available). The use of formaldehyde was restricted. The suppliers

TABLE II Code of conduct for suppliers

- **Legal:** All IKEA suppliers are required to adhere to their national laws. They must also comply with laws and regulations established by international conventions concerning the protection of the environment, working conditions and regarding child labour.

- **Working Conditions:** IKEA code of conduct included provisions that are based on the UN Declaration of Human Rights, 1948, the International Labor Organization (ILO) Declaration on Fundamental Principles and the Rights at Work, 1998, and the Rio Declaration on Sustainable Development, 1992.

  Suppliers must – provide a healthy and safe working environment for employees; pay the legal minimum wage and compensate for overtime; if housing facilities are provided, ensure reasonable privacy, quietness and personal hygiene.

  Suppliers must not - make use of child labour or bonded labour; discriminate; use illegal overtime; prevent workers from associating freely with any workers' association or group of their choice; accept any form of mental or physical disciplinary action, including harassment.

- **Environment and Forestry:** All IKEA suppliers are required to minimize damaging effects to the environment, which may result as a consequence of their activities.

  Suppliers must- reduce waste and emissions to air, ground and water; handle, store and dispose of hazardous waste in an environmentally safe manner; contribute to the recycling of materials and used products; use solid wood from known areas and, if possible, from sources that are well managed and preferably independently certified as such.

  Suppliers must not - use or exceed the use of substances forbidden or restricted in the IKEA list of 'Chemical Compounds and Substances; use wood originating from national parks, nature reserves, intact natural forests or any areas with officially declared high conservation values, unless certified.

Source: Compiled from IKEA Social and Environmental Responsibility Report, 2004.

also had to ensure that all the wood used for IKEA products came from forests that were certified by the FSC.

To ensure that its 'code of conduct' was met, IKEA appointed nearly 80 auditors across its offices in several countries. The auditors prepared a checklist that contained about 90 criteria like child labor, forestry and working conditions that the suppliers had to fulfill. The auditors monitored the suppliers and provided consultations. They also frequently conducted informed as well as surprise inspections. According to IKEA, more than 1500 audits were done every year. IKEA also conducted several third party audits of the suppliers, through agencies such as KPMG.[49] Any supplier who did not comply with IKEA requirements was trained and given suggestions for improvements. They

were then made to develop action plans and were given a time frame to bridge the gap. However, repeated violations of IKEA's requirements resulted in the termination of association with the supplier

In mid 2003, IKEA introduced key performance indicators (KPIs) to gauge its social and environmental performance. Some KPIs were IWAY approval of suppliers, IWAY fulfillment, number of IKEA audits conducted, number of third party audits conducted, total number of timber used, different modes of transport used and reduction in CO_2 emissions. As of late 2005, IKEA was still under the process of establishing KPIs for determining its CSR performance.

IKEA made an effort to develop the suppliers towards meeting its stringent requirements. The company believed that social responsibility went along with its environmental ethic. The company extended this responsibility towards the supplier as well. For instance, one of IKEA's European suppliers was close to shutting down its operations due to significant reduction in demand for an electrical component that the supplier manufactured. However, IKEA's designers discovered a new use for the outdated mold. As a result, a candle holder was created. Similarly, another supplier in Nehoiu, Romania, upgraded his factory with the help of a loan from IKEA. The factory, previously, had no ventilation system or air filters. This resulted in poor working conditions, so poor that workers had to leave the windows open even when it was snowing.

Most of the IKEA's efforts towards becoming a socially and environmentally responsible company were driven by the top management. In 2002, the Swedish Association of Environmental Managers[50] honored Dahlvig, IKEA Group president and CEO, with its 'Award of Good Environmental Leadership.' Summing up IKEA's efforts, Dahlvig said, "We're moving in the right direction, but we must remain humble. We should remain humble about what has been accomplished so far, because there is so much more that still remains to be done. We cannot change the world on our own. All we can do is to take small steps in the right direction."[51]

Additional readings and references

1. "The Natural Steps: Organizational Case Summary: IKEA," www.naturalstep.org, February 1998.
2. "IKEA and Greenpeace Join up to Protect Ancient Forests," www.djc.com, November 25, 1999.
3. Susan Reda, "Conservation Efforts Bring Cost Savings, Community Benefits to Major Chains," www.informinc.org, 1999.
4. "IKEA, Green Mountain Energy Company and Sun Power Electric Bring Solar Electric Power to the Greater Pittsburgh Community," www.eere.energy.gov, October 30, 2001.
5. "IKEA", www.bsdglobal.com, 2001.
6. "The Bible vs. the IKEA Catalogue – Which is Winning Hearts?" www.martinrothonline.com, August 22, 2002.
7. Linda Hales, "Throw Old Stuff Away! New Ads Deride Attachment to Worn-out Things," www.sfgate.com, September 28, 2002.
8. "IKEA Helps Support UNICEF's Play based Programs for Children," www.unicefusa.org, July 21, 2003.
9. "Sir Roger Moore Launches UNICEF-IKEA Initiative," www.unicef.org.uk, October 23, 2003.
10. Oliver Burkeman, "The Miracle of Almhult," www.guardian.co.uk, June 17, 2004.
11. "IKEA and the Environment," www.icsc.org, December 2004.
12. "IKEA Ltd—Safer Streets, Safer Shopping," www.bitc.org, 2004.
13. "A Company with Scandinavian Values," www.scandinavica.com.
14. "IKEA Builds with Environmental Stewardship in Mind," Roofing Quarterly, www.roofing.tectonicdirectory.com, August 2005.
15. Liz Stevens, "IKEA Does Good While Looking Good," www.dfw.com, September 10, 2005.
16. Richard M. Barret, "IKEA San Diego Supports 'Green' Movement by Developing Stricter Manufacturing and Supply Standards," www.sddt.com, September 13, 2005.
17. Warren McLaren, "IKEA's Environmental and Social Reports," www.treehugger.com, October 14, 2005.
18. "Expanding in the US, Swedish Retailer IKEA Plans to Grow Pacific Northwest Presence with Portland Store as Region's 2nd," www.pdc.us, October 20, 2005.
19. "Nike, IKEA and the Body Shop have Committed to Eliminating PVC from their Products," www.buyblue.org, October 28, 2005.
20. Karen Clothier, "IKEA Rocks," www.workerbees.typepad.com, November 21, 2005.
21. "IKEA Children's Holiday Gift Program Benefits Save the Children & UNICEF," www.furninfo.com, November 22, 2005.
22. "IKEA Canada Joins Global Campaign to Help Raise $2 Million for UNICEF & Save the Children," www.ikea.com, November 2005.
23. "The Wal-Mart Model: Is It Sustainable?" www.cbr.cam.ac.uk, December 2005.
24. "IKEA Stoughton and Zipcar Team to Create Unique Car Sharing Program," www.zipcar.com, December 08, 2005.
25. "Corporate Social Responsibility and Low Prices at IKEA," www.duurzaamondernemen.nl.
26. "IKEA Implements New Lennox' L Series® R-410A Units," www.lennoxcommercial.com, 2005.
27. "IKEA," www.planetark.org, 2005.
28. Suzanne J Konzelmann, Frank Wilkinson, Charles Craypo and Rabih Aridi, "The Export of National Varieties of Capitalism: The Cases of Wal-Mart and IKEA."
29. IKEA—Social and Environment Responsibility Report, 2003.
30. IKEA—Social and Environment Responsibility Report, 2004.
31. www.unicef.org.

32. www.wwf.com.
33. www.ikea.ca.
34. www.epa.gov.
35. www.ikea.com.

Notes

1. Barret, Richard M., "IKEA San Diego Supports 'Green' Movement by Developing Stricter Manufacturing and Supply Standards," www.sddt.com, September 13, 2005.

2. "IKEA," www.bsdglobal.com, 2001.

3. The Outstanding Sustainable Style Achievement (OSSA) Awards recognizes the outstanding social and environmental efforts across diverse style and design industries. The OSSA is awarded by the Sustainable Style Foundation (SSF), an international, non-profit organization that provides information, resources and innovative programs that promote sustainable living and sustainable design.

4. Brominated fire retardants (BFRs) are widely used in a number of consumer products to prevent fire-related injury and property damage. Polybrominated diphenyl ethers (PBDEs), a type of BFR, are persistent in the environment and are capable of accumulating in the tissues of animals, fish and human beings. They also cause neurological damage and learning disabilities in children and can cause cancer in adults.

5. The BUPA Healthy Communities award is given by the Business in the Community (BITC) organization headquartered at London, UK. The BITC consists of 700 member companies, both local as well as global. BITC's aim is to inspire, challenge, engage and support business in continually improving its positive impact on society.

6. Reda, Susan, "Conservation Efforts Bring Cost Savings, Community Benefits to Major Chains," www.informinc.org, 1999.

7. "Social and Environmental Responsibility: President's Message," www.ikea.com, 2005.

8. Smaland literally means 'Small Country.' It is a province in southern Sweden.

9. Formaldehyde is an important chemical used widely to manufacture building materials and numerous household products. It is also a by-product of combustion and certain other natural processes. Formaldehyde, by itself or in combination with other chemicals, serves a number of purposes in manufactured products. For example, it is used to add permanent-press qualities to clothing and draperies, as a component of glues and adhesives, and as a preservative in some paints and coating products. Formaldehyde is colorless, pungent-smelling gas. It can cause watery eyes, burning sensations in the eyes and throat, nausea, and difficulty in breathing in some humans exposed at elevated levels

(above 0.1 parts per million). High concentrations may trigger attacks in people with asthma.

10. PVC is a widely-used plastic. The world over, 50% of PVC manufactured is used in construction. As a building material, PVC is cheap and easy to assemble. Despite appearing to be an ideal building material, concerns have been raised about the environmental and human health costs of PVC. It is believed to cause skin related problems and even cancer. Cumbustion of PVC also releases toxic gases such as carbon dioxide and carbon monoxide.

11. "The Natural Steps: Organizational Case Summary: IKEA," www.naturalstep.org, February 1998.

12. Greenpeace is an independently funded organization that works to protect the environment. It seeks to protect biodiversity in all its forms, prevent pollution of the earth's oceans, land, air and fresh water, end all nuclear threats and promote peace, global disarmament and non-violence. Established in 1971, Greenpeace is a global environmental organization operating in more than 27 countries with over 2.5 million members around the world.

13. The BLLF-P is a non-government organization (NGO) in Pakistan. It works towards preventing bonded labor and slavery.

14. The Reebok Human Rights (RHR) award recognizes young activists who have made significant contributions to human rights causes through nonviolent means. The award aims to generate positive international attention for the recipients and support their efforts. Since 1988, more than 60 recipients from over 35 countries have received the award. The RHR Award is given by Reebok, a global shoes and sports wear manufacturer through the RHR Foundation. The RHR Award was established in 1988.

15. The United Nations Children's Fund employs more than 7000 people across 157 countries in the world. It is an international organization that works towards children's rights, their development and protection. UNICEF was created in December 1946 by the United Nations to provide food, clothing and health care to European children affected by the Second World War. UNICEF became a permanent part of the UN in 1953 and has since been undertaking projects for the development of children worldwide.

16. UP is a Northern state in India. It is the most populous and the fifth largest state in India. Lucknow is the capital city of UP. UP consists of 70 districts.

17. The 'carpet belt' of UP includes districts such as Mirzapur, Allahabad and Bhadohi.

18. www.ikea.com.

19. Established in April 1948, the WHO is the United Nations special agency for health. Headquartered at Geneva in Switzerland, the objective of WHO is the attainment of good health by all people. According to WHO, health is defined as the state of complete physical,

mental and social well-being and not merely the absence of a disease or infirmity.

20. CREDA is an organization based at Mirzapur in Uttar Pradesh, a northern state in India. It aims at abolition of child labour through education and social mobilization. The empowerment of rural women is also given priority.

21. An undersea earthquake measuring between 9.0 and 9.3 on the Richter scale occurred in the Indian Ocean on December 26 2004. This earthquake generated a tsunami (series of giant waves) that killed approximately 275,000 people, making it the deadliest disasters in modern history. The worst affected countries were Indonesia, Sri Lanka, Thailand and Southern India.

22. Roger George Moore was born in October 1927. He is an English actor best known for the portrayal of two fictitional English action heroes, Simon Templar in the television series The Saint from 1962 to 1969, and as James Bond in the phenomenally successful series from 1973 to 1985. He was knighted in June 2003. He has been a UNICEF ambassador since 1991.

23. "Sir Roger Moore launches UNICEF-IKEA initiative", www.unicef.org.uk, October 23 2003.

24. Acquired Immuno Deficiency Syndrome is the most severe case of the Human Immunodeficiency Virus (HIV). It is a human disease characterized by progressive destruction of the body's immune system. AIDS is currently considered incurable; where treatments are not available (mostly in poorer countries) most sufferers die within a few years of infection.

25. Established in 1919 'Save the Children' is a US based independent organization. It is a member of the International Save the Children Alliance, consisting of 27 national Save the Children organizations working in more than 100 countries. These organizations work towards the welfare of children.

26. "IKEA Canada Joins Global Campaign to Help Raise US$ 2 million for UNICEF & Save the Children," www.ikea.com, November 2005.

27. "The Natural Steps: Organizational Case Summary: IKEA," www.naturalstep.org, February 1998.

28. Karl-Henrik Robert is one of Sweden's foremost cancer scientists who, in 1989, initiated an environmental movement called TNS. His research on damaged human cells provided a platform for his interest in environmental questions. At the launch of TNS, Robert distributed educational material to every household and school in Sweden. Thereafter, he initiated a number of independent professional networks to support the framework of TNS. Major Swedish companies such as IKEA, Electrolux, Swedish McDonalds, construction companies, insurance companies, banks and a large number of other business corporations and municipalities began to incorporate the TNS framework into their business practices.

29. Founded in 1999 in Boston, Massachusetts, Zipcar is a membership based car-sharing company, providing automobile rental to its menbers. Zipcars has over 50,000 consumers and currently operates more than 900 vehicles in ten states including metropolitan Boston, New York City, San Francisco and Washington, DC.

30. "IKEA Stoughton and Zipcar Team to Create Unique Car Sharing Program," www.zipcar.com, December 08 2005.

31. "Corporate Social Responsibility and Low Prices at IKEA," www.duurzaamondernemen.nl.

32. The Forest Stewardship Council (FSC) is an international, not-for-profit organization to promote responsible management of the world's forests. FSC brings people together to find solutions to the problems created by bad forestry practices and to reward good forest management. FSC members consist of a diverse group of representatives from environmental and social groups, the timber trade and the forestry profession, indigenous people's organizations, corporations and community forestry groups.

33. Well-managed forests are forests that are sustainable. These forests provide raw material such as wood, bark and roots from its ecosystem without the degradation of the quality of the forest and without a decline in the yield of raw material over time.

34. Established in 1960, WWF is an international organization that aims at conservation of nature and its inhabitants. It has grown into the largest privately financed international conservation organization in the world with activities in more than 100 countries. Besides working towards conservation of endangered species, WWF also aims at controlling devastation of forests, forest management and oceans.

35. Chlorine-free paper is an environmentally preferable alternative to paper bleached with chlorine. Chlorine and its derivatives (such as chlorine dioxide) are the most common bleaching agents used by the pulp and paper industry. They are harmful to the environment, particularly the aquatic environment. Chlorine is used to give paper its white appearance and to remove lignin, an element of wood fiber that yellows paper when exposed to sunlight.

36. Old growth forests are forests whose natural cycles of growth have not been disturbed by logging, building roads or clearing. It is also known as 'original' or 'ancient' or 'natural' forest. It includes big old trees, young trees, mammals, insects, birds, frogs, rocks, fungi, dead trees, reptiles and countless other living and non-living things. Old growth forests provide many important ecological services which ensure the ongoing health and stability of the environment. These include maintenance of hydrological (water) cycles, climate regulation, soil production and fertility and protection from erosion, nutrient storage and cycling, pollutant breakdown and absorption and potential source for genetic material for new drugs and food crops.

37. American Forests was established in 1875. It is a world leader in planting trees for environmental restoration, a

pioneer in the science and practice of urban forestry. American Forests works to protect, restore and enhance the natural capital of trees and forests. It is headquartered in Washington DC.

38. A compactor is a closed container or machine in which waste materials are collected and compressed to reduce space.

39. "IKEA and the Environment", www.icsc.org, December 2004.

40. Mercury is a heavy, toxic and volatile silvery conducting metal, which is liquid at room temperature. It is used in making batteries, thermometers and barometers, and also used in the industrial processes (e.g. chlorine production). Much of the mercury in the environment stems from natural sources (e.g. volcanoes, glaciers, oceans and seas). Mercury can accumulate in the environment and can be toxic when inhaled. It is known to cause serious ailments.

41. Green Mountain Energy Company is a US based retail provider of cleaner electricity. The company produces electricity from sources such as wind, water and natural gas. It was established in 1997 and is headquartered at Austin in Texas.

42. Headquartered at Westborough, Massachusetts, Sun Power Electric is a division of the Conservation Services Group (CSG). Sun Power Electric designs, installs, operates and maintains solar electric power plants. In addition, the CSG offers renewable energy education, training, policy consulting and Renewable Energy Certificate services. Founded in 1997, it was the first all-photovoltaic (PV) utility in the US.

43. "IKEA, Green Mountain Energy Company and Sun Power Electric Bring Solar Electric Power to the Greater Pittsburgh Community," www.eere.energy.gov, October 21, 2001.

44. HVAC refers to the heating, ventilation, air conditioning system installed in a building to regulate temperature. This includes air conditioning plants, chillers or refrigerants and ducting systems, which ensure the uniform transfer of the cold or hot air, as the case may be throughout the building.

45. Prior to 2002, HVAC units used refrigerants R-22, which caused depletion of the ozone.

46. Lennox Industries is a leading provider of climate control solutions for heating, air conditioning and refrigeration markets in over 100 countries. The company is focused on three key businesses: Heating and Cooling, Service experts and refrigerants. The company was established in 1895 in the US.

47. A refrigerant is a chemical that produces a cooling effect. Air conditioning systems contain R-22 or R-410A refrigerant. R-22 is regulated by international controls under the Montreal Protocol and in the US by the Environmental Protection Agency. It is scheduled to be in production until the year 2020. Today, more and more air conditioning systems contain R-410A as a refrigerant. R-410A absorb and release heat more efficiently than R-22, hence compressors with R-410A run cooler than R-22 systems, reducing the risk of burnout due to overheating.

48. "IKEA Implements New Lennox L Series® R-410A Units," www.lennoxcommercial.com, 2002.

49. KPMG is a global company providing audit, tax and advisory services. The company operates in 148 countries. KPMG was formed in 1987 with the merger of Peat Marwick International (PMI) and Klynveld Main Goerdeler (KMG) and their respective member firms.

50. The Swedish Association of Environmental Managers is a professional organization for environmental managers with the aim of developing environmental management in the Swedish industry and economy. The association was founded in February 1994. The NMC has 158 members which represent a broad spectrum of the Swedish commercial and industrial sectors, e.g., engineering industry, forestry, chemistry, energy, commerce, transportation, and finance.

51. "A Company with Scandinavian Values," www.scandinavica.com, 2004.

PART

iii

PROCESSES

FIGURE AIII Business ethics and corporate social responsibility

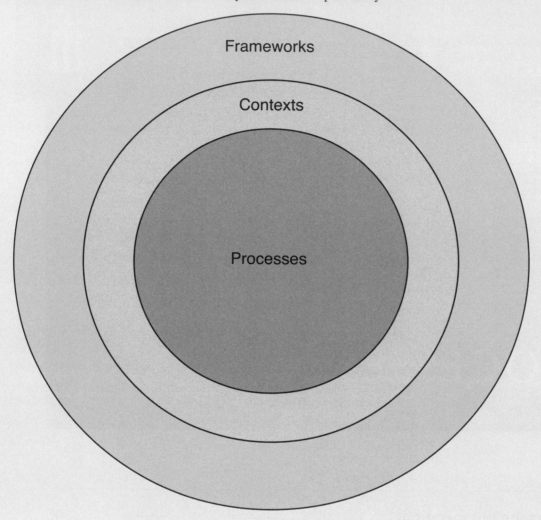

We have spent some time looking at concepts and the contextual factors that affect decisions relating to corporate social responsibility and business ethics. In Part III we look at practices and processes, the decisions themselves, and their effects and impacts. It is important, however, to bear in mind the conceptual and contextual backdrop to these practices. As we have indicated earlier, each decision can only be evaluated in terms of how it fits with the circumstances in which it occurs. Equally, each process or practice only works in virtue of the circumstances in which it exists, as it is these that actually provide the mechanisms for it to operate. Inevitably, given the wide range of different processes and practices affecting an organization, this part of the book has more chapters. In all of them, however, the setting provided by the frameworks and contexts described earlier are highly relevant.

Perhaps the most influential process is how an organization is governed, how the most senior managers, directors or trustees in the organization take account of the views and interests of others when taking decisions. One key potential problem or weakness with governance is the frequent failure of senior directors to take account of factors that others may have brought to their attention. Another is the risk that directors, being the most power-ful actors in an organization, can often make decisions that further their own interests at the expense of others. In terms of pay, share prices or access to benefits it is the directorate of a company that can give itself greatest access to these, often more than the shareholders, for whom, theoretically, the directors are working.

One key practice in relation to ethics and responsibility in organizations is the manner in which performance in these respects is measured. A range of different approaches can be adopted, including audits, codes and bulleted lists of good practice. Closely related to this are the internal processes of management of values in organizations – discourse, cognitive or virtue related. And this in turn reflects the ethics adopted when people and operations are managed internally.

Externally, the main issue for organizational responsibility is how fairly an organization deals with its key stakeholders – its customers and its suppliers. Fair principles of trade are thus critically important for corporate responsibility. Beyond stakeholders is the issue of how the organization behaves with respect to the natural world, and how this reflects environmental philosophies as well as fundamental ethical principles. And finally, we will look at how the organization gives something back to society at large – to targeted groups as much as to the wider population.

GOVERNING ORGANIZATIONS

INTRODUCTION

The most influential individuals for an organization are generally those entrusted to run it. Inevitably this creates substantial ethical responsibilities, for with the considerable power that a senior manager has to direct and control organizational performance comes opportunities for a wide range of actions that can fulfil or violate ethical requirements. Overall, the governance of an organization is the key factor affecting organizational success or failure, and this directly affects the interests of a wide range of dependent stakeholders – employees, customers, smaller shareholders and often also smaller suppliers are all highly dependent on how an organization fares, without having much opportunity to exercise significant influence on decisions. For example, those at the apex of an organization have the opportunity to confirm their own pay, which can lead to abuse by overpaying those who may not merit excessive reward. Similarly, the directors of a company can often benefit substantially from decisions relating to mergers, even when this is not in the interest of other stakeholders: one example of this is a conflict of interest where a director can influence the company to place orders with a supplier with which he or she has an interest, say as part-owner. And as it is the senior management of an organization that develops and directs its overall strategy, so they are responsible for its overall success or failure, and the impact that this will have on other stakeholders.

Ethically, therefore, directors have responsibilities to act for the benefit of other stakeholder groups, members of which may have little power to control events and who rely on the trustworthiness of the directorate, including not to misuse their position solely for their own benefit. As far back as ancient Greece there was the question: 'Who governs the governors?' Who can control those who are specifically placed in positions to control an organization?

Among the issues that this responsibility creates are the processes of consultation with other stakeholders as a means of representing and taking into account their interests, the manner in which directors are appointed and rewarded, and the balancing of the interests of shareholders with other stakeholders. In this chapter we will see how different national approaches give greater or lesser prominence to these issues and to specific stakeholder groups.

DEFINING CORPORATE GOVERNANCE

What is corporate governance? Although there is a wealth of different explanations, some reflecting the national and cultural variations discussed below, and many overlapping in coverage, the term is even today not well understood. For many it carries the association of meetings of boards of directors. While this is a central mechanism of governance, we shall see later that it may not be the determinant of effectiveness of governance processes. We shall adopt a definition given by Margaret Blair:

> ... *the whole set of legal, cultural, and institutional arrangements that determine what publicly traded corporations can do, who controls them, how that control is exercised, and how the risks and returns from the activities they undertake are allocated.*[1]

Interest in corporate governance has become progressively more acute as scandals such as BCCI, Sumitomo and Enron have unfolded. But also there has been growing disquiet as to whether systems in any country are able to cope with the increased complexity, volatility and technical sophistication of modern business. Doubts have been cast on the abilities of auditors, directors and regulators to exercise the appropriate level of control to ensure that companies are run soundly.[2]

The matter of how organizations are governed has fluctuated in emphasis and level of attention during the history of industrial organization. Not surprisingly, when economies are doing well, the benefits that industries and trade bring tend to dull arguments over accountability or control. And conversely, it is when economies are in difficulty, such as recession, that public calls for greater responsibility and for reform or greater control over organizations become more frequent and receive more interest.

Even a few years, or in some cases just some months, can sufficiently change the outlook for the global economy to alter substantially the attitude towards and expectations of companies and the way in which they are governed. It is not an accident that the first major study into corporate governance in the United States[3] was published in 1932, and specifically addressed issues that had arisen since the 1929 Crash. Similarly, the influential Cadbury Report[4] in the United Kingdom was published following the early 1990s recession.

So far as the present debate is concerned, this radically changed in just a few years. The situation of the early 2000s was one of rising economic activity, with some excessive increases in prices in specific areas (notably land and property), but this was accompanied by a continued and almost uninterrupted period of 15 years of economic growth. The economic collapse of 2007–09 was not unpredicted (by some at least) and has had disproportionate impacts, with banking, finance, property and motor manufacture experiencing very hard times, and areas such as low-cost retail in many cases finding increased sales. It has, however, focused attention again on the way in which companies, especially banks, have been managed. The first symptom of the economic downturn was the sudden crisis affecting low-cost mortgages in the United States (the 'sub-prime' market). But the general crisis in banking that followed indicated that so far from this being a problem affecting a couple of rogue institutions, whole waves of major finance houses had adopted highly risky lending policies. In the United States, United Kingdom, Japan and other countries many banks have had to be bailed out in one way or another – nationalization in some cases, enforced takeover in others. Iceland in particular was almost wrecked economically in 2008 by the performance of its large banks, which had become major destinations for offshore investment.

This has created a recent trend for governments to become larger players in their economies than had been customary over the last few decades. The major developed Western economies have, since the 1980s, tended to reduce the role of the state as a participant in commerce. Mixed economies have slowly been giving way to more market-based ones. However, as a response to serious problems with banking and motor manufacture, the United States and the United Kingdom, in particular, have taken into public ownership several major banks and car companies. This phenomenon has been less pronounced in other countries, although the role of governments as final resort providers of credit, for example, has increased their influence over commercial activity.

A central problem that these failures have underlined is that even in well-developed economies with regulatory systems that were perceived to be effective (such as the US Sarbanes-Oxley Act) it has proved difficult for those with major interests in a corporation's actions to either be protected from excessive risk or even to be aware that such risks were being incurred at all. While there have been some high-profile cases of fraud or other forms of illegal activity, the major banking problems have been the result of otherwise well-regarded firms simply not paying sufficient regard to the nature of the risks they were running, and in some cases not understanding exactly what those risks were. Many shareholders and major investors (including, in the case of the Icelandic banks, many large UK local authorities) were quite unaware of how risky their investments actually were, because the degree of risk was unappreciated (as well as in some cases being deliberately under-reported).

This illustrates a classic issue with governance, especially on the Anglo-Saxon approach – the so-called *agency problem*. Noted as long ago as 1776 by Adam Smith, this is the perception that an agent (i.e. someone you pay to carry out services on your behalf) is unlikely to take as much care over the area that they are entrusted with as the person who actually owns it. In this case the 'agent' is the director, acting on behalf of other shareholders. We will discuss the agency problem later in this chapter.

In reality the fluctuations in interest in the phenomenon of governance do not change the fact that all organizations are governed in some way or another, and therefore it is a legitimate question for all of them as to whether they are governed effectively. However, the impact of the economic cycle means that when governance and corporate behaviour are under critical scrutiny then it is more likely that governments will act to improve – or at least be seen to attempt to improve – the integrity of how organizations run.

THE KEY FEATURES OF GOVERNANCE

Underlying these fluctuations in the level of concern over corporate governance is a cluster of interrelated ethical problems, for which a range of different solutions, and clusters of solutions, have been adopted (or have emerged) in different countries and at different times. These problems include:

- How to ensure that the governing body of an organization acts with integrity and operates for the good of the business.
- How to balance the influence upon decision making of shareholders and others with an interest in a business.
- How the governing body of an organization should protect each key stakeholder group.

The solution to these problems in reality can raise a wide range of other issues. For example, how far ownership should take precedence over other forms of involvement with an organization such as employment, or how far do national cultures and legal systems promote or inhibit certain approaches to governance, or, finally, what the balance should be between forms of investment that denote some kind of owner-like relationship (equity) as opposed to investments that are more loan-based? And these in turn bring forward the interrelationship between at the very least the following elements:

- The structure of the top level of an organization's management, its composition and membership, and the manner in which it organizes itself and reaches decisions.
- The national and (potentially) supranational legislation regulating and defining corporate governance.
- The political and historical traditions surrounding national cultural attitudes towards specific governance structures.
- The nature of the economies in which an organization operates, and the pressures they place on governance, and in particular the engagement of an organization with financial markets and other sources of funds.

In what follows we discuss some of the key elements of the various debates and developments in governance, bearing in mind these contextual features such as culture.

It should be noted that the debate over corporate governance has almost exclusively been about the running of companies – for-profit firms that can be described as being owned by a range of individuals via their shareholdings. The reasons for this will become clear in the later discussion, but in brief they revolve around the potential power of majority shareholders to enforce their views even to the detriment of others, and the potential weakness of fragmented groups of shareholders in the way that they can be dominated by managers and others. But clearly other organizational forms are also governed in one way or another. Partnerships, owner-managed firms, third sector (or 'voluntary') organizations, as well as neo-governmental bodies that are delegated powers by governments, such as (some) central banks or state-funded educational institutions, all have some kind of governing structure. While these will not be discussed directly in this chapter, many of the points about issues such as independence of directors could be applied in those organizational forms as well.

ETHICS IN PRACTICE

GOVERNING AN SME

Meyport Ltd is the management company for a small set of residential moorings for houseboats on a river in south-east England. Originally a cooperative set up by the (then) residents, it has changed over time: several of the original shareholders have moved away (but kept their shareholding), and new residents have arrived but have not been able to buy into the firm. The 'board of directors' is in reality a meeting of all the shareholders (six individuals) and the day-to-day business of the company is carried out by one of these who receives a small fee for doing so.

Recently the company has experienced acute difficulties with some of the non-shareholding residents. Some have (incorrectly) suspected the firm of profiteering as they have not disclosed the use of the fees residents pay. Others have demanded fuller levels of service, or they will refuse to pay their fees.

The company secretary wants to avoid litigation, and to resolve the issue as fairly as possible.

To what extent could renewing the company as a cooperative resolve these problems? What would be the risks of doing this? And what would be the costs?

THE NATIONAL AND INTERNATIONAL DIMENSIONS OF GOVERNANCE

In much of the English language literature on governance, the discussion has focused, unsurprisingly, on the debates, processes and practices of the systems of governance to be found in the United States and the United Kingdom. This has given rise to a dominance of the 'Anglo-Saxon' model of governance in much of the debate. This model focuses in the main on the primacy of shareholders and owners. The key issues therefore are how far the interests of shareholders can be protected, and how far the actions of dominant players (be these majority shareholders, the CEO or the chair of the board) will support or neglect the interests of others. However, it is by no means the only approach taken to governance. So-called 'European' models are based on the practices in the longest standing EU countries such as Germany or France. These reflect a different way of looking at organizations – not so much on the primacy of the shareholder so much as the *relationship between capital and labour*, and therefore they involve higher levels of employee involvement and often involve a larger role for debt, and in particular bank loans, as sources of finance compared with equity. In Asia there are different traditions again: the Japanese model focuses on consensus and building networks, and thus lays emphasis on issues such as long-term profitability and stable growth; in contrast, Indian practices tend (even with the major global-sized firms) to remain rooted in owner and even family management, while Chinese governance is dominated by the role of the state as an owner and an economic partner, as well as a regulator.

These different approaches involve widely differing forms of governance, different practices, different strengths and weaknesses. The matter is made significantly more complicated by the global nature of business. Many of the very largest global players now have the opportunity to locate their head offices in a country of their choice. Such a choice would inevitably be affected by consideration of many variables, such as the organization's presence in local markets, linkages with local upstream and downstream supply chains, performance of that economy and local labour rates. It would be unlikely that the governance regime was the highest consideration in such a list, but it would certainly be on the list. In which case it can theoretically occur that a company will register in a country with the legal system that is perceived as most suitable for the firm – which can easily degenerate into meaning the least demanding. Even within a single country such a phenomenon can occur: different US states have different regulations relating to company registration and governance; as a result the state with the lowest level of demand, Delaware, has become the state of registration for a disproportionately large number of the largest US multinationals. This phenomenon has sometimes been called the 'race to the bottom'[5] – that is, the potential advantage of low regulation becomes very attractive to US companies, so that the different states vie with each other for the opportunity of winning the registration fees by offering lower and lower standards.

The 'race to the bottom' has often been seen as a pressure on organizations to reduce standards. Just as the differences in employment legislation have been cited as one reason for the flight of lower-skilled jobs from Europe to Asia, so there is a corresponding potential for company registrations to move from higher regulated to lower regulated legislative environments. However, as mentioned above, regulatory stringency is only one of many reasons that might incline a company to register in one country rather than another. Other economic or even political factors will be at least as important. An analogy may be made with a case from industry regulation: during the post-war years more and more shipping companies registered their vessels, not in the countries of their head office, but via shell companies registered in countries with low levels of regulation, such countries becoming known as 'flags of convenience'. Among these, Liberia, Cyprus and the United Kingdom's Channel Islands were well known as opportunities for a company to avoid the more demanding maritime regulations of developed economies. But by no means all shipping firms did register in 'flag of convenience' countries. And even when they did, clear patterns developed in relation to traditional commercial links, so that US ships tended to be registered in Liberia, Greek ones in Cyprus, UK ones in the Channel Islands and so on. Regulatory ease may be a factor, but it is not a sole determinant of company registration: not everyone will race all the way to the bottom.

This is a specific manifestation of a general phenomenon of globalization, that companies seeking specific services and goods will search around the world for them at the lowest cost. This places great power in the very largest companies, which may have turnover and assets in excess of some national economies, for they may be in a position to dictate to countries as to what kind of regulation may be adopted (on pain of the company withdrawing from that economy). Of course, such lobbying is normal and is experienced by even the largest and strongest economies, as politicians seek to maintain or enhance their popular standing, and as organizations seek to maximize their influence in order to protect and increase their profits. The present situation, however, has become more acute with the rise to extreme levels of financial power of the handful of really large firms, so that Noreena Hertz[6] has even questioned the viability of national governments to remain in control of their economies.

It would seem, then, that the explosion of global trade and corporate operations has two distinct effects on governance: first, the exposure of firms to different and sometimes contrasting national approaches, with their different emphases; secondly, the temptation on corporations to exploit differences for their own immediate advantage, without regard to the rationale or potential value of the corporate legislation in any particular country.

What also needs to be noted is that governance practices and legislation are changing. As a result of the long period of US-led growth, many countries traditionally not sympathetic to the Anglo-Saxon model of governance, such as Germany or Japan, had, during the early 2000s, begun to question whether their approaches were part of the reason for

ETHICS AND YOU

GOVERNANCE IN DIFFERENT INDUSTRIES

Which approaches to governance would you think were most conducive to the commercial effectiveness of (a) a technical SME; (b) a large retail chain; and (c) a public utility such as a water company?

their less impressive economic performance, and as a result these two countries in particular have made legislative changes that make US-style corporate activity (such as hostile takeovers) more feasible. Similarly, the United Kingdom, traditionally antipathetic to employee participation at board level, has seen an increase in employee representation in governance in some selected cases. This is only partially as a result of its membership of the European Union (where participation is required in cases of larger pan-EU organizations); it has also come about, as in the case of United Biscuits in the mid-1990s, as a result of competitive pressure not in the goods market but in the labour market. How far this (gradual) trend towards convergence will survive the crash of 2007–09 remains to be seen, but it is unlikely that there will be a return to such strongly differentiated governance patterns as were evident in the last decades of the 20th century.

SHAREHOLDERS AND AGENTS

Perhaps the central issue of corporate governance is the question of what role should shareholders play in a limited company. Naturally in the early development of a firm, the entrepreneur is often both owner and manager, and most external funding is provided in the form of loans from banks or even friends and family. In this context, the owner-manager's responsibilities are to respect legislation and act with integrity in relations with other stakeholders such as employees or suppliers. While the *ethics* of this situation lie in common with larger firms, the operation is simpler in terms of accountability.

The issue develops as a company grows, and in particular at the point where the owner-manager decides to raise additional capital via providing shares in the firm. Once this happens, then the interests of managers and owners begin to divide. So, for example, there is the potential for a minority shareholder to be unable to overturn poor decision making by the majority shareholder. As the business grows, more shares are issued, and 'ownership' becomes ever more fragmented and diffuse. In tandem with this is therefore an ever greater distancing of ownership from control, and therefore we encounter the so-called agency problem – the issue of how far someone who does not own something will take care over it compared with someone who does. As Adam Smith put this in *The Wealth of Nations*: '… directors … being the managers rather of other people's money than of their own, it cannot be expected that they should watch over it with the same anxious vigilance with which the partners … watch over their own.'[7] This issue of the separation of ownership from control has become a centrepiece of governance and indeed of the theory of the firm in general. How can those who do not actually own a company nevertheless operate it in the best interests of those who do own it?

Now, there are at least two substantial qualifications to make with this argument. First, this problem locates the ethical exposure as lying primarily with shareholders. It neglects the interests of others. Although criticized over the years,[8] this remains a key feature of the ideology of the 'Anglo-Saxon' model of governance. This model depicts governance as being about the protection of shareholders' interests and the development of shareholder value. Managers and directors are indeed presented as the 'agents' of the owners/shareholders, and whose interests are less directly tied to the assets they manage than those owners. For in theory the 'agents' may walk away, while the owners have the responsibility to ensure that the company either runs effectively or, if this is not possible, is wound up. But, as with other considerations of the different interests and levels of exposure of distinct stakeholder groups, some 'agents' have greater exposure to the vicissitudes of a company than many shareholders. I may as an individual hold a few hundred shares in a multinational, representing, say, €1000. This is not a negligible amount to lose if the company collapses tomorrow. But employees, at senior or junior levels, will have a large amount of their personal domestic finances based on the prediction of a monthly salary, and the immediate loss of this may be a disaster for them. So whose interests are more at stake if the firm fails? Ethically, this argument suggests that it is more a matter of the *scale of exposure* to risk than of the subject so exposed.

Secondly, it may even be questioned how widely applicable such a problem really is. Adam Smith, after all, in his original discussion, was referring to the difference between a partnership and a company. And in any case he was expressing himself speculatively: hence his use of the language of *expectation*. There is, though, a logical gap between drawing a distinction between how partners and directors work, and inferring that the presumed lack of 'vigilance' of directors is a general phenomenon.

It may be contested how far individual shareholders do in fact exercise 'anxious vigilance' over their investments to a greater extent than directors and managers. In practice, of course, many directors are shareholders, and usually substantial ones. And where there have been suggestions for the reform of governance it has been mainly to water down the control of the majority shareholders and their appointed directors, in favour of the inclusion of more independent directors. Some of the well-known failures of governance discussed in much of the modern literature, such as the Maxwell case (see the

THINKING CRITICALLY ABOUT ETHICS

TRANSPARENCY

Robert Maxwell was one the Britain's most successful newspaper proprietors, owning, among others, the *Daily Mirror* and *Sunday Mirror*, two of the best-selling national papers. He was known for his hard-hitting style of management, combining both the roles of chair of the board of directors and managing director, and operating an aggressive stance with those who opposed his business policies, both internally and externally.

When he died in somewhat unexplained circumstances in 1994, it came to light that to conceal substantial debts of his group, he had secretly taken money from the employees' pension fund, which subsequently had become vastly reduced in value. His position as chairman and as MD had meant that he had been able to conceal this from other senior managers and directors, including, so they argued at their trials, his two sons who had been senior figures in the business.

How far would additional checks, such as more transparent reporting procedures, have made a difference to this behaviour? Would this have been substantially different had the company had a separate managing director?

'Thinking critically about ethics' box), arose not because of failures of *agency* but because of failures of ownership *integrity*.

Additionally, while it is true that directors and managers have a different relationship with the company than the shareholders do, as indicated above this does not create greater ethical deserts, just different ones. But more importantly, the implication of the idea that agency represents a *problem* is that it would be better for a firm to remain owner-managed or, if it needed more people and funding, to operate as a partnership. This is a controversial issue. It may be argued against this view that an agent might take *more* care over something with which they are entrusted, precisely because it is not theirs. For example, a director acting out of a sense of responsibility for shareholders such as large pension funds may well act with greater care than a family firm where the shareholders are connected by the ambiguous ties of kinship. However, given that an agent stands one step removed from the organization in comparison with an owner, it is not unreasonable to at least accept the possibility that they will have less concern over its fortunes compared with owners.

In practice, few larger organizations choose to remain as partnerships unless required to do so by legislation.[9] However, this does not imply that the agency problem is non-existent – it simply indicates that the problem is not so widespread as to undermine the basis of modern corporate business. This does not, though, cover over the fact that when agency is problematic it can lead to major reversals for a company, including complete collapse. So some issues remain, but this discussion underlines that it is not as overarching as the Anglo-Saxon model might depict.

SHAREHOLDING, OWNERSHIP AND CONTROL

As Berle and Means indicated in their 1932 study, there is a range of degrees of ownership and control of a company, which creates different kinds of governance problems. They identified five different levels, which still remain valid descriptors today:

- **Owner-management** – one individual or perhaps a family has full control and probably near-complete ownership of a firm.
- **Majority control** – an individual shareholder or a tight group control more than 51 per cent of the voting shares.
- **Control through legal devices** – an individual or group may lack majority control but through legal mechanisms such as holding shares with multiple votes, or through cross-shareholdings, they can still out-vote other shareholders.
- **Minority control** – shareholders assign the right to vote on their behalf to another, so that the latter can exercise a block vote (so called proxy voting).
- **Management control** – shareholding is too diffuse and uncoordinated to directly control the affairs of the company, and therefore the senior managers in effect exercise control.

There have been two further developments since the 1930s. One is the growth in power of institutional investors, notably pension funds, trust funds and other collective investment bodies. As Table 9.1 indicates, their proportion of share ownership (at least in the United Kingdom) has grown significantly since the 1960s, with the trend appearing to flatten during the early 2000s (although in the late 2000s the effect of the stock market collapse will have likely been to change this pattern, as investors engaged in a flight from equity). Institutional investors are legally required to aim to maximize the returns for their members, and in practice they tend to adopt highly cautious and highly diversified

TABLE 9.1 Financial institutional shareholdings as a percentage of UK ownership

Year	Financial institutional holdings
1963	30.3
1969	35.9
1975	48.0
1981	57.9
1989	58.5
1994	60.2
2001	51.3
2002	51.5

Source: Office of National Statistics 2003.

investment strategies. In some cases they do hold significant stock in certain companies, and certainly in collective terms the institutional investors in a company represent the most informed and best placed parties to be able to evaluate that company's corporate perform-ance and strategy. However, there has been a traditional reluctance on the part of these investors to exercise too active a role in influencing the direction of the firms in which they invest – an attitude for which they have often been criticized.[10]

A second development has been a change over the past 20 years in patterns of in-dividual shareholding. Three factors in the 1980s and 1990s provided growing op-portunities for individuals to purchase shares: deregulation of share trading; privatization of state assets; and demutualization[11] of organizations such as savings and loan funds, building societies, etc. As a result, many individuals who in previous decades would not have been in a position to buy and sell shares in companies could now do so regularly and with ease. However, these have generally been held for rela-tively short periods. In many cases individuals took advantage of preferential offers (e.g. of privatized state assets) and 'cashed in' not long afterwards. Consequently, their collective holdings do not represent a large proportion of corporate equity and in fact have diminished significantly over the last 40 years (see Table 9.2 for

TABLE 9.2 Private shareholdings as a percentage of UK ownership

Year	Private individual holdings
1963	54.0
1969	47.4
1975	37.5
1981	28.2
1989	20.6
1994	20.3
2001	14.8

Source: Office of National Statistics 2003.

TABLE 9.3 Different kinds of interest of different shareholder groups

Shareholder group	Kind of interest	Level of knowledge	Likely degree of voting power	Exposure to risk
Financial institution	Maximizing long-term value for trustees or pension fund	High external knowledge	Potentially high but usually conservatively conducted	Usually fairly low as investment highly diversified
Major investor with board membership	Maximizing profits and long-term stability	High internal and external knowledge	High and used to support corporate policy	Usually high
Large 'sleeping' investor	Regular stable returns and protection of capital	Low	Potentially significant but only delegated as proxy	Often significant
Speculator	Short-term profits	High external knowledge	Significant but rarely exercised for long-term value	Often high, and deliberately embraced
Small investors	Protection of capital and regular income	Low to medium	Low	Usually low

an indication of this trend). However, notwithstanding this reduction in individual shareholding, the current climate has focussed shareholders much more explicitly on what they can reasonably expect in the way of involvement with decisions and information about corporate performance. There have been some high-profile examples of small shareholders exercising their rights (for example to ask questions at general shareholders' meetings) showing that they can on limited occasions demonstrate an influence beyond their voting power.

Implicit in the above analysis is that different shareholder parties have different needs and interests, and are exposed to the risks of investment in different ways. Table 9.3 illustrates some of these shareholder groups and the variances between them.

The table illustrates the extent to which shareholders have the same interests, run the same risks, and behave similarly: and the answer is that often they will not. 'Shareholder value' then can, if uncritically employed, become a misleading concept. Although it refers to a common matter (the value that a company generates that is then attributable to its 'owners') it can be deemed to carry with it a suggestion that these parties share the *same kind* of interest in this value and that categorizing them together in this way identifies something over and above their company shareholding. This is not, of course, a rebuttal of the idea that corporate governance should have as one of its aims the preservation and growth of shareholder value, but it does undermine the Anglo-Saxon model's focus on this as the single most important element in corporate governance.

OWNERSHIP, EQUITY AND LOAN FINANCING

One of the single most evident differences between national systems of corporate governance is the attitude to the balance of *debt* (such as bank loans) as opposed to *equity* (i.e. funds raised from shareholders) in a company's finances,[12] and the effect this has on corporate strategy. Referring back to the Anglo-Saxon model, where shareholder value is seen as all-important, there is a trend towards keeping the proportion of equity shares high in a business, and keeping debt lower. The reason for this is that debt represents a fixed cost – each year such and such a percentage of the loan has to be repaid as interest, and usually there will be a loan agreement that also specifies a certain repayment of capital. This therefore automatically reduces profits without the directors having any opportunity to exercise any discretion to offset the payments. In contrast, equity funding does not in itself automatically commit a company to a given repayment, and therefore gives greater flexibility to declare a certain dividend rate or not. Additionally, although there is a presumption on a shareholder's part that a certain amount of profit will be distributed to them as a dividend, before this happens the profit is attributable to the performance of the company, and its generation can therefore be represented positively in public relations terms, as an achievement of the current management. This contrasts with the politics of corporate debt, which only appears on the profit and loss account as a part of expenditure, and thus not attributable to profit, and therefore not a success that can be presented so positively to the shareholders or to the public.

In contrast, many mainland European countries have traditions of higher debt ratios. This reflects a different conception of governance being more about maintaining stability, growth and a focus on a wider range of stakeholders (notably with the inclusion of employees). The corporation is thus less intent on maximizing short-term profits for shareholders and more focused on efficient management and distribution of benefits to several stakeholder groups. Furthermore the banks (the usual sources of debt financing) tend to have a conservatizing effect on decision making: one of the sources of criticism of institutional shareholders alluded to earlier was that they are unlikely to encourage risky corporate behaviour, even when that might promise good returns. In general, banking involvement in the capital structures of mainland European firms has had the impact of encouraging longer-term development and growth potential. Germany, for example, has traditionally had much higher levels of involvement by banks in their funding than the Anglo-Saxon countries; indeed this involvement goes beyond simply the major banks being owed money by companies, to the point where banks have become significant shareholders in many of their larger firms. Germany, and in a different way other European countries such as The Netherlands, have significantly different political attitudes towards wealth creation, and the relationship between capital and labour. Hence the attribution of trading surpluses to corporate profits is, while not irrelevant, less high profile an issue than with the United States, where a free market ideology is still almost an article of faith. Indeed, given that the three major German banks do have substantial shareholdings in many industrial companies, they may prefer to encourage higher debt-to-equity ratios (and thus channel corporate earnings even more towards stable predictable loan interest as a cost to the company) rather than rely on the higher risk, and in the later 2000s, not necessarily higher return, prospect of dividends.

The German model involves more than simply higher levels of debt; it also, as we will see later, involves greater levels of employee participation. But the net effect of this high level of bank involvement is not without its own drawbacks. The risk-aversion issue referred to above is one. Another is that the longer-term focus can lead to slower short-term growth patterns. In the long economic rise of 1994–2006 this came to be seen as a disadvantage as compared with the United States. However, the economic downturn has had less of an impact on conservative Germany than on risk-embracing USA, so the argument as to which model of governance is best for firm profitability and stability may well turn out to rest on when the question is put, and in what economic circumstances, rather than on a single answer.

Yet further differences in attitude towards debt and equity may be seen in the traditional Japanese approach to governance. The Japanese model is characterized by, above all, an emphasis on long-term stability and growth. Planning timescales are characteristically longer than in Europe or North America, and as a corollary of this, extensive cross-holdings exist, sometimes between organizations that are upstream or downstream in a specific supply chain, and sometimes simply in diversified conglomerates. While a sizeable number of individuals do have personal portfolios of shareholdings, in many cases these are dominated by shares in the company of their employer. National cultural patterns of seeing oneself as first of all a member of the collective, and only secondarily as an individual, mean that the traditional European-derived economic concept of the individual as the prime locus of decision making and possessor of value is not so evident in Japanese thinking. In contrast, the trend of Japanese collective social awareness has tended to place the greatest focus of governance practices on the maintenance and development of the firm as a common benefit to society. On this approach there is again less attention to the short-term increase in personal wealth. The key end in itself is long-term increases in wealth, for employees as much as for shareholders. The debt-to-equity ratio is therefore higher than with the Anglo-Saxon model, but also the direct equity holdings of banks are significantly higher. However, the role of the bank in Japanese governance goes beyond this. Wan and others[13] argue convincingly that banks are the major mechanism for corporate governance of Japanese firms, through a complex and subtle combination of lending, shareholding, involvement in conglomerate networks, social exchange and direct board membership. This close relationship banking approach has not, though, prevented Japan from continuing to experience a long economic slowdown, traceable right the way back to 1989. It could even be argued that the social aspects of relationships between bank representatives and corporate directors have undermined the formers' ability to curtail weak corporate strategic decisions, as to challenge senior managers directly would cause a loss of face that would be socially unacceptable in Japanese culture. One might also add that the Japanese banking system has seen a number of high-profile crises and failures over the past 15 years or so – for example, the restructuring of Nippon Credit in 1998 due to poor performance. So despite the apparent wisdom of the long-term strategy, it does not seem to work in practice any better than other governance approaches.

ETHICS AND YOU

THE EQUITY–DEBT BALANCE

Which approach to the balance between equity and debt would you regard as fairest and most suitable for (a) an internet company with few assets but whose shares are held by many of the staff; (b) a manufacturing firm where a large number of middle managers have share options; and (c) an entertainments company where most of the shares are held by two or three people (family members)?

None of these particular national solutions to the question of how to structure the capital base of a company is fault-free. The Anglo-Saxon model has a high risk–return potential, which in good economic times is seen as effective but in bad is seen as reckless. The German model is often overly conservative, while the Japanese approach can often be less effective due to the social pressures to avoid direct conflict. One aspect that is overlooked in this part of the debate over governance is the role of CEOs, which we will turn to a little later. But arguably the capital structure of the firm is less a *lever* of governance and more a *reflection* of the underlying attitudes towards corporate governance nationally as well as at firm level.

ARE SHAREHOLDERS OWNERS AT ALL?

Before we move away from shareholding, there is one final argument regarding the role of shareholders that merits attention. This is the view that in the modern global firm, capital employed is too vast for it to be sensibly managed by a tight group of individuals, and in practice it represents too large an amount of wealth for even the highest net worth individuals to have much of a stake in such a company. The typical large public company may have hundreds, even thousands of investors. Add to this that the financial institutions are themselves not owners but only acting as stewards of end-beneficiaries such as those drawing pensions, or small-scale savings fund investors, and the volume of individuals who at some point have some call on the wealth within a company can become even greater.

Those who hold stock via some kind of fund stand at arm's length from corporate decision making, and therefore although they may 'own' a tiny slice of the firm, they do not even have a tiny slice of the decision making, since this is operated for them by a third party, the representative of the financial institutions. This kind of indirect relationship has been dubbed 'fiduciary capitalism'[14] – the control of firms by financial intermediaries rather than by direct shareholders. A different kind of agency problem may be identified for such arm's-length financial stakeholding – not the gap in motivation *to take care* of an asset, but the gap in information *to know how* care may best be taken. The typical investor in a mutual fund may not even know exactly what proportion of their investment has gone towards purchasing so many shares in Company X, so many in Company Y and so on. Generally, investment strategies are indeed public knowledge, but in practice a typical small investor may not understand the implications of a 5 per cent holding in mining firms as opposed to a 3 per cent holding in entertainments, for example. And the risks involved in placing investments in high-growth technology funds as opposed to, say, more stable agricultural funds are difficult even for professional investors to gauge, let alone the small private investor.

Even in the case of the direct small shareholder, participation in decisions is difficult. General meetings of shareholders are naturally dominated by the largest shareholders and by the board of directors. These tend to aim at securing assent from such meetings for their chosen strategies, and therefore they naturally tend to inhibit protest from smaller shareholders who oppose those strategies. Given that the smaller shareholders by definition, have little voting power, the most influence they can have is by stimulating public debate, but even this is often constrained in practice, for the simple reason that the board controls not only large blocks of votes but also the conduct of the general meeting itself.

While legally the small shareholder can be described as an 'owner', and the mutual fund investor in most cases would not, in practice their relationship with a firm and how it is governed is indistinguishable – neither has much access to meaningful information, neither

ETHICS AND YOU

SHAREHOLDER 'VOICE'

What are the respective merits of virtue ethics or discourse ethics with respect to the need to increase shareholder 'voice'?

Would you prefer governance to be managed by those of generally good character (but who might be ineffective in dialogue), or by those who manifest the intent and the skills to engage effectively in dialogue (but who might not be quite so scrupulous morally)?

has much voice in corporate decision making, and neither has any prospect of increasing their influence or knowledge except by working collectively, and usually with intermediaries. To say, therefore, that one has 'residual claims'[15] in a company and the other not is, if not a false differentiation, at least a vacuous one. Our very idea of 'ownership' has built up around the image of an individual or a tightly coherent and small collective having possession of, knowledge about, and full rights over an asset. Large collectives stretch this image beyond what is reasonable to suppose – in terms of possession shareholders do not 'hold' the company, in terms of knowledge they lack the full picture or may not have the expertise to understand data supplied to them, and in terms of rights these are so splintered as to be negligible. Ownership in such cases amounts to little that can be exercised in practice. In the future this might point to managerial and fiduciary capitalism as the governance of the global players.

However, this is not necessarily a gloomy prospect. There are clear indications about how fiduciary capitalism can exercise some influence over corporate decision making. The State of California pension fund (CalPERS – the California Public Employees' Pension System) gives a voice to its members by a process of systematic targeting of poorer performers in its investment portfolio, publicly identifying these, writing formal statements and transparently requesting information on how such firms plan to improve performance.[16] Not all institutional investors operate so actively, but there are continued pressures on them from industry and membership lobby groups to take more assertive roles in the running of the companies in which they invest.

CROSS-ORGANIZATIONAL OWNERSHIP

The governance task with many firms is made complicated by the matter of cross-ownership. This is often presented as a major advantage in the case of Japanese conglomerates such as *Keiretsu* (business-based networks, usually involving some form of vertical integration) or the earlier family-based *Zaibatsu* networks. The close interrelationships that build up in these networks as a result of shared organizational cultures, shared financial interests and frequent contact through operational connections, are seen as a means of preserving the long-term commitment of employees and directors that is central to the Japanese approach to business.

Cross-ownership in mainland European firms tends to follow a different but still substantial pattern, with German firms, for example, owning an average of over 20 per cent of equity in other companies, Austria and France having over a third (33 per cent) and with Belgian cross-ownership amounting to over 35 per cent.[17] While this has similar motivation to the Japanese approach – namely the encouragement of consensus and of a stakeholder-wide perspective – it is looser in nature, as there are fewer other coordinating mechanisms compared to a *Keiretsu*. In both regions, however, the banks play a major role as active participants in the running of firms (at least, relative to Anglo-Saxon governance).

Part of the additional complexity is that the matter of ownership is made less transparent. Recall from the previous sections that someone may 'own' a tiny slice of a company either through directly being a shareholder, but also by virtue of having an investment, or even simply a savings plan with a mutual fund. Now suppose that one of the companies that the mutual fund invests in also holds shares in yet another company. Then the end-investor (the individual with a personal pension or savings plan) may be said to 'own' a yet smaller slice of that other company.

For the 'retail' investor (i.e. the private individual who is not an investment or business professional) this represents further distancing of possession from influence – typically they hold very small shareholdings anyway, and the dilution of ownership makes the miniscule just more so. However, for the more professional investor, with significant corporate expertise and substantial control of funds, this can present an opportunity for gaining greater leverage of their investment, often through the building of 'pyramids' of investment, where one company is part-owned by another, which in turn is part-owned by yet another, and so on. Bruner and Perella point out how easy it is for such pyramids to be controlled in an environment where there are many shareholders (and therefore lower thresholds for acquiring a controlling share in a company).[18] Suppose there are five companies worth €100 each, and that the current structure of shareholdings means that a 25 per cent share is sufficient to control any one of these. I purchase a €25 share of Company One. I then (now being in control of this company) use some of its capital to purchase a €25 share of Company Two. And then in turn I use €25 of Company Two's capital to buy a share in Company Three, and then do the same for Companies Four and Five. I now control five companies worth €500, for the outlay of just €25. Not only can this allow a great concentration of power in the hands of an individual or clique, but also it can create further ethical problems. In some countries, such as Italy, this kind of complex of shareholdings has made it almost impossible to deal with serious ethical issues such as tax-evasion and corruption, as the individuals ultimately responsible cannot be traced through the tangled network of shareholdings, and thus they cannot be called to account.

Cross-holding does present other potential vulnerabilities. Director A has the majority shareholding in Company X and a large (and influential) minority holding in Company Y, which supplies X with components: clearly the potential exists for A to exploit this, using inside knowledge to drive down Y's prices, which naturally benefits X. Perhaps more difficult to identify and regulate is the possibility of forms of restrictive trading or cartelization. Directors sitting on the boards of Companies X and Y can so influence decisions that external firms wishing to break into the supply chain for X may be frozen out by unfair specification requirements, delivery schedules, quality standards, etc. – all of which might have been developed specifically to help Company Y win contracts at the expense both of competing firms but perhaps also of the other shareholders of X, should Y's products be basically more costly than those of its competitors. Legislation does exist in many countries to try to prevent this kind of anti-competitive practice, but the existence of cross-holdings of shares, and therefore of cross-flows of information, make it relatively easy for such laws to be avoided (as opposed to being broken).

Cross-holding also creates other potential weaknesses, such as 'cosy' non-threatening relationships between companies. Director A in our example above may find it harder to challenge the decisions of Company Y specifically because a senior figure in Y is also a director of X as well. So there is the unspoken presumption that 'I'll make it easy for you if you make it easy for us'. This is often accentuated in the non-conflictual cultures of countries such as Japan, where disagreement has to be skilfully managed to avoid senior figures losing face. This is not to say that there is no disagreement in such environments, but rather that it could be subverted by one who was intent on reducing criticism of corporate choices.

This last point underlines one of the key features of much of the debates on governance. For there are many points at which there is a potential for someone to undermine the effectiveness of external or internal influences on how the firm is run – *if they were so motivated*. But this risk – which in legal terms looks like a huge hole in the system – is less of a problem if there is confidence that the personnel involved can be trusted, and can demonstrate morally good character. Perhaps here is a point at which virtue ethics is a necessary condition for good governance. We shall return to this issue when considering the structure and operation of governance processes, in particular the performance of boards of directors. In the next section, however, we will look at the second most widely considered stakeholder group in the matter of governance – the employees.

EMPLOYEE REPRESENTATION

While in the Anglo-Saxon countries the main task of corporate governance is usually conceived as how far shareholders' interests may be protected from controlling agents (i.e. managers), in other environments (Europe particularly) it is often seen as the matter of how shareholders and their agents can work effectively with the employed staff. In other words, the Anglo-Saxon concern is with capital, while the European concern is with both capital *and* labour.

In many European countries legislation requires that companies have *dual board* arrangements – systems where as well as a main board (usually controlled by the share-holders) there is a second board that represents employees' interests. Indeed, for larger pan-European firms it is a European Union requirement that some form of workers' representation is made at the governance level. These secondary boards usually have the right to be consulted, to receive information on corporate performance and plans, and often to give specific advice on those plans. There are differences in the degree of power accorded to such boards with respect to strategic decisions. Supervisory boards in The Netherlands, for example, have the authority to approve (or not) major strategic decisions, as well as approving the appointment or termination of main board directors, and to approve the issue of a dividend to shareholders. In this case, then, the influence of the supervisory board is substantial. But as with other discussions in this chapter, this can only be understood when set in its national culture and general approach to business. The Netherlands, along with the Scandinavian countries, is often depicted as a 'coordinated' economy,[19] one that emphasizes high levels of interaction and ideally consent between employees' representation and investors, and is highly employee focused with an elaborate approach to vocational training, a cultural aversion to redundancy, and well-established traditions of collective employee agreements as the main vehicle of industrial relations. In such an environment it is not surprising that worker representation is well structured and has substantial levels of authority.

The mainland European models of employee involvement in corporate decision making reflect the history of how workers became organized into collectives during the period when their respective economies industrialized, as a means of protecting employees from the excesses of capitalism. In contrast, east Asian approaches to governance reflect different histories and different cultural traditions. The Japanese approach, which we have discussed above, reflects the cultural expectation that consent and agreement is reached at all levels. Employee representation at board level is not seen as requiring separate arrangements, because of the unitarist belief that the organization is there to serve all interests, and does not represent a collision between different interest groups (as the European models imply). Indeed, so far as Japanese legislation is concerned, employees do not have any special status accorded them as stakeholders in corporate decision making. However, this is not a covert means of silencing employee participation, rather it reflects the general presumption that the employee is the centrepiece of the business. Great account is taken of core employees of Japanese firms (the so-called 'salarymen'). They used to have almost a guarantee of a job for life (until the bursting of the 'bubble economy' in the early 1990s) and there are almost family-like ties between fellow employees, as well as elaborate systems of internal promotion, so that many directors have come up through the ranks of the workforce. While it has been argued that this pattern is changing to reflect more Anglo-Saxon approaches,[20] it remains the case that the priority of the employee in corporate activity is culturally highly desired.

Governance in China places a wholly different emphasis on the role of the employee. In so far as the main organ of economic life is still the state, processes of governance of companies are still heavily regulated and influenced by government representation and policy. The transition to a market economy from a socialist one has led to reforms in many areas, but the underlying conception of the individual as being subordinate to the institution still dominates. China has a dual board system, but, unlike the European models, the supervisory board has little potential influence over the managerial board. In practice both are still heavily controlled by state appointees, who will be appointed or dismissed by state or party interests. So although theoretically employees should have a large say in the running of companies, in practice this is dependent on governmental processes and agendas.

Overall it is clear that there is a range of approaches to the involvement of employees in corporate decision making, with secondary board membership the most visible means for this. Employee involvement can thus take many forms – works councils, individual members of a unitary board, discussion or focus groups, suggestion schemes, as well as the secondary board approaches discussed above. Some of these media are more conducive to strategic issues than others, and some encourage employee-upwards communication rather than full two-way dialogue. However, it would be highly misleading to suggest that, say, the Anglo-Saxon model is less encouraging of employee participation than, say, the

ETHICS AND YOU

PARTICIPATION

You are the Director of Human Resources in a large, conservative but highly successful accounting firm. Traditionally the company has avoided too much employee participation, on the ground that the business is not so complex that it needs a wide range of different views on how it should run. The management style adopted by most of the key managers is friendly but highly autocratic.

The new CEO has asked you to consider introducing a system of employee consultation. She would like the firm to become more innovative and sees participation as a key step in this direction.

How will you advise her? What key steps would you take?

Japanese. The presumption is that good management will operate as a throughput for employees' views to be channelled up to the board. Of course, the more steps in a chain of communication the more likely that a message will be filtered and distorted. But equally there are critiques of formal communication structures: the dominance of formal employee collectives such as trade unions, for example, can accentuate union-sympathized ideas at the expense of union-disapproved ones.

THE ROLES OF GOVERNMENT

The third key stakeholder in corporate governance is the state. Nowhere is its role more evident than in China: '... the stock market is operated by the state, regulated by the state, legislated by the state, and raises funds for the benefit of the state by selling shares in enterprises owned by the state'.[21] However, while the Chinese government is still by far the dominant player in its economy, still holding some 84 per cent of corporate equity, it does so through several different mechanisms, which have been argued to have a substantially differential effect on corporate performance.[22] Indirect state control has been seen as less effective than direct control, and region-wide corporations are seen as more effective than so-called town-village enterprises (TVEs). As with earlier discussion of other elements of governance, this needs to be placed in a cultural context. Chinese business behaviour is profoundly influenced by the obligations inherent in personal relationships – so-called *guanxi* – as well as by a strong sense of the value of family relationships. Both of these have a strong bearing on how governance operates, as well as creating potential ethical vulnerabilities. *Guanxi* has been criticized as having a potential for leading to corruption,[23] and the potential of family loyalty to turn into nepotism is clear. But what they indicate is that the role of government, while all-important at the highest corporate level, may have less impact at lower levels of the management of a business, and where smaller enterprises are concerned.

At the other extreme is the attitude of the United States, where the ideology of the free market has led to an aversion to too much government intervention. Economic liberalism suggests that the role of government is primarily to create a regulatory framework, a fair playing field, within which corporations should be free to do whatever their ingenuity and enterprise can develop, to secure profits for their owners. However, this too needs to be taken in its cultural context: despite its espoused free-market philosophy, many parts of the United States are values dominated – much of its history is dominated by the 'pioneer' spirit, which reflected the self-reliance of those who populated the central and western states in the 19th century. This kind of perception sees the government as a remote element that did not historically provide very great services for the people. Add to this the federate nature of the USA, as a cluster of states that have in some respects quite different practices, and it can be seen that government is not perceived as positively or as supportively as it might be in, say, a typical European country.

In fact this is as misleading as the Chinese perception of the state as all-encompassing. Government regulation goes well beyond simply providing a framework, and government involvement in some areas of the American economy – such as steel production or more latterly in supporting the problematic main car manufacturers – is as interventionist as in many European economies. And to a vast degree the US federal government is an economic player as a purchaser, for defence, for scientific development and for provision of a range of public services. While the latter are small in comparison with other developed countries, in absolute terms they are still substantial. This indicates that government has a

ETHICS IN PRACTICE

GOVERNANCE IN SOUTH AFRICA

The system of governance in South Africa has been heavily influenced by two reports by Mervyn King – one in 1994 and another in 2002.[24] These have also influenced governance in other African countries. Among other things, the 2002 report emphasizes the socio-political context of governance structures, and that national and regional contexts and cultures are significant for the effectiveness of whatever governance protocols may be in place.

EXTRACTS FROM THE 2002 CODE

38. Governance in any context reflects the value system of the society in which it operates. Accordingly, it would be pertinent to observe and to take account of the African worldview and culture in the context of governance of companies in South Africa, some aspects of which are set out as follows:

38.1. Spiritual collectiveness is prized over individualism. This determines the communal nature of life, where households live as an interdependent neighbourhood.

38.2. An inclination towards consensus rather than dissension, helps to explain the loyalty of Africans to their leadership.

38.3. Humility and helpfulness to others is more important than criticism of them.

38.4. In the main, African culture is non-discriminatory and does not promote prejudice. This explains the readiness with which Africans embrace reconciliation at political and business levels.

38.5. Co-existence with other people is highly valued. The essence of Ubuntu (humanity) that cuts across Africa is based on the premise that you can be respected only because of your cordial co-existence with others.

38.6. There is also an inherent trust and belief in fairness of all human beings. This manifests itself in the predisposition towards universal brotherhood, even shared by African-Americans.

38.7. High standards of morality are based on historical precedent. These are bolstered by the close kinship observed through totem or clan names and the extended family system.

38.8. An hierarchical political ideology is based on an inclusive system of consultation at various levels. The tradition of consultation as practised by the chiefs since time immemorial should form the basis of modern labour relations and people management practices.

38.9. Perpetual optimism is due to strong belief in the existence of an omniscient, omnipotent and omnipresent superior being in the form of the creator of mankind.

Source: European Corporate Governance Institute (http://www.ecgi.org/codes/).

This extract demonstrates the religious, political and cultural assumptions in this approach to corporate governance, even though in many respects the details of the King reports resemble much Western practice.

significant potential role to play in the governance of firms. That it does not is a political choice rather than a structural mechanism.

This brings out a general point about the role of national governments in the process of corporate governance – that there is a range of different moves that a government can make as tools of policy that can encourage or discourage corporate behaviours. Purchasing, as we saw with the environment, is a major and almost subliminal potential lever. In other areas, taxation policy is used to modify individual or corporate behaviour. Legislation, while the most immediate form of government involvement, is thus by no means the only way to influence business. Due to the ideology of the free market, the US government tends to avoid too high a profile in using legislation to modify corporate governance – even the well received Sarbanes-Oxley Act (see next section) was contested at the time of its inception. Europe is by comparison almost trigger-happy in the extent to which its countries pass laws covering many aspects of corporate behaviour, including the structure of governance processes. Oriental models, as we have seen, may differ significantly from each other in respect of legal structures but resemble each other significantly in the way in which cultural assumptions underpin the specific features of how government interacts with business.

BOARDS OF DIRECTORS

In most works on governance the structure and operation of the board of directors is one of the first things that is discussed. Our decision to hold off on this until later in the discussion is to indicate how many other variables can affect the work of the board. There has been much research on the effectiveness of different approaches to boards,[25] but in our view these studies tend to underrate the cultural, political, economic and historical complexities that make different governance approaches difficult to properly compare. Nevertheless, in all circumstances some form of controlling collective is a central aspect of how a firm is governed.

Boards of directors are usually composed of a chair, as well as the most senior manager (usually called the chief executive officer – CEO – or managing director), other significant shareholders and those with other interests (bank appointees, employee representatives) and independent directors. As we have seen already, legislation in some countries requires there also to be a secondary board that represents other interests (usually employees), and in other countries specific employees, such as a chief finance officer, may be expected to attend board meetings. It is generally required nowadays that there also be an audit committee that oversees corporate financial performance, and often there will be committees relating to matters such as the appointment and remuneration of directors. In different countries there are distinct legal responsibilities of directors. In Germany, for example, there is a requirement for the board to consider the effectiveness of the company in addressing the interests of a range of stakeholders, while in the United Kingdom and the United States the requirement is primarily shareholder focused.

In the unitary board approach, a primary concern is the concentration of power. The Cadbury Report recommended that the chair and the CEO roles always be held by distinct individuals, as a means of protecting the corporation from a 'rogue' individual exercising too much power. But even when roles are distinct, there is the possibility of a small coterie of individuals working together to flout ethical or legal requirements: the Enron case, where both the chief executive and the chief finance officer were complicit in the scandal, demonstrated that the sheer existence of potential checks and balances does not guarantee ethical corporate behaviour.

In theory the role of the independent director (called in the United Kingdom the 'non-executive' director) is to provide an unbiased evaluation of corporate plans and performance. The independents are meant to be individuals with appropriate strategic knowledge and experience, and sufficient standing in the industry to command respect among their peers, and in particular among the other directors. This group of directors could then act as a brake on reckless or unethical actions on the part of the 'executive' directors (CEO, chair, etc.) and provide an appropriate counterweight to the powerbase of the executives. The conception of the 'friendly critic' is intended to capture the ideal attitude of the independent director as a source of informed advice and challenge, but in a supportive and constructive environment.

In practice there has been considerable doubt as to how far independents have fulfilled the challenge aspect, as opposed to the supportive: independents have in general been seen as insufficiently robust and often sit in 'cosy' relationships with chairs of the board. One reason for this is appointment: it is rare indeed for a company to advertise for independent directors. Far more often the appointment operates via social networks. In some cases a retiring director may nominate someone they know, or another member of the board – and often this is the chair – will propose a name. The potential here for finding someone who possesses the same attributes as the rest of the board is significant. Many studies of recruitment in general talk of 'halo' and 'clone' effects: the disproportionate influence of someone with a significant positive attribute, and the tendency for people to choose someone who is like themselves. The practice of setting clear, measurable specifications for the appointment of a director is obviously one way in which these pitfalls may be avoided, though this is not often adopted.

Even when someone fulfils a person specification, if they have been introduced by an existing board member then there can easily be an implicit psychological obligation of the new director to be supportive of whomever may have introduced them. One can see that this obligation could be magnified in a culture where social obligations are substantial – so a culture with attitudes such as *guanxi* or the 'old school tie'[26] can be easily prone to subversions of governance despite structural enhancements. Appointment may also reflect other social patterns that are accepted but do not on the face of it directly enhance the quality of governance. In France there is a phenomenon called *pantouflage*,[27] the drift of senior government officials from public service to private sector directorships. This finds particular favour in France due to the elite status of those who have received their higher education in the so-called '*grandes écoles*' – ivy-league style institutions that more or less guarantee entry into higher civil service or good business appointments in France. This tendency has been criticized not only because of the exclusive and potentially discriminatory effect of such traditions, but also of the corrupting effect on both government and industry, as those who benefit from the trend may well be too close to both sectors to be able to objectively evaluate either. Also there is the potential for the public servant, in the years of their government career prior to early retirement, being prone to the corrupting effect of wishing to make themselves appear suitable for particular directoral appointments.

Another potential drawback concerning the effectiveness of independent directors is sheer availability. In a lot of industries there are not that many individuals who combine good strategic experience and industry knowledge with a standing and reputation for integrity, and who are able to devote appropriate time to the role. And this is without the argument that in general sufficient time for an independent to really fulfil their roles is not often invested. Bavly points out that many independents devote about two days per month to their role, whereas it is generally presumed that a new CEO needs 100 days to fully understand their task – on this basis it would take five years before an independent truly understood the business.[28] Unsurprisingly, in some industries there are many cross-directorships – director A on the board of Company One is the chair of the board of Company Two, which has, as an independent director, the chair of Company One. This practice is common among Japanese conglomerates, though in that case it is a

ETHICS IN PRACTICE

CORPORATE SPYING

In July 2009 two executives at Deutsche Bank were dismissed, and German prosecutors opened an enquiry into the possibility that the bank had secretly spied on members of the board of directors. It was suspected that two directors had been leaking confidential information to an active and critical shareholder of the bank.

In 2006 the CEO of Hewlett Packard was required to resign after allegations that the company had used illegal surveillance methods to discover whether board members had been leaking information.

deliberate policy to cement a range of close business interlinkages, and in reality such directorships are not presented as independent. The difficulty with European or Anglo-Saxon boards is that independents are expected to be genuinely independent, and this is less easy to maintain if the same people appear on different boards. However, when directors are seen as robustly independent, this can sometimes be viewed as a threat by the company. Mistrust of directors is becoming more prevalent, as non-executive directors are manifesting greater independence (see the 'Ethics in practice' box).

One response to the availability issue is to water down the competence requirements: in the United Kingdom, where politicians can legally have significant outside professional interests, it is often seen as a valuable asset to have a politician on the board, in the belief that this may provide the firm with a 'hot line' to senior government decisions, whether or not they have solid business capabilities. Senior economic journalists or business academics are often appointed as directors, and while these groups may have greater knowledge than the politicians, they are less likely to have the experience of dealing with acute professional conflicts that would be expected to arise in a suitably balanced board.

The other major problem with directors is their own performance and remuneration. There are few direct measures of the performance of a director: in the economic crisis of 2007–09, a number of banking executives and directors insisted upon exercising their full contractual rights to performance bonuses, even though in practice their companies had performed at an exceptionally poor level – as the terms on which such contracts had been drawn up were very vague, there was insufficient basis for the companies to refuse these. Again we see evidence in this of 'cosy' relationships, where it is assumed that directors would add value to the business, and therefore it would be unnecessary, or even discourteous, to tie them down to specific targets and measures.

The passing of the so-called Sarbanes-Oxley Act in the United States[29] was a milestone in the regulation of boards of directors, for it set out explicit obligations for directors to confirm financial accounts, and it laid down additional requirements for audit committees of boards. It also specified significant additional responsibilities for auditors, who had been found particularly wanting in the Enron case. Nevertheless, despite the criticism that this would shackle US businesses unnecessarily, it has also been criticized severely from the opposite side, on the basis that the concessions that the Act makes towards shareholder value as the cornerstone of governance, and the consequent emphasis on the independence of directors, cannot change the deep-rooted attitudes of directors that allowed Enron and the other major scandals of the 2000s. Aglietta and Reberioux

comment scathingly: 'The Sarbanes-Oxley Act, far from attacking the root of evil, ferti-
lizes it.'[30] Their view is that the real problems are based on the conception of what they
call 'shareholder sovereignty' – in other words the elevation of shareholders to be the
most fundamental object of value in the stakeholder complex. As we have seen, this is an
acute critique of Anglo-Saxon approaches, and implicitly of those countries in other regions that are attracted towards converging on that approach, but it does not deal adequately with the more value-based approaches evident in east Asia, which, though flawed
in their own ways, avert the major catastrophes of corporate greed.

So far as remuneration is concerned, in previous decades it was not uncommon for directors to be appointed on what was called a 'rolling' three-year contract: by this was meant
that at the end of each year the contract was renewed for another three years'. In effect this
represented a contractual commitment to pay a director three year remuneration upon
termination of their contract. Although this has become less prevalent, there remains
significant disquiet about directors' pay: simply that directors often receive disproportionately large payments for doing relatively little, and often without having a significant impact on corporate performance. In several countries codes have been produced and reports
published on mechanisms for improving directors' pay, but despite these there has been
little impact on levels of remuneration.

One mechanism that has not been employed directly might be to introduce a specific
value of *corporate service*, as both a motivating factor and also a source for measurement
of performance. By analogy with the concept of public service, which has guided (albeit
incompletely) government employees, this could provide a basis for the debate on performance and reward of directors to be conducted in an environment that goes beyond
legal requirements but is not firm-specific (as many codes of conduct tend to be).

THE FUTURE OF GOVERNANCE

We have approached the matter of governance comparatively. What we have seen is that
there are value-based approaches in some east Asian countries, approaches such as those
in the United States and the United Kingdom that elevate the shareholder above all else,
and mixed approaches that try to balance the interests of owners and employees. None is
flawless, and each certainly runs a risk of placing too much reliance on trust.

In the early 2000s, the continuing growth of the US economy – despite the failures of
WorldCom and Enron – led many to question whether the Anglo-Saxon model may be
the most effective for corporate performance. Developments in mainland Europe, in
Japan and even in China suggested that shareholder value, and the unitary board
approach, might become a standard for international governance practice. However, the
reversals of 2007 and 2008 have undermined this assumption. The failures of banking
have been worldwide, but most acute in countries following Anglo-Saxon style governance practices.

In terms of future governance, it is clear that a corporate responsibility perspective, evident in the efforts on many sides to create or renew structures and legislation, has failed to
get to the root of the weaknesses in governance. Our suggestion of a value of 'corporate
service' is unlikely to find legislative support, and for that reason alone is unlikely to find
much favour in litigious environments. But it reflects the point that in much of the discussion what we have seen are failures of value and integrity. In other words, these are ethical
failures, and likely to persist unless and until social norms encourage a greater sense of
integrity in business.

SUMMARY

- There are contrasting approaches to governance emanating from Anglo-Saxon, continental European and Asiatic cultures.

- The three key groups influencing the effectiveness of governance processes are shareholders, employees and government.

- Internationally operating firms face the need to manage within different governance frameworks.

- Legislation such as the Sarbanes-Oxley Act in the United States has been criticized as not attacking the root problems of governance.

- The operations of boards of directors are a key element of governance – issues that undermine their ethical soundness include potential conflicts of interest and recruitment of too like-minded individuals.

QUICK REVIEW QUESTIONS:

1 The discussion in this chapter has been almost entirely related to companies. How far do you think an approach such as the Anglo-Saxon model could be adapted for a not-for-profit organization?

2 What steps would you think are appropriate to attempt to develop greater levels of integrity in non-executive directors?

3 In what ways would you suggest that governance models or practices be amended so as to avoid the serious corporate reversals that have been seen in most governance regimes?

CASE STUDY: THE RUSSIAN WAY OF CORPORATE GOVERNANCE

BY FLOYD NORRIS
(Published 5 April 1999)

As Russia pleads with the International Monetary Fund for money to keep it from defaulting on its international debts, the country's government seems to believe that an IMF seal of approval will lead to a resumption of the flow of private capital into the country. Don't bet on it.

To understand why private investors should be hesitant, consider the case of Yukos, Russia's second-largest oil producer, which is run by Mikhail Khodorkovsky, a well-connected Russian oligarch.

The tale is a complex one, in which paper is shuffled as rapidly as aces in a game of three-card monte, in which judges with no apparent jurisdiction issue rulings, and in which oil is sold for absurdly low prices.

The losers are investors in the three oil companies that Yukos controls, known as Yuganskneftegaz, Samaraneftegaz and Tomskneft. Once those were hot stocks; now they are all but unsaleable. An investment of US$3000 at the end of 1996, divided

▶

equally among the three, would have grown to more than US$11,000 by the following August. Now it is worth about US$150, down 98 per cent.

World oil prices are depressed, and Russia's economy is in crisis. But those factors are not enough to account for the decline in share prices, in which one subsidiary that produces oil worth US$2 billion a year now is valued at about US$22 million. The price has tumbled as it became clear that the shareholders would not benefit from the sale of that oil.

This has happened despite Russian laws that purport to provide protection for minority investors by giving them representation on corporate boards and the right to veto deals smacking of conflict of interest.

At shareholder meetings of the three subsidiaries last month, plans were approved to allow Yukos to buy oil from the subsidiaries for three years at US$1.50 a barrel, about a tenth of the world oil price. Those meetings also approved issuing huge quantities of shares to unnamed investors in return for promissory notes issued by other Yukos subsidiaries. That will dilute the rights of other shareholders.

What happened to the Russian laws giving rights to minority holders? Groups of such owners had vowed to defeat the proposals, but they were barred from voting. A judge had ruled that since the minority holders all planned to vote the same way, they must be in league with one another and therefore in violation of anti-trust laws because they had not registered as such. The minority shareholders were not invited to the hearing that led to the ruling.

The shareholders managed to get another judge to rule that they could vote at one of the meetings. But his ruling was simply ignored.

Mr Khodorkovsky claims the whole fight is about Western investors who have illegally acted in concert and are trying to block good management, but the investors say that the Yukos actions are appalling even by Russia's low standards. 'No one can believe that anyone would be so blatantly crude', complains Michael Hunter, the president of Dart Management and a director of one of the subsidiaries, adding that Dart underestimated the level of corruption when it made its investments.

John Papesh of Misoli Enterprises, an affiliate of Dart, argues that 'This brazen asset grab takes the violation of Russian law and international standards of corporate governance to a new low.'

If the Russian government does nothing to protect the shareholders, it will send a clear message. But even an honest government cannot protect investors without help.

The Yukos tactics are reminiscent of the fight for control of the Erie Railroad in 1867 and 1868. Cornelius Vanderbilt tried to buy a majority of the stock, only to find that directors led by Jay Gould were printing more shares. Both sides got judges to issue rulings, amid suspicions of bribery. For a time, Gould could not enter New York except on Sunday, when the custom of the time barred people from being arrested. The minority shareholders, most of them from England, were treated badly.

None of that kept the United States from becoming the world's premier economy. Along the way such abuses led to the rise of J. P. Morgan, whose early power came from the fact that English investors trusted him.

If Russia is ever to become an economic success story, its oil will play an important role. But before that happens, a Russian Morgan – someone who understands Russian capitalism and earns the trust of overseas investors – will have to come along to assure that a dollar invested is not sure to become a dollar stolen. The Yukos affair shows Russia is a long way from that goal.

STUDY QUESTIONS

1 What are the governance issues that arise from this case?

2 Were the concerns of the foreign minority shareholders justified?

3 What should the Russian government have done?

4 Research what happened to Mikhail Khodorkovsky after the article was written. Was this an acceptable answer to concerns about corporate governance?

NOTES

1. Blair (1995), p. 3.
2. Cf. Bavly (1999), who gives a powerful critique, as an American auditing 'insider,' of the capability of the governance system to be effective in controlling corporate performance.
3. Berle & Means (1932).
4. Cadbury (1992).
5. Cf. Blair (1995), p. 23.
6. Hertz (2002).
7. Smith (1776) Book 5, Chapter 1.
8. For example, by Kay & Silberston (1995).
9. As, for example, in some countries, law firms are required to remain fully liable to their clients.
10. Cf. Short and Keasey (2005) for a summary of the evidence relating to institutional investor behaviour in the United Kingdom.
11. Demutualization – transforming an organization such as a building society or savings and loan fund, in which each retail saver has a voting stake, into a standard company where shares are bought and sold by individuals or institutions, and where savers may have no shares at all in the firm.
12. Generally known as the gearing ratio.
13. Wan *et al.* (2005).
14. Cf. Holton (2007).
15. That is, a claim on a part of the total net value of a company should it cease trading instantaneously.
16. For more detail on the CalPERS approach, cf. Bavly (1999) Chapters 7 and 8.
17. Goergen, Manjon & Renneboog (2005).
18. Bruner & Perella (2004).
19. Cf. Poutsma & Braam (2005).
20. Araki (2005).
21. Walter & Howie (2003).
22. Liu & Sun (2002).
23. Though the argument is not settled. Cf. Provis (2007).
24. Reports of the King Committee on Corporate Governance, 1994 and 2002. Institute of Directors.
25. That governance as currently practised under the Anglo-Saxon approach is unable to achieve significant improvements in company effectiveness is a key part of the argument of Dan Bavly (1999). Among the many other studies, one interesting piece focuses on the changes in oriental systems and how far this has affected corporate performance – see Nowland (2008).
26. A British term referring to an historical – and to some extent anecdotal – tendency on the part of corporate leaders in the United Kingdom to be partial to appointing people who had attended the same school or college (and thus wear the same uniform tie).
27. Another sartorial metaphor – in this case the idea that someone shuffles from employment in one sector (government) to another (private sector directorship) so easily that they do not even need to change their slippers (in French *pantoufles*).
28. Bavly (1999) Chapter 6.
29. As with much US legislation, the colloquial name for the Act refers to the two senators who sponsored it.
30. Aglietta & Reberioux (2005), Chapter 8.

REFERENCES

Aglietta, M. and Reberioux, A. 2005. *Corporate Governance Adrift*. Edward Elgar.

Araki, T. 2005. Corporate governance, labour and employment relations in Japan. Chapter 10 in Gospel, H. and Pendleton, A. (eds) *Corporate Governance and Labour Management*. Oxford: Oxford University Press.

Bavly, D. 1999. *Corporate Governance and Accountability*. Quorum Books.

Berle, A. and Means, G. 1932. *The Modern Corporation and Private Property*. Harcourt Brace.

Blair, M. 1995. *Ownership and Control*. The Brookings Institution.

Bruner, R. and Perella, J. 2004. *Applied Mergers and Acquisitions*. Wiley Finance.

Cadbury, A. 1992. *The Financial Aspects of Corporate Governance*. London: Gee Publishing.

Goergen, M., Manjon, M. and Renneboog, L. 2005. Corporate Governance in Germany, in Keasey, K., Thompson, S. and Wright, M. (eds) 2005. *Corporate Governance*. Chichester: John Wiley.

Gospel, H. and Pendleton, A. (eds) 2005. *Corporate Governance and Labour Management*. Oxford: Oxford University Press.

Hertz, N. 2002. *The Silent Takeover*. Arrow Books.

Holton G 2007. http://www.policyinnovations.org/ideas/innovations/data/investor_suffrage.

Kay, J. and Silberston, A. 1995. Corporate Governance. *National Institute Economic Review*, August, 84–97.

Keasey, K., Thompson, S. and Wright, M. (eds) 2005. *Corporate Governance*. Chichester: John Wiley.

Liu, G. and Sun, S. 2005. The class of shareholdings and its impacts on corporate performance: A case of state shareholding composition in Chinese publicly listed companies. *Corporate Governance: An International Review*, Vol. 13, No. 1, 46–59.

Nowland, J. 2008. Are East Asian companies benefiting from Western board practices? *Journal of Business Ethics*, Vol. 70, 133–150.

Poutsma, E. and Braam, G. 2005. Corporate governance and labour management in the Netherlands. Chapter 6 in Gospel, H. and Pendleton, A. (eds) 2005. *Corporate Governance and Labour Management*. Oxford: Oxford University Press.

Provis, C. 2007. *Guanxi* and conflicts of interest. *Journal of Business Ethics*, Vol. 79, 57–68.

Short, H. and Keasey, K. 2005. Institutional shareholders and corporate governance. In Keasey, K., Thompson, S. and Wright, M. (eds) 2005. *Corporate Governance*. Chichester: John Wiley.

Smith, Adam (original 1776). *The Wealth of Nations*. Oxford Paperbacks.

Walter, C. and Howie, F. 2003. *Privatising China*. Chichester: John Wiley.

Wan, W., Hoskisson, R., Kim, H. and Yiu, D. 2005. Network opportunities and constraints in Japan's banking industry. In Keasey, K., Thompson, S. and Wright, M. (eds) 2005. *Corporate Governance*. Chichester: John Wiley.

AUDITING AND REPORTING SOCIAL PERFORMANCE

LEARNING OBJECTIVES

After studying this chapter you should be able to:

- Depict the emergence and development of voluntary initiatives over time.
- Compare and contrast different types of voluntary codes.
- Appreciate the challenges of social accounting.
- Give an overview on the drivers and practice of social and environmental reporting including the principles that underpin good reporting.
- Explain the role of external assurance in social accounting and reporting.

INTRODUCTION

The willingness of states to regulate corporate behaviour has varied over time depending on political affiliations, ideology and economic conditions. As an alternative to binding regulation, companies have been encouraged to adopt voluntary principles and codes of conduct, especially on issues involving corporate activity in foreign countries. In this chapter we look at the voluntary measures that companies have taken to manage their social and environmental impacts. The chapter starts with an overview of voluntary codes and then moves on to discuss the principles and practice of social accounting and reporting.

OVERVIEW OF VOLUNTARY INITIATIVES

Corporate activity is regulated by states as the holders of ultimate physical and sovereign authority in our current world. Even when international organizations like the World Trade Organization make decisions that apply to more than one country, the provisions are effective only insofar as they are implemented by states. In general, implementation takes place through the adoption and enforcement of appropriate laws. States are therefore the main regulators of corporate activity, even in today's world of globalization. As was seen in the chapter on business and human rights, national laws and regulation may even control corporate behaviour beyond domestic borders resulting in extraterritorial jurisdiction. For example, the United States has strict laws banning illicit payments to foreign officials and these laws influence the behaviour of American companies operating abroad. In this chapter, however, the focus is on the voluntary codes and initiatives that are sometimes seen as an alternative to binding legislation. Voluntary measures are often preferred by companies that see them as more flexible and less costly than regulation, but also by governments that do not wish to burden the business community with extensive legislation and bureaucracy.

The first wave of voluntary codes in the 1970s was driven by the newly independent states that sought to control the power of foreign companies. In addition to introducing laws at the national level, these governments also advocated the international regulation of multinational enterprises. Standards adopted at the international level were seen as a way of ensuring that developing countries gained from the growth of international business without disadvantaging any one country that set restrictions on foreign investment. The newly independent states were also keen to act in concert to gain leverage against foreign companies that were regarded as a continuation of colonial exploitation.[1]

If the first wave of codes was driven by the governments of the south, the second wave in the 1990s was supported by a variety of actors from the north. It was now the large, well-known companies in the clothing, retailing and natural resources sectors that adopted codes to protect their reputation against allegations of misconduct in developing countries. In this context, voluntary codes were seen as a way of assuring consumers and other stakeholders that companies were taking action to address environmental and labour concerns. At the same time, northern governments took the lead in the development of industry-wide norms and in this way sought to ensure that companies complying with higher standards would not lose opportunities to their less principled rivals.[2]

ETHICS IN PRACTICE

CLEAN CLOTHES CAMPAIGN

The Clean Clothes Campaign was launched in 1989 in The Netherlands. Since then, it has become an alliance of trade unions and other non-profit organizations from 12 European countries. The aim of the Clean Clothes Campaign is to support garment workers in developing countries by seeking to improve their working conditions. The organization has lobbied companies to use their power to ensure that labour rights are upheld in their supply chains. It has also developed a code of conduct for this purpose and pressures retailers and manufacturers to adopt the code. Not many have done so, but the code is an example of the standards that emerged in the 1990s, setting out principles for corporate conduct. In addition to the code, the Clean Clothes Campaign educates and mobilizes consumers, lobbies government authorities and provides direct support for workers demanding better working conditions.

The Clean Clothes Campaign is one of the most successful organizations that emerged in response to concerns over labour conditions in the apparel and garment sector in the 1990s. Nevertheless, its work has not gone unchallenged. In 2007 the organization was summoned before a court in India for alleged defamation relating to information it had published on its website about labour rights abuses in a garment factory in India. Even though the case was later dropped, it demonstrates the continuing pressure on companies to comply with labour standards.

Source: Clean Clothes Campaign 2009. Available from http://www.cleanclothes.org, accessed 10 July 2009.

The content of voluntary codes has shifted over time. The codes launched in the 1970s by inter-governmental organizations were seen as a way to regulate international business and were therefore generic in nature. In contrast, the more recent codes have often applied to a single company or a group of companies sharing similar characteristics, making the content of codes relatively specific. Moreover, the early codes mainly applied to companies and their immediate subsidiaries, while the later codes extend beyond fully owned entities to suppliers and other business partners. This shift reflects the fact that corporate scandals have involved the behaviour of sub-contractors in developing countries rather than the direct activities of Western companies.

Finally, while the focus of codes in the 1970s and 1980s was on anti-bribery measures, the more recent codes have centred on labour and environmental issues. A study from 2000 found that 60 per cent of company-specific codes included statements on labour standards and 59 per cent on environmental issues, while only 23 per cent of the codes addressed the issue of bribery.[3] In contrast, an earlier study from 1978 found that more than half of the codes studied included statements on bribery and questionable payments. The content of codes also varies across sectors. For example, labour issues are a more prominent concern for companies that outsource their production to foreign countries in search of lower production costs than for companies that invest in highly skilled and expensive technological projects in the oil and gas sector.

DEVELOPMENT OF CODES OVER TIME

The first codes of conduct were initiated by countries that became independent in the years following the Second World War. These countries had a critical attitude towards foreign investment after years of colonial rule. They questioned the structure of world trade and the way it created pockets of wealth without raising the living standards among the poor in Asia, Latin America and Africa. For example, the dependency school of thought argued that richer countries exploited poorer ones by expecting unlimited market access while maintaining high import tariffs that made it difficult for companies from poorer countries to use their comparative advantage. The political and military power of a small number of countries upheld the system and made newly independent states dependent on the technological and financial strength of Western companies. The arguments of the dependency theorists were reinforced by a number of scandals involving Western companies in foreign countries. The activities of International Telephone and Telegraph (ITT) in Chile were particularly influential in drawing attention to the behaviour of Western investors. ITT, a large American telecommunications company, was critical of Salvador Allende's government for nationalizing parts of the country's mineral resources in the early 1970s. Concerned about its investment in the country, ITT allegedly supported Allende's overthrow by colluding with the Central Intelligence Agency (CIA) and financing opposition parties in Chile.

The critical attitude towards foreign investment led many developing countries to adopt regulations that sought to direct revenue and other benefits from foreign investment towards domestic growth.[4] Some countries, including Mexico, India and Iran, went further by expropriating the assets of foreign companies and nationalizing whole sectors. It was typical for the period to invest in the creation and support of domestic industries through subsidies and other measures that protected local companies against their foreign rivals. These measures were underpinned by the assumption that governments could channel revenue from foreign investment to areas where it contributed to national wealth.

The confidence in the central role of the government was influenced by the socialist and communist ideologies promoted by the Soviet Union and China. The oil crisis of 1973 further showed that countries of the south could take a stance against the interests of industrialized countries and have an impact on the world economy.

In addition to national regulation, developing countries sought to regulate foreign investment at the international level. By the 1970s, they formed the majority of member states in the United Nations General Assembly and used this power to promote the development of international standards on foreign investment.[5] The International Labour Organization, for example, adopted the Tripartite Declaration of Principles Concerning Multinational Enterprises and Social Policy, while the United Nations set up a Centre on Transnational Corporations with the aim of developing a general code of conduct for multinational enterprises. There was hence considerable pressure and activity within the United Nations to ensure that international business followed some basic principles and guidelines. As is usual, however, the documents were left for governments to implement and hence dependent on state approval and endorsement.

Standards for foreign investment were also adopted outside the United Nations system. These initiatives were less well received because developing countries had had little involvement in their development. For example, the OECD Guidelines for multinational Enterprises, first adopted in 1976, were interpreted as a defensive move on the part of northern governments to show some responsiveness to the concerns of developing countries without the introduction of more fundamental measures. Similarly, the code introduced by the International Chamber of Commerce in 1972 was seen as a way to avoid the adoption of more far-reaching and binding standards.[6] This criticism shows that codes are most authoritative when they are created by neutral organizations and involve all relevant parties.

ETHICS IN PRACTICE

ADIDAS SUSTAINABILITY PRINCIPLES

Our core values–Performance, Passion, Integrity, Diversity – inform our principles of sustainability, which helps us set standards for our social and environmental performance. They are:

Legislation

We adhere to social and environmental laws, directives and guidelines while continually improving upon our own contribution to a sustainable society.

Management

We aim to:

- Analyse, evaluate and assess the social and environmental impact of new products, technologies and processes at the design and development stage.
- Set up clear targets, formulate an action plan and monitor progress.
- Publish the results.

Supplier and customer relationships

We expect suppliers' activities to be compatible with our Workplace Standards. We work in partnership with them to improve our collective performance. We encourage our business customers to take a proactive stance on the social and environmental impact of their own activities.

Support

We support social and environmental projects and develop partnerships with businesses and organizations whose direct and indirect output contributes to a sustainable society.

Stakeholder dialogue

We aim to listen, respond and interact with all stakeholders in an atmosphere of mutual trust and respect. We provide them with appropriate information related to the social and environmental performance of the group on a regular basis.

Source: Adidas 2009. Available from http://www.adidas-group.com/en/sustainability/mission_and_values/sustainability_principles/default.asp, accessed 12 July 2009.

The 1970s also saw the first company-specific codes of conduct. This trend started in the United States where companies began to adopt codes in response to negative publicity surrounding their operations in foreign countries. The codes were voluntary in nature and varied from generic declarations of values to more substantial statements of self-regulation. A study of almost 200 codes in 1978 found that more than half of them covered payments to foreign officials. Indeed, many companies introduced a code of conduct to discourage bribery after the US Congress enacted the Foreign Corrupt Practices Act in 1977. This new law was introduced in the context of scandals involving questionable payments to officials in foreign countries. A code of conduct was seen as useful in communicating a corporate position on illicit payments to both internal and external stakeholders.

By the 1980s, many countries had changed their approach to foreign investment by moving away from state intervention and relaxing restrictions that had been introduced earlier to regulate the behaviour of foreign investors.[7] The atmosphere of pro-trade measures explains why the work on the code for multinational enterprises within the United Nations stopped and was never finalized.[8] Public pressure for the adoption of corporate codes also lessened and fewer voluntary codes were adopted by the corporate sector. It was not until the scandals of the 1990s that voluntary codes saw their renaissance. As discussed earlier in this book, many companies had invested heavily in branding that contributed to loftier margins, but also created vulnerability to negative publicity. In this context, voluntary codes were a way of protecting corporate image against damaging allegations of misconduct.

Levi Strauss, a company known all over the world for its jeans, was one of the first to adopt a voluntary code that set the terms of its relations with foreign suppliers. Other clothing manufacturers and retailers followed the example by introducing their own codes and participating in sector-specific initiatives in order to introduce common standards of behaviour. Corporate codes were also supported by government-led initiatives. For example, UK Prime Minister Tony Blair launched principles on transparency to encourage resource-rich developing countries to publicize the payments they received from the oil, gas and mining industries in the form of taxes, royalties and other payments. Such initiatives sought to create a level playing field so that Western companies would not lose business to competitors that were not facing similar pressures on ethical behaviour.

FORMS OF VOLUNTARY CODES

Company-specific codes

Codes of conduct can be unilaterally adopted by companies. The number of such codes has grown aggressively since the 1990s. Company-specific codes often cover issues relating to labour rights, consumer protection and the environment.[9] They also tend to refer to more widely accepted principles or standards. For example, many codes include a reference to the Universal Declaration of Human Rights or other documents adopted within the United Nations. Such references place a company's commitments into a wider context, but their meaning is not always clear. For example, given that the principal responsibility for the respect of human rights rests with states, it is not clear what authority and roles companies have in relation to the protection and promotion of human rights (see Chapter 7).

Multi-stakeholder initiatives

The number of joint initiatives launched by companies, non-governmental organizations, trade unions and governmental bodies has increased over time. These initiatives are often seen to go back to the 1992 Rio Conference on Environment and Development. The Rio Declaration encouraged collaboration between different actors and its follow-up process has seen a proliferation of partnerships between private and public sectors. The 2002 Johannesburg Summit has been seen as a climax for this trend even though the interests of corporate and non-governmental sectors seemed to conflict at the actual meeting. Well-known multi-stakeholder initiatives include the Forest Stewardship Council, ISO 14000 and Social Accountability 8000.

It is perhaps interesting to note that governments often play a facilitating role in multi-stakeholder initiatives. Many of the initiatives have been promoted by one or more governments and they seem to provide a neutral platform for other actors to come together. Despite the credibility of the multi-stakeholder initiatives, only a small number of companies have been actively involved. One hurdle has been the cost and complexity of monitoring mechanisms. As a result, Peter Utting from the United Nations has proposed a move to complaint-based systems as this would decrease costs for individual companies, improve transparency, and allow focus on key issues rather than the setting up of processes and bureaucracy that may work against the principles underlying the initiative.

Multi-stakeholder initiatives do not need to be adopted by companies. Some multi-stakeholder initiatives, like the Extractive Industry Transparency Initiative (EITI), address states rather than companies, though companies may play a role in the implementation of initiatives. For example, EITI expects participating governments to be transparent about payments they receive from companies in the form of royalties and other payments, but companies are also encouraged to publicize this information to improve transparency. Moreover, even when multi-stakeholder initiatives are targeted at companies, companies may use them as a reference and source of guidance instead of becoming a participant. Because of this, initiatives often have influence beyond their membership as they provide guidance and a standard against which companies can assess their performance.

Inter-governmental normative instruments

Principles and standards governing corporate conduct have also been developed within inter-governmental organizations. These standards include documents agreed upon by the International Labour Organizations (ILO), the OECD and the World Trade Organization.

While there is some agreement on the standards developed within the first two organizations, vigorous debate has taken place about the inclusion of social and environmental clauses in trade agreements negotiated within the WTO. It is the developing rather than industrialized countries that have resisted the introduction of social and environmental criteria in trade agreements. The criteria have been perceived as informal barriers to trade that would weaken the competitive position of developing countries.

Standards developed within inter-governmental organizations generally carry more weight than voluntary codes adopted by companies or industry associations. This is because international organizations are composed of member states that have the authority to implement and enforce any standards ratified by them at the national level. Regulation of international business therefore relies on the willingness and ability of states to implement the commitments they make as members of international organizations. The standards also carry more weight because they set common standards of behaviour and in this way ensure that no company is disadvantaged from applying more demanding and therefore costlier standards.

SOCIAL ACCOUNTING

Social accounting first emerged in the 1970s, but its recent popularity dates from the 1990s when a number of companies carried out a social 'audit' to assess and demonstrate their social and environmental performance. One of the first companies to do so was The Body Shop, as described in the nearby 'Ethics in practice' text box. The new audits were a way for companies to assess their social and environmental impact and introduce systems to measure and manage their influence in society. As the profession of social accounting was only emerging, many companies involved academics and independent consultants to assist in the development of approaches for collecting, recording and presenting relevant information. Over time, however, the biggest four accounting firms have become the main providers of professional services in the area, though some smaller consultancies have also survived and produced important thinking and standards in social accounting and auditing.

Social accounting refers to the process of collecting, recording and assessing information on social and environmental performance. The process often results in a summary published in report form. Gap, for example, produces a 'social responsibility' report on an annual basis. In comparison to financial accounting, social accounting is still a new field and lacks consistent terminology. The terms 'accounting', 'auditing' and 'reporting' are often used interchangeably and no clear definitions have yet been established. In financial accounting, 'auditing' refers to an independent review of an organization's financial statements, while 'reporting' involves the communication of the statement to internal and external stakeholders. Both terms are used in a more flexible way in the context of social accounting, but their meaning is likely to become more established over time. In this chapter, accounting, auditing and reporting are used as separate terms relating to distinct processes.

THINKING CRITICALLY ABOUT ETHICS

WHO ARE KEY REPORT READERS?

The readers of corporate social responsibility reports may not be the same as the readers of financial statements. Who, in your view, are the main readers of social and environmental reports?

Similarly to financial accounting, social accounting is about answering two questions: 'what' is accounted and 'who' is the information produced for?[10] The questions are inter-related as the decisions on 'what' are affected by 'who' the expected users of social and environmental data are. While financial information is mainly produced for the use of managers, lenders and investors, social and environmental information is relevant for a more diverse group of organizational stakeholders. Because of this, it is important for companies to consult their stakeholders when deciding on the scope of accounting. Indeed, the extent to which stakeholders are engaged and included in the process is essential for the quality and credibility of social accounting. In general, the scope of accounting should reflect both stakeholder concerns and organizational characteristics, including industry type, social impacts and business risks.

Once the scope of accounting has been established, relevant information needs to be collected, recorded and evaluated in a systematic way. Some of this information may already exist, but it has to be compiled and analysed for the purpose of social accounting. For example, organizations are likely to have information on staff turnover, which can be used as an indicator of employee satisfaction. Similarly, companies may already have information on gender and levels of pay that can be employed for the purposes of social accounting. In addition to data that already exist, organizations may also need to collect new information. For example, organizations would not normally have systematic in-formation on their public policy positions and lobbying activities, but this data could be used for the purpose of social accounting.

In general, it has been challenging for companies to find reliable information and indicators for social performance. For example, how can a company's impact on governmental policy be verified and measured when so many factors influence policy making? Because of the nature of data on social impacts, information is likely to consist of a mix of quantit-ative and qualitative data. The apparent subjectivity of qualitative information has meant that it has been important to present information in a context that evaluates its reliability. For example, stakeholder and expert views may be sought to assess a company's impact on governmental policy. Nevertheless, the fundamental challenge of social accounting re-mains in quantifying issues that are essentially qualitative in nature.

When companies first engaged in social accounting, few guidelines existed on social and environmental indicators. The situation has now changed and many sources provide guidance and measures for social accounting. For example, the EU Eco-Management and Audit Scheme (EMAS) is a set of indicators on environmental performance and the Global Reporting Initiative (GRI) provides guidelines for measuring both environmental and social impacts. The International Organization for Standardization has also devel-oped guidelines for social accounting; this signals the slow maturing of the field.

ETHICS IN PRACTICE

THE BODY SHOP SOCIAL AUDIT

The Body Shop was one of the first companies to carry out a 'social audit' in the 1990s. It had a strong repu-tation as an ethical company that had campaigned for a number of social causes, but the authenticity of its commitments had also been questioned. For example, it had been claimed that the company benefited from its opposition to animal testing without making clear that its products included ingredients tested on animals by other companies. The company's initial reaction to the allegations was defensive, but it later decided to carry out an audit in order to address the concerns in a more constructive manner. The audit benefited from the commitment of the company's leader to ethical auditing. Anita Roddick, founder of The Body Shop, had raised the issue in her autobiography and felt strongly about producing an environmental and social audit.

The audit was designed in collaboration with the New Economics Foundation that had developed an auditing methodology based on participative research techniques and organizational development literature. The audit started with a review of the company's policies against which performance would be evaluated. A decision was also made about the scope of the audit, which was limited to human stakeholders in the United Kingdom and countries where the company had suppliers. This meant that the audit excluded some important stakeholders, including the natural environment and constituency groups in the United States, but these stakeholders were included in later cycles of auditing.

The audit was designed around 11 categories including values and mission, stakeholder relations, environment, and contributions to social change. A further 39 subject areas were identified for assessing the company's performance. Overall, the company consulted about 5000 people for the audit through focus groups, surveys and interviews. The audit also considered quantitative and qualitative information provided by departments across the organization. External verifiers were given access to any conversations or data collected from stakeholders to improve the transparency and reliability of the process. For the same reason, survey data was analysed by independent researchers before it was forwarded to The Body Shop audit team.

The 300-page audit report was entitled *Values Report*. It was structured around different stakeholder groups to promote dialogue and clarity about the company's response to specific stakeholder concerns. It also included a summary of the company's performance in the 39 subject areas that had been reviewed. Each area was given a rating on a scale from one to five, and both positive and negative performance was acknowledged. According to The Body Shop, it is better to 'draw attention to your faults than have your critics do it' (The Body Shop, 1998, p. 14). The report of the external auditor was also made available and included a critical summary of the verification process. Subsequent to the publication of the report, stakeholders were consulted again to hear their views on the audit results and review the scope, content and process of auditing.

Sources: Sillanpaa, M. 1998. The Body Shop Values Report – Towards Integrated Stakeholder Auditing. *Journal of Business Ethics*, Vol. 17, 1443–1456.
The Body Shop 1998. *The Body Shop Approach to Ethical Auditing*. The Body Shop.

DRIVERS FOR SOCIAL AND ENVIRONMENTAL REPORTING

Many developments have made social and environmental reporting attractive to the business community. First, the emergence of ethical investment funds has prompted companies to publish reports as a way of communicating their performance to potential investors. Some funds have also used their shareholder rights to promote social and environmental reporting. For example, Morley Fund Management expects all companies listed on FTSE 100 to publish an environmental report. When no report is issued, Morley votes against the adoption of the company's annual accounts.[11] To date, ethical investment has been most prevalent in Europe and North America, but it is also gaining popularity in emerging markets, especially in Singapore and Malaysia. As it becomes more widespread, social and environmental reporting should increase in tandem.

More generally, reporting is an efficient way of communication and it is expected to reduce the resources spent on answering requests concerning social and environmental performance.[12] Such requests have increased with the number of ethical investment funds and other stakeholders that have put pressure on companies to consider their wider impacts in society. The main socially responsible investment companies and research institutions in North America have now agreed to consult sustainability reports before asking companies to fill out surveys and questionnaires.[13] Reporting should therefore decrease the number of information requests received by companies, whether originating from investors or other stakeholders. It also has the benefit of improving corporate communications by enhancing the quality and consistency of responses.

Finally and perhaps most importantly, governments have taken measures to encourage companies to produce responsibility reports. France, for example, requires companies listed on the French stock exchange to disclose information on social and environmental issues. Similar regulation has been introduced by Denmark, The Netherlands and Hong Kong. Other countries have also considered mandatory reporting, but decided against it. Instead, some have introduced voluntary guidelines (e.g. Canada) or required companies to include a statement on their social and environmental impacts in their annual report (e.g. the United Kingdom[14]). Moreover, a number of governments have combined mandatory requirements with practical assistance. In Japan, for example, the government has promoted environmental reporting by making it mandatory and establishing a scheme that helps companies to have their report verified by a third party.[15]

GROWTH IN REPORTING

Corporate responsibility reporting involves the disclosure of information on social and environmental performance. According to the Global Reporting Initiative (2006), a report should provide a balanced and reasonable representation of an organization's performance including its positive and negative impacts on society. Corporate responsibility reports are therefore similar to financial reports in the sense that they are designed to give an account of an organization's activities over the reporting period. Corporate responsibility reports are however aimed at a wider range of stakeholders – including non-governmental organizations, employees and government agencies – than financial statements, which are mainly targeted at shareholders and potential investors. Financial reporting also differs from social and environmental reporting because most countries have established standards determining the content and format of financial statements, while only a few countries have introduced comparable legislation on social reporting.

The number of social and environmental reports published by companies grew quickly from fewer than 100 in 1993 to more than 1500 in 2003.[16] By 2008, the majority of the largest companies in the world were producing sustainability reports.[17] As to geographical regions, European companies have been most active in reporting by publishing more than 50 per cent of all the reports between 1990 and 2003.[18] As shown in Figure 10.1, many North American companies also issue reports, while reporting is less common outside industrialized countries and particularly rare in Africa and the Middle East. In Latin America, Brazilian companies have been the leaders in social and environmental reporting, while companies from other countries have been slower to engage in reporting. In Asia, Japan and Hong Kong have taken the lead in reporting, but the focus is now on China where the first companies released reports in 2008.[19]

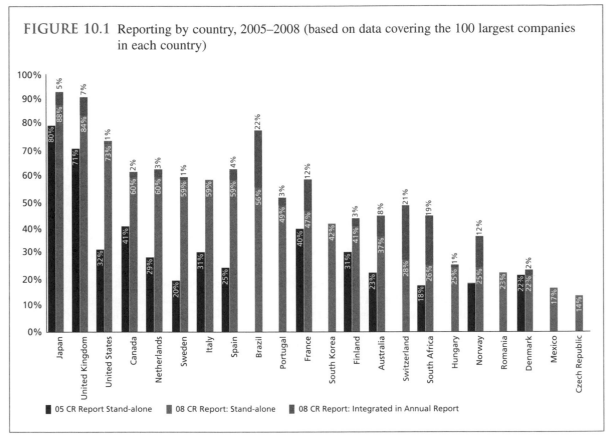

FIGURE 10.1 Reporting by country, 2005–2008 (based on data covering the 100 largest companies in each country)

05 CR Report Stand-alone   08 CR Report: Stand-alone   08 CR Report: Integrated in Annual Report

Source: KPMG (2008).

While many of the largest companies in the world now produce sustainability reports,[20] smaller companies have found it more difficult to find the resources for social accounting and reporting. The expense and complexity of collecting and compiling data have been the main factors inhibiting smaller companies from producing reports. Some observers believe that the development of common standards and best practice will make it less costly for smaller companies to publish social and environmental reports as they will not need to invest in the creation of standards and methodologies.[21] In general, it is likely that small and medium-sized companies from countries where reporting is mandatory will show example to their equivalents in other countries.

THE GLOBAL REPORTING INITIATIVE

The first social and environmental reports were of variable quality and lacked comparability over time and across companies. Even though the principle of transparency and disclosure of corporate performance was generally well received, many reports were immediately

DO THE GUIDELINES INCREASE REPORT CREDIBILITY?

The use of the Global Reporting Guidelines is expected to improve the credibility of reporting. Have you ever paid attention to whether a corporate social responsibility report complies with the Guidelines? In your view, how important is it for report credibility to follow the Guidelines?

criticized after being published. As a consequence, both companies and their critics called for standards and guidance on reporting. The United Nations Environmental Programme (UNEP) had already provided a framework for environmental reporting, but further steps towards a cohesive standard were taken by the Coalition for Environmentally Responsible Economies (CERES) based in Boston, United States. It was CERES that launched the Global Reporting Initiative (GRI) to develop more specific and widely accepted guidelines on social and environmental reporting. The initiative soon gained the support of UNEP, which provided a global platform for extensive consultations with diverse actors.

In 2000, the Global Reporting Initiative launched the Sustainability Reporting Guidelines to provide standards for collecting, compiling and presenting data on the economic, social and environmental impacts of organizational activity. In addition to the generic Guidelines, the Global Reporting Initiative also produces sector supplements designed to assist companies in applying the Guidelines to a specific sector. For example, sector supplements exist for the financial sector, logistics and transport, and public agencies. Since their initial launch, the Guidelines have been the subject of extensive review and have become the most influential initiative on sustainability reporting. According to research carried out by KPMG, the majority of companies producing reports base them on the Guidelines.[22] The success of the Guidelines shows that agreement can be established in a field that is often characterized by confrontation and disagreement between the business sector and its critics. It also demonstrates that a combination of generic standards combined with guidance for specific sectors and active engagement with relevant parties can produce a framework that is acceptable and useful for a variety of actors.

The Sustainability Reporting Guidelines apply to organizations of any size, sector and location. They consist of two types of principles and a set of standard disclosures. The first set of principles provide guidance on the content of sustainability reports and in this way determine what topics to include in a report and why. The four principles on report content are reviewed in some detail below as they illustrate the rationale and drivers behind the Guidelines and reporting in general. The second type of principles pertain to the quality of reporting. These principles are outlined in the next 'Ethics in practice' text box. They are designed to help companies to provide information in a thorough, balanced and meaningful way against the criticism that sustainability reports are window-dressing exercises seeking to portray companies in a positive light. Finally, the standard disclosures include a set of economic, social and environmental indicators that companies can use to give an account of their performance. It is the standard disclosures that have offered companies clear guidance on the type of data they can collect in order to assess and demonstrate their performance. For example, the standard disclosures include an indicator on non-discrimination and recommend companies to provide information on the total number of discrimination incidents and actions taken in response to such incidents.

The Guidelines recommend that companies make available general information on their strategy and corporate governance to provide a background against which information on economic, social, and environmental performance can be assessed. It is noteworthy that the Guidelines also require companies to disclose information on economic performance. Because this information is presented in a more evaluative and accessible way than data in financial statements, it can provide a clear and more critical overview of a company's financial performance, market presence and economic impact, resulting in many investment analysts now consulting sustainability reports to gain a better understanding of the opportunities and risks faced by companies.

PRINCIPLES ON REPORT CONTENT

Materiality

The principle of materiality is important in addressing the criticism that sustainability reports do not always disclose information on topics that stakeholders have been most concerned about. Accordingly, if a company is criticized for the safety of its products, the issue should be discussed in a comprehensive way in the sustainability report. In general, reports should include information on any significant impacts the organization has on the economy, society and the natural environment. Materiality is hence defined by a mix of internal and external considerations. For example, key policies, values and competences of the organization should be taken into account when assessing the materiality of information. Moreover, issues and topics raised by external stakeholders should be considered and included as salient. The Guidelines also advise companies to prioritize material topics by providing more detailed and measurable information on them.

Stakeholder inclusiveness

The principle of stakeholder inclusiveness reflects the importance of stakeholder thinking and invites companies to engage with a broad range of stakeholders to identify their expectations and concerns that should be addressed in the report. Companies are also advised to document and disclose the process of stakeholder consultation to enhance the transparency and credibility of reporting. The principle of stakeholder inclusiveness seems intuitive but is less clear than it seems. For example, given that most customers and employees are unlikely to read the sustainability report or even be aware of it, should companies give equal attention to the concerns of these stakeholders in comparison to those who will read the report? The Guidelines suggest that all stakeholders should be taken into account for determining report content, but the focus should be on those stakeholders who are expected to read the report. Also, it should be explained how the conflicting interests and expectations of stakeholders have been prioritized and balanced. Companies should also be mindful of the fact that the interests of stakeholder groups may be articulated and promoted by other stakeholders who will consult the sustainability report even when the actual stakeholder does not.

Sustainability context

The third principle on report content invites companies to present information in relation to local, regional and global standards so that the company's overall sustainability performance can be assessed in comparison to some benchmarks. Presenting information in a broader context helps the company to evaluate its performance, but also makes it easier for the report reader to do the same. For example, many governments and international organizations have set pollution targets that companies can use to provide a point of comparison for their own efforts. Similar standards exist on labour conditions and other social issues including human rights.

Completeness

Finally, information presented in sustainability reports should be sufficiently extensive to enable report readers to assess the company's performance in the reporting period. Completeness includes the three aspects of scope, boundaries and timing. Scope pertains to the inclusion of all the relevant issues based on stakeholder consultation and evaluation of any other significant impacts the organization has on society. Report boundaries refer to the range of activities included in the report in the sense of subsidiaries, joint ventures, suppliers and other entities over which the organization has some control. This control may vary over issues. For example, companies may have some influence over the environmental practices of their suppliers, but they are less likely to have control over the ownership of these organizations. Finally, reports should include all the issues that have arisen over the reporting period and also involve consideration of the organization's long-term impacts that accumulate over time.

ETHICS IN PRACTICE

PRINCIPLES ON REPORT QUALITY

Balance

The report should discuss positive and negative aspects of the organization's performance so that it provides an unbiased overview of the company. Factual information should be clearly distinguished from more interpretive material.

Comparability

Information should enable comparison over time and in relation to competitors if possible. This means that information should be reported over time and in a consistent way so that it can be used for comparison.

Accuracy

Information should be precise and sufficiently detailed. Quantitative information should be collected, analysed and presented in a reliable way, while qualitative information should be explained clearly and with justification.

Timeliness

Reports should be regular and presented in a timely manner for stakeholders to consider them in their decision making. Reports are normally produced annually and events should be covered in the report that follows their occurrence.

Clarity

Information should be presented in a way that is understandable and accessible. Technical jargon and unnecessary detail should be avoided to enhance the clarity of the report. Information should also be easy to locate.

Reliability

Procedures used in the compilation of information should be explained and disclosed so that the quality of how the data were collected and analysed can be assessed. Information included in the report should be supported by records kept by the organization.

Source: Global Reporting Initiative (2006).

EXTERNAL ASSURANCE

External assurance is one of the topical issues in sustainability reporting at the moment. It refers to the verification of report content and quality by independent external organizations. Assurance is important because it enhances the trustworthiness of reporting. According to the Association of Chartered Certified Accountants (2004), 'organizations that fail to obtain assurance for their reports are likely to face issues of credibility'.

Many observers have noted that the growth in sustainability reporting and transparency on the part of the business community has not resulted in increased levels of confidence and trust among the critics of corporate behaviour'[23] Instead, reports have been seen as biased documents written in promotional language and lacking coverage of key areas of concern. Assurance has been seen as a way to ensure and convince stakeholders that the content and quality of reported information is truthful and balanced. Assurance of sustainability reports is however new and organizations providing related services have often been learning by doing, which has cast doubt on the quality of the assurance practice itself. Nevertheless, the field has developed quickly and there are now a variety of assurance standards that should improve the credibility of the practice.

According to KPMG's survey on reporting in 2008, the number of companies using formal assurance is increasing with 40 per cent of Global Fortune 250 companies providing assurance statements in their sustainability reports. In general, companies from European countries are more likely to use external assurance than companies from other regions, with the exception of South Korea. The findings of the KPMG survey show that assurance varies across sectors and is most prevalent for companies that are subjected to stakeholder scrutiny and consumer pressure. For example, all of the largest companies in the mining sector use external assurance, which may be explained by the considerable attention the sector has experienced from non-governmental organizations. At the same time, only a small percentage of retailers, construction companies and forestry companies provide assurance statements in their reports; these sectors have also attracted less attention than, say, apparel and clothing.

In addition to independent assurance, a number of companies have asked experts and stakeholder panels to make statements about social accounting and reporting procedures. In 2008, about 27 per cent of Global Fortune 250 companies producing sustainability reports provided such statements in their reports.[24] The practice is therefore a fairly common way of improving the credibility of reporting. The statements are typically made by individual experts, academics or members of a local community, but companies have also set up panels consisting of representatives from different fields to provide views on reports and the underpinning process of collecting and analysing data. The panels often include members from non-governmental organizations and in this way provide companies with valuable feedback and connections to the non-profit sector. Despite the insightfulness of expert and panel statements, they do not signal assurance of report content and are easily subjected to the criticism of window-dressing.

Concerns have been raised about the use of external assurance in social accounting and reporting. More specifically, some observers have criticized them for managerial capture, referring to their use as management tools rather than real, externally verified audits of organizational performance. Accordingly, social accounts published by companies 'only look, smell, and quack like accountability because too many have swallowed a bland and incorrect definition of accountability'.[25] In reality, third party auditors are rarely in a position to comment on whether social reports cover all substantial issues and risks because of the limited knowledge we have about social and environmental matters.

SUMMARY

- Voluntary initiatives have emerged in two waves. The first wave resulted from the efforts of newly independent states to control the behaviour of foreign companies that were seen as a continuation of colonial exploitation. The second wave was prompted by the scandals of the 1990s that threatened the reputation of Western companies by linking them to misconduct in developing countries.

- Voluntary codes vary, from instruments adopted by single companies to initiatives developed within international organizations. Any code signals commitment to certain standards of behaviour, but the initiatives that include representatives from governments, international organizations and the non-profit sector generally carry more weight.

- Social accounting involves the assessment of information on an organization's social and environmental performance. Because it has not always been clear who the users of this information are, it has been difficult to define the scope and boundaries of social accounting. It has also been challenging to find reliable indicators for social and environmental performance.

- Social and environmental reporting has increased in response to growing demands on how corporations manage their impact on society. The demand is not only coming from critical non-governmental organizations, but also from government authorities and ethical investors. As a result, social and environmental reporting has developed into a practice that presents corporate performance in relation to stakeholder concerns and wider societal objectives.

- Use of external assurance is driven by the desire to improve the credibility of social and environmental reports in the eyes of sceptical stakeholders. The role of external verifiers is to assure that information presented in company reports is truthful, material and backed with evidence.

QUICK REVIEW QUESTIONS:

1   What are the main ways in which the voluntary codes adopted since the 1990s differ from those introduced earlier?

2   What are the expected benefits of social accounting and reporting?

3   Social and environmental reports are sometimes seen as window-dressing. What measures have been taken to improve the credibility of reporting?

CASE STUDY: SUSTAINABLE PALM OIL–A CHALLENGE

Palm oil is an increasingly common raw material used in food and non-food products. According to Friends of the Earth, one in every ten products found in an average supermarket contains palm oil in some form. For example, chocolate, margarine, crisps, washing power, shampoo and cosmetics may contain traces of palm oil. The demand for palm oil has recently increased because of its use as a bio-fuel that is mixed with diesel. As a result, palm oil is now the second most consumed oil after soybean oil in the world.

Palm oil is made from the fruit of the oil palm tree that can only be cultivated in tropical areas. It is cheaper to produce than many other vegetable oils because the palm oil tree produces several crops a year and yields a fairly large harvest by hectare. Palm oil is also attractive because it can be stored at room temperature without becoming rancid. For these reasons, palm oil now accounts for more than 20 per cent of the consumption of edible oil in the world and its overall share is still growing.

Farming of palm oil is linked to the loss of rainforests in Malaysia and Indonesia where tropical forests and peatland are cleared for palm plantations. Some non-governmental organizations fear that within the next 15 years almost all of the rainforests in the two countries will have disappeared. Deforestation is also expected to contribute to the disappearance of rare species of wildlife including the orangutan and Sumatran tiger. It will also escalate climate change by increasing the amount of greenhouse gases in the atmosphere. The destruction of forests and plantations has also led to the displacement of peoples and loss of their livelihood.

The supply chain of palm oil production involves several steps. The trees are grown in large plantations that send the fruits to centralized mills where oil is extracted from them. The oil is then shipped to refineries that are located in producer or consumer countries. It is in the refineries where the oil is processed into a range of products that are commonly used. The oil is sold by traders who are mainly based in Singapore. Companies like Unilever are important customers to major traders,

but there are also smaller brokers involved in the business.

The Roundtable on Sustainable Palm Oil was set up by a small group of companies and the World Wildlife Fund (WWF) in 2001 to establish standards for producing and procuring palm oil in a sustainable manner. Even before then, some companies had sought ways to address the issue. Migros, a Swiss retailer, had been particularly active in seeking to move away from the use of non-sustainable palm oil. The company's efforts were restricted by the limited availability of sustainable oil for commercial use. Migros' solution was to cut the overall use of palm oil by replacing it with other ingredients when possible.

The Roundtable includes manufacturers, growers and traders that form the supply chain of palm oil production. It has established a code of conduct and a supply chain certification system to support the growth and sourcing of sustainable palm oil. The code of conduct is a statement of commitment rather than a set of standards. As such, it signals intent rather than adoption of new policies and working methods. In comparison, the certification system is a more comprehensive instrument that sets forth principles on sustainable palm oil production and their implementation. It distinguishes between four methods through which sustainable palm oil can be brought to the market and includes regular auditing and a grievance procedure. The performance of the certification system is yet to be tested as it was only launched in 2008, but non-governmental organizations have already found weaknesses and problems in the system. Greenpeace, for example, has argued that companies using palm oil in their products have 'no way of knowing whether or not the palm oil they are using is from rainforest destruction'. This is because the origin of palm oil is difficult to trace. A buyer of palm oil can therefore never be fully certain of its source. An additional problem has been the segregation of sustainable oil from other oils in the supply chain of palm oil farming and production. One of the main reasons for this is that the oil is stored in shared containers in south-east Asia and Europe before being sold forward.

▶

Greenpeace argues that the Roundtable is creating 'the illusion of sustainable palm oil'. Instead, it is calling for government action to stop the destruction of rain forests. Greenpeace is focusing on the Indonesian government, which has been called upon to introduce a moratorium on converting forests into plantations. Non-governmental organizations have also lobbied for the restoration of rain forests and peatlands, which would reduce greenhouse gas emissions and provide a home for endangered species. Moreover, Friends of the Earth is calling for government legislation in countries in which the end-products are sold. According to the organization, legislation is needed because only a few companies would take action on a voluntary basis.

STUDY QUESTIONS

1 The Roundtable on Sustainable Palm Oil is a multi-stakeholder initiative. What actors need to be part of the initiative for the problem to be addressed in an effective way?

2 What is hindering the development of sustainable practices in the production of palm oil?

3 What developments have to take place to make the production of palm oil more sustainable?

SOURCES

Friends of the Earth 2004. *Greasy Palms: Palm Oil, the Environment and Big Business*. Available from www.foe.co.uk, accessed 8 April 2009.

Greenpeace 2007. *Cooking the Climate*. Available from www.greenpeace.org, accessed 8 April 2009.

Roundtable for Sustainable Palm Oil 2009. Available from www.rspo.org, accessed 8 April 2009.

NOTES

1   Jenkins (2001).
2   Jenkins (2001). See also Gordon & Miyake (2000); Utting (2000).
3   Gordon & Miyake (2000).
4   Jenkins (2001).
5   Jerbi (2009).
6   Jenkins (2001).
7   Ibid.
8   See Richter (2001).
9   Gordon & Miyake (2000).
10 Gray (2000).
11 ACCA (2004).
12 Willis (2003).
13 ACCA (2004).
14 http://www.frc.org.uk/.
15 ACCA (2004).
16 Ibid.
17 KPMG (2008).
18 ACCA (2004).
19 KPMG (2008).
20 Ibid.
21 ACCA (2004).

22 KPMG (2008).
23 Dando & Swift (2003).
24 KPMG (2008).
25 Gray (2000).

REFERENCES

ACCA (Association of Chartered Certified Accountants) 2004. *Towards Transparency: Progress on Global Sustainability Reporting 2004*. Certified Accountants Educational Trust.

The Body Shop 1998. *The Body Shop Approach to Ethical Auditing*. The Body Shop.

Dando, N. and Swift, T. 2003. Transparency and Assurance: Minding the Credibility Gap. *Journal of Business Ethics*, Vol. 44, No. 2–3, 195–200.

Global Reporting Initiative 2006. *Sustainability Reporting Guidelines*. Amsterdam: Global Reporting Initiative.

Gordon, K. and Miyake, M. 2000. *Deciphering Codes of Corporate Conduct: A Review of their Contents*. Working Papers on International Investment, No. 1999/2. Organization for Economic Cooperation and Development, March.

Gray, R. 2000. Current developments and trends in social and environmental auditing, reporting and attestation: a review and comment. *International Journal of Accounting*, Vol. 4, 247–268.

ILO undated. Corporate Codes of Conduct. Bureau for Workers' Activities. Available from http://actrav.itcilo.org/actrav-english/telearn/global/ilo/code/main.htm, accessed 12 July 2009.

KPMG 2008. *KPMG International Survey of Corporate Responsibility Reporting 2008*. KPMG International, October.

Jenkins, R. 2001. *Corporate Codes of Conduct: Self-Regulation in a Global Economy*. United Nations Research Institute for Social Development. Technology, Business and Society Programme Paper No. 2, April.

Jerbi, S. 2009. Business and Human Rights at the UN: What might happen next? *Human Rights Quarterly*, Vol. 31, 299–320.

Richter, J. 2001. *Holding Corporations Accountable: Corporate Conduct, International Codes, and Citizen Action*. London and New York: Zed Books.

Sillanpaa, M. 1998. The Body Shop Values Report – Towards Integrated Stakeholder Auditing. *Journal of Business Ethics*, Vol. 17, 1443–1456.

Willis, A. 2003. The Role of the Global Reporting Initiative's Sustainability Reporting Guidelines in the Social Screening of Investments. *Journal of Business Ethics*, Vol. 43, No. 3, 233–237.

Utting, P. 2000. *Potential and Limits of Voluntary Initiatives*. Report of the UNRISD Workshop, 23–24 October. Geneva: UNRISD.

MANAGING ETHICS INTERNALLY

LEARNING OBJECTIVES

After studying this chapter you should be able to:

- Identify and evaluate a range of mechanisms by which organizations attempt to manage their ethics.
- Identify key underpinning factors that contribute to, or can inhibit, the effectiveness of such mechanisms.

INTRODUCTION

In earlier chapters we have looked at ethical theories and the organizational factors that can affect how ethics works in organizations. In this chapter we shall look at what is, for practical purposes, the most direct matter for a manager, namely the opportunities to manage ethics in their organization. Underpinning this is the interaction between what individuals hold to be of value to them, and how organizations process matters of value. The ambiguous nature of 'value' has been mentioned before. In this context there is a tension between what is valuable for an organization and what for individuals. We used the phrase 'the survival imperative' to reflect the fact that in general organizations have an in-built logic to maintain their existence, and this can often completely override morals. In this chapter this imperative is taken as given, and what is mainly being discussed is how, within that logic, organizations can rule themselves to their best interests without compromising the interests of others.

MANAGING CORPORATE ETHICS

One question here is what exactly is meant by *corporate* ethics? Clearly it cannot be identified with the ethics of the totality of the workforce, as many of these may have ethical attitudes that are quite at variance with those of their employer (but suppress those differences). But it must be more than the official presentations of corporate values – as Argyris acknowledges when he draws the distinction between the espoused and the real values of an organization.[1] In this latter point there is an analogy with individual values – often these are not entirely clear to the outside world. Indeed, sometimes they may be unrecognized by the individuals themselves, so that an action in a novel ethical context may represent a *discovery*, as much by the actor as by others. So maybe the lack of a clear definition of 'corporate' ethics is not a damning weakness. In what follows we will assume that it does make sense to talk of the ethics of a corporation, and that this is not to be simply identified with official corporate policy or with some collective of employee attitudes. This inherent vagueness is actually a strength of organized behaviour, as we shall see later.

Another issue is exactly what we mean by talking of *managing* corporate ethics. One natural interpretation of this, implicit in the language of shared values,[2] is that the organization attempts to get some kind of uniformity of action, whereby all employees, if not exactly behaving identically, can at least be seen as embodying the same core values. At a minimum level this may be plausible, for example where a firm has a prohibition on employees accepting large gifts from clients, and the job of managing corporate ethics would in this case be to ensure that people do in fact refrain from accepting such gifts.

At a deeper level, however, there are potential problems with this interpretation of managing corporate ethics. As we have seen at some length in discussing ethical theories and concepts, ethics is not simply a matter of prescribing certain behaviour and how far people do in fact adhere to such prescriptions. With consequential approaches it is about the style of reasoning people use, and how far they look at long-term *outcomes* of their acts. With deontological approaches it is about the *structure* of people's thinking about reasons and actions, while with virtue ethics it is not about actions as such at all, but about the *kind of person* someone is. What this indicates is that the idea of managing corporate ethics is a more problematic area than the simple identification of some acts that are to be embraced and others that are to be avoided. Whichever of the main approaches to ethics is adopted, the question of how a corporation manages its ethics is about how it manages its employees' attitudes, their perceptions, their reasoning and their underpinning values. And in turn this requires some approach to issues such as understanding long-term consequences, about how a choice may have implications beyond the specific case, and about what kind of person the organization has who does, or does not, act in a certain way.

This goes beyond what is normally expected of corporations and their relationships with employees. Most firms have detailed systems of operational rules, and these are commonly assumed to cover the majority of situations that might have some ethical content. Thus company policies on areas such as non-discrimination, how to communicate with customers, use of company equipment for personal purposes, and health and safety are often presumed, in combination with the requirements of local laws, to cover the main body of ethical situations that employees are likely to encounter. In some cases a firm goes further and has a code of ethics or a code of conduct (the 'Ethics in practice' text box on Bharti Airtel gives one example of this).

CODE OF CONDUCT FOR BHARTI AIRTEL

Integrity and ethics

- The partners will conduct all its dealings in a very ethical manner and with the highest business standards.
- All partners with a business relationship with Bharti Airtel shall comply with the highest level of integrity and ethical practices.
- The partners will provide all possible assistance to Bharti Airtel in order to investigate any possible instances of unethical behaviour or business conduct violations by its employees. Partners will disclose forthwith any breach of these provisions that comes to their knowledge to allow for timely action in their prevention and detection.
- Partners will adopt appropriate processes to prevent offering any illegal gratification in the form of bribes or kickbacks either in cash or in kind in the course of all dealings with us. Any instances of such violations will be viewed in a serious manner and Bharti Airtel reserves the right to take all appropriate actions or remedies as may be required under the circumstances.
- All partners are required to confirm their compliance to ethical dealings on an annual basis by signing a certificate to this effect as per Bharti Airtel's standard annual certificate.
- Any ethical or integrity issues observed or encountered while dealing with Bharti Airtel shall be brought to the notice of Bharti Airtel's senior management or the Head of Internal Audit immediately.

Environment, health and safety

- Suppliers dealing with Bharti Airtel shall comply and adhere to all laws, regulations and guidelines on environment, health and safety.
- Suppliers will ensure that all new service offerings as well as new product designs are in compliance with the relevant environmental regulation and guidelines, at the time of implementation at Bharti Airtel.

Protection of intellectual property

The partners:

- Shall comply with the guidelines for use of the trademarks and trade names notified by the Company (including but not limited to 'Bharti' and 'Airtel') and shall not use the Company trademarks and trade names without the prior written consent of the Company.
- Shall, under no circumstances, advertise or use Bharti Airtel's name to market its own product or associate its company with Bharti Airtel. If a partner spots any counterfeit or infringing Company product/service, the partner shall immediately notify Bharti Airtel.
- Shall not reproduce, in whole or in substantial part, any copyrighted work in hard copies, prints, video or electronic copies in violation of the copyright laws including the Bharti Airtel Partner Manual.

Bharti Airtel's intellectual property also resides in trade secrets or know-hows. Trade secrets are technical, commercial or other information unknown to the public, which can bring economic benefits to its owner. Documents that contain trade secrets and available to the Partner shall be safeguarded and not shared by the Partner with any third party without prior written consent of Bharti Airtel.

Domestic and international trade controls

Suppliers shall understand and follow applicable domestic and international trade control and customs laws and regulations, including, but not limited to those relating to licensing, shipping and import documentation and reporting and record retention requirements.

Conflict of interest

Suppliers will ensure they do not engage in any personal dealings with Bharti employees, especially those that they interact with on Bharti business matters.

The most telling ethical questions, however, surface when a situation arises that goes beyond these policies and procedures. This is when an individual has to draw on their internal attitudes and values. By definition, these are not easy for a company to assess. True, there are available psychometric assessments that purport to evaluate aspects of a person's personal ethics.[3] However, even if accurate, these are limited to broad interpretations of an individual's values and do not pretend to predict behaviour in complex novel situations.

Unsurprisingly, therefore, the idea of managing corporate ethics tends to resolve itself down to the development of incentives, mechanisms and dialogues that will make individuals more motivated in general to be ethically more aware and more responsible. There is a potential weakness here in the kinds of ethical positions that are often assumed by companies, and thus in the manner in which people's values might turn into actions (and the 'Lying at work' text box provides an illustration of this).

Another side to this discussion is that it is the senior executive, who has a wide range of knowledge power and responsibilities, who has therefore the widest range of potential areas of action, and therefore has the widest range of areas of opportunity to act without ethical responsibility. And often it is precisely these individuals for whom the question of managing their ethics within the organization is not raised (often because it is they who are doing the managing themselves).

ETHICS IN PRACTICE

LYING AT WORK

Everybody accepts that lying is wrong, prima facie. Yet how people adhere to or violate this in their work depends on the manner in which this value combines with other motives and considerations, such as self-protection or organizational efficiency. In an anonymous study of workers in the northeastern United States, William Keep (2009) identified several different reasons why people might lie at work.

As well as efficiency and self-protection, also prominent were intentions to buy time for an organization, or to avoid conflict. Keep noted the direct contrast between what people do and the prescriptions embodied in codes, which tend simply to require honesty in all dealings.

MANAGING VALUES

Another key distinction to be drawn is between the management of ethics by an organization and the management of values. As the terms suggest, the former is concerned with behaviour while the latter is about people's internal perceptions, attitudes, feelings and beliefs. Many discussions about ethics focus on values specifically because these are seen as the key determining factor of someone's behaviour – all other things being equal, someone who values highly, say, tolerance, will act in a tolerant manner.

It is not quite as simple as this, however. All things are rarely equal: in business as in life there are often other pressures relating to one's own sense of well-being or security. Many cases of violation of ethical principles come down to a belief on the part of an individual that the security of themselves or those close to them are under threat. Also, values sometimes conflict: being kind to someone may on occasion involve lying to them. Yet a further issue is about the nature of practical reason – the move from a statement of value to a conclusion as to what to do involves often a range of additional steps, some of which embody further assumptions.

The kind of dilemma seen in the 'Ethics and you' text box is common enough, and a move that maintains commercial performance while adhering to the letter (but not necessarily the spirit) of a rule is also a common enough response. As seen in discussion of Keep's study of US workers, there are several specific reasons why people might lie at work. But while this is a low-level failure of integrity, much the same approach underlies many of the more serious corporate failures – auditing firms that ask set questions but fail to continue with the more probing follow-ups that might reveal corporate accounting problems, for example, or investment managers who ensure that they are told enough to be able to produce evidence to investigators that their firm complies with financial regulations but may deliberately not follow something up when they suspect that their investment staff may be in violation.[4] An anecdote reported in *Forbes* in 2006 illustrates a similar case: the then (now disgraced) senior ethics officer for Hewlett Packard, Kevin Hunsaker, asked a senior HP investigator if a supplier was acting ethically – the response from the investigator was that the supplier's actions were 'on the edge'; to which Hunsaker is reported to have said

ETHICS AND YOU

AN EXAMPLE OF A PRACTICAL DILEMMA

1 Jatin values honesty very highly.

2 Jatin's boss asks him to tell a waiting customer that a product is safe.

3 Although Jatin knows a lot about the many safety features of the product, he does not know definitively whether the product is completely safe or not, and his boss has just left the shop.

4 Jatin asks the customer if he has any specific concerns about the product.

5 He responds to each individual question truthfully.

6 The customer seems to be under the impression that Jatin has confirmed that the product is safe, though that general question is not asked, and Jatin does not volunteer that he does not know.

Has Jatin answered honestly? To the letter of the definition of not lying, yes. But clearly there is a failure of integrity, in that he has allowed the customer to be deceived.

'I shouldn't have asked.' In other words, he did not want to be in possession of evidence that he would have to act on, even though he had sufficient suspicion that all was not well.

The point about this example is that the individual there acts in a manner that they would argue represents an example of honesty – so there is an implied assumption here, that to answer truthfully, though not present the whole truth about a subject, is still an example of honesty. In this example the value of honesty is not enough to produce meritorious behaviour. Something more is needed (and was found lacking). The underlying *virtue* of honesty is more than the behaviour of simply telling the truth, involving in addition the taking of steps to ensure that people are not deceived.

Managing values, therefore, is relevant to managing ethics, but operates in unclear ways. For one, as seen above, the move from value to act can require a number of additional steps. For another, statements of value are often vaguely expressed, so that it becomes a controversial matter whether a particular action represents a confirmation or a violation of a value, as seen in the 'Right to work' text box. There are various ways to resolve this issue: one might be to argue that one or other side is confused. Another might be to accept that a concept such as the right to work is vague and admits of different means of being made concrete. This latter, of course, concedes the point that values are not action-guiding in the sense in which they are often presumed to be.

At this point one might ask, why worry about values then? Why not focus solely on behaviour and actions, and not care too much about the motives from which they spring? This position could only be justified from a consequentialist position, since approaches such as virtue ethics require a specific positive orientation to ethically worthy acts. However, even on a view such as utilitarianism, it is implausible. Someone may do x on one occasion because they think that *in these specific circumstances* x will bring about the greatest good of the greatest number (for example), even though they do not hold an underpinning value towards x-like actions in general. But on subsequent occasions some extraneous factor may lead them to act differently, and not do x, on the ground that they believe that on these other occasions the act will *not* bring about the greatest good of the greatest number. So the ethical importance of a certain *kind* of action cannot be consistently pursued on this view. The conclusion of this argument would therefore be that values have no role in guiding actions; the only value that would do so is the basic consequential value (in the case of utilitarianism, this would be the overriding value of avoiding pain and increasing pleasure).

In practice this is not the way we think of ethics or values – we expect people to act honestly, kindly, fairly, and we expect this to be not only a feature that we can recognize in their behaviour but also to be a part of their thinking and decision making. Ethically worthy action is not just the achievement of the right ends but the achievement of the right ends for the right reasons.

THINKING CRITICALLY ABOUT ETHICS

THE RIGHT TO WORK

Work is valuable for many reasons – it provides economic livelihood, it gives people an identity, it defines communities. For this reason many have claimed that individuals have a *right* to work – to be involved in gainful employment.

So, when workers go on strike to protest against redundancies, they may in some cases claim that they are doing so in virtue of their recognition of the right to work. However, some who decide *not* to strike may claim the same right to work, on the basis that they want to carry on working even if others withdraw their labour.

Managing values, then, is both relevant to the management of ethics but also unclear in its application. There is a further argument against too much reliance on the management of values, though. This is that an employer may have the right to expect people to behave in certain ways, but do they have the right to compel people to *feel* in certain ways as well? This goes back to the idea that values are private issues, while actions are what is public and therefore what matters. But while in principle there may be something to this argument, in practice it would be implausible to expect that someone would completely sublimate their own values in favour of those of their employer in a really serious matter. Indeed, there are ample examples that demonstrate the frequency with which personal principles can and do withstand organizational imperatives – whistle-blowing, as we shall see a little later, is one, just as is principled resignation, or direct refusal to carry out certain tasks. The fact that such acts do occur, at least on some occasions, indicates that people's personal values cannot be insulated from their actions when at work, and therefore the idea that an organization should not consider these as part of what the worker brings to their job is misplaced. This is not the same as saying that an organization can require people to hold certain values, but it does place the onus on an employee to give an account of how their personal values are compatible with the organizations practices and policies. 'I was only following orders' can never, therefore, be a defence against the charge of unethical behaviour.

A related polarity with regard to the management of values is the compliance–commitment opposition. In general, because what is generally publicly assessed is the complex of actions and outcomes of a corporation, behavioural compliance with set rules and procedures is a key target of the management of ethics in most organizations. But sheer compliance can mask an individual's underlying values, as we have seen above. Achievement of a deeper engagement, or even an identification with the values of a corporation is generally regarded as preferable, for the reasons that in novel or uncertain situations someone's commitment to a given set of values may well help them to reach sound conclusions even when regulations are not helpful.

For the reasons given earlier, this is not easy to measure and often not at all easy to achieve. Individual values are private, and thus by definition only as open as people choose to disclose to us. For another, we are inconsistent beings, and sometimes act out of weakness, self-deception or self-preservation. So our stated values may not often be our real ones, but also our explicit behaviour may also at times be misleading as to what our long-term latent values are.

The last area to discuss in this section, and perhaps the most problematic, is the belief that values should be *shared* in an organization. The rationale for this view is based on

THINKING CRITICALLY ABOUT ETHICS

EMPLOYEE ATTITUDES

How far should an organization concern itself with the values of individual employees? Clearly, if someone holds attitudes that might encourage people to act illegally, or in a manner that grossly undermines the mission of the organization, then that would be a legitimate source of concern – if these attitudes were expressed.

But what of lower-level attitudes that do not fit easily into organization's mission? What of attitudes that someone keeps private? What of views that are legally and socially acceptable but conflict with those of the organization, such as a committed and actively lobbying vegetarian who nevertheless works as, say, an accountant for a fast food burger chain?

the idea that since an organization is a collection of people working towards a commonly accepted set of goals, it makes sense for them to have a commonly accepted set of values as well. The sharing would, so this argument runs, then, make it easier for individuals to agree on operational and other matters.

There are, though, good reasons for *not* having too great a sense of shared values in an organization. The shared values argument seems to presume a simple linear chain of operations, where all employees cluster around a single process that does not change too dramatically. Modern organizations, on the other hand, are complex and involve a diversity of people, sophisticated networks of operations, and often rapidly evolving challenges and responses. One of the most important aspects of the management of change is consultation, not to eradicate dissent, but to discover key factors that leading decision takers may not know about, or may have misconstrued. If consultation is effective, then this should result, at times, in the consultees making clear that a proposed change should not be undertaken. Often, doubtless, this might simply be for operational reasons (such as the employees pointing out to management that they, the latter, have not realized that a certain kind of plant and equipment has been superseded by incremental additions to current inventory). But at times it may also be a matter of employees, or others, making clear to senior decision makers that a certain course of action would not be ethically acceptable. This therefore will normally require a certain amount of difference in values between those decision makers and those with whom they consult. If not, then the organization runs the risk of 'groupthink'[5] – the phenomenon whereby a collection of people fail to be sufficiently critical of poor proposals, due to actual or desired collective intellectual conformity.

Shared values are often an aim of organizational culture change programmes. However, it is not always realized that the evidence for such values is behaviour, and as we have seen above, and in Chapter 3 when discussing ethical philosophies, there is a substantial gap between what someone does and what they actually value. In most cases, *absolutely* held values influence behaviour in the same way that relative but *strongly held* values will do. Also ethical decision making often takes into account a whole range of intermediate assumptions – as the 'Practical dilemma' text box illustrated. So although culture change is a popular management technique, it is unlikely to achieve changes in people's values.

Another aspect of this is the role of diverse opinions and views as a source of richness in organizational knowledge management. The tendency of recruiters to appoint individuals who mirror their own features is an example of this issue – the idea in this case being that the appointment of 'clone' employees reduces the 'gene pool' of dialogue, as too many people will share the same views, and therefore fail to employ the right degree of critical evaluation and challenge to corporate wisdom. In some occupations critical debate is central to professional practice.

THINKING CRITICALLY ABOUT ETHICS

DIALOGUE AND DEBATE IN MEDICINE

A standard practice in medical practice, especially among hospital doctors, is the presentation for debate of specific cases. The two related aims of this are firstly professional development of individuals, and secondly enhancement of general professional standards of practice. This process cannot operate effectively unless there is not only an open forum where even junior doctors can express their opinions and challenge accepted norms, but also sufficient diversity of opinion for there to be people who are able to conceive of such challenges.

In the following sections we shall move away from underlying processes to the organizational methods used to manage ethics and values.

ETHICS OFFICERS AND COMMITTEES

A phenomenon seen with increasing frequency is the ethics officer. In North America, the Ethics and Compliance Officer Association (ECOA) has over 1300 members covering a wide range of industries. In India, multinational corporations such as Tata Motors have active and influential ethics officers reporting to the board of directors. Ethics officers are often seen as a key internal regulatory function within an organization, reconciling business and individual values. As the ECOA expresses this role:

> *An Ethics Officer is such a leader in the area of business conduct. The Ethics Officer is tasked with integrating their organization's ethics and values initiatives, compliance activities, and business conduct practices into the decision-making processes at all levels of the organization.*[6]

Note that this organization pairs ethics with compliance. In many cases the driver for appointing an ethics officer is less about enhancing values than it is about avoiding legal proceedings. Meeting legal requirements – complying with them – is often therefore a key function of this role. In areas such as finance, the role is more likely to be a named compliance officer, placing explicit priority on staying within the law. One reason for this is that financial regulatory authorities often require finance houses to have executives internal to the firm who are working to avoid legal infringements. A consequence of this, however, is an embodiment of the managerial folk-wisdom that what gets measured gets managed – the evidence of the banking crisis of 2008–09 has been that ethical expectations concerning responsible lending have not been given much attention, whereas the legal regulations governing banking procedures have been attended to, to the letter.

However, there are different interpretations of what is involved in the role of an ethics officer. Consider the following, taken from the code of conduct of a sub-group of the British Psychological Society:

> *The role of the Ethics Liaison Officer and Social Policy Officer has been created to ensure that all SGCP members have access to up-to-date information about ethical and social policy issues. ... It is not the intention of the SGCP that the Ethics Liaison and Social Policy Officer will provide specific advice or guidance to members ... However, it is the responsibility of the Ethics Liaison and Social Policy Officer to ensure that members understand how to source this type of advice ...*[7]

While this role is not exactly titled identically to that described by the ECOA, it is clear that this is the closest equivalent, and the explanation given of the role strongly indicates that a more general role is not present in this organization. Other examples of ethics officers also demonstrate the wide range of interpretations of the role. For example, the ethics officer of the Israeli army, Brigadier General Eli Shermeister, has a responsibility to uphold specific values, but also has a major public relations role, often speaking to the media defending the actions of his country's military forces.

This latter example, perhaps more overtly than the others, emphasizes a perennial difficulty with understanding the actions of organizations in relation to ethics: is it for show or for real? As we saw in Chapter 4 with 'greenwashing' it can be very tempting for an organization to treat a question of values as an opportunity for positive self-promotion, rather than as a trigger for ethical change. To be fair to many organizations, the kinds of arguments offered in favour of being more ethical often focus on reputation management and positive PR, so it is not unexpected if this can muddy the waters of what values the organization really embodies.

As well as a question mark over the *definition* of the role of ethics officer, there is the question of the *influence* of the role. This is often considered from the point of view of where in the organization structure the role is placed. However, while this is a significant issue, it is not the only factor influencing how effective an ethics officer may be. Senior management commitment is not guaranteed by giving an ethics officer a place on the board. The informal processes of an organization can often subvert the official structure – a less senior member of staff may seek to by-pass an ethics officer and communicate directly with the managing director for example, or some executives with apparently equal influence to the ethics officer may in fact have greater sway due to personal affiliations, working in a core value-generating part of the business, or simply greater forcefulness in decision-making arenas.

A further factor that affects how much impact an ethics officer may have is the question alluded to earlier of what is the driving force for the establishment of the role. If the reasons are related to reputation management this is clearly problematic. But it can also be argued that the close association with compliance actually works against the ethical dimension. In the words of Kent Greenfield, 'The law . . . merely imposes a price for illegal behaviour. If the corporation is willing to pay, then no problem with illegality.'[8] The point of this argument is that legal requirements are not motivationally overriding in the way that ethical ones can be. If something is a legal requirement then it is still open to someone to violate it if they are prepared to accept the consequences of sanctions. With moral issues the parallel argument does not apply. If someone chooses to violate ethical or moral standards then there are no sanctions in the same manner. The main consequence of an ethical transgression is that someone has acted immorally. Although ethical motivation is often weaker than, say, motives to avoid fines, it cannot be overruled.

Even more criticisms have been made of the idea of ethics officers. The well-known scandal where Hewlett Packard was discovered to be colluding in the illegal collection of information about its staff has been pointed out as a clear example of failure of the ethics officer role, for it was Hunsaker himself, as ethics officer, who was central in the scandal. The implication of this is to raise a question whether ethics officers are an effective group. But this is probably too hasty a judgement on the role. Granted, if one expects ethics officers to achieve major ethical change in an organization's ethics single-handedly, then the role is insufficient. But this is too high an expectation. Even with highly effective recruitment and selection procedures there is a risk that someone may be appointed to such a role who is not suitable. But more broadly than this, it is rash to consider that any individual role, even that of chief executive, can single-handedly transform an organization.

For this reason, ethics officers often work in coordination with a committee. In for-profit and not-for-profit organizations ethics committees may exist for several different purposes. In governance terms, many countries require corporations to have financial audit committees overseeing not only the details of an audit but also the contextual circumstances, such as whether the same auditing firm has been employed several years running, or whether the firm has any other commercial connections with the corporation. In medical or other professional industries ethics committees exist to deal with specific issues of staff conduct. In universities, similarly named committees often cover research matters, while in local councils ethics committees may deal with the conduct of elected representatives, or abuse of legal powers.

One advantage about a committee is that automatically there is a greater centre of gravity for the management of ethics – more people are involved, and ethics becomes not simply one individual's name on a company tree but a more substantial item. And while there is a significant danger of a committee being self-serving or impotent, in financially demanding corporations this is unlikely to last long – at regular intervals questions are asked such as, 'What is this committee for?'

Notwithstanding this, a committee can also become marginalized. One key issue that will greatly affect its performance will be its place in the hierarchy of decision-making mechanisms in the corporation. The 'Ethics in practice' text box, quoting an extract from the minutes of a meeting of the ethics committee of the Global Fund, illustrates this issue. Committees are specifically designed to allow representatives from different parts of an organization to come together to make decisions. As such they are inevitably prone to the delays and complications that this brings. For example, they can easily become weighed down with the need to refer matters from one committee to another, to consult across several layers of an organization.

ETHICS IN PRACTICE

ETHICAL DECISION-MAKING PROCESSES: AN EXAMPLE

Look at this extract from a board report of the Global Fund:

PART 3: OFFICE OF THE INSPECTOR GENERAL WHISTLE-BLOWING HOTLINE – Information

1 *At its Thirteenth Meeting, the Board approved the Whistle-blowing Policy for the Secretariat and Governance Bodies of the Global Fund and the In-Country Whistle-blowing Policy (the 'Whistle-blowing Policies'). The Whistle-blowing Policies cover the reporting of allegations of misconduct in relation to the operations of the Global Fund. Individuals may make such allegations anonymously or may choose to disclose their name confidentially for the purposes of follow-up. The Whistle-blowing Policies state that all reports should be provided to the Office of the Inspector General ('OIG') to allow independent treatment and follow-up.*

2 *At the Fifteenth Board Meeting, the Ethics Committee expressed concern that the OIG had made little progress towards the establishment of a whistle-blower hotline. Noting this, the Board requested the OIG 'to implement an independent, confidential and technically robust reporting hotline to support the Whistle-blowing Policies, as a matter of urgency' (the 'Whistle-blowing Hotline').*

3 *In a letter dated 22 May 2007, the Inspector General Ad Interim of the Global Fund, Ken Langford, informed the Chair of the Global Fund Board that the former Inspector-General had negotiated a contract for the establishment of the Whistle-blowing Hotline, but the contract had not been signed by the Global Fund due to the 'low capacity of the OIG to handle the reports of wrongdoing.' Mr Langford therefore suggested to the Chair of the Board that 'it would be more appropriate to defer specific action on this point until the new Inspector-General has arrived', with the assurance 'that any reports received by the OIG through other channels' would be 'followed up as best as possible'.*

4 *The Ethics Committee is disappointed that the OIG has not established the Whistle-blowing Hotline in accordance with the urgent request made by the Board at its Fifteenth Meeting. However, the Ethics Committee expects that the Whistle-blowing Hotline will be implemented, as a matter of urgency, by the new Inspector General.*

Question: How can these processes be made more efficient?

Source: Global Fund website (www.theglobalfund.org/documents/board/16/GF-BM16_09_Report_EC.pdf), accessed April 2009.

This tendency for committees to become bureaucratic and consequently ineffective is more pronounced the larger the organization, whatever economic sector it is in. Mainly this is due to the opportunity for an ineffective committee to persist for longer periods in a large organization where cost-efficiency is more easily dispersed around many functions. However, the effectiveness of an ethics committee may be enhanced by association with specific practices. Notable among these is the ethics audit. Ethics auditing is often similar in structure and operation to the process of environmental auditing discussed in an earlier chapter. Indeed often the two are identified. Nevertheless the ultimate purpose of the two types of audit are, while related, distinct. An ethical audit can potentially apply to each and every action of an organization. While in general most corporate actions do have an eco-logical/environmental dimension, the scope of the environmental audit is restricted to a more narrow range of criteria.

More influential than an internal ethics audit is measurement against an external standard. One of the prime reasons for this is simply the reputational impact of the measurement – it is public to competitors, clients and regulators. One example of this is the ethical measure-ment standard of the French association, Cercle Ethique des Affaires (see the 'Ethics in practice' text box). This follows a format for the award of the standard that will be familiar to those organizations that have engaged in ISO 9000 or 14000 accreditation. An advantage of this is that competences built up to meet one set of accreditation processes can then be harnessed to meet other related processes: this is no small matter, as in most cases there is a large cost to preparing an organization for accreditation by ISO or similar standards, in terms of paperwork, enhancing practices, communicating the process across a firm, etc.

Overall, the existence of ethics officers and committees does not guarantee that an organiza-tion will be effective at managing its ethics or values. They are mechanisms that will combine with other factors, such as industry culture, management commitment and related HR elements such as the structure of the reward package. As we have seen above, they can be subverted and function as smokescreens to cover or distract from unethical behaviour, and they can also func-tion as PR exercises. Notwithstanding these drawbacks, they clearly have, when located within the appropriate context, a potential to support and enhance an organization's ethics.

ETHICS IN PRACTICE

AN ETHICAL MEASUREMENT STANDARD

Qualéthique®

The Cercle d'Ethique des Affaires is a non-governmental organization the object of which is to promote ethical professional practices. It has developed the Qualéthique® Label to identify enterprises and other organizations that make a commitment to respecting its principles, both in their governance and functioning.

The criteria applied in the Label Qualéthique® concern: respect for persons, protection of the environ-ment and natural resources, the recognition of cultural and intellectual values, an ethical approach to financial matters and to good quality information and communication. Enterprises awarded the Label thereby can demonstrate to their partners and other parties an assurance of probity.

The Label Qualéthique® supports an enterprise's ethical capital. It thus can represent a major competi-tive advantage. It is awarded by the Cercle d'Ethique des Affaires, following an evaluation by certified experts, who are controlled according to ISO norms.

Source: http://www.cercle-ethique.net, accessed April 2009 (translation: authors).

WHISTLE-BLOWING

Perhaps the most acute manifestation of the manner in which an organization manages its ethics is in its handling of whistle-blowing. Among the many definitions of this idea, the following is probably a standard expression:

Whistle-blowing involves (1) intentional disclosure of information to which the individual has privileged access; (2) what is disclosed relates to wrongdoing or malpractice; (3) the disclosure is intended to rectify the malpractice.[9]

Key to this definition is that the information is not in the public domain and the action of 'blowing the whistle' is with good intentions. Many early commentators noted the negative attitude on the part of senior executives and managers towards whistle-blowing, often on the ground that this was a deliberate act of destructiveness, usually by aggrieved employees or recent ex-employees. In a series of papers, some dating to more than 25 years ago, Miceli and Near[10] demonstrated clearly that much (probably most) whistle-blowing is not conducted for destructive reasons, and is usually carried out by employees who are particularly loyal to the basic vision and values of the organization. Notwithstanding this, anecdotes still abound of employees treated as enemies by their employers for blowing the whistle, and it remains one of the riskiest acts for an employee to undertake.[11]

Recognizing the social value of whistle-blowing, many governments have passed legislation that in some way or another protects an employee when they make a disclosure that is in society's interest. Several of the states of Australia passed laws in the 1990s; the USA's Sarbanes-Oxley Act carries direct protection and even mandatory provision for whistle-blowing to take place via telephone hotlines; and during the early 2000s a cluster of countries followed suit with similar provisions. The precise form that the protection takes depends on the manner in which the employee makes the disclosure.

There are different ways to model the manner in which public interest disclosure takes place. Many writers divide the phenomenon into internal and external: the former being where an employee makes a disclosure within the organization, perhaps to someone higher up, or to a compliance or ethics officer or committee; the latter kind is where the employee goes directly to an external body, such as a government or industry regulatory body, or to a legal body or even the media. A more complex model has been formulated by Park *et al.*[12] They identify three categorizations of whistle-blowing:

- internal or external (as discussed above)
- formal or informal (formal being the use of established lines of reporting, as opposed to an individual taking a personal initiative to inform someone else)
- anonymous or identified (withholding or disclosing one's identity when blowing the whistle).

From these three divisions Park develops eight different types of whistle-blowing (internal-formal-anonymous; external-formal-anonymous; internal-informal anonymous; etc., through to external-informal-identified). Not all of these merit extensive discussion, but the main value of this is that it indicates that even within the definition given earlier of whistle-blowing, there are different forms that can reflect different motives and may well lead to different consequences for the whistle-blower. For example, the UK's Public Interest Disclosure Act requires an individual to have made efforts to communicate the issue via formal internal channels before any external disclosure can be protected under that law.

ETHICS IN PRACTICE

WHISTLE-BLOWING SYSTEMS

Anglo-Gold Ashanti is a gold mining company based in Ghana. It has a whistle-blowers' hotline, managed externally by Deloitte and Touche. Employees may contact the hotline, called 'Tip-Offs Anonymous' and disclose matters of concern.

The Anglo-Gold website advises individuals how they can preserve their anonymity, as well as reminding them of the internal communication procedures that they may follow.

Source: Anglo-Gold Ashanti website: http://www.anglogoldashanti.com/Additional/GeneralInfo/Confidential+Reporting.htm.

Not all public disclosure of private organizational information is justifiable. The discloser needs to have a strong justification that the information merits being made public. This requires them (a) to have sound reasons for believing that it is morally right to bring the information to the public; (b) to have a justified belief that unless they make a disclosure the information will not become public; and (c) to have good reasons to suppose that the scale of the wrongdoing is sufficiently large that the damage done to the organization's reputation via public disclosure is justified. Shaw adds the requirement that the disclosure is made from the right moral motive.[13] While this is appropriate in terms of how we might encourage individuals to think about making such disclosures, it is not a useful issue when it comes to dealing with people who make disclosures, for the basic reason that motives are relatively private and often not always clear even to the actors. An individual who has attempted to blow the whistle internally and been rebuffed, or even threatened, is likely to already feel some resentment to their employer. How exactly they can disentangle their unjustified desire to get back at their manager from the justified desire to see wrongdoing corrected and wrongdoers punished is often too difficult to resolve.

Of these requirements, perhaps the one that will often generate most dispute is the view that the scale of the issue merits disclosure, even when there is likely damage done to the organization's reputation. In practice, almost all disclosures of internal corporate wrongdoing will damage the organization. In the case of the Enron/Arthur Andersen affair, this proved to be a terminal blow. In such a case the company goes bust, but then many quite innocent employees lose their jobs and suffer major loss through no fault of their own. But even when the company survives, its relationships with many stakeholders will suffer – creditors, bankers, shareholders, government bodies and clients will all be very wary of dealing with the organization, and will be likely to strike harder bargains in terms of loans, contracts and other commercial involvement.

Part of the difficulty with this requirement is that the evaluation of the action will bring in many more issues than those perceived by the senior management of the organization. Disclosure of a bribe made to secure a contract, for example, might rectify a situation in which only a relatively small amount of value has been transferred, for only a relatively small benefit. But in societal terms, much more is at stake – the trustworthiness of the organization (or a least those directly involved in the offering or taking of the bribe), the possibility that a criminal act has taken place (with the expectation that criminal actions merit punishment of individuals irrespective of the actual scale of wrongdoing), as well as the corrosive nature of such actions on public morality. These are not matters pertinent to the economic value of the bribe for the organization – in the case of a bribe the organization's action can be very easily nullified by the money being repaid and the contract being placed elsewhere. The consequences thus become substantially bigger than the action itself. For this reason, if no other, many organizations will attempt to repress public disclosures, taking the view that the scale of the 'transaction' would not justify the size of the retribution.[14]

An example of disclosure

Another side to this is the calculation of potential consequences of making a disclosure, especially where there is some degree of uncertainty about the ethical justification. In the late 1990s there was a major controversy in the United Kingdom over a vaccine for young children that provided a combined protection against measles, mumps and rubella (the vaccine is commonly know as MMR). This had become the vaccine of choice for parents in the United Kingdom, with thousands of doses being administered. A team of researchers led by Dr A. Wakefield published an article questioning whether the MMR vaccine might cause childhood autism. This would fall into the category of formal external identified whistle-blowing, on the Park categorization. Notwithstanding the fact that the article was published in the leading medical journal,[15] it was subsequently shown to the satisfaction of the scientific community that the statistics on which the original paper was based were quite incorrect. However, the impact on public opinion has been dramatic, with continued concern being expressed by parents' groups. Autism is a life-long incurable condition, and the natural desire of parents is to minimize the risks of harm coming to their children. As a result many parents have been reluctant to have the MMR vaccine administered to their children – and as a consequence measles in particular has risen significantly in the United Kingdom, with the expected small proportion of such cases leading to major complications for some children. Part of the issue in this case has been that the statistical arguments refuting the claims of Dr Wakefield are not easy to express simply, whereas his original paper presented a stark correlation (in 8 out of the 12 cases his team had considered the children involved had developed autism after receiving the MMR vaccine).

Was the disclosure justified in this case? Certainly there was a public interest, and this was potentially substantial. Dr Wakefield had some reasons to believe that a correlation might indicate a causal connection, though this was never directly asserted, and some members of his team expressed greater doubt than he over the issue. Since then the research has been castigated as 'junk science' on account of the weak statistical basis for the argument. At the time, however, the argument was good enough for a leading academic journal to accept the paper. This represents a difficult example where there are arguments in both directions over the justification of the public disclosure. Probably the key issue is whether the initial appearance of a correlation justified the public disclosure. The incorrectness of Dr Wakefield's position did in fact lead to some serious repercussions, though had the factual claim turned out to be correct then he would probably have been hailed as a maverick hero. Additionally there is the role of public media, where people who may not be experts will report on scientific matters.[16] A whistle-blower is not likely to be able to control the public dissemination by others of what is disclosed – in some cases the media may find something not at all interesting and not report it, in others it may receive headline coverage. Hence the public 'damage' of disclosure is not entirely attributable to the whistle-blower – though they should be able to foresee that some media publicity will ensue from their actions.

One last issue about whistle-blowing legislation is whether it actually helps at all? Lewis has questioned the effectiveness of the UK's Public Interest Disclosure Act. More importantly, a question has been raised about the obligation that such legislation places on the individual.[17] If such protections exist, they make disclosure easier, and therefore there is less justification for not doing so. This is especially so where the organization has

ETHICS AND YOU

WOULD YOU BLOW THE WHISTLE IN THIS CASE?

Marek works for an IT software house. He discovers that there is a serious flaw in one of their main products, that is used by military forces in combat situations. The flaw could lead to soldiers in the field underestimating the degree of risk in certain operations. The product has in the main been sold to the forces of minority rebel forces involved in long-term civil wars.

Marek has raised the matter with his line manager who has assured him that they are working on the problem, but it may be a few weeks before it is resolved.

developed its own whistle-blowing code of practice. Therefore this can sometimes place a greater obligation on individuals to make such disclosures – the *right* to disclose turns into the *duty* to disclose, as Tsahuridu and Vandekerckhove (2008) argue. What this implies is that an organization can turn around wrongdoing, and blame those employees who failed to blow the whistle for the persistence of a wrong practice. The very protection that public interest disclosure intends to engender turns out to place further pressures on employees.

Overall, whistle-blowing can happen for various reasons and can take different forms. The underlying value of legal protection of those who make such disclosures is clear, but in specific cases there can be areas of uncertainty that render this difficult to evaluate ethically.

ORGANIZATIONAL INFORMATION ETHICS

The phrase 'information ethics' is commonly used to refer to the ethical issues that relate to computing and the use of the internet. In this chapter we will look at a different sense of the term, in which it refers to the ethics on the manner in which information is controlled, passed around parts of an organization, restricted or released, and how this may be a factor in the management of ethics and values of a corporation. In this respect this section follows naturally on from the previous discussion on whistle-blowing, for it is usually due to restraints on information that corporate wrongdoing gets concealed and, eventually, disclosed publicly.

Information that relates to an organization's activities, and that has been generated by means of the actions of that organization, may well be claimed by the organization as being its own property. Clearly this includes items such as advertising slogans, reports, software packages, published materials such as websites or books, even particular colour schemes. It is clear that such items are the direct creation of the organization, through its employees, and form part of its natural activity. These are the stuff of intellectual property, to which we will return in the next section.

However, this attitude, that information is automatically the property of an organization, and thus subject to organizational rules, can easily be extended to cover a range of areas for which the argument of ownership is much less compelling. Consider, for example, the disclosure of corporate plans. Clearly there are many cases where there is a good commercial reason for these not to be disclosed in the public domain, and as an extension of this it can be reasonable in some cases, where the plans involved very market-sensitive initiatives, for the information to be restricted to a narrow group of individuals and not to be passed on. Look, however, at the 'Ethics and you' text box, and consider your views on each of the examples there, before carrying on reading.

THE LIMITS TO CONFIDENTIALITY

Which of these do you think is a legitimate area for an organization to restrict access, and how far should that restriction go (e.g. need-to-know disclosure, general internal disclosure but not to be communicated to outsiders, restrictions to specific groups of workers internally, communication only with line manager, etc.)

1 salaries of middle managers

2 health and safety records

3 calculations used to compile annual company financial returns

4 aggregated statistical records of customer complaints

5 specific customer complaints

6 engineering information such as plant design, production specifications

7 general summaries of disciplinary actions

8 personal information about staff

9 market research data

10 internal promotions and succession plans.

In practice, every one of these has been regarded by some organization as a legitimate object of a high level of restriction, notifiable only to one's line manager or to those whom that line manager authorizes.
  Do you agree?

It is difficult to lay down hard and fast indications of what kinds of information might be the subject of some level of internal secrecy. In different industries different things can provide a competitive advantage, and therefore can become important areas to keep away from competitors. However, some items of knowledge may well be of public interest, even when they are competitively sensitive. The safety records of a particular piece of equipment, for example, may quite likely be of great value to a competitor, but may also be of great interest to the public. An individual considering seeking employment with that particular company may well want to know how safe are the processes that she or he might be asked to work with. A rival company will want to know about the safety records because that may tell them a lot about the company's internal costs, about their levels of activity or about their likely change plans for the future. It may be legitimate for an organization to try to avert the competitor's discovery of this information, but not to prevent members of the public knowing – and once information is in the public domain all attempt to restrict it is fruitless.

But this does not explain the great variations in levels of restriction on information between different organizations, even within the same industry. For example, in several large investment banks to disclose one's own salary to others is regarded as gross misconduct, on the ground that this undermines the individual salary negotiation that is a key component of their reward strategy. In other banks, however, salaries of the most senior executives may be seen on the bank's intranet, and in many public sector organizations salary scales are public information. It would be rash to condemn the first practice as simply a manifestation of a power culture that aims at control of employees above all. However, it needs to be demonstrated just how destructive this would be of the bank's position for the information to become public.

Secrecy serves many purposes for an organization. As long ago as 1979 the role of secrecy as a means to control the corporate environment had been noted.[18] It can also be a means of internal control as well – for example of resource allocation processes. Yet another intention may be to limit legal liability: as alluded to earlier in this chapter, there are cases where a manager may wish not to be seen as in possession of what has sometimes been called 'guilty knowledge' – knowledge that, once one is in possession of it one is obliged to act on.[19]

Information is a key source of power, and power is a key resource for a manager. Unsurprisingly, then, the control of information is a tempting stratagem for a manager. One answer to this dilemma might be to return to the idea of proportionality, the concept that the scale of an organization's (genuine) needs to protect itself supports greater or less intervention. So if it could be legitimately argued that disclosure of salaries might significantly undermine the organization (for example by making it easier for competitors to 'poach' good-quality employees) then secrecy with regard to this issue can be justified. And where there is some potential for damage, but at a lower scale, then while some restriction on disclosing salary details might be justified, an all-out prohibition about ever revealing such details would not be.

A further dimension of the management of information is the role of the professional worker. Professionals tend to have two loyalties – to their employer and to their chosen profession. They often look to their professional association as the source for their career development, as the source of new practice and as the ultimate determinant of standards of their performance. Indeed whistle-blowing actions often are prompted by reference to standards set out by professional bodies.

Many professionals share more information than their employers even realize. One of the authors had the experience of discussing with HR managers the use of 'job clubs' – meetings where managers from different companies shared information about salary levels, as a means of benchmarking; when the following week this was mentioned to the corresponding chief executives the latter protested that their HR staff would never do such a disloyal thing, even though this was an established practice across most organizations in that industry.

As a means of managing values and ethics, the control of information is not generally effective. Such controls can often be effective in creating high levels of employee compliance with explicit rules, though as we have seen earlier, this is not especially useful except in contexts where unexpected novel situations rarely present themselves, and thus established regulations can be relied on to help determine choices in all situations. In general, the freer the flow of information, the more likely the development of a learning organization, which will tend to be more conducive to ethically useful practices such as open discussion of clashes of values.

INTELLECTUAL PROPERTY AND THE FREE MOVEMENT OF IDEAS

The main issues of intellectual property properly belong in the chapters on fairness in trading. However, there are significant aspects of this that relate to the management of values and ethics in an organization. In effect, intellectual property legislation can be used as an extreme example of how information is controlled and managed in an organization – in this case by the simple expedient of declaring it to be the legal property of the firm.

Intellectual property has many definitions. The World Intellectual Property Association (an agency of the United Nations) defines it thus:[20]

Intellectual property (IP) refers to creations of the mind: inventions, literary and artistic works, and symbols, names, images, and designs used in commerce.

Intellectual property is divided into two categories: Industrial property, which includes inventions (patents), trademarks, industrial designs, and geographic indications of source; and Copyright, which includes literary and artistic works …

It is clear that employees of organizations may often develop intellectual items, be these logos, new technologies, designs and other similar entities that have been generated solely in virtue of their employment, during their paid time, and using corporate resources (including training). These it would be difficult for an individual to argue are not the property of the corporation. However, many actions are more problematic.

One of the main reasons to employ people from outside the company is that they bring their experience from other firms. Where this may be represented as simply experience and skill then there is no 'property' aspect, but as soon as there is the matter of knowledge that has been developed within that organization, then there is a question of whether the individual may take it with them. Legislation on these issues varies greatly around the world, with the United States taking a strong line on such knowledge being the property of the firm, and European legislation generally being (a little) less restrictive.

The relevance of this concept in this chapter is the manner in which it can restrict free expression of ideas. An idea on reducing carbon emissions developed by an employee of a major environmental consulting firm is of obvious societal value, yet technically (legally) it would probably be argued to represent property of the firm.[21] While there are often ways around the restriction (e.g. by subtle variations in a technique or concept that then can be used to argue that the later version is not a pure copy of the original) it means that activities such as open discussion of techniques and practices may in certain cases be restricted.

This has resulted in organizations using this argument to suppress public discussion of practices, and to lay claim to personal developments made by employees. The university is a particularly problematic kind of institution, where individuals are often developing ideas and technologies that may have substantial economic value, but where it is difficult to clearly differentiate where what they have done is part of their paid employment and part of their natural curiosity: university academics are notoriously maverick in their approach to their work, often working on ideas purely out of curiosity without any direct link to their 'official' tasks, and it can thus be difficult to define where their paid work ends

THINKING CRITICALLY ABOUT ETHICS

INTELLECTUAL RIGHTS

Janet works for a candle manufacturer, as a production supervisor. There is a running problem with misshapen, defective candles. In her spare time Janet works out a system that will cut the number of defects by 80 per cent. Just as she is about to implement this she is made redundant. She is subsequently employed by a competitor, who implements her ideas, but the original employer hears of this and claims that the system belongs to them and may not be used.

Legal considerations aside – who has the moral right over this idea?

and their hobby begins. It then becomes a disputed matter if an academic decides to commercialize for themselves a technique or invention that might arguably be the property of the university.

Yet a further potential development of this, so far not exploited by corporations such as universities, might be to claim that the expressed opinions of employees, if developed within their work, might be described as corporate property. This is hardly likely to apply where a footballer decries a referee, but it may be more arguable where a researcher working for a political lobbying firm expresses a view about a certain policy, for this could well have been an opinion developed as a direct result of their work. Tenuous though this might be, it is not impossible. In a world where even biological organisms have been patented, it is not beyond conception that opinions may also be claimed as the rightful property of organizations. This issue is raised in this chapter as there is a potential for this kind of attitude – towards the intellectual activity of employees as subject to the control of the business – to develop opportunities for the organization to constrain the activities of employees.

ETHICAL CHANGE MANAGEMENT

The final section in this chapter deals with the potential for change management as a trigger for the enhancement of a corporation's ethics. Ethics programmes are popular mechanisms for attempting to change the behaviour of an organization as a whole, by creating awareness, common language and collectively recognized actions and targets. Such programmes will normally require a series of interconnecting elements, including:

- an explicit statement of values
- a code of conduct covering a range of different areas of activity
- identification of an ethics champion at a senior level or ethics officer function
- corporate communication, training and development
- reporting and whistle-blowing systems
- monitoring and remedial systems.[22]

This, however, needs to be set into a general organizational context. The pre-existing culture of the organization, and how strong a hold this has on people's behaviour, is important. So is the general pressure of the business and the industry: the KPMG survey of integrity[23] identified that pressure to deliver results is the highest perceived reason for unethical conduct by employees. A further issue is the general pattern of psychological contract within the business – an organization where many staff feel well rewarded in non-financial as well as financial terms will be one where there is greater propensity to embrace changes. The problem mentioned earlier with respect to culture change also applies here, in that there is a substantial gap between the evidence we have for people's values (aspects of their behaviour) and what they do in fact value.

The well-known models of change originally propounded by Kurt Lewin have an important role in understanding how an organization's ethics can be explicitly changed by programmes or managerial initiatives.[24] One of Lewin's models deals with inertia and drift. It is often difficult to build up commitment to change due to an attachment to the status quo, and it can be difficult to maintain a change due to a lack of commitment to the new system. Lewin depicted the change process in terms of the metaphor of freezing. The initial position is one that has persisted for some time and with which people are familiar, even when not entirely happy. This very familiarity requires that a proposed change needs to be justified. Lewin posited that the first stage in this process is to adopt activities that build up a recognition of the need for change – what he called unfreezing activities. Only when there is an acceptance that change is necessary should the change be made. But then the new situation needs to be reinforced – refreezed, in Lewin's terminology – to ensure that people do not drift back to the earlier arrangements. This requires monitoring and confirmation of results in the new situation, rewards and if necessary sanctions to ensure that the commitment to the new situation is maintained.

Lewin's model is extremely popular and has been used in countless change programmes. It does help to focus on the processes to erode resistance to change and then to build up resistance to drift. However, it does oversimplify the process of *value* change. Unlike corporate behaviour, values will always matter to people. They are tightly bound in with our conceptions of our own identity. Being so central to our being they naturally resist change – rightly so, as one would be suspicious of someone who was easily able to switch from one value set to a different one. So the processes of changing ethics are altogether more involved than those of changing, say, approaches to managing customer relationships (though even this has its ethical dimension).

What complicates this is that values can resist change in different dimensions. In some cases an individual may feel sufficiently strongly about a particular example that they are prepared to modify the locutions that express their values but will not shift on the particular example. Someone may for example believe that lying in public statements must always be wrong, and will therefore be prepared in argument to modify lots of aspects of how they express this, so long as they are able to retain the claim that lying in public statements is wrong. In other cases, someone may be less attached to a particular evaluative example, but may feel strongly about the particular language in which values are expressed. They may, then, be prepared to easily revise their views about which examples fall under a certain ethical prescription, but not to change the format of the value as they express it. In the former case, then, the resistance is about concrete application, while in the latter it is about conceptualization.

These therefore represent different ways in which values may resist change.[25] The management of these thus requires quite different approaches. The person strongly attached to a certain example may well be relatively unresistant to different ways of expressing the values in question, and therefore the standard methods of consultation and discussion will not make much difference here. On the other hand, the person attached to a particular concept of value may be difficult to argue with, but act with flexibility in terms of direct application. In this case debate is less likely to be effective compared to experience and reflection. What this discussion underlines is that the management of values is not susceptible to single-strategy approaches: there may need to be as many approaches as individuals.

A further aspect of ethical change is that the process ought to reflect the values. In general, change management is seen as more effective when there is a high degree of consultation, where a wide range of stakeholder needs are taken into account and where conflicts are kept to a minimum. This is an ideal that often finds itself confounded by the commercial necessity for change to happen quickly. Be that as it may, change that involves little consultation, or misleading consultation, is often perceived negatively by individuals, and can be self-defeating.

SUMMARY

- The manner in which people reason about ethics is complex and often obscure – people can often agree about something for entirely different reasons.
- Many ethical arguments rest on a wide range of assumptions, and are therefore difficult to read.
- Some ethical terminology is ambiguous; hence managing debates on responsibility in business can be problematic.
- It is not always ethically desirable to aim for all members of an organization to have shared values – some difference and value conflict can be constructive.
- Ethics officers are a growing phenomenon – however, these roles can vary widely in their scope and support from senior management.
- Whistle-blowing protection procedures are a common mechanism for public interest disclosure, though they have been criticized for being ineffective.
- Information and intellectual property can be a means of securing leverage over individual and corporate behaviour.
- Ethical change initiatives are another common means of attempting to manage ethics and values, though these tend to reflect existing cultures more than achieve profound change.

QUICK REVIEW QUESTIONS:

1   What kinds of role can an ethics officer take in an organization, and what is likely to make them most effective?

2   Apply Park's categories of whistle-blowing to a case you know well, and evaluate what kind of stance was taken by the individual concerned.

3   What do organizational approaches to the management of information tell you about their overall approach to the management of values and ethics?

CASE STUDY: THE ETHICAL BRA

BY NOSHUA WATSON

Sri Lankan lingerie manufacturer MAS Holdings has proved that a philanthropic culture is not a barrier to healthy profits.

The apparel industry is frequently accused of roaming the world in search of the lowest costs, which may involve using child labour and sweatshop factories. The stigma of being involved with unethical sub-contractors can tarnish a brand for years. Major brands such as Victoria's Secret, Gap, Marks & Spencer and Nike want to protect their reputations as well as their margins by complying with ethical manufacturing initiatives, and they've turned to MAS Holdings, a US$650 million apparel manufacturer based in Colombo, Sri Lanka.

MAS has set the global apparel industry standard for compliance by developing Women Go Beyond, a programme to educate and empower its 92 per cent female workforce.

Most corporate social responsibility (CSR) programmes have little to do with a company's strategy, but MAS is trying to differentiate itself strategically from a horde of low-cost competitors throughout the developing world.

Founded in 1986 by brothers Mahesh, Ajay and Sharad Amalean, MAS took advantage of textile trade quotas imposed by the international Multi-Fibre Agreement (MFA) in 1974, which placed restrictions on the export of textiles from the developing world to developed countries. By specialising in lingerie and intimate apparel, MAS was able to focus on a niche market where the quota was more generous. The company subsequently became Victoria's Secret's largest supplier.

Mahesh, the eldest brother, current chairman and former CEO, says: 'We focused our business on manufacturing intimate apparel when the rest of the country decided to generalize in the products that they manufactured.'

Plants in nine countries (another way to beat the country-based textile quotas) have allowed the brothers to maintain production of more than 44 million bras a year and employ 35,000 people despite Sri Lanka's ongoing civil war. Over the years, MAS has generated double-digit annual revenue growth while avoiding sweatshop conditions and spending 3–4 per cent of costs on employee and philanthropic programmes.

It provides transport to work, free meals, medical care and on-site banking at all its plants. It also funds hospitals, schools and scholarships in the rural villages where its plants are located. Mahesh says: 'We believe strongly that if the people we work with have their basic needs taken care of, they are freer to concentrate on the work at hand and bring out their best.'

MAS broke the mould by basing its operations near villages so that workers, mostly female, would not have to leave their families and move to cities.

More usually, women in their late teens would move away from their home villages to the free-trade manufacturing zones where they would live in crowded hostels. By building its plants in rural villages, MAS provides local employment and allows workers to remain with their families.

The competitive environment changed in 2005 when the MFA expired (and which by then had been placed under the jurisdiction of the WTO) ending the textile quotas, paving the way for more open, global free trade. Within six months, Chinese textile exports to the EU and the United States increased by 534 per cent and 627 per cent respectively. Sharad Amalean, CEO and middle brother, says that they were not discouraged: 'These days, it's not just the price. You go to a country because of the service and flexibility.'

The Amaleans were already committed to operational efficiency because their customers demanded it. The plants had implemented Six Sigma (a manufacturing process designed to eliminate defects) and MAS had been the first Asian apparel plant to use SAP enterprise software. But even at maximum efficiency MAS could produce orders in multiples of only 10,000 units and so could not compete with Chinese plants, which push out batches of 100,000.

Instead, MAS spent more on CSR. Its most strategic assets were intangible – a history of fair labour practices and community service, adherence to the United Nations Global Compact on corporate values and its own MAS standard of workplace values (see above). In 2003, the Amaleans hired Ravi Fernando from the pharmaceutical industry as CEO of marketing and branding. Fernando saw the company's labour and philanthropic track record as something worth promoting. However, nearly every board member at MAS was trained as an accountant or engineer, and all were opposed to spending money on a marketing gambit.

Despite their lifelong commitment to fair work practices, Mahesh was the only brother to see the potential of Fernando's Go Beyond programme. Ajay, who oversees the design, human resources, finance and IT functions, says: 'To be honest, I was disappointed because we had done it for the last 15 years. When we first started the company, we didn't know about CSR. It was just the right thing to do.'

Fernando persisted. 'I said: "Look at all our operational excellence features and rate them. Compare it with our customers' top 10 list of vendor needs." It became clear that there was not much left for us to fight the battle on.' He won over Mahesh Amalean, Deepthi de Silva, director of human resources, and two more board members. In August 2003, the board agreed to allow an internal programme that focused on the workers. Fernando and de Silva researched the best practices at each plant and developed a four-point Go Beyond framework to be the standard at each of the 17 apparel plants: career advancement, work–life balance, rewarding excellence and community action.

Under the supervision of a Go Beyond Champion at each site, every plant is required to offer English, IT and financial management classes, and any other offerings that fit within the framework. 'Go Beyond helps individuals enhance their own skill sets and empowers them to feel that their careers are not limited to stitching a garment,' says de Silva. 'It gives people the ability to take more responsibility and make more decisions on behalf of the company and the customers.'

The programme includes a beauty, health and hygiene certificate sponsored by Unilever, in addition to classes on reproductive health, domestic violence, traditional crafts and starting a home business. Fernando had hoped to reach two plants per week, but ultimately it took seven months to roll out the programme to every site. In the first year, the 17 plants held 290 presentations that were attended on average 3.7 times by each worker.

At the end of 2004, each plant chose an Empowered Woman of the Year at a gala event in Colombo. To benchmark the programme's progress, MAS hired a research firm to produce a survey each year. Fernando says: 'Ninety per cent of the workers and managers are aware of the programme, but only 40 per cent said they have been genuinely affected so far. Even so, that's 14,000 people. But we have more to do.'

The response from industry activists, NGOs and the media has been positive.

'I don't think MAS appreciated throughout the firm, at all levels, the non-technical aspects of labour relations. Over the last few years, this has really changed,' observes Gowrie Ponniah, an anti-child labour activist and representative of the International Labour Organization in Colombo.

Now, says Ponniah, other Sri Lankan apparel firms are interested in Go Beyond. MAS has won the American Apparel and Footwear Association award for excellence in social responsibility and has been hailed by the UN Global Compact as an exemplar of best practice. Yet the attention raises watchers' expectations of MAS. De Silva agrees: 'We aren't likely to slip up because we are watching the radar closely. If we do slip up, we will pay the price.'

However, MAS continues to flourish. 'After the MFA ended, we expected prices to plummet,' says Sharad Amalean. Instead, MAS' annual growth is in double digits. After Go Beyond started, all four of their major customers – Victoria's Secret, Gap, Marks & Spencer and Nike – increased their business with MAS and made it a strategic vendor in their production plans. In general, major brands concentrate 70 per cent of their orders with fewer than 20 manufacturers, but use several hundred different factories for the remainder of their merchandise. With so many suppliers, ethical sourcing takes considerable effort, but is justified by increasing consumer demand for socially responsible, sustainable and fair-trade products.

Gap inspects every factory in its supply chain for speed, innovation, cost and social responsibility standards, and rejects about 15 per cent of them each year. Dan Henkle, senior vice-president of global compliance and governance at Gap Inc., explains: 'We hope that we can begin to relay more information to our customers about how our products are made and that it may eventually get factored into buying decisions.'

MAS is now a respected strategic vendor, but competition from China and India remains the biggest challenge. In other industries, a firm might target specific competitors, but in the apparel industry, it's the country that matters. Fernando explains: 'Countries' labour laws differ. In China, you can start work at the age of 14. In Sri Lanka, you can't be fully employed until you're 18.' MAS has four plants in India, all of which have the Go Beyond programme, and it is exploring in China.

MAS has also invested in its supply chain and expanded into materials and design and product development. As Mahesh says: 'We've gone from being a contract manufacturer, where we're given a design, materials and a tech pack, to being able to provide our customer with a fully integrated solution.

The retail market is extremely competitive and they need to focus on that and leave the rest to the vendor base. MAS best practices have already attracted attention. Nearly 80 MAS middle managers have been tempted away by its closest Sri Lankan rival, Brandix Apparel. De Silva says: 'It can be imitated, but MAS is the first one. We're seen as the leader. But I would like to see people aligned with sustainability and put their money where their mouth is and make a commitment.'

Fernando's goal is to add a new element to the Go Beyond programme every six months. The community philanthropy dimension didn't fit well within the Go Beyond framework as plant managers were defensive about what they had always done on a local basis. But MAS customers were attracted to the way in which the programme involved the local communities.

As a result, Gap committed US$150,000 over three years to Gap Go Beyond, which includes classes about sustainable development at 20 schools, university scholarships for local youth and entrepreneurship workshops for local women business owners. 'MAS makes continuous efforts to go beyond the basics,' says Henkle. 'We thought that the programme would have more impact if it could be extended to benefit women in the community.' Now, Nike and Marks & Spencer Go Beyond programmes are in the works.

Ultimately, Fernando thinks that emulation adds to the greater good. 'If a global organization comes to us and says it wants Go Beyond labels to be the global standard for ethical apparel, we will say no problem, because immediately you will have a level playing field.'

STUDY QUESTIONS

1 What aspects of ethical human resource management does the case illustrate?

2 Board members resisted the Go Beyond programme. Why was this and what was needed for the programme to go ahead?

3 What benefits has social responsibility initiatives brought to MAS Holdings?

NOTES

1. Argyris (1992).
2. A concept that goes back at least a quarter of a century – cf. Peters & Waterman (1982).
3. For example, the 'Giotto' psychometric instrument purports to measures an individual's virtues.
4. Though presumably this would only occur when the managers did not believe that the violation was serious. Related to this are some of the many examples of poor practice by the now-defunct Arthur Andersen auditing firm, where auditors had some anecdotal awareness of problems in cases such as the Sunbeam and Baptist Foundation but did not press the issue to gain the formal evidence that would then appear in their reports. Cf. Ferrell *et al.* (2008), pp. 359 ff.
5. As described by Janis (1972).
6. ECOA website (http://www.theecoa.org//AM/Template.cfm?Section=Home), accessed April 2009.
7. Extract from Special Group of Coaching Psychologists (SGCP, part of the British Psychological Society): code accessed via website (http://www.sgcp.org.uk/), April 2009.
8. Quoted by the online compliance magazine *Sox*: http://www.soxfirst.com/50226711/corporate_eth ics_and_law.php
9. Adapted from Tsahuridu & Vandekerckhove (2008).
10. Best summarized in their book (Miceli & Near, 1992).

11. Shaw provides several prominent recent examples, such as Coleen Rowley, vilified for going public over the attempt by the US FBI to cover up their failures to prevent the 2001 Twin Towers attacks (Shaw, 2005, Chapter 8).
12. Park *et al.* (2008).
13. Shaw (2005), Chapter 8, p. 299.
14. Not a justified position, however, and reminiscent of many excuses made by petty criminals attempting to offset the scale of burglary or mugging for example.
15. *The Lancet.*
16. Though in fairness, many leading TV stations and newspapers do employ science graduates to be their scientific reporters.
17. Tsahuridu & Vandekerckhove (2008).
18. Erickson *et al.* (1979).
19. Hopkins (2009) argues that often the concern to reduce legal liability is misplaced.
20. Source: WIP website (http://www.wipo.int), accessed April 2009.
21. Though the precise nature of an item of 'intellectual' property has been hotly debated. For an example of the debate cf. Paine (1991), where she argues that intellectual property is not to be treated in the same manner as physical property.
22. Adapted from Ferrell *et al.* (2008), Chapter 8.
23. KPMG (2008). *KPMG Forensic Integrity Survey.*
24. Originally in Lewin (1946), but better presented in standard OB texts such as Mullins (2007).
25. A fuller account of the resistance of values to change may be found in Griseri (1998).

REFERENCES

Argyris, C. 1992. *On Organisational Learning*. New York: McGraw-Hill.
Erickson, P., Kukuk, C., Flynn, J. and Morgan, B. 1979. Organizational secrecy and environmental control. *Society*, Vol. 16, No. 4, 46–51.
Ferrell, O., Fraedrich, J. and Ferrell, L. 2008. *Business Ethics*. Houghton Mifflin.
Griseri, P. 1998. *Managing Values*. London: Palgrave.
Hopkins, A. 2009. *A Corporate Dilemma: To Be A Learning Organisation or to Minimise Liability?* National Research Centre for OHS Regulation, Australia, Working Paper 43.
Janis, I. 1972. *Victims of Groupthink*. Houghton Mifflin.
Keep, W. 2009. Furthering organizational priorities with less than truthful behavior. *Journal of Business Ethics*, Vol. 86, 81–90.
Lewin, K. 1946. *Field Theory in Social Science*. Routledge.
Miceli, M. P. and Near, J. P. 1992. *Blowing the Whistle: The Organizational and Legal Implications for Companies and Employees*. New York: Lexington Books.
Mullins, L. 2007. *Management and Organisational Behaviour*. Seventh edition. London: FT-Pitman.
Paine, L. 1991. Trade secrets and the justification of intellectual property: A Comment on Hettinger. *Philosophy and Public Affairs*, Vol. 20, 247–263.
Park, H. *et al.* 2008. Cultural Orientation and Attitudes Toward Different Forms of Whistleblowing: A Comparison of South Korea, Turkey, and the U.K. *Journal of Business Ethics*, Vol. 82, 929–939.
Peters, T. and Waterman, R. 1982. *In Search of Excellence*. New York: Harper & Row.
Shaw, W. 2005. *Business Ethics*. Thompson Wadsworth.
Tsahuridu, E. and Vandekerckhove, W. 2008. Organisational Whistleblowing Policies: Making Employees Responsible or Liable? *Journal of Business Ethics*, Vol. 82, 107–118.

RESPONSIBILITY IN MANAGING PEOPLE AND OPERATIONS

LEARNING OBJECTIVES

After studying this chapter you should be able to:

- Identify key ethical issues that arise with the range of operational areas of an organization's value chain.

- Evaluate the key ethical and strategic risks involved in different responses to these issues.

INTRODUCTION

In earlier chapters we have looked at aspects of managing ethics and the contextual factors that influence ethical decisions. In this chapter we shall look directly at the content of day-to-day management of different operational aspects of organizational realities, identifying ethical issues in each area and some of the various responses that may be made to these. The intention in this chapter is not to provide a tick list of issues and answers, but rather to provide the reader with sufficient awareness that they can deal with both recognized and novel ethical challenges, and can formulate answers to these that suit the particular circumstances in which they arise. As people are the heart and soul of an organization, a large part of the chapter will be concerned with this dimension of ethical management, though there will be discussion of other functions such as supply chain management and the management of information.

MANAGING PEOPLE ETHICALLY

Organizations can be seen as no more than groups of people working more or less collectively in a manner that is roughly focused on the achievement of some commonly recognized targets. It is not surprising then that people management is at the heart of organizational management, at least as much as the meeting of the needs of those who benefit from the organization's services or produced goods.[1]

It is important to note the scope of this section. 'People' management can cover a wide range of different groups, tasks and relationships. The people of an organization can include, among others:

- established employees on open-ended contracts of employment
- those on short-term contracts
- independent workers who supply services to the organization
- voluntary workers, such as interns, charity workers, or students on placement
- employees of strategic partners.

Each of these groups has a different stake in the performance of the organization, and their members have different expectations. For example, the short-term contracted worker is concerned with each party meeting the specific defined objectives of the contract, but is not necessarily focused on what opportunities the firm may offer in the future. In contrast, the permanent employees are more likely concerned with long-term survival of the organization than on its immediate performance – indeed there have been cases where permanent employees have foregone wages in order to ease the financial pressure on a firm in financial trouble.

At first sight one might question exactly the responsibilities of an organization to voluntary workers – surely if something affects them that is not ethically acceptable, then are they not free to cease providing any service for that organization? However, although it is true that voluntary workers can more easily walk away from an organization than those who are in a contractual relationship, it remains the case that while someone is involved with the work of an organization the firm has ethical responsibilities to them and for them. For example, a voluntary worker is still entitled to be communicated with honestly, and still has rights not to be treated unfairly.

Equally one might query the relevance of a firm's ethics for the employees of its strategic partners – surely this is the business of the partner? However, it is common for employees of strategic partners to work directly together – so operational issues such as health and safety, equality of treatment, or protection of their basic human rights, would all be of equal relevance to both sets of employees. In addition, the fortunes of partner organizations are interlinked in the success of the joint venture they undertake, so reckless actions by the managers of one partner could well place at risk the livelihoods of the employees of the other partner.

As well as treating broadly the scope of the people covered by 'people management', one should also recognize the breadth of the range of tasks and responsibilities involved in people management. Some writers[2] have tended to construe the 'people' side in the light of the generally accepted content of human resource (HR) management – recruitment, performance, reward, developing staff, dealing with grievances, etc. As we saw in Chapter 11, there are areas such as change management that go beyond the traditional HR boundaries. More importantly, as well as these 'personnel' areas, there are day-to-day line managerial issues that raise significant ethical questions – for example delegation of unpopular tasks, motivation of staff, or communication of difficult managerial decisions. Our focus is therefore both on the 'personnel' issues such as recruitment or rewards, *and* on the more line management people management issues such as team management, and balancing individual needs and team and organizational needs.

TRADITIONAL HUMAN RESOURCE ISSUES

We shall first look briefly at some of the specific HR areas and identify some of the ethical issues that these raise. HR as a function is intended to ensure that an organization has sufficient people working for it, using their skills appropriately to achieve the organization's goals, and ensuring that sufficient is provided for workers' needs that they make an appropriately valuable contribution to the work of the organization. In order for this to happen, ideally a range of elements needs to be in place, including, for example:

- Individuals have been recruited in the right numbers and with the appropriate skills to perform the duties expected of them.

- People working for the organization feel sufficiently rewarded to work with a reasonable degree of motivation, diligence and commitment – this includes financial reward, tangible non-financial rewards and also psychological, intangible rewards such as a feeling of recognition.

- People are supported, trained and encouraged to perform at a sufficient level; where performance is insufficient then steps are taken to rectify the situation.

- Efforts are made to maintain and enhance the capability and commitment of employees as individuals and as a collective.

Taking the first level requirement for the HR function – namely the provision of sufficient staff with sufficient skill to do the work – there are several areas that can raise substantial ethical issues. The equality of treatment of potential employees is one of the most immediate. In many countries practices in the past tended to favour specific national or cultural groups, so that it would be easier for someone of a certain race, or religion, or class or gender, to get a good job. Many governments have passed legislation over the last 30 years that has prevented these forms of discrimination, though this is not universal.

One of the issues with fair treatment of staff is that a multinational corporation may find that what is entirely acceptable, desirable even, in one country or culture may be unacceptable in another. For example, in the rural areas of countries such as Pakistan and Afghanistan, it is not only legal for children of a relatively young age to work, it can often be that these provide a major source of income to the household. This is in direct contrast with the urban centres of these countries, and with many of the more developed economies, where

ETHICS IN PRACTICE

DISCRIMINATION WITHIN THE LAW

Indonesia for many years had legislation that allowed direct discrimination against members of minority ethnic groups. Recent legislation has prohibited this in many contexts, but discrimination by individual government officials or bodies is still allowed.

Malaysia has also enacted legislation to widen equality measures, but while it states explicitly that 'there shall be no discrimination against citizens on the ground only of religion, race, descent or place of birth' it leaves unstated, and therefore ambiguous, the role of women.

Source: AsiaPacific Forum (http://www.asiapacificforum.net); Constitution of Malaysia, Part II (Fundamental Liberties 8 (2)).

the concept of a childhood freed from arduous responsibilities and focused on growth and development is well established. In these latter cases, the idea of children having to work instead of attending school, and having to bear the responsibility of providing some of the income for their family, is deemed unacceptable. These cultural variations have led to some of the more well-publicized concerns with multinational firms. How far should a company go along with cultural norms, and how far should they challenge them?

This creates more than one dilemma for a firm, and these echo some of the issues discussed with respect to the role of companies in social and political as well as economic development, such as the role of Total Oil in Burma. For one thing, there is the risk that whatever benefit has accrued to a community as a result of the economic involvement of a multinational may be lost if the company is required by public opinion to withdraw. For another, there is the uncertainty of whether the company's actions or pressure will change things, or might they even make matters worse. And thirdly there is the uncertainty of whether withdrawal will simply leave a space for a competitive rival to enter and carry on the very practices that are in dispute.

As with earlier dilemmas, we see here not simply problems with competing values, but also cognitive issues such as assessment of how likely it is that certain actions will have certain consequences. In particular, in cases such as these, the imaginative capacity of companies or individual managers to find solutions that satisfy both sets of competing values is a key means of avoiding a dilemma. The more successful initiatives in this respect have been able to formulate compromise solutions to this kind of dilemma – such as providing employment opportunities but also supporting local educational initiatives.

REDUNDANCY AND OPENNESS

One of the most frequent and most difficult ethical dilemmas where staffing is concerned is the management of redundancy. Often a manager is required not to disclose that redundancies are likely for some time, perhaps because this will reduce confidence in a troubled company still further, or because it might have an impact on share prices, or on the willingness of creditors to wait for payment.[3] So there can be good commercial reasons for not disclosing the possibility that staff may have to be 'released'. How far can this be balanced against the natural right of individuals to be communicated the truth, or with the virtue of honesty?

ETHICS IN PRACTICE

THE AGA KHAN DEVELOPMENT NETWORK

The Aga Khan Development Network (AKDN) is a collection of initiatives operating in countries such as Tadjikistan, Afghanistan and Mozambique, which have as their object the economic and cultural development of those countries. An Aga Khan University has been set up across three central Asian countries, and various commercial projects have been set up to generate local economic development, including services such as micro-finance. The local nature of the development, allied to the non-discriminatory nature of the Network, means that individuals at the lowest levels in these countries can benefit directly from the work of the AKDN.

Source: AKDN (www.akdn.org).

Different ethical positions suggest different kinds of responses here. A consequentialist approach will involve the weighing up of the different alternative courses of action and an evaluation of the respective merits of each. This process is implicit in legal principles that may be cited in this kind of issue, such as the concept of *proportionality* – the idea that a company may violate a virtue such as honesty to the extent that such benefit as it obtains outweighs the detriment experienced by others such as employees. It is also implicit in management concepts such as stakeholder management, as discussed earlier.

But this does have its problems. So far as proportionality is concerned, it is difficult to reconcile the degree of damage done to individuals with the risk to an organization. Loss of one's job is a major economic loss to the vast majority of employees. For one individual the impact is very substantial indeed. While in absolute terms the scale of the loss is minor compared with the risk of openness to a company, in *relative* terms the scale may be greater. In some cases there might be a common basis of measuring the difference – for example, if there is a substantial risk that if the company admits openly that redundancies are under consideration then this may reduce confidence so far that a larger number of redundancies will have to be made than would otherwise have been the case. Whether such common bases for measuring such actions would always be available is unlikely however.

Taking a deontological approach to this issue would at first sight lead to a simpler, if less commercially practical, response. Deception is wrong, and therefore this counts against such an act. However, a closer analysis of the case makes this less simple. Deception is indeed wrong, but then so is recklessly prejudicing the jobs of other employees by overly public communications, or cutting the earnings of shareholders by making statements that could reduce share prices, or placing loans at greater risk of non-payment. All the factors that would be evaluated as part of a consequentialist reckoning of the overall total value of alternative courses of action are still relevant for the deontologist. Although here they are not measured and assessed in any quantitative or structured manner, they still need to have some account taken of them. A Kantian version of deontology may base the answer to this in some principle of reason – could I consistently accept that the deception be adopted in all such cases, or would this lead to the breakdown of corporate communications? In similar fashion a Rawlsian test might be to ask whether I would find tolerable the position of being the person most disadvantaged by such an act of deception. While superficially the first of these looks like a more objective test than the second, it nevertheless rests on a personal judgement of what would count as 'consistent' and on how far a practice might break down or be sustainable.

It is important to see that these are not simple alternatives, however. One cannot justifiably choose on one occasion to adopt a Rawlsian test and on another to carry out a utilitarian style analysis of a situation. To do so could lead to the charge of using whatever principle serves one's own ends without demonstrating a clear commitment to any. In practice managers may well attempt to deal with the issues pragmatically, based on a risk assessment of which kind of response is likely to minimize both damage to the organization and preserve at least some degree of dignity for the employee. There is a range of different ways in which fundamentally the same response can be carried out, and crucially it may be in the detail of what is done that there lies a successful response. For example, a manager may decide that after all some deception is justified to protect the organization, but they may act in a way that gives them the earliest opportunity to be open to staff, and indeed at such time they explain the reasons for the earlier withholding of information. It can be that it is where it is clear that a manager has taken seriously the rights of employees, *even when these are not fully respected*, that their actions in not communicating openly may be accepted by even those who have been deceived.

ETHICS AND YOU

REDUNDANCY, FIFO, LIFO, PERFORMANCE OR COMMITMENT?

When large-scale redundancies are announced, it is common practice for a firm to consult with employees' representatives (in the main trade unions) to agree a rational basis on which to make the redundancies. Several sets of criteria are in common use: (1) FIFO (First In First Out), is less frequently used but is often attractive where there are many long-standing employees at the top of their pay scale, hence their leaving will significantly ease the salary bill; (2) LIFO (Last In First Out), is often seen as fair in that those employees who have been with the company the least length of time have less personal stake in the company; (3) Measured Employee Performance is based on the view that the firm would prefer to keep the best workers; and (4) Commitment, often measured in terms of disciplinary record, is also based on an argument that the organization will try to keep people who will work well.

Which of these is ethically most defensible, in your view? Which would you adopt if you were a senior HR manager?

HUMAN RESOURCE PLANNING AND STAFFING LEVELS

The sheer management of overall workforce levels creates several different areas of potential ethical risk. For example, it is common, especially where an organization is trying to hold down its costs, for vacancies to be left unfilled for extended periods of time. In some cases this is partially remedied by the appointment of an 'acting' replacement (someone already on the staff asked to take on the role temporarily) but whether this is the case or not, usually the period of the unfilled vacancy places substantial extra demands on other staff. For example, where there is a vacancy for a member of a team of four which is unfilled for a period of time, often the work will be shared between the others, so that each individual is required to do about 33 per cent more work than their standard workload. This is tolerable for a short period of time, but can be highly stressful for longer periods.

But over and above the stress, there is an argument about whether or not it is *fair*. In effect, the decision not to appoint a replacement can in this kind of case be a covert attempt to get other people to do extra work for no extra pay – the saved salary is not normally redistributed to the staff working extra but simply treated as extra contribution to the organization's financial surplus. In concrete examples, this issue would need to be weighed up in combination with other factors such as the financial pressures on the firm, the opportunities for staff to leave and get other jobs, the extent to which the firm may have provided greater than expected benefits or conditions to staff in the past, and so on. But this does not eliminate the point that there is something that is not fair about asking people to do extra work – it simply underlines that this is one of many factors to take into account when making the decision.

This kind of case brings up another potential ethical situation, in that if someone is asked to take up the vacant role in a temporary or 'acting' capacity, there are often increased expectations created by this. Usually the person who takes on an 'acting' position is from a lower level in the organizational hierarchy. The offer of an acting position is generally seen as a statement by management that an individual is showing signs of being able to take up such a role as a permanent responsibility. In other words, the person in an acting role is

ETHICS AND YOU

TEMPORARY ACTING POSITIONS

How would you resolve the acting capacity issue described in the text? Suppose you had a vacant post that is difficult to fill, and one person who is reasonably competent but not outstanding who could occupy it on a temporary basis until the post is filled. They accept the role, but it is clear as time goes on that (a) they are growing in their belief that they will be made permanent in this role and (b) they are making several significant mistakes that suggest to you that they will not be suitable to fulfil this role on a permanent basis.

In their normal post they are fairly successful, very popular, and they have shown great commitment to the firm in times past, doing additional work without receiving commensurate reward.

How would you manage this situation? What are the key operational and ethical factors that need to be taken into account?

assumed, sometimes by themselves, sometimes by others, to be in line for promotion. In particular there is an assumption that if someone is in an acting position for more than the minimum period needed to fill the job on a permanent basis then they are being groomed for that very post. It can be convenient for a manager to allow their member of staff to believe this, as it is very likely to be a spur to their motivation. However, over and above cases where the manager is clearly acting without integrity (say when they allow the staff in an acting role to think they have a chance of the permanent role when in reality the manager has no intention of giving it to them) there are also often grey cases. For example, a manager may offer someone an acting position, and at that time point out that there is no guarantee of getting the permanent post. But as time goes on the ambitious staff member who is acting the role will naturally continue to evaluate their prospects for promotion and seek to interpret the responses from their manager. Unless their expectations are carefully managed it can easily be that the belief grows in their minds and in others that the job will be theirs. Not always is this a result of unethical managerial practice – it is incumbent on individuals in such positions to maintain a balanced view of their prospects, for sometimes sheer hope outweighs realism in someone's view of their future; also sometimes the supporters of the person in the acting post may provide misguided encouragement without knowing in reality how well someone is actually doing in the role. Nevertheless, this carries at the least a risk that someone will act in the belief that they are on a promise of the job when this is not going to happen: and when this is the case it is incumbent on managers to prevent the expectation becoming unreasonable.

RIGHTS AND DISCRIMINATION

The general management of staff covers a wide range of issues with potentially ethical dimensions. One broad category that covers many of these is the concept of human rights at work, and in this section we shall consider some aspects of this.

We have seen the role of the Universal Declaration of Human Rights in earlier chapters (in particular Chapter 7), in relation to corporate social responsibility initiatives and the role of corporations in different regimes and in the treatment of local communities. Several elements of human rights have been isolated that relate specifically to employees – notably the right to be treated fairly and equally to others, the right to free association and collective representation, the right to freedom to be politically active or to participate in a certain religion, the right of members of disadvantaged groups (including minority races, the female gender, those with disabilities) to be treated appropriately and irrespectively of their ability to fulfil the requirements of a job, as well as general rights of respect and freedom from ill-treatment or harassment.

These rights are dealt with very differently in different countries. Part of the explanation for this is cultural – differences in cultural values mean that some of these rights matter more or less in some societies than in others. The US culture embodies a 'pioneer' spirit (dating back to the colonization of the country by those of European descent in the 19th century), which often leads to an attitude that each individual is responsible for their own destiny, and therefore needs less legal support for issues such as employment protection. Hence there remains in US legislation a principle that an employer may dismiss employees without notice and without needing to provide a good cause.[4] In contrast, European traditions reflect the history of that continent in terms of continual inward as well as outward migration, and many unforeseeable events such as wars, or the growth of empires that expand to absorb neighbour countries, and the consequent redrawing of national boundaries. As a result many European cultures place greater emphasis on social support, reflecting a belief that individuals are often prey to events outside of their control. Hence in the European Union there is a blanket requirement that employment is protected. Any US-style 'fire at will' policy is barred, and in its place organizations are required to consult with employees, seek alternative employment if someone is redundant and provide financial compensation – all these being mechanisms to provide support for the employee.

Similar points may be made about other rights – such as the rights of women, which are conceived differently in different countries, or the need for legislation to protect older people's rights, given that different cultures have widely contrasting attitudes towards the elderly.

Of all the areas of people management that raise ethical issues, probably unfair discrimination is the most prevalent and most difficult. Discrimination grew up when humans were concentrated in smaller and more isolated communities than today, when social roles were more fixed, and when there were fewer formal legal rules and a greater emphasis on social norms. It was socially useful to be more trusting of those with whom one had a close social link, and less so with those who were socially distant or who did not conform to a defined social role. As social roles carried a great deal of power with them, this attitude of a stable categorization of others became a way to dominate and subject some groups by others. And eventually this turned into outright unfair treatment of weaker social groups by stronger ones, so that by the beginning of the 19th century there was a huge scale of subjection of non-industrialized peoples by the industrialized ones, a substantial difference in the fortunes of women as compared to men, great differences in the quality of life experienced by the poor in comparison with the more affluent, and so on. Ultimately, the worst outcome of this was mass murder under a pretext of 'ethnic cleansing'.

In modern times the trend towards explicit equality between all members of society has eroded this attitude towards social differentiation, so that on a wide range of dimensions there are efforts on the part of many countries to build in social protections for specific disadvantaged groups. However, the above description is a very general one, and indicates that there are potentially very many ways in which socially dominant groups will use personal features to maintain control over others.

This gives rise to two related difficulties that beset anti-discrimination legislation. First, it is specific to particular social groups. It is true that the most grievous and unjustifiable forms of unfair discrimination have been based on race and gender, and therefore legislation that solely relates to these has provided a substantial advancement of general social equality. However, there remain many groups for whom there is limited or no protection. Non-citizens, such as illegal immigrants, enjoy far fewer rights than citizens. Those without jobs or homes often find that they are not treated equally with people from more stable social situations. Members of socially eccentric groups, such as fringe religions, may not receive the same protection as those with more orthodox beliefs. As different groups are recognized as being unfairly discriminated against, so legislation has been added to protect each of these groups.[5] However, this piecemeal strategy has led to some groups being clearly protected (at least in law) and others who seem to have equal moral right not being so protected.

Many corporations have moved to a more embracing approach on the basis of more unspecified values, where the general diversity of a firm's workforce and client base is celebrated, as opposed to the more defensive approach of equal opportunities. The HSBC text box provides extracts from one such policy. One interesting aspect of this extract, however, is that while in the earlier part of the extract a series of general statements are made about diverse groups, there remains the perception that different groups ought to be identified specifically, as per the second part. What is also interesting in this example is that some features have been mentioned there that would not normally be protected in law – regional accents, for example, or physical appearance. There is a slight ambivalence here in terms of the generalized nature of diversity, and the need to reassure certain disadvantaged groups that they are protected.

However, the second aspect of discrimination is that it is not as easy to eradicate as legislation might indicate. In many European countries there has been legislation banning

ETHICS IN PRACTICE

EXTRACTS FROM THE EQUALITY AND DIVERSITY STRATEGY OF HSBC

We know that employing and managing diverse people gives us a more rounded and balanced organization and makes us more adaptable to new situations. This is not simply about gender, ethnicity, disability or age: it is about open-mindedness, embracing non-conformity and creating balanced teams. Respect for individuals of all types will inspire loyalty in both employees and customers, which will have a direct line of sight to the achievement of business goals.

Competitive edge can be gained from the variety present in our workforce and customer base, and specific attention to market variation, in, for example:

■ age, (length of) experience
■ gender, sexuality
■ race, religion, culture, nationality
■ physical ability and appearance
■ outside, non-employment, activity and interests
■ personality
■ educational background
■ regional or other accents.

Source: HSBC (http://www.hsbc.co.uk/1/2/about/diversity-values).

discrimination against women or against members of minority ethnic groups for three decades or more, and yet still the vast preponderance of people in senior positions in companies, in government and in prominent social positions remain white males. Various attempts have been made to combat this less overt discriminatory trend – for example, the concepts of indirect and institutional discrimination have been developed to identify and help combat this form of inequality. What the legal forms of redress have not adequately addressed, however, is the deep-seated nature of social discrimination, wrong as it may be. The discussion earlier of the genesis of social discrimination indicates that there are long-term origins of how people perceive and deal with those whom they regard as 'other'. Compliance with rules that forbid the unequal treatment of 'others' is certainly an advance, but it is not the whole battle. Those with discriminatory attitudes towards a certain group will doubtless submerge these, consciously or unconsciously. But such attitudes are even more problematic when submerged, as their influence then goes unacknowledged.

One aspect of how dominant social groups may maintain their dominance, and thus disadvantage others, even when each individual within the dominant group is aware of and consciously intends to avoid discriminatory behaviour, is that even when discriminatory behaviour is regulated and legislated against, *discriminatory thinking* is much harder to avert. There is a strong body of thinking that asserts that the modern organization is not simply male dominated in terms of the gender of those in prominent positions, but that the way in which these operate reflects male thinking. Male-oriented, militaristic metaphors abound in modern business – strategy and tactics, campaigns, hostile takeovers. 'Masculine' personality features create an organizational environment in which internal managerial competition is more accepted than inclusive consultation: we shall look a little later at the link between this and bullying, but suffice to note here that an issue such as the provision of discursive space, for women as well as men to express themselves and to be listened to, is a critical success factor for making organizations more gender-equal.[6]

In general the remedies for unfair discriminatory behaviour are not dissimilar from those for other aspects of bad practice in people management: clear definition of the targets

THINKING CRITICALLY ABOUT ETHICS

INDIRECT AND INSTITUTIONAL DISCRIMINATION

- **Indirect:** when a requirement or condition is set that, although grammatically general, in practice is distinctly harder for a member of a discriminated group to meet than for others and is not justifiable in terms of operational needs – e.g. to require that the successful candidate for a middle management role be no older than 35 and have had at least five years' experience as a manager is significantly harder for many women to meet than for any man, because many women will have taken a career break in their late 20s or early 30s to have children.

- **Institutional:** when the sum total of a range of organizational policies collectively makes it more difficult for members of one disadvantaged group to succeed than for others – e.g. where candidates for promotion need to have undertaken a development programme in advance, and where the requirements for entry to the programme rule out those without certain qualifications, even though these are not necessary for successful fulfilment of the managerial role.

What features of the organization's culture might exacerbate or inhibit these forms of discrimination?

to be attained, organization-wide dissemination of good practice, direct and explicit senior management commitment, consultation and training for all, a set of rules that are clear to follow and actively enforced, and an explicit process of monitoring and enhancement. This kind of package we have seen in previous chapters, in relation to environmental management and the management of organizational values, and it mirrors general change methodology as developed for example in relation to quality management.

The remedies for discriminatory thinking, however, are less easy to set out, as these require large-scale changes to individual psychology, and in some cases the unearthing of long-standing attitudes that go back many generations. For this there is even greater need for senior management commitment, but in addition there needs to be a recognition of how deeply rooted some attitudes may be. Periodic backlashes against 'political correctness' often represent a misinformed response to anti-discrimination, based on individuals' resentments about attitudes that they have suppressed and hear criticized constantly, but which they still privately 'hold' in an unconscious manner. This is psychologically more difficult for the individual to deal with because the simple expression of, say, racially discriminatory attitudes is clearly socially and morally unacceptable. But within many who overtly conform to the prevailing norms there may remain atavistic, unformed but corrosive feelings about the rights and benefits accruing to different groups – feelings that become less rational because they are inhibited from public expression. A common anecdote is of the individual who says 'I'm not racist but…' and then goes on to say something that is clearly highly racist. What is happening in such cases is that someone recognizes the public prevailing attitude, and thus they do not wish to identify themselves as contravening the accepted public norm, but they want to express a feeling that they still hold internally in some way, and acknowledge privately to be discriminatory. The remedies for this are not always to be located in organizational policies or practices. Much of this is society-wide, and latent discrimination against different groups may often be fanned by populist politicians or media fashion. Some effect is achieved by the clear drive for anti-discriminatory behaviour, and the role of training consultation and development has had some influence. But it would be naïve to presume that this is an issue that can be successfully resolved with a new policy – it is a matter of social evolution over decades at the very least.

VIOLENCE AT WORK

Bullying and harassment are unequivocally banned in law and by organizational policy in the vast majority of situations, yet they remain frequent causes of sickness, stress and low productivity, and every year in every country there are many cases taken to law over these

ETHICS AND YOU

THE BOUNDARIES OF EQUAL OPPORTUNITY

The HSBC diversity policy cited earlier refers to physical appearance, regional accent and personality. These are not areas covered by current legislation.

How far do you feel that these areas should receive the same level of attention as those that are covered by the law?

Should they be issues that an organization should concern itself with at all?

issues. In general, the remedies for these are much clearer than those for discrimination, since no one has ever suggested that violence in the workplace is a good thing. So the existence of codes of practice, hotlines for disclosure and an attitude of support for potential victims, are all well-placed mechanisms for combating this. There are, however, some issues that merit discussion with regard to violence at work.

The first issue is what counts as violence. The text box sets out a range of different activities, all of which are detrimental to an individual's standing in an organization. Each reader may have a different reaction to this list. Most people would regard physical assault as violence and always to be avoided, though in at least some cases, for example in some cultures, so far as adolescent boys and young men are involved, it can be almost a form of 'sparring' – light-hearted play-fighting that carries no intent to harm. Not that this is intended as grounds for tolerating it in an organization, for the simple reason that it can be almost impossible to distinguish this from assaults where there is definitely an intention to harm or intimidate. But it does indicate that even the most blatant examples of violent behaviour may contain greater ambiguity than is often supposed. At the other extreme, some might well say that while avoidance of eye contact with someone, or ignoring them socially, are negative phenomena, they are not really an act of violence. However, for some people the result of dealing with someone who avoids social contact with them can be a feeling of being threatened, of being intimidated by an engagement where the other person appears to refuse to display their true feelings. Metaphorically, some might regard this as a form of violence.

The point of this argument is to indicate that there is a greater level of interpretation and psychology in the definition of violence than many discussions in the literature would indicate. Catley and Jones have identified at least four different forms that violence might take: physical acts of violence; violent speech acts; structural physical violence; and structural symbolic violence.[7] One example of the last form that they cite is the refusal of governments to allow the speaking of minority languages, as a form of domination of

THINKING CRITICALLY ABOUT ETHICS

THE DIVERSITY OF VIOLENCE

Consider the following:

- physical assault
- threats to assault someone
- dismissal of someone's credibility by suggesting they are stupid
- denigration or ridiculing of someone on grounds such as height or appearance
- practical jokes that emphasize someone's weaknesses
- refusal to give someone the opportunity to make a contribution to a discussion
- marginalizing someone's contributions
- failing to take seriously someone's ideas
- avoidance of eye contact
- ignoring someone.

Are all of these examples of violence? In all circumstances? In none?

minority or colonized peoples. Their point is that while violence is more than simple physical violence, it is still a substantial concept and should not be dismissed as undecidable. Nevertheless, the implication of this is that violence is not easily subjected to behavioural rules and regulations. Of course, these do need to be there, to inhibit the operation of any of the forms of behaviour cited in the text box and more, when these are used to intimidate or harm others. The difficulty is that at the lower end, at least, some such behaviours are ambiguous and in some contexts may be harmless, while in others they may be used with unethical intent.

One way to deal with this issue – though hardly to resolve the dilemma – is to look at it from a virtue-ethical perspective. Some acts are done by people wishing to intimidate or harm, though this is not at all easy to establish with great assurance. But we could argue that if someone is motivated by, say, the virtue of kindness, or by that of respecting others, then their actions are unlikely to carry such an intention. Care needs to be taken with this – an unscrupulous individual might use this as a defence of what was in fact a deliberate attempt to harm or intimidate. But this is not actually an argument that can be used to justify or criticize specific acts, so much as an explanation of what may underlie individual actions. The rectification of violence lies only partially in rules – though these remain important – but also in continued development of human sensitivities to the potential effects of their behaviour.

The remedies for violence, in the workplace as elsewhere, lie in transparent reporting systems, support for disclosure, clear rules and sanctions, and also in the attention paid to those who perpetrate violent acts. Few people are simply violent. Some people are bullies because they have been bullied or abused in childhood. Others act violently as some kind of defence against some phenomenon that they perceive – rightly or wrongly – as a threat to them. Just as many actions can be violent, so also many events can be perceived as a threat: the risk of losing one's job, but also the risk of incurring the displeasure of one's boss, of prejudicing the good opinion of others, even the possibility of being publicly embarrassed. Often the remedy for these lies in a combination of clearly applied rules and the management of individuals' anger.

In this and the preceding sections, we have looked at some of the key ethical issues relating to the management of people. We have not sought to provide a comprehensive discussion of all relevant issues, but in the main to consider those where there is some degree of conceptual lack of clarity with regard to the manner in which they are managed. One theme that has come out in these discussions is that in organizational terms a joint approach is generally needed – on the one hand compliance with stated rules and policies is an important starting-point, but on the other it is important to accept that this is a starting point only, and that the development of values, sometimes on a very long-term basis, is also required.

ETHICS IN MARKETING

The aim in this section is to provide examples of how marketing relates to ethics and corporate responsibility. Unlike fairtrade and ethical investment, marketing is a corporate function similar to operations and finance. It is discussed in this chapter because marketing practices seem to attract considerable criticism compared to other corporate functions. Indeed, marketing is often seen by critics as the unscrupulous side of business activity. Instead of reviewing concerns relating to each dimension of the marketing mix (product, price, place and promotion), the focus in this section is on a smaller number of issues that have given rise to controversy. As will be seen, issues such as deception and privacy apply to more than one element of the marketing mix.

Promotion of materialism

Marketing is often associated with the promotion of consumerism and artificial needs that are argued to impoverish modern societies. Indeed, this is perhaps the most fundamental criticism presented about marketing as it discredits the practice as something that is essentially detrimental for the development of our societies. Accordingly, marketing creates artificial wants and desires that lead to feelings of insecurity, inadequacy and dissatisfaction. One example of this aspect of marketing is the promotion of role models that arguably perpetuate unhealthy or racial stereotypes with potentially life-threatening consequences. Somewhat surprisingly, a number of well-known sociologists have stepped in to defend marketing and challenged the critics for their patronizing and elitist approach.[8] In what follows, both sides of the argument are discussed.

John Kenneth Galbraith, a renowned economist, has argued that marketing is harmful because it creates artificial needs and leads to an unproductive use of societal resources. Galbraith is of the view that in affluent societies, people focus on the satisfaction of higher order wants and desires that are artificial in the sense that people can go without them. For example, we do not need chocolate to survive, but many of us have developed a liking for it. Galbraith argues that people entertain artificial needs for two reasons. First, it is common for human beings to compare themselves to others and seek to copy their peers. This behaviour is generally useful because it helps communities to establish shared values and norms. Secondly, people are increasingly influenced by marketing that creates and sustains artificial needs. This trend is particularly noticeable in societies where companies need to persuade people to consume the supply that exceeds demand. Galbraith therefore suggests that marketing plays an essential role in the creation of artificial needs. He also goes further by proposing that the goods and services created to satisfy artificial needs contribute little to society. Instead, marketing and advertising result in a move of resources from meaningful and beneficial areas of consumption to the satisfaction of wants and desires that bring little benefit to society.

A further concern about marketing is that it seems to equate personal happiness with consumption and material possessions. Accordingly, people now define who they are by the shops they use and purchases they make. Such behaviour is not new, but a number of authors are of the view that it now dominates our society and poses a threat to democracy. Benjamin Barber (2007), for example, argues in his book *Consumed* that advertising and branding promote a culture of infantilization that encourages adults to follow the lifestyle

ETHICS IN PRACTICE

SKINNY MODELS PROMOTE UNHEALTHY IDEALS

Fashion designers and magazines have been criticized for using underweight models in photo shoots and on catwalks. The critics argue that in so doing, they promote unhealthy role models and ideas of what is a normal body weight. The debate culminated in 2006 when a model died during a show after not eating for days. Since then, many fashion weeks have banned 'size zero' models, but there are still designers and people in the industry who believe that ultra-thin models present clothes in a better way.

of adolescents. What is more, people have become focused on 'me' at the expense of 'we' as evidenced by declining interest in politics and voting. As a result, people are less active in challenging their government on meaningful grounds. Instead, people use their time in consuming, which has become the principal way of defining their identity. In such a world, having the most recent gadget or model is a way of establishing who you are and relating to others.

Criticism of marketing as promotion of consumerism has been challenged on economic, practical and political grounds. First, it has been argued that society benefits from the construction and satisfaction of artificial wants because the process generates employment and economic growth.[9] Accordingly, marketing plays a role in the generation of wealth by creating demand, even though the nature of this demand is seen as undesirable by some. Secondly, people have become more educated and literate about advertising and are active participants rather than passive victims of consumer society. Consumers have learned to be critical about advertising and make conscious choices that contribute to their identity in the modern world. Consumption is hence a way of satisfying needs for personal and social identity rather than an empty pursuit of some goal that can never be reached.[10] Finally, an excessive control of people's wants and desires is a feature of totalitarian rather than democratic societies. The idea of democracy is underpinned by the freedom of opinion, and even though the exercise of this freedom may lead to a situation where people embrace values and behaviour that are seen as unwanted by some, no preferences should be imposed on individuals unless they behave against the principles of democracy. It is elitism to say that a liking for art and literature is more important than following trends in fashion.

Deception in marketing

It is sometimes argued that deception and lying are an acceptable part of business activity. A. Z. Carr, for example, argued that business is similar to a game of poker where the rules are different from the rules of everyday life. Without examining the strengths and weaknesses of this argument in more detail, suffice it to say that deceptive and fraudulent marketing is unlawful in many jurisdictions. What is more, failing to disclose and communicate information that enables consumers to make informed choices can be illegal depending on the risks involved. For example, Ford's failure in the 1990s to be clear about the risks of driving a Ford Explorer with certain Firestone tires resulted in a US lawsuit that was finally settled for over US$50 million.

Marketing is deceptive if it misrepresents product characteristics or fails to communicate some important information to the consumer. Deception can apply to any aspect of marketing. Pricing, for example, can be deceptive in many different ways. One of the most typical 'tricks of the trade' is to set the price just below the next round number at, say, 9.99. Even though this pricing tactic can be seen as relatively harmless, it is based on persuading the consumer to buy a product by making it look cheaper. Similarly, product packaging can be misleading if it exaggerates the size of the product. Food retailers have been criticized for using this technique, but it is also common in many other sectors.

False or deceptive marketing can take many forms, from puffery to omission of important information:

- *Literal* deception pertains to untruthful statements or representations of the product. For example, fast food restaurants have been criticized for deceiving their customers with photos that do not contain the same ingredients as the real product. Some companies are now using words like 'help' to ensure that their statements are not literally false. This practice can still be criticized on ethical grounds as even though it may be literally correct to say that a face lotion 'helps fight signs of ageing', it may still be misleading to the consumer.

- *Puffery* involves an exaggeration of product qualities. For example, Gillette's slogan of 'the best a man can get' is misleading in the sense that it is not sufficiently specific or substantiated by research. Nevertheless, such statements have become acceptable in the context of advertising as people have become more literate about advertising slogans. In today's world, many overstatements go unnoticed, with the exception of a few jurisdictions that have taken a stricter stance on puffery. Also, in some cases, it is companies that file complaints against each other for gaining competitive ground.

- *Implied* deception concerns messages that are communicated without making explicit statements about product qualities or impact. For example, alcohol adverts have been criticized for suggesting that drinking makes one happy and successful, because they often portray a group of people having a good time. Such adverts have been perceived particularly negatively because of their appeal to and impact on young people. Similarly, the fashion industry has been criticized for promoting an unhealthy image of the female body by using underweight models in their adverts.

- Finally, *omissive* deception involves the exclusion of information on important qualities or risks associated to the product. The best-known examples of this were tobacco adverts before they were required by law to state the effects of smoking on health. In the 1960s, a tobacco advert would not have said 'tobacco kills' or 'smoking while pregnant can harm your baby' even though tobacco companies were aware of the harmful effects of smoking. Omission may also involve the intentional exclusion of price information from products and services, though this is now regulated in many countries.

Concerns over privacy

Marketing practices have given rise to diverse concerns over consumer privacy. For example, consumers may be wary of giving out personal details that might make them targets of advertising campaigns. More generally, there is a concern about the misuse of private information including identity theft and financial fraud. Some marketing practices can also be seen to reduce the private space we have as individuals living in the modern world. Naomi Klein made this argument in her book *No Logo*. Accordingly, advertising and branding have invaded spaces that were previously seen as public or private including schools, hospitals and art. Government regulation has emerged to protect consumers against unsolicited marketing and security of personal data,[11] but concerns still exist over the issue of marketing and privacy. In what follows, two types of issue relating to privacy are discussed. The first involves direct marketing and the way in which promotional activities penetrate our private space and time. The second pertains to the information companies collect and use for marketing purposes.

Boundaries of direct marketing Direct marketing concerns promotional activities targeting consumers and organizations directly without the use of public media. Most of us have experienced direct marketing by receiving a sales call from a company or being given promotional material on the street. Another example of direct marketing involves the delivery of paper mail to households in a particular geographical area. This type of direct marketing is often the main form of advertising for restaurants and other small enterprises that seek to target their advertising to local customers. Consumers can refuse direct marketing, but this is not always easy and can be unpleasant, inconvenient and costly in terms of time.

An interesting case of direct marketing is junk e-mail. When it first emerged, there was an outcry against the practice by people and organizations whose inboxes were filled with unsolicited messages. Software and regulation were soon introduced to control spam and after a few high-profile court cases against companies spreading junk email, the controversy seems to have disappeared. Nevertheless, the practice has also changed the way in which organizations deal with e-mail and most will now have software to block spam. Moreover, e-mail users have become accustomed to the occasional adverts they receive electronically. Similarly to conventional junk mail, electronic spam has become an element of our daily lives with implications on our behaviour and views over the boundaries of our privacy.

Collection and use of private information Many companies collect some information on their customers and use it to market their products. The development of information technology has enhanced this practice and given rise to new concerns over how information is gathered, stored and used. The cards many supermarkets have launched to collect information on the shopping habits of their customers are one example of this dimension of concerns over privacy. Critics note that supermarkets may know more about us than close family members because they have information about what, where and when we buy. For example, if a person only shops at the stores of one supermarket chain, their physical moves and shopping habits can be traced with some accuracy. Indeed, some supermarkets stock their selves on the basis of this information to satisfy their customers and improve sales.

In addition to loyalty cards, the internet is another relatively new source of concerns over how private information is collected and used. In contrast to supermarket cards, information on the internet is often collected without explicit notice or acknowledgement from the consumer. For example, online technology can track a user's history, preferences, online activity and transactions through cookies without notifying the user. The internet also allows the collection of real-time data that updates a user's profile every time he or she visits a website, downloads material or uses a browser. Few consumers are aware of the extent of information that can be collected in this way and therefore have little control over the data that exist on them.

Another area of concern relates to how information collected on the internet is used. Internet companies may, for example, sell consumer databases to other companies that use them for direct marketing. Such information may include contact details, financial information and usage data. Even though consumers may be able to opt out from a database, it is often difficult to do. Personal information is also used to tailor websites to individual tastes and preferences. For example, Amazon.com recommends books to its customers on the basis of search criteria and transaction information. Such personalization is becoming

ETHICS IN PRACTICE

LOYALTY CARDS AND PRIVACY

Loyalty cards are used to determine what people buy and when. This information is then employed to place new products next to the ones that are regularly bought by some groups of customers. Are you comfortable with this practice? Do you think it invades your privacy or are you happy that you may be introduced to new products in this way?

increasingly widespread in the online world.[12] Even though some users may find this type of customization acceptable and even useful, there are also consumers who feel that the practice is invading their privacy.

In general, internet users may not be aware of the extent of information collected on them and lack control over how the information is used. Nevertheless, surveys suggest that most internet users are concerned about privacy, especially when information is considered sensitive and the user is not familiar with the organization handling the information.[13] Companies are becoming increasingly aware of this and some have reduced the amount of information they gather on their users. Companies can also subscribe for seals certifying that they apply certain principles to what information is collected and used.[14] These types of certifications and government-imposed regulation are likely to increase in the future to address concerns over privacy and online fraud.

ENTREPRENEURIAL ETHICS

The common stereotype of entrepreneurship is of an individual having an idea or seeing an opportunity and using their initiative, creativity, judgement and often also bravery in bringing this successfully to market. At first sight values do not seem to intrude in this picture, save the values of business achievement. However, this view can and has been contested. Venkataraman has described ethics and entrepreneurship as 'two sides of the same coin: the coin of value creation and sharing.'[15] Harmeling and others have shown how closely ethical values and the drive to develop new businesses figure in the thinking and recollections of well-known entrepreneurs.[16] Most people do not simply start a business because they want to be an entrepreneur – they start up a business in a field that they enjoy and see as valuable to society. For example, many of the great IT companies of the last 50 years – such as Microsoft, Netscape, Google and eBay – started as garage hobbies that grew beyond their founders' original wildest dreams. So, built in to the very process of starting a business is a sense of value – a belief that people will benefit from purchasing an item, using a certain service, or finding a new application for a technology.

Entrepreneurs share with small business owners some specific ethical issues. One key aspect about the small and rapidly growing business is that there is often little in the way of time or cash available for non-operational needs. The entrepreneur who has a difficult team member, for example, may be too busy to deal properly with the HR need that this involves, and they may not perceive the potential financial risks that a poorly handled personnel issue runs.[17]

Related to this is the fact that a rapidly growing business has limited resilience against reverses, as usually finances are tight and production or delivery deadlines are often less flexible than with a larger firm (due to the reduced negotiating power of the smaller player). The perception that a firm may be under threat of going under is a common justification for decisions that lack sufficient ethical justification. In a new venture this risk is almost constant until the business gets established, and therefore this kind of justification can be deployed at many points in the early stages of development of the business. Nick Molina, founder and CEO of the telecoms company Let's Talk Cellular, expressed it as follows: 'Sometimes when you're backed up against the wall, your instincts take over, and you do what you have to do to survive.'[18] His phrase 'up against the wall' exemplifies a version of that attitude towards the business environment we have called 'the survival imperative', but to an extreme degree that is often associated with entrepreneurs – that the external business world is a hostile place in which businesses can be wrecked, almost the archetypal Darwinian struggle between competitors, where a business cannot falter for even a moment lest events sweep it away. Doubtless some environments are indeed like this – retail electronics (where Molina started) is notoriously competitive. But not all new ventures operate in such competitive arenas: the rise of many good new internet businesses is less to do with direct competition than with the development of an inventive and original new idea: operations such as Google or Facebook rose quickly because they were attractive new applications, not because they outraced competitors.

Due to attitudes such as that expressed by Nick Molina, it is commonly felt that entrepreneurs are 'different' ethically – that they approach ethical issues differently from those operating in large firms. It is certainly likely that in order to succeed with bringing new ventures to fruition entrepreneurs will often need to approach issues in a more opportunistic manner. In some cases they may even lack the same degree of cognitive moral development that people working as employees for larger firms display. Vyakarnam[19] has, however, identified *situational* challenges for entrepreneurs that might lead them to react differently: the asymmetries in information inherent in entrepreneurial activity; the priorities assigned to different stakeholders; and the conflicts of interest of distinguishing one's personal interests from those of the company one has set up. It is true that finally he also includes personality factors that lead someone to become an entrepreneur (such as risk taking, and drives for success and achievement). Critical here, though, is that three of these four issues are not directly about entrepreneurs themselves, but about the *context* in which they operate.

Related to this is the growing literature on the two related fields of entrepreneurial and small business ethics,[20] where there remains a debate on the difference of these from larger corporate ethics. In general, many of the *concerns* are the same – the need to satisfactorily meet responsibilities towards the range of direct stakeholders, questions of virtue such as how far to balance honesty with prudence, or issues such as the evaluation of different kinds of outcome from business activity. The *scale* and *scope* of these, however, represents a key difference. As stated earlier, the margins of tolerance in a smaller business are much narrower than those for an established corporation, as are the timescales for decisions. Also, the smaller organization usually is in a relatively weak position vis-à-vis customers, regulators and suppliers. While all these may lend some impression of justification to the attitude expressed by Molina above, the personality of the entrepreneur remains a key factor: as noted earlier, not all are without integrity, though their drive to establish a new venture, and the perception of the external environment as potentially threatening, can result in a 'bunker'-type defensiveness that can lead individuals to cut ethical corners. Conceivably, though, the real question is not so much whether entrepreneurs are 'different' so much as whether enterprise requires people to act differently.

THINKING CRITICALLY ABOUT ETHICS

HOW MUCH ALLOWANCE SHOULD BE MADE FOR ENTREPRENEURS

Entrepreneurs create new ideas, new jobs, new services and generate new sources of wealth for a society.

Should we perhaps make allowance for the creativity and drive of these individuals? Might we overlook some of their foibles on the ground that a greater good is achieved by their development of new ventures? Should we thus judge them by less demanding standards of integrity?

SAFETY

Safety impacts on organizational activity in a range of ways, affecting different stakeholders. There is the safety and health of those who work for or supply an organization, as well as the safety of the goods and services delivered by the organization to its customers; there are the safety implications of whatever level of impact the organization makes on the natural environment. Also, though less discussed, are the questions of the health of those who direct an organization and those who depend on its successful functioning.

Health and safety is a well-established field of people management. As such it is attended by the usual machinery of such elements of HR, including codes of practice, international standards, national legislation, elaborate training programmes and consultancy models. Figure 12.1 is a screenshot of the website of NIOSH (National Institute of Occupational Safety and Health), the Malaysian government-backed institute for health and safety at work, which is a good indication that this field is now at least as elaborated in the newer Asian developed economies as in the older Western ones. What is interesting in this figure is the range of health and safety activities it offers: certification, other training programmes, a forum for discussion, research opportunities, consultancy and many other facilities.

Institutes such as NIOSH, coupled with legislation at national and international levels, have raised substantially the level of awareness of potential risks and hazards involved in most occupations. A risk-based approach is often adopted as the prime legal means of dealing with safety in the workplace. 'Risk-based' in this context refers to the balancing of organizational effort against the scale of probability and the potential impact of any damage (or 'hazard'). A substantial but extremely unlikely hazard should, on this approach, not

FIGURE 12.1 The NIOSH website

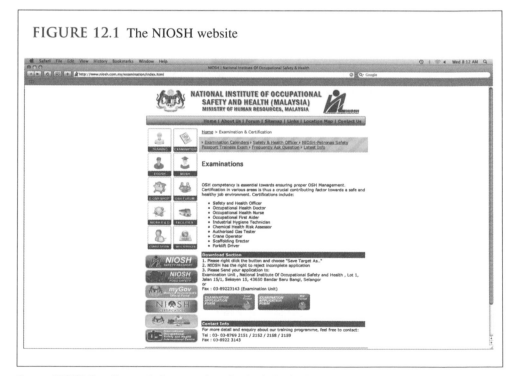

Source: NIOSH (http://www.niosh.com.my/examination/index.html).

require as much attention as a significant but much more likely one. So, although the hazard of an office block disintegrating is vast, the likelihood is very low, and therefore this should receive less preventative attention than the risk of people contracting respiratory disease from faulty air-conditioning systems (a relatively frequent hazard). This approach is usually perceived as a means of enabling employers to manage risks to safety without prejudicing their ability to carry on their business, and this tends to be regarded as a duty for employers, not just a convenient opportunity.

In general, while the employer is required to provide as safe an environment as they can reasonably achieve in the competitive environment, some work, such as mining, remains a dangerous occupation. To make this as risk-reduced as, say, office work, would require vast investment, which would raise the cost base of the industry, and thus the price to customers, by a substantial multiple. Hence, rather than cripple the industry, legislators and courts have in some countries put a balance between what is reasonable for an organization to do in the circumstances and what level of hazard someone is risking in carrying out certain tasks. This allows companies to carry on their business but does not absolve them from fulfilling social responsibilities. However, there are potential shortcomings with such an approach. What is deemed reasonable at one time may not be seen to be so later: social expectations and norms change over time, so any decision today is always subject to a potential critique in the future. Norms also vary across cultures, so any multinational organization has the dilemma of deciding which set of norms to follow. This has often led to charges of social dumping – firms choosing to move investment and operations to countries with lower safety standards (or employment protection) to the detriment of countries where there is greater protection.

In some cases, however, the onus is not placed on the employer but is given to the employee. Notably in South African legislation on safety in the mining industry, employees have a legal right to refuse to do dangerous tasks, and also have a right to know if others have refused these before. While this is not carte blanche for someone to pick and choose what they want to do (what counts as 'dangerous' is clearly spelled out) it creates a different balance of responsibility. In many countries in other ways it is assumed that there is a collaboration between employer and employee in respect of safety, for in most cases activities cannot be completely specified to the extent that someone's actions are completely controlled. In most operational situations there is some degree of employee discretion, and with this comes a degree of employee responsibility.

Notwithstanding all this, even in those countries that pride themselves on their health and safety provision, there remain many accidents and occupational injuries and illnesses each year. In 2007–08 in the United Kingdom, which has one of the strongest occupational

THINKING CRITICALLY ABOUT ETHICS

SHOULD EMPLOYEES HAVE THE RIGHT TO REFUSE DANGEROUS JOBS?

It can be argued that the South African position on the option of employees to refuse dangerous tasks is a fair move, in that it allows individuals to decline tasks about which they are unhappy.

However, it can be countered that in fact what this does is shift at least a part of the burden of establishing whether something is safe or not to the individual, who will not have the same infrastructure to process information on risks.

safety records, there were 2.1 million work-related accidents, and over 200 fatalities at work. Similar statistics apply in the rest of the European Union, and in other developed nations such as Japan, and the United States.[21]

How can this happen? Clearly one reason is simply that some employers are insufficiently concerned about the safety of their employees or others to follow established good practice, or even may feel that they can violate legislation and escape scot-free. A related issue is that many employees often underestimate the degree of risk or hazard in an activity, and fail to take adequate precautions even though their employer has suggested these. More prevalent is the relative weakness of government regulation. The existence of an inspectorate is common in many countries, but the criteria they work to are often difficult to enforce, and the recording systems that provide the critical flow of information are usually flawed in several ways.

One aspect of this is that casual workers are often not formally entered onto registers of employees, and hence accidents or injuries to these are often overlooked. Casuals usually only work for one organization for a relatively short period of time, so if there is a condition that takes time to manifest itself then it becomes much harder to argue that this is a result of a working practice in a given organization that the individual worked for perhaps months or years ago. Not all aspects of temporary work fall into this category, however: Hernanz and Toharia, in a study comparing temporary workers in Italy and Spain, have argued that in many cases of temporary contract work, there are not direct differences between the prevalence of accidents in the workplace compared with established permanent workers.[22] Against this, however, is the evidence of the ILO, that in the rapidly developing BRIC countries many people are coming to heavy industrial work for the first time and are at an especially acute risk of injury. As stated by Jukka Takala, director of the ILO's 'Safework' programme:

This is happening because in the newly developing countries workers are often coming out of the rural areas, with few skills and very little training in safe work practices. Most have never worked with heavy machinery, and some have little or no experience with industrial hazards such as electricity, so they don't know how dangerous these things can be. Yet these are elements of the kinds of jobs that are available for low skilled workers in rapidly industrializing countries.[23]

Related to the recording of safety is the employment of illegal migrants. In much of the globe there are people who have illegally entered a country. By definition they are not likely to want their status or even existence to be made known to government authorities, so when they experience an accident they have a motive for this not to be reported. In some cases unscrupulous employers exploit this by refusing to improve working conditions, but even where this is not the case, it is easy for an unofficial employee to be left out of reporting systems. Add to this that in some countries the reporting of accidents to migrants, even legal ones, is not encouraged,[24] and there are many substantial ways in which government statistics under-represent the degree of risk in the workplace. The underpinning point here is that while many well-motivated employers will take steps to protect their employees, where they do so in excess of what the government is likely to regulate or manage they may well be putting their firm(s) at competitive disadvantage in comparison to other companies with less ethical concern. It is clear that there exist sufficient management tools to reduce occupational safety risks to an acceptable level. These tools and systems, however, suffer from incomplete implementation, in the main stemming from poor recording practices, and they sometimes reflect varying social attitudes.

INTELLECTUAL PROPERTY AND COMMON GOODS

In a previous chapter we looked at the potential for intellectual property legislation to be used to exercise control over values. This final section will not cover the full range of issues relating to intellectual property, but will focus on two key and related ethical questions, namely the open/proprietary debate in the IT industries, and the use of intellectual property legislation to distort markets.

The debate over open source versus proprietary software has raged in internet circles for some years. By 'open source' is meant software that is presented to the public freely. In most cases this means in a form in which anyone with the appropriate skills may freely modify it, for example to customize it to specific needs, or sometimes to develop an improvement.[25] This approach therefore treats a piece of software as public property. Perhaps the best known piece of open software is the Linux operating system, though there are many other applications that are also available. In contrast, a proprietary source is one where an application may not be modified without the explicit consent of the originator – usually where the application is acquired by members of the public they are only licensed to use it and do not actually own a copy. The computing giants, such as Apple and Microsoft, require users to confirm agreement to a number of conditions before being able to use an application – one of these is generally agreement not to attempt to modify the software.

Legally it is clear that the IT corporations are fully within their rights to do this. Part of their argument is that modifications are not necessarily improvements, and this could damage their brand. Commercially there is a different argument, namely that from time to time a software house will want to improve and re-release their software to the public, and if it were open source this would make it difficult to generate appropriate revenues to justify the process.

The counter-argument is that morally such developments should be the property of all, and that major developments in IT, principally the internet, have only come about because of an openness on the part of innovators such as Tim Berners-Lee.[26] Furthermore, this argument goes, the development of packages such as Microsoft Office, or Apple iTunes, are only able to exist because of openly sourced earlier developments. Related with this is a profound philosophical view of the nature of knowledge and how it should be possessed by society. The traditions of academia, stretching back well over two millennia, have been for open presentation of ideas and technological developments, made freely available, not only as a good for all, but also because the free and open discussion of ideas is a most efficient method for their development and enhancement. This attitude has been reflected in the recent emergence of the Creative Commons (see text box), a movement that seeks to liberate creative and intellectual development from too great a reliance on corporate ownership.

Creative Commons came about as a direct reaction to the growth of intellectual property legislation allowing corporations to lay claim to many creative and intellectual outputs. In one case it was even suggested that a company might be able to patent a gene, although in practice this really indicated that one particular process of identifying a gene was patented (the confusion arose because the process described was the only existing method to identify a gene at that time). The fact that this could be attempted, though, coupled with actions such as the artist Yves Klein patenting a particular colour,[27] indicates that much of what we would call the common intellectual heritage of the world is becoming the property of big business.

It is doubtful that the Creative Commons movement would have needed to come into being had it not been for some excessive applications of patent and intellectual property

> ## THE CREATIVE COMMONS
>
> The organization summarizes its aims and activities as follows:
>
> *Creative Commons is a nonprofit corporation dedicated to making it easier for people to share and build upon the work of others, consistent with the rules of copyright. We provide free licences and other legal tools to mark creative work with the freedom the creator wants it to carry, so others can share, remix, use commercially, or any combination thereof.*
>
> ### Creative Commons licences
>
> - *Attribution*: You let others copy, distribute, display and perform your copyrighted work — and derivative works based upon it — but only if they give credit the way you request.
> - *Share alike*: You allow others to distribute derivative works only under a licence identical to the licence that governs your work.
> - *Non-commercial*: You let others copy, distribute, display and perform your work – and derivative works based upon it – but for non-commercial purposes only.
> - *No derivative works*: You let others copy, distribute, display and perform only verbatim copies of your work, not derivative works based upon it
>
> Source: Creative Commons website (http://creativecommons.org/).

law, that restricted artists designers and inventors. Notoriously, some technologies have been patented by companies, only for them to 'sit' on these and use their ownership to prevent dissemination. In other examples, trade names have been used to restrict activities: a small local butchers in Scotland called McDonald's (a common Scottish name) was subject to litigation by the global hamburger chain on the ground that he was violating the use of their brand. Perhaps the most striking example of corporate control over ideas and technologies has been the protracted negotiations between the largest drugs companies and several African governments, in order to enable the citizens of the latter to benefit from drugs to deal with HIV, TB and other related chronic illnesses that these poorer nations cannot afford to distribute on a national scale. IP has also been used to control artists in the creative directions they wish to develop, sometimes by preventing their existing work being disseminated in the manner that they hoped for.

The conclusion of these points is that intellectual property legislation has been used to distort markets, and to hinder the free spread of information. The widespread practice of music file sharing via the MP3 format is another example of how far corporate needs are not respected by the public – or put another way, how corporate intentions do not match the interests of their customer base. The music case illustrates how the growth of the internet has changed the issues of intellectual property – in practice now it is extremely difficult to completely control copyright or patents once these get into the public domain.

Against all of this the corporate argument is simply that a huge amount of investment is needed in the knowledge industries to develop new ideas, and this has to be recouped in some way. The teenager who downloads a free version of a new album is often ignorant of how much has gone into it – including recording, production, songwriting, performing, advertising and promotion. What is more, in many countries there is little attempt to try to control violations of copyright, so that many books, music albums and videos may be obtained at a low price (and often a low copied quality), thus undermining the standard pricing of these items, and representing a loss of revenue to the companies that made them. Corporations, even large market leaders, need to have paying customers in order to be able to continue their activities. Free music would, on this view, lead eventually to no music, or at least an industry so fragmented that it would revert to a cottage industry style of operation, with little resources for global dissemination.

Perhaps the solution to this particular dilemma is for revenue to be attached, not to specific songs or albums, but to *access*, via licensing. So instead of an individual paying €1 per track downloaded (which the average teenager will try to subvert for both economic and social reasons), they may pay an annual fee for access to a catalogue or playlist of songs, which they can access as freely as they wish. The point of this is that this example indicates that corporate ownership has been based in the past on control over content, which has in turn been construed as sales of single items such as copies of recorded performances or books. The internet has created an environment in which many multiples of an item may be generated digitally in no time at all, and disseminated over a wide geographical area, often beyond the reach of a specific piece of intellectual property legislation. The strategic response to this should be based on the provision of a sound alternative that does not substantially intrude on the freedom of individuals to access content, but guarantees a steady and reliable stream of revenue for the company. This can only happen if the intrusion is not too much – i.e. if the companies are prepared to accept a more modest level of income than was the case with the CD market in the 1990s. Otherwise the Creative Commons movement will be the focus for much higher levels of consumer reaction against corporate profits.

SUMMARY

In this chapter we have looked at a range of issues that pertain to the day-to-day operations of an organization – the management of people, of the supply chain, and related areas such as intellectual property. We have not attempted to be exhaustive, but to identify areas that highlight key issues. In much of the discussion we have seen close interrelationships between ethical issues and established organizational practices, such as quality systems and strategic pricing. While this does not provide strong support for the idea that 'good ethics is good business' it does indicate that the image of ethics as a distinct field with its distinct concerns is not a complete account of its role in corporate life.

- People management is intrinsically linked to many ethical issues: human beings are at the heart of ethics and carry a unique value, and therefore all aspects of their management – recruitment, delegation, staff planning, redundancy and safety – carry potential for ethical good or ill.

THINKING CRITICALLY ABOUT ETHICS

EXTENDING COMMONS AND INTELLECTUAL PROTECTION

In the text we have identified a potential resolution of the music file sharing dilemma based on an alternative pricing model.

How far do you think this could be extended to other examples of distorted intellectual protection, such as excessive use of trademarking, or the resistance of drug companies to allow generic medicines to be used as an alternative to their proprietary brands?

- Intellectual property can be used as a method to enhance or inhibit the openness that is often crucial to sound ethical discourse.

- Marketing is associated with a range of ethical concerns because it is often the main corporate function that interacts with the consumer.

- In response to the criticism that marketers create artificial needs that bring little benefit to society and lead to perpetual dissatisfaction, defenders of the function have argued that the critics are underestimating the consumer and the way in which consumption and identity are linked in today's world.

QUICK REVIEW QUESTIONS:

1 Identify three themes that underpin and illustrate ethical issues in human resource management. Give examples.

2 Why is discrimination a controversial issue? Examine the question from a conceptual and practical point of view.

3 Some authors have argued that marketing is unethical because it promotes consumerism. Discuss.

4 What are the differences between direct, indirect and institutional discrimination, and how might organisations deal with each of these three forms?

5 What are the different forms of deception in marketing and how should firms work to minimise each of these?

6 What are the advantages or disadvantages of a company adopting a creative commons approach?'

CASE STUDY: FORCED LABOUR IN MALAYSIA – WHO IS RESPONSIBLE?

Local Technic Industry is a small Malaysian company manufacturing parts for hard-disk drives. Its customers include well-known companies from across the world, although the company discloses little information about its clients. The majority of its 160 employees come from poorer countries in the region including Indonesia, Bangladesh and Cambodia. According to *Newsweek*, the migrant labourers live in a situation that can be characterized as forced labour and the company's managers are aware of the plight of their workers. An executive told *Newsweek* that the labourers 'have been fooled hook, line and sinker', but that it is the fault of dishonest labour brokers, not the company.

In general, the migrant labourers in Malaysia are recruited by labour brokers who often lure people with gifts, working papers and false promises. Some workers pay brokers directly, but others learn about the brokers only when they arrive to the country and are told to pay a fee amounting to US$1000 per person.

The newcomers are also informed that they will not be able to return home before they have paid the broker. As a result of this practice, a Bangladeshi employee of Local Technic earns a monthly net pay of US$14 after deductions for room, board, taxes and a broker's fee. If he spends none of this, he earns a meagre US$168 a year. Moreover, his freedom of movement is limited until he has paid the fees to the broker.

As a relatively wealthy nation, Malaysia is a country of destination for many migrant workers in south-east Asia. Malaysia has about 2.5 million foreign workers, most of whom come from countries in the same region. Many of the migrant workers are not allowed to change employers; if they do, they are classed as illegal aliens and subject to imprisonment and flogging before being expelled from the country. Because employers are expected to confiscate the passports of guest workers and report escapees to the authorities, foreign labourers exercise little choice about their employment and can therefore be regarded as victims of forced labour.

The International Labour Organization defines forced labour in reference to two main factors: absence of consent and threat of punishment. First, forced labour concerns situations where the worker has not given informed consent due to being subjected to psychological or physical duress, debt bondage or, as is the case with workers in Malaysia, deceit. Secondly, forced labourers are threatened by violence, arrest or deportation if they refuse to work. A Malaysian non-governmental organization, Tenaganita, has estimated that 65 per cent of human trafficking in Malaysia is for forced labour.

Until recently, Malaysia had not enacted laws that could be used to protect the victims of forced labour or prosecute those responsible for it. Victims of forced labour and trafficking have been rescued due to action by foreign embassies. Illegal migrants are generally arrested and deported without being identified as victims. As a result, the US Department of State has criticized the country and encouraged the government to take measures to eliminate human trafficking. What is more, Malaysia has allegedly become a transit point for trafficking. There have also been reports about some government officials being complicit in helping traffickers by providing them with forged documents. In 2007, the Malaysian parliament passed a law to abolish human trafficking. The Anti-Trafficking in Persons Act should make it easier for the authorities to pursue and prosecute traffickers as well as to protect their victims. The new Act provides for sentences of up to 20 years in prison, fines and caning. Victims will be offered support by way of medical care and half-way shelter houses. What is more, they will not be charged for illegal immigration. Mohamed Nazri Abdul Aziz, Minister in the Prime Minister's Department, has said that the 'law will address the concerns raised about human trafficking and (provide) armed enforcement agencies with the tools to fight it.'

STUDY QUESTIONS

1 How far should a company like Technic be expected to investigate the legal status of employees sourced by independent brokers?

2 What, in virtue-ethical terms, are the main problems in this case?

3 What organizationally based mechanisms are necessary to help ensure the success of the recent legislation passed by the Malaysian government combating forced labour?

SOURCES

Wehrfritz, G, Kinetz, E. and Kent, J. 2008. Bottom of the barrel, *Newsweek*, 15 March. Available from http://www.newsweek.com/id/123481, accessed 31 March 2008.

The HumanTrafficking.org project. Available from http://www.humantrafficking.org/countries/malaysia, accessed 1 April 2008.

This case study was prepared using only publicly available sources of information for the purposes of classroom discussion.

NOTES

1. We shall look at the ethics of managing customers and clients in the next chapter.
2. For example, Fisher and Lovell, and Winstanley and Woodall.
3. And, less ethically, the willingness of debtors to pay the firm what they owe.
4. Though a whole raft of US legislation ensures that dismissal may not be on grounds such as racial origin or trade union activity.
5. In most countries this is usually on a relatively slow timescale however.
6. See Simpson & Lewis (2007) for a discussion about this aspect of gender equalization in organizations.
7. Catley & Jones (2002).
8. Baudrillard (1998).
9. Hayek (1976).
10. Baudrillard (1998).

11. Sheenhan & Hoy (2000).
12. Chellappa & Sin (2005).
13. Sheenhan & Hoy (2000).
14. Caudill & Murphy (2000).
15. Venkataraman (2002).
16. Harmeling *et al.* (2009).
17. Such as discrimination or unfair dismissal litigation.
18. Quoted in Seglin (1998).
19. Vyakarnam *et al.* (1997).
20. Though there are some differences, such as the fact that some entrepreneurs only build up businesses to a point and then sell them on: sometimes called *serial* entrepreneurs.
21. Source: Eurostat (http://epp.eurostat.ec.europa.eu).
22. Hernanz & Toharia (2006).
23. ILO (2005).
24. For example, the statistics of occupational injuries and accidents in Egypt specifically exclude accidents to those who are normally resident outside the country (source ILO).
25. This oversimplifies – in practice the Open Source Initiative adds other specifications, such as non-discrimination, non-restriction and absence of any specific technological tie-in. See the website of the Open Source Initiative: http://www.opensource.org/docs/osd.
26. Who famously made HTML, his creation, available freely to all. It is estimated that one of his other developments – the use of the @ sign as part of the protocol of e-mail addresses – would have made him a multi-millionaire had he even only charged 0.01 of a US cent per usage.
27. A particularly deep shade of blue, which is now known, unsurprisingly, as Klein Blue.

REFERENCES

Barber, B. 2008. *Consumed*. W.W. Norton.

Baudrillard, J. 1998. *The Consumer Society: Myths and Structures*. Sage.

Carr, A. Z. 1968. Is business bluffing ethical? *Harvard Business Review*, January–February, Vol. 46, No. 1, 143–153.

Catley, B. and Jones, C. 2002. Deciding on violence. *The Journal of Philosophy of Management*, Vol. 2, No. 1, 25–34.

Caudill, E. and Murphy, P. 2000. Consumer online privacy: Legal and ethical issues. *Journal of Public Policy and Marketing*, Vol. 19. No. 1, 7–19.

Chellappa, R. and Sin, R. 2005. Personalization versus privacy: An empirical examination of the online consumer's dilemma. *Information Technology and Management*, Vol. 6, No. 2, 181–202.

Fisher, C. and Lovell, A. 2005. *Business Ethics and Values*. London: FT-Prentice Hall.

Galbraith, J. K. 1958/1999. *The Affluent Society*. Fifth revised edition, 1999. Harmondsworth: Penguin.

Harmeling, S., Sarasvathy, S. and Freeman, R. 2009. Related debates in ethics and entrepreneurship. *Journal of Business Ethics*, Vol. 84, 341–365.

Hayek, F. 1976. *Law, Legislation and Liberty*. London: Routledge and Kegan Paul.

Hernanz, V. and Toharia, L. 2006. Do temporary contracts increase work accidents? A microeconometric comparison between Italy and Spain. *Labour*, Vol. 20, No. 3, 475–504.

ILO (Dr J Takala) 2005. *Decent Work: Safe Work*. International Labour Office.

Klein, N. 2001. *No Logo*. Flamingo.

Seglin, J. 1998. True Lies Inc.com (online magazine): http://www.inc.com/magazine/19981015/1107.html.

Sheenhan, K. and Hoy, M. G. 2000. Dimensions of privacy concern among online consumers. *Journal of Public Policy and Marketing*, Spring, 62–73.

Simpson, R. and Lewis, P. 2007. *Voice Visibility and the Gendering of Organizations*. London: Palgrave.

Venkataraman, S. 2002. Stakeholder value equilibration and the entrepreneurial process. *Business Ethics Quarterly*, The Ruffin Series, Special Edition, No. 3, 45–57.

Vyakarnam, S., Bailey, A. and Myers, A. 1997. Towards an understanding of ethical behaviour in small firms. *Journal of Business Ethics*, Vol. 16, 1625–1636.

Winstanley, D. and Woodall, J. 2000. *Ethical Issues in Contemporary Human Resource Management*. London: Palgrave.

ENVIRONMENTAL RESPONSIBILITY

LEARNING OBJECTIVES

After studying this chapter you should be able to:

- Evaluate the relevance of certain key principles for decision making in relation to environmental responsibility.

- Identify contextual issues for strategic decisions relating to environmental management.

- Evaluate certain optional solutions to organizational environmental issues.

- Identify key features of environmental measurement systems.

INTRODUCTION

In Chapter 4 we looked at the concepts surrounding the debates over the environment. The current chapter is intended to focus on practical features of the debate that affect the degree of environmental responsibility on the part of organizations.

A further contrast between the two chapters is the structure of the discussion. The general discussion of philosophical positions on the environment was presented as a series of alternative positions, some of which overlap, some of which can sit in parallel and some of which are clearly opposed. This chapter is based around some key themes relating to the strategic decisions that an organization might take with respect to environmental management and protection.

FRAMING THE LINK BETWEEN BUSINESS AND THE ENVIRONMENT

There are several ways to frame the various activities and considerations relating to the link between organizational activity and environmental responsibility. Many discussions[1] focus mainly on private sector firms. However, while market economies are dependent on the development and performance of companies and partnerships, state bodies can and do have a significant impact on the environment, in terms of legislation and policy initiatives, as a major employer, as a major investor and facilitator of inward investment, as well as through regulatory and enabling functions. Third sector organizations perhaps play a smaller role, though some of these are influential: for example, environmental lobbyists or ecological protection organizations have a direct relevance. So all sectors have some degree of impact on the environment that needs explicit management.

Terminology such as 'environmental management' can mislead the reader into supposing that this is a different thing altogether from general operational and strategic management. It will become apparent that this is not so, and that managing environmentally is simply managing, but with a recognition, on the part of managers, of the importance of the environment for that task. It is thus possible to adapt standard strategic business management models to reflect the green agenda. Beaumont and others[2] have shown how the range of the models typically encountered in a strategic management course (Boston matrix, generic strategies, industry analysis, value chain analysis, PESTL) may be applied to include an element of environmental content. It should be noted that such approaches reflect approaches discussed earlier that see business and environmental protection as compatible – 'bright green' positions that are optimistic about the possibility of combining business imperatives with environmental responsibility.

In keeping with the main themes of the book, the key point of reference in this chapter is the idea of strategic decision making. A strategic decision may be mapped out in many ways and one of these is as follows:

- identifying principles and vision
- clarifying the context
- evaluating potential solutions
- implementing and measuring the impact of decisions.

The following sections will not cover these aspects exhaustively, but will focus on the key issues in environmental management that relate to ethics and responsibility.

ETHICS AND YOU

ENGAGEMENT BETWEEN BUSINESSES AND ENVIRONMENTALISTS

It may seem impractical to reflect for too long on the more far-reaching environmental positions – 'deep' and 'dark' green approaches – in relation to business practices. However, it is likely that at times organizations will encounter influential stakeholders who adhere to one of these more demanding environmental philosophies.

What kinds of options could you use to successfully engage with a 'deep' or a 'dark' green activist who opposes your organization's plans?

PRINCIPLES: RESPONSIBILITY AND PRECAUTION

Two principles relating to decisions underpin much discussion of environmental management and regulation. The first of these is the notion of responsibility, in particular the idea that those who damage the eco-system are liable to pay to clean up or offset the effects of their actions. The second is the idea that we should protect first and then investigate later – sometimes called the principle of precaution, sometimes more bluntly summarized as 'better safe than sorry'.

Who pays for environmental damage?

We looked at the metaphor of the 'tragedy of the commons' in Chapter 4. The issue of liability for environmental damage is reflected in much environmental literature by the principle that 'the polluter pays'. If a company pollutes the atmosphere or the land by their activity, then they should bear the costs of a clean-up. This principle has been supported in policy statements by the Organization for Economic Cooperation and Development (OECD) and in the Rio Declaration.

While a defensible principle in itself, there are limitations in its operation. It is clear how to allocate responsibilities in major environmental disasters such as the wreck of the Exxon Valdez. However, the issue also covers wider issues such as the continuing erosion of natural resources, for which causal responsibility is harder to establish. For example, it is the collective impact of some activities undertaken by *many* agents – such as the release of gases into the atmosphere, or to use rightfully owned land until its fertility is exhausted – that make some natural resources more scarce and more costly to extract or exploit. Some of these impacts on the environment, on a day-to-day basis, are almost imperceptible, but when repeated daily for decades become major erosions of natural amenity. Also, how far should an individual company or industry be required to pay for environmental damage that may persist for many years? In the case of nuclear power stations the environmental damage may last for thousands of years, which would in practice make both the impact and the financial implications of the damage incalculable.

This point could easily be distorted by those wishing to avoid responsibility for environmental damage they have knowingly brought about. For a firm trying to formulate its environmental strategy, however, it creates wider issues, for what appears to be harmless may be part of a much wider pattern, in which many agents contribute to environmental problems.

A counter-argument to the polluter pays principle might be that it is the responsibility of *society* to pay for environmental impacts. The basis of this argument is that it is society that gains or loses from the economic activity of business, and should it desire to eliminate a negative consequence of economic activity then it is the choice of society rather than one of business, just as when society chooses to avail itself of positive consequences the businesses whose activity may have created these are not consulted or deemed to have a right to be involved in the choice. General Motors charges people to buy cars, but cannot charge society for the advantages we gain from being able to travel long distances easily. And equally, the argument goes, it should not have to pay for people using their cars irresponsibly: we do not ask car manufacturers to pay every time a drunk driver causes an accident, so why should they when people do not take care to drive fuel-efficiently? The free market argument here is that business should be at liberty to operate within the legal framework that society develops, and that where there are undesirable effects of business activity then society as a whole should take responsibility to eliminate these.

Underpinning this debate is a basic philosophical view over agency, reward and responsibility. The general trend of Western thinking since the time of Aristotle has been that it is the *agent*, the person who has committed an act, who is morally responsible for that act and its consequences. Hence the model of action that this presumes is that an agent makes a choice based on their own knowledge and motives, and then the primary responsibility for, and benefit of, that action accrues to them specifically. Such a model may be critiqued on several grounds. One concern is how far we should take responsibility for things that we know will in part result from what we did, but also rest on the actions of others. How can we deal effectively with something that we can reasonably assume will result from what we do, but we do not intend it to occur? For example, the Christian theological debate on whether war could ever be justifiable used the principle of 'double effect' as a way of marking that an agent may act in a certain way for a given reason, and yet they may bring about other outcomes that are reasonably predictable but not wished (e.g. the deaths of innocent non-combatants in war). Hence arms manufacturers are not normally held responsible for wars, nor are food producers for obesity. Another issue is whether we have enough knowledge to predict the ethically relevant consequences of an act, such as producing a certain kind of car. In the modern world the trail of consequences from a corporate act may stretch far beyond what is generally foreseeable, and hence beyond what even the strictest consequentialist could reasonably expect of agents. A conclusion of this latter point is therefore that those who initiate actions cannot be held entirely liable for all the outcomes, only those which were reasonably foreseeable.

The implication of the agency argument is that while an oil company might be held liable for immediately attributable results of a spillage, such as damage to seashore or physical injury to fish and birds, they cannot be responsible for results that lie far in the future, such as cancers in humans that may develop partially as a result of the oil spillage. However, this position can only be sustained because we cannot have enough confidence

THINKING CRITICALLY ABOUT ETHICS

DOUBLE EFFECT

The principle of 'double effect' is the idea that I may be justified in doing something that brings about morally bad or unacceptable consequences if (a) the action I engage in is for a morally worthwhile end; (b) I did not intend, though I may have foreseen, the unacceptable consequences; (c) the purpose or end that I seek to achieve is a direct result of the action, while the unacceptable effects are incidental; (d) the good is sufficient to compensate for the bad effects. A typical application of this principle is the argument that it may be acceptable to engage in an activity as part of warfare, say bombing a munitions factory in the heart of a city, that one can foresee will happen to kill a small number of innocent civilians; whereas to deliberately target killing innocent civilians, maybe by bombing the city when one could put the factory out of action by other means, even as part of superficially the same kind of action, would not be justifiable.

Would this provide a basis for, say, a paper company to justify its cutting down of forests – perhaps arguing that they do not intend the destruction of the forests, but it is not their business to replant trees on land that they may have only been licensed to collect timber from by the government?

Could it justify the decision of a company to continue to use paper invoices rather than electronic, on the basis that electronic invoices are more often disputed and therefore consume disproportionately more resources?

about the trail of causes between oil spillage and cancer. If by some fortunate scientific development one were able to establish that a certain incidence of an illness was directly attributable to a corporate action, even if that act had occurred decades earlier, then responsibility – and compensation – would be held to be attributable to the agent (in this case the corporation).

The principle that those who cause damage, even when this is many years ago, should pay to remedy or compensate for it is well established. It was seen, for example, in the long drawn-out court cases over smoking tobacco and lung cancer, and in similar cases involving asbestos exposure and asbestosis. In both of these cases there was a long gap in time between action and the illnesses they caused, yet in both examples courts in several countries established that the corporations involved were the causes of the illness and therefore responsible.

The suggestion that society should pay for environmental damage, then, is not relevant when causation can be clearly demonstrated – for in those cases the agent (i.e. the cause of the damage) can be identified and responsibility attributed. The net result of this set of arguments is that the idea of society, rather than individual polluters, paying for pollution is misplaced. Common natural resources will diminish without active moves to create greater senses of individual corporate responsibility, and the basic principles of agency imply that corporations should be liable for what environmental degradations are attributable to their activity.

For organizations, the main issue here is that a simple line of responsibility is difficult to establish, but this should not lead decision makers to assume that such causal lines cannot or will not be established. In the next section we will look at a principle that, among other things, can represent a means for organizations to prevent excess liability for their actions.

Precautions

Another key principle that has been debated in the context of environmental protection is the so-called precautionary principle. This is based on the idea that the potential severity of the consequences of global warming indicates that we may be safest assuming that some damage has occurred as a result of human activity, and then working to reducing this,

---

ETHICS IN PRACTICE

POLLUTER PAYS IN JAPAN

The Japanese Environmental Restoration and Conservation Agency (ERCA) levies a tax on specific industries that produce soot and smoke as part of their operations. A smaller tax is levied on automobiles for the same purpose. With this levy they make payments to compensate those who have suffered health damage as a result of atmospheric pollution in those areas that until 1988 were classified as highly polluted.

The principle is explicitly stated that 'expenses should be burdened by the concerned who causes air pollution' [*sic* in English translation].

A formula is used to calculate liabilities for past pollution as well as present. Emissions are reported on a voluntary declaration basis, much as company finances are for corporation tax purposes.

Source: ERCA (http://www.erca.go.jp).

rather than adopting a view that we need to wait until the science has been more strongly established before doing anything: 'When an activity raises threats of harm to human health or the environment, precautionary measures should be taken even if some cause and effect relationships are not established scientifically. In this context the proponent of the activity, rather than the public, should bear the burden of proof.'[3]

This contrasts with the general approach to managing risks – namely that a decision is generally held in abeyance until sufficient data has been collected to support a robust evaluation of the risks in terms of hazard scale and probability. However, on such a risk *management* model a practice might exist unchecked until such time as (a) it has already caused some environmental damage and (b) this has been accepted to be the case through socially legitimate decision making or juridical processes. Given that these take time, it could mean that the damage has gone on for an extended period. On a *precautionary* basis such damage does not occur.

Delay has been a key feature of several long legal disputes over health and environmental risks. Aggressive denial of human-caused global warming by a small part of the science community is one example. The long drawn-out legal battles have meant that companies have been able to carry on practices unchecked as yet, whatever the final outcomes might be. Parallel with this are the extended legal cases over smoking tobacco and lung cancer – the cigarette manufacturers were able to stave off bans on sales and advertising in the Western world long enough to switch their major marketing activities to the developing countries (where smoking is at an all-time high).

Although at first sight precaution would seem to be essentially a rule of efficiency, it is actually compatible with several ethical approaches. Seen from a consequentialist perspective, precaution is a practice likely to avoid undesirable results. From a virtue perspective it expresses a virtue of prudence, while from a deontological standpoint it represents the deferral of gain until the relevant action is justified.

Carolan[4] has underlined an important theme concerning precautions and environmental protection, namely that there is a limited range of positions that characteristically find expression in the debate over when to proceed with controls and when not. Minorities often have less influence in political debates in a country, and are thus likely to have fewer opportunities to have sufficient 'voice' in debates over environmental opportunities and controls. This is not through deliberate censorship (at least not generally) so much as via a failure of consultative and discursive processes to create the appropriate space for all

ETHICS IN PRACTICE

GM FOOD AND THE SUPERMARKETS

GM foods have not, in general, resulted in significant health hazards so far. Indeed there remain significant parts of the scientific establishment that express confidence that GM can result in safe foods that can flourish in relatively unfavourable conditions.

However, the public in general, and many in the environmental movement, are less confident that GM foods are safe. Consequently many supermarkets have publicly stated that they will not offer GM foods for sale. In 1999 virtually the entire supermarket industry in Germany banned GM in a matter of weeks, including Lidl, Aldi, Tengelmann and Spar. Other European countries have also followed this example in recent years.

Is this the precautionary principle, or simply response to market demand?

relevant views to be taken into account. Often it is only by concerted action that disadvantaged communities can be included in environmental development. Some companies, such as BP, have set up structured consultation processes – one example of an outcome of this is the formation of micro-financial support by the company to support agricultural and environmental development in Angola.

CONTEXT: SOCIAL, POLITICAL AND LEGAL ASPECTS

In the preceding section we looked at two key principles relevant to strategic environmental decisions. Before solutions can be formulated and evaluated, however, it is important to establish some of the context within which decisions are made. We will look briefly at some of the characteristic elements of the political social and legal context of environmental protection and how this relates to business.

Environmentalism and colonialism

In Chapter 3 we discussed briefly the concept of 'discourse' ethics – the idea that businesses should create the conditions for effective dialogue and debate with key stakeholders. One precondition of this is the space for discussion to be available. This in turn reflects power relationships between those seeking a voice and those able to provide the space for a voice to be heard. In the debates and policy arenas in which global environmental issues are considered, the relative power positions of key nations has become a critical factor. We will look at the north–south power relationship, and what this implies for environmental decision making.

The term 'colonialism' carries a somewhat outdated tone, with its nuances of the affluent and powerful northern countries dominating the poorer developing countries of the south. However, in the context of environmental management there is a live and lively debate relating to the way in which environmental issues may reflect those international imbalances of power, which can easily give rise to differences of definition, of emphasis and of practice.

At one level the argument here is that the global moves towards environmental responsibility reflect narrowly focused, Western-dominated perspectives, interests and world views. As was observed at the Second International Indigenous Forum on Climate Change at The Hague in November 2000:

> ... the measures to mitigate climate change currently being negotiated are based on a worldview of territory that reduces forests, lands, seas and sacred sites to only their carbon absorption capacity. This worldview and its practices adversely affect the lives of Indigenous Peoples and violate our fundamental rights and liberties, particularly, our right to recuperate, maintain, control and administer our territories which are consecrated and established in instruments of the United Nations.[5]

Behind this is the view that the very idea of 'the environment' carries a technical, Western-scientific perspective that is alien to many indigenous conceptions of the relation between humans and the rest of the globe. One example of this is the variation between different world-views, and the views of knowledge they express or imply, and in turn the implications for technology. This may be seen in Breidlid's[6] discussion of the interrelationship between spirituality and science on some African world-views.[7] This contrasts with the characteristic western/northern modernist perspective whereby the natural world is treated as inert matter, without a spiritual dimension, to be investigated and then mastered by technology. The contrast is between holistic views of the natural world and human life, and models that represent the two fields as distinct.

One result of this is that the environmental debate is seen as not relevant by many indigenous peoples. For example the highly influential Johannesburg Declaration on Sustainable Development[8] omits extended discussion of the role of *indigenous knowledge and skill* in sustainable development. At the level of global corporate operations, built on Western science and technology, this may seem irrelevant, but the meaning, and therefore value, of environmental impacts and indeed environmental solutions needs to be cast in a cultural context. For example, if a particular piece of land is regarded as inert then there is only a technical argument about using it for developing housing. If it is seen as sacred then the very community that might benefit from such housing may be those who find it offensive.

In most cases global businesses have extensive non-Western operations. To take one aspect of this: the vast majority of staff employed in a given country will be that country's nationals. To continue the example of African countries, a Western oil company attempting to implement an environmental responsibility programme in Africa will need to acknowledge that the education necessary for its staff to carry out the programme may rest on what the latter will see as alien principles. This is emphatically not to suggest that local staff cannot acquire the knowledge and skills necessary to carry out such activities, but it is to point out that what is seen by the Western executive as the application of knowledge that has grown out of their own personal societal assumptions, is for the local member of staff an imposed world-view, one that contrasts with what they may have grown up with. The contrast is not with what one individual knows and what another does not, rather it is between knowledge that one individual regards as a natural component of their socially accepted world-view and what the other has come to accept as an addition, a grafting, onto a substantially different way of intellectually engaging with the world. Implementation is difficult enough when working with shared cultural assumptions, but can become excessively hindered when those who are tasked with putting a programme into practice have a world-view that is not fully compatible with the changes envisaged.

This has significant implications for approaches to environmental management based on stakeholder engagement or discourse ethics. For in the case of stakeholder engagement, the key decision maker may simply not *understand* what matters for other stakeholders. Part of the struggle for many minority groups is simply to find space in the stakeholder nexus to be noticed and understood, what Holzer calls 'stakeseeking'.[9] So far as discourse-ethical environmental management is concerned, there is a parallel issue, which Gail Whiteman has called 'the voice effect'.[10] This refers to the differences in both understanding and participation with respect to consultation over the environment and the rights of indigenous citizens. As well as different ideas of what constitutes science, some minorities approach self expression and public discussion in a very different manner from Western-style legalism. This is again not simply a north/south divide issue – indigenous groups in North America and Europe have experienced difficulties in their involvement with consultative processes intended to ensure environmental protection.[11] The natural mode of interaction and communication in many of these indigenous cultures is not compatible with the highly rule-governed approach of many judicial processes, especially as these affect the environment. Indeed, the very shift from the term 'nature' to that of 'environment' reflects a change in perspective from a realm that carries, for many, positive overtones of involvement to one that is more technical and scientific in connotation.

Society and environmental damage

The damage that business is causing for the environment is not a matter simply of poor strategic decisions by companies. Social practices, the behaviour of consumers within their particular culture, are central factors in the impact on the eco-sphere. However, public understanding of science is very restricted, and hence the ordinary consumer can often act in ill-informed ways. For example, in northern European countries, where traditionally there has been a high level of environmental *awareness*, this has not always translated itself into citizens' *actions*. Noorgaard[12] describes how rural Norwegians appear to engage in collective denial of the realities of global warming – to confront these would require a comprehensive rethinking of their way of life. Understanding of risks to the environment needs also to be brought into connection with an awareness of potential remedies. Consumer behaviour is directly affected by what they believe needs to be done but also by what they think can be done. For example, Kotchen[13] studied people's willingness to pay for secure disposal of pharmaceuticals (as opposed to practices such as washing unwanted medications down the sink into the public drainage system), finding that there was a direct link between behaviour/willingness and their awareness of the risks and costs of each practice.

What these examples illustrate is that to understand the complex of factors that have led to the present situation of potentially severe trauma to the global eco-system, we need to see how *corporate activity* links directly with *social practice*. In consequentialist terms the matter of remediating environmental damage requires not only change in corporate operational practice but also in raising public awareness of environmental solutions and the costs and benefits of these. This also implies *duties* and *virtues* for society as well as for corporations – environmental protection is not solely a responsibility of companies but of all involved in production and consumption. One imperative, then, in addressing the problems of the environment, is not just to find ways to remedy damage and stop specific practices happening in the future. It is also about educating the public to be able to make more informed evaluations of the scientific evidence. This imperative is not, however, the sole responsibility of one set of agents. Rather it involves the manner in which information comes to public understanding via government, businesses, academia, the broadcast media and the worldwide web. And this is not solely about creating access to information, it is at least as much about creating the right cultural context for this information to make sense in human terms.

ETHICS IN PRACTICE

CONSUMER WATER USAGE

Domestic water usage involves high levels of waste – over-flushed lavatories, taps left running or dripping, washing small quantities of dishes in the same amount as large quantities.

Colgate-Palmolive has developed a system that helps the domestic as well as the business consumer to improve their water efficiency. The 'water footprint' identifies the full range of impacts that water has in a range of activities. It involves examining both the water consumption of production processes and consumer usage patterns, linking the latter also to energy usage, and is planned to be implemented in water-stressed areas of the globe equally with areas where water is less scarce. As a result consumers can monitor their own water usage and manage this accordingly.

Source: Colgate (colgate.com).

Legislative frameworks

Environmental management operates within a range of institutional fields, and among these perhaps uppermost is a legislative framework. This can work at several levels:

- Local level – by-laws, community specific regulations; sub-national rules.

- National level – laws requiring or forbidding certain behaviours, regulations and principles.

- Cross-national – laws affecting trade or political communities of countries such as the North American Free Trade Association, the European Union, or the ex-Soviet Community of Independent States.

- International – voluntary agreements such as the Law of the Sea.

A feature of corporate environmental behaviour is that legal differences between different countries provide an opportunity for companies to reduce their costs by shifting operations from highly regulated to lower regulated legislative regions. This can be categorized as a form of 'social dumping' – i.e. the passing of socially undesirable phenomena such as pollution from more developed countries to poorer ones, usually by transfer of investment. This aspect of corporate behaviour is made more complex when viewed on a regional basis. For example, the European Union's Directive on Environmental Liability (which, officially, came into force in 2007) will affect the whole 27 member states – however, EU Directives are notoriously implemented at different speeds by different members, so that a national competitive edge can be maintained by a country adopting a slower implementation speed than other member states.

In general, environmental issues are perceived as a cost to companies, and therefore, in keeping with standard shareholder value orientation, many firms will aim to comply with legislation but will rarely attempt to exceed it. Sharfman et al,[14] adopting an institutional theoretic perspective, have identified a range of external factors that can lead to higher-level global environmental performance; however, it is not clear to what extent their analysis of big international players can apply to smaller and medium-sized firms. There are, certainly, good reasons why some firms do in fact go beyond existing legislation, including:

- The firm realizes that the legislation is too weak and chooses to move to a higher specification in advance of the change in the law.

- The firm is able to present itself to customers as ecologically responsible, thus deriving some competitive advantage for their actions.

- The firm is seeking to avoid foreseen potential litigation.

- The firm sees potential cost-efficiencies by adopting environmentally responsible processes.

- The mission and vision of the firm leads them to identify environmental responsibility as consistent with their strategy.

Daily and others[15] have identified four key determinants of what they call 'organizational citizenship behaviour directed towards the environment' (OCBE) – environmental concern, organizational commitment, perceived supervisory support and perceived corporate social performance. Their theoretical work is not only interesting because of the internal factors that they identify but also because they locate *corporate* responsibility clearly as a resultant of *individual* responsibility. So as well as factors such as corporate strategy, mission and vision identified above, individual elements such as ethical commitment also provide part of the motivation for organizations to go beyond mere compliance with legislation.

ETHICS AND YOU

KEEPING TO THE LEGAL MINIMUM

How far should a company go in exceeding the existing legislation in one particular country, particularly where other countries have more demanding laws?

One argument is that there should be clear limits on environmental initiatives taken autonomously by firms. Given that some firms may well choose to stay exactly at the legal minimum, there is always the potential of losing competitive advantage – and thus diminishing the value for shareholders – by being too ethical. Furthermore, there may be good reasons why the law is not any more demanding. Also managers are stewards of companies, acting on behalf of the shareholders, and thus they have a duty to preserve the value of the company for those shareholders, even if they would prefer to act with greater altruism.

How far are you persuaded by this argument? When should a company choose to stay at the legal minimum, and when ought it to exceed legal requirements?

How businesses or individuals respond to legislation may vary, due to denial, deliberate evasion and often simply to avoid encountering a first mover disadvantage. The example of the split in the oil industry, between the environmental collaborators (e.g. BP) on the one hand and those more sympathetic with existing industry standards (e.g. Exxon) on the others reflects corporate desire to gain competitive advantage, but also difference in attitude to law, as well as in perception of the scientific facts.

Another aspect of compliance with legislation is the manner in which public debates influence the evolution of new policies. Maguire and Hardy[16] take the example of the evolution of the Stockholm Convention on Persistent Organic Pollutants (CFCs, DDT, etc.) and indicate the roles played not only by new knowledge and perspectives, but also by the manner in which these integrate with existing ideas and practices, so that the resulting policy emerges from a complex of negotiation and debate at several levels, as well as by direct intervention by key players. The institutional context is therefore a critical feature of the evolution of law and policy.

In this section we have looked at some key themes of three aspects of the business context, as these relate to the environment – the political context, the social and the legal. This is not at all exhaustive but indicates some of the important factors that need to be taken into account when formulating decisions. The next section will look directly at two characteristic solutions to environmental problems.

SOLUTIONS TO ENVIRONMENTAL PROBLEMS

Direct reduction approaches

The earlier 'light green' style strategies developed for dealing with environmental problems were based on the aim to directly reduce environmental damage, and this remains the dominant train of practice today. The basic concept is to identify the source of environmental damage and then either reduce it directly or find means to offset it. 'Plant a tree' programmes, recycling points and cleaner manufacturing processing are all examples of this. These tend to be linear activities where the citizen or company carries out an action that will contribute to the damage remediation envisaged. More recent developments have taken this a step further, involving the citizen or company more directly in the processes which give rise to the environmental problem.

Energy generation is a good example of these developments. The gradual increase in renewable energy generation (using solar, wind or underground heat sources) at the end-user point in the network has created opportunities for electricity not only to be created for users themselves, but also for any surplus to be sold back to the national network. Thus not only do end-users become self-sufficient, they may contribute to reductions in overall non-renewable energy consumption. As well as the reductions in direct network-based consumption, there are additional benefits of such distributed energy generation (such as low leakage due to short transmission lines).[17] The point of this example is that it involves the end-user as an actor in the supply chain. This changes the nexus of responsibility – no longer is energy production solely the responsibility of the energy utility companies – as well as creating new opportunities for greater energy efficiency. It reflects also the growing trend towards high levels of customized services and products, where end-users take a much greater role in areas such as specification of requirements. This takes into account the issue discussed in the previous section, of society's role in environmental protection or harm. Additionally this kind of process increases dialogue, the frequent absence of which has been a running theme through our discussion.

One of the perceived weaknesses of such approaches, however, is that unless they are followed through in a concerted fashion in society, they can be ineffective. Paper and glass recycling points are common sights in many cities currently, but they have not in themselves made a large impression on the environment. Partially this is because they are not universally used, and partially because the volumes are small in comparison with corporate waste.

We have seen examples of government regulation of corporate environmental behaviour, as well as government-inspired standards intended to directly reduce environmental problems. However, the free-market environmentalist camp argues that these problems are actually the *result* of defects in law and government regulation. On this view, a negative consequence such as the air pollution resulting from a company burning lots of fossil fuels should be transformed into a direct cost to the company by the polluter pays principle – the argument being that the company has had the direct benefit of using clean air to 'wash' out its waste gas, and therefore this should be accounted for within the company's profits. In an early example of environmental economics, Ronald Coase argued that the process of attributing such costs to those firms that incur them (thus making them internal costs for that firm) would drive greater efficiency and thus provide a financial incentive for greater environmental responsibility.[18] Some have gone further and argued that natural resources will always have a potential to

ETHICS IN PRACTICE

THE CANBERRA ELECTRICITY FEED-IN SCHEME

In common with other states in Australia, the government of the Australian Capital Territory surrounding Canberra (ACT) operates an electricity purchase scheme, whereby domestic homes that generate solar energy may sell this to the electricity grid at an appropriate rate per watt.

Unlike other schemes, which pay users for the surplus energy they generate, the ACT pays users at a premium rate for *all* the energy they generate, selling electricity back to the consumer at the standard rate. This 'feed-in' scheme treats each domestic solar generator as in effect a component of the electricity network.

How fair is this on consumers? Would they be better off with a buy-back scheme?

experience a 'tragedy of the commons' unless in private ownership, when the owner will have an incentive to maintain and encourage the long-term value of the resource.[19]

There are various government attempts to regulate corporate environmental responsibility, though these are themselves problematic. For example, led by Finland, a number of northern European countries have introduced carbon taxes as a means of controlling emissions. However, this does not take account of the complexity of the chemistry of carbon in the atmosphere, placing the full economic cost of carbon emission on the originator of the emission, but not taking account of contributory influences of other actors (e.g. suppliers of materials that may lead to greater levels of emissions). Carbon elimination is not a uniform matter in any case. Due to differences in prices of many items across country boundaries, the cost of eliminating a tonne of carbon dioxide in one country may be significantly different from in another country. So there may be an incentive for a company operating in one country to reduce its carbon emissions, while not for its operations in another country.

Trading approaches

The theoretical basis of reduction strategies is clear and uncontroversial, even though it may lead to difficult assessments in practice. In contrast, the more recent development of trading-based responses to environmental issues has generated a substantial degree of dispute, with pro- and anti-environmentalists on each side of the debate as to whether trading is an appropriate way forward.

The trading alternative to direct taxation or regulatory control is to create *market mechanisms* to control emissions that cut across country boundaries. The primary market mechanism that has been set up to control environmental pollution is the phenomenon of emissions trading, established as a provision of the Kyoto Protocol.

Essentially the basic idea of emissions trading is that countries[20] are allocated certain allowances to carry out a certain activity – such as the emission of gases into the atmosphere – up to a certain limit. Each country has the opportunity either to make full use of its allowance, or, should it not use all the allowance, it can 'sell' its allowance to another country – in effect it transfers, for a price, the unused part of its allowance to some other country that may have used all of its own allowance and wishes to use more. While carbon trading has received the greatest attention, there are trading systems for other gases such as nitrogen oxide, as well as for other environmental issues such as water quality.

The process clearly involves several potentially controversial steps. The allocation of emissions allowances is based on political and economic decisions on the part of the Kyoto signatories, which can be argued to reflect the interests of the more powerful economies at the expense of the weaker ones. Many of the largest energy-consuming companies, and their governments, have lobbied hard to get a system that is generous to them. Carbon limits and pricing have therefore not yet made significant impact on the total volume of emission of CO_2 into the ecosphere.

There are further issues with environmental trading. The market exists because of global inequalities. Should the developing countries reach similar production levels to the developed, then there will be little or no differences in carbon usage, and therefore no imbalances to trade against. Also, the really poor populations of the world, with less access to infrastructure and major processing capability, are not in a position to enter the carbon trading process. However, their less deprived country-people, already perhaps disproportionately affluent, may well take the financial benefits of carbon trading.[21] So trading might alleviate the environment at the cost of increasing global poverty.

Yet another criticism is that the 'price' of an emissions credit may look like a free-market issue, but the players are not equal in power. For an underdeveloped country, the opportunity to get foreign currency such as dollars or euros is a critical requirement for international trade. For the more developed country, the difficulty of operating on a lower level of emissions may be annoying, and clearly represent some degree of financial costs, but the stronger economy will have other resources and facilities at its disposal that could, in extremis, be used to offset the emissions – for example, switching from fossil fuels to nuclear, or buying energy directly from other countries without attempting to generate it internally.

As with carbon taxation, the costs of eliminating emissions varies between countries, depending on their technological development, on the national stock of other resources, and even on the skill-base of the workforce. However, credits may be bought from other countries as an alternative to the search for more efficient modes of production. So the trading system may mask or even undermine the efficiencies that are normally held to be associated with markets. Similar points about the potential inefficiency of credit-based systems have been made relating to energy trading credits within one national boundary.[22]

George Monbiot has offered a different strand of argument with the current approach to carbon trading. He sidesteps the technical, consequentialist arguments about efficiencies. Instead he offers the point that if one were to take trading seriously, then the underlying cost–benefit analysis might lead a company – or a government – to deliberately aim for the environmentally damaging course of action, if this were shown to be cost-effective compared to more responsible actions. In other words, using cost and price as a basis for re-forming the use of carbon around the globe could well backfire:

> So, for instance, in the Stern report, we saw Sir Nicholas Stern costing everything from the price of eggs to human life and producing a social cost of carbon of $30/ ton.... the unacknowledged and unrecognized consequence of his methodology is that if it turns out that the dollar profits to be made from burning fossil fuels are greater than the dollar losses identified as a result of climate change, under his methodology, you then conclude that it makes economic sense to kill people.[23]

One might question Monbiot's assumption here, that dollar profits would outweigh the losses, but his point is only superficially about the detail of financial comparisons. Under-pinning this is a deontological position regarding the way human life is valued in economic

THINKING CRITICALLY ABOUT ETHICS

ENVIRONMENTAL 'TRIAGE'

An additional environmentally related decision is to adopt a *triage* strategy with respect to environmental problems. This is based on the concept used in hospital emergency facilities, where a decision is made about where action will be most effective. Priority is given to the cases where action has the best chances of success. Crudely, a patient who is most likely to die gets less treatment than one where there is a good chance of survival.

By analogy, in dealing with species extinction, environmental triage would focus attention on species where there is a good chance of rescuing them from extinction. Species that are at extreme risk of extinction might be 'sacrificed' so that conservation resources are focused where they may have the best chance of success.

Are there any other ethical considerations that should be taken into account in deciding which species might be saved and which left to go extinct?

terms. This is a philosophical argument rather than a technical one. But it underlines that the debate on trading reflects once more a partial, one-sided perspective on what is valuable in society.

Emissions trading has been established as part of the Kyoto Protocol, and will be part of the future of environmental management for some decades to come. However, as the above discussion indicates, it is itself problematic, and arguably will not provide the key incentives to reduce pollution, but simply spread the liability more evenly around the globe. Perhaps, then, the more incisive response may after all be the more extreme free-market view, whereby it is the enforcement of property and liability legislation that will lead to an effective market mechanism to control environmental responsibility.

ENVIRONMENTAL MEASUREMENT AND MANAGEMENT

In the previous section we looked briefly at two key types of action that might be taken to reduce environmental deterioration. In practice the most common, and most effective, act that an organization can take is to measure its environmental performance. Measurement is a standard way to assess performance and then evaluate the success of other environmental decisions. It also has the advantage of certifying levels of performance, as well as making the process of becoming greener more transparent to all stakeholders. We will look briefly at some approaches, but this is inevitably highly selective.

In general, the measurement of environmental performance occurs within a range of contextual factors:

- national and trans-national legislation
- the dynamics of a particular industry and the inclinations of its key players
- the implications of specific environmental outcomes on performance and, for a profit-seeking firm, on competitiveness
- the levels of resource that enable such measurement
- the social structures within which such measurement is carried out and disseminated to society at large.

Unsurprisingly, perhaps the most influential factors have been the development of legislation encouraging or even requiring environmental measurement, and the impact on environmental factors on competitiveness. Government facilitation is crucially dependent on international competitiveness, on general prosperity and on available infrastructure. To take one example, India, one of the two fastest growing economies in the world in the 2000s, has been perceived as only having slowly developed environmental practices.[24] Part of this is reflected in the lower number of ISO 14000 registrations in India as compared with China, though this in turn probably reflects the rapid growth of the urban poor population, and thus the urban micro-business sector, in India. But in general India is a country with dispersed political power, some of which resides as much in individual states as in central government. In contrast, China, though not regarded as so environmentally conscious as its neighbour, has a more centralized government with more sweeping nationwide powers – hence decisions about issues such as ISO 14000 have a wider and more direct impact than in India where there would be greater debate over the issue.[25]

Environmental reporting works differently in different industries. For example, Bolivar, in a study of how Spanish firms used the internet for environmental reporting, found that his two sample industries (the resource and the utilities industries) behaved quite differently in terms of areas such as interaction with the public over environmental reports or disclosure of internal mechanisms such as corporate environmental codes.[26] Similarly, Ramus and Montiel found significant variations industry-wide between services, manufacturing, and oil and gas.[27] One source of explanation for such variations may be found in institutional theory[28] – essentially one would expect players in the same industry to perform similarly with respect to an issue such as the environment because they are subject to the same institutional forces: the same lobby and pressure groups, the same government departments, the same nexus of the 'five forces' of the industry. This may go some way towards explaining differences, but not entirely. Pulver,[29] for example, found that within the oil production industry there was a clear split with respect to environmental policy between ExxonMobil and others on the one hand, and BP and Royal Dutch Shell on the other, with the former players set on a policy of non-response to the environmental lobby, and the latter on greater cooperation and substantial investment in renewable energy. But crucially this was *not* based on institutional pressures or even on operating and commercial needs. Rather it was explained in terms of the manner in which different threads of scientific knowledge were incorporated into the respective firms' internal decision processes – essentially, then, the difference between these players in the same industry was determined by the differences in the scientific networks that the key executives in these companies were involved with.

Environmental measurement can bring a range of advantages for an organization, including:

- demonstration of progress towards achievement of environmental targets
- demonstration of compliance with external goals set by governments and industry-wide consortia
- collection of examples of practice as a means of organizational learning
- identification of areas for further attention and improvement.

In carrying out environmental measurements and reporting, a range of steps for collecting information and interpreting it for action will tend to reflect general methods for measuring and improving organizational performance. It has been noted that ISO 14000, the international environmental standard, is based on ISO 9000, the international standard for quality in general.[30] In that respect this emphasizes that environmental management in general is not different in kind from general operational management, and that the key issue is primarily one of intentions and ends rather than of systems or processes.

In addition, as Young and others have pointed out,[31] measurement requires certain preliminary elements, such as the identification of aspects that are measurable, selection of measures that are comprehensible to the target audience, and that are appropriate over a sufficient timescale to allow management actions to be implemented and themselves evaluated. These are not value-neutral matters. The selection of one measure over another is an indication, even in some cases a determination, of key priorities. A common adage in the area of organizational measurement is that '... what gets measured gets managed', that is that targets are only ever expressed in terms of how they can be measured, and it is only what is targeted that receives significant managerial attention. So measurement is not only a means of finding out about an organization, it is also a way to fix what will receive managerial attention. Also, the decision about how the results of this may be disseminated and communicated is at the same time a choice as to how the firm will engage with its audiences and markets. So the decision of a firm such as BP to include material from its environmental self-evaluations in advertisements reflects not only a desire to have environmental responsibility associated with the BP brand but also to present the firm to the public as one capable of bearing scrutiny in this respect.

There are several approaches to environmental measurement and evaluation, including:

- Environmental auditing: the regular, formal collection of information to evaluate environmental performance, covering key processes across the whole value chain.

- Environmental impact assessment (EIA): data collection similar to auditing, but often with a future perspective to help evaluate proposed projects.

- Life-cycle assessment: '. . . an analysis covering every stage and every significant environmental impact of a product from the extraction and use of raw materials through to the eventual disposal of the components of the products and their decomposition back to the elements.'[32]

These tend to adopt similar processes – formally structured data collection instruments covering inputs and/or outputs across a range of factors relevant to the process model of the organization. Reports tend to be technical in nature, but this can mask the ability of key players such as senior directors to ensure that the questions that get asked are the ones that they would like asked. One disadvantage about these approaches is that the structures tend to be imposed from without, and reflect the interests of a narrow group of stakeholders. The interests of customers or affected communities are often dealt with not in terms of what they actually feel but in terms of the processes that the organization adopts to consult – in other words a top-down approach rather than an inclusive one.

Ecological footprint

Related with these measurement methods is the idea of an ecological footprint. 'Footprint' is less a methodology of collecting data than a way of representing and interpreting data once collected. Two versions of this are commonly used: carbon footprint and ecological footprint. In each case an attempt is made to express the aggregate of environmental demands in terms of a single index value – in the first case of output of carbon dioxide, and in the second a more comprehensive estimate of consumption of land. Such a measure can therefore provide quick comparisons between land use in, say, urban France and in rural Australia.[33] This is therefore very convenient for public education. The ecological footprint represents the amount of land that would be required to sustain a given lifestyle or production of a particular item – so this includes not only the land necessary for production, but also that required to cope with outputs such as carbon dioxide from air travel.

Inevitably there are potential shortcomings of such a measure – assumptions of technology used to absorb carbon emissions, or the incommensurability of different regional environmental inputs. However, the concept can provide a valuable snapshot to stimulate further investigation. In its more developed forms ecological footprint can thus provide a view of the full supply chain involved in the production of a good or service.

Footprint is one of a whole raft of indexes that can cover many different aspects of ecological sustainability – species persistence, consumption of specific resources. As Singh points out,[34] however, most of these indexes tend to focus on either environmental, economic or social aspects of sustainability, whereas in terms of managing human activity in order to protect the environment all three need to be seen, and thus evaluated, as integrated systems. Footprint, in contrast, can provide a general means of making overall comparisons between corporations, industries, individual domestic units and even whole nations.

Standardized environmental management tools

Environmental management systems (EMS) have become a growth industry in recent years, with consultancies aplenty providing methodologies and frameworks. There are several similar key benchmark systems in common use, such as the European Eco-Management and Audit Scheme (EMAS) and the International standard ISO 14000.

One kind of approach that does differ from these more process-oriented systems is the inclusive strategy adopted by the Netherlands Environmental Assessment Agency, as described by de Vries and others.[35] This approach does not address the specific activities of firms on a predefined set of dimensions or measures. Rather it is based on a distillation of the views of a wide range of stakeholders as to the key areas, which are brought together as scenarios, and then used as a basis for environmental policies. Although the model is presented by de Vries as a policy-driving mechanism, it can also be seen as a firm-regulating methodology: the firm can identify the stakeholders it wishes to work with, and then allow their views to generate views and scenarios that then can be used to evaluate proposed strategic options.

At the time of writing there is no evidence that this has been carried out by companies as yet, but it remains an interesting possibility. One of the key merits of such an approach is that it overcomes the potential objection to much environmental management that it is too 'top-down' – that is that there is a disconnect between those who take environmental protection action and those on whose behalf the actions are taken. We have seen one version of this issue with the 'colonial' discussion. It has been raised in other contexts, too – Carolan[36] has asked the simple question, 'Whose nature are we preserving?' with the unstated implication that not all stakeholder groups will have the same view on what needs to be protected. Taking full account of a stakeholder-wide perspective environmental management is on this approach a key objective, one that is absent from some of the schemes discussed below.

The ISO 14000 family of standards covers a wide range of distinct aspects of an EMS, including auditing and LCA, plus labelling, product specification and performance evaluation (what are not explicit here, although covered in the detail particularly of the auditing standards, are environmental *actions* – matters such as energy efficiency and discharge/waste management). Central to this family of standards is ISO 14001, which specifies the requirements for an effective environmental management policy. This builds on the international quality standard ISP 9000 which requires the formulation and implementation of a quality policy.

The Eco-Management and Auditing Scheme (EMAS) was developed in the 1990s by the European Union. It provides specifically that organizations conduct the following:

- environmental review
- establish an effective EMS
- carry out environmental auditing
- provide a publicly accessible statement of environmental performance.

It is important to note that standards such as EMAS or ISO 14000 are, in legal terms, voluntary. No organization is bound to seek these. However, the government in many countries can act as an influence over environmental responsibility beyond its role as a legislator. For example, a government procurement policy may specify that companies wishing to tender for government contracts are required to have ISO registration.

ISO 14001 and EMAS in their different ways require transparency of information with respect to policy and implementation, for the advantage of a wide range of stakeholders.

Transparency may have PR and reputation-building appeal for corporations, but may also have reputation-destructive potential, and represent an additional cost to be set against profits. Not surprisingly firms often use several strategies to manage EMS-related information to enhance their reputations and to minimize damage to the same. In a study of Spanish firms and their response to legal environmental reporting requirements, Criado-Jimenez[37] and others, taking an *impression management* perspective, found that firms will, in order to improve their position vis-à-vis their more powerful stakeholders, use different techniques depending on circumstances. For example, as well as simple non-compliance, companies may adopt passive acquiescence, avoidance by concealing non-compliance, or they may directly challenge standards by dismissing the legitimacy of such regulations. In general, Criado-Jimenez found that there was more emphasis placed on concealment rather than outright challenge (and one could speculate that this might partially be because the latter carries an element of risk that the firm might lose the argument and thus be forced to comply with regulation).

Scientific drawbacks to environmental measurement

Measurement in this area is not without its difficulties, however. It is relatively straightforward to define (though not necessarily to implement) some human-impacting measures, such as air, noise or water pollution, or the loss of species that are highly human-visible, such as the panda. But the eco-system is highly complex, with high levels of integration of causalities, which can lead to so-called 'butterfly' and 'catastrophe' effects – phenomena that arise from highly complex systems that, while determinate, are too complex for human beings to properly comprehend.

Shaw gives a good example of the kind of integrated and systematic knock-on effects in the natural environment:[38] in the 1990s wolves were reintroduced into the US Yellowstone Park, after a long period of absence. When this happened, the elk that the wolves naturally preyed upon moved for safety on to higher ground, which then meant that the places they had formerly used for grazing and now relinquished became more conducive to the growth of certain trees (aspen and cottonwoods primarily), which in turn stabilized river banks, which led to reduced river water temperature, which in its turn led to increased numbers of river trout. Other consequential effects, such as changes in the balance of coyotes, songbirds and rodents, can also be traced to the reintroduction of the wolves. One change that on the face of it might have only limited impact, but led to a whole raft of associated changes.

The above example is of a single change and its impact on a complex system. But human activity may be making several changes simultaneously, and some of these may, when combined, lead to what is called a 'cocktail' effect: namely that one change accentuates the impact of another.[39] Chemicals are known to interact significantly – carcinogens occurring

ETHICS AND YOU

CARRYING OUT ENVIRONMENTAL ASSESSMENTS

You are the manager of a national subsidiary of a global marketing firm. What managerial steps do you need to take in order to plan for an effective environmental assessment of the firm's carbon footprint?

What might be strategic challenges resulting from the outcome of such an assessment? What internal processes are needed to ensure that the firm draws the full benefit from the assessment?

ETHICS AND YOU

A DILEMMA

ABC Corp produces a chemical that on its own is relatively inert, but can produce an extremely toxic gas when it comes into contact with certain rare metals. There are no known applications than might create such a risk. On standard measures the process comes out as sound. It would be easy not to make any mention of the potential toxicity to potential client firms, and to disclose the risk could make clients nervous. On the other hand, not doing so would be highly negligent should, by some mistake, the chemical be applied to the metals in question.

Can you get out of this dilemma without prejudicing the health of others or the sales of your firm?

at low levels in some foods, for example, are known to become more dangerous when interacting with chemicals found in other foods. Furthermore, chemicals and physical changes when combined may also have some degree of cocktail effect. Combinations of chemicals or physical changes can also reduce an effect. The complexity of the systems, and the corresponding complexity of the science involved, has made the debate over this particular aspect of pollution difficult to resolve to a sufficient degree to provide a clear guide for corporate action.

Cocktail, butterfly and catastrophic phenomena all indicate that there may be unpredictability (on a human scale, not a logical one) in even highly deterministic systems. This therefore creates a difficulty for the practices of environmental measurement discussed previously. For one thing, it suggests that until humans have a much more comprehensive knowledge of all outputs of our activity, we cannot be that confident of the collective impacts of our lifestyles on the natural world. Measurement presumes some stability in order for appropriate changes in one variable to be a useful indicator of changes in one or more other variables. This stability may be theoretical, or (as in the case of measurement of length) be a physical reference point. But until there is a clear understanding of how the key environmental variables change, environmental measurement will remain problematic.

The precautionary principle applies here, therefore. In this context, then, this implies that while we do not know what is going on clearly, until we do it is safe to assume that there are serious issues to be resolved. Organizations engaging in economic activity of whatever kind, therefore, may need to adopt much wider data-collection policies, in order to be able to make reasonable estimates of the likely effects of their actions. Governments may need to require much higher levels of data collection and data integration in order to be able to interpret the trends in human-generated changes in the eco-sphere. The costs of this are substantial, and are one of the reasons offered earlier why corporations would naturally seek to avoid what they would regard as excessive environmental measurement. However, given both the 'polluter pays' and precautionary principles it naturally behoves firms to take steps to reduce their exposure to future liabilities.

SUMMARY

■ There is a duality of influence on the environment on the part of government – as legislator but also as employer, purchaser and investor.

- The free-market environmental position has provided a series of strong arguments in favour of specific kinds of response to the question of how to create greater environmental responsibility.

- Measurement is highly problematic in this field, and social practices play a significant role as well as corporate ones in the many different approaches taken to this task.

- A further issue is how democratic environmental protection is – do all stakeholders have sufficient say in the process?

- There is a 'colonial' question that environmental management as currently conceived seems almost to require a continued disparity in wealth between the north and the south.

One continuing theme in this discussion has been the interdependence between what might be called the 'macro' considerations – the corporate social responsibility, if you will, as opposed to the 'micro' ones, the ethical motives and choices of individuals and groups. Sound environmental practice clearly requires both.

QUICK REVIEW QUESTIONS:

1 What are the underlying assumptions of the 'polluter pays' principle?

2 What arguments would you adopt to persuade a manufacturing firm to adopt the precautionary principle?

3 What are the main arguments *against* emissions trading systems?

CASE STUDY: CARREFOUR GOES GREEN IN CHINA

Carrefour is the second largest retailer in the world after Walmart. It has stores in more than 30 countries and generated a net income of €1.9 million in 2007. It employs almost half a million people across over 15,000 stores in Europe, Asia and Latin America. In the future, it seeks to expand its operations in large national markets including China, Indonesia, Brazil and Turkey.

Carrefour entered China in 1995 with the opening of a store in Beijing. Despite the novelty of the idea of supermarkets in the country, Carrefour expanded its presence relatively quickly and operated more than 70 stores by 2006. The stores were a successful mix of East and West in the sense that they combined the Western concept of a clean and well lit store with checkout counters, with the Eastern variety and freshness of food. Carrefour's strategy of working together with local partners

was also successful in avoiding regulation targeted at foreign companies.

Location is important for retail stores as shoppers often become regular uses of stores that are closest to them or otherwise conveniently located and this is why retailers often own the land on which their stores are built. In China, Carrefour decided to work together with local partners despite the importance of store location. Instead of owning the land and buildings itself, Carrefour found local partners that owned the land and the buildings, while holding ownership of the display equipment, lighting, refrigeration systems, and other fixtures and fittings inside the buildings.

When Carrefour first entered China, green issues were not high on the agenda of the Chinese government. Over time, however, the government has become increasingly sensitive to environmental issues as a result of increasing consumption of energy and the reliance of the country on foreign sources of energy. Also, due to the exchange rate between the US dollar and the yuan, imports from foreign countries are relatively expensive and raise the overall cost of energy in China. As a result, the Chinese government issued new regulation in 2006 on the energy efficiency of new construction projects. China's engagement in international organizations and events including the World Trade Organization and the Olympics has also increased its awareness of environmental issues.

Despite the legislation on energy efficiency in the construction sector, reality of aggressive developers, lack of technological knowledge, expensive materials and corruption have made the implementation of the regulation weak. In the retail sector, the owner of the land and builder of the facilities would pay for the cost of green features, while the benefits of lower energy consumption are assumed by the tenant. As a result, the local developers have few incentives to fight the hurdles of building greener stores and it is widely believed that the new buildings do not meet the international standards of green technology.

Meanwhile, Carrefour has been increasingly targeted by environmental groups. This attention on Carrefour and other well-known retailers does not only concern their operations in Western countries but also in emerging economies such as China. For example, Greenpeace has found genetically engineered rice from Carrefour stores in China and demanded that the company takes immediate action on the issue. Concerns have also been raised by local residents living close to large stores about the noise and air pollution caused by the proximity of supermarkets.

At the same time, Carrefour has begun to pay more attention to the cost of the energy it is using to run its operations. Even though energy costs do not constitute a high proportion of the company's turnover, the increasing price of energy is starting to influence the low profit margins found in retailing. Several studies have showed that energy efficiency has a significant impact on the profitability of the sector. As a result, Carrefour has started testing different energy saving solutions across its stores in different countries. For example, it has tried the use of solar panels in Spain. Moreover, in 2006, it formed a new department with a mandate to bring the different initiatives and solutions together into a new corporate-wide strategy on sustainability. It also announced the opening of a new 'Green Store' in Beijing, China. The store would use renewable sources of energy and the most advanced technologies available to reduce energy consumption. These plans were implemented through a mix of 'green' equipment, energy management systems and building design.

Carrefour was not alone in seeking to introduce more environmentally friendly stores in China. Other foreign retailers in the country were also taking steps to make their business greener. The local competitors were slower to adopt environmentally friendly policies, but some of them had started to launch initiatives that reflected their increasing awareness of environmental issues, although this was limited by their lack of experience and focus on market share and financial performance.

STUDY QUESTIONS

1 What kinds of measures of environmental responsibility would you suggest Carrefour use? What would be the strengths and the drawbacks of your choice?

2 How can Carrefour best manage its supply chain in China and other regions to maximize environmental performance?

3 Does Carrefour involve all its key stakeholders sufficiently in its attempts to be more environmentally responsible?

SOURCES

Carrefour 2009. Available from http://www.carrefour.com, accessed 9 March 2009.

Schotter, A., Beamish, P. and Klassen, R. 2008. *Carrefour China: Building a Greener Store.* Richard Ivey School of Business, The University of Western Ontario, Canada.

NOTES

1. For example, Cairncross (1995).
2. Beaumont *et al.* (1994); Hutchinson & Hutchinson (1997); Welford (1996).
3. Raffensperger and Tickner (1999).
4. Carolan (2007).
5. IIFCC (2000).
6. Breidlid (2009). See also Odora Hoppers (2002).
7. Much as religion was held to be relevant to science in pre-Renaissance Christianity, and, in different ways, in some versions of Islam.
8. United Nations (2002).
9. Holzer (2008).
10. Whiteman (2009).
11. For example, Antunes *et al.* (2008) examined five water projects in Europe and concluded that '...the purpose of participation was still limited to providing accountability rather than contributing to the substance of policy. The real impacts of participation stood only for the minimum required level of informing the public; there was no true involvement and collaboration of the interested parties in the evaluation processes.'
12. Noorgaard (2006).
13. Kotchen *et al.* (2009).
14. Sharfman *et al.* (2004).
15. Daily *et al.* (2008).
16. Maguire and Hardy (2006).
17. See Karger and Hennings (2007).
18. For which he received the Nobel Prize for Economics in 1991. Cf. Coase (1960).
19. A well-established online source of free-market environmentalism may be found at *The Commons Blog* (http://commonsblog.org/about_commons.php).
20. At least, those countries that have signed up to the Kyoto Protocol.
21. For a discussion of these and related issues, cf. Lohmann (2007).
22. See Singh (2007) for a discussion of energy credit systems in India and potential inefficiencies.
23. Quoted in Wittneben (2008).
24. A useful overview of environmental development in India may be found in Sawhney (2004).
25. We do not intend to suggest that China is more environmentally responsible than India in general, simply to note the variance in one key environmental element.
26. Bolivar (2007).
27. Ramus and Montiel (2005).
28. See, for example, DiMaggio and Powell (1983).
29. Pulver (2007).
30. Which in turn is derived from the principles of quality management advocated by Deming.
31. Young (1996).
32. Welford (1996).
33. Wood and Garnett (2009) provide an interesting application of this concept to indigenous people in northern Australia.
34. Singh *et al.* (2008).
35. de Vries and Petersen (2009), though the two authors freely acknowledge the cooperation of others in their modelling.
36. Carolan (2006).
37. Criado-Jimenez *et al.* (2008).
38. Shaw (2005), p. 402.
39. So-called to reflect the fact that in alcoholic cocktails the mixing of different kinds of alcohol can multiply the intoxicating effect by a factor greater than simply the addition of the amounts of alcohol in themselves.

REFERENCES

Antunes, P. *et al.* 2009. Participation and evaluation for sustainable river basin governance. *Ecological Economics*, Vol. 68, 931–939.

Beaumont, J., Pedersen, L. and Whitaker, B. 1994. *Managing the Environment.* Butterworth-Heinemann.

Bolivar, M. 2007. Evaluating Corporate Environmental Reporting on the Internet: The Utility and Resource Industries in Spain Business and Society. Sage OnlineFirst, August 2007.

Breidlid, A. 2009. Culture, indigenous knowledge systems and sustainable development: A critical view of education in an African context. *International Journal of Educational Development*, Vol. 29, 140–148.

Cairncross, F. 1995. *Green Inc.* Earthscan.

Carolan, M. 2006. Conserving nature, but to what end? *Organization and Environment*, Vol. 19, 153–170.

Carolan, M. 2007. The precautionary principle and traditional risk assessment. *Organization and Environment*, Vol. 20, 5–24.

Coase, R. 1960. The Problem of Social Cost. *Journal of Law and Economics*, Vol. 3, No. 1, 1–44.

Crabtree, L. and Hes, D. 2009. Sustainability uptake in housing in metropolitan Australia: An institutional problem, not a technical one. *Housing Studies*, Vol. 24, 203–224.

Criado-Jimenez, I. *et al.* 2008. Compliance with Mandatory Environmental Reporting in Financial Statement: The Case of Spain. *Journal of Business Ethics*, Vol. 79, 245–262.

Daily, B., Bishop, J. and Govindarajulu, N. 2008. A conceptual model for organizational citizenship behaviour directed toward the environment. *Business and Society*. Sage OnlineFirst March 2008.

de Vries, B. and Petersen, A. 2009. Conceptualising sustainable development. *Ecological Economics*, Vol. 68, 1006–1019.

DiMaggio, P.W. and Powell, W.W. 1983. The iron cage revisited: Institutional isomorphism and collective rationality in organizational fields. *American Sociological Review*, Vol. 48, 147–160.

Food Standards Agency 2002. *Review of the Risk Assessment of Mixtures of Pesticides and Similar Substances*. HMSO.

Holzer, B. 2008. Turning Stakeseekers Into Stakeholders. *Business and Society*, Vol. 47, No. 1, 50–67.

Hutchinson, A, and Hutchinson, F. 1997. *Environmental Business Management*. New York: McGraw-Hill.

IIFCC 2000. Proceedings of the Second International Indigenous Forum on Climate Change.

Karger, C. and Hennings, W. 2007. Sustainability evaluation of decentralised electricity generation. *Renewable and Sustainable Energy Reviews*, Vol. 13, 583–593.

Kotchen, M. *et al.* 2009. Pharmaceuticals in wastewater: Behavior, preferences, and willingness to pay for a disposal program. *Journal of Environmental Management*, Vol. 90, 1476–1482.

Lohmann, L. (ed) 2007. *Carbon Trading*. Dag Hammerskjold Foundation.

Maguire, S. and Hardy, C. 2006. The emergence of new global institutions: A discursive perspective. *Organization Studies*, Vol. 27, 7–29.

Noorgaard, K. 2006. We don't really want to know. *Organization and Environment*, Vol. 19, 347–370.

Odora Hoppers, C. (ed) 2002. *Indigenous Knowledge and the Integration of Knowledge Systems*. New Africa Books.

Ortiz, O. *et al.* 2009. Sustainability based on LCM of residential dwellings: A case study in Catalonia, Spain. *Building and Environment*, Vol. 44, 584–594.

Pulver, S. 2007. Making Sense of Corporate Environmentalism. *Organization and Environment*, Vol. 20, 44–83.

Raffensperger, C. and Tickner, J. (eds) 1999. *Protecting Public Health and the Environment: Implementing the Precautionary Principle*. Island Press.

Ramus, C. and Montiel, I. 2005. When are corporate environmental policies a form of greenwashing? *Business and Society*, Vol. 44, No. 4, 377–414.

Roberts, P. 1995. *Environmentally Sustainable Business*. Paul Chapman Publishing.

Sawhney, A. 2004. *Environmental Management Problems in India*. Ashgate Publishing.

Sharfman, M. P. *et al.* 2004. A model of the global and institutional antecedents of high level corporate environmental performance. *Business in Society*, Vol. 43, No. 1, 6–36.

Shaw, W. 2005. *Business Ethics*. Belmont: Thompson Wadsworth.

Singh, A. 2007. A market for renewable energy credits in the Indian power sector. *Renewable and Sustainable Energy Reviews*, Vol. 13, 643–652.

Singh, R. K. *et al.* 2008. An overview of sustainability assessment methodologies. *Ecological Indicators*, Vol. 9, 189–212.

Stewart, I. 1990. *Does God Play Dice? The Mathematics of Chaos*. Blackwell.

United Nations 2002. *Declaration on Sustainable Development* ('Johannesburg Declaration') UN.

Welford, R. (ed) 1996. *Corporate Environmental Management*. Earthscan.

Whiteman, G. 2009. All my relations. *Organization Studies*, Vol. 30, 101–120.

Wittneben, B. 2008. George Monbiot on management research and climate change. *Organization and Environment*, Vol. 26, 76–81.

Wood, R. and Garnett, S. 2009. An assessment of environmental sustainability in Northern Australia using the ecological footprint and with reference to indigenous populations and remoteness. *Ecological Economics*, Vol. 68, 1375–1384.

Young, C. W. 1996. Measuring Environmental Performance in Welford, R. (ed), *Corporate Environmental Management*. Earthscan.

GIVING BACK TO SOCIETY

LEARNING OBJECTIVES

After studying this chapter you should be able to:

- Explain how corporate charitable activity has evolved over time.
- Describe the phenomenon of strategic philanthropy and identify some of the controversies surrounding the trend.
- Explain why some companies donate more strategically than others.
- Discuss the drivers and main forms of employer-supported volunteering.
- Describe the concrete programmes that companies carry out in local communities and evaluate the criticism that has been presented about these projects.

INTRODUCTION

It has been established in previous chapters that companies engage in many ways with their surrounding communities. Until now, the focus has been on how businesses can be managed in a responsible way in terms of their internal policies and business-related processes such as supply chain management. In this last chapter we will examine the specific ways in which the private sector has used its resources to 'give back to society'. The chapter starts with a brief overview of the history of philanthropy, before discussing how corporate philanthropy has become more strategic and professional over time. Cash and in-kind donations are then reviewed as the main forms of corporate philanthropy. The chapter concludes with an examination of employee volunteering and other ways in which companies have engaged in a more active way with communities.

OVERVIEW OF CORPORATE PHILANTHROPY

Corporations and business leaders have donated substantial sums of money to charitable causes for hundreds of years. With the coming of the industrial revolution, many businessmen of the 19th century were well known for their charitable giving and became important philanthropists, donating money to diverse social causes. Charitable giving was important because charities and the church were the main providers of welfare services until the state assumed the function at the beginning of the 20th century. Those with no family or with strong religious beliefs were particularly likely to donate large sums of money to charity. For example, George Cadbury (1839–1922), owner of a chocolate factory in the United Kingdom, became an important bene-factor driven by the principles of the Quaker religion. He donated a large part of his personal fortune to charitable causes and established Bourneville, a village that provided a leafy altern-ative to the congested and unhealthy housing available for the working class in the city.[1]

Many early business leaders believed that the interests of society and business were interlinked and that companies could only thrive in affluent societies. The underlying motivation behind Ford Motor Company's 'five dollar a day wage' may thus have been compassion for the workforce, but it also reduced rates of absenteeism and turnover that were threatening the company's competitive position. The wage also enabled Ford to turn its workforce from labour to potential customers. The example of Ford demonstrates the interconnectedness of societal and business interests. The bond was famously highlighted by Charles Wilson, President of General Motors, who was queried about his loyalties when appointed Secretary of Defense in the Eisenhower administration: 'What is good for the United States is good for General Motors'. While one might question whether the motives for such attitudes were consequential in nature or sprang from a more deontological atti-tude, it is clear that they led to substantial corporate contributions to charities.

ETHICS IN PRACTICE

BILL GATES

Bill Gates is well known for founding Microsoft, one of the most successful and largest companies in the world. He has a reputation of being a demanding and confrontational manager who expects his employees to be able to articulate and defend their positions. He has also topped the *Forbes* list of the richest people in the world more than 15 times. In 1999, his personal fortune exceeded US$100 billion. In addition to his business activities, Gates is also an important philanthropist who has made donations worth billions of dol-lars. Many of the donations are channelled via the Bill and Melinda Gates Foundation established in 2000. Gates himself is now working full-time for the foundation after stepping down from the chief executive position at Microsoft in 2000. The foundation focuses on the areas of health and education including HIV and malaria. Compared to other similar organizations, it has a more business-like and transparent approach to charitable work. For example, a benefactor can follow how her money is spent by the foundation.

Sources: BBC News 2004. *Profile: Bill Gates*. Available from http://news.bbc.co.uk/1/hi/business/3428721.stm, accessed 17 July 2009.

Cronin, J. 2005. *Bill Gates: Billionaire philanthropist*. BBC News. Available from http://news.bbc.co.uk/1/hi/business/3913581.stm, accessed 17 July 2009.

Governments took responsibility for the social welfare function only from the beginning of the 20th century when it became clear that the needs of the industrial society could not be addressed by charity alone.[2] Thereafter, instead of simply providing social welfare, charitable organizations often became pioneers in developing solutions to problems such as poverty, homelessness and addiction. They have been particularly well placed to help individuals who have fallen outside normal support services or need only temporary help, but charities have limited reach and resources to tackle more structural and society-wide issues. More recently, the ability of governments to address social problems has weakened and led to the re-privatization of many welfare services. Even though the services may now be based on public policy and legislation, it is increasingly typical that they are delivered by companies or charitable organizations.[3]

The history of corporate giving in the United States shows that corporate philanthropy is not without controversy. Emerging from the Second World War as leaders of the war effort, many American executives saw themselves as 'corporate statesmen' with public responsibilities.[4] Donations were however made by business leaders as private individuals because of legal restrictions that prohibited the involvement of corporations in social affairs. The restrictions had been imposed on business to cut workplace abuses at the end of the 19th century. Moreover, business was not trusted in balancing the interests of diverse societal actors without prioritizing their own. The situation changed only in 1953 when a court ruled against a shareholder who had contested a donation made to Princeton University by a manufacturing company. The ruling legitimized donations to charitable causes and enabled companies to engage in broader programmes of corporate giving. As a consequence, many firms established private foundations through which donations were channelled to a wide variety of causes. The donations were often disconnected from core business activities. Bankers, for example, would give to arts rather than something that was closer to their line of business.[5] The dissociation was welcomed by those who criticized business for deriving benefits from philanthropic donations, but it also eliminated a natural bond between companies and the communities in which they operated.

More recently, the pendulum of corporate giving has swung back to more strategic donations. The pressure on governments to cut public sector spending has resulted in demands for companies to assume a greater role in society. At the same time, shareholders are expecting higher returns on their investments even though competition has increased.[6] As a consequence, companies are becoming progressively more strategic in their giving. Arco, a US petroleum company, was one of the first to adopt a more strategic approach by funding and forming alliances with environmental groups that helped the company to develop responses to green issues. In the absence of similar contacts, Exxon, another US

ETHICS IN PRACTICE

COMMUNITY COMMITMENT AT FALABELLA

Falabella is one of Latin America's biggest retail chains. In 2006 it received prizes for its support for IT in education; it was involved in rehousing people living in deprived camps, supported the national Chilean 'one child – one bed' campaign to eradicate child homelessness, created a number of jobs for disabled people and contributed 200 million pesos (approximately US$500,000) in the national charitable telethon. While these sums are not large in comparison with the firm's turnover, the activities, and the prominence given to them in corporate literature, reflect the importance that many companies around the world are placing on this aspect of their responsibilities.

petroleum firm, was unable to form constructive relationships with environmental activists that criticized the company's management of the Exxon Valdez oil spill in 1989. Until then, the Exxon Education Foundation had been one of the most admired foundations because it had been run independently from the company's business interests.[7]

The important role of business is not limited to Europe and the United States. Other regions have seen similar engagement of business leaders in social welfare. For example, Telemar, a Brazilian company, supplies schools with access to the internet. Between 2004 and 2006, almost 2000 schools benefited from Telemar's help.[8] Similarly, Li Ka-Shing, a well-known businessman in Hong Kong, set up a private foundation to channel money from his many companies to various charitable causes. When SARS broke out in 2003, Li Ka-Shing gave a donation of a million oranges to the local healthcare sector.[9] Finally, the Tata Group, a large Indian conglomerate, gives away between 8 and 14 per cent of its annual net profits to charity.[10] In recognition of the company's long-standing contributions to philanthropic causes, the chairman of the group was awarded the Carnegie Medal of Philanthropy in 2007.

THE OXYMORON OF STRATEGIC PHILANTHROPY

Managers of firms with established and high-value giving programmes believe that philanthropic activities are becoming increasingly strategic.[11] The word 'philanthropy', however, refers to behaviour motivated by concern for others and the society at large. The term 'strategic philanthropy' may therefore seem contradictory by implying that donations to charitable causes should serve other, more strategic goals instead of being motivated by the desire to 'do good'.[12] Should not philanthropy be driven by altruism as opposed to the egotistic pursuit of self-interest suggested by the word 'strategic'? In this section, we will see that strategic philanthropy has come to denote two different types of behaviour. While one of these is in line with the altruistic meaning of the word philanthropy, the other refers to behaviour that is driven by a mix of motives of which altruism is just one.

It was argued earlier in this chapter that companies are facing increasing pressures to align charitable donations with business interests. Charitable giving is hence expected to serve the dual role of advancing both societal and business goals. There are many examples of companies that have done this successfully. Pfizer, for example, has collaborated with non-profit organizations to build infrastructure that allows people in remote communities in developing countries to have access to medicine against trachoma, a preventable cause of blindness. In this way, the company has provided a social benefit by enabling people to obtain medication,

THINKING CRITICALLY ABOUT ETHICS

DOES IT MATTER THAT BUSINESS IS NOT TRULY PHILANTHROPIC?

The word 'philanthropy' originates from ancient Greek where it means love for humanity. In order to be truly philanthropic, corporate giving should therefore be motivated by altruism. Often, however, this is not the case as charitable donations are made for a mix of reasons. Yet, does it matter? What should be the basis on which corporate giving is assessed: underpinning motivations, impact of donations or some other criteria?

STRATEGIC PHILANTHROPY IN PRACTICE

Take a company that you know well, and identify ways in which it might use its competitive advantages to develop strategic philanthropic activities.

What benefits could this bring (a) to communities and (b) to the company?

but it has also gained business benefits by creating an infrastructure that can be used for distributing its other products.[13] Charitable activity can also advance business interests by increasing the company's name recognition, boosting employee morale and productivity, and improving cooperation between business units.[14] Arguably, this type of strategic philanthropy is not in line with the purely altruistic meaning of the word. Instead, it presents corporate giving as something that can be engineered to serve multiple purposes.

In contrast, the term 'strategic philanthropy' has also been used to refer to the general mobilization of corporate resources in support of charitable causes. Accordingly, corporations should 'play a leadership role in social problem solving' and donate not only money but also managerial advice and technological support.[15] In the words of Michael Porter and Mark Kramer (2002), companies should make use of their distinctive strengths to maximize the value of their philanthropic contributions and align their donations with their resources and expertise. For example, Nokia could use its knowledge of telecommunications and mobile technology to help an educational institution to design a programme in the management of telecommunications business. This type of strategic behaviour is in line with the altruistic meaning of the word philanthropy. Instead of aligning business interests with social goals, it asks companies to think how they can make the best use of their resources to advance social goals. In this context, philanthropy is strategic because corporate resources are used in the best possible way for the good of society, not because philanthropy can also advance business objectives.

PATTERNS OF GIVING BEHAVIOUR

There is evidence to suggest that philanthropy becomes more strategic over time as it develops into a more common and customary phenomenon among the business community. In countries where philanthropy is a relatively new phenomenon, patterns of giving seem to reflect the personal interests of managers rather than more strategic business goals.[16] In these contexts, corporate leaders are patrons who seek to gain the goodwill of their workers and the general public by being generous. The patron may, for example, pay for a new football field to win sympathy in the local community.[17] In countries where corporate giving is more established, philanthropy is often an independent organizational function managed by professionals who seek to balance the profit-seeking objectives of their organizations with the needs of the society.[18] From this it follows that the overall approach to philanthropy is more strategic even though the top managers may still have their pet projects and charitable causes that are less clearly aligned with organizational goals.

In general, managers seem to play a role in how corporations approach corporate giving. Research has found that the more discretion a manager has over corporate giving, the more likely it is that his or her individual preferences and qualities influence the size and target of donations. For example, the more highly a manager values service to community, the more generous the corporate donations are[19]. Managers may also prefer to focus on the effectiveness rather than the target of giving. For example, while Bill Gates has consistently donated significant amounts of money to health-related causes, Warren Buffet, a well-known investor and financial expert, gave a sizable proportion of his personal fortune to the Bill and Melinda Gates Foundation because he believed it was well managed.

Some authors suggest that exposure to public scrutiny can be a driver of corporate giving because managers expect charitable donations to create general goodwill and influence.[20] Research provides support for this argument by showing that firms with close ties to the public spend more on philanthropy than firms with less contact with the public.[21] Moreover, it seems that media attention has the greatest impact on rates of giving,[22] though public scrutiny can also result from government attention and civil society pressure. Overall, charitable donations can be seen as a strategic response to public scrutiny. Indeed, managers themselves report being more strategic about their donations when exposed to public attention.[23]

THINKING CRITICALLY ABOUT ETHICS

WHO RECEIVES DONATIONS?

In many countries, religious organizations receive a large proportion of individual and corporate donations (see Figure 14.1). This trend reflects priorities and drivers for charitable giving, but it also raises questions about the impact of donations. What might be some of the concerns people have about donations to religious organizations and what is your personal view on this issue?

FIGURE 14.1 Recipient organizations, 2008

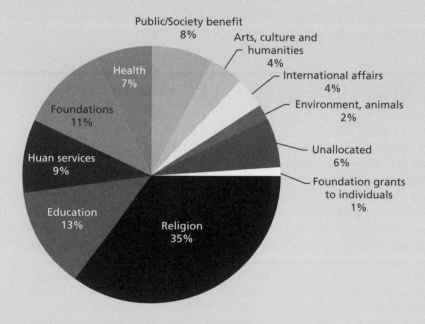

Owning USA 2009: The Annual Report on Philanthropy for the Year 2008.

ETHICS AND YOU

PHILANTHROPY AND RECESSION

How would you encourage a corporation to maintain its level of corporate giving in a time of economic downturn? What strategic benefits could you point to that would persist even when profits are down?

Research also suggests that industry has an effect on corporate giving. One study found that industries with important social and environmental externalities, such as tobacco and alcohol, donate more money to charitable causes than companies in other industries, though this seems to be true for only those companies with a strong consumer focus.[24] The same study finds that companies in emerging industries such as computer software donate less money to charitable causes than companies in more mature industries. Based on this, it can be argued that corporate giving is strategic in the sense that it is the socially and environmentally sensitive industries that are most likely to seek reputational benefits by donating money to charitable causes.

Finally, evidence suggests that charitable donations increase as profit-motivated business expenditures increase.[25] Big spenders are therefore also big spenders in philanthropy! The relationship is particularly strong between philanthropic contributions and advertising expenses, suggesting that companies may expect to gain name recognition and other advertising benefits from donations to charitable causes.[26] No relationship has however been found between the size of donations and financial performance.[27] Instead, donations seem to increase when companies have more resources available in the form of cash flow, making money available and accessible for more discretionary use.[28] It therefore seems that companies 'give back to society' when they have readily available resources to do so.

PHILANTHROPY AS BUSINESS

The rise of strategic philanthropy has taken place in parallel to a more business-like and professional approach to charitable giving. As part of this trend, banks and asset management companies that have started to offer related services and individuals with a financial background have set up consultancies to apply their expertise to philanthropy. For example, some of the largest banks including Citigroup, JP Morgan and UBS provide advice to private and corporate customers on philanthropic investment. The banks offer their services to help donors to identify charities, structure grant agreements and supervise the implementation of arrangements. Some also collect and publish data that can be used for designing philanthropic programmes. For example, New Philanthropy Capital founded by two Goldman Sachs' bankers publishes research reports on subjects such as education, health and communities.[29] One of the main goals of the reports is to ensure that donations go to charities 'with the best results'. New Philanthropy Capital also has a 'charity selector' that helps aspiring philanthropists to find a charity based on a mix of criteria ranging from the social cause to the risk involved in delivering the expected results.

In addition to advice on grant-giving and social causes, more engaged forms of philanthropy have emerged as a result of donors who wish to play a more active role in the charitable sector. Venture philanthropy,[30] for example, is based on the principles of venture capital investment that offer organizations managerial and technical support in addition to

ETHICS IN PRACTICE

PROJECT LOOK!

Project Look! is a non-profit organization that fosters children's understanding of art by working together with schools and galleries in California. It has received support from Social Venture Partners, reputable venture philanthropists in the United States. The venture capitalists invested in Project Look! because of the ambitious leader who sought to professionalize and grow the organization. Social Venture Partners helped by providing management and leadership support, a better technology platform, improved financial and accounting systems and a funding plan. After five years, the budget of Project Look! had doubled from US$400,000 to US$800,000 and it employed a larger staff with strong infrastructure.

Source: Nauffts, M. 2002. Paul Shoemaker, Executive Director, Social Venture Partners. *Venture Philanthropy in a Changed World*, 16 September 2002. Available from http://foundationcenter.org, accessed 17 July 2009.

capital funding and loans. Venture philanthropists seek to build close relationships with the charities they support in order to provide access to resources and expertise that might not otherwise be available to charitable organizations. These philanthropists often sit on the charity's trustee board to monitor their investment and give advice on strategy, marketing and any other expertise that senior managers may benefit from. Similarly to venture capital firms, venture philanthropists seek to engage with smaller and less established charities that aspire to grow and improve the management of their resources. With the help of long-term funding and business-like advice, charities can focus on building their core activities instead of spending time on short-term projects that depend on volatile funding.

Does a more business-like approach to charitable giving then work? Venture philanthropists themselves urge caution as social problems are often less quantifiable and more complex than standard business issues.[31] For example, poverty, child abuse and homelessness are areas where it is particularly challenging to find solutions through business thinking. As a venture philanthropist has noted, 'there is a reason why the market isn't there'.[32] There is also a danger that money is channelled to social causes that are amenable to commercial solutions while other, equally important causes are neglected.[33] It is true that there is room for corporate and private giving to become more efficient and better targeted.[34] Nevertheless, many examples have shown that creativity and innovation originating from the private sector can offer new solutions to old problems.

Finally, philanthropy may have developed into a financial service offered by large banks and asset management companies, but many of the smaller organizations have struggled to make a profit and are themselves supported by generous sponsors. It can therefore be asked whether venture philanthropists are changing philanthropy or whether philanthropy is changing them. Nevertheless, the emergence of support services in philanthropy is a signal of the maturing and professionalization of the field.

CASH AND IN-KIND DONATIONS

Today, corporate giving is an established practice around the world. The largest corporate donors give away hundreds of millions of dollars on an annual basis, as can be seen from Table 14.1. Indeed, cash donations are one of the most important forms of corporate

TABLE 14.1 Top US cash givers

Company	Money given 2002 (US$ millions)
Wal-mart Stores	156.0
Ford Motor	129.8
Altria Group	113.4
SBC Communications	100.0
Exxon Mobil	97.2
Target	87.2
Wells Fargo	82.3
Citigroup	77.8
Verizon Communications	75.0
Pfizer	73.8

Source: *BusinessWeek* 2003. Available from http://www.businessweek.com/magazine/content/ 03_48/b3860617.htm, accessed 11 November 2008. (Ranking is based on data voluntarily submitted by S&P 500 companies.)

philanthropy in addition to in-kind giving and employee volunteering. The target of these donations ranges from local sports clubs and nationwide programmes to international development projects. The latest trend involves an increasing number of companies making donations to inter-governmental organizations including the World Health Organization and UNICEF.

Even though the largest donors are responsible for the bulk of corporate giving in absolute terms, many smaller and middle sized companies also donate 1–2 per cent of their pre-tax earnings to charity. Donations are attractive to companies because they are often tax-deductible and in this way decrease the overall tax paid by companies. For example, charitable donations have been tax-deductible in the United States since the 1935 Revenue Act that released restrictions on corporate giving. Nevertheless, many top managers say that they are keener to improve the effectiveness of corporate giving than promote numerical targets,[35] which shows the commitment of these leaders to charitable causes.

In addition to cash, companies also donate products and other goods. General Mills, for example, gives away packaged food including Cheerios and Wheeties to food banks across the United States,[36] Similarly, Merck has donated over 300 million prescribed amounts of Mectizan to treat river blindness.[37] In general, in-kind donations seem to be typical for industries selling products that are amenable for giving.[38] As can be seen from Table 14.2, the largest in-kind givers include four pharmaceuticals and three software companies. The products of these companies are more suitable for giving than, say, weapons or alcohol. Nevertheless, there is room for companies to become more innovative about their in-kind donations. For example, car manufacturing companies could donate vehicles to the United Nations field missions in developing countries.

TABLE 14.2 Top US in-kind givers

Company	In-kind 2002 (US$ millions)	Gifts as per cent of revenues
Eli Lilly	204.8	1.848
Pfizer	528.0	1.631
Parametric Technology	9.6	1.294
Merck	575.0	1.110
McGraw-Hill	49.0	1.023
Oracle	95.0	1.003
Microsoft	207.1	0.730
Tribune	34.0	0.631
Adobe Systems	4.5	0.387
General Mills	22.6	0.215

Source: *BusinessWeek* 2003. Available from http://www.businessweek.com/magazine/content/03_48/b3860620.htm, accessed 11 November 2008. (Ranking is based on data voluntarily submitted by S&P 500 companies.)

Many companies have set up foundations through which they donate money to charitable causes. The foundations are registered as charitable organizations with a requirement to use any profit or surplus for charitable purposes. They typically receive an initial donation from the founding company. For example, the Shell Foundation was set up with a US$250 million endowment from Shell. Contributions can also be made on a regular basis. This is the case for the Vodafone UK Foundation, which receives an annual donation from Vodafone UK and the Vodafone Group Foundation. Foundations may also hold equity in a company and get revenue through dividends and trade in shares. The Bertelsmann Foundation, for example, owns 58 per cent of Bertelsmann, one of the largest media companies in Germany.[39] Companies may also give office space and administrative assistance to their foundations as supplementary support. In return, foundations may be responsible for the charitable activities of the sponsoring company. The linkages between companies and foundations can therefore be close. Nevertheless, many foundations are run independently from their corporate sponsor. Indeed, one motivation for setting up a foundation is to ensure that corporate giving is free from business interests.

EMPLOYEE VOLUNTEERING

Employee volunteering has become an increasingly popular way for business to engage with their surrounding communities. The law firm Linklaters, for example, has a programme through which its employees volunteer for local community projects across its 30 offices worldwide. In London, its lawyers and staff from the marketing and human resources department act as mentors to formerly homeless people who seek to set up their own business. The company promotes the volunteer programme to its employees in many ways, but one of the most successful channels has been a desk calendar with photos of different community investment programmes.[40] In general, employee volunteering is a way in which business can make a contribution to society, but it also benefits companies by building contacts to local community, enhancing reputation and providing a better understanding of the external environment.

Volunteering is a well established phenomenon, but it has received a boost from recent government initiatives encouraging employers to set up volunteering schemes. Volunteering programmes have also gained popularity after industry leaders have launched innovative initiatives. The next Ethics in Practice case provides an example of such a volunteering opportunity provided by IBM. The rise in volunteering has also resulted from better awareness among employers about the benefits of volunteering. In general, an increasing number of businesses are viewing volunteering as an opportunity to motivate and train their employees in addition to establishing the company as part of the community. As a consequence, an increasing number of companies are carefully managing and controlling their volunteering programmes.

ETHICS IN PRACTICE

IBM CORPORATE SERVICE CORPS

IBM introduced a new volunteering programme called Corporate Service Corps in 2008. Over 5000 employees applied to the programme when it was first launched making it one of the most popular employee initiatives in the company's history. A successful applicant from China, Qing Xia Zhang, hopes that the project broadens her business viewpoint and makes a difference in the Philippines where she will work with small and medium-sized businesses in rural communities.

The programme involves a month's stay in an emerging economy where IBM employees participate in projects that have been designed to make use of their skills. The programmes combine socio-economic goals with information technology, as demonstrated by the following examples:

- Izmir, Turkey: work with local chambers of commerce and city councils to promote economic, social and democratic progress.

- Arusha, Tanzania: market research and strategy development for a micro-finance organization to expand its services to entrepreneurs.

- Danang City, Vietnam: the design of training programmes in IT management to assist the local Chamber of Commerce in supporting small and medium-sized enterprises.

The projects are chosen together with a small group of non-profit organizations that specialize in arranging volunteering opportunities for people with a private sector background. The role of the partner organizations is to help IBM to identify suitable projects. The partners also provide training that involves learning about local customs, culture and political situation.

The Corporate Service Corps programme is part of IBM's Global Citizen's Portfolio, which aims to enhance the skills and expertise of the company's employees. It is expected to produce benefits for the company by bringing together employees who otherwise might not meet. This is one of the reasons why each project involves a team of eight employees from different countries and business units. When the employees return, they are expected to share their experiences with their colleagues. In this way, the benefits of the programme are communicated across IBM.

Source: IBM's Corporate Service Corps heading to six emerging countries to spark socio-economic growth while developing global leaders (2008). *IBM Press Release*, 26 March 2008. Available from http://www-03.ibm.com/press/us/en/pressrelease/23743.wss, accessed 6 September 2008.

Research[41] on volunteering suggests that people volunteer for different reasons. Some may have an altruistic desire to 'help people', while others act on more egoistic motives to satisfy psychological needs and develop their skills. In general, more women than men take part in volunteering activities, except for political volunteering. Age is also significant; studies have found that people over 50 are more likely to volunteer than younger people who may be busy with building their careers and starting a family. Volunteering may also be an opportunity to express and transmit core values to others. This is why people with strong religious beliefs are likelier to volunteer than those with more secular values. Finally, people are also more likely to volunteer if they have some direct contact with community organizations. Parents with school-aged children, for example, may donate time to education-related activities.

Little research has been carried out on why some employers are more interested than others in supporting employee volunteering. Existing evidence suggests that larger firms are likelier to promote employee volunteering than small and medium-sized companies. For example, approximately 70 per cent of the largest companies in the United Kingdom have some kind of an employer-supported volunteering programme, while only 20 per cent of medium-sized businesses and 14 per cent of small companies have a volunteering scheme. Surveys also suggest that organizations in the field of finance and public administration are most likely to support employee volunteering, while construction and retail sectors offer only a few opportunities for their employees to engage in volunteering activity.[42] A mix of reasons therefore seems to determine whether a company has a volunteering scheme.

Volunteering can take a variety of forms for diverse objectives. Some of the most common forms of volunteering are highlighted in Table 14.3. Typically, volunteering involves the donation of time to community work, whether during work hours or on employee's own time. Some forms of volunteering can require a substantial time commitment from the volunteer and his or her employer. For example, secondments are usually organized for at least three months, mainly because it takes some time before a volunteer understands a community project well enough to make a substantial contribution. Other forms of volunteering may be especially suitable for senior level employees. For example, mentoring and board membership are activities that are seen to require senior level involvement. Finally, there is an

TABLE 14.3 Forms of volunteering

Type	Description
Unpaid work	Volunteers donate time to work in community projects with the agreement of their employer
Team challenge	An event where a group of employees tackle a problem in the community
Development assignment	Assignments involve completing a specific project in a charity
Secondment	An employee is transferred to a community organization while being paid by a company
Mentoring	Regular advice given by a company employee to a community member
Board membership	Corporate employees serve as board members in community organizations

increasing demand for volunteering opportunities that provide clear benefits for the employer. For example, team challenges, where a group of employees tackles a community problem, are popular because they benefit the employer by building team spirit and skills.

As already seen, volunteering can be beneficial for companies by way of increased employee morale, networking and reputation in community. In addition, though, a global survey carried out in 2002[43] suggests that some of the most important benefits of volunteering as identified by business people include the feeling of giving something back to the community. The 'ability to give something back' was seen as the most important benefit by 77 per cent of senior managers and 68 per cent of employees who responded to the survey.

COMMUNITY PROGRAMMES

An increasing number of companies have specially designed community programmes through which they coordinate cash donations, in-kind gifts and employee volunteering. Such programmes tend to be delivered by large companies in the oil, gas and mining sectors and focus on the areas of healthcare, education, economic development and infrastructure. For example, companies may invest in improving levels of education through sponsoring the construction and renovation of schools, providing pupils with physical and educational material, and paying towards the salaries of teachers. Similarly, they may contribute to the development of health services by supporting campaigns on vaccination, hygiene and sanitary education. In general, community programmes represent an effort to direct corporate resources towards selected areas of focus rather than spontaneous projects.[44] They also enable companies to have a more strategic impact on the social and economic development of communities.

Even though the largest community programmes are likely to be found in developing countries where host governments have limited resources to build infrastructure and provide welfare services,[45] some companies have important community programmes in industrialized countries as well. These programmes range from training and education of young people in disadvantaged communities to the support of social movements on a national scale. The programmes in industrialized countries have seen a revival after civil society groups have started to inspect corporate behaviour. Placed under increasing scrutiny, companies found that they had few links to local communities and that it would take time to create these networks. This was in part due to the fact that the connection between businesses and local communities had originally weakened when corporate ownership became dispersed and increasing amounts of capital were raised through minority shareholders who did not necessarily have any links to the areas where companies had their physical facilities. As a result, the power of corporations grew, but the bond to the local communities weakened. It is only after the big corporate scandals of the 1990s that many companies began re-establishing their relations to local communities.

Collaboration with non-governmental organizations, educational institutions and other societal groups is becoming typical in running community programmes.[46] An example of this is the partnership project between Rio Tinto, a mining company, and the World Wildlife Fund to establish a national approach to the conservation of frogs in Australia.[47] The role of companies in such projects varies from financial sponsorship to engagement in the design and delivery of projects. The degree of corporate involvement is often influenced by the attitude of managers. While some seek to have a higher degree of control over the programmes and therefore become more involved, others

PHONE SHOPS IN DISADVANTAGED COMMUNITIES

Many townships in South Africa have phone shops operated from converted shipping containers. These shops are part of the community programme launched by Vodacom, the largest mobile phone company in the country, to provide access to telecommunications services in disadvantaged communities at affordable rates. The programme currently involves 4400 phone shops that are run by more than 1800 entrepreneurs. In addition to providing access to communication services, the shops also offer business opportunities in communities where employment is otherwise difficult to find. Each shop is operated by an entrepreneur whose start-up costs Vodacom has covered. The company also provides training and other support for the entrepreneurs.

Source: World Resources Institute 2009. *Digital Dividend*. Available from http://www.digitaldividend.org/case/case_vodacom.htm, accessed 17 July 2009.

engage less because they believe there are organizations that are better equipped to deal with social and environmental issues. In addition to the company or a project partner, local community groups may also play a role in the management of community programmes. It is, however, more typical to consult the beneficiaries of community programmes before and during their implementation to ensure that they address real community needs.

Community programmes have been criticized for being attempts to build corporate reputation while ignoring larger problems relating to corporate operations. Programmes have been viewed in a negative light particularly when companies have been seen to present information about them in response to other concerns. For example, said an inhabitant from the Sudanese area where Talisman Energy, a Canadian oil company, had a community development programme: 'It is not a question of how many schools are built or how adequate they are... What good are these schools to you when you can be shot, burned and killed in the villages?'[48] This criticism demonstrates that company efforts to contribute to the realization of social and economic development can be viewed as futile in a situation where basic physiological and safety needs are not being satisfied. It also suggests that in order to avoid criticism, companies should address the main issues associated with their operations in a particular community.

DO MOTIVES MATTER?

Given that corporate–community relationships have often only improved in the wake of scandals, it can be argued that this is a form of defence rather than genuine altruism.

Does this matter, however? In what circumstances do you think the difference might be important? And how might you use either the defensive position or the altruistic to persuade a corporation to be more involved in community programmes?

Community programmes have also been criticized because government agencies have used them for their own purposes. For example, because the schools, clinics, wells and other facilities built by Talisman Energy in Sudan were located in garrison towns rather than in rural areas, they were condemned for encouraging displacement and change of traditional living patterns.[49] It has also been alleged that the programmes enabled northerners to settle in the area in place of the southerners who had been forced to move, which is why the community programmes were sometimes referred to as 'programmes of displacement'.[50] This criticism shows that corporate efforts to contribute to community development can be, or can be seen as, detrimental to the good of the community even when 'the company seem to want to do what is right'.[51] The criticism also shows the difficulty of running community programmes in a situation where the government is not respecting its basic human rights obligations. As a result, community programmes may become tools in the pursuit of some other objectives by the host government.

SUMMARY

- Corporations and business leaders have donated substantial sums of money to charitable causes for hundreds of years. Over time, corporate giving has become increasingly strategic in the sense that it is being tied to business objectives. The field has also progressively become more professionally managed.

- Altruistic philanthropy allows corporate managers to pursue charitable goals that are not linked to corporate interests or performance. Firms that use philanthropy as a strategic tool manage their donations in the way they manage most other spending decisions and link them to performance objectives.

- Corporate giving is driven by both altruistic and strategic motives. Historical evidence suggests that philanthropy becomes more strategic over time as it develops into a distinct corporate function. Industries that are subjected to public scrutiny and important societal externalities are most likely to approach philanthropy in a strategic way.

- Employee volunteering usually involves the donation of time to community work. Many governments have encouraged employer-supported volunteering as a way of enhancing social cohesion and supporting community development. Businesses have also begun to appreciate the benefits of volunteering.

- Companies may establish community programmes to coordinate their charitable activities in a particular area. These programmes often seek to improve the social and economic situation in a particular community where corporate facilities are located. They have attracted some criticism as unsatisfactory responses to more pressing problems relating to internal conflict or other forms of violence.

QUICK REVIEW QUESTIONS:

1 Explain how corporate philanthropy has developed over time.

2 What are the main forms of corporate philanthropy?

3 Philanthropy is becoming a business in its own right. Discuss the benefits and disadvantages of this trend for society.

CASE STUDY: THE COLOUR OF MONEY

BY EMILIE FILOU

(RED) is unique in its scale and application, but is this business model the future of corporate giving?

It has become a familiar sight: Bono, in his conspicuous red shades, flanked by the world's rich and famous, promoting the latest product to join his (RED) campaign to fight HIV/Aids in Africa. It could be a film premiere or a celebrity endorsement. And, of course, a celebrity endorsement is what it is, but of a very special kind. (RED) is not a product, nor is it a charity.

It's a business model designed to create a sustainable – and substantial – flow of private sector funds to HIV/Aids projects in Africa. A unique blend of business, philanthropy and PR, it could revolutionize the uninspired world of corporate social responsibility.

The premise is simple: a percentage of the profits from (RED) product sales goes to HIV/Aids projects, while the rest is retained by the participating corporations. On the surface, it's nothing new: win-win scenarios and enlightened self-interest have been talked about for as long as the corporate social responsibility debate has been around. But (RED) is unique in its scale and application.

It is the brainchild of Bono and Bobby Shriver, lawyer and local politician, member of the Kennedy clan and brother-in-law of Arnold Schwarzenegger, governor of California. Bono and Shriver had already founded DATA (Debt, Aids, Trade in Africa) in 2002, a multinational NGO aimed at helping Africa through debt relief and trade.

Their plan with (RED) was to create a credit card that would help raise funds to fight HIV/Aids in Africa and raise awareness of the plight of the 40 million people infected worldwide by HIV/Aids. They approached American Express (Amex) in 2003 and, slowly, the plan evolved into a broader concept.

Thanks to their philanthropic activities, Bono and Shriver persuaded five more high-profile partners to climb on board: Gap, Armani and Converse at the launch, and Motorola and Apple later on. Each partner has designed a (RED) product or collection, with a percentage of the profits going to the Global Fund and the rest to their coffers. All have signed a five-year agreement with a guarantee of exclusivity in their sector. The initiative was unveiled at the World Economic Forum in Davos last year and launched in the UK in March 2006.

Set up in 2002 by former UN secretary-general Kofi Annan to fight HIV/Aids, tuberculosis and malaria worldwide, the Global Fund was, in the words of its executive director Richard Feachem, 'the world's biggest kept secret until (RED) came out'. With an asset base of US$10 billion, it received over 95 per cent of its funds from public sector donors and little attention from the rest of the world.

Feachem says that private funding had been a tough nut to crack because of three main difficulties. The contributions had to be large enough to have an impact and had to be sustainable, so that the fund did not have to spend its resources in soliciting donors every year.

Third, the donations should not detract from other worthy causes. So (RED) came as a blessing. 'It was love at first sight,' says Feachem. 'Bobby and Bono came up with the concept of the credit card, and built into it was scale: this could be millions of dollars, it could be good for the company and therefore sustainable. It was completely new and would not steal from other causes.'

The UK was a logical starting point for (RED). Home to Live Aid, Bob Geldof and the Body Shop, British consumers have long been attuned to ethical consumerism. In 2005, the ethical goods industry was worth £29.3 billion, overtaking for the first time the retail market for tobacco and alcohol. During its research on (RED), Amex identified 1.5 million 'conscience consumers', predicted to grow to 4 million by 2009.

The UK was also a good target market for (RED) partners. For Amex, the ethical consumer represented a significant departure from its older male clientele, while Motorola had the opportunity to enter a niche market, out of Nokia's reach. Armani used London Fashion Week to launch its capsule (RED) collection, and for Gap (RED) was an opportunity to reassert its ethical responsibility after sweatshop scandals had tarnished its image. In the 2005 Ethical Reputation Index, Gap had been ranked as the 12th worst corporate by consumers for business ethics.

In this context, one of (RED)'s main successes is the creation of a high-profile social issue umbrella brand. Anita Roddick's Body Shop was perhaps the first example of social branding, and Fair Trade, which guarantees minimum prices for producers, has also become a household name over the past few years. But (RED)'s uniqueness lies in bringing iconic brands together under its own flag.

Craig Smith, senior fellow in marketing and ethics at London Business School, says that one of the obstacles Fair Trade encountered early on was the issue of quality. If its coffee tasted like dishwater, no one would buy it, save, perhaps, a dedicated few. With (RED), he says, consumers do not have to compromise on quality or price. The brand and reputation are guaranteed, and that has taken social branding to a new level. In fact, this is arguably (RED)'s greatest contribution to the HIV/Aids cause: the high profile has given sufferers a much needed boost of positive publicity.

(RED)'s other achievement is financial: US$20 million has been raised for the Global Fund so far. Most of the money has gone to two projects – in Rwanda and Swaziland – that provide training for healthcare professionals to prevent mother-to-child transmission of the HIV virus, voluntary counselling and testing for the prevention of the disease, and anti-retroviral therapy for HIV/Aids sufferers. Extra projects will be added to the (RED) portfolio as funds increase.

(RED) is reticent to the point of coyness about how much its partners receive from the sale of their products. It agreed not to disclose information about partners' individual contributions to, and gains from, the scheme. All that is known is the consumer's contribution – how much from each item goes to the fund (see above).

Tamsin Smith, (RED)'s president in the US, defends the decision, saying she does not want to create a hierarchy within the partners. 'We are in this together. There is no company that is more

(RED) than another, and I would not want one of our partners to feel less valued.'

Feachem is similarly diplomatic. 'There is a discussion about how much is being put in the public domain. My preference would be to put it all out there, but some partners might say: "We are small in money, but huge in commitment and we do not want to feel like a minor partner". We have to tread carefully.'

Few would criticize the fact that the corporations involved take something out of the scheme. This is the very essence of sustainability. The worry, which stems directly from the lack of transparency, is that they may be taking more than their perceived 'fair share'. Anton Kerr, senior policy adviser of the International HIV/Aids Alliance, argues, for instance, that the high-profile public relations 'halo effect' – the extension of the overall (RED) impression to the company – and the extra non-(RED) business that corporations generate as a result of the publicity should be enough for them.

And good PR they are getting. Karen Fraser, who runs the Fraser Consultancy and produces the Ethical Reputation Index, found that 60 per cent of the people who had heard of (RED) said that their opinion of (RED) clothing brands (Armani, Gap, Converse) had improved; 48 per cent also thought better of Amex, which had ranked as the ninth worst offender on the Index.

However, Tamsin Smith says that good PR will not be enough to ensure (RED) stays at the forefront of what consumers want. 'We are asking them to create a complete sub-brand, a special campaign, a new everything. We want Motorola's latest phones, Apple's brand-new Nano. Companies would not be able to sustain that investment for five years if they gave all their profits away.' Alexis Dormandy, executive board member for (RED) in Europe, says that it is a simple case of enlarging the pie before cutting it.

What is difficult to establish is whether (RED) has been a success. Smith says that its objective for 2006 was to launch and establish a global brand. That has been achieved, but the next stage is vague: 'Our future vision is to attract new partners in targeted industry categories, continue with the global roll-out beyond UK and America, and with the core goal of raising sustainable funds for the Global Fund in the fight against Aids in Africa,' she says.

So what does US$20 million mean? Compared with the level of public funding the fund receives it is a drop in the ocean, but it represents a four-fold increase in private sector contributions. 'We don't want to make monetary objectives because we are not tied to money-specifics. We want a long-term plan, not just to get the most money in one year,' says Smith.

John Knell, director of the Intelligence Agency and who regularly works with charities on their business plans, says that (RED)'s reluctance to set targets (or make them public at least) might stem from a desire to protect the project from negative publicity. 'If it set a target of US$20 million and made only US$10 million, the story would be about it not reaching its target.'

But what about this year? And in five years' time? 'Whatever the sensitivity, you should at some point know what to expect,' says Knell. 'Targets drive aspirations and they drive business.' (RED) partners should be used to challenging targets in their everyday work, and Dormandy is a seasoned businessman, familiar with the demands of P&L, thanks to a career that has taken him to the likes of McKinsey and Virgin.

(RED), by its own admission, still has the feel of a start-up. 'The last thing we are is a finished and polished product,' says Tamsin Smith. 'We don't have the perfect formula yet. We are still a furious band of crazy warriors.' Indeed, with a staff of only 12 stretched across the Atlantic – its headquarters are in Los Angeles, its main market is in the UK and it raises funds for an organization based in Switzerland – one gets the picture. The trouble is that this hardly conveys the sense that (RED) is going to take over the world, if that is what it wants to do.

As for the partners, although they won't state precisely what they are getting from (RED), early indications suggest that their involvement has been positive. Motorola says it wants to turn (RED) into a mainstream product and Armani is reported to be pleased with the demand for its collection. All partners launched in the US last October, with the exception of Amex. Because of the complexity of repayment schedules, it takes 18 to 24 months to judge whether a credit card scheme is successful. But if it turns out to be a success, Amex says it will consider other markets.

Most (RED) products are now available online, and (RED) has started partnerships with Yahoo! and Google to raise its profile. MySpace, where the (RED) community now numbers more than 800,000 members, has also played a vital role in spreading the word.

However, despite this, Fraser says research done by her consultancy shows that only about a quarter of the UK adult population was aware of the project six months after its launch. (RED) products remain decidedly niche and upmarket. It has also had to fend off criticism that it exploits western consumers: if people really cared about HIV/Aids in Africa, they wouldn't need a credit card to go on a guilt-free shopping spree. But Dormandy says that (RED) is designed to attract precisely those well-intentioned people who never quite get around to doing anything about their good intentions.

(RED) also faces the challenge of maintaining the uniqueness of its brand as it expands. Dormandy says it has been a feat of marketing genius to combine each individual brand with the (RED) label. 'Our partners are trying stuff they have never done before. It's not a trivial marketing task to pull off,' he says. In fact, Motorola is rumoured to have ditched an advertisement for its (RED) phone made by (RED)'s advertising agency Mother. The ad shows two naked black bodies emerging from a lump of flesh being worked on a potter's wheel, a marked move away from its more usual techie branding – and perhaps a move too far.

Partners have also opted for different strategies. Apple and Motorola, for instance, offer identical (RED) and non-(RED) products, while other brands have opted for specific (RED) items. Smith says that the partners know best what to do in their market, but what is eclectic in a group of six may become chaotic with more partners and products.

The real litmus test will come in four years' time when current partners will have to decide whether to renew their contracts. Only then will we be able to judge whether Bono's idea heralded a new era of corporate social opportunity.

STUDY QUESTIONS

1   Were you aware of RED before reading this case? How is awareness important for the project?

2   What aspects of RED are strategic for the companies participating to the initiative?

3   What has happened to RED since the case was written? Was it deemed successful by the participating companies and have they renewed their commitment?

SOURCE

http://www.managementtoday.co.uk/search/article/636366/the-colour-money/.

NOTES

1. Owen (1965), pp. 434–442.
2. Owen (1965).
3. Drucker (1984).
4. Reich (1998).
5. Smith (1994).
6. Reich (1998); Vogel (1986).
7. Smith (1994).
8. Maung (2006).
9. Einhorn, (2003).
10. http://www.carnegiemedals.org/news/2007.html, accessed 19 January 2009.
11. Saiia *et al.* (2003).
12. Gan (2006).
13. Porter & Kramer (2002).
14. Smith (1994).
15. Smith (1994).
16. Sanchez (2000).
17. Sanchez (2000).
18. Saiia *et al.* (2003).
19. Buchholtz *et al.* (1999).
20. Gan (2006).
21. Fry *et al.* (1982).
22. Gan (2006).
23. Saiia *et al.* (2003).
24. Brammer & Millington (2003); Burke *et al.* (1986).
25. Fry *et al.* (1982); Seifert *et al.* (2004).
26. Fry *et al.* (1982).
27. Griffin & Mahon (1997); Seifert *et al.* (2003).
28. Buchholtz *et al.* (1999); Seifert *et al.* (2004).
29. New Philanthropy Capital (2008). Available from http://www.philanthropycapital.org/, accessed 6 November 2008.
30. John (2007).
31. Jack (2007a).
32. Jack (2007a).
33. Jack (2007a).

34. Jack (2007b).
35. Burke *et al.* (1986).
36. Conlin *et al.* (2003).
37. Brice (2005).
38. Conlin *et al.* (2003).
39. This arrangement makes Bertelsmann takeover proof as the foundation owns the majority of its shares.
40. Ramrayka (2006).
41. Bussell & Forbes (2002).
42. Hardy (2004).
43. *Engage Survey* (2002).
44. Burke *et al.* (1986).
45. Eweje (2006).
46. Burke *et al.* (1986).
47. Humphreys (2000).
48. Christian Aid (2001), p. 29.
49. Gagnon & Ryle (2001).
50. Christian Aid (2001), p. 27.
51. Harker (2000).

REFERENCES

Brammer, S. and Millington, A. 2003. The evolution of corporate charitable contributions in the UK between 1989 and 1999: Industry structure and stakeholder influences. *Business Ethics: A European Review*, Vol. 12, No. 3, 216–228.

Brice, A. 2005. Donating medicines to developing countries: A major commitment for NJ pharmaceutical companies. *New Jersey Business*, 1 January 2005. Available from http://www.allbusiness.com/north-america/united-states-new-jersey/1082604-1.html, accessed 11 November 2008.

Buchholtz, A., Amason, A. C. and Rutherford, M. 1999. Beyond resources: The mediating effect of management discretion and values on corporate philanthropy. *Business and Society*, Vol. 32, No. 2, 167–187.

Burke, L., Logsdon, J. M., Mitchell, W., Reiner, M. and Vogel, D. 1986. Corporate community involvement in the San Francisco Bay area. *California Management Review*, Vol. 28, No. 3, 122–141.

Bussell, H. and Forbes, D. 2002. Understanding the volunteer market: The what, where, who and why of volunteering. *International Journal of Non-Profit and Voluntary Sector Marketing*, Vol. 7, No. 3, 244–257.

Christian Aid 2001. *Scorched Earth*. Online. Available from http://www.christian-aid. org.uk, accessed 15 June 2006.

Conlin *et al.* 2003. The corporate donors. Special report – Philanthropy. *BusinessWeek*, 1 December 2003. Available from http://www.businessweek.com, accessed 13 October 2008.

Drucker, P. F. 1984. The new meaning of corporate social responsibility. *California Management Review*, Vol. 26, No. 2, 53–63.

Einhorn, B. 2003. Asia: Hong Kong is priming the pump. *BusinessWeek*, 1 December 2003. Available from http:/www.businessweek.com, accessed 13 October 2008.

Engage Survey 2002. International Business Leaders Forum. Available from http://www.iblf.org/docs/engage/survey.doc, accessed 7 October 2008.

Eweje, G. 2006. The role of MNEs in community development initiatives in developing countries: Corporate social responsibility at work in Nigeria and South Africa. *Business and Society*, Vol. 45, No. 2, 93–129.

Fry, L. W., Keim, G. and Meiners, R. E. 1982. Corporate contributions: Altruistic or for-profit? *Academy of Management Journal*, Vol. 25, No. 1, 94–106.

Gagon, G. and Ryle, J. 2001. *Report of an Investigation into Oil Development, Conflict, and Displacement in Western Upper Nile. Sudan*, October.

Gan, A. 2006. The impact of public scrutiny on corporate philanthropy. *Journal of Business Ethics*, Vol. 69, 217–236.

Griffin, J. J. and Mahon, J. F. 1997. The corporate social performance and corporate financial performance debate: Twenty-five years of incomparable research. *Business and Society*, Vol. 36, No. 1, 5–31.

Hardy, R. 2004. *Employer-supported Volunteering and Giving: Findings from the 2001 Home Office Citizenship Survey*. Home Office Research Study 280. Home Office Research, Development and Statistics Directorate, October 2004.

Harker, J. 2000. *Human Security in Sudan: The Report of a Canadian assessment mission*. Prepared for the Ministry of Foreign Affairs. Ottawa, January.

Humphreys, D. 2000. A business perspective on community relations in mining. *Resources Policy*, Vol. 26, 127–131.

Jack, A. 2007a. Philanthropy: More may not be better. *FT.com Reports*. Available from http://www.ft.com, accessed 13 October 2007.

Jack, A. 2007b. The business of philanthropy: Intermediaries have the skill to help. *FT.com Reports*. Available from http://www.ft.com, accessed 13 October 2007.

John, R. 2007. Venture Philanthropy. Available from http://www.philanthropyuk.org/AGuidetoGiving/Informationsheets/Venturephilanthropy, accessed 7 November 2008.

Maung, Z. 2006. Latin America: Brazil's private sector – what community service really means. *Ethical Corporation*, 14 December 2006. Available from http://www.ethicalcorp.com, accessed 10 November 2006.

Nevin-Gattle, K. 1996. Predicting the philanthropic response of corporations: Lessons from history. *Business Horizons*, May–June, 15–22.

Owen, D. 1965. *English Philanthropy*. Cambridge, MA: The Belknap Press of Harvard University Press.

Porter, M. and Kramer, M. R. 2002. The competitive advantage of corporate philanthropy. *Harvard Business Review*, December, 78–92.

Prochaska, F. 1988. *The Voluntary Impulse: Philanthropy in Modern Britain*. London and Boston: Faber and Faber.

Ramrayka, L. 2006. Putting profits back into the community. *The Guardian*, 6 November 2006. Available from http:/www.guardian.co.uk, accessed 13 October 2008.

Reich, R. B. 1998. The new meaning of corporate social responsibility. *California Management Review*, Vol. 40, No. 2, 8–17.

Saiia, D. H., Carroll, A. B. and Buchholtz, A. K. 2003. Philanthropy as strategy: When corporate charity 'begins at home'. *Business and Society*, Vol. 42, No. 2, 169–201.

Sanchez, C. M. 2000. Motives for corporate philanthropy in El Salvador: Altruism and political legitimacy. *Journal of Business Ethics*, Vol. 27, 363–375.

Seifert, B., Morris, S. A. and Bartkus, B. R. 2003. Comparing big givers and smaill givers:financial correlates of corporate philanthropy. *Journal of Business Ethics*, Vol. 45, 195–211.

Seifert, B., Morris, S. A. and Bartkus, B. R. 2004. Having, giving, and getting: Slack resources, corporate philanthropy, and firm financial performance. *Business and Society*, Vol. 43, No. 2, 135–161.

Smith, C. 1994. The new corporate philanthropy. *Harvard Business Review*, May–June, 105–116.

Vogel, D. 1986. The study of social issues in management: A critical appraisal. *California Management Review*, Vol. XXVIII, No. 2, 142–151.

Whetten, D. A., Rands, G. and Godfrey, P. C. 2001. What are the responsibilities of business to society? In Pettigrew, A., Thomas, H. and Whittington, R. (eds), *Handbook of Strategy and Management*. London: Sage Publications.

INTEGRATIVE CASE STUDIES: CASE STUDY III.1

RED BULL OR BLACK DEVIL?

BY DR. MICHEL PHAN, ESSEC BUSINESS SCHOOL, PARIS-SINGAPORE

Twenty-one years ago, in 1987, Dietrich Mateschitz, an Austrian entrepreneur, launched a small business in Austria with one product that would consequently revolutionize the beverage industry. Red Bull was born and has created a new soft drink category: energy drinks. It quickly became the market dominator around the world in its category. Sold mostly in bars, nightclubs, sporting events, supermarkets and convenience stores, the beverage embodies that which is unique, stylish and mysterious. Targeting masses of young consumers around the globe, Red Bull successfully implemented highly adapted marketing strategies to appeal to the same target market throughout the world. However, despite this immediate success, there was much controversy surrounding its consumption which had resulted in its ban in many countries, namely Norway, Denmark, Uruguay (Reuters, 14 August 2008). France has only authorised its sale since May 2008.

A bull's market

Red Bull is a yellow carbonated beverage that technically qualifies as an energy drink. It has been described by critics as "cough syrup,"[1] "tinny and medicinal,"[2] and subsequently is known for its sweet flavor. Moreover, it is widely known for the caffeine-energy boost that it provides. Its main ingredients are: water, sugar, taurine, glucuronolactone, vitamins B12, niacin, inositol and caffeine.[3] Taurine is an amino-acid found in meat, fish and humans. Glucuronolactone is a carbohydrate produced by the body, and is said to increase metabolic rate. Caffeine is a natural stimulant found in other common beverages, such as coffee and tea.[4] Red Bull is said to contain 80 milligrams of caffeine, similar to a cup of coffee.[5] In terms of sugar, Red Bull contains the same amount of sugar as a can

of soda. It is packaged in an 8.3 fluid-ounce blue and silver colored can. The "slim" design of the packaging sets this energy drink apart from other beverage categories. In the United States, the usual 12-ounce soda can looks outdated and unsophisticated in comparison. Featured on the face of the can are two bulls with interlocked horns, a most imposing image. The sleek silver can is the "anti-Pepsi" statement. Although the can is smaller, it implies a "concentrated experience."[6]

Red Bull targets extreme sports athletes, young socialites and students in college. Its growing popularity in bars and nightclubs has created a trend for mixing it with alcohol. The company denies that this is a marketing tactic, and insists that they target people who need energy. Despite common concerns that the beverage may be associated with health risks, especially when used as an alcoholic mixer, Red Bull promises that it "revitalizes body and mind . . . improves performance. . . . increases endurance . . . improves concentration and increases reaction time."[7] Red Bull's savvy distribution strategy truly sets it apart from other beverages in its category. Initially, upon US entry, they had relied upon established distributors such as Coca-Cola and Pepsi for their distribution channels. Today, Red Bull has small distributors who work solely with their product. Local "consumer educators" are hired to promote and distribute the product to new consumers within that area.[8]

European origin

In the early 1980's, Dietrich Mateschitz was intrigued by the syrups consumed by business executives in Asia to gain additional energy and decided to work with a Bangkok based pharmaceutical company to create his own energy drink. This concoction, called "Red Bull Krateng Dang" was sold in Asia. In 1984, Mateschitz set up a company in Austria to introduce his energy drink to the European market. In 1987, after Mateschitz refined the product to be less syrupy and added carbonation, he then launched Red Bull in Austria. By 1993, Red Bull was selling more than 35 million cans a year and Mateschitz decided to introduce the product into Germany, the Netherlands, Switzerland, and the UK in 1994. In 1995 the product was brought into Eastern European countries. Red Bull continued to expand into Australia and Brazil and by 1997 Red Bull charged into the United States market.[9] By August 2002, Red Bull controlled 70% of the fast growing energy drink category, selling 1 billion cans and bottles the previous year, up from 100 million in 1997.[10] By 2007, Red Bull has sold 3.5 billions of cans in 143 countries[11] with a total sales turnover of US$ 4.2 Billion, twice the sales of 2004. An international presence in over so many countries qualified Red Bull as a global player. However, this edgy energy tonic found itself in the midst of controversy and negative publicity. For instance, in Sweden (and previously in Japan) the drink could only be sold in pharmacies.[12] The product was considered as a medicine, and therefore classified as a drug. Sweden's National Food Administration adopted this policy following the incident of a young woman who had consumed the product with alcohol and suffered from dehydration resulting in death; two other deaths tied to Red Bull were under investigation in Sweden. A death was linked to Red Bull in Hong Kong, where a British man mixed it with a pitcher of vodka and died. Greek health officials issued a warning to avoid mixing Red Bull with alcohol, and in conjunction with exercise. "Just one can of the popular energy drink Red Bull can increase your risk of heart attack or stroke and the effect was seen even in young people. The caffeine-loaded beverage causes blood to become sticky, a pre-cursor to cardiovascular problems such as stroke."[13] Spokespeople for Red Bull have responded by asserting that the company does not promote mixing the product with alcohol; however Austria and Australia are among the few countries where warning labels on the product exist. Labels on cans sold in Austria warn that unsuitable levels of caffeine make the product inappropriate for children. In Australia, Red Bull cans require the health warning, "This food is not recommended for children, pregnant or lactating women and individuals sensitive to caffeine".[14]

Red Bull global consumer profile

Red Bull generally caters to the same group of consumers globally. Red Bull's primary consumers fit into the age bracket of 16-29 years.[15] This age demographic lends itself to the youthful, energetic image that the company portrays through its sales force and its brand meaning. To maintain a steady flow of new consumers, they set an aggressive goal of getting a "new generation of 16-year-olds on board every year."[16] Although the youth market does not usually have as much disposable income as older generations, the Red Bull consumer is not price-sensitive. The value of the Red Bull brand name justifies the higher price. There are many different "needs" that the beverage can fulfil, but these all relate back to the simple need for energy. Socialization needs cater to a certain "in-crowd"; a group of young consumers, possibly of college age or older, who utilize the beverage for its trendy appearance and mysterious reputation. A college student was quoted as saying, "It's really a kind of fashionable drink. You see the fashionable sorority girls buying their can of Red Bull… It's like, 'Look, I can afford to pay $3 for this ridiculous drink.'"[17] These individuals consume the product most often in bars or nightclubs, where it is often mixed with alcohol for a more desirable effect.

Extreme athletes are another targeted group within the age cohort. Their consumption relates to the actual need for energy during high-endurance exercise and activity. The psychological effect of participating in risky alternative sports activities, such as snowboarding, cliff-diving, car-racing and street luge, makes this consumer ideally suited to the product itself. The energy boost, combined with the "health risks" associated with mass-consumption of high-caffeine and sugary beverages truly fit the reputation of the young extreme athlete who is willing to take risks. Sponsoring promotional events that these athletes can identify with is a smart means of communication. Some events include: Red Bull Air race game in Porto, Formula 1 motor racing with Sebastian Vettel and Sebastien Bourdais as the car drivers, Red Bull X fighters (motorbike racing), NASCAR race in the USA, and Red Bull X-Alps (paragliding competition) to name a few.[18] Similarly, Red Bull has a universal appeal to the DJs and "raver" dancers who are known to dance all night long in discos and clubs. The energy required to stay up all night makes this group of young music fans ideal consumers to use Red Bull.

Red Bull Music Academy was founded as a global forum where aspiring club DJs could meet to discuss skills and music. At these sports and music venues, Red Bull cleverly places their product in the hands of many potential new customers, but does not directly promote it. The goal is to create brand awareness among new consumers that fit their target markets without obvious sales tactics. The goal is to create brand awareness globally.

Distribution tactics

When Red Bull was launched in the USA in 1997, the company divided the country into eight decentralized sales-units and expanded on a city-by-city basis. Red Bull did not use mass marketing but instead each of the eight units was responsible for creating distribution channels, making sales calls, and developing targeted marketing plans.[19] Red Bull's differentiated global strategy utilizes a sales force that caters specifically to each target market in each area. Red Bull hires "hip locals" who drive around in Red Bull logoed cars offering free samples and promoting the product in popular venues. This dedicated sales force finds the trendy "hot spots" in each particular market and through high-end promotions can put their product into the hands of their target market. The plan of expansion into new markets was unique to Red Bull. When Red Bull enters a new market, they scout out accounts at popular venues frequented by the target market. Red Bull then picks only five venues to introduce their product. At this point, Red Bull develops consumer education teams. For example, on college campuses, Red Bull employs student brand managers who are responsible for getting the product into the hands of their peers. These students are essentially brand extensions of Red Bull's ambassadors; they embody the ideal Red Bull consumer. In addition, Red Bull finds small distributors who will dedicate themselves to the product and deliver it in Red Bull-branded vans. Red Bull requires distributors who carry other products to employ a separate sales force to handle their drink.[20] Red Bull's hard work in establishing distribution channels independent of larger brands, for example Coke and Pepsi, is rewarded in the loyalty achieved from the distributors who represent their product exclusively. Red Bull as a company is truly self-sufficient. It is one product, with one united driven sales force, represented by distributors who only handle their account, and engage in purely secretive marketing strategies. To compete with Coca-Cola and Pepsi while keeping up with changes in consumer's preferences, Red Bull launched its own cola version in a limited number of countries and a sugar free version[21] [see Exhibit 1]:

Red Bull continues to dominate the energy drink market in the USA and throughout the world. Despite the negative publicity surrounding this product, many young people are still consuming Red Bull in mass quantities without paying any attention to its potential harm and it is surprising that consumers do not demand more information about post-consumption effects prior to purchase. What exactly are the health risks (or benefits) associated with mass consumption? Certainly this has been a market success, especially in the USA, but regulatory obstacles could hinder future growth as more information is obtained (if possible).

Presumed innocent—ethical questions

"Ross Cooney, 18, was a healthy basketball player, but died in 2000 just hours after drinking Red Bull. The student from Limerick, Ireland, died after sharing four cans of the drink with friends before a basketball game. At his inquest, the coroner called officials from the Austrian-based company to give evidence about their product. They said that no adverse effects had been proven in connection with the drink. The inquest jury later ruled that the teenager had died as a result of Sudden Adult Death Syndrome, but called for an inquiry into high-caffeine energy drinks."[22]

Energy drinks have exploded into the global market. Their unique characteristic makes them difficult to classify between foods and dietary supplements. Red Bull has managed to fall through the regulatory cracks in many of its international markets and has taken this to its advantage. In the United States, for example, the FDA did not issue any warning for Red Bull despite suspicious correlations between deaths and injury related to the drink. According to the FDA, average amounts of ingredients are used,

EXHIBIT 1

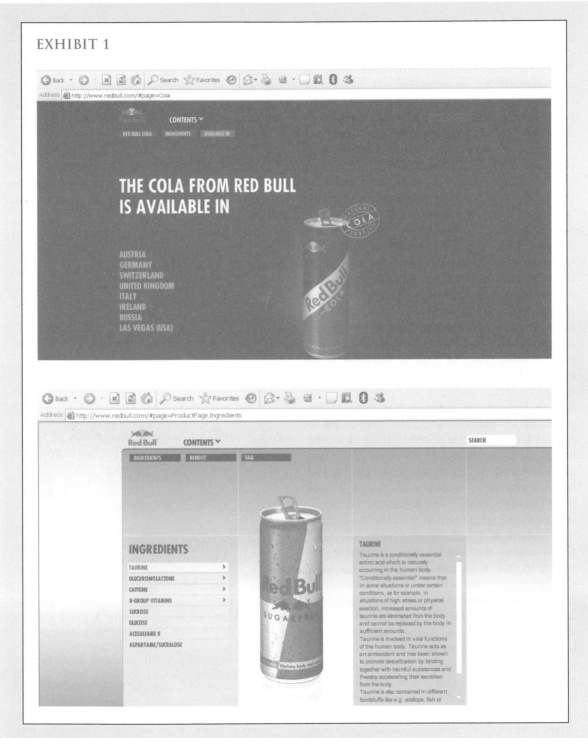

Source: "Unilever and Water – Towards Sustainability," www.unilever.com, 2003.

enabling Red Bull to be classified under the food category.[23] Additionally, research has not been conducted to prove health risks associated with Red Bull.[24] The lack of cohesive information about the long-term effects for teenagers and adolescents raises some ethical questions with regard to targeting young consumers. Red Bull avoids using ephedrine and guarana, which are potentially hazardous ingredients in competitor drinks and instead uses products with FDA approval such as caffeine and taurine.[25] Consumers of the product are encouraged by the FDA and Red Bull officials to exercise "common sense" and not to misuse the product. Several health experts in the United States and abroad believe there are potential harmful effects from Red Bull consumption, especially when mixed with alcohol. Medical experts claim that alcohol is a depressant, which affects the nervous system, while caffeine (coupled with other ingredients) is a stimulant. The combined effect can lead to heart failure.[26] Alcohol poisoning and dehydration are other concerns because Red Bull masks feelings of drunkenness and drowsiness with alertness. Consumers may use an excessive amount without realizing their intoxication. Lynn Willis, professor of pharmacology and toxicology at Indiana University School of Medicine, described energy drinks as "drugs sold as food."[27] Beyond the United States, in 2000, the Irish government requested further research into Red Bull following Ross Cooney's death.[28] The British Dietetic Association responded by increasing research efforts to raise awareness. The European Union is supposed to investigate the issue as well, responding to several deaths linked to the drink in Sweden. Compared to the size of the market, the phenomena of injury and death are extremely rare.[29] Despite its success, Red Bull's long-term effects are still unknown. The potential market success is tarnished by some basic ethical questions that have yet to be answered. Is Red Bull really concerned about the health of its consumers? Is it similar to the tobacco industry in the United States: marketing a product it knows is detrimental to the health of the young cohort it targets? Where is the line drawn between successful marketing strategies and corporate social responsibility? Red Bull's vague responses to these issues, either on their web site or in interviews, do not shed any light. Should Red Bull be subjected to stricter regulations? Will they continue to dominate the market with a potentially hazardous product expanding their market share infinitely? Only time will tell if Red Bull market savvy strategies can withstand the threat of regulations and investigations around the globe.

Discussion questions

1   Discuss the advantages and disadvantages of Red Bull's distribution and targeting strategy in the United States.

2   How could Red Bull have effectively and actively dealt with the rumors of health risks and deaths associated with the drink?

3   What other target markets Red Bull may have neglected? What are the potential of those "untapped" markets?

4   Should (or should not) Red Bull be concerned by Corporate Social Responsibility (CSR) issues? Given the unknown information regarding its safety, is it moral to give free samples to young consumers?

Acknowledgements: Sincere thanks to Nancy Crook, Erika Gonzalez, and Rachel Gordon for their valuable research assistance.

Notes

1. (2001, February 21). Red Bull Energy Drink—The BevNET.com Review. Retrieved October 22, 2002 from the World Wide Web: http://www.bevnet.com/reviews/redbull/

2. (2001, February 28). Popular drink Red bull runs around Ohio State U. campus. *The Lantern,* Retrieved October 22, 2002 from Lexis-Nexis Academic Universe on the World Wide Web: http://web.lexis-nexis.com/univ

3. Gustafson, Kristi L. (2001, June 14). Have yourself a Bull. *The Times Union,* P2. Retrieved October 23, 2002 from Lexis-Nexis Academic Universe on the World Wide Web: http://web.lexis-nexis.com/univ

4. (4 August 2002). Energy drinks pack real punch. *The Times-Picayune.* Retrieved October 24, 2002 from Factiva on the World Wide Web: http://global.factiva.com/en/arch/

5. Perkins, Rachel. (2002, January 15). Ball State U.: Experts suggest mixture of alcohol, popular energy

drink may pose health risks. *Daily News.* Retrieved October 24, 2002 from Factiva on the World Wide Web: http://global.factiva.com/en/arch/

6. Rodgers, Anni Layne. (2001, October). It's a (Red) Bull Market After All. Retrieved October 24, 2002 on the World Wide Web: http://www.fastcompany.com/build/build_feature/redbull.html/

7. Salkin, Allen. (2000, November 12). Noticed; Conveniences: Caffeine Cocktails. *The New York Times,* (9) 9. Retrieved October 20, 2002 from Lexis-Nexis Academic Universe on the World Wide Web: http://web.lexis-nexis.com/univ

8. Hein, Kenneth. (2001, May 28). A Bull's market. Retrieved October 24, 2002 from ProQuest database (Periodical abstracts) on the World Wide Web: http://proquest.umi.com

9. Red Bull GmbH. (2002, October 11). Hoover's Company Profiles. Retrieved. October 25, 2002 from ProQuest database (Periodical abstracts) on the World Wide Web: http://proquest.umi.com

10. Newbart, Dave. Safety of Trendy Club Drinks Questioned. (2002, January 22) Chicago Sun Times. Retrieved October 20, 2002 from ProQuest database (Periodical abstracts) on the World Wide Web: http://proquest.umi.com

11. Imaginascience Reuters, 2008: http://www.sur-la-toile.com/article-6090-Boissons-energisantes-(red-bull)-et-risque-d-infarctus.html

12. Henning, Justin. (2002, September 9). Controversy Swirls over Red Bull. University Daily Kansan. Retrieved October 20, 2002 from ProQuest database (Periodical abstracts) on the World Wide Web: http://proquest.umi.com

13. Reuters, 2008: http://www.reuters.com/article/health-News/idUSSYD5846120080815?feedType=RSS&feedName=healthNews

14. Irvine, Martha. (2001, December 20). Debate Brewing Worldwide over safety of Popular 'Energy Drink'. Retrieved October 20, 2002 from ProQuest database (Periodical abstracts) on the World Wide Web: http://proquest.umi.com

15. Hein, Kenneth. (2001, May 28). A Bull's market.

16. (2002, May 11). Business: Selling energy; Face value. *The Economist.* Retrieved October 20, 2002 from ProQuest database (Periodical abstracts) on the World Wide Web: http://proquest.umi.com

17. Walker, Rob. (31 August, 2002). Bull Marketing. *Australian Financial Review.* Retrieved October 20, 2002 from Lexis-Nexis Academic Universe on the World Wide Web: http://web.lexis-nexis.com/univ

18. www.redbull.com

19. Hein, Kenneth. (2001, May 28). A Bull's market. Retrieved October 24, 2002 from ProQuest database (Periodical abstracts) on the World Wide Web: http://proquest.umi.com

20. Hein, Kenneth. (2001, October 15). Red Bull Charging Ahead. Brandweek. Retrieved from October 262, 2002 from ProQuest database (Periodical abstracts) on the World Wide Web: http://proquest.umi.com

21. www.redbull.com

22. Maxime Frith, The Independent Newspapers "European court backs ban on Red Bull over health concerns", 7 February 2004.

23. Feher, Stephanie. (2001, February 28). Popular Drink Red Bull runs around Ohio State U. Campus.

24. Newbart, Dave. Safety of Trendy Club Drinks Questioned. (2002, January 22) Chicago Sun Times

25. Morman, Todd. (2002, March 21). Jitters for Sale or Legal Speed in a Can?

26. Kiang, Kylene. (2002, February 5). Red Bull Mix may lead to Death some say.

27. Johnson, Nancy. (2001, January 17). Blast in a Can Drinks promise energy, memory, but do they deliver?

28. Devine, Michael. (2000, November 17). We Need EU Drink Research.

29. Morman,Todd.

STARBUCKS CORPORATION: BUILDING A SUSTAINABLE SUPPLY CHAIN*

Over the last several years, Starbucks has instituted a new purchasing philosophy. We have done this because it is the right thing to do – for farmers, for our people, and for our business. Because we have persuaded our customers to pay high prices for quality roasted coffee, we are able to pay high prices for green unroasted coffee. We also believe that the high prices we pay for coffee allow us to be a potential force for positive reform in every part of our supply chain.

— Orin Smith, Former President and CEO; and Dub Hay, SVP, Coffee, Starbucks Corporation[1]

Starbucks Corporation was the world's largest specialty coffee retailer, with $6.4 billion in annual revenue for the fiscal year ended October 2, 2005. The company continued to expand the number of retail stores worldwide, and consistently saw strong growth in the sales and net profits (see Exhibits 1 and 2). Since going public in 1992, its stock appreciated more than 4,000 percent after adjusting for stock splits.

In the 1990s, the specialty coffee industry experienced gigantic growth, fueled largely by the coffee-drinking habits of college graduates and other educated professionals. In the previous few years, however, a worldwide oversupply of lower-grade coffee had depressed the world's market prices, making it difficult for coffee farmers to earn enough revenue to cover the cost of production. Although Starbucks only purchased the highest quality Arabica coffee and paid premium prices, all farmers suffered from the oversupply of coffee (see Exhibit 3).

By the end of 2005, Starbucks was at a challenging point in its history. It boasted more than

10,000 stores—up from 676 a decade before—and roasted 2.3 percent of the world's coffee. Each day it opened an average of four stores and hired 200 employees. To support such a high growth rate, it was clear that an integral part of the company's future success would come from meeting increased demand through a secure supply of high-quality coffee beans. Coffee beans constituted the bread and butter of Starbucks' business—the company had to ensure a sustainable supply of this key commodity. Consequently, Starbucks partnered with Conservation International, an environmental nonprofit organization, to develop C.A.F.E. Practices (Coffee and Farmer Equity Practices). C.A.F.E.'s goals were to contribute to the livelihood of coffee farmers and to ensure high-quality coffee for the long term. This initiative was based on three principles: (1) a sustainable supply of high quality coffee beans, provided by a stable source of coffee farms with farmers who were not exploited by their trading partners, (2) lands farmed with environmentally sound methods, and (3) families that live in healthy, secure and supportive societies. Such farmers would be more inclined and able to invest in productivity improvement tools and activities, and in their communities, thereby promoting a source of stable and sustainable coffee supply.

Company background

Starbucks was founded in 1971 when three academics—English teacher Jerry Baldwin, history teacher Zev Siegel, and writer Gordon Bowker—opened a store called "Starbucks Coffee, Tea, and Spice" in Seattle. The partners named the company in honor of Starbuck, the coffee-loving first mate in Herman Melville's Moby Dick. The company's logo is a two-tailed mermaid encircled by the store's name.

By the early 1980s, the company had four Starbucks stores in the Seattle area and had showed profitability every year since opening. However, the roles of the founders underwent major changes. Zev Siegel left the company, Jerry Baldwin took over day-to-day management and functioned as CEO, and Gordon

---

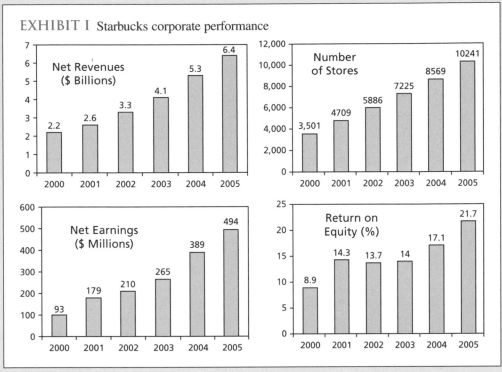

EXHIBIT I Starbucks corporate performance

Source: Starbucks Annual Reports.

EXHIBIT II Starbucks' statement of earnings

Fiscal Year Ended	Oct 2, 2005 (52 Wks)	Oct 3, 2004 (53 Wks)	Sept 28, 2003 (52 Wks)
STATEMENTS OF EARNING DATA			
Net revenues:	$5,391,927	$4,457,378	$3,449,624
Company-Operated retail	673,015	565,798	409,551
Specialty:	304,358	271,071	216,347
Licensing			
Foodservice & other			
Total specialty	977,373	836,869	625,898
Total net revenues	**6,369,300**	**5,294,247**	**4,075,522**
Cost of sales including occupancy costs	2,605,212	2,191,440	1,681,434
Store operating expenses	2,165,911	1,790,168	1,379,574
Other operating expenses	197,024	171,648	141,346
Depreciation & amortization expenses	340,169	289,182	244,671
General and administrative expenses	357,114	304,293	244,550
Subtotal operating expenses	5,665,430	4,746,731	3,691,575
Income from equity investees	76,745	59,071	36,903
Operating income	**780,615**	**606,587**	**420,850**
Interest and other income, net	15,829	14,140	11,622
Earnings before income taxes	796,444	620,727	432,472
Income taxes	301,977	231,754	167,117
Net earnings	**$494,467**	**$388,973**	**$265,355**

Source: Starbucks Form 10K, p. 23 (filled 12/16/2005).

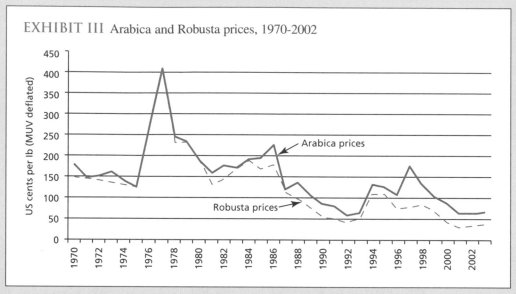

EXHIBIT III Arabica and Robusta prices, 1970-2002

Source: Data retrieved February 12, 2007, from Global Financial Data.

Bowker remained involved as owner while devoting most of his time to other business ventures.

In 1982, Baldwin recruited Howard Schultz, vice president and general manager of U.S. operations for Hammarplast, a Swedish maker of stylish kitchen equipment and housewares, as head marketing and retail stores supervisor. Schultz's biggest idea for the future of Starbucks came during the spring of 1983 when the company sent him to Milan, Italy, to attend an international housewares show. While walking from his hotel to the convention center, Schultz spotted an espresso bar and went inside to look around. The cashier beside the door nodded and smiled. The barista (counter worker) greeted Howard cheerfully, then gracefully pulled a shot of espresso for one customer and handcrafted a foamy cappuccino for another, all the while conversing merrily with those standing at the counter. On Schultz's return from Italy, he shared his revelation and ideas for modifying the format of Starbucks stores with Baldwin and Bowker. But instead of winning their approval, Schultz encountered strong resistance. After many failed efforts trying to persuade Baldwin and Bowker, Schultz decided to leave Starbucks and planned to open espresso bars in high-traffic downtown locations that would emulate the friendly, energetic atmosphere he had encountered in Italy. Schultz

left Starbucks in late 1985 to open his first II Giornale store a year later.

In March 1987, Jerry Baldwin and Gordon Bowker decided to sell the whole Starbucks operation in Seattle—the stores, the roasting plant, and the Starbucks name. Schultz raised capital and immediately bought the company. The new name of the combined companies was Starbucks Corporation. Howard Schultz, at the age of 34, became Starbucks' president and CEO.

In 2005, Starbucks had more than 10,200 company operated & licensed stores in more than 35 countries. The stores offered coffee drinks and food items, as well as beans, coffee accessories, teas, and music. Starbucks operated more than 5,200 stores in ten countries (80 percent in the U.S.), while licensees operated more than 2,800 units in 28 countries. U.S. licensed stores were located primarily in shopping centers and airports. The company also owned and licensed the Seattle's Best Coffee and Torrefazione Italia chains in the U.S. (more than 100 shops). In addition, Starbucks marketed its coffee through grocery stores and licensed its brand for other food and beverage products.

The specialty coffee industry and the Starbucks coffee supply chain

Since the 1980s and especially in the 1990s, the specialty coffee industry grew dramatically. Many experts felt that the differentiated coffees supported by the specialty industry would continue to expand at a much faster rate than conventional coffees. However, the definition of specialty in the United States continued to be refined. By 2005, it included coffees that were not necessarily high quality and were otherwise only distinguished by being flavored (e.g., chocolate, cinnamon, and hazelnut, etc.) and served as an espresso or milk-based beverage. The industry began to redefine "specialty" to reflect more of a quality orientation (see Exhibit 4). Also called "gourmet" or "premium" coffee, specialty coffee was made from exceptional beans grown only in ideal coffee-producing climates. It tended to feature distinctive flavors, shaped by the unique characteristics of the soil in which it was grown. Specialty coffee became one of the fastest growing food service markets in the world. The percentage of adults in the U.S. that consumed specialty coffee daily increased from 9 percent in 2000 to 16 percent in 2004, and 56 percent of adults claimed to be occasional consumers. The total specialty coffee market was estimated to be $9.62 billion in 2004.[2]

In 2004, there were an estimated 18,600 specialty coffee outlets in the United States.[3] Starbucks' success had prompted a number of ambitious rivals to scale up their expansion plans. Observers believed there was room in the category for at least two or three other national players. (See Exhibit 5 for Starbucks' key competitors.)

EXHIBIT IV Specialty coffee factoids

- Specialty coffee is defined as a coffee that has no defects and has a distinctive flavor in the cup.

- Specialty coffee, a term that refers to the highest-quality green beans roasted by true craftspeople, is surprisingly affordable. One cup costs about 24 cents (based on 50 cups/lb @ $ 12/lb)—making it cheaper than bottled water.

- Every day, Americans drink more than 300 million cups of coffee; 75% of those cups are home-brewed.

- In 2005, 15 percent of the adult American population enjoyed a daily cup of specialty coffee.

- Like wine and honey, specialty coffee has a unique flavor thanks to the micro-climates that produce it.

- In 1683, one pound of coffee in New York was worth as much as four acres of land.

- To be considered truly fresh, coffee should be ground right before brewing and brewed within three to seven days of roasting.

- Surprisingly, a 1 oz. espresso contains less caffeine (approx. 40 mg) than a regular 8 oz. serving of drip coffee (approx. 85 mg). In fact, in the espresso brewing method, water is in contact with the grounds for only 20 to 25 seconds and extracts less caffeine than methods that put water in contact with the grounds for several minutes.

- Strong-tasting coffee has no more caffeine than its weak-tasting counterpart. Caffeine contributes no taste; it's a product of the type of bean, water-to-coffee ratio, and brewing method.

- Seventy percent of the world's coffee production is the Arabica species.

- Thanks to some popular commercials, most of us believe that coffee originated in Colombia or Brazil. Not so; it originated in Ethiopia.

- The global coffee industry employs more than 20 million people.

- It takes approximately 42 coffee beans to make an average serving of espresso.

Source: "Specialty Coffee Factoids," Specialty Coffee Association of America, http://www.scaa.org/pdfs/specialtycoffeefacts.pdf (February 6, 2007).

Coffee beans could come from all over the world—about 50 percent came from Latin America, 35 percent from the Pacific Rim, and 15 percent from East Africa. Most of the coffee producers were small to medium-sized family-owned farms. Some farms were able to process their coffee beans, but most sold their outputs to processors through local markets (mills, exporters or cooperatives). The processors turned coffee "cherry" into parchment or green coffee, and then sold it to suppliers who were exporters or distributors. These suppliers provided many services to processors and farmers, such as marketing, dry milling, technical coffee expertise, financing, and export logistics.

Starbucks also purchased coffee through agents from individual estates and producer associations in addition to suppliers, or directly

---

EXHIBIT V Starbucks' main competitors

Caribou Coffee (http://www.cariboucoffee.com)

The company owned and operated the second largest non-franchised coffee chain in the U.S. (behind Starbucks), with about 300 stores in 12 states and the District of Columbia. The outlets, designed to resemble ski lodges and Alaskan cabins, offered a wide variety of coffee blends as well as specialty coffee drinks. The company also sold whole bean coffee and related brewing supplies. Caribou Coffee was founded in 1992 by John and Kim Puckett. Crescent Capital, the private equity arm of First Islamic Investment Bank, bought a 70 percent stake in Caribou Coffee in 2000—the ownership was later increased to almost 90 percent.

Diedrich Coffee (http://www.diedrich.com)

Diedrich Coffee had more than 515 coffeehouses in the U.S. and 13 other countries. The nation's #2 coffeehouse company (behind Starbucks), Diedrich's outlets operated under the brands Diedrich Coffee, Gloria Jean's, and Coffee People. The company also supplied wholesale coffee to restaurants (such as Ruby Tuesday and Ruth's Chris Steak House), office coffee suppliers, and other hospitality and specialty retail customers. Chairman Paul Heeschen controlled 32 percent of Diedrich Coffee.

Dunkin Brands (http://www.dunkinbrands.com)

A division of wine and spirits maker Allied Domecq, it franchised more than 12,000 quick-service eateries, including Dunkin's Donuts, Baskin-Robbins, and Togo's. With about 6,000 locations (more than 4,400 in the US), Dunkin was the world's leading chain of doughnut shops and Baskin-Robbins was a leading seller of ice cream and frozen snacks with its more than 5,400 outlets (about half are located in the US). Dunkin's Togo's shops (more than 400 West Coast units) served a variety of made-to-order sandwiches. About 1,100 locations offer a combination of the company's brands. In 2005 Dunkin's parent company was taken over by Pernod Ricard.

Others

In addition, numerous restaurants were picking up on the growing popularity of specialty coffees and had installed machines to serve espresso, cappuccino, café latte, and other coffee drinks to their customers. Starbucks also faced competition from nationwide coffee manufacturers such as Kraft General Foods (the parent of Maxwell House), Procter & Gamble (the owner of the Folger's brand), Sara Lee, and Nestlé, the latter two also distributed their coffees through supermarkets. There were also a number of specialty coffee companies that sell whole-bean coffees in supermarkets.

Source: "Coffeehouses and Donut Shops - US - February 2005," Mintel Reports, Mintel International Group Limited.

from the processors. (Exhibit 6 gives a simplified picture of the supply chain of green coffee to Starbucks.)

C.A.F.E. Practices

Despite its domination of the specialty coffee industry, Starbucks did not use its purchasing power as a way to squeeze its coffee suppliers in order to improve margins. Instead, the company decided to use its market power as a way to implement social change within its supply chain through C.A.F.E. Practices. C.A.F.E. Practices was a way for Starbucks to ensure a sustainable supply of high quality coffee beans, which was an essential component of Starbucks' business. The initiative built mutually beneficial relationships with coffee farmers and their communities. It also helped to counteract the oversupply of low-grade coffee on the world's market, which suppressed prices making it difficult for farmers to cover the cost of production. When Starbucks implemented C.A.F.E. Practices, it had six objectives in mind:

1 Increase economic, social, and environmental sustainability in the specialty coffee industry, including conservation of biodiversity.

2 Encourage Starbucks suppliers to implement C.A.F.E. Practices through economic incentives and preferential buying status.

3 Purchase the majority of Starbucks coffee under C.A.F.E. Practices guidelines by 2007.

4 Negotiate mutually beneficial long-term contracts with suppliers to support Starbucks' growth

5 Build mutually beneficial and increasingly direct relationships with suppliers.

6 Promote transparency and economic fairness within the coffee supply chain.

C.A.F.E Practices was a set of coffee buying guidelines designed to support coffee buyers and coffee farmers, ensure high quality coffee and promote equitable relationships with farmers, workers, and communities, as well as to protect the environment (see Exhibit 7). It was not a code of conduct or a compliance program. Instead, it was a way of doing business that was aimed at ensuring sustainability and fairness in the coffee supply chain. This sustainability and fairness was achieved through a set of global guidelines for Starbucks suppliers and a set of incentives to reward farmers and suppliers who followed those guidelines. The guidelines consisted first of a set

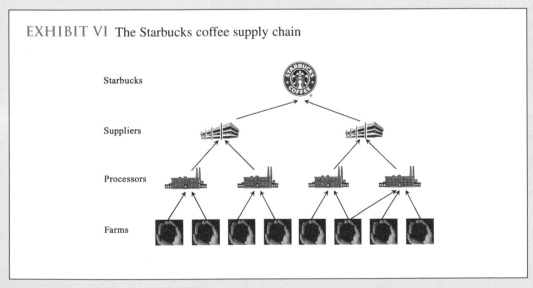

EXHIBIT VI   The Starbucks coffee supply chain

Starbucks

Suppliers

Processors

Farms

Source: Starbucks. Reprinted by permission.

of prerequisites, which had to be met in order to be considered for the C.A.F.E. Practices initiative. These prerequisites set a minimum standard for Starbucks suppliers, including coffee quality and economic transparency. The transparency prerequisite meant that suppliers were expected to illustrate economic transparency on the amount of money that was ultimately paid to farmers.

After the initial prerequisites had been met, suppliers were graded based on a set of environmental and social criteria. All suppliers were evaluated not just on their performance, but also on their supply networks of farms. Farmers were rewarded for coffee growing and processing practices that contributed positively to the conservation of soil, water, energy, and biological diversity, and had minimal impact on the environment. Also, C.A.F.E. Practices encouraged farmers and others to make sure that workers' wages met or exceeded the minimum requirements under local and national laws. Effective measures were required to ensure workers' health and safety and provide

---

EXHIBIT VII C.A.F.E Practices self-evaluation checklist

Product Quality – Required

- Green Preparation - Prerequisite
- Cup Quality - Prerequisite

Economic Accountability - Required

- Demonstration of Economic Transparency
- Equity of Financial Reward
- Financial Viability

Social Responsibility

Hiring Practices and Employment Policies:
- Minimum/Living Wage/Overtime Regulation*
- Freedom of Association/Collective Bargaining
- Vacation/Sick Leave Regulation
- Child Labor/Discrimination/Forced Labor*

Worker Conditions:
- Access to Housing, Water and Sanitary Facilities
- Access to Education
- Access to Medical Care
- Access to Training, Health & Safety

Coffee Growing - Environmental Leadership

Protecting Water Resources:
- Watercourse Protection
- Water Quality Protection

Protecting Soil Resources:
- Controlling Surface Erosion
- Improving Soil Quality

Conserving Biodiversity:
- Maintaining Coffee Shade Canopy and Natural Vegetation
- Protecting Wildlife
- Conservation Areas and Ecological Reserves

EXHIBIT VII (Continued)

Environmental Management and Monitoring:
- Ecological Pests and Disease Management and Reducing Agrochemical Use
- Farm Management and Monitoring Practices

Coffee Processing - Environmental Leadership

Wet Milling
- Minimizing Water Consumption
- Reducing Wastewater Impacts

Water Conservation:
- Waste Management Operations/Beneficial Reuse

Energy Use:
- Energy Conservation/Impacts

Dry Milling

Waste Management:
- Waste Management Operations/Beneficial Reuse

Energy Use:
- Energy Conservation/Impacts

Source: Starbucks. For more information, see "C.A.F.E. Practices: Generic Evaluation Guidelines," Starbucks Coffee Company, November 9, 2004, http://www.scscertified.com/csrpurchasing/docs/CAFEPracticesEvaluationGuidelines 110904English.pdf.

them with adequate living conditions. Based on their performance, as measured against the environmental and social criteria, suppliers might earn up to 100 percentage points in C.A.F.E. Practices.

Under C.A.F.E. Practices, farms, mills, and suppliers had to illustrate equitable payments to those who worked for them or sold to them. They had to demonstrate economic accountability and document their hiring and employment practices. Scores were audited by an independent verifier, and licensed by Scientific Certification Systems, a third-party certification company that provided independent analysis and certification of a wide range of environment sustainability and food safety achievements.[4] Since the verifier was independent of Starbucks, the cost of the verification had to be negotiated between the supplier and the verifier. However, there was no cost to the supplier to submit a C.A.F.E. Practices application to Starbucks.

In order to qualify for C.A.F.E. Practices supplier status, suppliers had to be independently verified and meet minimum Social Responsibility criteria. Points above 60 percent increased the status of the supplier. For scores above 60 percent, the supplier qualified as a Preferred supplier and would gain preference in future Starbucks coffee purchases. Additionally, suppliers who earned scores above 80 percent would qualify as Strategic suppliers and would earn a Sustainability Conversion Premium of $0.05 per pound of coffee for one year.[5] In order to encourage continued improvement, Starbucks also offered an additional Sustainability Performance Premium of $0.05 per pound of coffee to suppliers who were able to achieve a 10-point increase above 80 percent over the course of a year.

Besides the price premium for Strategic Suppliers, C.A.F.E. Practices allowed Starbucks to buy from preferred suppliers first, paying high prices and offering preferential contract terms to those with the highest scores. The premium prices helped coffee farmers make profits and support their families, despite a global glut in the coffee bean industry. Additionally, Starbucks provided access to affordable credit to coffee farmers through various loan funds. They invested in social development in coffee producing countries and collaborated with farmers through the Farmer Support Center in Costa Rica to provide technical support and training. If a supplier failed to meet C.A.F.E. Practices criteria, Starbucks sponsored information sessions in coffee growing regions for farmers. (See Exhibit 8 for a description of a farmer benefiting from the C.A.F.E. Practices program.)

Benefits to Starbucks

Even though the direct benefits of C.A.F.E. Practices helped suppliers and farmers, Starbucks received significant indirect benefits from the program. The program strengthened Starbucks' supply base, improved its marketing ability, and increased its visibility into the supply chain. Therefore, the benefits of C.A.F.E. Practices extended all the way through the supply chain, from the farm to the end consumer.

Supply base

On the supply base side, the program served to lock in strategic and high quality suppliers. This consistent, quality supply could provide Starbucks with a competitive advantage over other coffee roasters in the industry. Since suppliers would have invested resources in complying with Starbucks programs, they would have an incentive to remain with Starbucks and would face switching costs should they try to demonstrate their excellence to another coffee roaster. The large pool of high quality suppliers would also smooth supply fluctuations by providing a base supply of high quality growers. Since Starbucks' long purchase cycle included signing purchase agreements before the crop had even been harvested, any reduction in supply uncertainties and fluctuations could

---

EXHIBIT VIII Success story of a coffee farmer: Investment payoff for C.A.F.E, Standards

For years, the Santa Teresa farm did well enough by producing regular extra-prime coffee rather than higher quality specialty grade. But that changed when world coffee prices hit rock bottom several years ago. Ervin Pohlenz Cordova, the son of the farm's owner, wasn't earning enough for his crops to cover the farm's expenses. The farm nearly went bankrupt.

Cordova was introduced to Starbucks through his exporter and discovered he could earn more by producing higher-quality coffee. Santa Teresa is located in Chiapas, Mexico, an area known for its optimal altitude, fertile soil and shade trees—perfect coffee-growing conditions. Some investments were needed to improve quality and implement sustainable farming practices, a commitment Cordova was willing to make, despite initial resistance from his elderly father.

It took three years before the coffee grown on Santa Teresa farm reached Starbucks quality standards. Along the way, the exporter worked with Cordova on implementing quality improvements. In 2003, Starbucks signed a three-year contract to buy all of Santa Teresa's high-quality coffee at premium prices and added a provision that earmarked funds for social improvement and environmental protection projects to benefit the farm. Cordova's accomplishment is now the pride of his father.

The Starbucks contract gives Pohlenz security in knowing he has a buyer for his future crops and one that contributes to the quality of life on Santa Teresa farm. "Now I feel that I will work my entire life as a coffee producer because my farm is sustainable," he said. Clearly, Cordova's investment is paying off. And for Starbucks, we gain a wonderful source of high quality coffee grown under sustainable conditions. Cordova is a firm believer in C.A.F.E. Practices, and his goal is to become a Starbucks preferred supplier in 2005.

Source: "Starbucks—Corporate Social Responsibility Report, FY04," Starbucks Corporation.

lead to better planning of future supply in the form of faster procurement. C.A.F.E. Practices could also improve Starbucks' reputation among suppliers, which would make it easier to expand into purchasing in different countries or locations.

In the long run, C.A.F.E. Practices also sought to buffer against a form of bullwhip effect that existed in the coffee industry supply chain. As coffee sales increased during the 1990s with the growth of Starbucks and the specialty coffee industry, suppliers and farmers began to respond with a huge increase in the amount of land dedicated to coffee farming. The resulting glut of coffee beans on the market led to decreased prices and a shortage of high quality coffee. Such fluctuations in price and supply were common in commodity products that faced very long supply response times. In order to combat price and supply volatility, the C.A.F.E. Practices initiative induced longer-term supply relationships with a consistent set of suppliers. Starbucks was hopeful that this program would reduce its susceptibility to price and supply volatility in the global coffee market.

Marketing

On the marketing side, C.A.F.E. Practices supported Starbucks' socially responsible goals. While C.A.F.E. Practices were not yet widespread and were not directly marketed to customers, an increased awareness of Starbucks corporate social responsibility (CSR) practices could help justify Starbucks' premium prices. C.A.F.E. Practices would allow Starbucks to market its coffee as procured through a highly selective process that ensured only the highest quality beans. Awareness of this program might encourage other coffee roasters to join in the C.A.F.E. Practices program; however, Starbucks would be known as the inventor of the program. They might also be able to brand their practices and sell the know-how to other roasters that were looking to implement similar initiatives. Such widespread expansion of the program would simply serve to extend its benefits towards creating a base of high quality coffee beans. With each improvement in the supply of beans, Starbucks achieved more flexibility in being able to charge premium prices at its stores.

C.A.F.E. Practices also improved employee morale by creating an atmosphere of social responsibility that they could be proud of.

Supply chain visibility

Finally, C.A.F.E. Practices increased the visibility of Starbucks' supply chain by demanding documented and verified product and financial flows through its suppliers' supply chains. In the past, Starbucks had very poor visibility into their supply base, as coffee farmers and processors were not very technologically sophisticated or mature in their business processes. By increasing the transparency of their supply base, Starbucks would be able to gain a better understanding of the needs and the conditions of their suppliers. The increased visibility would also allow Starbucks to improve its relationships with growers, who before had been isolated from them due to intermediaries—coffee exporters and distributors—that came between the two sides.

On a more practical note, increased visibility in the supply chain could allow Starbucks to better predict supply shortages as they arose. Since the majority of Starbucks coffee was grown in developing countries in Latin America, Africa, South America, and Southeast Asia, Starbucks had a significant risk of supply shortage due to regional instability. Without visibility into the supply base, Starbucks did not have a good way to predict the impact of regional instability to its coffee supply. With increased visibility, an outbreak of regional instability could be linked to a particular quantity of expected coffee supply, giving Starbucks advance notice of the need to find alternate sources of coffee. This could allow Starbucks to be proactive in managing supply disruptions even before they arose.

Corporate social responsibility

Starbucks provided various resources to promote and help farmers comply with the guidelines of C.A.F.E. Practices and ensure sustainability. In January 2004, the company opened a farmer support center called the Starbucks Coffee Agronomy Company in Costa Rica that contained a team of experts in soil management and field-crop production (agronomists), and in coffee quality and sustainable practices. These experts collaborated directly with farmers and suppliers in Central America and provided services to farmers and suppliers in Mexico and South America. This helped build long-term and strategic relationships with members in the supply chain who were committed to the sustainable production of high-quality coffee. They also administered C.A.F.E. Practices, oversaw regional social programs, and engaged with local government on sustainability issues.

Starbucks also bought certified or eco-labeled coffees that had been grown and sold in ways that helped preserve the natural environment and/or promote economic sustainability. There were three such types of environmentally sustainable coffee purchased by Starbucks:

- *Conservation coffee* (shade-grown): Starbucks, through its partnership with CI (a nonprofit organization dedicated to protecting global biodiversity), encouraged coffee farmers to use traditional and sustainable cultivation methods. The basic aim was to protect shade trees, which were often stripped away and replaced with tight rows of coffee trees on large coffee plantations. This not only destroyed the habitats of numerous species but also resulted in lower coffee production.

- *Certified organic coffee:* This coffee was grown without the use of synthetic pesticides, herbicides, or chemical fertilizers to help maintain healthy soil and groundwater.

- *Fair trade certified coffee:* Through a licensing agreement with TransFair USA, Starbucks tried to ensure that coffee farmers were fairly compensated for their crops. The Fair Trade Certified Coffee label certified that the coffee met Fair Trade criteria. These criteria focused primarily on price and other sustainable needs. Fair Trade Certified coffees only came from democratically owned cooperatives, not large farms or coffee pulled across supply channels.

In order to improve farmers' access to financing, Starbucks provided loan funds to several organizations to ensure that farmers could obtain affordable loans and to help them gain some financial ability to improve their agriculture techniques. In 2004, Starbucks committed $6 million to several loan programs. The importance and alignment of this upstream support component was highlighted in a quote from Shari Berenbach of Calvert Foundation: "Starbucks has taken a leadership position by aligning its investment capital with the company's mission and products to create more sustainable coffee growing communities."

Finally, Starbucks worked with local farmers to understand the greatest needs of their rural communities, which often lacked basic necessities such as adequate housing, health clinics, schools, good roads, and fresh drinking water. Starbucks collaborated with these farmers to develop projects that helped meet their needs, especially in areas where the company bought large volumes of coffee. In fiscal 2004, the company contributed nearly $1.8 million for 35 social programs.

C.A.F.E Practices implementation

There were two main challenges facing C.A.F.E. Practices implementation that could potentially be addressed with better integrated information technologies. First, since some members of the supply chain had very poor information systems, it could be very difficult to gain economic transparency—a key goal of C.A.F.E. Practices—from these members. Second, as C.A.F.E. Practices were updated and refined, it became a daunting job to effectively communicate the revised requirements and practices to farmers, suppliers, and other members of the industry.

In addition, it had been a very labor-intensive and slow process to evaluate farmers for scores in the C.A.F.E. program. Auditors had no choice but to travel to the farms, which were often located in barely accessible areas.

The company was in the process of developing an internal system to track compliance with C.A.F.E. Practices, and link such data to support procurement. The plan was to integrate the C.A.F.E. Practices data, at the time stored in spreadsheets, with the more versatile database, and to then link the data with its procurement system, together with other information systems on quality data.

To Starbucks, it seemed that a more comprehensive information system was needed to support a large-scale implementation of C.A.F.E. Practices.

Future of C.A.F.E Practices

As Starbucks embarked on the aggressive expansion of C.A.F.E. Practices towards meeting its goal of supplying the majority of its coffee through the program by 2007, there were a number of internal and external challenges. Internally, Starbucks would have to address its information system issues. Externally, Starbucks had to find an effective way to communicate and interface with its low-tech suppliers.

The opportunity, however, was tremendous. If Starbucks was able to overcome the implementation issues that it faced, C.A.F.E. Practices could go a long way towards improving the sustainability of its coffee supply chain while at the same time improving Starbucks' image as a socially responsible corporation.

Notes

1. This case is based oh interviews with the following Starbucks representatives: Dub Hay, Vice President of Coffee Procurement; Brooke Brown, Project Specialist, Coffee; Stephane Erard; and Michelle Richardson. All subsequent quotes and references are from these interviews or information provided by Starbucks unless otherwise noted.
2. "Specialty Coffee Retail in the USA 2005," Specialty Coffee Association of America, https://www.scaa.org/pdfs/news/specialtvcoffeeretail.pdf (February 5. 2007).
3. Ibid.
4. "About SCS," Scientific Certification Systems, http://www.scscertified.org/about.html (March 1, 2007).
5. On average, Starbucks paid about $1.20 per pound of coffee. "Starbucks - Corporate Social Responsibility Report, FY04," Starbucks Corporation, p. 15.

LIFEBUOY "SWASTHYA CHETNA": UNILEVER'S SOCIAL MARKETING CAMPAIGN

"Swasthya Chetna is not about philanthropy. It's a marketing program with social benefits. We recognize that the health of our business is totally interconnected with the health of the communities we serve and if we are to grow sales of our brand, we have to increase the number of people who use soap."[1]

– Harpreet Singh Tibb, Senior Product Manager for Lifebuoy, Hindustan Lever Ltd, in 2005.

"Unilever believes that one of the best and most sustainable ways it can help to address global social and environmental concerns is through the very business of doing business in a socially aware and responsible manner."[2]

– Unilever, in its report *"Global Challenges – Local Actions", in 2005.*

Lifebuoy leaves its stamp on India

In April 2006, Lifebuoy, a leading soap brand manufactured and marketed by Hindustan Lever Limited (HLL), the Indian arm of the fast moving consumer goods (FMCG) major, Unilever, became the first brand in India to be featured on a postal cover. On the occasion of World Health day, on April 7, 2006, the Minister of State for Communications and IT, Government of India (GoI), Dr Shakeel Ahmed, released a special Lifebuoy "Swasthya Chetna Postal Cover" (*Refer to Exhibit I for a picture of the Lifebuoy "Swasthya Chetna Postal Cover"*). The Department of Post under the Ministry of Communications issued this Special Postal Cover in recognition of the work done by HLL to increase awareness about health and

hygiene, through its Lifebuoy 'Swasthya Chetna' ('Health Awakening') program in rural India (*Refer to Exhibit II for the Lifebuoy "Swasthya Chetna" logo*). Speaking on the occasion, Chief Post Master General of the Maharashtra[3] Circle, K Noorjehan, said, "I congratulate Lifebuoy and Hindustan Lever for initiating and assiduously implementing this socially beneficial movement."[4]

Lifebuoy's "Swasthya Chetna" (LSC) was a five-year health and hygiene education program launched by HLL, in 2002, in eight states across India. The objective of this program was to educate around 200 million people in rural and urban areas about the importance of adopting good 'health and hygiene' practices. The program spread awareness about germs and their adverse effects on health, and how proper 'health and hygiene' practices, such as bathing and washing hands with soap could prevent diseases like diarrhea. "Our number one aim is to challenge the misconception that 'visibly clean' is 'hygienically clean'. And we are working with parents and children, health educators, teachers, community leaders, and government agencies to spread the word,"[5] said Caroline Harding, Global Brand Director, Health Brands, Unilever. In the process, HLL sought to increase the sales of Lifebuoy soaps by convincing these people to use soaps more frequently and also to create new users for its brand.

HLL launched the LSC program in villages where media penetration was negligible. The people of these villages were educated through lectures, demonstrations, visual aids such as flip charts and interactive quizzes. Various media vehicles were used in the program including cinema vans, wall paintings, weekly markets, fairs, and festivals. The initiative started with communication to schoolchildren, which was extended to their parents and other adults, and culminated in the formation of sustainable health clubs by the local people. The whole process took around two to three years. HLL had committed US$ 5.4 million for this five-year program.[6] The program was implemented by Ogilvy Outreach,[7] while Weber Shandwick (WS),[8] one of the largest public relations (PR) agencies in the world, provided the PR support.

EXHIBIT 1 Lifebuoy "Swasthya Chetna postal cover"

Source: www.unilever.com.

EXHIBIT II Lifebuoy "Swasthya Chetna" logo

Source: Dr. Brigitte Tantawy Monsou, "SoL Sustainability Consortium." solsustainablility.org, April 27, 2005.

By the end of 2005, HLL had covered more than 18,000 villages in these eight states. The sales of Lifebuoy grew by 20 percent in 2003-04 with strong sales reported from the eight states where the program was being implemented. In 2005, the Lifebuoy brand grew by 10 percent and this growth was expected to continue in 2006. The program also received a lot of positive media attention.

According to HLL, LSC was not a philanthropic activity, but a marketing program with a social benefit. HLL sought to grow the Lifebuoy brand in India by attracting those consumers who never used soap. In the process, the company sought to bring about a behavioral change by convincing people to use soaps more frequently, thus creating more users for its brand. Given the overall success of the LSC program in India, Unilever initiated a similar program in Bangladesh. Unilever also planned to replicate this program in five African countries in the near future.

Background note

Hindustan Vanaspati Manufacturing Company, the first Indian subsidiary of Unilever was established in 1931. (*Refer to Exhibit III for a brief note on Unilever*). However, many of Unilever's popular brands like 'Lifebuoy', 'Pears', 'Lux', 'Vim', and 'Dalda' were already available in India. In 1933, Lever Brothers India Ltd. was set up followed by the establishment of another subsidiary United Traders Ltd. in 1935. In 1956, these three subsidiaries merged to form HLL.

In the 1990s, HLL consolidated its leadership position in the FMCG market through a number of mergers and acquisitions like the merger of Tata Oil Mills Company[9] (TOMCO) with HLL, the formation of Brooke Bond Lipton India Ltd. (BBLIL),[10] and the merger of Pond's (India) Ltd.[11] with HLL. HLL also formed joint ventures with Kimberley-Clark Corporation[12] and Lakmé Ltd.[13] (Lakmé).

In the late 1990s, many of HLL's star brands faced intense competition from domestic and international rivals. For instance, its soap brands, such as Lux, Lifebuoy, and Liril, which together accounted for almost 70 percent of the Rs. 35 billion market in India, faced increased competition from low-priced soap brands of companies like Nirma Ltd. Brands in other categories such as Pepsodent, Close-Up, and Fair & Lovely, too faced similar competition. In 2000, HLL lost market share across various categories. It examined its brand portfolio thoroughly and decided to concentrate its resources behind 30 of its key brands, termed as "power brands", out of its 110 brands. These brands were selected using various criteria such as size, brand strength, brand relevance, competitive advantage, and potential for growth. HLL also realized that if it wanted to drive the growth of its brands, it had to focus its efforts on the vast rural market.

Though HLL had started increasing its presence in the rural market since the mid-1980s, it mostly used traditional modes to reach out to the rural consumer i.e., wholesalers, retailers, and van campaigns to induce the village retailers to stock its products. The downside was that, areas which could not be reached by these motor vehicles were not catered to. In 1998, HLL launched "Project Streamline" to enhance control over the rural distribution by appointing appointed Rural Distributors attached to sub-stockists, who were expected to increase distribution in the neighboring villages through unconventional modes like tractors, bullock carts, etc. This project helped HLL in extending its rural reach to about 37 percent in 1998 from 25 percent in 1995.

In 1998, HLL initiated a rural home-to-home effort 'Project Bharat', to increase use of personal care products among the rural population. Low-unit price packs of personal care products were introduced and microcredit[14] was provided to villagers through the local banks. HLL trained

---

EXHIBIT III A brief note on Unilever

Unilever, an Anglo-Dutch company, was formed in 1930 by the merger between British soapmaker Lever Brothers and Dutch margarine producer Margarine Union. For tax reasons, the merged unit formed two separate entities – Unilever Plc in London and Unilever NV in Rotterdam, the Netherlands. By the start of the new millennium, Unilever had become a leading manufacturer and marketer of consumer product brands in foods, beverages, cleaning agents, and personal care products. Some of its big brands are Knorr, Lipton, Flora, Becel, Bertolli, Slimfast, Hellmann's, Birds Eye, Omo, Domestos, Surf, and Radiant. Its personal care brands include Dove, Vaseline, Sunsilk, Signal, Rexona, AXE, Lux, Pond's, and Lifebuoy. Unilever's revenues for 2005 were €39.67 billion (just over US$50 billion) and it employed more than 206,000 people around the world.

Source: Compiled from various sources.

them to utilize this credit to buy the company's products and sell them at a profit. In late 1999, HLL engaged Ogilvy Outreach to take care of its rural communication campaign. As the media penetration in rural areas was just 57 percent, unconventional media strategies were used. Messages were presented through wall paintings, colorful flyers, entertaining jingles, and traveling cinema vans. The messages were longer and had a local flavor. Live shows were organized at village fairs to promote the company's brands.

In 2001, HLL introduced a rural initiative called 'Project Shakti'. Initially, it worked with 13,000 underprivileged rural women, training them in skills to become entrepreneurs distributing HLL products. In 2002, it started LSC for promoting the use of soaps to wash hands in rural areas. In late 2003, HLL was engaged in the process of piloting `I-Shakti', an IT-based rural information service that provided solutions to key requirements of the rural people in areas of education, vocational training, agriculture, health and hygiene.[15] In 2005, HLL had around 25,000 such entrepreneurs under its fold.[16] In the same year, it launched Pureit, a water purifier product, in India.

HLL's revenues for 2005 were Rs.110.61 billion (as of December 31, 2005) and its net profit was Rs. 14.08 billion.[17] As of August 2006, HLL, in which Unilever held a 51 percent stake, was the largest FMCG company in India, with a large number of brands in its portfolio. (*Refer to Exhibit IV for a list of HLL's brands*).

Lifebuoy and health

Lifebuoy was initially launched in India in 1895, within one year of its launch in the UK. It was the flagship soap brand of Unilever (*Refer to Exhibit V for Lifebuoy's logo*). In the 1930s, Unilever started the "Clean hands help guard health" campaign in the US to encourage consumers to make their hands germ-free by using Lifebuoy. The success of this campaign prompted HLL to start a similar initiative in India in 1935, and by 1940, Lifebuoy had become the market leader in the personal wash category in India. Ever since its launch, Lifebuoy had had a strong association with health and well-being and Unilever engaged in activities which

reinforced this association. For instance, during the Blitz[18] of London in 1940, the people of London could avail of free emergency mobile washing facilities provided by Lifebuoy. There were also Lifebuoy vans, which were equipped with hot showers, soaps, and towels. In India, HLL's ad campaigns for Lifebuoy too reinforced the association of the brand with health and hygiene, and Lifebuoy was firmly positioned as a brand for healthy and hard-working men.

In 1964, the Lifebuoy brand underwent a major transformation in India, with a change in product formulation, shape, and packaging. The new soap was in the shape of a red brick bar and cresylic-perfumed.[19] The new ad had the jingle '*Tandurusti ki raksha karta hai Lifebuoy . . . Lifebuoy hai jahaan tandurusti hai wahaan*' (Lifebuoy protects one's vitality . . . where there is Lifebuoy there is vitality). The jingle became very popular over the next few decades. All the ad spots showed the model playing some form of sports and was followed by a shot of him enjoying a bath with Lifebuoy, thus reinforcing the brand's association with health and hygiene. Notwithstanding competition from other economical soaps such as Tomco's bathing soap, and Det bathing bar, Lifebuoy remained the market leader. It had mass appeal and 70 percent of its sales came from rural areas and towns.[20]

Until the early 1990s, the bath soap market in India was categorized into three segments – Premium, priced above Rs.11; Popular, priced between Rs.7 and Rs.11, and Carbolic soaps, which were priced below Rs.6. Lifebuoy was the market leader in the carbolic soaps segment. In 1992, Nirma Ltd. launched Nirma Bath Soap that was very similar to Lifebuoy, at half the price of Lifebuoy. The success of the Nirma Bath Soap also brought new competitors into the market. In the late 1990s, the emerging 'discount segment'[21] brands started eroding the market shares of the 'popular' and 'carbolic' segment brands. This was evident from the fact that in 2001, when the premium and popular segments posted growth rates of three percent and one percent respectively (in volume terms) over the previous year, the 'discount segment' grew by 15 percent. At the same time, the carbolic soaps segment, dominated by Lifebuoy, registered a negative growth rate of

EXHIBIT IV List of HLL's brands

Category	Sub-Category	Brands
Home and Personal Care	Personal Wash	Lux, Lifebuoy, Liril, Hamam, Breeze, Dove, Pears, Rexona
	Skin Care	Fair & Lovely, Pond's
	Laundry	Surf Excel, Rin, Wheel
	Hair Care	Sunsilk Naturals, Clinic Plus
	Oral Care	Pepsodent, Close-up
	Deodorants	Axe, Rexona
	Colour Cosmetics	Lakme
	Ayurvedic Personal and Health Care	Ayush
Foods	Tea	Brooke Bond, Lipton
	Coffee	Bru
	Foods	Kissan, Knorr Annapurna
	Ice Cream	Kwality Wall's
Hindustan Lever Network	Home and Personal Care	Detergents (Lever Home), Home cleaning (Lever Home), Personal care & cosmetics for women (Aviance), Soaps (Ayush Spa range, Aviance and Denim Xclusive), Oral care (Mentadent), Health care (Ayush Spa), Male grooming (Denim xclusive), Kids Care (Little Animalz)
	Food	Children's nutrition (Ayush Poshak Rasayana), Ready-to-cook rice meals (Indus Valley)
Exports	Home and Personal Care	Lux, Lifebuoy, Pears, Fair & Lovely, Dove, Vaseline, Close-Up, Pepsodent, Signal
	Tea	Brooke Bond, Brooke Bond Red label, Brooke Bond Taj Mahal, Lipton, Lipton Yellow Label, Lipton Green Label, Lipton Brisk, Lipton 3-in-1 premix, Chinese Rickshaw
	Marine Products	Ocean Diamond, Ocean Excellence, Shogun, Hima, Gold Seal, Tara and Prima
	Rice	Gold Seal Indus Valley, Rozana and Annapurna
	Castor	Topsol
Water Purifier		Pureit

*The list is not exhaustive

Source: www.hll.com.

5 percent. Consumers preferred the 'discount soap' brands due to their affordability, softer texture, and better fragrance when compared to the hard and rugged carbolic soaps.

The increased penetration of the communication media into rural areas also impacted the sales of Lifebuoy. As rural consumers became aware of the wide range of soaps available in the market, some of them changed their brand preference. The increasing involvement of women in purchase decisions of household goods was also viewed as a reason for the fall in the sales of carbolic soap brands like Lifebuoy. Women preferred the newer, softer, and more fragrant soaps. Lifebuoy's overtly

EXHIBIT V Lifebuoy logo

Source: www.hll.com

masculine image too didn't help in this regard. In 2001, Lifebuoy's market share (in value terms) fell to 12.5 percent from 15.4 percent in 1997.[22] The decline in the overall soap market by 10 percent further affected the sales of the brand.

In 2002, HLL decided to reposition the brand by moving away from the personal hygiene plank to the family health plank. Lifebuoy started a repositioning exercise to shed its masculine image and appeal to women as a health soap for the entire family. Accordingly, changes were brought about in the formulation, size, shape, weight, and packaging of the soap. The product formulation was changed from a hard carbolic soap to a softer total fatty matter (TFM) soap with a refreshing fragrance. Four new variants were introduced – Lifebuoy Strong, Lifebuoy Fresh, Lifebuoy Gold, and Lifebuoy Naturals. The marketing communication was also changed to appeal to the women in the household. However, many analysts felt that HLL was confusing its consumers with its brand extensions. For instance, its Lifebuoy talc could cannibalize its deodorant brands, while some variants of Lifebuoy soap, such as Lifebuoy Naturals were not in line with Lifebuoy's 'health' positioning.

In 2002, HLL started a five-year rural marketing program called Lifebuoy "Swasthya Chetna" (LSC) and the 'Healthy Hindustan' campaign in 2003 in urban areas. After the re-launch of

Lifebuoy in 2002, sales volumes increased by 30 percent. In addition, its market share grew from 15.5 percent (as of March 2002) to 17.6 percent (as of December 2003).[23] HLL also introduced a herbal variant of Lifebuoy and Lifebuoy Talc, a talcum powder, in 2003.

In 2004, HLL started another repositioning exercise for Lifebuoy. The soap was given a more curved shape for 'easy grip' and the pack was changed to look more contemporary. (*Refer to Exhibit VI for pack-shots of Lifebuoy soap*). A number of variants of Lifebuoy with new formulations were introduced over the next two years, including Lifebuoy Clear Skin, a premium soap for clear skin and prevention of acne.

HLL said that the two repositioning exercises in 2002 and 2004 were undertaken to mark a "deliberate shift from the male, victorious concept of health to a warmer, more versatile, more responsible benefit of health for the entire family"[24] and to target the "housewife with a more inclusive 'family health protection for my family and me' positioning."[25] In 2005, Lifebuoy was still the leading bathing soap brand in India with a market share of 18.8 percent.[26]

For Unilever, Lifebuoy was a strong regional brand that was mainly sold in Asia and parts of Africa. Lifebuoy was a market leader in all the Asian markets where it was sold, and had positioned itself

EXHIBIT VI Pack-shots of Lifebuoy soaps

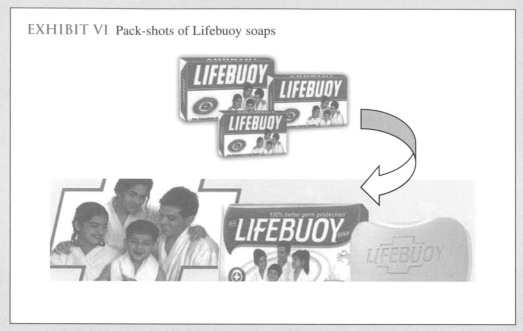

Source: www.hll.com

on the 'health and hygiene' platform. In 2005, Lifebuoy received the award of 'Citizen Brand' in Indonesia for its handwashing program. Walter Gibson (Gibson), the bioscience group leader, Research & Development, Hygiene & Personal Care, Unilever, summed up the aspect of Lifebuoy's positioning when he said, "Lifebuoy aims to reach everyone. Positioned as an aspirational product but is accessible to all. Lifebuoy is not focused particularly on the poor – it is about health for everybody. Lifebuoy positioned as a product to continue your life: saves you from disease, rejections etc. lets you continue to live your life, protection etc. Studies on measurement on recognition of brands and what they stand for, i.e., brand of Lifebuoy recognition of protection and fear from germs has gone up."[27]

Initiating a behavior change

It is estimated that across the world, diarrhea results in the death of about 3 million children each year.[28] In India, around 600,000 children die every year on account of diarrhea.[29] Diseases like diarrhea also lead to loss of workdays that directly affect labor productivity in rural India. However, diarrhea can be prevented by adopting the simple practice of washing one's hands with soap. Unilever, being a partner to the Global Public-Private Partnership for Handwashing with soap (GPPP-HW), decided to support the program initiative in India. (*Refer to Exhibit VII for a note on the GPPP-HW program*).

HLL started the LSC program with a new brand vision for Lifebuoy – 'to make a billion Indians feel safe and secure by meeting their hygiene needs'.[30] LSC was designed to change the behavior of those rural and urban consumers, who were infrequent users of soap. HLL's senior product manager for Lifebuoy, Harpreet Singh Tibb (Tibb) said, "People believe that 'visible clean' is 'safe' clean and hence tend to overlook simple hygiene practices such as washing hands with soap. But the fact is that there are invisible pathogens, which are responsible for many infectious diseases. We hence aim to educate people on the presence of invisible germs and raise concern on their consequences."[31]

The LSC campaign targeted the rural community and encouraged them to practice good personal hygiene habits, such as bathing with soap and using soap regularly for washing hands after defecation and before taking meals. The key

EXHIBIT VII A public-private partnership for handwashing

Diarrhea is estimated to kill over three million children every year. A study conducted by the World Bank[32] in 1998 in Guatemala, Bangladesh, and the USA, showed that mortality due to diarrhea could be reduced by 48 percent by washing hands with soap and water. Though it was well known that hands should be washed with soap after contact with human excreta and before handling food, it was not universally practiced. The problem was worse in developing countries where diarrhea was a major killer. With the aim "to reduce the incidence of diarrheal diseases in poor communities through Public-Private Partnerships (PPPs), promoting handwashing with soap",[33] the Global Public-Private Partnership for Handwashing with soap (GPPP-HW) was conceptualized in 2000.

The GPPP-HW project was launched by the World Bank, the London School of Hygiene and Tropical Medicine (LSHTM),[34] the United States Agency for International Development (USAID),[35] The United Nations Children's Fund (UNICEF),[36] World Health Organization (WHO),[37] etc., and the three biggest multi-national corporations (MNC) producing soap: Unilever, Procter & Gamble Co.[38] (P&G), and Colgate Palmolive Co.[39] The partnership aimed to market soap by targeting urban and rural poor people, and changing their behavior and attitudes toward handwashing. At the country level, the governments who controlled access to the potential markets too joined in the partnership. GPPP-HW strove to combine the expertise and resources of the soap industry with the facilities and resources of governments to promote handwashing with soap.

India was a potential market as half a billion people did not have access to proper sanitation, but the cost of reaching this highly scattered market was prohibitive for any company. So it was planned that the cost would be underwritten and facilitated by the GPPP-HW.[40]

In early 2001, HLL initiated the experimental "handwashing" campaign in Kerala, in partnership with the Indian Soap and Toiletries Manufacturers' Association (ISTMA), along with UNICEF, the LSHTM, and a various non-governmental organizations (NGOs).[41] However, HLL had to abandon the program in Kerala due to criticism from activists, who felt that the company was more interested in selling soap rather than promoting any health benefits. Notwithstanding this initial setback, HLL formally launched the LSC program in eight states of India in 2002.

Source: Compiled from various sources.

communication elements consisted of educating the target audience about the presence of germs and their role in causing diseases. The target audience was also educated about the role of handwashing with soap in preventing diseases like diarrhea. HLL wanted to position Lifebuoy as "a soap that kills germs, and an affordable prevention tool."[42] The program was test launched in 2001, when there was a 9-10 percent decline in the Indian soap market had severely impacted Lifebuoy.[43] Hence, HLL wanted to spur the growth of Lifebuoy by increasing the usage frequency and creating new users from among people who had never used soaps.

The program was formally launched on May 9, 2002, in eight states (Madhya Pradesh, Chhattisgarh, Jharkhand, Bihar, Uttar Pradesh, Maharashtra, Orissa, and West Bengal) across India. HLL had committed €4.5 million (US$ 5.4 million) to fund the campaign for five years.[44] The program aimed to reach 200 million people through this five-year program.

A multi-phase interactive program

Initially, the objective of trying to change the behavior and attitudes of rural consumers proved to be a tough challenge. The LSC program was a multi-phase initiative and it took around three years to complete all the phases of the campaign. It was a highly interactive campaign that aimed to educate people about germs and their consequences on health, using one-to-one interaction, outdoor media, PR, and a variety of community-based events for children, mothers, and other adults (*Refer to Figure 1 for Lifebuoy "Swasthya Chetna" – an interactive approach, and Figure 2 for the communication process in LSC*).

The LSC teams consisted of two members specially trained in communication – a health development facilitator (HDF) and a health development assistant (HDA). The HDF and HDA traveled from village to village and school to school, educating the community through meetings, classroom lectures, and demonstrations. Each team covered 24 villages in a month and 72 villages in a quarter. There were four direct contacts in a year to facilitate the behavioral change from "no relevance" to "habit formation."[45] The primary audience was schoolchildren (8-13 years) and the

secondary audience was the parents of these schoolchildren and key influencers like the village head, village community representatives, health workers, and schoolteachers. Subsequently, follow-up visits and communication were undertaken at periodic intervals to reinforce the learning.

The initiative was rolled out in each village after the permission of the village elders had been obtained. In the first phase, the teams visited schools to teach children about germs and the importance of washing hands with soap. Children were educated with the help of a 'Glo-germ demonstration', visual aids such as flip charts with pictorial stories, and quizzes with attractive prizes. In the 'Glo-germ demonstration', children applied a white powder to the palms of their hands before washing it with only water. The hands washed with water were then held under ultra-violet (UV) light and the powder glowed where dirt still remained. The children then repeated the process using soap, and the UV light did not show any trace of dirt. This visual demonstration effectively

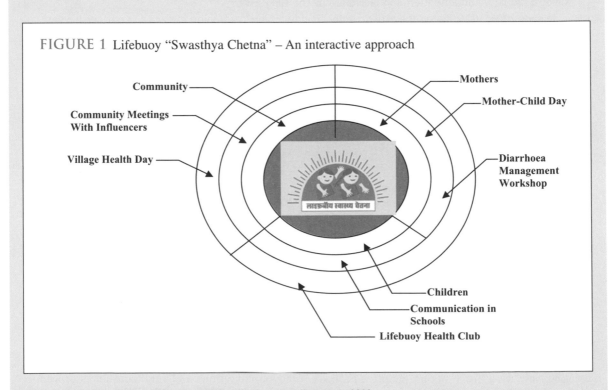

FIGURE 1 Lifebuoy "Swasthya Chetna" – An interactive approach

Source: "Unilever and Water – Towards Sustainability," www.unilever.com, 2003.

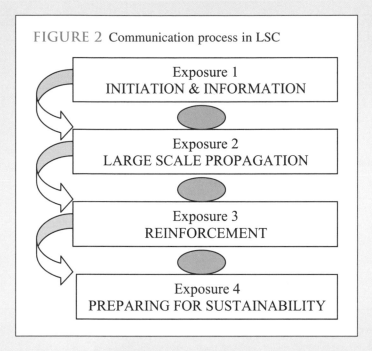

FIGURE 2 Communication process in LSC

Exposure 1
INITIATION & INFORMATION

Exposure 2
LARGE SCALE PROPAGATION

Exposure 3
REINFORCEMENT

Exposure 4
PREPARING FOR SUSTAINABILITY

Source: "PPP for Handwashing Global Learning Workshop," www.globalhand-washing.org, March 2005

demonstrated that washing hands without soap was not enough. The team also held interactions with key influencers of the community (*Refer to Exhibit VIII for a picture of the campaign for health and hygiene and Exhibit IX for the a picture of the 'Glo-germ demonstration'*).

In the second phase, after about two months, the team returned with toys for children who had saved the Lifebuoy soap wrappers. They also brought certificates and medals for those children who had won the "most neat and clean person" badge, which had been initiated by the LSC team in the earlier visit, most often. An LSC team member said, "The concept caught on so well that at first we intended the badge for just one person, but the children decided to make that a rotating thing. It was a great motivator for them."[46] In the second phase, the school conducted a 'Swasthya Diwas' (Health Day) event for parents and the other villagers. The children were used as influencers, and with their help the HDF interacted with the parents and educated them about good health and hygiene practices and their impact on the community. Children participated in "Glo-germ demonstrations"

and acted out stories and songs regarding the benefits of handwashing with soap. The LSC team also gave prizes to those children who had actively participated in this event.

In the third phase, the LSC team visited the villagers in their houses and convinced the mothers of young children to attend a health education session where the benefits of handwashing were reinforced. The local health workers were also part of this session and they gave the children a height and weight check. These periodic contacts with the villagers reinforced the message and ensured that the villagers internalized the messages.

In the final stage, health clubs were set up with volunteers comprising children and their parents. These volunteers were responsible for organizing events such as community bathing at the village pond. By setting up the health clubs, the program aimed to transfer the ownership of this initiative to the community itself. The objective was to present the activity as the villagers' self-initiative, and the HDF relinquished his/her active role and acted as a facilitator.[47] Tibb explained, "We talk to elders of the village, mothers, community representatives,

EXHIBIT VIII Campaigning for health & hygiene

Source: www.ogilvyindia.com.

EXHIBIT IX Glo-germ demonstrations

Source: "PPP for Handwashing Global Learning Workshop," www.globalhandwashing.org, March 2005.

medical practitioners, even the teacher of the local school. When we visit villages, we are welcomed into people's homes to see the actual practice of health and hygiene. We see for ourselves how many people are using the soap and when. Villagers welcome us because they believe we are doing something good for them – it's not just about commercial interest."[48]

The media vehicles used in the program consisted of cinema vans, wall paintings, weekly markets, fairs, and festivals (*Refer to Exhibit X for a wall painting of Lifebuoy*). Cinema vans were the most popular medium where popular movies were shown with product advertisements. Promotional schemes were also designed for Lifebuoy. For people with low income, an 18-gram bar of *Lifebuoy* soap was introduced, enough for one person to wash their hands once a day for 10 weeks.[49]

To ensure the effectiveness of the campaign, Tibb visited the villages in which the program operated, every three months. 'Before and after' studies were conducted to measure awareness of germs, concerns for health and hygiene, and the impact of the campaign on behavior and attitudes. "We see impacts only a few months after our first village visit -- people are able to recall the campaign's key health and hygiene messages,"[50] said Tibb.

WS helped to take this social initiative to the GoI. It was WS that suggested to HLL that it should have the program endorsed by the government to achieve a better media outreach. WS worked to get the government to endorse the program as this would lend more credibility to the campaign and make it more effective. Arijit Sengupta (Sengupta), vice-president at WS, said, "We, as an agency, initiate a lot of non-media activities for our clients and expect it to bring in even more value to them. And looking at the dedication and enthusiasm of Lifebuoy for this prestigious social campaign, it was very important for us to implement the same to make it effective. As the vision of the brand is to make one billion Indians feel safe and secure, LSC is instrumental to translate that vision into reality and we helped them achieve that."[51]

In the first year of the program's launch, 150 LSC teams who were well versed in the local

EXHIBIT X Wall painting of Lifebuoy

Source: www.ogilvyindia.com.

language visited around 9,000 villages. Another 9,000 villages were visited the following year. In 2004 and 2005, HLL focused on introducing new phases to these 18,000 villages. By the end of 2004, the campaign reached 70 million people, including 20 million children. The cost to HLL was US$ 2.7 million. By the end of 2005, the campaign had reached around 18 000 villages.

The company contended that the LSC program had helped expand Lifebuoy's market by winning over new customers, while at the same time furthering its corporate social responsibility (CSR) agenda. "This will help us grow the soap market in India and at the same time have a positive impact on the health of people living in rural India,"[52] said Tibb.

Impact of the program

In 2003-04, the sales of Lifebuoy grew by 20 percent. According to Unilever, the sales of Lifebuoy were showing "directly attributable growth"[53] as sales from the eight states where the program operated was particularly strong. In 2005, the sales of the brand grew by 10 percent. "Swasthya Chetna isn't about philanthropy; it's an outstanding example of business with a purpose. Our vision is to build cleaner, more hygienic, and ultimately healthier communities, and the health of our business in the last few years demonstrates the power of this approach,"[54] said Rajeev Shukla, Regional Brand Development Director for Lifebuoy in Asia and Africa.

By the end of 2005, the campaign had touched 86 million rural consumers and registered a 30 percent increase in their awareness of germs, 20 percent increase in understanding the association of germs with diseases, and an increase in current user base by 33 percent compared to pre-campaign status in activity villages.[55] "Before *Swasthya Chetna* came to my school I didn't know about germs or that diseases can be prevented by washing hands with soap. Now I wash with soap whenever I can and my friends and I are telling everyone about hidden germs and how soap can help you stay well,"[56] said Julie, a schoolgirl in a village in Orissa.

The program received a lot of attention from the media as well as the government. Unilever

Bangladesh adopted the HLL model in 2003, and by the end of 2004, 3,100 villages in Bangladesh had been covered. In addition to this, Unilever gained valuable insights on how to implement such public-private partnerships (PPPs) and market its products to the underprivileged segments of the society (*Refer to Table I for lessons learnt by Unilever from the LSC program*).

The accolades

On the whole, the program received positive coverage by the national as well as international media. *The Financial Times*[57] reported, "New distribution channels have been developed for the (LSC) program, with representatives that are part salespeople, part health workers sent to villages to teach schoolchildren the importance of hand washing with soap.[58] Many analysts applauded the program and cited it as an example of how a socially beneficial program could help improve the revenues of the brand. In his book, *The Fortune at the Bottom*

TABLE I Lessons learnt by Unilever from
the LSC program

- Soap needs to be divided into smaller portions in order to make it affordable for local populations;

- Cultural differences have to be taken into account and made to work for you – washing with soap has become a kind of ritual, i.e., it has been accepted;

- Multi-stakeholder relationships should be used as a tool to ensure that the social and educational aspects of the project are clear to the public;

- There should be transparency about the company's role to show that the company is not just doing this to make money;

- Local actors should be engaged to help in the process, as they have a lot of influence.

Source: "The Business of Health – the Health of Business," www.iblf.org, February 2006.

of the Pyramid: Eradicating Poverty Through Profits (2005), management guru C.K. Prahalad[59] cited the example of HLL's LSC to show how companies could sometimes find it in their own interests to help solve some of the problems of the poor, which had traditionally been addressed by the public sector. By increasing awareness among the poor rural masses, HLL not only succeeded in convincing villagers to use a product that protected them against disease, but also was rewarded by way of increased sales of Lifebuoy.

The GoI also acknowledged HLL for the good work it had done in implementing LSC in rural India, when India Post[60] released a special Lifebuoy "Swasthya Chetna Postal Cover" on the occasion of World Health Day on April 7, 2006.

Tibb too received major recognition for his effective handling of Lifebuoy and the LSC program. In 2002, he received the Unilever Directors' Enterprise Award for the successful relaunch of the Lifebuoy brand, and in the following year, he was given the Chairman's Enterprise Award, in recognition of the more than 20 percent value growth of Lifebuoy in 2002-03.

Some criticisms

In early 2001, HLL initiated a handwashing program in Kerala as part of the GPPP-HW. But its initiative in Kerala faced protests from some antiglobalization activists. Critics argued that HLL's campaign had more to do with selling soap than to do with social benefits. The choice of Kerala as a state for the program was severely criticized. The critics contended that people in Kerala were educated and had high health indices, and did not have the need for such a program. Scientist and environmentalist, Vandana Shiva (Shiva) was very vocal in her criticism of the initiative. "If Kerala has been chosen for the World Bank project claiming to reduce diarrheal deaths in spite of having the lowest incidence of childhood diarrhea, quite clearly the project is not about "saving lives" but merely about "selling soap."[61]

In addition to environmental activists, even a few doctors and local newspapers were part of the resistance (*Refer to Table II for the main points of criticism against LSC*). HLL failed to

---

TABLE II The main points of criticism against LSC

- The choice of Kerala for the program in view of its already high human development indicators.
- Unclear link between handwashing and health improvement.
- The potential adverse effect on the indigenous and local soap industry by increasing the market share of multinational soap companies.
- The suggestion that the state government was capitulating to World Bank pressure.

Source: "Unilever Fighting Disease Clean Handed," www. wbcsd.com, 2005.

---

make any headway with the government of Kerala. After many discussions on the issue spread over a few months, the program was abandoned in August 2003.

Other initiatives for Lifebuoy

The handwashing campaign was extended to urban areas in August 2003 with the "Healthy Hindustan" campaign. For this, HLL partnered with McDonald's[62] Western India across cities like Mumbai, Pune, Ahmedabad, and Vadodara to educate children about the benefits of handwashing with soap. Children who visited select stores of McDonald's between August 15 and September 15, 2003, received a booklet on hygiene tips, played germ buster games, and also viewed the 'Glo-germ' demonstration. The effort was supported by an ad campaign.

In the aftermath of the Tsunami[63] in Asia, in December 2004, Lifebuoy bars were distributed in relief packages in Southern India, Sri Lanka, and Indonesia to help prevent the spread of infectious diseases that generally became an epidemic following such natural catastrophes. In 2005, over 200,000 bars of Lifebuoy soap were donated to UNICEF and the International Committee of the Red Cross (ICRC)[64] to support their earth-quake relief operations in Northern India and Pakistan.

In May 2005, HLL started the "Save the child campaign" for Lifebuoy, to support the World Health Organization[65] (WHO) approved oral rehydration salts (ORS)[66] campaign to combat diarrhea in India. Under the campaign, select wrappers of Lifebuoy soaps had amounts of money in denominations of Rs.50, Rs.500, Rs.5000, or Rs.1 lakh[67] printed inside. On sending the wrapper to the company, the consumer received the amount printed inside the wrapper. HLL contributed an amount equivalent to the prize money given under this campaign (approximately Rs.5 million) to the USAID-funded WHO-ORS campaign. Dr. Massee Bateman of USAID said, "We are happy to be associated with Lifebuoy in this effort to save Indian children from diarrhea. The common nature of this ailment causes us to overlook the significance of this serious public health problem – where it causes the death of one child every minute in India. Fortunately, simple means to prevent and treat diarrhea are available to us – washing hands with soap to prevent diarrhea and giving ORS to treat diarrhea being two of the most important ones."[68]

In August 2005, as heavy rains brought Mumbai to a standstill, HLL donated a total of 150,256 soaps to UNICEF, People for Change,[69] Tata Institute for Social Sciences[70] (TISS) and BehtarBharat.com[71] for distribution among the poor people to prevent the outbreak of diarrhea. Ashok Venkatramani, Vice-President, Skin Care, HLL, said, "We are happy to provide support to the organizations and their effort to extend the necessary health facilities for the underprivileged and through this act, we hope to make a positive contribution to the health of the community. The brand has also been educating people on the importance of hand wash with soap and water, and how this simple act can help reduce diarrhea by 47 percent. This is yet another effort in this direction."[72] These activities firmly reinforced the brand association of Lifebuoy with health and the association of Lifebuoy as a 'do-gooder' brand.

To reinforce its brand association with killing germs and protecting health, Lifebuoy for the first time engaged in a co-branded promotion with the big budget film 'Krrish',[73] in 2006. The partnership involved printing pictures of Krrish on the Lifebuoy packs and giving away Krrish merchandise with Lifebuoy. An HLL official explained, "We chose Lifebuoy over the other brands since the brand is all about protection and Krrish's character is also about protecting the world from enemies."[74]

Outlook

By 2005, LSC was regarded as India's single largest health and hygiene education program.[75] Changing the behavior of people, particularly in the rural areas was a big challenge for LSC, as these behaviors were deeply rooted. Tibb said, "It takes a long time to change habits, so the project needs to take a long-term view."[76] However, LSC had succeed in getting its 'health and hygiene' agenda rolling in more than 17,000 villages. In 2006, the LSC program was being extended to another 10,000 villages in the eight states. HLL was also in discussion with the GoI to extend this program to other states and beyond the previously intended five-year duration of the program.

With the success of this campaign, the management committee at Unilever recommended to the board that CSR be integrated with its other businesses as well. Unilever was also exploring the commercial viability of its Pureit water purification product in India.[77] This was based on WHO estimates that 80 percent of all diseases in developing and emerging countries, including cholera and typhoid, were water-related and that access to safe drinking water was scarce.

Analysts too felt that PPPs like LSC could solve many problems in the world. In this case, the private sector interest was to expand the market for soap while the public sector interest was in promoting health. While the public sector could provide access, reach, and scalability to the program, the private sector had the necessary skills and marketing acumen to change behavior. They also noted that companies were gradually moving away from corporate philanthropy to PPPs that increased the financial bottom line of the company, while providing benefits to the society.

Additional readings and references

1. "HLL Plans Rural Campaign to Reposition Lifebuoy – to Pitch on Hygiene Platform," www.thehindubusinessline.com, February 12, 2002.
2. "A fresh lease of Lifebuoy?" Business Standard, February 25, 2002.
3. Vandana Shiva, "'Saving Lives or Destroying Lives?' World Bank Sells Synthetic Soap & Cleanliness to Kerala: the Land of Health and Hygiene," www.mindfully.org, September 23, 2002.
4. Nisha Lahiri, "Message with a Healthy Cause – Marketing Hygiene through Community Projects, Class Lectures," www.telegraphindia.com, October 9, 2002.
5. Mahalakshmi, "HLL's I-Shakti exploits the power of women", *The Financial Express*, August 01, 2003.
6. "Lifebuoy launches 'Healthy Hindustan' Campaign," www.indiainfoline.com, 2003.
7. "Unilever and Water – Towards Sustainability," www.unilever.com, 2003.
8. Gayatridevi N and A.V Vedpuriswar, "Unilever in India – Building and Nurturing Brands," www.icmr.icfai.org, 2004.
9. Gayatridevi N, "Unilever in India – Rural Marketing Initiatives," www.icmr.icfai.org, 2004.
10. "PPP for Handwashing Global Learning Workshop," www.globalhandwashing.org, March 2005.
11. Dr. Brigitte Tantawy Monsou, "SoL Sustainability Consortium," solsustainablility.org, April 27, 2005.
12. "HLL and USAID Join Hands to Save Indian Children from Diarrhoea," www.newdelhi.usembassy.gov, May 25, 2005.
13. HLL, "Analysts & Press Meet," www.hll.com, July 30, 2005.
14. "Lifebuoy Joins Campaign against Diarrhoea in Mumbai," www.thehindubusinessline.com, August 13, 2005.
15. "I Didn't Know Soap Could Save Lives. I Didn't Even Know About Germs." www.unilever.com, 2005.
16. SS Srikanti, Jitesh Nair, "Lifebuoy, Successful Repositioning and Re-launch of an Established personal Care Brand," www.icmr.icfai.org, 2005.
17. "Unilever Fighting Disease Clean Handed," www.wbcsd.org, 2005.
18. "Hygiene Factors Provide Opportunities for Private Sector," Financial Times, www.undp.org, January 26, 2006.
19. "The Business of Health – the Health of Business," www.iblf.org, February 2006.
20. "HLL's Lifebuoy becomes first Indian Brand to have a Special Postal Cover," www.domain-b.com, April 7, 2006.
21. "Lifebuoy's Rural Health and Hygiene Programme Acknowledged on World Health Day," exchange4media.com, April 8, 2006.
22. "Soap Leaves its Stamp on Health and Hygiene," www.cybernoon.com, April 8, 2006.
23. "Weber Shandwick Carries HLL's Social Initiative to the Government," www.agencyfaqs.com, April 2006.
24. University of Handwashing, "Workshop Report (Vol. I): Key Lessons and Challenges," www.globalhandwashing.org, May 1-2, 2006.
25. Purvita Chatterjee, "HLL to Ride on Movie Krrish to Market Lifebuoy," www.thehindubusinessline.com, June 24, 2006.
26. "Examination of Witnesses (Questions 320 - 339)," www.parliament.uk, July 23, 2006.
27. "Harpreet Singh Tibb – India," www.unilever.com/ourvalues/environmentandsociety/ people_profiles/harpreet_singh_tibb.asp, 2006.
28. "Have No Fear with Lifebuoy," www.unilever.com/ourbrands/healthyliving/ havenofearwithlifebuoy.asp, 2006.
29. "India: Lifebuoy Promotes Handwashing with Soap to Improve Health," www.unilever.com, 2006.
30. "Lifebuoy's Swasthya Chetna – Awenening to One's Health," www.ogilvyindia.com, 2006.
31. "Our Approach to Health and Hygiene," www.unilever.com, 2006.
32. "Preventing Disease," www.unilever.com, 2006.
33. www.en.wikipedia.org.
34. www.finance.google.com.
35. www.hll.com.
36. www.ogilvyindia.com.
37. www.unilever.com.

Notes

1. "Unilever Fighting Disease Clean Handed," www.wbcsd.org, 2005.
2. "I Didn't Know Soap Could Save Lives. I Didn't Even Know About Germs," www.unilever.com, 2005.
3. Maharastra is a state in central India.
4. "HLL's Lifebuoy Becomes First Indian Brand to Have a Special Postal Cover," www.domain-b.com, April 7, 2006.
5. "Have No Fear with Lifebuoy," www.unilever.com, 2006.
6. "India: Lifebuoy Promotes Handwashing with Soap to Improve Health," www.unilever.com, 2006.
7. Ogilvy Outreach was the non-profit arm of Ogilvy & Mather, a leading advertising agency in the world with a presence in more than 120 countries. It was set up in 1994 with the objective of reaching people who lived in the media dark corners of rural India.
8. Weber Shandwick is one of the leading PR and communications management firms in the world, with a

presence in 72 markets. (Source: www.webershanwick.com)

9. The Tata Oil Mills Company (TOMCO) was in the business of manufacturing and selling soaps, detergents, and cooking oils. It was established in 1917 by the Tatas, a respected business group in India.

10. Brooke Bond India and Lipton India merged in July 1993 to form Brooke Bond Lipton India Limited (BBLIL).

11. Pond's India Ltd. had been present in India since 1947. It became a part of Unilever after Unilever's acquisition of Chesebrough Pond's USA in 1986.

12. Kimberly-Clark Corporation is a US-based company engaged in the manufacture and marketing of a wide range of health and hygiene products. Some of its popular brands are Kleenex (facial tissue), Kotex (feminine hygiene product), and Huggies (disposable diapers). In 1994, it formed Kimberly–Clark Lever Limited, a joint venture with HLL to manufacture and sell disposable diapers and feminine care products.

13. Lakmé Limited was a Tata company that was into the manufacture and sale of cosmetic products. In 1995, it formed a joint venture called Lakmé Lever Limited with HLL. In 1998, Lakmé Limited sold its brands to HLL and divested its 50 percent stake in the joint venture.

14. Microcredit involves providing small loans to people who are too poor to qualify for loans from traditional banks. Microcredit enables very poor people to take up self-employment projects that generate income for them and sustain their livelihood.

15. Mahalakshmi, "HLL's I-Shakti Exploits the Power of Women," The Financial Express, August 01, 2003.

16. http://www.hll.com/citizen_lever/project_shakti.asp.

17. http://www.hll.com/mediacentre/annualreport2005.pdf.

18. The Blitz was the continuous bombing of the UK by Germany between September 7, 1940 and May 16, 1941.

19. Cresylic-perfumed soaps have a disinfectant perfume.

20. "HLL Relaunches Lifebuoy, Eyes Strong Growth," http://www.my-india.net, February 13, 2002.

21. The 'discount segment' in the soap market emerged in the mid-1990s as various companies launched soaps in the market that were priced 10 percent to 15 percent lower than the popular soaps. This was facilitated by the 40-50 percent fall in prices of vegetable oils during that period. The prominent brands in this segment were Godrej No. 1 and Breeze (another HLL brand).

22. "A Fresh Lease of Lifebuoy?" Business Standard, February 25, 2002.

23. "Presentation," http://www.hll.com/investor/presentation/2004/ ICICI-IndiaUnlimited2004-forweb.pdf, March 2004.

24. "Lifebuoy," www.hll.com/ brands/lifebuoy.asp.

25. "Lifebuoy," www.hll.com/ brands/lifebuoy.asp.

26. HLL, "Analysts & Press Meet," www.hll.com, July 30, 2005.

27. University of Handwashing, "Workshop Report (Vol. I): Key Lessons and Challenges," www.globalhandwashing.org, May 1-2, 2006.

28. "Unilever: Fighting Disease Clean-handed," www.wbcsd.org, 2005.

29. "Lifebuoy's Campaign to Promote ORS; Smriti Irani to Support Cause," www.indiantelevision.com, May 28, 2005.

30. "Preventing Disease," www.unilever.com, 2006.

31. "Lifebuoy Launches 'Healthy Hindustan' Campaign," www.indiainfoline.com, 2003.

32. The World Bank Group, headquartered in Washington, DC, USA, is a group of five international organizations responsible for providing finance and advice to countries for the purposes of economic development and poverty reduction, and for encouraging and safeguarding international investment. The group and its affiliates have local offices in 124 member countries. (Source: www.en.wikipedia.org)

33. "The Global Public-Private Partnership for handwashing with Soap," www.globalhandwashing.org.

34. The LSHTM is a leading and internationally recognized postgraduate institution in Europe for public health and tropical medicine. It is associated with the World Health Organization (WHO).

35. The USAID is an independent federal agency in the US government organization responsible for most non-military foreign aid.

36. UNICEF, headquartered in New York City, USA, is a body of the United Nations, that provides long-term humanitarian and developmental assistance to children and mothers in developing countries.

37. WHO, headquartered in Geneva, Switzerland, is an agency of the United Nations, acting as a coordinating authority on international public health.

38. Procter & Gamble Co. is a global corporation based in Cincinnati, Ohio, USA, that manufactures a wide range of consumer goods.

39. Colgate-Palmolive Co., with its international headquarters in New York City, USA, is an MNC in the business of consumer products such as soaps, detergents, and oral hygiene products.

40. "Baroness Chalker of Wallasey," www.nuclearspin.org.

41. NGOs are private or nonprofit organizations that are not affiliated with a governmental body or institution.

42. "Lifebuoy's Swasthya Chetna – Awakening to One's Health," www.ogilvyindia.com, 2006.

43. "HLL Plans Rural Campaign to Reposition Lifebuoy – to Pitch on Hygiene Platform," www.thehindubusinessline.com, February 12, 2002.

44. "India: Lifebuoy Promotes Handwashing with Soap to Improve Health," www.unilever.com.

45. "PPP for Handwashing Global Learning Workshop," www.globalhandwashing.org, March 2005.

46. Nisha Lahiri, "Message with a Healthy Cause – Marketing Hygiene through Community Projects, Class Lectures," www.telegraphindia.com, October 9, 2002.

47. "Lifebuoy's Rural Health and Hygiene Programme Acknowledged on World Health Day," exchange4media.com, April 8, 2006.

48. "Harpreet Singh Tibb – India," www.unilever.com/ourvalues/environmentandsociety/people_profiles/harpreet_singh_tibb.asp.

49. "Unilever Fighting Disease Clean Handed," www.wbcsd.com, 2005.

50. "Harpreet Singh Tibb – India," www.unilever.com/ourvalues/environmentandsociety/people_profiles/harpreet_ singh_tibb.asp.

51. Weber Shandwick Carries HLL's Social Initiative to the Government," www.agencyfaqs.com, April 2006.

52. "Hygiene Factors Provide Opportunities for Private Sector," Financial Times, www.undp.org, January 26, 2006.

53. Dr. Brigitte Tantawy Monsou, "SoL Sustainability Consortium," solsustainablility.org, April 27, 2005.

54. "Have No Fear with Lifebuoy," www.unilever.com/ourbrands/healthyliving/havenofearwithlifebuoy.asp.

55. "Lifebuoy's Swasthya Chetna – Awakening to One's Health," www.ogilvyindia.com.

56. "I Didn't Know Soap Could Save Lives. I Didn't Even Know About Germs." www.unilever.com, 2005.

57. The *Financial Times* is a leading international business newspaper printed in 22 cities around the world.

58. "Hygiene Factors Provide Opportunities for Private Sector," Financial Times, www.undp.org, January 26, 2006.

59. CK Prahalad, world-renowned management expert and professor of Corporate Strategy at the University of Michigan, USA. He, alongwith Gary Hamel propounded the concept of 'core competency' in 1990.

60. India Post (formerly the Department of Posts), is the government owned and operated postal system in India. It functions under the Ministry of Communications and Information Technology.

61. Vandana Shiva, "'Saving Lives or Destroying Lives?' World Bank Sells Synthetic Soap & Cleanliness to Kerala: the Land of Health and Hygiene," www.mindfully.org, September 23, 2002.

62. McDonald's is the world's largest chain of fast-food restaurants.

63. The Tsunami (a series of waves generated when a body of water, such as an ocean is rapidly displaced on a massive scale), which hit the coastal areas of many Asian countries on December 26, 2006, was one of the deadliest natural disasters in modern history that left a total of 229,866 persons lost, including 186,983 dead and 42,883 missing.

64. The ICRC, based in Geneva, Switzerland, is a private humanitarian institution having a unique authority based on the international humanitarian law of the Geneva Conventions to protect the victims of international and internal armed conflicts. (Source: www.en.wikipedia.org)

65. The World Health Organization (WHO) is a specialized agency of the United Nations, which deals with health issues like combating infectious diseases and promoting the general health of people across the world.

66. Oral rehydration salts (ORS) consist of a solution of salts and other substances such as glucose or molasses, which is administered orally for combating dehydration caused by diarrhoea.

67. Ten lakhs is equal to one million.

68. "HLL and USAID Join Hands to Save Indian Children from Diarrhoea," www.newdelhi.usembassy.gov, May 25, 2005.

69. People for Change is an NGO supported by popular Indian TV actor, Smriti Irani.

70. The TISS was established in 1936, as the Sir Dorabji Tata Graduate School of Social Work. It was the first school of social work in India. Renamed as TISS in 1944, it is a deemed university in India and considered a center of excellence, contributing relevant education and research, toward the national agenda of sustainable, participatory, and equitable development. (Source: www.tiss.edu)

71. BehtarBharat is a non-profit organization dedicated to the development of communities and infrastructure programs in India. (Source: www.en.wikipedia.org)

72. "Lifebuoy Joins Campaign against Diarrhoea in Mumbai," www.thehindubusinessline.com, August 13, 2005.

73. 'Krrish' is a popular Bollywood movie, which released in June 2006 in India. The movie has Hindi film actor Hrithik Roshan in the lead role as a superhero.

74. Purvita Chatterjee, "HLL to Ride on Movie Krrish to Market Lifebuoy," www.thehindubusinessline.com, June 24, 2006.

75. www.hll.com/mediacentre/7April06_Lifebuoy_Swasthya_Chetna_postal_cover.doc

76. "Harpreet Singh Tibb – India," www.unilever.com/ourvalues/environmentandsociety/people_profiles/harpreet_ singh_tibb.asp.

77. "Our Approach to Health and Hygiene," www.unilever.com.

JOHN MACKEY AND WHOLE FOODS MARKET

BY NANCY F. KOEHN AND KATHERINE MILLER*

John Mackey stepped away from the microphone and walked swiftly out of the ballroom of the Fairmont Hotel in Santa Monica, California.[1] To some at the 2003 annual shareholders meeting of Whole Foods Market, it looked like the CEO was storming off the floor.[2] He had just broken off a heated exchange with an animal rights activist, Lauren Ornelas, who had interrupted the gathering to criticize the living conditions of the ducks sold in his chain of natural-foods supermarkets.[3] In an impassioned voice, Ornelas described the treatment of the birds at Grimaud Farms, a Whole Foods supplier.[4] Their beaks were clipped to keep them from pecking each other, she said, and their factory-like living quarters were so dismal that they never had a chance to swim.[5] After a few minutes, Mackey—who was himself a vegetarian—had had enough. "We have the best animal standards in the country," he told her. "Go bother somebody else."[6]

By 2003, Whole Foods Market, the target of Ornelas's campaign, was the largest natural and organic supermarket in the world.[7] The company's 145 stores offered everything that the often-monotonous floors of a conventional supermarket did not—tantalizing arrangements of fruits

and vegetables, cheeses and chocolates, hot prepared dishes, and freshly baked bread, all free of artificial preservatives, additives, sweeteners, and coloring.[8] The organic foods on prominent display were held to federally regulated standards that prohibited conventional fertilizers, pesticides, additives, and other agrichemicals. From the time Mackey founded the first store with his girlfriend in 1980, he had been in the business of promoting less processed, healthier, more sustainable food.[9] In the 11 years since Whole Foods had gone public, it had helped bring concerns about the way food was produced—including how animals were raised and slaughtered, how fish were harvested, how produce was farmed, and how other staples were brought to market—out of the counterculture and into the American mainstream. The growing organization had also influenced how consumers thought about their own health and well-being in relation to food quality.

Increasingly and perhaps ironically, however, Mackey's chain was coming under attack from activists like Ornelas who believed that the foods sold under an organic banner should embody an even higher ideal. When Mackey left the ballroom at the Fairmont, followed swiftly by a band of senior executives and shareholders, that might have been the end of the story.[10] But Ornelas was persistent, and after the meeting, she tracked Mackey down and convinced him to give her his e-mail address.[11] At first, their electronic exchanges seemed unproductive.[12] "I didn't understand why [activists like Ornelas] were so passionate about this issue," Mackey said. "I perceived them as our enemies. Now, the best way to argue with your opponents is to completely understand their point of view."[13] So after a few weeks of communicating with Ornelas, Mackey stopped his e-mails to her and started reading books on livestock treatment.[14] One of them was philosopher Peter Singer's *Animal Liberation*, originally published in 1975, a tome considered by many to be the bible of the animal rights movement today and one of the earliest indictments of animal testing and factory farms.[15]

After three months of self-imposed study, Mackey decided that not only did he understand

*Professor Nancy Koehn and Research Associate Katherine Miller prepared this case. This case was developed from published sources. HBS cases are developed solely as the basis for class discussion. Cases are not intended to serve as endorsements, sources of primary data, or illustrations of effective or ineffective management.

Ornelas's viewpoint, he agreed with it.[16] The Whole Foods CEO then adopted an almost completely vegan diet, shunning not just steak and bacon but all foods produced from animals, including eggs and cheese.[17] He invited Ornelas, his former adversary, to help him change the standards for meat suppliers at Whole Foods.[18] In 2005, the company donated $550,000 to launch an independent nonprofit organization, the Animal Compassion Foundation, dedicated to helping farmers "achieve a higher standard of animal welfare excellence while still maintaining economic vitality."[19] Whole Foods also collaborated with farmers and organizations like People for the Ethical Treatment of Animals (PETA) and the Humane Society of the United States to develop a system of Animal Compassionate Standards for its meat and poultry products.[20] Grimaud Farms, the source of Ornelas's original complaint, remained committed to supplying Whole Foods. In 2004, the California-based poultry farm began to plan a space where its ducks could swim.[21]

Agriculture's organic roots

In 1980, when John Mackey opened the first Whole Foods Market, the organic and natural-food products that his store promoted were considered part and parcel of a radical hippie lifestyle. More than 25 years later, most supermarkets still label an apple grown with chemicals "conventional" and its naturally grown counterpart "organic," but the history behind both kinds of farming belies this distinction. Food products are considered organic if they have been raised with ecological controls for weeds and pests—barring most chemicals—and if livestock have not been treated with pharmaceuticals, including regular antibiotics and hormones.[22] While the movement for organic agriculture is relatively young, dating back to the 1940s, the techniques used in organic food production are as old as any human civilization. Before the advent of chemical fertilizers and pesticides, organic apples were, by default, conventional food. It was not until the mid-20th century, when the use of such chemicals became commonplace in a food chain dominated by huge agribusiness corporations, that a new word was needed to define food grown in a more traditional way.

For most of human history, men and women around the world sustained their families by hunting and gathering wild forms of food.[23] Only relatively recently, within the last 11,000 years, did humans begin to domesticate some wild varieties of plants and animals.[24] Between 8500 B.C.E. and 2500 B.C.E., early societies around the world—from the Fertile Crescent to Mesoamerica, from China to New Guinea—domesticated species as varied as olives, wheat, sunflowers, squash, and sugar cane.[25] Organized food production led to population growth and more complex societies, which, in turn, spurred agricultural advances such as large-scale irrigation.[26] The seasonal nature of most crops allowed societies to exploit farming labor in the off-season for other pursuits.[27] Additionally, the storage of surplus provisions freed whole classes of people from food production for the first time.[28] Some worked as specialized craftsmen constructing public works, some served as soldiers or mercenaries, some created sculpture and paintings, and others turned to commerce.[29] A few groups—the ruling classes—did not work at all. With the rise of agriculture, civic life, art, science, religion, trade, and warfare flourished.[30]

Early farmers developed a range of techniques to nourish the soil their crops depended on and to make their labor more efficient. In the Old World, large mammals like horses and cows were domesticated and used to till fields that were sown with one type of seed, and thus harvested one crop.[31] Growing only one crop depleted the soil of certain nutrients, and the manure of livestock was used as a natural fertilizer. In the New World, with no domesticated animals large enough to pull a plow, fields were tilled by hand and planted with a variety of crops at once.[32] The Wampanoag Tribe of North America, for instance, planted corn, beans, and squash together.[33] Corn fed on nitrogen in the soil, the beans replenished the nitrogen, and the broad leaves of the squash blocked out the sunlight, preventing weeds from taking root.[34] In India, farmers developed a system of composting to fertilize the land and grow surplus crops.[35] The basic techniques of both the Indian and Wampanoag farmers are used by many organic farmers today.

Between 6000 and 3500 B.C.E., agriculture took root in west and central Europe when domesticated crops like wheat and peas arrived from the

Fertile Crescent.[36] Around 2500 B.C.E., the Celts from mainland Europe arrived in what is now England and brought with them cows, sheep, pigs, and a system of mixed farming, raising livestock together with cereal crops.[37] Because cereal crops suffered from low yields and rapidly exhausted the soil's natural nutrients, farmers throughout Europe learned to alternate the growth of spring grains with winter wheat and a year of rest.[38] When a field lay fallow, livestock were allowed to graze on it and spread their manure.[39] In the Middle Ages, English farmers—like the Wampanoag Indians in North America—discovered that legumes, such as peas and beans, enriched the land on which they grew.[40] Although nobody knew it at the time, manure and legumes made such effective fertilizers because both replenished the supply of life-giving nitrogen in the soil.[41]

The agricultural revolution

For much of the pre-industrial period, the number of people in England and in Europe as a whole had grown only gradually. Whenever population swelled, it was almost inevitably checked by infant mortality, war, disease, and, most important, a relatively constant food supply.[42] The technology and trade patterns of the time were no match for the power of the elements or epidemics like the plague. In most societies, two consecutive years of bad harvests brought catastrophe, as famine ushered in disease and widespread death.[43] When the crops failed, people turned back to hunting and gathering whatever they could—acorns, wild fruit, even grass.[44] In particularly dire circumstances, people sometimes ate human flesh.[45] Historian Fernand Braudel calls this period, when the ebb and flow of population in relation to the food supply kept life in a virtual balance, the biological *ancien regime*.[46] This regime held sway in both Europe and Asia until about the time of the Industrial and Agricultural Revolutions. From the time of the Roman invasion in 43 C.E. until 1750, the peak of the English population was approximately 5.7 million.[47]

By the 1700s, the farming methods in most parts of the world had been refined for hundreds—in some instances, thousands—of years. For better or worse, these practices were utterly transformed by the Industrial and Agricultural Revolutions that began in the early 18th century. English farmers at this time had more animal power than farmers elsewhere, claimed more land for farming, and increased sustainable crop yields substantially with the intensive use of nitrogen-fixing plants, such as clover, in place of fallow fields.[48] The old practice of dividing commonly held fields into strips for subsistence farming was replaced in the late 1700s, when a series of acts passed by the British Parliament accelerated the enclosure of lands for large, privately owned farms.[49] While the consolidated farms were more efficient, many small, subsistence farmers were displaced and forced to the cities as laborers.[50] These drastic—and at times wrenching—increases in productivity, in turn, drove unprecedented demographic changes. With previous limits on agricultural production broken, the English population nearly tripled to 16.6 million by 1850.[51]

Beginning in the 1820s and 1830s, mechanical advances such as the seed drill and the threshing machine boosted the efficiency of the English farmer even further.[52] So, too, did steam-powered pumps, which helped drain large areas of marsh and enabled farmers to claim previously unusable land.[53] Traction engines, which came into widespread use in the 19th century, plowed fields 20 times faster than men or oxen ever could.[54] Taken together, these developments meant that many fewer farm workers were now needed to produce the same amount of food, freeing labor for urban industries.[55] In the cities, rising populations stepped up demand for ever more food and thus more innovation.

In addition to these managerial and mechanical efficiencies, English agriculture in the 19th century also saw the advent of chemical innovations. In 1840, in his monograph *Chemistry in its Application to Agriculture*, German chemist Justus von Leibig isolated three nutrients—nitrogen, phosphorous, and potassium—responsible for plant growth.[56] In effect, Liebig argued that the complex ecological relationship between the soil, plant growth, and plant and animal waste could be replicated and improved with the application of mineral salts.[57] Twenty years later, England was producing tens of thousands of tons of this "chemical manure."[58] The new chemical technology received a further boost in 1909, when German chemist Fritz Haber discovered how to turn atmospheric nitrogen into a usable form, paving the way for synthetic fertilizer in the form of ammonium nitrate.[59]

From 1840 to 1940, the use of mineral salts as chemical fertilizers in Europe and the United States increased steadily.[60] But it skyrocketed at the end of World War II when several war-related developments spurred the use of synthetic compounds in farming.[61] Ammonium nitrate had been used in weapons production during the conflict, and in 1947, the U.S. Department of Agriculture (USDA) began using the excess supplies as fertilizer.[62] Nerve gas research in the war effort produced variants of DDT and other poisons which had recently been proven effective as pesticides, and many of these were later applied to crop fields.[63] By the 1950s, thanks to Liebig's discovery and the technical improvements that sped chemical production, synthetic fertilizers had become the norm, and agriculture production surged accordingly. Between 1935 and 1965, the number of corn bushels per acre produced by a typical farm more than tripled.[64]

The confluence of synthetic fertilizers and pesticides, hybrid seeds, motorized farm equipment, and government policy in the postwar years led to the first industrial American farms. Early in the 20th century, the U.S. government began to regulate farming as an industry, establishing credit institutions for farmers and offering subsidies on imported synthetic fertilizer.[65] From 1910 to 1990, the acreage of the average farm expanded more than threefold, and increasingly, farmers began to specialize in one or two products.[66] In 1900, a farm grew or raised an average of 5.1 commodities.[67] Nine decades later, the average farm produced 1.8.[68] Not surprisingly, the number of individual farms shrank dramatically during this period, from 5,740 to 1,925.[69] The productivity gains wrought by the Agricultural Revolution, along with the consolidation of farmland, dramatically affected the lives of millions of Americans. At the dawn of the 20th century, nearly 40% of the country's men, women, and children lived and worked on farms.[70] At its close, less than 2% did.[71]

Economies of scale allowed large, specialized commercial farms to dominate many areas of American agriculture. Corporate farms, also known as agribusinesses, did not necessarily manufacture food any more cheaply than a family farm, but such enterprises could control the food supply system—from the land itself to food additives, production plants, and marketing—in a way that smaller farms could not.[72] Many of the biggest agribusinesses today grew up in the early to mid-20th century. The agribusiness heavyweight ConAgra, which was created when four Nebraska flour mills merged in 1919, increased its sales from $50 million to $500 million between 1960 and 1974.[73] Tyson Foods, today the largest meat-processing company in the world, had its start in the Great Depression when John Tyson, a chicken farmer in Arkansas, devised a way to transport his poultry to Chicago.[74] By the mid-1970s, conglomerates as diverse as Standard Oil and Kaiser Aluminum had subsidiaries in agribusiness.[75] By 1992, the largest 10% of American farms controlled 76% of farmland by acreage and 70% of the value of farm product sales.[76]

By the mid 20th century, chemical fertilizers and pesticides had outpaced time-honored practices such as crop rotation and manure distribution on the vast majority of American farms, introducing a mechanical aspect to the farmer's relationship with the environment.[77] These same innovations, however, also enormously extended the yield of finite farmland, and by such extension, enabled continuous population growth.[78] Supported by the scale of corporate farms—many with global reach—world population continued to grow so quickly that, by the 1970s, many experts believed that agricultural industrialization had reached a point of no return. In 1971, the U.S. Secretary of Agriculture, Earl Butz, said: "We can go back to organic farming if we must—we know how to do it. However, before we go in that direction, someone must decide which 50 million of our people will starve."[79] The geographer Vaclav Smil contends that without the invention of chemical fertilizers, two out of five humans living today would not exist.[80]

The organic movement

The increased use of synthetic fertilizers and pesticides, along with the emergence of corporate farms in the early 20th century, alarmed a range of scientists, politicians, environmentalists, and activists of many stripes. One of the first such observers was the British agronomist Sir Albert Howard. Howard had spent the years from 1905 to 1930 studying agricultural practices in India and conducting experiments in chemical-free farming.[81] As synthetic fertilizers gained ground in western nations, he began arguing for holistic, environmentally conscious farming in place of "artificial" practices.[82] In 1940, Howard's book, *An Agricultural Testament*, warned that

> The slow poisoning of the life of the soil by artificial manures [chemical fertilizers] is one of the greatest calamities which has befallen agriculture and mankind.... The flooding of the English market with cheap food, grown anywhere and anyhow, forced the farmers of this country to throw to the winds the old and well-tried principles of mixed farming....The spraying machine was called in to protect the plant; vaccines and serums the animal; in the last resort the afflicted livestock are slaughtered and burnt. This policy is failing before our eyes.[83]

Although science had not yet clearly identified the risks associated with chemical farming, Howard argued that industrial farming techniques posed real harm not only to the land, but also to people who consumed the products grown in this way. He was joined by other voices in England, including nutritionist and physician Robert McCarrison, who had observed the effect of different regional diets in Southeast Asia, and Lady Eve Balfour, the first president of Britain's Soil Association.[84] Around the time Howard was writing, however, other groups had latched onto traditional farming as a tool for less virtuous—in some cases, hateful—aims.[85] In the 1930s, fascist right-wing publications lauded organic farming as a return to a "natural ideal" that rejected Jews and non-whites along with the industrial byproducts of modernization.[86] While this strain survives today—Terry Nichols, one of the terrorists involved in the Oklahoma City bombing, was once an organic farmer—it was largely superseded by organic activists with radically different values.[87]

Before the end of World War II, Howard's ideas spread to the United States, and his book became a touchstone for the burgeoning organics movement.

In the early 1940s, American health-food enthusiast and founder of the magazine *Organic Gardening and Farming*, J. I. Rodale, who was a fan of Howard's work, first gave chemical-free food the name "organic."[88] Rodale hoped that commercial farmers would take an interest in organic methods.[89] But for more than 20 years, his readership was limited to backyard gardeners, including a large number of first-generation immigrants.[90] Nevertheless, toward the end of the 1960s, hippies and others embracing alternative lifestyles began to take an interest in ecology, and subscriptions to Rodale's magazine rose.[91] As collective interest in organic food gathered steam, Howard's ideas found a new audience and newfound popularity. In 1971, the critic Wendell Berry published an essay on Howard's work in an underground magazine called the *The Last Whole Earth Catalog*.[92] For a growing group of people concerned about the environmental effects of industrialization, organic agriculture held enormous appeal.

During the same time, a range of agronomists, biologists, and other scientists was studying the broader effects of chemical pesticides and fertilizers. In 1962, zoologist Rachel Carson published *Silent Spring*, a book that exposed the environmental dangers of some chemical pesticides, including DDT, and helped raise ecological awareness.[93] Highly publicized disasters heightened the urgency of environmentalists' claims.[94] In November 1966, the *New York Times* trumpeted "New York Caught in Poison Balloon" as a cloud of noxious exhaust gases formed over the city.[95] By 1969, the Cuyahoga River in Cleveland was so polluted that it (famously) caught fire.[96] Against this backdrop, some environmental activists saw organic agriculture as a way to fight back against industrial pollution. As one pseudonymous contributor to the *Rat*, an underground New York paper, noted, "an attack against environmental destruction is an attack on the structures of control and the mechanisms of power within a society."[97]

In addition to being a choice about personal health and the environment, growing or purchasing natural and organic food also became a form of political expression.[98] Some anti-capitalist cooperatives adopted organic food, as did some antiwar activists, who noted the links between chemical weapons and agrichemicals.[99] (Some of the companies that produced chemical weapons used in the Vietnam War, including Agent Orange, were also large producers of chemical pesticides.)[100] As critic Warren Belasco explained, "beyond defining the content of food, natural [food] was a state of mind, a symbol of opposition to mass production, efficiency, rationalization, limits."[101] As passionate as opponents of industrial farming were, they remained a tiny (but vocal) minority in the United States. Indeed, despite a myriad of protesting voices and efforts, annual pesticide use in the U.S. grew rapidly in the postwar years, climbing from 200,000 pounds in 1950 to 1.1 billion pounds in 1986.[102] With the growing proliferation of chemicals, medicines, and other additives to the food chain, conventional farming moved further and further away from traditional or organic methods.

At the same time, proponents of various ideologies appropriated organic food for sometimes conflicting causes. The meaning of "organic" agriculture required constant redefinition, and in some quarters it became contentious. Could the milk from a cow fed on conventionally grown grain be organic?[103] What about farmed fish? Should organic produce always be grown on family-run, sustainable farms? Could an industrial farm be organic?[104] Was "organic" a way of life, or only a way to grow food? When Mackey opened the first Whole Foods Market in 1980, there was no consensus among farmers, consumers, or government officials on any of these issues. Even today, the debate surrounding organic food remains alive and well.

Industry expansion and regulation

Until the 1970s, when some private organizations began developing organic certification services, there were no set guidelines to define what "organic" meant, and no consumer protections against fraud.[105] Organic products were relegated mainly to small health-foods stores and cooperatives patronized by a small but faithful customer niche. In the 1980s, states such as Washington issued their own certification requirements, but there was still no national reference.[106] Finally, in 1990, the U.S. Congress passed the Organic Foods Production Act to establish a set of federal standards to regulate the

small, growing industry.[107] In 1992, a National Organic Standards Board was appointed to help advise and draft regulations for the USDA.[108]

The task of the National Organic Standards Board was complicated by continuous developments in agricultural science. The first targets of organic advocates—fertilizers, pesticides, and fungicides—were no longer the only synthetic products used on industrial farms. The application of medicine and other forms of biotechnology to livestock drew similar protest. Crops grown with synthetic fertilizer and pesticides were used to feed animals as well as humans. Vaccines were developed to protect farm animals from disease, and antibiotics became a common additive in their feed.[109] Critics feared that overuse of antibiotics in animals could lead to resistant strains of disease in humans, and in the 1990s, one drug used in poultry did produce an antibiotic-resistant strain of salmonella.[110] In 1994, the FDA approved the use of synthetic bovine growth hormone (BST), which farmers used to boost milk production and which some medical experts believed contributed to breast and prostate cancer.[111]

For nearly 10 years, the National Organics Standards Board met to address questions ranging from the acceptability of genetically modified crop species to the use of sewage sludge as a fertilizer.[112] In 2001, the USDA published the Final Organic Rule, cementing standards for certified organic food.[113] By October 2002, all food marketed as "organic" in the United States had to comply with the new national standards, which included certification for all growers, handlers, and food processors.[114] For crops, this included the prohibition of synthetic fertilizers, sewage sludge, and pesticides.[115] Certified organic fields were also required to have buffer zones to protect against contamination by substances from conventional farms.[116] In livestock, antibiotics and growth hormones were banned, but the use of some vaccines was permitted.[117] All animals had to be fed with organically grown products and had to have access to the outdoors.[118]

The national standards also outlined acceptable methods for managing soil fertility, weeds, pests, and disease.[119] To replenish nutrients in the soil, for instance, farmers could practice crop rotation by varying the type of plant grown on an area of land in sequential seasons.[120] Under certain conditions, they could spread compost or animal manure as a natural fertilizer.[121] Fields could be weeded by hand, and farmers could introduce natural predators in place of pesticides to prey on crop pests.[122] To ward off outbreaks of disease among livestock, preventive tactics included nutritious, vitamin-rich feed and outdoor exercise.[123] All organic farmers had to keep detailed records of their practices in order to maintain USDA certification.[124] In turn, they had the right to market their products to the steadily growing throng of shoppers who sought out the organic label.

Although the Organic Foods Production Act of 1990 made no health claims about products designated as organic, links between conventional agrichemicals and environmental pollution were already beginning to multiply.[125] In 1989, the National Academy of Sciences found that more than half of the nation's water pollution could be attributed to the application of chemical fertilizers.[126] A 1990 expose on Alar, a growth chemical used on conventionally grown apples that was declared carcinogenic by the EPA, produced a temporary jump in the demand for organic food.[127] However, many conventional growers and retailers were still skeptical of the potential market for organic produce.[128] In the early 1990s, suppliers and consumers generally regarded organic products as inferior and unreliable, too "crunchy" for the mainstream. Myra Goodman, a co-founder of the organic producer Earthbound Farm, recalled that in 1993, "Costco wanted our prewashed spring mix, but they didn't want organic...To them, organic sent the wrong message: high price and low quality."[129] Between 1992 and 1997, the acreage devoted to certified organic production increased by 111%, but still made up only 0.2% of total U.S. cropland.[130]

But the idea of organic as a fringe, eccentric product would not outlast the 1990s. In this decade, sales of organic food grew on the order of 20% per year.[131] Between 1997 and 2005, sales of organic food climbed from $3.5 to $13.8 billion, and organic penetration—or the share of organics in total food sales—rose from 0.81% to 2.48% (total food sales at grocery stores and supermarkets in the same period rose from $444

to $557 billion).[132] While organics still made up a small percentage of total food purchases, they offered substantially higher profit margins and attracted wealthier consumers.[133] Estimated profit margins for natural-foods retailers averaged about 5%, compared with 1% to 2% for traditional supermarkets.[134] As purchases of organic products rose and their profitability became more evident, the profile of organic retailers also began to shift. Consumers could choose to buy organic food from an expanding universe of retailers that included independent natural and health-food stores, local cooperatives, farm stands, and, increasingly, supermarkets and grocery chains. By 2000, conventional supermarkets sold more organic foods than any other single channel, edging out natural-food retailers for the first time.[135] In April 2006, the world's largest retailer, Wal-Mart, announced its own organic initiative with plans to double organic offerings in many stores through partnerships with big-name brands such as Del Monte and Ragu.[136] This was the dynamic landscape in which John Mackey and his young company operated.

John Mackey and Whole Foods Market

John Mackey was born in 1953 in Houston, Texas.[137] His childhood had been called "conventional," but from an early age he exhibited a headstrong, competitive spirit.[138] Mackey played basketball in high school, and when he was cut from the team, he convinced his parents to move to a new school district so he could have a chance to play.[139] After graduating from high school in 1971, Mackey attended two colleges—the University of Texas and Trinity University—but dropped out before receiving a degree from either one.[140] In 2004, Mackey summed up that period of his life:

Before I started Whole Foods Market I attended two universities, where I accumulated 130 hours of electives, primarily in philosophy and religion, and ended up with no degree. I never took a single business class. I actually think that has worked to my advantage in business. I spent my late teens and my early twenties trying to discover the meaning and purpose of my own life.

My search for meaning and purpose led me into the counter-culture movement of the late 1960s and 1970s. I studied eastern philosophy and religion at the time, and still practice both yoga and meditation. I studied ecology. I became a vegetarian (I am currently a vegan [a vegetarian who also avoids animal products and byproducts]), I lived in a commune, and I grew my hair long and beard long. I'm one of those crunchy-granola types. Politically, I drifted to the Left and embraced the ideology that business and corporations were essentially evil because they selfishly sought profits.[141]

When Mackey was in his early 20s, he worked in a natural-foods store in Austin while living at a vegetarian housing co-op.[142] "It was the first time I realized what you ate could affect how you felt," he said.[143] With then-girlfriend Renee Lawson Hardy, he decided to open his own health-food store and restaurant in a three-story Victorian mansion in Austin, Texas.[144] Mackey and Lawson Hardy raised $45,000 to open the store, called SaferWay, including $20,000 from Mackey's father and $7,000 from an inheritance that Lawson Hardy had received.[145] After Mackey and his girlfriend were kicked out of their apartment for keeping food products there, they decided to live on the third floor of the SaferWay building.[146] "Renee and I would take showers in the Hobart dishwasher in the restaurant, you know, using the spray hose," Mackey said.[147]

In spite of their frugality and commitment, the first year of the business was difficult and frustrating for the young entrepreneurs. Customers had trouble finding parking, and the restaurant was losing money.[148] Mackey recalled:

Operating a business was a real education for me. There were bills to pay and a payroll to be met, and we had trouble doing either because we lost half of our initial $45,000 of capital in our first year. Our customers thought our prices were too high, and our employees thought they were being underpaid, and we were losing money. Renee and I were only being paid about $200 a month and the business was a real struggle. Nobody was very happy . . .[149]

Still, because SaferWay carried products that other natural-foods stores refused to stock, such as refined sugar, it gradually caught on with a broader range of customers.[150] In its second year, the store turned a small profit, and Mackey set his sights on opening another store.[151] Again, he turned to his father for capital, this time asking for $50,000.[152] In response, William Mackey proposed a challenge: if John could find an investor to match him, he would pledge half the amount.[153] John Mackey met the condition within days, persuading a SaferWay customer to put up $25,000.[154] He also convinced the owners of the neighboring Clarksville Natural Grocery, Craig Weller and Mark Skiles, to join him in the new venture.[155] Mackey explained:

They were a competitor but they were friends of mine. So I didn't go up there and threaten them and say, "Join with us. We're gonna drive you out of business." I went up there and said, "We're gonna open a 10,000-square-foot store about a mile from here. Wouldn't it be a lot more fun to join forces together? Rather than compete? When our store's gonna be four times bigger than yours?" And they saw the logic of that argument.[156]

Mackey called his new store Whole Foods Market, and it opened September 20, 1980.[157] With 19 employees and 12,500 square feet, this store was much bigger than SaferWay and most other health-food stores.[158] Its size allowed it to offer more variety—it carried more organic products, but also mainstream staples like red meat—than most health-food retailers, and unlike its smaller rivals, the store became a viable alternative to conventional supermarkets for one-stop shopping.[159] Then, just as the new store was getting on its feet, disaster struck. The worst flood Austin had seen in 70 years swept through the city on Memorial Day 1981, killing at least 13 city residents and causing an estimated $20 million in damages.[160] Cars in the neighborhood where Whole Foods was located could be seen floating down the streets.[161] Mackey's store was uninsured and sustained a loss of more than $400,000 in inventory and equipment.[162] With the help of supportive customers, vendors, and investors, Whole Foods Market reopened in just four weeks.[163] The federal government offered a $250,000 small business loan, enabling the young company to stay afloat financially.[164]

Building the business

In the early 1980s, as the business grew, Mackey and his colleagues worked to refine the broader objectives of the enterprise they were building and, at the same time, to understand the ways in which the enterprise itself was shaping them. In 1985, a group of 60 Whole Foods workers volunteered to join Mackey on a series of retreats aimed at distilling and articulating the mission of the business.[165] By the end of the year, they had crafted a document called the "Declaration of Interdependence."[166] That declaration was largely a reflection on the company's five core values: (1) selling the highest quality natural and organic products available; (2) satisfying and delighting customers; (3) supporting team member excellence and happiness; (4) creating wealth through profits and growth; and (5) caring about communities and the environment.[167] During the next two decades, these values were codified in a series of operating and organizational strategies that came to define the business in an expanding, changing market.

Quality standards

The quality standards at Whole Foods reflected its commitment to first-rate healthy food in a variety that could satisfy picky gourmet shoppers.[168] While it shunned artificial colorings, flavorings, sweeteners, preservatives, and hydrogenated oils, the chain carried meat, fish, and packaged foods that met company standards.[169] Conventional products were not prohibited, but organic and natural-food products were preferred. As Whole Foods' business grew, it became a major distributor and promoter of organic foods. The company also played a prominent role in the movement for national organics standards. In the late 1990s, Margaret Wittenberg, the Vice President of Global Communications and Quality Standards at Whole Foods, served as the sole retail representative on the National Organic Standards Board while the federal organic recommendations were being drafted.[170] Whole Foods was also the lone retailer represented on the USDA

Advisory Committee on Agricultural Biotechnology, formed in 2000 to help inform federal policy related to issues such as the use of genetically modified crops.[171]

Mackey had never restricted his stores to products that would satisfy his own vegetarian—and later, vegan—diet, but he frequently ordered increasing oversight of the suppliers of animal products. In 2003, Whole Foods demanded that the duck supplier Grimaud Farms stop dealing with a foie gras producer because Whole Foods opposed the force-feeding of ducks necessary to produce the delicacy.[172] (That producer, Sonoma Foie Gras, later sued Whole Foods).[173] Soon after, it also required the supplier to develop better conditions for its own ducks.[174] In 2006, based partly on a study citing lobsters' ability to feel pain and on concerns about the conditions in which lobsters were kept from the moment of capture to the moment of sale, Whole Foods stopped selling live lobsters in its stores.[175] An exception was later made for the store in Portland, Maine, but only when it found a supplier that could transport and treat the crustaceans more humanely.[176]

In the wake of Mackey's encounter with Ornelas and his reconsideration of specific factory farming practices, Whole Foods began to develop Animal Compassionate Standards for every animal product carried at the chain. The new guidelines required "environments and conditions that support the animal's physical, emotional, and behavioral needs."[177] For instance, ducks had to have access to the outdoors and to a swimming area, as well as comfortable accommodations during transport (enough room to sit naturally without hitting their heads).[178] Standards for pigs recommended that piglets stay with their litter mates from birth to slaughter, and forbid weaning a piglet from its mother before it was 28 days old.[179] The company also restructured its Quality Standards to include a species-specific rating system, ranging from one (benchmark) to five (animal compassionate gold standard).[180] Eventually, customers would be able to view this rating whenever they purchased eggs, milk, steak, and other animal products.[181]

For customers concerned about food quality, Whole Foods served a critical filtering function. The company grappled with the definition of organic and the ethics of animal husbandry and passed its expertise and beliefs on to consumers in the end products that it sold. As grocery consultant Bill Bishop, quoted in *Newsweek*, put it, "What everyone is really looking for is a mother . . . . Whole Foods assumes the responsibility of taking care of you in a somewhat maternalistic way— everything in their store has been edited."[182] Whole Foods had strict health standards, but it also liked to treat its customers and honor their tastes for baked goods, chocolate, and other indulgent products. Mackey was known to joke that "we're Whole Foods, not holy foods."[183] And Mackey himself, whom the *New York Times* dubbed a "yoga-practicing-vegetarian-libertarian who admires Ronald Reagan and prefers *The Wall Street Journal* editorial page to this newspaper's," seemed to personify the delicate balancing act of a store that carried both organic spinach and organic cheese puffs.[184]

Customer delight

The products stocked at Whole Foods were carefully displayed. A stroll through a typical store revealed fresh-baked individual pastries, a veritable vista of artisanal cheese, and trademark mounds of colorful organic produce. The premium the company put on the customer experience was apparent in the design of the stores, which were characterized by wide aisles and attractive displays. The layout of each store was designed to give top billing to the fresh produce section. Many of the foods in this area were marked with information describing the place and even farm of origin, and sampling opportunities were frequent all over the store. In most stores, customers could enjoy hot prepared food in a sit-down dining area. Nearby, suggestion boards solicited their input.[185] Some locations even offered luxuries like massage services and valet parking.[186]

The shopping experience at each Whole Foods store was unique in the natural foods and conventional grocery retailing industries. At the time when Whole Foods entered the national market, conventional supermarkets stocked their offerings in crowded, fluorescent-lit aisles.[187] Processed, packaged foods often dominated the center of these conventional stores, where big-name brands dictated the arrangement of shelf space. The relentless emphasis on low prices was a far cry from Whole Foods' tempting, feel-good gourmet selection.[188] Mackey observed: "Shopping for groceries for most people is like a chore. It's like doing the laundry or taking out the garbage. [But Whole Foods strives] to make shopping engaging, fun and interactive. Most Americans are in a kind of eating rut."[189]

In fact, the idea of grocery shopping as entertainment was part of what distinguished Whole Foods. In the spring of 2005, the company celebrated its 25th anniversary with the opening of a new flagship store in Austin, where a chocolate fountain, wine tasting area, and sushi bar trumpeted the "delight" it promised its customers.[190] The 80,000 square-foot store promised to showcase all that the business had become known for—creative, attractive, natural and organic grocery products and prepared foods—on the grandest scale yet. When the store opened, one company vice president, Bruce Silverman, called it a "food amusement park."[191] According to Silverman, customers were so astonished at the variety, abundance, and overall presentation of the food that many "walk[ed] around the store, just saying 'Oh my God . . . This place should be against the law.'"[192]

The opening of the Austin flagship store in 2005 was one of many milestones for Whole Foods. The same year, the company broke onto the Fortune 500 list at number 479 and also reached number 30 on the *Fortune* list of the 100 best companies to work for.[193] Sales in 2005 totaled $4.7 billion, more than twice those in 2001, and comparable store sales growth had grown in the double digits for eight consecutive quarters.[194] After opening 15 new locations, Whole Foods could claim 175 stores in 30 states, the District of Columbia, Canada, and the United Kingdom.[195]

Mackey attributed the performance of his company to the way it created value for all of its stakeholders: "customers, team members, investors, vendors, communities, and the environment."[196] He believed that the firm's focus on all of these constituents, particularly customers, was directly connected to its innovation and growth. "In the profit-centered business, customer happiness is merely a means to an end: maximizing profits," he said. "In the customer-centered business, customer happiness is an end in itself, and will be pursued with greater interest, passion, and empathy than the profit-centered business is capable of."[197]

Team members

Each Whole Foods store employed between 40 and 650 employees, known as team members, who were organized into self-directed teams.[198] Every team was responsible for an individual product or service area, such as seafood, prepared foods, and customer service, and reported to a team leader who worked closely with store management, or "store team leaders" as they were known within the company.[199] Front-line team members played a pivotal role in distinguishing Whole Foods from other grocery retailers. They were chosen and trained for knowledgeable, friendly service, and in Whole Foods' decentralized management model, they did more than stock shelves and scan items. They also participated in a range of operational decisions at the store level.[200] With input from store team leaders, for instance, individual employees were empowered to decide what products to stock in their section.[201] Many team members were drawn to Whole Foods by its commitment to organic agriculture and the environment and wanted to share in the company's mission.[202] Others came for the competitive wages, benefits, and stock options available at all position levels. Still others were attracted by the relative latitude and impact of their work at Whole Foods.

The employment system at Whole Foods worked on a democratic model and encouraged transparency. At each store, potential team members could apply to one of up to 13 teams.[203] Current team members played an important role in the hiring process. They interviewed and voted on prospective colleagues.[204] A candidate required a two-thirds majority of department team members to be hired.[205] Because high-performing teams could earn up to $2 extra an hour, current employees were motivated to hire productive workers.[206] Other key decisions depended on team member input. In 2003, for example, all benefit options, including health insurance and store discounts,

were selected by a company wide vote.[207] Mackey and his senior team encouraged the flow of information up, down, and across the organization. Whole Foods' open-book policy gave all team members access to its financial records, including compensation information for other employees; an employee in the bakery or at the meat counter could view the salary of his peers, his supervisor, and even the CEO.[208] Caps on executive salaries limited management compensation to eight times the pay of average employees. (In succeeding years, the cap increased to 10, 14, and finally 19 times the average pay, to keep the company competitive. In 2007, Mackey permanently reduced his own annual salary to $1).[209]

The company's Declaration of Interdependence stated that "'Us versus them' thinking has no place in our company. We believe that the best way to [build positive and healthy relationships among team members] is to encourage participation and involvement at all levels of our business."[210] Whole Foods supported its claims to employee empowerment with competitive benefits: free medical coverage for full-time workers (or 90% of the company's workforce) and options for dental, vision, disability, and life insurance.[211] The company also offered paid time off and emergency funds for team members in need.[212] The vast majority of company stock options—94%—went to non-executive staff, including front-line employees.[213] This ratio was nearly reversed in other U.S. companies, where, on average, 75% of stock options went to top executives and 25% to the rest of the workforce.[214] Employee empowerment was evident in other aspects of the company's culture. At the end of every company meeting, including board of directors meetings, for instance, team members participated in a ritual that Mackey called "appreciations," when participants were encouraged to thank or praise others publicly for their work.[215]

Whole Foods promoted the philosophy of a "shared destiny" to all team members. Broadly speaking, this meant that no one deserved entitlements, and everyone shared a collective fate.[216] This philosophy was evident in the retailer's treatment of top management: like everyone else, they flew coach class, and had to follow strict limits on business expenses.[217] Every four weeks, team productivity was evaluated and those with the best performance shared in the company's profits.[218] Mackey's view of value creation reflected the democratic, inter-dependent nature of his employment model:

> *I'm a businessman and a free market libertarian, but I believe that the enlightened corporation should try to create value for all of its constituencies. From an investor's perspective, the purpose of the business is to maximize profits. But that's not the purpose for other stakeholders—for customers, employees, suppliers, and the community. Each of those groups will define the purpose of the business in terms of its own needs and desires, and each perspective is valid and legitimate.*[219]

Value creation

Throughout the 1980s, Mackey and his team slowly, steadily expanded the company's reach, opening new stores and acquiring existing natural-foods retailers. In 1984, four years after founding his business, Mackey opened his first store outside Austin—in Houston, Texas.[220] In 1986, the company purchased Bluebonnet Natural Foods Grocery in Dallas, Texas. In 1988, it acquired the Whole Food Company in New Orleans (the term "whole food" referred to foods that were processed or refined as little as possible).[221] The Louisiana store was already 14 years old at the time of the acquisition and had achieved sales of more than $1 million per year with the help of employees who were all company stockholders.[222] At the end of the 1980s, in 1989, the company opened a West Coast location in Palo Alto, California.[223] By this time, as Fleur Hedden, then the vice president of marketing, noted, "We no longer position ourselves as an alternative . . . We are mainstream."[224]

The company's stores attracted mainstream customers, many of whom would not have set foot in natural-food co-ops. With the profusion of information available in stores and in company literature, Whole Foods invited these customers to buy its values along with its products.[225] "We didn't change to conform," Mackey said.

"The world came in our direction...driven by the quality and authenticity of what we do."[226] The influx of SUV-driving patrons upset some customers who believed that buying and eating organic food were inseparable from a socially and environmentally conscious lifestyle.[227] But Mackey believed that a bigger market for Whole Foods meant a bigger impact for organic, regardless of who the customers were. "Whole Foods is not a business for a clique, or for the elite," he said. "We wanted the philosophy of the stores to spread throughout the culture. We wanted to change the world."[228]

By 1991, the company operated 12 stores with total annual sales of $92.5 million.[229] The next year, Whole Foods went public, raising $23 million at a split-adjusted price of $8.50 a share.[230] It was the first retailer born of the countercultural natural-foods movement to conduct an IPO.[231] Mackey vowed that going public would not compromise the company's values. "Wall Street isn't going to corrupt Whole Foods Market," he said. "We're going to purify Wall Street."[232] In fact, many of the practices that Whole Foods aimed to continue were unconventional for a company of its size. At the time of the IPO, executive pay—including Mackey's—was limited to 10 times the pay of an average Whole Foods team member; by comparison, in 1990 the average CEO at a major company made 85 times the amount of an average American factory worker.[233] (By 2004, the Whole Foods salary cap had risen to 14 times average pay, while chief executive pay nationwide had soared to 431 times the salary of an average worker).[234]

Throughout the 1990s, Mackey's bet that well-educated consumers would pay more for the products that Whole Foods offered—foods free of artificial additives, sweeteners, colorings, and preservatives, and organic whenever possible—paid off handsomely. From 1993 to 1997, the number of Whole Foods stores nearly doubled from 42 to 76, and annual sales climbed from less than $500 million to more than $1.1 billion.[235] During the same period, Whole Foods' revenues climbed 96% or 18% per year compounded.[236] Between 1999 and 2003, by comparison, total grocery sales in the U.S. grew about 13%, a compound annual growth rate of 2.5%.[237] Whole Foods was more profitable than many, much larger supermarket chains. In 2006, it earned almost $200 million on sales of $5.8 billion or about three percent.[238] By comparison, Safeway with sales of $40 billion earned about 2% or $870 million.[239] Ten years after its initial public offering, with sales approaching $2.7 billion, Whole Foods was added to both the NASDAQ-100 and S&P MidCap 400 indices.[240] And after opening its first store in Toronto, Canada in May of 2002, the chain claimed an international reach.[241]

Caring for the environment and communities

Whole Foods' management believed that local and global communities and the natural environment were, like investors, stakeholders in their enterprise. In addition to its support of organic agriculture, the company employed a range of environmentally friendly practices such as composting spoiled produce for use in gardens and farms.[242] When a new store was constructed, green techniques—methods for reducing the amount of virgin material used and toxic waste produced—were implemented whenever possible.[243] Construction materials included recycled steel, biodegradable linoleum, and tiles made from recycled glass bottles.[244] Whole Foods was the first retailer to build a supermarket that met the environmental standards of the LEED (Leadership in Energy and Environmental Design) Green Building Rating System.[245] In 2006, the company made the largest corporate purchase of wind credits in the history of the United States, enough to offset 100% of its total electricity use.[246]

Whole Foods encouraged philanthropy and outreach in the communities it served and throughout the world. Team members were paid for time spent performing community service.[247] A minimum of 5% of after-tax company profits was donated to charity each year.[248] Individual stores could also host "five-percent days," on which 5% of store sales would be donated to a local charity.[249] In 2005, the profits of two five-percent days were used to establish two Whole Foods foundations, the Animal Compassion Foundation and the Whole Planet Foundation, which was dedicated to fighting poverty

through assistance to entrepreneurs and microloans to the poor in developing countries.[250] It worked with Muhammad Yunus, the 2006 winner of the Nobel Peace Prize and founder of the Grammen Trust, who had pioneered the use of microcredit in 1977.[251] By the end of 2005, the Whole Planet Foundation had provided more than $375,000 in small business loans to 2,200 women in Costa Rica, where Whole Foods bought bananas and pineapple, and Guatemala, where growers for Whole Foods produced high-quality coffee.[252]

Expanding the market

Like Whole Foods, natural-foods stores across the United States tapped into an increasing consumer interest in organics. In the 1990s, Whole Foods grew partly through careful acquisition of some of the most successful natural-food chains. In October 1992, just after Whole Foods went public, it purchased Boston-based Bread & Circus, a chain owned by the Irish-born Anthony Harnett. Harnett and his wife, who had opened their first natural-foods store in Dublin so that they could find acceptable food for their new baby, had bought the New England chain in 1975.[253] In its early years, Bread & Circus applied a strict definition to its "natural" foods, and in 1987 briefly prohibited sales of alcohol, chocolate, and coffee.[254] Though Harnett later relented, at the time he claimed that "the items in question are addictive drugs that have no place in a whole foods supermarket."[255] The chain became famous throughout the Northeast for products such as wild blueberries, shiitake mushrooms, and whole milk in glass bottles.[256] By 1987, it was doing $27 million in annual sales and counted Julia Child among its devoted customers.[257] (Bread & Circus enjoyed such a strong reputation in its region that the New England stores did not assume the Whole Foods name until 2003, 11 years after the acquisition.)[258]

Soon after buying Bread & Circus on the East Coast, Whole Foods made another major acquisition in the West. The 1993 purchase of Mrs. Gooch's Natural Foods Markets in Los Angeles cemented Whole Foods' position as the nation's largest natural-foods retailer.[259] After a few smaller acquisitions, the company bought another

East Coast retailer, Fresh Fields, which had a large presence in the Washington, D.C. area.[260] Rather than impose its own corporate culture on its new chains, Whole Foods made it a point to incorporate some of the strategies that had made these regional competitors popular in the first place.[261] Unlike Bread & Circus, for instance, Whole Foods had never banned substances like white flour or coffee. But some of the aspects that Bread & Circus was known for—hormone-free meat, a fish counter, and fresh produce—complemented and enhanced the existing Whole Foods philosophy.[262]

In the 1990s, Whole Foods also grew by opening new stores in selected areas where management believed that a market existed for natural and organic foods.[263] When building a new store, the company focused on premium real estate sites in urban locations. It preferred large formats, ranging from 25,000 to 50,000 square feet.[264] As Whole Foods executives scouted out new sites, they concentrated on areas with a high density of college graduates, reasoning that people with a better understanding of pesticide dangers would be willing to pay a higher premium for its chemical-free products.[265] In fiscal year 1993, the retailer opened new stores in Raleigh, Chicago, Ann Arbor, and San Antonio.[266] From 1996 to 2000, Whole Foods built a total of 50 new stores and opened another 40 through acquisitions.[267]

As the number of Whole Foods stores across the country increased, Mackey and his team worked to create an organization that could meet surging customer demand for safe, healthy food while remaining true to the company's core values. By the late 1990s, Whole Foods could no longer rely solely on small, scattered independent farms to source its stores. Like any large supermarket, it needed a central infrastructure and a dependable supply chain. Part of the capital from the company's initial public offering in 1992 was earmarked to expand and relocate what was then its only regional distribution center.[268] Less than 15 years later, Whole Foods stores were supported by a range of centralized facilities, including nine regional distribution centers, seafood processing facilities, a national meat purchasing office, and a specialty coffee procurement and roasting operation.[269]

In 2006, wholesale suppliers and vendors at the local, regional, and international levels supplied the regional distribution centers that ultimately supplied individual Whole Foods stores.[270] Twenty-two percent of the company's purchases were made through United National Foods, a third-party supplier, which provided dry and frozen goods.[271] This allowed Whole Foods to focus its internal efforts on the perishable products for which it was most well known—produce, prepared foods, seafood, and meat.[272] Although the majority of Whole Foods' purchases were made at the regional or national level, each store had the power to buy directly from local producers, and consequently every store had a slightly different product mix.[273] The design of each store, along with its product offerings, reflected the tastes of the community where it was located.[274]

By September of 2006, sales at all stores had climbed to $5.6 billion.[275] The company operated 186 stores: 177 in the United States, three in Canada, and six in the United Kingdom.[276] While revenue and profits were up, same-store sales growth had declined to 11% from a 2004 peak of 14.9%.[277] In February 2007, the store announced plans to buy one of its biggest rivals, Wild Oats, for $565 million.[278] Wild Oats, a natural-foods grocery founded in 1987 in Boulder, Colorado, had a strong presence in markets where Whole Foods was less established: the Pacific Northwest, the Rocky Mountain region, and Florida.[279] As the second-largest natural-foods supermarket in the nation, with 110 locations and $1.2 billion in annual sales, Wild Oats was Whole Foods' most ambitious acquisition yet.[280] In fact, some investors worried that the project might be too ambitious, a brash attempt to meet Mackey's goal of $12 billion in total sales by 2010 and a potential indicator of a downturn in the company's organic growth.[281] Mackey maintained that the merger—the 18th in the chain's history—would ultimately bolster the company's position in an increasingly competitive market.[282] "We need each other," he said.[283]

Breaking the mold

As the founder and CEO of a Fortune 500 company who unabashedly proclaimed that "love is the only reality," Mackey was something of a maverick.[284] Of all the unconventional methods that Mackey incorporated into his business, one of the most distinctive was his management style. "Our leadership is decentralized," Mackey said. "Each store is divided into teams, and team members are like people in a band within a tribe—they are empowered to do what needs to get done. They don't waste time waiting for the chief back at headquarters to give them orders."[285] Where Mackey saw a united tribe powered by independent initiative, however, others saw chaos. One former Whole Foods executive remarked that "Mackey is hardly a manager at all . . . he's an anarchist."[286]

Mackey was convinced that the individual freedoms and positive reinforcement in his model guaranteed better, faster innovation than the old-school competition. "The corporation was modeled after the great centralized organizations of their times—armies and the Catholic Church," he said. "These hierarchical models of organization are not well adapted anymore."[287] According to the entrepreneur, decentralization, including employee empowerment and individual store decision-making authority, would allow Whole Foods to evolve along with shifts in the marketplace.[288]

The top-down structure typical of large corporations was not the only standard that Mackey rejected. He was also an opponent of the labor unions that had come into being with late 19th and early 20th century corporations. A democratic-socialist turned libertarian, Mackey first came into conflict with unions in 1990, when Whole Foods acquired a co-op in Berkeley, California.[289] Mackey believed that union demands had helped sink the co-op, and when Whole Foods took it over, it did not hire any of the former employees.[290] In response, the new Whole Foods was picketed by the United Food and Commercial Workers local.[291] The Berkeley Labor Commission charged that Whole Foods paid $1 to $5 less than comparable supermarket employers.[292] Whole Foods maintained that its pay was competitive, and while Mackey defended the rights of workers to unionize, he also was adamant in his conviction that unionizing was "not in [the company's] best interest or [the employees'] best interest."[293] In a 2005 interview, Mackey explained that

Unions as they evolved in the United States became very adversarial, untrusting, and opposed to the success and prosperity of the business. This is my major objection to unions today—they harm the flourishing of the business for all the stakeholders. Instead of cooperation between stakeholders, they focus on competition between management and labor. Instead of embracing the notion of the "expanding pie" vision of capitalism—more for everyone, or win-win—they frequently embrace the zero-sum philosophy of win-lose.[294]

Some of Mackey's more colorful comments characterized unionization as "like having herpes." "It doesn't kill you," he said, "but it's unpleasant and inconvenient, and it stops a lot of people from becoming your lover."[295]

When, in 2002, workers at a Whole Foods store in Madison, Wisconsin voted to join a union, they were the first—and, as of 2007, the only—store in the company to do so.[296] The next year, however, the Madison store's staff overwhelmingly petitioned to withdraw from union membership.[297] An employee interviewed at the time cited dissatisfaction with the union's health plan and promotions structure, which, unlike Whole Foods' merit-based system, was based on seniority.[298] Industry experts agreed that, as Whole Foods continued to grow, it would become an increasingly attractive target to union organizers, but Whole Foods was just as committed to remaining non-union.[299] "The whole labor union idea that labor and capital are at war with each other is nonsense," said Mackey. "They're partners to create value."[300]

Spoils of success

By the dawn of the 21st century, mainstream demand for organics had reached unprecedented levels, attracting the attention of conventional growers, distributors, Wall Street, and the business press. Customers had the choice of nearly twice the number of local farmers' markets selling fresh produce than had existed 10 years earlier.[301] At the same time, conventional supermarkets like Wegmans and Kroger were increasing their own organic selections and were copying signature

Whole Foods strategies in customer service and prepared foods.[302] Finally, Wal-Mart's much-heralded entry into low-priced organic produce in 2006 was backed by planned organic development from suppliers like General Mills and PepsiCo.[303] The world's largest retailer quickly became the world's biggest seller of organic milk.[304] With concern mounting over increased competition in the organics market, in 2006 Whole Foods' stock price declined 40%.[305]

As a rule, organic food cost more to produce than conventional food, especially when it was grown on small, family-run farms rather than industrial complexes. Old-fashioned labor, such as weeding by hand, was more expensive than spraying a chemical herbicide.[306] Without powerful chemicals, potential damages to crops from natural pests could also be more costly.[307] The prices at Whole Foods had long reflected this difference, earning it the tongue-in-cheek nickname "whole paycheck." But Mackey viewed the cost of natural food as a trade-off and defended his chain's prices in a 2006 interview with a reporter from the television program *60 Minutes*: "It might be a little more expensive, but you're getting a better tasting, higher quality food that's going to be better for your health and better for the environment."[308] A year earlier, he had compared Whole Foods products to Starbucks coffee and luxury cars, saying that "if Americans want to eat higher quality, they can pay for it."[309]

As competition from lower-priced rivals intensified, however, Whole Foods management seemed bent on bucking the "whole paycheck" reputation. In 2006, for example, the company ran a 12-week advertising campaign in *The New York Times* that proclaimed, "More of the good stuff. For less than you think."[310] The company also planned to promote its private-label brands, including 365 Organic Everyday Value™, and to expand the product offerings of those lines.[311] Mackey, who had built his company largely on the idea that consumers would pay for the added value of healthy food, claimed that competition from Wal-Mart in particular had so far had little effect.[312] In explaining the 2006 fall in the company's stock price, he pointed out that same-store sales growth had fallen only after years of double-digit increases.[313] Still, Mackey confirmed that price competition had become a new priority

for his chain. "We're being more aggressive on price," he said. "If [a competitor carries] the exact same product, then we're going to sell it at a matching or lower price."[314]

The price pressure at Whole Foods stemmed largely from competition with a single chain, Trader Joe's. Like Whole Foods, Trader Joe's aimed to cater to well-educated consumers and courted them with a mix of gourmet and natural or organic foods. The chain's non-union employees were, like the team members at Whole Foods, compensated with above-union wages and generous benefits, including a pension plan.[315] Unlike Mackey's company, however, Trader Joe's made rock-bottom prices the center of its strategy.[316] Since the 1970s, buyers for the store had been seeking out low-priced suppliers from Singapore to the Czech Republic, and by 2003 about 80% of Trader Joe's products were private label.[317] Store offerings varied depending on the current supply, and while Trader Joe's was famed for cheap wines—customers affectionately referred to one line as "Two-Buck Chuck"—it did not attempt to compete with supermarket selections of produce and meat.[318] Since 1978, the California-based chain had been privately owned by one of Europe's richest merchant families, the Albrechts, whose other holdings included the discount giant Aldi.[319] And at $4.5 billion, Trader Joe's estimated sales in 2006 were not far behind Whole Foods, which posted sales for the same year at $5.6 billion.[320]

Mackey was acutely aware of the threat Trader Joe's posed for his company. In early 2007 he explained Whole Foods' response, saying, "we've recently taken to just matching all their prices across the board."[321] But he also spoke optimistically about the stimulus such rivalry provided:

Competition is a good thing. Competition forces you to get better—otherwise, you get complacent. You can never own a customer, you can only rent them for a little while. It's like a one-day lease, and they can break it anytime they want to. You have to continue to innovate, you have to continue to do a better job, or your customers are going to go shop somewhere else . . . Whole Foods is using [this competition] to help make us a better company.

We think that's a good thing. We're a company that doesn't really sit still.[322]

Characteristically, he was also relatively unconcerned about Wall Street's valuation of his company:

Our stock was very highly valued, and [the 2006 drop] took some air out of the tire, and now we're more reasonably valued. As long as we continue to do a good job and we're innovative and creative, if we're able to continue to successfully meet our customers' needs and desires, our company's going to continue to flourish and the stock price will take care of itself. I can't afford to say...that I don't care, but we do manage the business for the long term.[323]

A new consumer consciousness

In the face of mounting pressure from investors and competitors, Whole Foods also found itself compelled to justify its policies to a demanding coterie of shoppers. Over the years, customers who saw organic agriculture as part of a larger social and political agenda, or who simply romanticized the idea of a natural-foods store, became critical of some Whole Foods policies, including Mackey's opposition to unions and the company's use of large-scale suppliers. The organic label alone was no longer enough to satisfy some eco-conscious consumers, who now factored local farmers, sustainable production, and humane treatment of animals into their buying decisions.[324] The size and decadence of the new stores alienated other organics fans, leading to the provocative *New York Times* headline, "Is Whole Foods Straying From Its Roots?"[325] An article in the *New Yorker* quoted an organic grower and former Columbia University nutritionist on the increasing disillusionment with businesses, such as Whole Foods, that critics termed "corporate organic":

When we said organic, we meant local. We meant healthful. We meant being true to the ecologies of the regions. We meant mutually respectful growers and eaters. We meant social justice and equality.[326]

For those faithful to the idea of organic as it emerged in the 1960s—a way of life that rejected conventional food systems, industrial farms, agrichemicals, even militarization—shopping at Whole Foods posed a unique dilemma. The company had undoubtedly helped to bring organic produce to the mainstream, introducing millions of consumers to food grown without artificial fertilizers and pesticides. But to do so, it had adopted some economies of scale that seemed incompatible to many with the values of the counterculture that had originally supported organics.

One of the most controversial consequences of these scale economies was the rise of the industrial organic farm—a development that 20 years earlier would have seemed an oxymoron. To many organics consumers, the word "organic" signaled a method of farming that rejected both the chemicals and the livestock crowding of conventional, industrial-scale farms. In this ideal, an organic farm was a small enterprise, perhaps family-run, and a model for environmental and animal compassion standards. But industrial organic farms, some of them owned by companies as large as General Mills, Kraft, and Coca Cola, increasingly stocked the organic sections of many supermarkets, including Whole Foods.[327] Journalist Michael Pollan visited and reported on the reality of these organic farms in his best-selling book *The Omnivore's Dilemma*, published in 2006. In the process, he dealt some strong words to Whole Foods. At Petaluma Poultry, a Whole Foods supplier, he described organic chickens raised in houses that "resemble[d] military barracks."[328] Although the chickens technically had access to a door outside, due to fear of infection the door was closed until two weeks before the birds were slaughtered.[329] At some industrial organic dairies, the cows were fenced into dry lots, not pasture, and milked three times a day.[330]

Pollan spoke for many when he lamented that "the word organic has been stretched and twisted to admit the very sort of industrial practices for which it once offered a critique and alternative."[331] Supermarkets like Whole Foods and corporate organic farms like salad supplier Earthbound Farm found themselves at the center of an intensifying debate about the enterprises they had struggled to create. Had mainstream demand for organic created a monster? Should organic grocers refuse to deal with large farms? If so, should organics consumers accept high prices and limited, sporadic supply? As Drew Goodman, co-founder of Earthbound Farm, commented, "the only way we can sell organic produce at a reasonable price is by moving it into a conventional supply chain the moment it's picked."[332]

For those who charged his company with selling out, Mackey had a swift response: "America has a romance with small businesses. And it has mistrust of the large businesses. Whole Foods is out to prove that wrong. I don't see any inherent reason why corporations cannot be just as caring and responsible as small businesses."[333] But the problem with a large corporation that relied on industrial organics, according to Pollan and other critics, had less to do with the romance of a small farm than with environmental sustainability. While organic farming was supposed to benefit the environment, sourcing stores around the country with produce from a single industrial farm required an enormous amount of fossil fuel. According to David Pimental, a Cornell ecologist quoted in Pollan's book, shipping an organic salad from California to the East Coast consumed 57 calories of fuel energy for every one calorie in the salad itself.[334] And Mackey himself acknowledged that on the basis of taste, local was sometimes a better choice: "I would probably purchase a local nonorganic tomato before I would purchase an organic one that was shipped from California," he said.[335]

Logistically, supplying Whole Foods customers purely with local produce, particularly, say, in the Northeast during winter, would be virtually impossible. But as Mackey pointed out in a response to Pollan, Whole Foods and other natural-foods stores were instrumental in creating a market for local organic farmers in the first place, long before organics began to hit the mainstream.[336] While 22% of the company's top produce suppliers were corporate farms in 2005, he noted, 78% were still independent or family-run.[337] Mackey also suggested that "a strictly local foods philosophy is not a very compassionate philosophy," as it prioritized local products at the expense of struggling farmers in other countries.[338] Still, in the months after Pollan's book came out in early 2006, Whole Foods introduced a series of initiatives designed to

encourage more local trade: all stores were required to buy from at least four local farmers; some would have Sunday farmers' markets in their parking lots; and the company would give low-interest loans to local farms to the tune of $10 million annually.[339]

The view from the top

On a rainy evening in February 2007, Mackey found himself seated next to Michael Pollan on the journalist's home turf at the Graduate School of Journalism at U.C. Berkeley. The CEO and the author had engaged in an open dialogue on Mackey's blog from the time Mackey first read Pollan's book and posted a response. Less than a year later, the two came together for a public talk on the social, ethical, and economic considerations of organic farming and the future of Whole Foods.

Before a sold-out crowd of over 2,000 students and spectators, Mackey opened the talk with a presentation he called "The Past, Present, and Future of Food." To embark on a debate about the future of farming, he first took the audience back thousands of years, outlining the evolution of human agriculture from the era of the hunter-gatherers to the rise of industrial farms and a new phase he called the "ecological era."[340] He talked about global warming and the obesity epidemic in the United States and showed a graphic video of the conditions that animals lived in on corporate farms. After placing the story of Whole Foods within the broader history of the natural-foods movement, Mackey talked about the concerns his company would face in the future: support of local foods, food artisans, ethical trade, sustainable farming, and animal welfare.

After an hour, Mackey sat down to field questions from Pollan and the audience. Some wanted to know about the stock performance or how the company viewed competition from Wal-Mart. But Mackey also faced questions that went straight to the heart of the tension between the recent success of organics in the mainstream market and the belief system of the movement's early followers. As Pollan noted, the prices at Whole Foods often fed charges of elitism by its critics. Organic and other healthy, non-processed foods were the most expensive items in conventional grocery stores, and while America was "getting somewhere as a culture in improving the diet of people who have money, there [were] a lot of other people."[341]

Mackey put the problem in a larger context. Americans spent only 8% of their disposable income on food, less than any other contemporary society and less than U.S. consumers had 30 or 40 years earlier. If American consumers bought only organic products, he claimed, they would spend about 15% of their incomes on food, about the same fraction as Europeans in 2007 did. Budget shoppers, he continued, could spend less on produce by purchasing products in season and looking for Whole Foods' private-label goods. American culture was steeped in prepared, ready-to-go meals, but for those willing to cook, the same dishes could be made for considerably less money. In the end, Mackey argued, "it's really just about making choices."[342]

The CEO went on to say that he believed consumers would make healthy choices, and that the "factory farm" model for raising livestock was fated for collapse. The practices in these large factory farms, particularly in regard to animals raised and slaughtered for meat, had long been shielded from the public eye. As long as there was no viable alternative, consumers had been complicit in averting their gaze from the suffering that such practices inflicted on other sentient beings—cows, pigs, lambs, chickens, ducks, and geese. Mackey believed that the initiatives of new organics entrepreneurs, many supported by Whole Foods, in tandem with the rise in consumer consciousness would lead to an ethical revolution in the agricultural industry:

When people really have an alternative they'll look. Right now they're afraid to look because they don't want to become vegetarians or vegans, so they'd rather not know . . . I believe that when we create an alternative so that people can buy humanely raised animal products, that they will really become outraged at the factory farms, [that this issue will] come out of the closet then. The journalists that don't want to write about it right now will write about it, a critical mass will be built up, and things will change pretty quickly. It'll tip.[343]

Mackey's assessment of American consumers reflected his own path as an entrepreneur, executive,

and human being. For almost three decades, Whole Foods had been grappling with the ethical and environmental aspects of the products it sold. In formulating and redefining the retailer's quality standards, Mackey had had to balance his own evolving dietary beliefs with consumer demand and insufficient or unacceptable supply. "There [were] no simple answers," he said. "God didn't come down and give us our values—humans had to forge them."[344]

In their eyes, the enterprise that Mackey and his team had created was, along with the values they had incorporated into it, a step apart from both conventional business models and anti-capitalist counterculture. As Mackey said:

The business model that Whole Foods has embraced could represent a new form of capitalism, one that more consciously works for the common good instead of depending solely on the "invisible hand" to generate positive results for society. The "brand" of capitalism is in terrible shape throughout the world, and corporations are widely seen as selfish, greedy, and uncaring. This is both unfortunate and unnecessary, and could be changed if businesses and economists widely adopted the business model that I have outlined here.

To extend our love and care beyond our narrow self-interest is antithetical to neither our human nature nor our financial success. Rather, it leads to the further fulfillment of both. Why do we not encourage this in our theories of business and economics? Why do we restrict our theories to such a pessimistic and crabby view of human nature? What are we afraid of?[345]

Notes

1. The description of this meeting draws on Charles Fishman, "The Anarchist's Cookbook," *Fast Company*, issue 84, July 2004. Viewed November 6, 2006 at http://www.fastcompany.com/magazine/84/wholefoods.html.
2. Fishman, "The Anarchist's Cookbook."
3. Fishman, "The Anarchist's Cookbook."
4. Fishman, "The Anarchist's Cookbook."
5. Fishman, "The Anarchist's Cookbook."
6. Fishman, "The Anarchist's Cookbook."
7. The structure of this section also draws on Fishman, "The Anarchist's Cookbook."
8. Fishman, "The Anarchist's Cookbook."

9. Fishman, "The Anarchist's Cookbook."
10. Fishman, "The Anarchist's Cookbook."
11. Fishman, "The Anarchist's Cookbook."
12. Fishman, "The Anarchist's Cookbook."
13. Fishman, "The Anarchist's Cookbook."
14. Fishman, "The Anarchist's Cookbook."
15. Fishman, "The Anarchist's Cookbook."
16. Fishman, "The Anarchist's Cookbook."
17. "The exceptions are eggs laid by his own chickens which roam free at his property outside Austin, and goat cheese made by a local farmer who 'Mr. Mackey has ensured on a personal visit' 'treats the animals very well.'" Katherine Griffiths, "The Interview: John Mackey, Founder, chairman and chief executive of Whole Foods Market," *The Independent*, September 24, 2005.
18. Fishman, "The Anarchist's Cookbook."
19. Lynne Miller, "Animal Rights Group Split on Whole Foods' Initiative," *Supermarket News*, February 7, 2005. Viewed April 14, 2007 at www.factiva.com.
20. John Mackey, "An Open Letter to Michael Pollan," Whole Foods Market website, http://www.wholefoods.com/blogs/jm/archives/ 2006/05/an_open_letter.html, viewed March 23, 2007.
21. Fishman, "The Anarchist's Cookbook."
22. "Organic Farming and Marketing," Economic Research Service, USDA, http://www.ers.usda.gov/ Briefing/Organic/. Viewed April 3, 2007.
23. John Mackey and Michael Pollan, "The Past, Present, and Future of Food," speech given on February 27, 2007, at the University of California at Berkeley School of Journalism, http://webcast.berkeley/event_details. php?webcastid=19147&p=1&ipp=15&category=, accessed March 2007.
24. Jared Diamond, *Guns, Germs, and Steel: The Fates of Human Societies* (New York: W.W. Norton & Company, 1999), 86.
25. Diamond, *Guns, Germs, and Steel*, 100.
26. Diamond refers to this cycle as a "chicken or the egg" argument: food production may have led to larger populations and complex societies, or large populations may have led to increased food production. In any case, food production stimulated societal complexity, and vice versa. See Diamond, *Guns, Germs, and Steel*, 284-285.
27. Diamond, *Guns, Germs, and Steel*, 284-285.
28. Diamond, *Guns, Germs, and Steel*, 284-285.
29. Diamond, *Guns, Germs, and Steel*, 284-285.
30. John Mackey and Michael Pollan, "The Past, Present, and Future of Food."
31. Diamond, *Guns, Germs, and Steel*, 128.
32. Diamond, *Guns, Germs, and Steel*, 128.
33. "Unit on Corn, Beans, and Squash," Wampanoag Tribe of Gay Head, http://www.wampanoagtribe.net/ Pages/Wampanoag_Education/corn, viewed April 5, 2007.
34. "Unit on Corn, Beans, and Squash," Wampanoag Tribe of Gay Head.

35. Samuel Fromartz, *Organic, Inc.* (New York: Harcourt Books, 2006), xvii.
36. Diamond, *Guns, Germs, and Steel*, 101.
37. T. Bedford Franklin, *A History of Agriculture* (London: G. Bell and Sons Ltd, 1948), 25.
38. Franklin, *A History of Agriculture*, 44. See also Fernand Braudel, "Corn and crop rotation," *Capitalism and Material Life 1400–1800* (New York: Harper and Row, 1967), 74-77.
38. Franklin, *A History of Agriculture*, 44.
40. Mark Overton, "Agricultural Revolution in England 1500–1850," BBC History, http://www.bbc.co.uk /history/british/empire_seapower/agricultural_revolution_01.shtml, viewed March 20, 2007.
41. Overton, "Agricultural Revolution in England 1500–1850."
42. Braudel, "The Weight of Numbers," *Capitalism and Material Life 1400–1800*, 53.
43. Braudel, "The Weight of Numbers," *Capitalism and Material Life 1400–1800*, 38.
44. Braudel, "The Weight of Numbers," *Capitalism and Material Life 1400–1800*, 42.
45. Braudel, "The Weight of Numbers," *Capitalism and Material Life 1400–1800*, 42.
46. Braudel, "The Weight of Numbers," *Capitalism and Material Life 1400–1800*, 1-54.
47. Overton, "Agricultural Revolution in England 1500–1850."
48. Overton, "Agricultural Revolution in England 1500–1850."
49. Franklin, *A History of Agriculture*, 38-50 and 131-144.
50. Franklin, *A History of Agriculture*, 139.
51. Overton, "Agricultural Revolution in England 1500–1850."
52. Overton, "Agricultural Revolution in England 1500–1850," and William N. Parker, "On a certain parallelism in form between two historical processes of productivity growth," *Two Centuries of American Agriculture*, Vivian Wiser, ed. (Goleta, CA: The Agricultural Historical Society, 1976), 112.
53. Franklin, *A History of Agriculture*, 111.
54. Bruce Robison, "All Change in the Victorian Age," BBC History, http://www.bbc.co.uk/history/british/victorians, viewed April 17, 2007.
55. Overton, "Agricultural Revolution in England 1500–1850."
56. Michael Pollan, *The Omnivore's Dilemma: A Natural History of Four Meals* (New York: Penguin Press, 2006), 146.
57. Richard Merrill, "Toward a Self-Sustaining Agriculture," *Radical Agriculture*, ed. Richard Merrill (New York: New York University Press, 1976), 296.
58. Merrill, "Toward a Self-Sustaining Agriculture," *Radical Agriculture*, 296.

59. Pollan, *The Omnivore's Dilemma*, 42.
60. Merrill, "Toward a Self-Sustaining Agriculture," *Radical Agriculture*, 297.
61. Merrill, "Toward a Self-Sustaining Agriculture," *Radical Agriculture*, 297.
62. Pollan, *The Omnivore's Dilemma*, 41.
63. Merrill, "Toward a Self-Sustaining Agriculture," *Radical Agriculture*, 287.
64. United States Department of Agriculture, "Trends in U.S. Agriculture, published by USDA-NASS," "U.S. Corn Yields, 1900-1999," http://www.usda.gov/nass/pubs/trends/cornyields.csv, viewed March 1, 2007.
65. Bruce L. Gardner, *American Agriculture in the Twentieth Century* (Cambridge: Harvard University Press, 2002), 186–187.
66. Gardner, *American Agriculture in the 20th Century*, 58.
67. Gardner, *American Agriculture in the 20th Century*, 61.
68. Gardner, *American Agriculture in the 20th Century*, 61.
69. Gardner, *American Agriculture in the 20th Century*, 61.
70. "Trends in U.S. Agriculture," U.S. Department of Agriculture, http://www.usda.gov/nass/pubs/ trends/farmpopulation.htm, viewed April 17, 2007.
71. "Trends in U.S. Agriculture," U.S. Department of Agriculture, http://www.usda.gov/nass/pubs/ trends/farmpopulation.htm, viewed April 17, 2007.
72. Nick Kotz, "Agribusiness," *Radical Agriculture*, 43-44.
73. Ray A. Goldberg, Carin-Isabel Knoop, and Carlos Gonzalez, "ConAgra, Inc.: Across the Food Chain," April 6, 1999, HBS case no. 999-010.
74. "Tyson Foods, Inc." Hoovers, http://premium.hoovers.com/, viewed April 17, 2007.
75. Kotz, "Agribusiness," *Radical Agriculture*, 41.
76. Gardner, *American Agriculture in the 20th Century*, 66.
77. Pollan, *The Omnivore's Dilemma*, 45.
78. See Pollan, *The Omnivore's Dilemma*, 42–43.
79. Cited in Fromartz, *Organic, Inc.*, 24.
80. Cited in Pollan, *The Omnivore's Dilemma*, 43.
81. *Oxford Dictionary of National Biography* (online version), "Sir Albert Howard," viewed April 12, 2007.
82. Warren J. Belasco, *Appetite for Change* (Ithaca: Cornell University Press, 1993), 70. See also the *Oxford Dictionary of National Biography*, "Sir Albert Howard," and Pollan, *The Omnivore's Dilemma*, 146–148.
83. Sir Albert Howard, *An Agricultural Testament*, 220.
84. Fromartz, *Organic, Inc.*, 14-15.
85. Fromartz, *Organic, Inc.*, 17.
86. Cited in Fromartz, *Organic, Inc.*, 17.
87. Fromartz, *Organic, Inc.*, 17.
88. Pollan, *The Omnivore's Dilemma*, 142.
89. Belasco, *Appetite for Change*, 71.
90. Belasco, *Appetite for Change*, 71.
91. Pollan, *The Omnivore's Dilemma*, 142.
92. Pollan, *The Omnivore's Dilemma*, 145.

93. Fromartz, *Organic, Inc.*, 21.
94. Fromartz, *Organic, Inc.*, 21-22.
95. Stuart H. Loory, "'Conspiracy' of Nature's Forces Is Blamed for Smog: New York Caught in Poison Balloon," *The New York Times*, November 26, 1966.
96. Fromartz, *Organic, Inc.*, 22.
97. Cited in Belasco, *Appetite for Change*, 21.
98. Pollan, *The Omnivore's Dilemma*, 143.
99. Pollan, *The Omnivore's Dilemma*, 143.
100. Pollan, *The Omnivore's Dilemma*, 143.
101. Belasco, *Appetite for Change*, 40.
102. Belasco, *Appetite for Change*, 139.
103. Pollan, *The Omnivore's Dilemma*, 155.
104. Pollan, *The Omnivore's Dilemma*, 155.
105. Carolyn Dimitri and Catherine Greene, "Recent Growth Patterns in the U.S. Organic Foods Market," Agriculture Information Bulletin No. (AIB777), Economic Research Service, U.S. Department of Agriculture, September 2002, 8.
106. Miles McEvoy, "Organic Regulations for Washington and the United States," Washington Tree Fruit Postharvest Conference, March 13 and 14, 2001. Viewed April 4, 2007 at http://postharvest.tfrec.wsu.edu/ PC2001K.pdf. See also Dimitri and Greene, "Recent Growth Patterns in the U.S. Organic Foods Market," p. 8.
107. Dimitri and Greene, "Recent Growth Patterns in the U.S. Organic Foods Market," 8.
108. "National Organic Standards Board," USDA website, http://www.ams.usda.gov/nosb/, viewed April 20, 2007.
109. Gardner, *American Agriculture in the Twentieth Century*, 26.
110. Randall Pinkston, "Profile: Concern mounting over antibiotics entering food chain," CBS Morning News, March 12, 2007. Viewed March 20, 2007 at www.factiva.com.
111. Gardner, *American Agriculture in the Twentieth Century*, 26. See also "Advocacy Groups Hope Codex Ruling Leads to RBGH Suspension," *FDA Week*, March 2, 2007. Viewed March 20, 2007 at www.factiva.com.
112. National Organic Standards Board, http://www.ams.usda.gov/nosb/, viewed March 5, 2007.
113. National Organic Standards Board, http://www.ams.usda.gov/nosb/, viewed March 5, 2007. See also "Organic Industry Timeline," Whole Foods Market, http://www.wholefoodsmarket.com/issues /organic/timeline.html, viewed March 5, 2007.
114. Dimitri and Greene, "Recent Growth Patterns in the U.S. Organic Foods Market," 8.
115. James E. Austin and Reed Martin, "Organics: Coming Center Stage?" HBS No. 907-045.
116. National Organic Program Standards, The National Organic Program, U.S. Department of Agriculture,

http://www.ams.usda.gov/NOP/NOP/standards/
FullText.pdf, viewed March 5, 2007.

117. National Organic Program Standards, The National
Organic Program, U.S. Department of Agriculture,
http://www.ams.usda.gov/NOP/NOP/standards/
FullText.pdf, viewed March 5, 2007.

118. National Organic Program Standards, The National
Organic Program, U.S. Department of Agriculture,
http://www.ams.usda.gov/NOP/NOP/standards/
FullText.pdf, viewed March 5, 2007.

119. See William A. Sahlman and Alison Berkley Wagonfeld,
"Earthbound Farm," HBS No. 807-061 (Boston: HBS
Publishing, 2006).

120. National Organic Program Standards, The National
Organic Program, U.S. Department of Agriculture,
http://www.ams.usda.gov/NOP/NOP/standards/
FullText.pdf, viewed March 5, 2007.

121. National Organic Program Standards, The National
Organic Program, U.S. Department of Agriculture,
http://www.ams.usda.gov/NOP/NOP/standards/
FullText.pdf, viewed March 5, 2007.

122. National Organic Program Standards, The National
Organic Program, U.S. Department of Agriculture,
http://www.ams.usda.gov/NOP/NOP/standards/
FullText.pdf, viewed March 5, 2007.

123. National Organic Program Standards, The National
Organic Program, U.S. Department of Agriculture,
http://www.ams.usda.gov/NOP/NOP/standards/
FullText.pdf, viewed March 5, 2007.

124. National Organic Program Standards, The National
Organic Program, U.S. Department of Agriculture,
http://www.ams.usda.gov/NOP/NOP/standards/
FullText.pdf, viewed March 5, 2007.

125. Fromartz, *Organic, Inc.*, 25-29.

126. Fromartz, *Organic, Inc.*, 25.

127. Pollan, *The Omnivore's Dilemma*, 153.

128. Pollan, *The Omnivore's Dilemma*, 153.

129. Cited in Pollan, *The Omnivore's Dilemma*, 163-64.

130. Catherine Greene, "U.S. Agriculture Gaining Ground,"
Economic Research Service, U.S. Department of
Agriculture, *Agricultural Outlook*, AGO-270, April
2000, p. 2. Viewed March 5, 2007 at http:// www.ers.
usda.gov/publications/AgOutlook/apr2000/ao270d.pdf.
See also Catherine Greene, *U.S. Organic Farming
Emerges in the 1990s: Adoption of Certified Systems*,
Agricultural Information Bulletin No. 770, Economic
Research Service, U.S. Department of Agriculture,
2001, p. 23. Viewed March 5, 2007 at http:// www.ers.
usda.gov/publications /aib770/aib770.pdf.

131. Fromartz, *Organic, Inc.*, xvii.

132. 2006 Manufacturer Survey, Organic Trade Association,
http://www.ota.com/pics/documents/ short%20over
view%20MMS.pdf, viewed March 5, 2007.

133. Daren Fonda, "Organic Growth," *TIME* magazine, August
12, 2002. Viewed April 14, 2007 at www.time.com.

134. Matt Milder, "Wild in the Aisles," *TheDeal.com*,
September 18, 2006. Quoted by James E. Austin and
Reed Martin in "Organics: Coming Center Stage?"
HBS No. 907-405.

135. Dimitri and Greene, "Recent Growth Patterns in the
U.S. Organic Foods Market," p. 8.

136. Katherine Bowers, "Wal-Mart Seeks Sustainability,"
Supermarket News, April 24, 2006. Viewed March 5,
2007 at www.factiva.com.

137. Wendy Zellner, "Peace, Love, and the Bottom Line:
How ex-hippie John Mackey built a natural-foods
empire," *BusinessWeek*, December 7, 1998. Viewed
December 1, 2006, at www.factiva.com.

138. "John Mackey: Not Your Average Grocer," *60 Minutes*
(CBS) interview with correspondent Dan Rather, June 4,
2006. Trancsript viewed April 14, 2007 at http://www.
cbsnews.com/stories/2006/05/31/60minutes/
main1671466.shtml.

139. "John Mackey: Not Your Average Grocer," *60 Minutes*
(CBS).

140. Zellner, "Peace, Love, and the Bottom Line."

141. John Mackey, "Winning the Battle for Freedom and
Prosperity," originally a speech at FreedomFest in
May, 2004. Viewed March 1, 2007 at http://www.
wholefoods.com/blogs/jm/archives/2006/02/winning_
the_bat.html.

142. Zellner, "Peace, Love, and the Bottom Line."

143. Zellner, "Peace, Love, and the Bottom Line."

144. Zellner, "Peace, Love, and the Bottom Line." See also
Fishman, "The Anarchist's Cookbook."

145. Zellner, "Peace, Love, and the Bottom Line."

146. "History of Whole Foods Market," Whole Foods
Market website, http://www.wholefoodsmarket.com /
company/history.html, viewed March 1, 2007. See
also Fishman, "The Anarchist's Cookbook."

147. Fishman, "The Anarchist's Cookbook."

148. Zellner, "Peace, Love, and the Bottom Line."

149. "20 Questions with Sunni's Salon," http://www.endervidual-
ism.com/salon/intvw/mackey.htm, viewed March 1, 2007.

150. Zellner, "Peace, Love, and the Bottom Line."

151. Zellner, "Peace, Love, and the Bottom Line."

152. Zellner, "Peace, Love, and the Bottom Line."

153. Zellner, "Peace, Love, and the Bottom Line."

154. Zellner, "Peace, Love, and the Bottom Line."

155. Zellner, "Peace, Love, and the Bottom Line." See also
"History of Whole Foods Market," Whole Foods
Market website, http://www.wholefoodsmarket.com/
company /history.html, viewed March 1, 2007.

156. "John Mackey: Not Your Average Grocer," *60 Minutes*
(CBS).

157. "History of Whole Foods Market," Whole Foods
Market website, http://www.wholefoodsmarket.com/
company/history.html, viewed March 1, 2007.

158. "History of Whole Foods Market," Whole Foods
Market website, http://www.wholefoodsmarket.

com/company/history.html, viewed March 1, 2007.

159. Zellner, "Peace, Love, and the Bottom Line."

160. "Austin, Tex., Flood Damage is Estimated at $20 Million," *The New York Times*, May 28, 1981. Viewed April 4, 2007 at www.factiva.com. See also "History of Whole Foods Market," http://www.wholefoodsmarket.com/ company/history.html, and "13th Texas Flood Victim Found," *The New York Times*, June 3, 1981, viewed April 25, 2007 at www.factiva.com.

161. Arnold Garcia Jr., "Ten years ago, a sunny day turned to horror," *Austin American-Statesman*, May 19, 1991. Viewed April 14, 2007 at www.factiva.com.

162. "History of Whole Foods Market," Whole Foods Market website, http://www.wholefoodsmarket.com/ company/history.html, viewed March 1, 2007.

163. "History of Whole Foods Market," Whole Foods Market website, http://www.wholefoodsmarket.com/ company/history.html, viewed March 1, 2007.

164. Kim Tyson, "SBA office for loan applications opens today," *Austin American-Statesman*, December 28, 1991.

165. Jon Gertner, "The Virtue in $6 Heirloom Tomatoes," *The New York Times Magazine*, June 6, 2005. Viewed November 17, 2006 at www.factiva.com.

166. "Declaration of Interdependence," Whole Foods Market website, http://www.wholefoodsmarket.com/ company/declaration.html, viewed March 6, 2007.

167. "Our Core Values," Whole Foods Market website, http://www.wholefoodsmarket.com/company/corevalues.html, viewed April 20, 2007.

168. Per the Whole Foods Market 2006 Annual Report, the company mission is to "promote the vitality and well-being of all individuals by supplying the highest quality, most wholesome foods available."

169. Gertner, "The Virtue in $6 Heirloom Tomatoes."

170. Whole Foods Market 2006 Annual Report.

171. "Sustainability and our Future," Whole Foods Market website, www.wholefoodsmarket.com. Viewed April 16, 2007.

172. Michelle Machado, "Whole Foods Animal Treatment Rules May Affect Stockton, Calif., Duck Supplier," *The Record*, November 9, 2003. Viewed March 23, 2007 at www.factiva.com.

173. Michelle Machado, "Whole Foods Animal Treatment Rules May Affect Stockton, Calif., Duck Supplier," *The Record*, November 9, 2003. Viewed March 23, 2007 at www.factiva.com. For lawsuit, see Marian Burros, "Organizing for an Indelicate Fight," *The New York Times*, May 3, 2006. Viewed March 23, 2007 at www.factiva.com.

174. Fishman, "The Anarchist's Cookbook."

175. Louis Wittig, "Lobsters v. Whole Foods," *The Daily Standard*, June 28, 2006. Viewed March 22, 2007 at www.factiva.com. For Maine exception, see Clarke Canfield,

"Whole Foods makes an exception to no-lobster rule in Maine," Associated Press Newswires, February 7, 2007. Viewed March 22, 2007 at www.factiva.com.

176. "Maine Whole Foods to sell live lobsters," *The Columbus Dispatch*, February 9, 2007. Viewed March 23, 2007 at www.factiva.com.

177. "Animal Compassionate Standards," Whole Foods Market website, http://www.wholefoodsmarket.com/ products/meat-poultry/qualitystandards.html, viewed March 23, 2007.

178. "Whole Foods Market Natural Meat Program and Animal Compassionate Standards for Ducks," Whole Foods Market website, http://www.wholefoodsmarket. com/issues/animalwelfare/ducks.pdf, viewed March 23, 2007.

179. "Whole Foods Market Natural Meat Program and Animal Compassionate Standards for Pigs," Whole Foods Market website, http://www.wholefoodsmarket. com/issues/animalwelfare/pigs.pdf, viewed March 23, 2007.

180. "Farm Animal and Meat Quality Standards," Whole Foods Market website, http://www.wholefoodsmarket. com/products/meat-poultry/qualitystandards.html, viewed March 23, 2007.

181. "Farm Animal and Meat Quality Standards," Whole Foods Market website, http://www.wholefoodsmarket.com/products/meat-poultry/qualitystandards. html, viewed March 23, 2007.

182. Daniel McGinn, "The Green Machine," *Newsweek*, March 21, 2005. Viewed March 5, 2007 at www.factiva. com.

183. Patricia Kilday Hart, "Hitting the Organic Jackpot by Making Shopping a State of Mind, the Whole Foods Market Chain Has Become a Giant among Natural-Foods Retailers," *The Boston Globe*, March 16, 2003. Viewed March 23, 2007 at www.factiva.com.

184. Gertner, "The Virtue in $6 Heirloom Tomatoes."

185. For Whole Foods' description of its stores, see its 2006 Annual Report, p. 11.

186. Whole Foods Market 2006 Annual Report.

187. Gertner, "The Virtue in $6 Heirloom Tomatoes."

188. Gertner, "The Virtue in $6 Heirloom Tomatoes."

189. "John Mackey: Not Your Average Grocer," *60 Minutes* (CBS).

190. Natalie Gott, "Whole Foods offers new ingredient to grocery shopping—fun," *Associated Press Newswires*, May 22, 2005. Viewed March 5, 2007 at www.factiva.com.

191. Gott, "Whole Foods offers new ingredient to grocery shopping—fun."

192. Gott, "Whole Foods offers new ingredient to grocery shopping—fun."

193. "Company Timeline," Whole Foods Market, http:// www.wholefoodsmarket.com/company/ timeline.html, viewed March 5, 2007.

194. Whole Foods Market 2005 Annual Report.

195. Whole Foods Market 2005 Annual Report.

196. John Mackey in "Rethinking the Social Responsibility of Business," *Reason*, October 1, 2005. Viewed March 20, 2007 at www.factiva.com.

197. Mackey in "Rethinking the Social Responsibility of Business."

198. Whole Foods Market 2005 Annual Report.

199. Whole Foods Market 2005 Annual Report.

200. Whole Foods Market 2005 Annual Report.

201. Fishman, "The Anarchist's Cookbook."

202. Whole Foods Market 2005 Annual Report.

203. Fishman, "The Anarchist's Cookbook."

204. "Interviewing and Hiring," Whole Foods Market website, http://www.wholefoodsmarket.com/careers/hiring process2.html, viewed April 25, 2007.

205. Fishman, "The Anarchist's Cookbook."

206. Fishman, "The Anarchist's Cookbook."

207. "For Seventh Straight Year, Whole Foods Market Team Members Place Company on '100 Best Companies to Work For' List," Whole Foods Market website, http://www.wholefoodsmarket.com/company/pr_01-06-04.html, viewed March 20, 2007.

208. John Mackey, "Open Book Company," *Newsweek*, November 28, 2005. Viewed April 25, 2007 at www.factiva.com.

209. "Compensation at Whole Foods Market," Whole Foods Market website, http://www.wholefoods.com/blogs/jm/archives/2006/11/compensation_at_1.html, viewed March 7, 2007.

210. "Declaration of Interdependence," Whole Foods Market website, http://www.wholefoodsmarket.com/ company/declaration.html, viewed March 22, 2007.

211. "Whole Foods Market Benefits," Whole Foods Market website, http://www.wholefoodsmarket.com/careers/benefits_us.html, viewed March 22, 2007. For 90% figure, see "Whole Foods Market at Morgan Stanley Global Consumer & Retail Conference (transcript)," November 16, 2006. Viewed March 22, 2007 at www.factiva.com.

212. "Whole Foods Market Benefits," Whole Foods Market website, http://www.wholefoodsmarket.com/careers/benefits_us.html, viewed March 22, 2007.

213. Charles Fishman, "The Anarchist's Cookbook," *Fast Company*, July 2004. Viewed November 6, 2006 at www.fastcompany.com.

214. "Compensation at Whole Foods Market," Whole Foods Market website, http://www.wholefoods.com/ blogs/jm/archives/2006/11/compensation_at_1.html, viewed March 22, 2007.

215. Kilday Hart, "Hitting the Organic Jackpot by Making Shopping a State of Mind, the Whole Foods Market Chain Has Become a Giant Among Natural-Foods Retailers."

216. "Our Core Values," Whole Foods Market website, http://www.wholefoodsmarket.com/company/corevalues.html, viewed April 17, 2007.

217. Interview with Ralph Sorenson, March 16, 2007.

218. Fishman, "The Anarchist's Cookbook."

219. Mackey in "Rethinking the Social Responsibility of Business."

220. "History of Whole Foods Market," Whole Foods Market website, http://www.wholefoodsmarket.com/company/history.html, viewed March 1, 2007.

221. "History of Whole Foods Market," Whole Foods Market website, http://www.wholefoodsmarket.com/company/history.html, viewed March 1, 2007.

222. "History of Whole Foods Market," Whole Foods Market website, http://www.wholefoodsmarket.com/company/history.html, viewed March 20, 2007

223. "History of Whole Foods Market," Whole Foods Market website, http://www.wholefoodsmarket.com/company/history.html, viewed March 1, 2007.

224. Marian Burros, "A Growing Harvest of Organic Produce," *The New York Times*, March 29, 1989. Viewed November 16, 2006 at www.factiva.com.

225. Gertner, "The Virtue in $6 Heirloom Tomatoes."

226. McGinn, "The Green Machine."

227. Fishman, "The Anarchist's Cookbook."

228. Fishman, "The Anarchist's Cookbook."

229. Sarah Barnes, "Whole Foods Hits Wall Street Today at $17 Per Share," *Austin American-Statesman*, January 23, 1992. Viewed April 15, 2007 at www.factiva.com.

230. For stock price, see Seth Lubove, "Food Porn," *Forbes*, February 14, 2005. Viewed April 26, 2007 at www.forbes.com. For amount raised, see "History," Whole Foods Market, Hoover's, Inc., www.hoovers.com. Viewed April 26, 2007.

231. David Craig, "Economic worries strip 29.07 from Dow," *USA Today*, January 24, 1992. Viewed March 6, 2007 at www.factiva.com. See also Wendy Zellner, "Whole Foods Market: Moving Tofu into the Mainstream," *BusinessWeek*, May 25, 1992. Viewed November 8, 2006 at www.factiva.com.

232. Wendy Zellner, "Whole Foods Market: Moving Tofu into the Mainstream."

233. John A. Byrne, "The Flap over Executive Pay," *BusinessWeek*, May 6, 1991. Viewed March 6, 2007 at www.factiva.com. See also "Compensation at Whole Foods Market," Whole Foods Market website, http://www.wholefoods.com/blogs/jm/archives/2006/11/compensation_at_1.html, viewed March 6, 2007.

234. "Study Finds CEO Pay Has Soared Since 2001," *The Wall Street Journal*, August 31, 2005. Viewed March 21, 2007 at www.factiva.com.

235. Whole Foods Market 10-K Annual Report 1997. Viewed March 21, 2007 at http://www.wholefoodsmarket.com//investor/sec_archives.html.

236. Fishman, "The Anarchist's Cookbook." See also Whole Foods Market Annual Reports, 1999-2003.

237. Fishman, "The Anarchist's Cookbook." See also Whole Foods Market Annual Reports.

238. Whole Foods Market 2006 Annual Report.

239. Safeway 2006 Annual Report, http://shop.safeway.com/superstore/sixframeset.asp?page=investors, viewed April 18, 2007.

240. "Company Timeline," Whole Foods Market, http://www.wholefoodsmarket.com/company/ timeline.html, viewed March 5, 2007.

241. "Company Timeline," Whole Foods Market, http://www.wholefoodsmarket.com/company/ timeline.html, viewed March 5, 2007.

242. "How Green Are We?" Whole Foods Market website, http://www.wholefoodsmarket.com/issues/commitment-green2.html, viewed March 20, 2007.

243. "How Green Are We?" Whole Foods Market website, http://www.wholefoodsmarket.com/issues/commitment-green2.html, viewed March 20, 2007.

244. "How Green Are We?" Whole Foods Market website, http://www.wholefoodsmarket.com/issues/commitment-green2.html, viewed March 20, 2007.

245. "How Green Are We?" Whole Foods Market website, http://www.wholefoodsmarket.com/issues/commitment-green2.html, viewed March 20, 2007.

246. "Whole Foods Market Makes Largest Ever Purchase of Wind Energy Credits in the United States," Whole Foods Market website, http://www.wholefoodsmarket.com/company/pr_01-10-06.html, viewed March 20, 2007.

247. "Together, We're Making a Difference," Whole Foods Market website, http:// www.wholefoodsmarket.com/company/makingadifference.html, viewed April 25, 2007.

248. "Together, We're Making a Difference," Whole Foods Market website, http:// www.wholefoodsmarket.com/company/makingadifference.html, viewed April 25, 2007.

249. "Community Giving," Whole Foods Market website, http://www.wholefoodsmarket.com/company/community-giving.html, viewed April 25, 2007.

250. "Funding," Whole Planet Foundation website, http://www.wholeplanetfoundation.org/funding.html, viewed April 25, 2007. See also "Funding," Animal Compassion Foundation website, http://www.animalcompassionfoundation.org/funding.html, viewed April 25, 2007.

251. Whole Planet Foundation website, http://www.wholeplanetfoundation.org/, viewed March 20, 2007.

252. Whole Foods Market 2006 Annual Report.

253. Christina Robb, "Healthy, Wealthy and Wise," *The Boston Globe*, September 27, 1987. Viewed March 21, 2007 at www.factiva.com.

254. Chris Reidy, "For Chain, A Natural Evolution," *The Boston Globe*, June 3, 2003. Viewed March 21, 2007 at www.factiva.com.

255. Sheryl Julian, "Bread and Circus to Drop Caffeine, Alcohol from Shelves," *The Boston Globe*, February 18, 1987. Viewed March 21, 2007 at www.factiva.com.

256. Robb, "Healthy, Wealthy and Wise."

257. Robb, "Healthy, Wealthy and Wise."

258. "Massachusetts Bread & Circus stores to use Whole Foods name," *Associated Press Newswires*, June 3, 2003. Accessed March 21, 2007 at www.factiva.com.

259. "Company News: Acquisition Merges Largest Natural-Foods Retailers," *The New York Times*, May 13, 1993. Viewed November 16, 2006 at www.factiva.com.

260. "Company Timeline," Whole Foods Market, http://www.wholefoodsmarket.com/company/ timeline.html, viewed March 5, 2007.

261. McGinn, "The Green Machine."

262. McGinn, "The Green Machine."

263. Whole Foods Market 1999 Annual Report.

264. Whole Foods Market 1999 Annual Report.

265. Kristina Zimbalist, "Green Giant: How Whole Foods reinvented the supermarket by making organic produce a hot commodity," *Time*, April 24, 2006. Viewed March 5, 2007 at www.factiva.com.

266. Whole Foods Market 10-K Annual Report 1997. Viewed March 21, 2007 at http:// www.wholefoodsmarket.com//investor/sec_archives.html.

267. Whole Foods Market 2000 Annual Report.

268. Sarah Barnes, "Whole Foods prepares public offering of stock next week," *Austin American-Statesman*, January 18, 1992. Viewed March 21, 2007 at www.factiva.com.

269. Whole Foods Market 10-K Annual Report 2006. Viewed March 21, 2007 at http:// www.wholefoodsmarket.com//investor/sec_archives.html.

270. Whole Foods Market 2006 Annual Report.

271. Whole Foods Market 2006 Annual Report.

272. Whole Foods Market 2006 Annual Report.

273. Whole Foods Market 2006 Annual Report.

274. Whole Foods Market 2006 Annual Report.

275. Whole Foods Market 10-K Annual Report 2006. Viewed March 21, 2007 at http:// www.wholefoodsmarket.com//investor/sec_archives.html.

276. Whole Foods Market 10-K Annual Report 2006. Viewed March 21, 2007 at http:// www.wholefoodsmarket.com//investor/sec_archives.html.

277. Whole Foods Market Annual Reports 2004–2006.

278. James Covert and Janet Adamy, "How Whole Foods' Wild Oats Deal Is Unhealthy for Rivals," *The Wall Street Journal*, February 22, 2007. Viewed March 21, 2007 at www.factiva.com.

279. Andrew Martin, "Whole Foods Makes Offer for a Smaller Rival," *The New York Times*, February 22, 2007. Viewed March 22, 2007 at www.factiva.com.

280. Martin, "Whole Foods Makes Offer for a Smaller Rival." See also Kristi Arellano, "Rival to Buy Wild Oats," *Denver Post*, February 22, 2007. Viewed March 22, 2007 at www.factiva.com.

281. James Covert, "Whole Foods' Investors Cautious," *The Wall Street Journal*, March 7, 2007. Viewed March 22, 2007 at www.factiva.com. See also Gerry Smith, "Whole Foods CEO tries to calm investors," *The Atlanta Journal-Constitution*, March 6, 2007. Viewed March 22, 2007 at www.factiva.com.

282. Mike Duff, "Can Whole Foods Digest Wild Oats?" *DSN Retailing Today*, March 5, 2007. Viewed March 22, 2007 at www.factiva.com.

283. Andrew Martin, "Whole Foods Buys Smaller Rival," *The New York Times*, February 22, 2007. Viewed March 22, 2007 at www.factiva.com.

284. Gertner, "The Virtue in $6 Heirloom Tomatoes."

285. Jeff Nightbyrd, "Entrepreneur with philosopher's bent runs Whole Foods," *Austin American-Statesman*, June 17, 1993. Viewed December 1, 2006 at www.factiva.com.

286. Fishman, "The Anarchist's Cookbook."

287. Nightbyrd, "Entrepreneur with philosopher's bent runs Whole Foods."

288. Nightbyrd, "Entrepreneur with philosopher's bent runs Whole Foods."

289. Seth Lubove, "New Age Capitalist," *Forbes*, April 6, 1998. Viewed February 28, 2007 at www.forbes.com. For political views, see "20 Questions with Sunni's Salon," http://www.endervidualism.com/salon/intvw/mackey.htm, viewed March 1, 2007.

290. Lubove, "New Age Capitalist."

291. Michael Abramowitz, "Berkeley's New Age Shoppers Confront Old-Time Unionism in Organic Checkout Line," *The Washington Post*, Februrary 19, 1992. Viewed February 28, 2007 at www.factiva.com.

292. Abramowitz, "Berkeley's New Age Shoppers Confront Old-Time Unionism in Organic Checkout Line."

293. R. Michelle Breyer, "Labor practices draw praise and pickets," *Associated Press Newswires*, May 13, 1998. Viewed February 28, 2007 at www.factiva.com.

294. "20 Questions with Sunni's Salon," http://www.endervidualism.com/salon/intvw/mackey.htm, viewed March 1, 2007.

295. Jenny Little, "A Vegan Dealing in Dead Animals," *The Mail*, August 21, 2005. Viewed April 19, 2007.

296. "A Wal-Mart for the granola crowd," from *The Economist*, August 4, 2005. Viewed March 22, 2007 at www.factiva.com.

297. "Q4 2003 Whole Foods Market Earnings Conference Call—Final," Fair Disclosure Wire, November 12, 2004. Viewed March 22, 2007 at www.factiva.com.

298. Stephanie Turner, "Madison, Wis., Whole Foods Employees Want Out of Union," *The Wisconsin State Journal*, August 2, 2003. Viewed March 22, 2003 at www.factiva.com.

299. Katherine Field, "Making Retail Pay," *Chain Store Age*, July 1, 2006. Viewed March 22, 2007 at www.factiva.com.

300. Kilday Hart, "Hitting the Organic Jackpot by Making Shopping a State of Mind, the Whole Foods Market Chain Has Become a Giant Among Natural-Foods Retailers."

301. "Farmers Market Growth," United States Department of Agriculture, http://www.ams.usda.gov/farmersmarkets/FarmersMarketGrowth.htm, viewed March 29, 2007. See also John Cloud, "My Search for the Perfect Apple," *Time*, March 12, 2007. Viewed March 5, 2007 at www.factiva.com.

302. Marian Burros, "Is Whole Foods Straying from Its Roots?" *The New York Times*, February 28, 2007, www.nytimes.com. Viewed February 28, 2007.

303. Melanie Warner, "Wal-Mart Eyes Organic Foods, and Brand Names Get in Line," *The New York Times*, May 12, 2006. Viewed March 29, 2007 at www.factiva.com.

304. Warner, "Wal-Mart Eyes Organic Foods, and Brand Names Get in Line."

305. David Kaplan, "A natural in groceries finds the going tougher," *Houston Chronicle*, January 14, 2007. Viewed March 29, 2007 at www.factiva.com.

306. "Economist: Organic ag[riculture] fastest growing food market," AG answers: Business and Science of Agriculture, an Ohio State Extension and Purdue Extension Partnership, http://www.agriculture.purdue.edu/aganswers/story.asp?storyID=3877, February 11, 2005. Viewed March 29, 2007.

307. "Economist: Organic ag[riculture] fastest growing food market," AG answers: Business and Science of Agriculture, an Ohio State Extension and Purdue Extension Partnership, http://www.agriculture.purdue.edu/aganswers/story.asp?storyID=3877, February 11, 2005. Viewed March 29, 2007.

308. "John Mackey: Not Your Average Grocer," *60 Minutes* (CBS).

309. McGinn, "The Green Machine."

310. Lilly Rockwell, "Whole Foods Touts Its Prices," *Austin American-Statesman*, August 20, 2006. Viewed February 28, 2006 at www.factiva.com.

311. Rockwell, "Whole Foods Touts Its Prices."

312. Steven Gray, "Boss Talk: Natural Competitor—How Whole Foods CEO Mackey Intends to Stop Growth Slippage," *The Wall Street Journal*, December 4, 2006.

313. Gray, "Boss Talk: Natural Competitor—How Whole Foods CEO Mackey Intends to Stop Growth Slippage."

314. Gray, "Boss Talk: Natural Competitor—How Whole Foods CEO Mackey Intends to Stop Growth Slippage."

315. Larry Armstrong, "Trader Joe's: The Trendy American Cousin," BusinessWeek Online, European cover story, April 26, 2004. Viewed March 29, 2007.

316. Ellen Paris, "Brie, But No Budweiser," *Forbes*, October 2, 1989. Viewed March 28, 2007 at www.factiva.com.

317. Amy Wu, "A Specialty Store with a Discount Attitude," *The New York Times*, July 27, 2003. Viewed March 28, 2007 at www.factiva.com.

318. Pia Sarkar, "The tao of Trader Joe's," *The San Francisco Chronicle*, June 6, 2006. Viewed March 28, 2007 at www.factiva.com.

319. Deborah Orr, "The Cheap Gourmet," *Forbes*, April 10, 2006. Viewed March 28, 2007 at www.factiva.com.

320. Sales estimate from trade journal *Supermarket News*, quoted in Orr, "The Cheap Gourmet."

321. John Mackey and Michael Pollan, "The Past, Present, and Future of Food."

322. John Mackey and Michael Pollan, "The Past, Present, and Future of Food."

323. John Mackey and Michael Pollan, "The Past, Present, and Future of Food."

324. See Kim Severson, "Why Roots Matter More," *The New York Times*, November 15, 2006. Viewed December 18, 2006 at www.nytimes.com.

325. Burros, "Is Whole Foods Straying from Its Roots?"

326. Steven Shapin, "Paradise Sold," *The New Yorker*, May 15, 2006. Viewed February 1, 2007 at www.newyorker.com.

327. "John Mackey: Not Your Average Grocer," *60 Minutes* (CBS).

328. Pollan, *The Omnivore's Dilemma*, 171-173.

329. Pollan, *The Omnivore's Dilemma*, 171-173.

330. Pollan, *The Omnivore's Dilemma*, 139.

331. Pollan, *The Omnivore's Dilemma*, 157.

332. Pollan, *The Omnivore's Dilemma*, 166.

333. "John Mackey: Not Your Average Grocer," *60 Minutes* (CBS).

334. Pollan, *The Omnivore's Dilemma*, 167.

335. Cloud, "My Search for the Perfect Apple."

336. Mackey, "An Open Letter to Michael Pollan."

337. Mackey, "An Open Letter to Michael Pollan."

338. John Mackey, "Detailed Reply to Pollan Letter," Whole Foods Market website, http://www.wholefoods.com/blogs/jm/archives/2006/06/detailed_reply.html, viewed March 23, 2007.

339. Carol Ness, "Whole Foods, taking flak, thinks local," *San Francisco Chronicle*, July 26, 2006. Viewed February 28, 2006 at www.factiva.com.

340. John Mackey and Michael Pollan, "The Past, Present, and Future of Food."

341. John Mackey and Michael Pollan, "The Past, Present, and Future of Food."

342. John Mackey and Michael Pollan, "The Past, Present, and Future of Food."

343. John Mackey and Michael Pollan, "The Past, Present, and Future of Food."

344. John Mackey and Michael Pollan, "The Past, Present, and Future of Food."

345. "Rethinking the Social Responsibility of Business," reprinted from *Reason* magazine, John Mackey's blog, Whole Foods Market website, September 28, 2005, http://www.wholefoodsmarket.com/blogs/jm/archives/2005/09/. Viewed April 19, 2007.

THE HUMAN FACE OF HIV/AIDS

Contracts of employment are not just commercial transactions – they are transactions in social responsibility[1]
– Clifford Mkhize (Human Resources Manager)

"We almost woke up a little bit too late,"[2] said Clifford Mkhize with a wry smile, sitting in his 'no frills' conference room in industrial Durban, where he was discussing his company's response to the HIV/AIDS crisis. It was April 2005, and the consequences of the HIV/AIDS pandemic to the business sector were becoming increasingly obvious. The private sector was taking more responsibility for what had initially been regarded as a public health and social issue, as businesses became aware of the implications of its failure to take proactive steps to halt the epidemic.

The HIV/AIDS epidemic was seen by many analysts as a strategic socio-economic issue that would have an impact on the business environment over the next decade at least.[3] For investors doing business in South Africa and those looking to enter the market, HIV could pose as much of a risk to doing business in South Africa as economic factors such as exchange rate volatility and GDP growth.[4] Business vulnerability to increased costs from the disease was unquestionable.[5] Businesses

This case was prepared in 2002 by Research Associate, Clare Mitchell, with Senior Lecturer Margie Sutherland. It was updated in 2005 by Murray Cairns and Margie Sutherland. Although it is inspired by actual events, the names of all the parties involved and of the company, have been changed. The case is not intended to demonstrate ineffective or effective handling of an administrative situation; it is intended for classroom discussion only.

Printed with permission from Wits Business School and www. ecch.com.

in South Africa faced cost increases up to 3.2 times the annual salary of each employee infected with HIV[6] This excludes the cost of diminishing markets. For one beverage manufacturer it was predicted that annual sales volumes would fall by as much as 12.5% over the next 10 years.[7] due to the increased mortality rates in the country.

The results of a research project[8] initiated by the South African Business Coalition on HIV/ AIDS and conducted by the Bureau for Economic Research in 2004, indicated that employer response to the epidemic was linked to employer size, with small companies having done very little in the way of action against the epidemic. The survey also found that at 60% of mines and 50% of manufacturers surveyed HIV/AIDS had reduced labour productivity, increased absenteeism and led to higher employee benefit costs. Respondents in all sectors expected the impact on profitability to escalate in the next five years.

By 2005 Southern Africa was the worst affected sub-region in the world. An estimated 5.3 million people in this area were living with HIV at the end of 2003. The 2004 antenatal survey of pregnant women in South Africa showed a 28% HIV infection rate, as against 3% in the early 1990s[9]. It had been estimated that approximately 3 million people would die of HIV/AIDS related causes by 2010 in South Africa.[10]

South African president, Thabo Mbeki's stated uncertainty on a link between HIV and AIDS had led to heated debate over the issue, and had retarded the development of a comprehensive national HIV/AIDS policy for South Africa. On 17 April 2002, however, the official government policy changed, with a cabinet statement making it clear that government started from the premise that HIV caused AIDS.[11] In this statement government indicated its commitment to a universal roll-out plan for the drug nevirapine[12] to be given to pregnant women, as well as to providing a comprehensive package of care for sexual-assault victims. At the beginning of 2004 the government announced a plan for the provision of free ARVs in accredited public health clinics. As at October 2004, 19 500 were on treatment through this scheme.[13]

Company background

The company for which Mkhize worked was founded in 1948 and operated in a niche area as a subcontractor in the building industry. In 1996 it was listed on the Johannesburg Stock Exchange, in which year it diversified from its original core business. This strategy was not a success, however, and in 1999 the organisation was placed in liquidation. After a management buyout the company was able to continue business, but refocussed on its original niche area. Since then it has operated successfully as a subcontractor in the building industry and in 2005, employed 280 employees, of whom approximately 150 are skilled. Until 2000 the company had no formal position on AIDS, but it had introduced an HIV/AIDS policy shortly after the promulgation of the Employment Equity Act No 55 of 1998. The policy was brief and to the point, stating that no employee could be tested in anticipation of, or during, his or her employment with the company, without having given prior consent to the test, and that discrimination against employees living with HIV/AIDS was unlawful.

It was against this background that Mkhize devised and implemented his company's HIV/AIDS awareness and education programme. When planning and structuring the programme his initial response was to consult the experts. Having made contact with a professor of medicine who specialised in HIV/AIDS, Mkhize discussed with him the possibilities of delivering lectures to his company's workforce. Throughout their discussions Mkhize felt a niggling concern, however, that the talks would be too high powered, and he was not happy about the idea of using interpreters. He believed that interpreters needed to use words in the correct context for the audience to which they were speaking, and he was not sure that the interpreters would have the capacity to deliver on this score.[14]

Why was he outsourcing this particular project, he asked himself, when he not only spoke the language of the workers, but had always made a point of nurturing close relationships with so many of them? After pondering the matter a little further he concluded that he would be the best person to undertake the HIV/AIDS education programme for the company.

Having made this decision he set about an intensive course of self-education. Mkhize was fortunate that his wife was a general practitioner, who was able to teach him about the disease that she encountered "eight or nine times a day"[15] at her own workplace. Whilst she became his 'coach', he also obtained educational videos, and a copy of *AIDS: The Challenge for South Africa* by Whiteside and Sunter.[16] Once satisfied that he was sufficiently qualified to impart his knowledge to others, Mkhize implemented his education and prevention programme.

The programme

Over a period of 18 Fridays during 2003, 15 to 20 workers came to head office for one Friday each, where they were given breakfast and lunch, and taught firstly about company structure and business principles. "I coached them so that they could go back and be better employees",[17] said Mkhize. But after that initial hour, it was all AIDS. "It's quite easy. I draw a picture of a man with dots all over him and these are the CD4 cells. In red I show the cut where the HIV cells get in and then I show how they eat up all the CD4 cells. I explain to them that the CD4 cells are the soldiers and that they can no longer fight infections because they have been taken over by the enemy which are the HIV cells."[18]

Mkhize also discussed sexual transmission of the disease at these sessions and the company handed out condoms to employees from time to time. The main focus of his talks was methods of safer sex: for example, how to ensure that a condom would, in fact, perform the task it was intended to perform. The reason for this was, according to Mkhize, that his company operated in a high-risk industry because many of the contracts were performed outside of Durban. This meant that workers were seconded to places far from home for many months at a time. "Most of our staff members are in adulterous relationships,"[19] remarked Mkhize. He had little doubt that when they were away from home the workers had two or three different partners during the contract period. The simple fact of the matter was that prevention, rather than abstinence, had to be the focus of his teaching.

He also asked the workers to put their hands on the table during these sessions and noted how many of them had cut fingers. In this particular industry it was common to accidentally nick or cut a finger, and again he emphasised to the workers that cuts presented potential points of entry for the HI virus. He stressed the need to be vigilant about contact with any body fluids that might carry the virus.

One of Mkhize's chief goals was to teach the workers the importance of being tested and knowing their own HIV/AIDS status. He gave them pamphlets giving the details of nearby testing centres. He wanted them to know that the company would not discriminate against employees who were HIV positive but would, on the contrary, help them as much as it could. He hoped through education to create an atmosphere where people felt comfortable to talk about the disease, and to build up sufficient confidence for workers to approach him if they knew that they were infected.

Mkhize had repeated the training sessions in 2004 for all new employees. On World AIDS Day at the end of 2004 he had handed out red ribbons, condoms and new HIV/AIDs pamphlets to all members of staff. He was saddened to see many of these had landed up in the company dustbins.

The social and business dilemma

By April 2005 Mkhize knew of fifteen employees in the company who were HIV positive, all of whom had voluntarily admitted their condition to him in the course of the past 12 to 14 months. He told them he was sworn to secrecy, and believed that no one else in the company knew about their positive status. He estimated, however, that approximately 60% of his company's workforce was, in fact, living with HIV. How was he going to bridge the divide and encourage others to be tested?

He had looked through the company's records on numbers of employees who had died whilst being employed and noted that on average one employee had died per year from 1990 to 2000. Four had died in 2004, one in an industrial accident and the other three, all aged between 28 and 43, from pneumonia, diarrhoea and tuberculosis according to their death certificates. Mkhize had also found out that only one fifth of the company's employees were members of a medical aid scheme. The main reason for this was the expense of such schemes, and consequently those employees who earned small salaries were more reluctant to join medical aid schemes on account of the large deductions that would be made from their salaries every month. It was therefore only the more skilled employees who earned better salaries who actually belonged to medical aid schemes.

Should the company pay for the treatment of those employees who were HIV positive and who did not have medical aid coverage? Or could they get treatment for free under the government's anti-retroviral "roll out" programme? How did one access the clinics? Would the cost of non treatment of employees be higher than the cost of treatment? What would the impact of HIV/AIDS be on the profitability of the company over the next five years? Would or should the company provide different levels of care depending on the value of the employee to the company? These were some of the questions which Mkhize faced when confronting the problems presented by the HIV/AIDS pandemic. For a man like himself who took such an interest in the workforce, and who prided himself on his close personal relationships with his employees, it became a question of both personal and social responsibility.

The various conflicting interests that Mkhize had to juggle were poignantly highlighted by the cases of Michael and James.

Michael

Michael was a valuable employee. In fact he possessed the second highest level of technical qualifications that could be reached in his field of specialisation and he was the third highest paid foreman in the company. In February 2003, while overseeing a project to the value of R28 million in Kwazulu-Natal, Michael told Mkhize that he was HIV positive. At that stage he showed no signs of poor health and was perfectly able to do his job. Although Mkhize was obviously distressed and concerned for Michael, he was also pleased when he spoke to him. At last the silence had been broken, and he had someone who was 'apparently well', though HIV positive, whom he could try to help.

Mkhize consulted a private medical centre that specialised in treating HIV/AIDS patients and sent Michael there. He established that the cost of ARVs would be approximately R1 400 per month.[20] Michael fell within the 20% of the company's staff who were members of a medical aid scheme, but the HIV/AIDS policy of that scheme did not cover the cost of ARVs. Mkhize therefore set about seeking alternatives. He located a scheme that paid R25 000 per annum for ARVs. The catch, however, was that there was a nine-month waiting period during which time Michael would be obliged to contribute to the scheme, without receiving any benefits from it.[21]

Mkhize took Michael's case to his company's board of directors and asked that they consider two things: first, moving Michael to the other medical aid scheme and second, funding the cost of Michael's ARVs during the nine-month waiting period. Mkhize's motivating argument was that there was no one else in the company who could take over Michael's job, that Michael was steeped in the corporate culture of the company, and that quite apart from his academic qualifications he had such extensive practical experience that he was sufficiently important to the company to justify the expense.[22]

The board approved Mkhize's proposal on the basis that it would be more costly to the company to lose Michael than to pay for his medication. "This isn't about family losses only, but also about company losses",[23] noted Mkhize. He arranged for a company driver to collect the appropriate medication from the pharmacy every month and for it to be delivered safely to Michael at the contract site hundreds of kilometres north of Durban. The company also sent Michael for regular CD4 count checks, and ensured that his viral load was regularly monitored. Michael's health had deteriorated for a time, when his hands and feet were very painful and when he could only work at "90 percent capacity",[24] but since then he had recovered and was able to work to full capacity. Mkhize believed that Michael's future with the company would not be limited by his HIV status. His condition would be tolerated and, if it became necessary, the company would seek out projects that would best accommodate his state of health.

Mkhize noted that Michael's son was an apprentice with the company and once he knew of Michael's condition, he decided to fast track the son's development by sending him to the technikon to further his qualifications. The aim was to train him into his father's position as "he one day will be the breadwinner".[25] The company had always pursued a policy of employing family members of existing employees. They believed that this approach bred greater loyalty among employees, and so far they had not been disappointed. It was therefore a natural progression to pursue this policy in relation to people suffering from HIV/AIDS.

James

James was a senior store man in the company, who had a Store's Management Certificate, which he had obtained after being sent on a course by the company. Store men were always key figures in company projects because millions of rands' worth of stock passed through their hands during the course of any one project. Midway through 2003 James' health began to deteriorate and he was often off work with chronic diarrhea and also had a severe case of shingles. At the end of 2003 he was admitted to hospital suffering from tuberculosis and was put on a six month course of medication. Once his sick pay had been exhausted he was given leave without pay, on the understanding that his job would always be there for him.

In January 2004 James was better and came to see Mkhize. He told Mkihize that during his time in hospital he had learnt that he had AIDS, and said that he was ready to die. He was busy getting his affairs in order. He asked that his beneficiaries under the industry provident fund (the Fund) of which he was a member be amended. Mkhize ensured that this was done and suggested that James go home to recover, and said that he should come back to work when he felt ready to do so.

Contrary to all expectations James' condition improved, and two months later he reported for work, feeling a lot better. The company decided to give him the position of co-store man on their sites, where he would be able to fulfill the less demanding of the two store man roles. He earned the same salary as he had done previously. But when Mkhize saw James in April he was concerned that his health was once more deteriorating.

In June 2004 Mkhize heard about the government's roll-out of an ante-retroviral programme. Mkhize spent almost a week finding out how to get James onto one of these programmes. As James was not on medical aid, the company paid for James to have the requisite tests and it was discovered that James' CD4 cell count was 88 and his viral load was 187 000. Mkihze went with James to the roll-out clinic on five occasions and James was put onto a triple cocktail of anti-retrovirals which he received monthly, free of charge. Although for the first two weeks James felt nauseous and reported a lot of discomfort in his stomach area, by the end of the second month he was much better and said he was ready to take up the senior position again. The company had been awarded a huge contract in Empangeni and James was sent to set up the stores in October. Before relocating, James' CD 4 cell count had risen to 120, and his viral load was undetectable. The clinic said they would transfer James file to the roll-out clinic in Empangeni and he could continue his treatment there.

A month later James went to the clinic in Empangeni and found to his dismay that his file hadn't arrived. The nursing staff seemed overwhelmed with patients and said that without his file they could not dispense the daily medicines he needed. He was frustrated because the staff at the clinic didn't accept his word that he'd been receiving ARVs previously, and that he'd have to prove compliance once again by coming into the clinic for repeated visits before being put on a cocktail. Because of his frustration, and also because he was feeling so much better and knew his latest test results, he decided to follow up with his original clinic over the Christmas holiday period. In December he was unable to leave the site because the contract was running behind schedule, and operations continued without break.

In January James became desperately ill and sent a message to Mkhize that he wasn't going to be able to return to work. Various employees of the company visited James in his small home, which

they noted had no running water, and they reported to Mkhize that James was very ill and bound to die. No one mentioned the fact that James had AIDS, but Mkhize believed that it must have been apparent to them judging from the man's condition.

At this point Mkhize was faced with two options:

- he could dismiss James from the company and apply for sick or disability benefits from the Fund; or
- he could keep James on the company books as a contributing member of the Fund and apply for death benefits when he died.

In the case of sick or disability retirement the Fund would have paid out a sum of approximately R12 900 and nothing more. If Mkhize pursued the second option he knew that the death benefits available to James' beneficiaries would be in the region of R135 000. The only additional cost to the company would be that of James' monthly contributions to the Fund, which were approximately R100 per month.

Mkhize chose the second option and James died in March 2005. He had worked for the company since 1989. The company paid the family R5 000 as a contribution towards funeral expenses and the staff collected about R1 800 as a voluntary donation. The case would in due course come before the trustees of the Fund (of whom Mkhize was one), who had a discretion in terms of the rules of the Fund to determine exactly what amounts should be paid in what proportions to which beneficiaries.

Approximately sixty staff members attended James' funeral at a cemetery surrounded by low cost housing, shacks and traders selling second hand clothing and a wide range of food on the sandy pavements. Mkhize attended in person, even though he felt uncomfortable about going into such areas. But he felt it was very important that he should attend the funeral in both a personal and an official capacity, showing support for a member of staff who had died in these circumstances.

Mkhize seized James' funeral as an opportunity to address the people there, telling them that James had done nothing wrong – he had done nothing that any of them hadn't done, but he had been unlucky. Mkhize never mentioned the words AIDS or HIV, but everyone knew what he was talking about. While it was never officially mentioned at the company that James had died of AIDS, the cause of his death was obvious. His death certificate stated that he had died of 'natural causes'.

During the period leading up to James' death and at the time of the preparations for his funeral Mkhize had interacted extensively with his family. When he visited James at his home he became aware that he had two unemployed brothers who spent most of their time drinking. James was the sole breadwinner and had provided for his four young children, his wife who was ill in bed, his sister and his two brothers. Mkhize was well aware that this whole family unit, would be the poorer for James' death. He discussed the matter with his contracts' resources manager and between them they decided to offer James' two brothers positions in the company. When Mkhize telephoned them with this proposition they readily accepted. They were initially employed as general workers, but their progress was to be evaluated along the way.

This was a means by which "we could give them bread on their table without compromising company money",[26] said Mkhize. As he had already pointed out, it was part of normal company culture to employ family members of existing employees, and his actions in this particular instance had given away nothing about the true cause of James' death. The HIV/AIDS pandemic meant that Mkhize's contracts of employment had taken on new meaning. "Contracts of employment are no longer just commercial transactions – they are transactions in social responsibility," he noted.[27]

Conclusion

It was with some pride that Mkhize opened a file at the end of the meeting and paged to the Government Employment Equity Act returns that he had recently completed on behalf of his company. He pointed out that he had been able to sign off the fact that every employee of the company had been through his HIV/AIDS training sessions at some stage. He sat back on his chair, asked rhetorically, "But is it enough?" and smiled the same wry smile.

Questions

- Is Mkhize doing the right thing ?
- What elements should be in a company's HIV/AIDS policy ?
- How should a company implement an HIV/AIDS policy ?

Notes

1. From an interview by the authors, 16 April 2002.
2. *Ibid.*
3,4,7. The SA HIV/AIDS Scenario Deutsche Securities Equity Research 2004 T Njobe and G Smith.
5,6. HIV/AIDS: The costs to SA Business. Deutsche Securities Equity Research 2004. T Njobe and G Smith.
3. The Impact of HIV/AIDS on selected Business Sectors in South Africa, 2004. A survey conducted by the Bureau for Economic Research, funded by the South African Business Coalition on HIV & AIDS.
4. The Impact of HIV/AIDS on selected Business Sectors in South Africa, 2004. A survey conducted by the Bureau for Economic Research, funded by the South African Business Coalition on HIV & AIDS.
5. The Impact of HIV/AIDS on selected Business Sectors in South Africa, 2004. A survey conducted by the Bureau for Economic Research, funded by the South African Business Coalition on HIV & AIDS.
6. The Impact of HIV/AIDS on selected Business Sectors in South Africa, 2004. A survey conducted by the Bureau for Economic Research, funded by the South African Business Coalition on HIV & AIDS.
7. The Impact of HIV/AIDS on selected Business Sectors in South Africa, 2004. A survey conducted by the Bureau for Economic Research, funded by the South African Business Coalition on HIV & AIDS.
8. The Impact of HIV/AIDS on selected Business Sectors in South Africa, 2004. A survey conducted by the Bureau for Economic Research, funded by the South African Business Coalition on HIV & AIDS.
9. SAIRR Fast Facts December 2004.
10. The Impact of HIV/AIDS on selected Business Sectors in South Africa, 2004. A survey conducted by the Bureau for Economic Research, funded by the South African Business Coalition on HIV & AIDS.
11. Cabinet statement on HIV/AIDS, 17 April 2002. *[http://www.gov.za/speeches/cabinetaids.02.htm]*, (accessed 28 May 2002).
12. Nevirapine is a drug, the effect of which is to "reduce risk of *intrapartum* HIV-1 transmission from mother to child in pregnant women not taking antiretroviral therapy at the time of labour". Taken from the package insert.
13. SAIRR Fast Facts December 2004.

14. Interview by the authors 16 April 2002.
15. *Ibid.*
16. Whiteside A. and Sunter C. (2000): *AIDS The Challenge for South Africa*, Cape Town: Human & Rousseau (Pty) Ltd.
17. From interview by the authors, 16 April 2002.
18. *Ibid.*
19. *Ibid.*

20. In 2003.
21. *Ibid.*
22. *Ibid.*
23. *Ibid.*
24. *Ibid.*
25. *Ibid.*
26. *Ibid.*
27. *Ibid.*

EXHIBIT I   Global estimates of HIV and AIDS as of end 2003

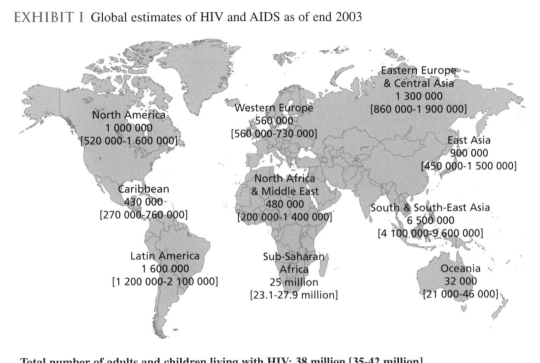

Total number of adults and children living with HIV: 38 million [35-42 million]

Number of people living with HIV			
	Total	37.8 million	[34.8-42.3 million]
	Adults	36.7 million	[32.7-38.8 million]
	Women	17 million	[16.8-18.8 million]
	Children <16years	2.1 million	[1.9-2.6 million]
People newly Infected with HIV in 2003			
	Total	4.8 million	[4.2-8.3 million]
	Adults	4.1 million	[3.6-5.8 million]
	Children <16 years	630 000	[670 000-740 000]
AIDS deaths in 2003			
	Total	2.9 million	[2.6-3.3 million]
	Adults	2.4 million	[2.2-2.7 million]
	Children <16 years	490 000	[440 000-680 000]

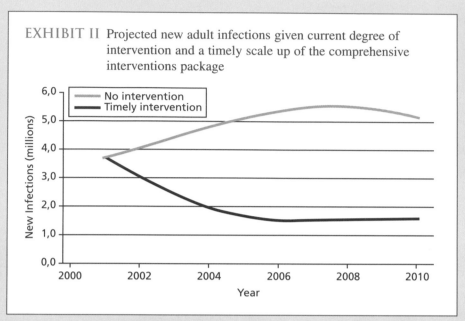

EXHIBIT II Projected new adult infections given current degree of intervention and a timely scale up of the comprehensive interventions package

Source: Stover J. *et al.* can we reverse the HIV/AIDS pandemic wih an expanded response? *Lancet* 2002).

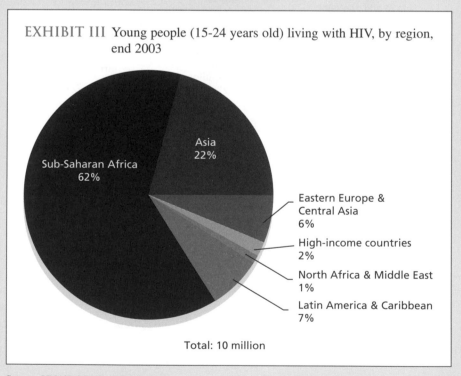

EXHIBIT III Young people (15-24 years old) living with HIV, by region, end 2003

Source: UNAIDS/Unicef/WHO, 2004.

GLOSSARY

Accounting is the process of collecting, recording and assessing information on organizational performance.

Agency problem the idea that someone entrusted with an asset will act with less concern than the person who owns the asset.

Anglo-Saxon model of governance the approach to governing organizations based on the pre-eminence of the interests of the shareholders

Assurance refers to the internal or external verification of corporate statements.

Auditing is an independent review of a statement made by an organization.

Barriers to trade are any policies or practices that obstruct free trade. Quality standards, for example, can be seen as a barrier to trade, but tariffs and import quotas are seen as more typical barriers to trade.

Bluewash refers to the use of the United Nations logo in corporate communications without a genuine commitment to the values promoted by the organization.

Bottom of the pyramid is the bottom quartile of the economic pyramid that categorizes world population by income.

BRIC economies the currently fastest growing developing countries – Brazil, Russia, India, China

Cadbury report a report on governance in the UK published in the early 1990s, amongst whose recommendations include that Chief Executive Officers should be a distinct role from that of Management Director.

Categorical imperative the Kantian idea that something is morally right to do whatever the circumstances, and whatever your interest or situation.

CEA Cercle Ethique des Affaires (France).

Certification refers to the confirmation of certain characteristics that goods or services have.

A charitable organization uses any resources including possible profits or surplus for benevolent goals.

Child labour refers to the employment of children below a certain age in work that is harmful for their dignity, future potential, or health. Minimum age levels vary by country.

Chinese walls the metaphor expressing how a company that deals with a client with two different services (e.g. as an accountant and as an auditor) can manage the potential conflict of interest involved.

Civil and political rights ensure that an individual can freely participate to civil and political life. They include the freedom of thought and conscience.

Civil society refers to voluntary activity outside the economic and political structures of society.

Codes of conduct are voluntary commitments that guide organizational policy and behaviour.

Commodity is a product that is sold without negligible qualitative difference. Crude oil, copper, salt and coffee beans are examples of commodities.

Competitive position refers to the characteristics of a company and its products in relation to competitors.

Consequentialism the philosophical idea that an action's moral rightness or wrongness is established solely by reference to its actual or supposed outcomes.

Co-operative an organization owned by its users and people who work for it.

Co-ordinated economy a national economy where the interests of the key different parites – mainly capital and labour – are well integrated and thus rarely in direct conflict: often applied specifically to Scandinavian countries.

Corporate governance the process by which an organization may be run at the very top.

Corporate social performance refers to the assessment of corporate activity against some social and environmental criteria.

Creative Commons an approach to intellectual property that seeks to ensure that those who originate ideas or technologies are recognized as such, without leading to the excessive ownership regime of standard copyright constrictions.

Code of ethics a document that sets out the moral expectations and procedures in an organization, with a view to encouraging or directing more morally right action.

Critical theory the range of theories that are based on the idea that probing of the social presuppositions of a concept can be a liberating process.

CSO Civil society organizations

'Deep', dark' 'light' 'bright' green a scale of philosophical approaches to environmental protection and support

Deontology the philosophical idea that an action's moral rightness or wrongness is based, not on its consequences, but on the nature of the action or on its motive.

463

Discourse ethics the idea that ethics should be based on processes of dialogue between different parties.

Dual board system of governance where as well as a board of directors, there is a second board that represents interests other than shareholders – usually the employees, but in some versions other stakeholders may also be included.

ECOA the Ethics and Compliance Officer Association (USA).

Ecological footprint a way of measuring the impact of an organization on the environment by presenting the total impact in a single representative value.

Economic and social rights ensure that an individual is able to life a dignified life. They include right to food and right to health.

Economic sanctions are penalties that are applied by a country or a group of countries to discourage unwanted behaviour. Typical sanctions include embargos and freezing of governmental or individual assets.

Egoism in ethics the idea that morality for any individual is to be understood in terms of the interests of that individual.

EMAS the European Eco-Management and Audit Scheme.

Emissions trading a system where each country has a set amout of permitted environmental pollution – if this is exceeded, a country may purchase unused permission from other countries; usually the direction of trade is for poorer countries to sell unused permission to richer, higher polluting countries.

Environmental auditing the process of identifying all the intakes of resource and outputs of pollution of an organization, by analogy with financial audits.

Environmental impact assessment a method of measuring environmental performance by evaluating the total impacts of a company.

Environmental 'triage' the idea that environmental damage such as species extinction be dealt with on an analogy with hospital emergency admissions, where the cases with the best chance of survival will be given priority over the more injured cases, where survival chances are lower.

Ethics committee a committee in an organization, usually of substantial seniority, that manages the ethics of that organization.

Ethics officer an employee of a firm whose job role is to manage and enhance the ethical soundness of the form's activities; often reports to an ethics committee.

Extraterritorial jurisdiction refers to the application of laws beyond national borders.

Fair trade refers to trade that seeks to improve the situation of low-income farmers and workers in developing countries.

Forced labour refers to work that a person is not free to leave because of threat of destitution, violence or other extreme hardship.

Free trade refers to absence of government interference in economic transactions.

FTSE4Good is a list of companies that meet certain social and environmental standards. It is jointly owned by the Financial Times and the London Stock Exchange.

Gaia hypothesis the idea that the earth is a single integrated organic whole.

Gearing, or debt-to-equity ratio the relation between the amount of capital in a company that is based on money brought in by selling shares in a company, as opposed to funds raised by taking out loans (e.g. from banks).

Global Compact is a network of companies that have signed up to respect ten principles relating to human rights and sustainability. The Global Compact was launched by Kofi Annan, former secretary-general of the United Nations and is still linked to the organization.

Greenwashing by analogy with 'whitewashing', the practice of some companies to include eco-friendly messages in their marketing communications, when these are not reflective of the reality of how that company deals with the environment.

Groupthink the tendency of a well integrated group of decisionmakers to converge towards agreement to the extent of inhibiting rational argument.

GHGs Greenhouse gases.

Guanxi a Chinese term referring to the importance of personal relationships in business dealings.

Human rights are entitlements held by all human beings irrespective of their characteristics. They embrace basic rights and freedoms including the right to life and freedom of thought.

Humanitarian organizations advance human welfare and well-being.

Hypernorms are fundamental values that are independent of culture and other local variations.

Indirect discrimination a practice that does not explicitly discriminate against specific demographic groups, but the net effect is to unfairly disadvantage members of such groups

Institutional discrimination the net effect of an organization's policies and practices where these unfairly disadvantage members of a specific demographic group.

ISO 14000 the International Standard on Environmental Management.

Intellectual property ideas, concepts, creative works and other items that are essentially non-material but are owned by a specific organization or individual.

Johannesburg Declaration on Sustainable Development statement of 37 principles agreed at the UN World Summit on Sustainable Development held in Johannesberg September 2002.

Keiretsu a Japanese term for conglomerates of firms that are closely integrated by ties of ownership and cross-trading.

King reports two influential reports on corporate governance in South Africa in the post-apartheid era which, amongst many things, place significance not only on pure economic goals but also include spiritual and related aims as relevant for business.

Kyoto Protocol the agreement signed in Kyoto committing signatories to a raft of emission control practices, including emissions trading; this came into force in the early 2000s.

Life-cycle assessment a means of measuring the environmental (and other) performance of an organization by estimating the overall net total of impacts over the full life of the processes measured; commonly used in evaluating building design.

Managerial capture refers to the use of external assurance for managerial purposes rather than their original purpose.

Materiality is a term relating to social and financial accounting. It refers to the importance of information included in social and financial statements. Information is material if it is likely to affect decision making.

Natural person is a legal term referring to a human being rather than a legal person that also includes organizations.

NIOSH National Institute of Occupational Safety and Health (Malaysia).

NGO non-governmental organization

Non-executive directors members of a board of directors who do not have a significant shareholding in the firm, and are recruited in theory to provide independent advice based on a good knowledge and expertise relating to the industry.

Non-governmental organizations are independent from governments in the sense that they exclude governments from membership or representation.

Open Source Initiative the initiative to produce computer software and systems that are free to the public, thus ensuring the continuing freedom of projects such as the world wide web from too much corporate protectionism.

OCBE Organizational Citizenship Behaviour directed towards the Environment.

Pantouflage the tendency of some senior civil servants to move directly from their government service to work in industry (France).

Para-state body (also quango) an organization that is ultimately owned and thus controlled) by a government, but may operate in a semi-autonomous manner.

PIDA Public Interest Disclosure Act (UK).

Positive and negative rights positive rights are rights to be able to do or be something, whereas negative rights are the freedom from constraint against doing or being something.

Philanthropy refers to efforts to promote human well-being, often through donations to charitable organizations.

Price level is an economic term referring to the general level of prices. Price level may be fixed in fair trade arrangements to guarantee a certain level of revenue for low-income producers and workers.

Principle of precaution the principle that where there may be substantial threats to the environment, it is safer to cease a practice first and then establish the precise degree of environmental damage that might be involved.

Principle of double effect the idea that in some cases, where a greater good is involved, an action that brings about ethically wrong outcomes may be tolerable if the individual does not directly wish those outcomes but they nevertheless are results of the action in question.

Principle of polluter pays the idea that the party that creates environmental damage should be the one to pay for whatever clean-up is involved.

Proportionality the principle that in an area such as human rights, an organization might in some cases be entitled to violate rights, but only in proportion to the scale of the potential damage to the organization that is thus being averted.

Race to the bottom refers to the argument that government deregulation aimed at attracting foreign investment will result in the deterioration of social and economic standards.

Rawlsianism the idea that a practice is just if we can tolerate even the worst outcomes of this for us personally.

Race to the bottom the tendency for firms to compete to adopt worse and worse practices where this provides some kind of competitive advantage such as reduced cost.

Rio Declaration the main statement agreed at the Earth Summit in Rio de Janiero and comprising 27 principles on the environment.

Sarbanes-Oxley Act an act passed in the USA in the 2000s, and imposing several new requirements on companies, in order to reduce the chance of major corporate failures such as Enron.

Social accounting is the process of collecting, recording and assessing information on social and environmental performance.

Social premium is a payment made in addition to the purchase price of fair trade products. It provides a secure source of income that enables communities to make long-term plans.

Social responsiveness refers to the actions that companies take to advance social and environmental goals. It is used in distinction to the normative concept of 'corporate responsibility'.

Stakeholder is an individual or a group of individuals that affect or can be affected by corporate activity.

State-seeking a feature of some minority ethnic groups, who seek to have some form of legitimate governmental structure by which their interests may be expressed and addressed.

Subjectivism in ethics the various approaches to ethics based on the idea that what is right is what I believe to be right.

Subsidiarity the idea that so far as possible, decisions be delegated to the lowest point where there is competence to judge the issues and implement the decision; associated with the view that in the European Union, the precise versions of union-wide principles be formulated at national level rather than at continental.

Supervisory board the second board in a dual system of governance; in some cases called the advisory board as this board tends not to have executive but only advisory capability.

Supply chain is the network of organizations that are needed to produce a certain product or service.

Tragedy of the commons an analogy suggesting that commonly held assets will not be conserved so effectively as those held by a specific body.

Unitarism the idea that a social entity such as a corporation be best seen as a locus of a single agreed set of values.

Unitary board the sole governing body of a corporation under the Anglo-Saxon approach to governance, under the control of the shareholders.

Utilitarianism a version of consequentialism that focuses on the idea that what is right is what produces the best overall outcome – sometimes called the greatest good of the greatest number; in the original form 'good' was identified with happiness or even pleasure.

Veil of ignorance test a key step in the Rawlsian argument: what would you choose (e.g. in a system of government) if you did not know what place in society you occupied?

Virtue ethics the idea that ethical rightness is best understood not in terms of the actions themselves but in terms of the character of those who act.

Whistleblowing the practice of making public information about corporate wrongdoing.

Zaibatsu a Japanese term that refers to family-based company networks.

INDEX